Dear Student:

You have chosen to begin a career as a business professional by majoring in a business discipline. If your experience is anything like mine, you will not regret your choice. Working in business leads to fulfilling and enjoyable experiences and relationships with interesting, quality people. Working in a company you admire that sells products or services in which you believe will enable you to feel positive about yourself, your contributions, and your professional life.

The MIS class is one of the most important classes in the business curriculum for twenty-first-century workers. Perhaps you have heard that many professional jobs are being outsourced overseas to countries like India and China. As you will learn in Chapter 1, it is primarily jobs involving routine work that are moving overseas. The U.S. demand for non-routine work and workers is expected to grow substantially throughout the first half of the twenty-first century. Robert Reich, former U.S. Secretary of Labor, states such workers must learn three behaviors: They must engage in abstract thinking, understand and be able to think in terms of systems, and be able to collaborate successfully. This course is key to learning all three of those behaviors. In fact, in Chapter 2 you will learn about information systems that can help you collaborate in team projects right now, while you are still in college. You will also have many opportunities to work collaboratively by doing the Collaboration Exercises at the end of each chapter.

A study done by the RAND Corporation states that twenty-first-century professionals must learn to innovate. In business, innovation is less often the invention of new technology than it is the creative adaptation of emerging technology to gain competitive advantages. Amazon.com did not invent Internet technology, but it applied that technology as an e-commerce pioneer. YouTube did not develop technology for low-cost data storage and communication, but it found an innovative way to use that technology to provide a revolutionary platform for sharing video.

This textbook was specifically designed to help you learn the three behaviors recommended by Reich and also to practice innovation. Each chapter begins with an interview of a business professional who explains a contemporary application of the chapter's content. These professionals are real people, working in real businesses, right now. Additionally, each chapter includes two boxed ***In Practice*** features; one involves innovation and a second involves the application of technology to business problems. Both set up end-of-chapter collaboration exercises for you and a team of students to perform. Additionally, each chapter has three thought-provoking, two-page discussions and activities called ***Guides***. These guides address practical business problems based on experiences in my own career. Perhaps you have formed the habit of ignoring boxes in textbooks. Do not ignore them here; in many ways, they contain the most important material for your future success.

Like all worthwhile endeavors, this course is work. That's just the way it is. No one succeeds in business without sustained focus, attention, desire, motivation, and hard work. It won't always be easy, and it won't always be fun. On the other hand, you will learn concepts, skills, and behaviors that will prepare you for a long and successful business career in the twenty-first century.

I wish you, as an emerging business professional, the very best success!

Sincerely,

David Kroenke

Seattle, Washington

THE GUIDES

Each chapter includes three *unique* guides that focus on current issues in information systems. In business, you will deal with similar issues, and you may be asked to recommend solutions to these problems. The content of each guide is designed to stimulate thought, discussion, and active participation to help YOU develop your problem-solving skills and become a better business professional.

A description for each category of guide is provided below, along with a page reference for its location in the chapter.

Ethics GUIDES

Ethical issues abound in business. As recent news stories indicate, some businesspeople are better than others at sorting through ethical conflicts. The **Ethics Guides** stimulate debate on how ethics apply to information systems issues. These guides will help you respond to future ethical dilemmas authentically and in a way that is consistent with your own values.

Security GUIDES

We live in an information age, and securing information is critical for business. The **Security Guides** highlight appropriate security skills and behaviors to protect valuable assets, both yours and those of your company. The following Security Guides appear where listed. In addition, Chapter 12 addresses the topic of information security.

Problem-Solving

GUIDES

Improving the quality of your thinking will improve any information system that you use, and your ability to use MIS in your career. The **Problem-Solving Guides** present ideas from cognitive science and apply them to MIS. Not only will you learn to use technology more wisely to attain your business goals, you will learn methods of how to better analyze and solve many other problems that life throws at you.

Opposing Forces

GUIDES

In almost any situation, you will find one or more people with opinions contrary to the generally accepted wisdom. The **Opposing Forces Guides** introduce you to someone who disagrees with one of the main ideas or methods in the chapter. (All of the people whose opinions are included in these guides actually exist.) More likely than not, you will encounter one or more such "contrarians" during your career. These guides help you learn to manage their opinions and respond effectively.

Reflections

GUIDES

In business, people will differ in their opinions and then "agree to disagree," meaning they will back off, reflect, and sometimes alter their viewpoints. In the **Reflections Guides**, I state some strong personal opinions. Every editorial expresses a justifiable opinion, but you should approach them with skepticism and a critical eye. Your task in reading them will be to respond to these opinions and discuss their merit.

Learning Aids for Students

We have structured this book so you can maximize the benefit from the time you spend reading it. As shown in the table below, each chapter includes various learning aids to help you succeed in this course.

RESOURCE	DESCRIPTION	BENEFIT	EXAMPLE
Guides	Each chapter includes three guides that focus on current issues in information systems. One of the three in each chapter addresses ethics.	Stimulate thought and discussion. Address ethics once per chapter. Help develop your problem-solving skills.	Dialing for Dollars, p. 260
Chapter-introduction Interviews	The topic of each chapter is introduced by a business professional working in IT or IS.	Learn the importance of the chapter topic from an expert. Observe the wide range of IS and IT careers.	Chapter 2, Lily Shen, p. 29. Chapter 3, Neil Miyamoto, p. 61.
Query-based Chapter Format	Each chapter starts with a list of questions; each major heading is a question; the Active Review contains tasks for you to perform to demonstrate you are able to answer the questions.	Use the questions to manage your time, guide your study, and review for exams.	Chapter 2, starting on p. 31 with "Q1 What Is Collaboration?"
In Practice Boxes	Each chapter includes two boxes. One asks you to apply the chapter's topic in a business situation. The second asks you to find innovative applications of systems or technology.	Transfer knowledge gained from the chapter to a practical business problem. Practice innovation.	Chapter 9, Business Intelligence in Practice, p. 332. Chapter 4, Microsoft Surface, p. 114.
Active Review	Provides a set of activities for you to perform to demonstrate you are able to answer the primary questions addressed by the chapter.	After reading the chapter, use the Active Review to check your comprehension. Use for class and exam preparation.	Chapter 2 Active Review, p. 56
Using Your Knowledge	These exercises ask you to take your new knowledge one step further and apply it to a practice problem.	Tests your critical thinking skills.	Question 1–6, pp. 85–86
Collaboration Exercises and Cases	These exercises and cases ask you to collaborate with a group of fellow students, using collaboration tools introduced in Chapter 2, on questions relating to the In Practice features in the chapter.	Give you practice in working with colleagues toward a stated goal.	Questions 1 and 2, pages 178 and 179

RESOURCE	DESCRIPTION	BENEFIT	EXAMPLE
Application Exercises	These exercises ask you to solve situations using spreadsheet (Excel) or database (Access) applications.	Helps develop your computer skills.	Exercise 1, p. 285; Exercise 2, p. 285
Case Studies	Each chapter includes a case study at the end of the chapter. Also, two additional case studies appear at the end of each part.	Requires you to apply newly acquired knowledge to real situations.	Case Study 7, The Brose Group, p. 286; Case Study 3-2, Laguna Tools, p. 377.
International Dimension	Each part (a sequence of three chapters) includes a discussion of the international aspects of the topics addressed in the part.	Understand the international implications and applications of the chapters' content.	International Dimension, Part 3, page 368.
Companion Website	Includes Self-Study Quizzes for each chapter and a Glossary. You will receive automatic feedback upon submitting each quiz.	Helps you cement your understanding of the material in the text.	*www.prenhall.com/kroenke*
Videos	(1) "Dee's Dilemma" presents six short episodes dealing with a marketing manager's challenge in creating a sales force blog. (2) Author Video Tutorials, in which David Kroenke further explains selected concepts from the chapters.	(1) Entertainingly demonstrates the need for all business professionals to understand technology in organizations. (2) Expands and relates chapter material and helps you develop deeper conceptual understanding of the chapter.	*www.prenhall.com/kroenke*
MyMISLab	A student and instructor portal that contains an Online Microsoft Office 2007 tutorial, SharePoint collaboration tools and assignments, a class-testing program tied to AACSB standards, and classroom and tutorial videos.	Expands the classroom experience with valuable hands-on activities and tools.	*www.mymislab.com*

Using MIS

second edition

Using MIS

David M. Kroenke
University of Washington

Upper Saddle River, New Jersey

Library of Congress Cataloging-in-Publication Data
Kroenke, David.
Using MIS / David M. Kroenke.—2nd ed.
p. cm.
Includes bibliographical references and index.
ISBN 978-0-13-813248-4 (pbk. : alk. paper)
1. Management information systems. I. Title.
HD30.213.K76 2008
658.4'038011—dc22
200704801

AVP/Editor-in-Chief: David Parker
AVP/Executive Editor: Bob Horan
VP/Director of Development: Steve Deitmer
Development Editor: Ann Torbert
Assistant Editor: Kelly Loftus
Media Project Manager: Cathi Profitko
Marketing Manager: Anne Howard
Marketing Assistant: Susan Osterlitz
Senior Managing Editor: Judy Leale
Associate Managing Editor: Suzanne DeWorken
Permissions Project Manager: Charles Morris
Senior Operations Specialist: Arnold Vila
Operations Specialist: Michelle Klein
Art Director: Kathy Mrozek
Interior Design: Kathy Mrozek
Cover Design: Kathy Mrozek, Ilze Lemesis
Cover Illustration/Photo: Shutterstock and iStockphoto
Director, Image Resource Center: Melinda Patelli
Manager, Rights and Permissions: Zina Arabia
Manager: Visual Research: Beth Brenzel
Manager, Cover Visual Research & Permissions: Karen Sanatar
Image Permission Coordinator: Richard Rodrigues
Photo Researcher: Nancy Tobin
Composition: Integra Software Services
Full-Service Project Management: BookMasters, Inc.
Printer/Binder: Quebecor World Versailles
Typeface: 10/12 Utopia

Credits and acknowledgments borrowed from other sources and reproduced, with permission, in this textbook appear on appropriate page within text.

Pearson Education LTD.
Pearson Education Singapore, Pte. Ltd
Pearson Education, Canada, Ltd
Pearson Education–Japan
Pearson Education Australia PTY, Limited
Pearson Education North Asia Ltd
Pearson Educación de Mexico, S.A. de C.V.
Pearson Education Malaysia, Pte. Ltd

10 9 8 7 6 5 4 3 2 1
ISBN-10: 0-13-813248-8
ISBN-13: 978-0-13-813248-4

Dedicated to Peter Snell,
a warm and gracious colleague, who is greatly missed

Brief Contents

Defines MIS, describes how MIS relates to you as a future business professional, and explains what you should learn in the course.

Explains the nature of collaboration, describes the use of collaboration tools, and explains how collaboration pertains to decision making, problem solving, and project management.

Describes reasons why organizations create and use information systems: to gain competitive advantage, solve problems, and support decisions.

Three chapters focus on key components of IT.

This chapter appendix discusses another type of network—internets—and explains how the Internet works.

Discusses IS within organizations, including functional and cross-functional systems.

Discusses IS among organizations, particularly e-commerce and supply chain systems.

Describes business intelligence and knowledge management, including reporting systems, data mining, and knowledge management systems.

Describes the processes for developing information systems.

Describes the role, structure, and function of the IS department; the role of the CIO and CTO; outsourcing; and related topics.

Describes organizational response to information security: security threats, policy, and safeguards.

Contents

Why MIS?

We begin this text with three introductory chapters. Chapter 1 defines MIS and describes how MIS relates to your future career as a business professional.

Chapter 2 discusses information systems for collaboration and presents knowledge that you can use immediately for team projects while in school. Finally, Chapter 3 explains how organizations use information systems to gain a competitive advantage and to improve business processes.

Before proceeding, reflect on the title of this text: *Using MIS*. Our goal is to help you learn to *use* information systems to accomplish your personal goals as a business professional and to accomplish the goals of the organizations in which you work. As you read, keep in mind that it is not enough just to learn the meanings of the terms presented in this text; you also need to learn how to successfully apply them to situations that will arise in your professional career.

1 MIS and You

STUDY QUESTIONS

Q1 What is MIS?

Q2 What should you learn from this class?

Q3 How can you use the five-component framework?

Q4 What is information?

Q5 What are the characteristics of good information?

Q6 What is the difference between information technology and information systems?

Q7 How can you enjoy this class?

Meet Kevin Hamilton

My career high:
Being hired as an IS graduate by Procter & Gamble.

My favorite business book:
Influence: The Psychology of Persuasion, by Robert Cialdini.

My very first job:
A Lotus Notes Certified Developer, where I created an interactive Web site used to collect and disseminate worldwide market measurement information.

My hero:
People who overcome difficult circumstances . . . such as working single mothers who put themselves through school or any poverty-level individuals who overcome structural, cultural, and even institutional disadvantages to succeed.

Kevin Hamilton graduated with a degree in information systems from the College of Business at the University of Texas, Austin, in 1999. He worked the next five years for Procter & Gamble in a variety of positions, initially as a Lotus Notes developer and then as an information systems manager on sales teams that supported major P&G customers such as K-mart and Fleming Distribution. He also splits his time at P&G working as a market research manager for the sales teams. After five years at P&G, he moved to Clorox, where he worked as the Marketing Information and Analytics Solutions manager for the company. He left Clorox to enter the MBA program at the University of Michigan, where he now studies corporate strategy and business economics and the use of information systems technology to help organizations achieve their strategic goals. At the time of this interview (June 2007), Kevin was completing a summer internship with Diamond Management and Technology Consultants, a firm that operates on the "intersection of business and technology."

On the need for this class:

"Why do future business professionals need this class? Well, in 2007 and beyond, every significant advance in business will involve technology. Whether you want to make healthy food faster, or design and build greener cars, or reduce costs in the supply chain, those opportunities will involve technology, and most will involve information systems in one form or another. Executives need to understand, recognize, and fully appreciate the power of technology—how it drives information flow and management and that it has become a key driver for revenue and margin improvement.

"Today, too many executives do not understand technology and, even worse, don't understand the importance of its role in business strategy. They are forced to trust the advice of others, and they may not know whom to trust. I think that's why companies make so many poor, in fact stupid, IS investments. Any business person who does understand the value of technology, and who knows enough to gauge the expertise of others, will have a competitive advantage. Knowledge of information systems is part of the core competency of any business professional today."

On future opportunities:

"The cost of data storage and data communications is so low, essentially free, that it is possible to move massive amounts of data around the world. Not just structured data, like order and shipment documents, but unstructured data, like voice and video. The result has been an enormous increase in globalization. With cheap data communication technologies, organizations collaborate across a broad spectrum of companies, people, opportunities, and cultures.

"Because of globalization, organizations can take advantage of low costs, worldwide. Developed countries like the United States just can't compete with routine products and skills. Anything that can be commoditized will go to the cheapest vendor, including routine white-collar work like preparing tax returns. If it's routine, it can be done at the cheapest source.

A mistake I wish I hadn't made:
As a kid from a poor home, I didn't understand the difficulty of college and the need for studying. I received a 1.6 GPA my first semester. Twelve years later, I still feel the ramifications. Lesson: Knock the work out of the park the first time, and life gets much easier after that.

What drives me:
Never again living paycheck to paycheck. Disproving the stereotype that African American men are only athletes, criminals, or rappers.

My motto:
Make it happen.

My pet peeve(s):
Being late for appointments. People interrupting me while I'm speaking.

Kevin Hamilton

"To compete, U.S. companies and workers must provide value to justify their relative high cost. I think innovation and service are the keys. If you and your organization are innovating, if you're developing new technologies or new ways of using new technologies, you can compete in the global workplace. Also, if you provide a nonroutine professional service, if you can apply your personal intellectual capital to emerging business opportunities, then you can compete."

On a career in information systems:

"I chose information systems because I could get a broad education in business—we had at least two courses in every business discipline—as well as technical knowledge about information systems.

"That background served me well. While I started in a technical position as a Lotus Notes developer, having a broad knowledge of business allowed me to be selected for jobs that required business knowledge. In my case, it was the combination of IS and marketing. At P&G, which by the way is a great company, I was the IS representative on a sales team. I served as the bridge between the P&G IT organization and the IT departments of customers like K-mart. At the same time, I was also a bridge between sales and marketing professionals on our team and the IT personnel in both companies.

"Information systems professionals work on a continuum between the poles of technology and business management. I started closer to technology and as my career advanced, I became less technical and more oriented to business. It helps to have a technical background, though. I can manage technical people because I know their issues, they know I understand their perspectives, what they're dealing with, and they trust me more because of that.

"There's such a wide breadth of career opportunities in IS. You can work in IS infrastructure, managing networks; you can build new information systems; as an IT-savvy business analyst, you can help business managers find innovative ways to accomplish their goals. During a career, you can do all of these and much more.

"In fact, you can do them all in a week. This past Monday, I met with the VP of marketing to determine what she wants to accomplish. On Tuesday, I met with the manager of Web development to see how we might go about meeting her needs. On Friday, I needed to bring all of that together in a project proposal for non-IT management. It's incredibly interesting."

On preparation for a future career:

"How would I advise someone to prepare for a career in business? Work on your 'soft' skills. Learn to get along, to be able to connect with different types of people. Be able to talk effectively with senior management in the morning and with junior developers in the afternoon. Be malleable. Understand what drives someone, what they want, what incentives they respond to. Business is the closest thing to politics. It's all about people and influence."

On IS as a major:

"Would I advise a student to become an IS major? It depends on what you want to do. I believe it's one of the best degrees because it's so broad-based. It sets you up for just about any career in business.

"You can start as a technical person, and later move into another part of the business. Unlike accounting or finance, where it's rare to leave your discipline, IS professionals can move among business disciplines. You might work in finance on one project and marketing on the next. Granted is not as simple as saying, 'OK, today I want to work on a brand-marketing campaign,' but the background in MIS allows for choice and flexibility. Three, four, or five years out you might discover that you really want to specialize in supply chain operations. If so, your knowledge of IS and your broadly based business background will open that door and set you up to succeed."

CHAPTER PREVIEW

If you are like most students, you have no clear idea of what your MIS class will be about. If someone were to ask you, "What do you study in that class?" you might respond that the class has something to do with computers and maybe computer programming. Beyond that, you might be hard-pressed to say more. You might add, "Well, it has something to do with computers in business," or maybe, "We are going to learn to solve business problems with computers using spreadsheets and programs like that."

None of these answers is more than partially correct. So, a good place for us to begin this course—and this book—is to answer the following two questions: What is MIS? And what should you expect to learn in this class?

Q1 What Is MIS?

MIS stands for **management information systems**, which we define as *the development and use of information systems that help businesses achieve their goals and objectives*. This definition has three key elements: *development and use, information systems*, and *business goals and objectives*. Let's consider each, starting first with information systems and their components.

Components of an Information System

A **system** is a group of components that interact to achieve some purpose. As you might guess, an **information system (IS)** is a group of components that interact to produce information. That sentence, although true, raises another question: What are these components that interact to produce information?

Figure 1-1 shows the **five-component framework**—the five fundamental components of an information system: **computer hardware**, **software**,[1] **data**, **procedures**, and **people**. These five components are present in every information system, from the simplest to the most complex. For example, when you use a computer to write a class report, you are using hardware (the computer, storage disk, keyboard, and monitor), software (Word, WordPerfect, or some other word-processing program), data (the words, sentences, and paragraphs in your report), procedures (the methods you use to start the program, enter your report, print it, and save and back up your file), and people (you).

Consider a more complex example, say an airline reservation system. It, too, consists of these five components, even though each one is far more complicated. The hardware consists of dozens or more computers linked together by telecommunications hardware. Further, hundreds of different programs coordinate communications among the computers, and still other programs perform the reservations and related

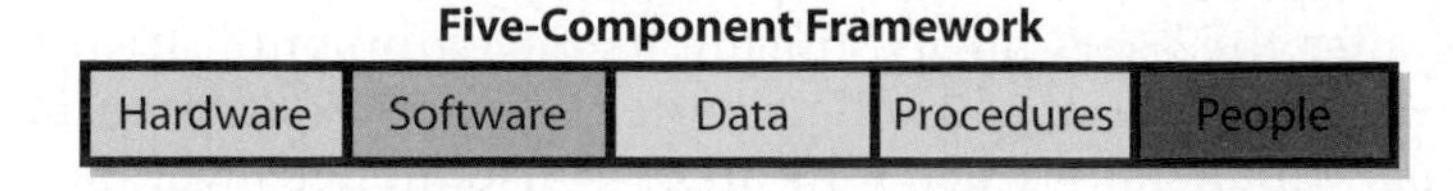

Figure 1-1
Five Components of an Information System

[1]In the past, the term *software* was used to refer to computer components that were not hardware (e.g., programs, procedures, user manuals, etc.). Today, the term *software* is used more specifically to refer only to programs, and that is how we use the term throughout this book.

services. Additionally, the system must store millions upon millions of characters of data about flights, customers, reservations, and other facts. Hundreds of different procedures are followed by airline personnel, travel agents, and customers. Finally, the information system includes people, not only the users of the system, but also those who operate and service the computers, those who maintain the data, and those who support the networks of computers.

The important point here is that the five components in Figure 1-1 are common to all information systems, from the smallest to the largest. As you think about an information system, learn to look for each of these five components. Realize, too, that an information system is not just a computer and a program, but rather an assembly of computers, programs, data, procedures, and people.

As we will discuss later in this chapter, these five components also mean that many different skills are required besides those of hardware technicians or computer programmers when building or using an information system. People are needed who can design the databases that hold the data and who can develop procedures for people to follow. Managers are needed to train and staff the personnel for using and operating the system. We will return to this five-component framework later in this chapter, as well as many other times throughout this book.

Before we move forward, note that we have defined an information system to include a computer. Some people would say that such a system is a **computer-based information system**. They would note that there are information systems that do not include computers, such as a calendar hanging on the wall outside of a conference room that is used to schedule the room's use. Such systems have been used by businesses for centuries. Although this point is true, in this book we focus on computer-based information systems. To simplify and shorten the book, we will use the term *information system* as a synonym for *computer-based information system*.

Development and Use of Information Systems

The next key element in our definition of MIS is the *development and use* of information systems. This course in particular, and MIS in general, are concerned with development because information systems do not pop up like mushrooms after a hard rain; they must be constructed. You may be saying, "Wait a minute, I'm a finance (or accounting, or management) major, not an information-systems major. I don't need to know how to build information systems."

If you are saying that, you are like a lamb headed for fleecing. Throughout your career, in whatever field you choose, information systems will be built for your use. To have an information system that meets your needs, you need to take an *active role* in that system's development. Even if you are not a programmer or a database designer or some other IS professional, you must take an active role in specifying the system's requirements and in helping manage the development project. Without active involvement on your part, it will only be good luck that causes the new system to meet your needs.

To that end, throughout this text we will discuss your role in the development of information systems. In addition, we devote all of Chapter 10 to this important topic. As you read this text and think about information systems, you should begin to ask yourself questions like, "I wonder how that system was constructed?" and "I wonder what roles the users played during its development?" If you start asking yourself these questions now, you will be better prepared to answer them once you start work, when financial, career, and other consequences will depend on your answers.

In addition to development tasks, you will also have important roles to play in the *use* of information systems. Of course, you will need to learn how to employ the system to accomplish your goals. But you will also have important ancillary functions as well. For example, when using an information system, you will have responsibilities for protecting the security of the system and its data. You may also have tasks for backing up data. When the system fails (most do, at some point), you will have tasks to perform while the system is down as well as tasks to accomplish to help recover the system correctly and quickly.

Achieving Business Goals and Objectives

The last part of the definition of MIS is that information systems exist to help businesses achieve their *goals and objectives*. First, realize that this statement hides an important fact: Businesses themselves do not "do" anything. A business is not alive, and it cannot act. It is the people within a business who sell, buy, design, produce, finance, market, account, and manage. So, information systems exist to help people who work in a business to achieve the goals and objectives of that business.

Information systems are not created for the sheer joy of exploring technology. They are not created so that the company can be "modern" or so that the company can claim to be a "new-economy company." They are not created because the information systems department thinks it needs to be created or because the company is "falling behind the technology curve."

This point may seem so obvious that you wonder why we mention it. Every day, however, some business somewhere is developing an information system for the wrong reasons. Right now, somewhere in the world, a company is deciding to create a Web site for the sole reason that "every other business has one." This company is not asking questions like, "What is the purpose of the Web site?" "What is it going to do for us?" or "Are the costs of the Web site sufficiently offset by the benefits?"—but it should be!

Even more serious, somewhere right now is an IS manager who has been convinced by some vendor's sales team or by an article in a business magazine that her company must upgrade to the latest, greatest high-tech Gizmo Version 3.0.[2] This IS manager is attempting to convince her manager that this expensive upgrade is a good idea. We hope that someone somewhere in the company is asking questions like, "What business goal or objective will be served by the investment in Gizmo 3.0?"

Again, MIS is the development and use of information systems that help businesses achieve their goals and objectives. Already you should be realizing that there is much more to this class than buying a computer, writing a program, or working with a spreadsheet.

Q2 What Should You Learn from This Class?

As a business professional in the twenty-first century, you need sufficient MIS knowledge to be an informed and effective consumer of information technology products and services. You need to be able to ask pertinent questions, you need to be able to correctly interpret the responses to your questions, and you need to have the knowledge to manage effectively and to make wise decisions.

You will relate to information systems in three fundamental ways. First, you will be a user of information systems, and for that you need to know enough to

[2]Gizmo 3.0 is a fictitious name. During your career, you will be confronted with many variations of "Gizmo 3.0." It may be the latest version of Windows. Or it may be a new kind of mobile communications technology; a new industry standard, like XML Web Services; or something else. These various gizmos may be just the solution for your situation, or they may be a complete waste of money. Learning how to discriminate one from the other is one of the major goals of this class.

accomplish your work. If you are an accountant, you will need to know how to use a spreadsheet, for example, to create financial statements or other documents. If you are a marketing analyst, you will need to know how to operate business intelligence systems to create the marketing information you will need. You also need to be able to express your requirements to IS professionals who will build new information systems for you.

Second, you may be a manager of a department, and in that role you will need to know enough to ensure that the people who work for you have the systems they need to accomplish their work. When new information systems are developed, you need to know how to ensure that the requirements of your department are considered appropriately. You also need to be able to judge the quality of the work that IS personnel produce on behalf of your department.

Finally, as Kevin Hamilton says in his interview, you need to be able to think strategically about information systems. How can information systems be used in new and innovative ways to accomplish the strategic goals of your organization? If your company chooses to be the lowest-cost widget vendor, you need to be able to actively and effectively participate in discussions about how information systems can play a role.

You will learn many new terms in this class. Such learning is fine, as far as it goes, but you need to go beyond basic definitions. For example, you will learn that a *CRM* is a customer relationship management system. But, you need to know how such a system will relate to you in, say, marketing or operations. You need to understand what responsibilities you have in developing such a system and to be able to consider how your current CRM could be improved to better accomplish your organization's strategy.

Innovation is such an important topic that each chapter contains an Innovation in Practice *box. Callouts like this one will remind you to stop and read that content. The* Innovation in Practice *box on page 9 discusses cognitive skills needed for innovation.*

Figure 1-2 presents the outline of this text. Note that the text consists of four parts of three chapters each. The parts address *why, what, who,* and *how*, respectively. Figure 1-2 shows the key questions addressed by each part. Again, for each topic, you need to know not just the definitions, but also how to use the knowledge to be a better manager and to find innovative ways of accomplishing your organization's goals and objectives.

Summary of MIS Course Content

	Knowledge Category	Key Questions	Location in Text
Why?	Why do we need information systems?	• What is the purpose of an information system? • How can you use, right now, information systems for collaboration? • How do organizations gain a competitive advantage with information systems?	Chapters 1, 2, 3
What?	What is the essential technology?	• How do organizations budget for computers? • What is the function of DBMS? • How does the Internet work?	Chapters 4, 5, 6
Who?	Who uses information systems?	• How do organizations use IS inside the organization? • How do organizations use IS across organizations? • How do information systems help decision makers?	Chapters 7, 8, 9
How?	How are information systems developed and managed?	• What process should be used to develop information systems? • How are IS resources managed? • How should security be managed?	Chapters 10, 11, 12

Figure 1-2
Summary of MIS Course Content

 INNOVATION IN PRACTICE

WORK SKILLS FOR THE 21ST CENTURY

> Rapid technological change and increased international competition place the spotlight on the skills and preparation of the workforce, particularly the ability to adapt to changing technologies and shifting product demand. Shifts in the nature of business organizations . . . favor strong nonroutine cognitive skills, such as abstract reasoning, problem-solving, communication, and collaboration.
>
> Lynn A. Karoly and Constantijn W. A. Panis, *The 21st Century at Work* (RAND Corporation, 2004), p. xiv.

The RAND Corporation is a think tank located in Santa Monica, California. For more than 60 years, RAND has published innovative and groundbreaking ideas, including the original design for the Internet. The RAND report quoted here predicts the shape of the future workplace and describes the skills required for workers in the twenty-first century.

According to these RAND analysts, demand will be strong for those who possess strong **nonroutine cognitive skills**, including abstract reasoning, problem-solving, communication, and collaboration. To succeed, workers will need to be comfortable with ambiguity and be willing to take risks and to experiment.

Much of your education has not prepared you for such work. If you are like many students, you are most comfortable with assignments that have definite answers like, "The train will arrive at the train station at 3:15 PM." But, according to Karoly and Panis, the question to which that statement is an answer is the sort of question that can be "solved" using a routine method. Such questions can be shipped via the global economy to a location where someone working for a very low wage can provide answers.

Instead, to justify your relatively high labor rate, you will need to answer questions like, "How can we use the Web to increase sales to teenagers in Eastern European countries?" or "How can we use information systems to improve supply chain efficiency and reduce our raw materials inventory by 15 percent?" These kinds of questions require communication, collaboration, willingness to experiment, and nonroutine thinking. Furthermore, the report continues:

> . . . technological change is expected to continue to propel demand for highly skilled workers who can develop the new technologies and bring them to market and who can exploit the new technologies in the production of goods and services." (Ibid., p. xviii).

As a business major, you are unlikely to develop new technologies, but you are very likely to use new technology in novel ways. Jeff Bezos did not invent the Internet, but he used Internet technology to create Amazon.com. He *exploited* Internet technology, and you will be given many opportunities to exploit new technology as well.

You need to become comfortable with ambiguity. You need to learn to think creatively to exploit technology in new ways. You need to be able to communicate and collaborate and be willing to experiment in ill-defined situations.

To help you learn these critical skills, each chapter of this book has a boxed feature titled *Innovation in Practice*, which presents ideas for the innovative application of the chapter's contents. Each box is linked to a collaborative exercise at the end of the chapter. *The related exercise for this chapter is Collaboration Exercise 1, found on page 25.*

Q3 How Can You Use the Five-Component Framework?

The five-component framework in Figure 1-1 can help guide your learning and thinking about IS, both now and in the future. To understand this framework better, first note in Figure 1-3 (next page) that these five components are symmetrical. The outermost components, hardware and people, are both actors; they can take actions. The software and procedure components are both sets of instructions: Software is instruction for hardware, and procedures are instructions for people. Finally, data is the bridge between the computer side on the left and the human side on the right.

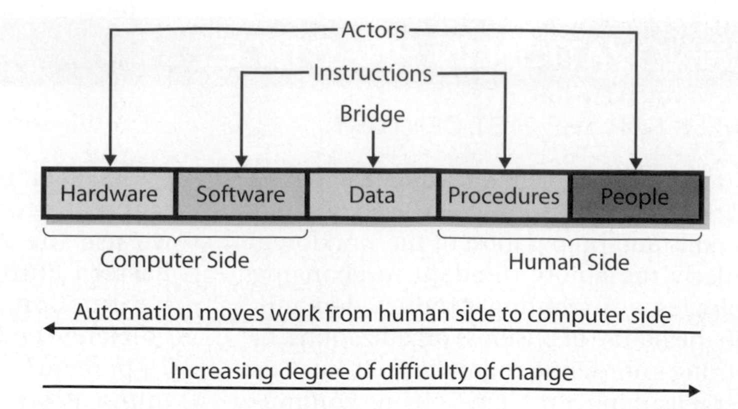

Figure 1-3
Characteristics of the Five Components

Now, when we automate a business process, we take work that people are doing by following procedures and move it so that computers will do that work, following instructions in the software. Thus, the process of automation is a process of moving work from the right side of Figure 1-3 to the left.

The Most Important Component—YOU

You are part of every information system that you use. When you consider the five components of an information system, the last component, *people*, includes you. Your mind and your thinking are not merely *a* component of the information systems you use, they are *the most important* component.

Consider an example. Suppose you have the perfect information system, one that can predict the future. No such information system exists, but assume for this example that it does. Now suppose that on December 14, 1966, your perfect information system tells you that the next day, Walt Disney will die. Say you have $50,000 to invest; you can either buy Disney stock or you can short it (an investment technique that will net you a positive return if the stock value decreases). Given your perfect information system, how do you invest?

Before you read on, think about this question. If Walt Disney is going to die the next day, will the stock go up or down? Most students assume that the stock will go down, so they short it, on the theory that the loss of the founder will mean a dramatic drop in the share price.

Each of the chapters in this text contains a Problem-Solving Guide *that presents ideas from cognitive science and applies them to business situations. We discuss thinking skills in an MIS book because improving your thinking improves the quality of every information system that you use. The first* Problem-Solving Guide, *on page 20, asks you to think about perspectives and points of view.*

In fact, the next day, the value of Disney stock increased substantially. Why? The market viewed Walt Disney as an artist; once he died, he would no longer be able to create more art. Thus, the value of the existing art would increase because of scarcity, and the value of the corporation that owned that art would increase as well.

Here's the point: Even if you have the perfect information system, if you do not know what to do with the information that it produces, you are wasting your time and money. The *quality of your thinking* is a large part of the quality of the information system. Substantial cognitive research has shown that although you cannot increase your basic IQ, you can dramatically increase the quality of your thinking. You cannot change the computer in your brain, so to speak, but you can change the way you have programmed your brain to work.

High-Tech Versus Low-Tech Information Systems

Information systems differ in the amount of work that is moved from the human side (people and procedures) to the computer side (hardware and programs). For example, consider two different versions of a customer support information system: A system that consists only of a file of email addresses and an email program is a very low-tech system. Only a small amount of work has been moved from the human side to the computer side. Considerable human work is required to determine when to send which emails to which customers.

In contrast, a customer support system that keeps track of the equipment that customers have and the maintenance schedules for that equipment and then automatically generates email reminders to customers is a higher-tech system. This simply means that more work has been moved from the human side to the computer side. The computer is providing more services on behalf of the humans.

Often, when considering different information systems alternatives, it will be helpful to consider the low-tech versus high-tech alternatives in light of the amount of work that is being moved from people to computers.

Understanding New Information Systems

The five-component framework can also be used when learning about new systems. When in the future some vendor pitches the need for a new technology to you, think about the five components. What new hardware will you need? What programs will you need to license? What databases and other data must you create? What procedures will need to be developed for both use and administration of the information system? And finally, what will be the impact of the new technology on people? Which jobs will change? Who will need training? How will the new technology affect morale? Will you need to hire new people? Will you need to reorganize?

Components Ordered by Difficulty and Disruption

Finally, as you consider the five components keep in mind that Figure 1-3 shows them in order of ease of change and the amount of organizational disruption. It is usually a simple matter to order new hardware and install it. Obtaining or developing new programs is more difficult. Creating new databases or changing the structure of existing databases is still more difficult. Changing procedures, requiring people to work in new ways, is even more difficult. Finally, changing personnel responsibilities and reporting relationships and hiring and terminating employees are both very difficult and very disruptive to the organization.

The Ethics Guide *in each chapter of this book considers the ethics of informations systems use. These guides challenge you to think deeply about ethical standards, and they provide for some interesting discussions with classmates. The* Ethics Guide *on page 14 considers the ethics of using information that is not intended for you.*

Q4 What Is Information?

Using the discussions in the last two sections, we can now define an information system as an assembly of hardware, software, data, procedures, and people that interact to produce information. The only term left undefined in that definition is *information*, and we turn to it next.

Definitions Vary

Information is one of those fundamental terms that we use every day but that turns out to be surprisingly difficult to define. Defining information is like defining words such as *alive* and *truth*. We know what those words mean, we use them with each other without confusion, but nonetheless, they are difficult to define.

In this text, we will avoid the technical issues of defining information and will use common, intuitive definitions instead. Probably the most common definition is that **information** is knowledge derived from data, whereas *data* is defined as recorded facts or figures. Thus, the facts that employee James Smith earns $17.50 per hour and that Mary Jones earns $25.00 per hour are *data*. The statement that the average hourly wage of all employees in the Garden Department is $22.37 per hour is *information*. Average wage is knowledge that is derived from the data of individual wages.

Another common definition is that *information is data presented in a meaningful context*. The fact that Jeff Parks earns $10.00 per hour is data.[3] The statement that Jeff Parks earns less than half the average hourly wage of the Garden Department, however, is information. It is data presented in a meaningful context.

Another definition of information that you will hear is that *information is processed data*, or sometimes, *information is data processed by summing, ordering, averaging, grouping, comparing, or other similar operations*. The fundamental idea of this definition is that we do something to data to produce information.

There is yet a fourth definition of information, which is presented in the *Problem-Solving Guide* on page 20. There, information is defined as *a difference that makes a difference*.

For the purposes of this text, any of these definitions of information will do. Choose the definition of information that makes sense to you. The important point is that you discriminate between data and information. You also may find that different definitions work better in different situations.

Information Is Subjective

Consider the definition that information is data presented in a meaningful context. What exactly is a *meaningful context?* Clearly, context varies from person to person. If I manage the Garden Department and you are the CEO, our contexts differ. To me, the average hourly wage of the Garden Department is information. To you, it is a data point—the average hourly wage of employees in one of your departments. To you, as CEO, information would be the average hourly wage of all employees in all departments, a list of all departmental averages presented in ascending order, or some other arrangement of the average wages in the context of the entire company.

Sometimes you will hear this same idea expressed as, "One person's information is another person's data." This statement simply means that information in one person's context is just a data point in another person's context. All of us have experienced this phenomenon one time or another when we excitedly report something to another person, only to have them suppress a yawn and say, "Yeah, so what?"

Context changes occur in information systems when the output of one system feeds a second system—a process illustrated in Figure 1-4. For example, suppose an information system in the manufacturing department produces a summary of the day's activity as its information. That summary is input to the general ledger system in the accounting

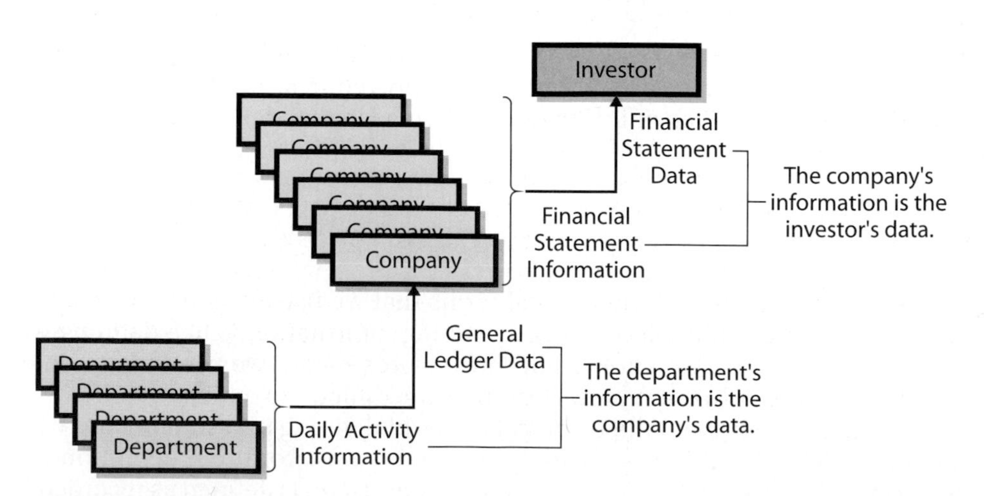

Figure 1-4
One User's Information Is Another User's Data

[3]Actually the word *data* is plural; to be correct we should use the singular form *datum* and say "The fact that Jeff Parks earns $10 per hour is a datum." The word *datum*, however, sounds pedantic and fussy, and we will avoid it in this text.

department, where the summary is just another data point. The general ledger system takes inputs from manufacturing, sales, accounts receivable, accounts payable, and so forth and transforms those data into the information that it produces, such as the monthly balance sheet and income statement. Those financial statements go to investors, where they become data points in the portfolios of the investors.

The bottom line is that information is always understood in a context, and that context varies from one user to another. Therefore, information is always subjective.

Q5 What Are the Characteristics of Good Information?

All information is not equal: Some information is better than other information. Figure 1-5 lists the characteristics of good information.

Accurate

First, good information is **accurate**. Good information is based on correct and complete data, and it has been processed correctly as expected. Accuracy is crucial; managers must be able to rely on the results of their information systems. The IS function can develop a bad reputation in the organization if a system is known to produce inaccurate information. In such a case, the information system becomes a waste of time and money as users develop work-arounds to avoid the inaccurate data.

A corollary to this discussion is that you, a future user of information systems, ought not to rely on information just because it appears in the context of a Web page, a well-formatted report, or a fancy query. It is sometimes hard to be skeptical of information delivered with beautiful, active graphics. Do not be misled. When you begin to use an information system, be skeptical. Cross-check the information you are receiving. After weeks or months of using a system, you may relax. Begin, however, with skepticism.

Timely

Good information is **timely**—produced in time for its intended use. A monthly report that arrives 6 weeks late is most likely useless. The information arrives long after the decisions have been made that needed that information. An information system that tells you not to extend credit to a customer after you have shipped the goods is unhelpful and frustrating. Notice that timeliness can be measured against a calendar (6 weeks late) or against events (before we ship).

When you participate in the development of an IS, timeliness will be part of the requirements you will ask for. You need to give appropriate and realistic timeliness needs. In some cases, developing systems that provide information in near real time is much more difficult and expensive than producing information a few hours later.

- **Accurate**
- **Timely**
- **Relevant**
  - To context
  - To subject
- **Just sufficient**
- **Worth its cost**

Figure 1-5
Characteristics of Good Information

Ethics

GUIDE

Ethics of Misdirected Information Use

Consider the following situations:

Situation A: Suppose you are buying a condo and you know that at least one other party is bidding against you. While agonizing over your best strategy, you stop at a local Starbucks. As you sip your latte, you overhear a conversation at the table next to yours. Three people are talking loudly enough that it is difficult to ignore them, and you soon realize that they are the real estate agent and the couple who is competing for the condo you want. They are preparing their offer. Should you listen to their conversation? If you do, do you use the information you hear to your advantage?

Situation B: Consider the same situation from a different perspective—instead of overhearing the conversation, suppose you receive that same information in an email. Perhaps an administrative assistant at the agent's office confuses you and the other customer and mistakenly sends you the terms of the other party's offer. Do you read that email? If so, do you use the information that you read to your advantage?

Situation C: Suppose that you sell computer software. In the midst of a sensitive price negotiation, your customer accidentally sends you an internal email that contains the maximum amount that the customer can pay for your software. Do you read that email? Do you use that information to guide your negotiating strategy? If your customer discovers that the email may have reached you and asks, "Did you read my email?" how do you answer?

Situation D: Suppose a friend mistakenly sends you an email that contains sensitive personal medical data. Further, suppose you read the email before you know what you're reading and you're embarrassed to learn something very personal that truly is none of your business. Your friend asks you, "Did you read that email?" How do you respond?

Situation E: Finally, suppose that you work as a network administrator and your position allows you unrestricted access to the mailing lists for your company. Assume that you have the skill to insert your email address into any company mailing list without anyone knowing about it. You insert your address into several lists and, consequently, begin to receive confidential email that no one intended for you to see. One of those emails indicates that your best friend's department is about to be eliminated and all of its personnel fired. Do you forewarn your friend? ■

Discussion Questions

1. Answer the questions in situations A and B. Do your answers differ? Does the medium by which the information is obtained make a difference? Is it easier to avoid reading an email than it is to avoid hearing a conversation? If so, does that difference matter?
2. Answer the questions in situations B and C. Do your answers differ? In situation B, the information is for your personal gain; in C, the information is for both your personal and your organization's gain. Does this difference matter? How do you respond when asked if you have read the email?
3. Answer the questions in situations C and D. Do your answers differ? Would you lie in one case and not in the other? Why or why not?
4. Answer the questions in situation E. What is the essential difference between situations A through D and situation E? Suppose you had to justify your behavior in situation E. How would you argue? Do you believe your own argument?
5. In situations A through D, if you access the information you have done nothing illegal. You were the passive recipient. Even for item E, although you undoubtedly violated your company's employment policies, you most likely did not violate the law. So, for this discussion, assume that all of these actions are legal.
   a. What is the difference between legal and ethical? Look up each term in a dictionary and explain how they differ.
   b. Make the argument that business is competitive, and that if something is legal, then it is acceptable to do if it helps to further your goals.
   c. Make the argument that it is never appropriate to do something unethical.
6. Summarize your beliefs about proper conduct when you receive misdirected information.

If you can get by with information that is a few hours old, say so during the requirements specification phase.

Consider an example. Suppose you work in marketing and you need to be able to assess the effectiveness of new online ad programs. You want an information system that not only will deliver ads over the Web, but that also will enable you to determine how frequently customers click on those ads. Determining click ratios in near real time will be very expensive; saving the data in a batch and processing it some hours later will be much easier and cheaper. If you can live with information that is a day or two old, the system will be easier and cheaper to implement.

Relevant

Information should be **relevant** both to the context and to the subject. Considering context, you, the CEO, need information that is summarized to an appropriate level for your job. A list of the hourly wage of every employee in the company is unlikely to be useful. More likely, you need average wage information by department or division. A list of all employee wages is irrelevant in your context.

Information should also be relevant to the subject at hand. If you want information about short-term interest rates for a possible line of credit, then a report that shows 15-year mortgage interest rates is irrelevant. Similarly, a report that buries the information you need in pages and pages of results is also irrelevant to your purposes.

Just Barely Sufficient

Information needs to be **sufficient** for the purpose for which it is generated, but **just barely so.** We live in an information age; one of the critical decisions that each of us has to make each day is what information to ignore. The higher you rise into management, the more information you will be given, and because there is only so much time, the more information you will need to ignore. So, information should be sufficient, but just barely.

Worth Its Cost

Information is not free. There are costs for developing an information system, costs of operating and maintaining that system, and costs of your time and salary for reading and processing the information the system produces. For information to be **worth its cost**, there must be an appropriate relationship between the cost of information and its value.

Consider an example. What is the value of a daily report of the names of the occupants of a full graveyard? Zero, unless grave robbery is a problem for the cemetery. The report is not worth the time required to read it. It is easy to see the importance of information economics for this silly example. It will be more difficult, however, when someone proposes the Gizmo 3.0 to you. You need to be ready to ask, "What's the value of the information?" "What is the cost?" "Is there an appropriate relationship between value and cost?" Information systems should be subject to the same financial analyses to which other assets are subjected.

Q6 What Is the Difference Between Information Technology and Information Systems?

Information technology and information systems are two closely related terms, but they are different. **Information technology (IT)** refers to the products, methods, inventions, and standards that are used for the purpose of producing information.

As stated in the previous section, an *information system (IS)* is an assembly of hardware, software, data, procedures, and people that produces information.

Information technology drives the development of new information systems. Advances in information technology have taken the computer industry from the days

The Information Systems in Practice *box below discusses types of workers in business organizations, especially symbolic-analytic workers.*

INFORMATION SYSTEMS IN PRACTICE

SYMBOLIC-ANALYTIC WORKERS

In the book *The Work of Nations,*[4] Robert Reich argues that globalization has forced a major change on U.S. corporations in the past 50 years. In the 1950s, U.S. corporations succeeded at the high-volume production of standardized goods and services. Since then, globalization has moved the production of standardized goods and services offshore to lower-cost vendors. According to Reich, ". . . the firms that are surviving and succeeding are shifting from high volume to high value" (p. 82). *High-value firms* are those that produce unique products tailored to particular customer demands, typically in low volume.

Reich identifies three categories of work: routine production services, in-person services, and symbolic-analytic services (p. 174). Workers who provide **routine production services** are employed by high-volume organizations. Such workers require few skills: they need to be able to read and perform simple calculations; they must be reliable and be able to take direction. Because of the low skills required, such jobs pay little, and many of them have moved offshore along with the high-volume production work.

In-person services are jobs that must be provided face-to-face. The tasks, like those of routine production workers, are simple and repetitive; these jobs require workers who can communicate, but otherwise the skills needed are low. Because they are provided in person, such jobs cannot be readily moved offshore. Examples of such jobs are waitresses, janitors, cashiers, hotel workers, house cleaners, and hospital attendants. Demand for such jobs will remain high, but the pay will be low.

Workers in the third category, **symbolic-analytic services**, are required by high-value organizations. They deal with information and apply abstract reasoning. They use these skills to identify customer needs, to determine innovative ways of meeting those needs, to find better ways to accomplish the organization's goals and objectives, and to do other nonroutine tasks. Such jobs need not be performed in person and can be performed offshore using modern communications facilities. However, because of the high value of such work, these jobs need not go to the lowest bidder. Instead, they will be performed by the people most qualified, worldwide.

Reich identifies three types of symbolic-analytic workers: problem-identifiers, problem-solvers, and solution brokers. **Problem-identifiers** process information to determine that something is not as it should be. **Problem-solvers** use technology and other assets to create problem solutions. **Solution brokers** link problem-identifiers with problem-solvers. They understand the underlying domain of the problem and of the solutions and are able to raise money and influence decision makers to create the solution.

These ideas are not abstract, pie-in-the-sky concepts. Reread the interview with Kevin Hamilton and note his statement, "This past Monday, I met with the VP of marketing to determine what she wants to accomplish. On Tuesday, I met with the manager of Web development to see how we might go about meeting her needs. On Friday, I needed to bring all of that together in a project proposal for non-IT management." The VP of marketing is a problem-identifier; she wants to change something about the marketing of her products. The manager of Web development is a problem-solver; he possesses the knowledge and expertise to use a Web-based information system to solve the problem identified by the VP of marketing. Finally, Kevin Hamilton is the solution broker. He is developing the budget, writing the justification, and creating the presentation materials to obtain the resources needed to create the solution.

Because you are reading this book, it is unlikely you want to be a routine production worker or an in-person service provider. Most likely, you want to be a symbolic-analytic worker—a problem-identifier, a problem-solver, or a solution broker.

Each chapter of this book includes a boxed feature, like this one, that explores the use of the chapter's content by symbolic-analytic workers. Each of these boxes continues with a collaborative exercise at the end of the chapter. *The exercise for this chapter, Collaboration Exercise 2, which explores the ways that problem-identifiers, problem-solvers, and solution brokers use information systems, will be found on page 26.*

[4]Robert B. Reich, *The Work of Nations* (New York: Alfred A. Knopf, 1991).

of punched cards to the Internet, and such advances will continue to take the industry to the next stages and beyond.

Moore's Law

Gordon Moore is the cofounder of Intel Corporation, the world's leading manufacturer of computer chips and other computer-related components. In 1965, he said that because of technology improvements in electronic chip design and manufacturing, "The number of transistors per square inch on an integrated chip doubles every 18 months." This observation is known as **Moore's Law**. Moore's prediction has proved generally accurate in the 40 years since it was made.

The density of transistors on a computer chip relates to the speed of the chip, and so you will sometimes hear Moore's Law expressed as, "The speed of a computer chip doubles every 18 months." This is not exactly what Moore said, but it comes close to the essence of his idea.

Dramatic Reduction in Price/Performance Ratio

As a result of Moore's Law, the price/performance ratio of computers has fallen dramatically for years (see Figure 1-6). The result has been that computers have shrunk from multimillion-dollar, room-filling machines in 1968 to $300 small desktop devices in 2007. Along the way, the availability of increased computing power has enabled developments such as laser printers, graphical user interfaces like Windows, high-speed communications, cell phones, PDAs, email, and the Internet.

In March 2003, Moore stated that he expects Moore's Law to hold for at least another 10 years. This means that computers will continue to become faster and cheaper through at least the early years of your career.

No one has been good at predicting what this means. The rapid rise of the Internet surprised even Microsoft cofounder Bill Gates. All we can say is that, because of the decreasing price/performance ratio, information technology will continue to change and improve, information systems will become even more powerful and effective, and businesses will find new ways of using these systems. The result should be further increases in worker productivity.

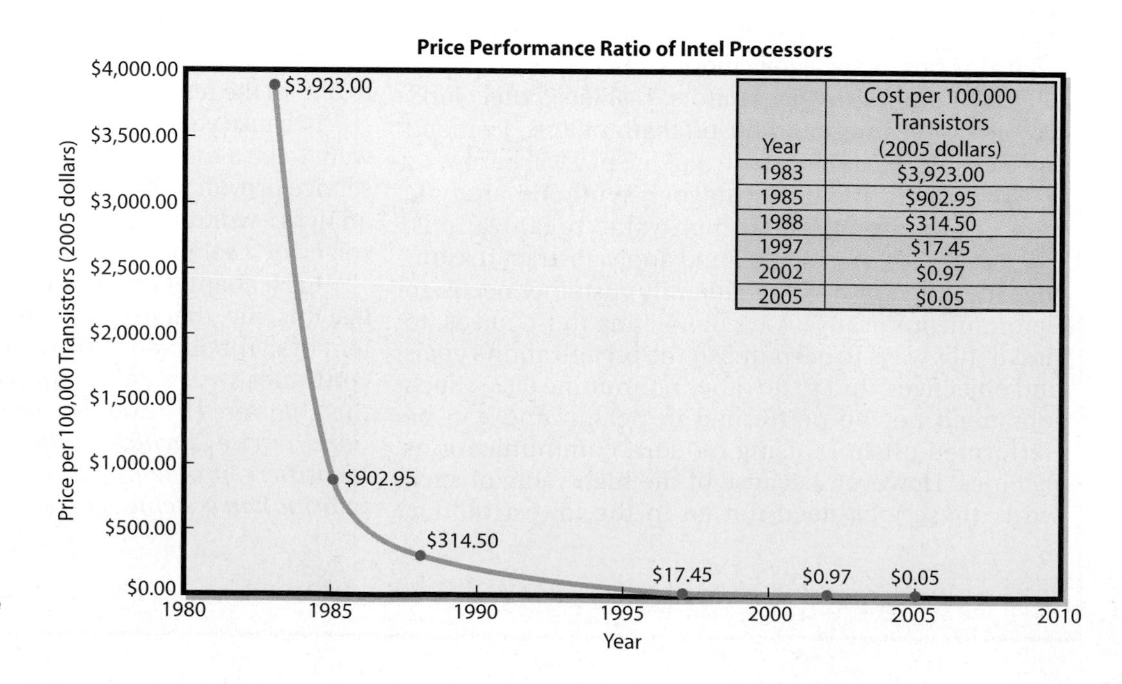

Year	Cost per 100,000 Transistors (2005 dollars)
1983	$3,923.00
1985	$902.95
1988	$314.50
1997	$17.45
2002	$0.97
2005	$0.05

Figure 1-6
Computer Price/Performance Ratio Decreases

All of this means that information systems will increase in importance throughout your career. The knowledge you gain here will benefit you for many, many years to come.

Q7 How Can You Enjoy This Class?

The best way to enjoy this class is to think seriously about it. IT and IS are incredibly important in business today. It will be worth your while to form your own opinions about what you read and to confront the opinions of others. The *Opposing Forces Guides* (another category of guides, that you will find in later chapters) and the *Problem-Solving Guides* will help you do that. In addition, many chapters conclude with an editorial, called a *Reflections Guide,* in which I express my personal ideas about material in the chapter. You may or may not agree with these ideas, but the activity of critically reading and considering them will help you marshall your thoughts and opinions about the chapter material.

Some chapters of this book conclude with an editorial, called the Reflections Guide. *These editorials express my personal ideas about material in the chapter. These ideas are just my opinions; you, the student next to you, and your professor may all disagree with them. The goal of the* Reflections Guide *is to stimulate your thinking about the chapter's contents. See the first of these, on page 22.*

Beyond such critical reading and thinking, the key to enjoying the class is to apply what you are learning to situations and organizations of interest to you. For example, think about the information systems around you. Consider your university's class enrollment system and ask as many questions as you can think of: What hardware, software, data, procedures, and people are involved? Who are the users? What procedures do they follow? How are those people trained? How do you suppose your class enrollment system was developed? Was it constructed just for your university? Was the software written in-house by university employees or was it purchased from vendors? Do other universities use this same system?

What information does the university gain from this system? Of course, the system schedules classes, but what other information does it produce? How could the university use that information in innovative ways? What can the university learn about trends in education? About trends in student goals and objectives? What information can it extract from this system to facilitate planning and budgeting?

Every day you touch dozens of information systems. Begin to ask yourself about the nature of those systems and how they impact you. What, besides the obvious, do they do? At the grocery store, is the information system that interprets the UPC codes on the items that you buy connected to the information system that processes your credit card? If so, could the credit card company refuse to allow you to buy certain items? Would they? Would it be legal if they did? Who owns the data about your grocery store purchases? What keeps the credit card company from selling the fact that you buy lots of ice cream to the Association of Dairy Farmers of America? Could your insurance company raise the premium on your health insurance because you buy lots of calorie-laden foods?

Less controversial, consider the information systems you encounter in the context of your major field of study. For example, if you are studying marketing, how could the marketing department of the grocery store use the purchase data to plan sales? Or how can management use the effectiveness of sales promotions? How can the grocery store use its information systems to control theft?

As you proceed through this class, learn to be curious about the information systems around you. Ask the employees of stores and restaurants what they think about the systems they use. How long have they had their information system? What did they do before it? How well do they like it? The more you apply the knowledge you gain in this class to your life, the more interesting it will be, and the more you will enjoy this class.

Problem-Solving

GUIDE

Understanding Perspectives and Points of View

Every human being speaks and acts from the perspective of a personal point of view. Everything we say or do is based on—or equivalently, is biased by—that point of view. Thus, everything you read in any textbook, including this one, is biased by the author's point of view. The author may think that he is writing an unbiased account of neutral subject material. But no one can write an unbiased account of anything, because we all write from a perspective.

Similarly, your professors speak to you from their points of view. They have experience, goals, objectives, hopes, and fears, and, like all of us, those elements provide a framework from which they think and speak.

Consider the statements in Kevin Hamilton's interview. Now examine the statements in the *Reflections Guide* on page 22. Both of those items contain what is obviously editorial, opinion-oriented material. When you read them, it is easy to recognize that they are written from strongly held points of view and therefore contain personal biases.

But consider statements that are less apparently opinions. For example, consider the following definition of information: "Information is a difference that makes a difference." By this definition, there are many differences, but only those that make a difference qualify as information.

This definition is not obviously an opinion, but it nevertheless was written from a biased perspective. The perspective is just less evident because the statement appears as a definition, not an opinion. But, in fact, it is the definition of information in the opinion of the well-known psychologist Gregory Bateson.

I find his definition informative and useful. It is imprecise, but it is a good guideline, and I have used it to advantage when designing reports and queries for end users. I ask myself, "Does this report show someone a difference that makes a difference to them?" So, I find it a useful and helpful definition.

My colleagues who specialize in quantitative methods, however, find Bateson's definition vapid and useless. They ask, "What does it say?" "How could I possibly use that definition to formalize anything?" or "A difference that makes a difference to what or whom?" Or they say, "I couldn't quantify anything about that definition; it's a waste of time."

And they are right, but so am I, and so was

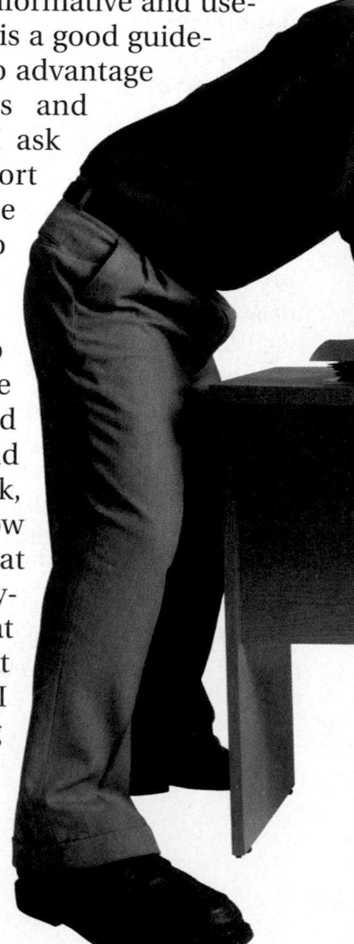

Gregory Bateson. The difference is a matter of perspective, and surprisingly, conflicting perspectives can all be true at the same time.

One last point: Whether it is apparent or not, authors write and professors teach not only from personal perspectives, but also with personal goals. I write this textbook in the hope that you will find the material useful and important and tell your professor that it is a great book so that he will use it again. Whether you (or I) are aware of that fact, it and my other hopes and goals bias every sentence in this book.

Similarly, your professors have hopes and goals that influence what and how they teach. Your professors may want to see light bulbs of recognition on your face, they may want to win the Professor of the Year award, or they may want to gain tenure status in order to be able to do some advanced research in the field. Whatever the case, they, too, have hopes and goals that bias everything they say.

So, as you read this book and as you listen to your professor, ask yourself, "What is her perspective?" and "What are her goals?" Then compare those perspectives and goals to yours. Learn to do this not just with your textbooks and your professors, but with your colleagues as well. When you enter the business world, being able to discern and adapt to the perspectives and goals of those with whom you work will make you much more effective. ■

Discussion Questions

1. Consider the following statement: "The quality of your thinking is the most important component of an information system." Do you agree with this statement? Do you think it is even possible to say that one component is the most important one?
2. This text claims that although it is not possible to increase your IQ, it is possible to improve the quality of your thinking. Do you agree? Whether or not you agree, give three examples that illustrate differences in quality of thinking. They can be all from one person or they can be examples from three different people.
3. Though it does not appear to be so, the statement, "There are five components of an information system: hardware, software, data, procedures, and people" is an opinion based on a perspective. Suppose you stated this opinion to a computer engineer who said, "Rubbish. That's not true at all. The only components that count are hardware and maybe software." Contrast the perspective of the engineer with that of your MIS professor. How do those perspectives influence their opinions about the five-component framework? Which is correct?
4. Consider Bateson's definition, "Information is a difference that makes a difference." How can this definition be used to advantage when designing a Web page? Explain why someone who specializes in quantitative methods might consider this definition to be useless. How can the same definition be both useful and useless?
5. Some students hate open-ended questions. They want questions that have one correct answer, like 7.3 miles per hour. When given a question like that in question 4, a question that has multiple, equally valid answers, some students get angry or frustrated. They want the book or the professor to give them the answer. How do you feel about this matter?
6. Do you think someone can improve the quality of his or her thinking by learning to hold multiple, contradictory ideas in mind at the same time? Or, do you think that doing so just leads to indecisive and ineffective thinking? Discuss this question with some of your friends. What do they think? What are their perspectives?

Reflections

GUIDE

Duller Than Dirt?

Yes, you read that title correctly: This subject can seem duller than dirt. Take the phrase, "development and use of IS in organizations." Read just that phrase, and you start to yawn, wondering, "How am I going to absorb 500+ pages of this?"

Stop and think: Why are you reading this book? Right now in the Sea of Cortez the water is clear and warm, and the swimming and diving are wonderful. You could be kayaking to Isla San Francisco this minute. Or, somewhere in the world, people are skiing. Whether in Aspen, Colorado, or Portillo, Chile, people are blasting through the powder somewhere. You could be one of them, living in a small house with a group of friends, having good times at night. Or, whatever it is that you like to do, you could be doing it right now. So, why are you here, where you are, reading this book? Why aren't you there?

Waking up should be one of your goals while in college. I mean waking up to your life. Ceasing to live according to someone else's plan and beginning to live your own plan. Doing that requires you to become conscious of the choices you make and the consequences they have.

Suppose you take an hour to read your assignment in this book tonight. For a typical person, that is 4,320 heartbeats (72 beats times 60 minutes) that you have used to read this book—heartbeats that you will never have again. Despite the evidence of your current budget, the critical resource for humans is not money, it is time. No matter what we do, we cannot get more of it. Was your reading today worth those 4,320 heartbeats?

For some reason, you chose to major in business. For some reason, you are taking this class, and for some reason, you have been instructed to read this textbook. Now, given that you made a good decision to major in business (and not to kayak in Baja), and given that someone is requiring you to read this text, the question then becomes, "How can you maximize the return on the 4,320 heartbeats you are investing per hour?"

The secret is to personalize the material. At every page, learn to ask yourself, "How does this pertain to me?" "How can I use this material to further my goals?" If you find some topic irrelevant, ask your professor or your classmates what they think. What's this topic for? Why are we reading this? What I am going to do with it later in my career? Why is this worth 1,000 (or whatever) heartbeats?

MIS is all-encompassing. To me that's one of its beauties. Consider the components: hardware, software, data, procedures, and people. Do you want to be an engineer? Then work the hardware component. Do you want to be a programmer? Write software. Do you want to be a practicing philosopher, an applied epistemologist? Learn data modeling. Do you like social systems and sociology? Learn how to design effective group and organizational

procedures. Do you like people? Become an IS trainer or a computer systems salesperson. Do you enjoy management? Learn how to bring all of those disparate elements together.

I've worked in this industry for almost 40 years. The breadth of MIS and the rapid change of technology have kept me fascinated for every one of those years. Further, the beauty of working with intellectual property is that it doesn't weigh very much; you don't wear yourself out moving symbols around. And you do it indoors in a temperature-controlled office. They may even put your name on the door.

So, wake up. Why are you reading this? How can you make it relevant? Jump onto Google and search for MIS careers or some other phrase from this chapter and see what you get. Challenge yourself to find something that is important to you personally, in every chapter.

You just invested 780 heartbeats in reading this editorial. Was it worth it? Keep asking! ■

Discussion Questions

1. Explain what it means to "wake up to your life."
2. Are you awake to your life? How do you know? What can you do once a week to ensure that you are awake to your life?
3. What are your professional goals? Are they yours, or are they someone else's? How do you know?
4. How does this class pertain to your professional goals?
5. How are you going to make the material in in this class interesting?

ACTIVE REVIEW

Use this Active Review to verify that you understand the ideas and concepts that answer the chapter's study questions.

Q1 What is MIS?

Identify the three important phrases in the definition of MIS. Name the five components of an information system. Explain why end users need to be involved in the development of information systems. Explain why it is a misconception to say that organizations do something.

Q2 What should you learn from this class?

Describe three different roles that you will likely have with regard to information systems. Name the role that Kevin Hamilton considers most important. Explain the structure of the 12 chapters in this book. Give two sample questions for each major part.

Q3 How can you use the five-component framework?

Explain the symmetry in the five components of an information system. Show how automation moves work from one side of the five-component structure to the other. Explain how the components are ordered according to difficulty of change and disruption. Name the most important component and state why it is the most important. Use the five-component model to describe the differences between high-tech and low-tech information systems. Explain how you can use the five components when considering new information systems.

Q4 What is information?

State four different definitions of information. Name the one that is your favorite and explain why. Explain how information is subjective; use the example in Figure 1-4 in your answer.

Q5 What are the characteristics of good information?

Create a mnemonic device for remembering the characteristics of good information. Explain why good information must fit each of the characteristics.

Q6 What is the difference between information technology and information systems?

Explain the difference between IT and IS. State Moore's Law and explain its importance to your future career. Explain how the trend in price/performance will impact business during your career.

Q7 How can you enjoy this class?

In your own words, state the purpose of this class. Explain why this class will be important to you during your career. List actions you can take to make this class more interesting to you. Read the *Reflections Guide* on page 22 and answer the questions in that guide.

KEY TERMS AND CONCEPTS

Accurate information 13
Computer hardware 5
Computer-based information system 6
Data 5
Five-component framework 5
Information 11
Information system (IS) 5
Information technology 16
In-person services 17
Just-barely-sufficient information 16
Management information systems (MIS) 5
Moore's Law 16
Nonroutine cognitive skills 9
People 5
Problem-identifiers 17
Problem-solvers 17
Procedures 5
Relevant information 16
Routine production services 17
Software 5
Solution brokers 17
Symbolic-analytic services 17
System 5
Timely information 13
Worth-its-cost information 16

USING YOUR KNOWLEDGE

1. Describe three to five personal goals for this class. None of these goals should include anything about your GPA. Be as specific as possible and make the goals personal to your major, interests, and career aspirations. Assume that you are going to evaluate yourself on these goals at the end of the quarter or semester. The more specific you make these goals, the easier it will be to perform the evaluation. Use Figure 1-2 for guidance.
2. Consider costs of a system in light of the five components: costs to buy and maintain the hardware; costs

to develop or acquire licenses to the software programs and costs to maintain them; costs to design databases and fill them with data; costs of developing procedures and keeping them current; and finally, human costs both to develop and use the system.

a. Over the lifetime of a system, many experts believe that the single most expensive component is people. Does this belief seem logical to you? Explain why you agree or disagree.
b. Consider a poorly developed system that does not meet its defined requirements. The needs of the business do not go away, but they do not conform themselves to the characteristics of the poorly built system. Therefore, something must give. Which component picks up the slack when the hardware and software programs do not work correctly? What does this say about the cost of a poorly designed system? Consider both direct money costs as well as intangible personnel costs.
c. What implications do you, as a future business manager, take from questions (a) and (b)? What does this say about the need for your involvement in requirements and other aspects of systems development? Who eventually will pay the costs of a poorly developed system? Against which budget will those costs accrue?

3. Consider the four definitions of information presented in this chapter. The problem with the first definition, "knowledge derived from data," is that it merely substitutes one word we don't know the meaning of (*information*) for a second word we don't know the meaning of (*knowledge*). The problem with the second definition, "data presented in a meaningful context," is that it is too subjective. Whose context? What makes a context meaningful? The third definition, "data processed by summing, ordering, averaging, etc.," is too mechanical. It tells us what to do, but it doesn't tell us what information is. The fourth definition, "a difference that makes a difference," is vague and unhelpful.

Also, none of these definitions helps us to quantify the amount of information we receive. What is the information content of the statement that every human being has a navel? Zero—you already know that. In contrast, the statement that someone has just deposited $50,000 into your checking account is chock-full of information. So, good information has an element of surprise.

Considering all of these points, answer the following questions:

a. What is information made of?
b. If you have more information, do you weigh more? Why or why not?
c. If you give a copy of your transcript to a prospective employer, is that information? If you show that same transcript to your dog, is it still information? Where is the information?
d. Give your own best definition of information.
e. Explain how you think it is possible that we have an industry called the *information technology industry*, but we have great difficulty defining the word *information*.

4. The text states that information should be worth its cost. Both cost and value can be broken into tangible and intangible factors. *Tangible* factors can be directly measured; *intangible* ones arise indirectly and are difficult to measure. For example, a tangible cost is the cost of a computer monitor; an intangible cost is the lost productivity of a poorly trained employee.

Give five important tangible and five important intangible costs of an information system. Give five important tangible and five important intangible measures of the value of an information system. It it helps to focus your thinking, use the example of the class scheduling system at your university or some other university information system. When determining whether an information system is worth its cost, how do you think the tangible and intangible factors should be considered?

COLLABORATION EXERCISES AND CASES

Collaborate with a group of fellow students on the following exercises.

1. Answer the following questions. Before you begin, consider part j, and if you can think of an innovative way of answering these questions, use it.

a. What is innovation?
b. Does innovation differ from creativity? If so, how?
c. Can people increase their creative ability? If so, how?
d. What is the relationship between creativity and intelligence?
e. Can creativity be measured? If so, how?
f. Is there such a thing as group creativity? Explain why or why not.
g. What work environments are conducive to innovation? What environments hamper innovation?
h. Why are tolerance for ambiguity and willingness to experiment important for innovation?
i. What characteristics of IS make it an especially rich field for innovation?
j. How can you use an innovative process to answer these questions?

2. Develop an answer to the following questions.
   a. Characterize the differences between a high-volume company and a high-value company. Give an example of each.
   b. What kinds of information does a high-volume company need? What kinds are required by a high-value company?
   c. Using your answer to part a and the five-component model, specify how you think the components of an information system vary between high-volume and high-value companies.
   d. Explain how routine production workers, in-person service providers, and symbolic-analytic service providers differ.
   e. What kinds of information do routine production and in-person service providers need? What kinds of information do symbolic-analytic service providers need?
   f. Using your answer to part e and the five-component model, specify how you think the components of an information system vary between routine production and in-person workers and symbolic-analytic workers.
   g. Explain how problem-identifiers, problem-solvers, and solution brokers differ.
   h. How do the information requirements vary among problem-identifiers, problem-solvers, and solution brokers?
   i. Symbolic-analytic workers compete in a global marketplace. Explain how information and information systems can be used to give a competitive advantage to problem-identifiers, problem-solvers, and solution brokers.

APPLICATION EXERCISES

1. The spreadsheet in Microsoft Excel file **Ch1Ex1** contains records of employee activity on special projects. Open this workbook and examine the data that you find in the three spreadsheets it contains. Assess the accuracy, relevancy, and sufficiency of this data to the following people and problems.
   a. You manage the Denver plant, and you want to know how much time your employees are spending on special projects.
   b. You manage the Reno plant, and you want to know how much time your employees are spending on special projects.
   c. You manage the Quota Computation project in Chicago, and you want to know how much time your employees have spent on that project.
   d. You manage the Quota Computation project for all three plants, and you want to know the total time employees have spent on your project.
   e. You manage the Quota Computation project for all three plants, and you want to know the total labor cost for all employees on your project.
   f. You manage the Quota Computation project for all three plants, and you want to know how the labor-hour total for your project compares to the labor-hour totals for the other special projects.
   g. What conclusions can you make from this exercise?

2. The database in the Microsoft Access file **Ch1Ex2** contains the same records of employee activity on special projects as in Application Exercise 1. Before proceeding, open that database and view the records in the EmployeeHours table.
   a. Seven queries have been created that process this data in different ways. Using the criteria of accuracy, relevancy, and sufficiency, select the single query that is most appropriate for the information requirements in Application Exercise 1, Parts a–f. If no query meets the need, explain why.
   b. What conclusions can you make from this exercise?
   c. Comparing your experiences on these two projects, what are the advantages and disadvantages of spreadsheets and databases?

CASE STUDY 1

Requirements Creep at the IRS

The United States Internal Revenue Service (IRS) serves more people in the United States than any other public or private institution. Each year it processes over 200 million tax returns from more than 180 million individuals and more than 45 million businesses. The IRS itself employs more than 100,000 people in over 1,000 different sites. In a typical year, it adapts to more than 200 tax law changes and services more than 23 million telephone calls.

Amazingly, the IRS accomplishes this work using information systems that were designed and developed in the 1960s. In fact, some of the computer programs that process tax returns were first written in 1962. In the mid-1990s, the IRS set out on a Business System Modernization (BSM) project that would replace this antiquated system with modern technology and capabilities. However, by 2003 it was clear that this project was a disaster. Billions of dollars had been spent on the project, and all major components of the new system were months or years behind schedule.

In 2003, newly appointed IRS commissioner Mark W. Everson called for an independent review of all BSM projects. Systems development experts from the Software Engineering Institute at Carnegie Mellon University and the Mitre Corporation and managers from the IRS examined the project and made a list of factors that contributed to the failure and recommendations for solutions. In their report, the first two causes of failure cited were:

- "There was inadequate business unit ownership and sponsorship of projects. This resulted in unrealistic business cases and continuous project scope 'creep' (gradual expansion of the original scope of the project)."
- "The much desired environment of trust, confidence, and teamwork between the IRS business units, the BSM organization [the team of IRS employees established to manage the BSM project], the Information Technology Services (ITS) [the internal IRS organization that operates and maintains the current information systems], and the Prime [the prime contractor, Computer Sciences Corporation] did not exist. In fact, the opposite was true, resulting in an inefficient working environment and, at times, finger pointing when problems arose."

The BSM team developed the new system in a vacuum. The team did not have the acceptance, understanding, or support for the new system from either the existing IRS business units (the future users of the system) or from the existing ITS staff. Consequently, the BSM team poorly understood the system needs, and that misunderstanding resulted in continual changes in project requirements, changes that occurred after systems components had been designed and developed. Such requirements creep is a sure sign of a mismanaged project and always results in schedule delays and wasted money. In this case, the delays were measured in years and the waste in billions of dollars.

In response to the problems that it identified, the IRS Oversight Board recommended the following two actions:[5]

- "The IRS business units must take direct leadership and ownership of the Modernization program and each of its projects. In particular, this must include defining the scope of each project, preparing realistic and attainable business cases, and controlling scope changes throughout each project's life cycle. . . ."
- "Create an environment of trust, confidence, and teamwork between the business units, the BSM and ITS organizations, and the Prime. . . ."

Sources: IRS Oversight Board, 2003, www.treas.gov/irsob/index.html; "For the IRS, There's No EZ Fix," *CIO Magazine,* April 1, 2004.

Questions

1. Why did the Oversight Board place leadership and ownership of the Modernization program on the business units? Why did it not place these responsibilities on the ITS organization?
2. Why did the Oversight Board place the responsibility for controlling scope changes on the business units? Why was this responsibility not given to the BSM? To ITS? To Computer Sciences Corporation?
3. The second recommendation is a difficult assignment, especially considering the size of the IRS and the complexity of the project. How does one go about creating "an environment of trust, confidence, and teamwork?"

   To make this recommendation more comprehensible, translate it to your local university. Suppose, for example, that your College of Business embarked on a program to modernize its computing facilities, including computer labs, and the computer network facilities used for teaching, including Internet-based distance learning. Suppose that the Business School dean created a committee like the BSM that hired a vendor to create the new computing facilities for the college. Suppose further that the committee proceeded without any involvement of the faculty, staff, students, or the existing computer support department. Finally, suppose that the project was one year late, had spent $400,000, was not nearly finished, and that the vendor complained that the requirements kept changing.

   Now, assume that you have been given the responsibility of creating "an environment of trust, confidence, and teamwork" among the faculty, staff, other users, the computer support department, and the vendor. How would you proceed?
4. The problem in question 3 involves at most a few hundred people and a few sites. The IRS problem involves 100,000 people and over 1,000 sites. How would you modify your answer to question 3 for a project as large as the IRS's?
5. If the existing system works (which apparently it does), why is the BSM needed? Why fix a system that works?

[5]The report identified more than two problems and made more than two recommendations. See the "Independent Analysis of IRS Business Systems Modernization Special Report" at *www.itsoversightboard.treas.gov.*

2 Information Systems for Collaboration

STUDY QUESTIONS

Q1 What is collaboration?

Q2 How can you use collaboration systems to improve team communication?

Q3 How can you use collaboration systems to manage content?

Q4 How can you use collaboration systems to control workflow?

Q5 How do businesses use collaboration systems for decision making?

Q6 How do businesses use collaboration systems for problem solving?

Q7 How do businesses use collaboration systems for project management?

Meet Lily Shen

My management style:
Laid back, as long as you maintain open communication lines.

My motto:
It never hurts to ask (politely, of course).

What I do when I'm not working:
Doing a home improvement project or watching HGTV to get ideas for the next home improvement project.

Lily Shen is a project manager at Hitachi Consulting in Dallas, Texas. She specializes in projects involving Microsoft products, focusing on business intelligence and SharePoint solutions. She and her teams work closely with clients worldwide. Currently, she manages a project that is implementing an enterprise reporting solution for an organization in China.

In high school, Lily enjoyed problem solving and programming classes. She also enjoyed working with different people and being active in various organizations. At the suggestion of her parents, she looked into information systems and decided that it would offer her a great opportunity to utilize both her technical and people skills.

On the nature of her job:

"I am always communicating in my job. Discussing issues, brainstorming ideas, participating in meetings, gathering requirements for users, providing status reports to project sponsers, communicating next steps, understanding road blocks, and so on. Communication is not just disseminating information; it is making sure that the intended message was conveyed and understood.

"On my current project, the end users are in China, and so we have more communication hurdles than most projects. There's a 13-hour time difference, which causes a delay in email. And not only do we have the normal communication challenges, we also have language and cultural differences which add to the difficulty."

On collaboration:

"A number of information systems facilitate our collaboration. We use Microsoft SharePoint to store, manage, and share all of the project's information. People go to a central location to obtain the documents they need, and using version control we know who changed a document, when it was changed, and what was changed. SharePoint also helps us manage workflow when tasks require approval.

"We often use NetMeeting to conduct meetings. With it, participants in the United States and China talk to each other while viewing the same computer display. Sometimes we use WebEx as well. Of course, we also do regular conference calls and email.

"Is collaboration the same thing as communication? No, I don't think so. Collaboration involves communication; I don't think you can collaborate without effective communication. But there is more to it. You collaborate by working

My pet peeve:
Reading long paragraphs in a PowerPoint presentation.

One thing you must know about information systems:
It is a people business. It's about establishing relationships, building trust, understanding needs, communicating, etc.... It is absolutely not an *Office Space* job.

One characteristic of a superior employee:
Attitude. Approaching any challenge with a good attitude is the first step toward accomplishing your goal.

Lily Shen

together on something, building something together. You need a plan, a goal, and you must coordinate your activities. And, if something does not work out exactly as planned, you communicate the changes and adjust accordingly."

On information systems for non-IS majors:
"Information systems are an integral part of every business person's life. Regardless of your specialty, you need to understand and use information technology to carry out your function. The more you know, the better you'll be able to perform your role and responsibilities.

"Suppose you're a product manager and your product isn't selling well. First, how would you know that? Would a reporting system provide you with that information? What if the system you have doesn't meet all your needs? How do you know what is possible without some knowledge of technology? You need to understand data—where it came from and how to get more of what you need."

On information systems as a career:
"I like information systems because of the variety. There are so many aspects to it. You can focus more on the technical side, or on the functional side, or anywhere in between. It is incredible how many options are available to you!

"And you never know what the next challenge will be. Maybe a key user is not a proponent of the new system and hinders you from gathering requirements. How do you overcome that hurdle? How do you collaborate with the user to get the necessary information?

"Or, what if technology doesn't work quite like you thought? Maybe there's a problem with the software, or maybe performance is unacceptable. What do you do? You're a bridge between the technical people and the users. Can the problem be fixed within reasonable costs? Or, can the requirements be changed and still be effective? It is just fascinating.

"And the job opportunities are great. Right now we can't find enough IS people. We're hiring worldwide."

Any advice for an IS major?
"Send me your resume."

CHAPTER PREVIEW

This chapter discusses information systems that facilitate collaboration. The knowledge you will gain from this chapter is useful to you, right now. If your college is like most, nearly every course involves some sort of team project. This chapter will teach you how to use information systems to increase the efficiency of your teamwork.

We begin with a brief discussion of the nature of collaboration and of the three key drivers of collaboration performance. Next we will consider how you can use information systems and technology to improve team communication, manage the team's work product, and control team workflow.

After that, we will consider collaboration in the context of business. We will examine how information systems improve collaboration for decision making, problem solving, and project management.

Q1 What Is Collaboration?

Collaboration occurs when two or more people work together to achieve a common goal, result, or work product. When collaboration is effective, the results of the group are greater than could be produced by any of the individuals working alone. Collaboration involves coordination and communication, but it is greater than either of those.

Consider an example of a student team that is assigned a term project. Suppose the team meets and divides the work into sections and then team members work independently on their individual pieces. An hour before the project is due, the team members meet again to assemble their independent pieces into a whole. Such a team evidences both communication and coordination, but it is not collaborative.

The Importance of Feedback and Iteration

Collaborative work involves feedback and iteration. In a collaborative environment, team members review each others' work product and revise that product as a result. The effort proceeds in a series of steps, or iterations, in which one person produces something, others comment on what was produced, a revised version is produced, and so forth. Further, in the process of reviewing others' work, team members learn from each other and change the way they work and what they produce. The feedback and iteration enable the group to produce something greater than any single person could accomplish working independently.

Learning how to collaborate is important. According to a study published by the RAND Corporation, the demand for those who have strong collaboration skills will explode in the twenty-first century.[1]

Critical Collaboration Drivers

The effectiveness of a collaborative effort is driven by three critical factors:

- Communication
- Content management
- Workflow control

Communication has two key elements. The first is the communication skills and abilities of the group members. The ability to give and receive critical feedback is particularly important. Work product can improve only when group members can criticize each other's work without creating rancor and resentment and can improve their contributions based on criticism received.

The second key communication element is the availability of effective communication systems. Today, few collaborative meetings are conducted face-to-face. Group members may be geographically distributed, or they may be unable to meet at the same time, or both. In such cases, the availability of email and more sophisticated and effective communications systems is crucial.

The second driver of collaboration effectiveness is **content management**. When multiple users are contributing and changing documents, schedules, task lists, assignments, and so forth, one user's work might interfere with another's. Users need to manage content so that such conflict does not occur. Also, it is important to know who made what changes, when, and why. Content-management systems track and report such data. Finally, in some collaborations members have different rights and privileges. Some team members have full **permissions** to create, edit, and delete content,

[1]Lynn A. Karoly and Constantijn Panis. *The 21st Century at Work* (Santa Monica, CA: RAND Corporation, 2004), p. xiv.

others are restricted to edit, and still others are restricted to a read-only status. Information systems play a key role in enforcing such restrictions.

Workflow control is the third key driver of collaboration effectiveness. A **workflow** is a process or procedure by which content is created, edited, used, and disposed. For a team that supports a Web site, for example, a workflow design may specify that certain members create Web pages, others review those pages, and still others post the reviewed and approved pages to the Web site. The workflow specifies particular ordering of tasks and includes processes for handling rejected changes as well as for dealing with exceptions.

The three collaboration drivers are not equally important for all collaborations. For one-time, *ad hoc* workgroups, it is seldom worthwhile to create and formalize workflows. For such groups, communication is the most important driver. On the other hand, formally defined workflow for a team of engineers designing a new airplane is crucial.

The Collaboration in Practice box below discusses the qualities and characteristics that make a good collaborator.

In the next three questions (sections), we will consider how you can use information to facilitate collaboration in your team projects at school. Read carefully and use the knowledge you gain here, tonight!

COLLABORATION IN PRACTICE

KEY CHARACTERISTICS FOR COLLABORATION

Researchers Ditkoff, Allen, Moore, and Pollard surveyed 108 business professionals on the qualities, attitudes, and skills that make a good collaborator. Their results, published in November 2005, found no significant differences in the top 10 qualities among the respondents' age, sex, experience, or occupation. All respondents seemed to agree for the top 10.

The following table lists the most and least important characteristics reported in the survey.

Three of the top seven characteristics involve disagreement: speaking an unpopular viewpoint (3), willingness to enter into difficult conversations (5), and skill at giving and receiving negative feedback (7). Note, too, that these three fall after enthusiasm for the

What qualities, attitudes, and skills help make a good collaborator?	Average	Overall Rank
Indispensable (3)		
Is enthusiastic about the subject of our collaboration.	4.4	1
Is open-minded and curious.	4.3	2
Speaks their mind even if it's an unpopular viewpoint.	4.0	3
Very Important (9)		
Gets back to me and others in a timely way.	3.9	4
Is willing to enter into difficult conversations.	3.9	5
Is a perceptive listener.	3.9	6
Is skillful at giving/receiving even negative feedback.	3.9	7
Is willing to put forward unpopular ideas.	3.8	8
Is self-managing and requires "low maintenance."	3.7	9
Is known for following through on commitments.	3.7	10
Is willing to dig into the topic with zeal.	3.7	11
Thinks differently than I do/brings different perspectives.	3.7	12

Not Relevant (9)		
Is well organized.	2.9	31
Is someone I immediately liked. The chemistry is good.	2.8	32
Has already earned my trust.	2.7	33
Has experience as a collaborator.	2.4	34
Is a skilled and persuasive presenter.	2.4	35
Is gregarious and dynamic.	2.4	36
Is someone I knew beforehand.	2.3	37
Has an established reputation in field of our collaboration.	2.2	38
Is an experienced business person.	1.9	39

Source: Survey, "What Qualities, Attitudes, and Skills Help Make a Good Collaborator?" from Mitch Ditkoff, Tim Moore, Carolyn Allen, and Dave Pollard, November 2005, *http://blogs.salon.com/0002007/stories/2005/11/18/theIdealCollaborativeTeamAndAConversationOnTheCollaborativeProcess.html* © 2006 Dave Pollard.

subject (1) and being open-minded and curious (2). The respondents seem to be saying, "You need to care, you need to be open-minded, but you need to be able to deal with conflict, effectively disagree, and receive opinions that are different from your own."

These results are not surprising when we think about collaboration as an iterative process in which team members give and receive feedback. During collaboration, team members learn from each other, and it will be difficult to learn if no one is willing to express unpopular or contentious ideas. The respondents also seem to be saying, "You can be negative, as long as you care about what we're doing." These collaboration skills do not come naturally to people who have been taught to "play well with others," but that may be why they were so highly ranked in the survey.

The characteristics rated *not relevant* are revealing. Experience as a collaborator or in business does not seem to matter. Being popular also is not important. A big surprise, however, is that being well organized was rated 31st out of 39 characteristics. Perhaps collaboration itself is not a very well-organized process?

This topic continues in Collaboration Exercise 1 on page 58.

Q2 How Can You Use Collaboration Systems to Improve Team Communication?

If you truly are going to *collaborate* on your team projects, if you are going to create work products (such as documents), encourage others to criticize those products, and revise those products in accordance with the criticism, then you will need to communicate. Similarly, if you are going to review others' work, make critical comments, and help them improve their product, then you will also need to communicate. So, improving communication capabilities is key to collaboration success.

Figure 2-1 (next page) summarizes technology available to facilitate communication. **Synchronous communication** occurs when all team members meet at the same time, such as with face-to-face meetings or conference calls. **Asynchronous communication** occurs when team members do not meet at the same time. Employees who work different shifts at the same location, or team members, like Lily Shen's, who work in different time zones around the world, must meet asynchronously.

Most student teams attempt to meet face-to-face, at least at first. Arranging such meetings is always difficult, however, because student schedules and responsibilities differ. If you are going to arrange such meetings, consider creating an online group calendar in which team members post their availability, week by week. Also, use the meeting facilities in Microsoft Outlook to issue invitations and gather RSVPs. If you

Figure 2-1
Information Technology for Communication

Synchronous		**Asynchronous**
Shared calendars Invitation and attendance		
Single location	Multiple locations	Single or multiple locations
Office appplications such as Word and PowerPoint	Conference calls Multiparty text chat Microsoft Groove Videoconferencing	Email Discussion forums Team surveys

Virtual meetings

don't have Outlook, use an Internet site such as Evite (*www.invite.com*) for this purpose. For face-to-face meetings, you will need little other technology beyond standard Office applications such as Word and PowerPoint. Given today's communication technology, most students should forgo face-to-face meetings. They are too difficult to arrange and seldom worth the trouble. Instead, learn to use **virtual meetings** in which participants do not meet in the same place and possibly not at the same time.

If your virtual meeting is synchronous (all meet at the same time), you can use **conference calls** or **multiparty text chat**. Some students find it weird to use text chat for school projects, but why not? You can attend meetings wherever you are, silently. In the next section, we will describe Microsoft Groove, a tool you should consider because it has easy-to-use multiparty text chat, along with several other useful features.

If everyone on your team has a camera on his or her computer, you can also do **videoconferencing** like that shown in Figure 2-2. Microsoft NetMeeting is one such product, but you can find others on the Internet. Videoconferencing is more intrusive than text chat; you have to comb your hair, but it does have a more personal touch. Sometime during your student career you should use it to see what you think.

In some (most?) classes and situations, synchronous meetings, even virtual ones, are impossible to arrange. You just cannot get everyone together at the same time. In this circumstance, when the team must meet asynchronously, most students try to communicate via **email**. The problem with email is that there is too much freedom.

Figure 2-2
User Participating in NetMeeting

Source: Courtesy of Zigy Kaluzny, Getty Images/Getty Images, Inc.

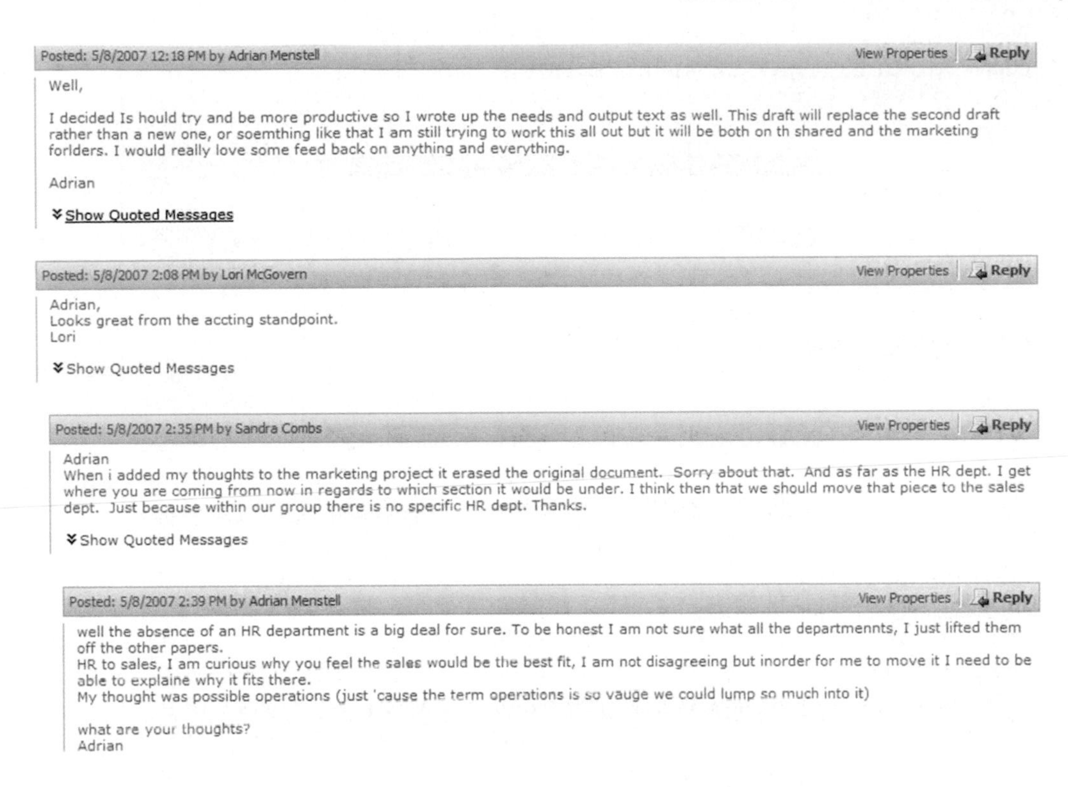

Figure 2-3
Example of Discussion Forum

Not everyone will participate, because it is easy to hide from email. Discussion threads become disorganized and disconnected. After the fact, it is difficult to find particular emails, comments, or attachments.

Discussion forums are an alternative. Here, one group member posts an entry, perhaps an idea, a comment, or a question, and other group members respond. Figure 2-3 shows an example. Such forums are better than email because it is harder for the discussion to get off track. Still, however, it remains easy for some team members not to participate.

Team surveys are another form of communication technology. With these, one team member creates a list of questions and other team members respond. Surveys are an effective way to obtain team opinions; they are generally easy to complete, so most team members will participate. Also, it is easy to determine who has not yet responded. Figure 2-4 (next page) shows the results of one team survey. ConfirmIt (*www.confirmit.com*) is one common survey application program. You can find others on the Internet. Microsoft SharePoint (discussed later) has a built-in survey capability.

Q3 How Can You Use Collaboration Systems to Manage Content?

The second driver of collaboration performance is content management. You and your teammates will need to share documents, illustrations, spreadsheets, and other data. The information systems you use for sharing content depend on the degree of control that you want. Figure 2-5 (next page) lists three categories of content-management control: no control, version tracking, and version management. Consider each.

Shared Content with No Control

The most primitive way to share content is via email attachments. It is easy to share content this way, but email attachments have numerous problems. For one, there is

Figure 2-4
Portion of Sample Team Survey

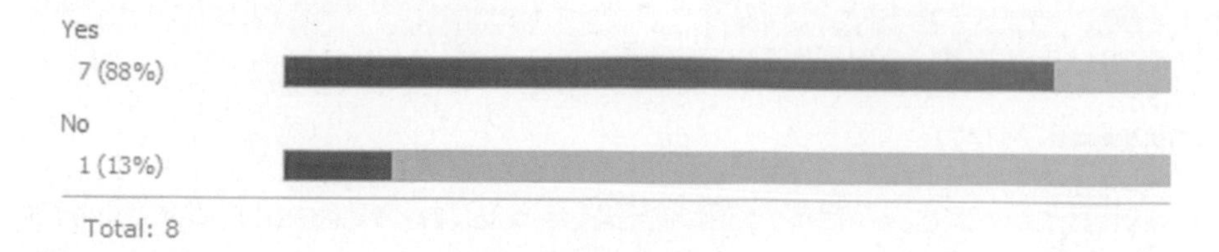
1. Have you read the Project 3 and 4 instructions from the power point slides? (Check box if yes)
Yes
7 (88%)
No
1 (13%)
Total: 8

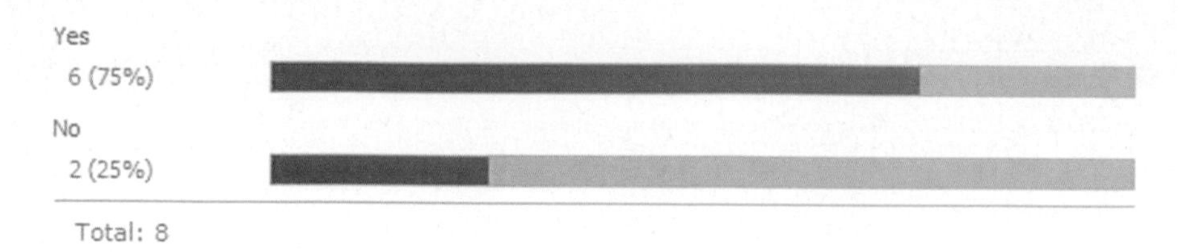
2. Do you understand the requirements for Project 3?
Yes
6 (75%)
No
2 (25%)
Total: 8

3. Do you understand the requirements for project 4?
Yes
7 (88%)
No
1 (13%)
Total: 8

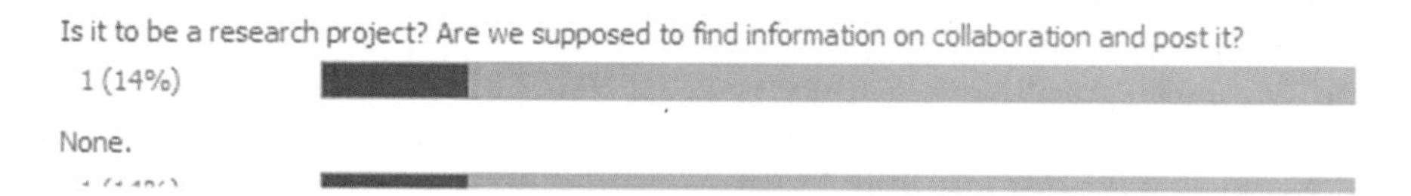
4. What confusions (if any) do you have in regards to Project 3?
Is it to be a research project? Are we supposed to find information on collaboration and post it?
1 (14%)
None.

always the danger that someone does not receive an email, does not notice it in his or her inbox, or does not bother to save the attachments. Then, too, if three users obtain the same document as an email attachment, each changes it, and each sends back the changed documents via email, different, incompatible versions of that document will be floating around. So, although email is simple, easy, and readily available, it will not suffice for collaborations in which there are many document versions or for which there is a desire for content control.

Another way to share content is to place it on a shared file server. You will learn more about servers in Part 2, but for now, just understand that a server is a computer that provides a service. In this case, the service is content storage. If your team has access to a file server, you can put documents on the server and others can download

Alternatives for Sharing Content		
No Control	Version Management	Version Control
Email with attachments Shared files on a server	Wikis Google Docs & Spreadsheets Microsoft Groove	Microsoft SharePoint

Increasing degree of content control

Figure 2-5
Information Technology for Sharing Content

them, make changes, and upload them back onto the server. Often a technology called **ftp** is used to get and put documents (discussed in Chapter 6).

Storing documents on servers is better than using email attachments because documents have a single storage location. They are not scattered in different team members' email boxes. Team members have a known location for finding documents.

However, without any additional control, it is possible for team members to interfere with one another's work. For example, suppose team members A and B download a document and edit it, but without knowing about the other's edits. Person A stores his version back on the server and then person B stores her version back on the server. In this scenario, person A's changes will be lost.

Furthermore, without any version management it will be impossible to know who changed the document and when. Neither person A nor person B will know whose version of the document is on the server. To avoid such problems, some form of version management is recommended.

Shared Content with Version Management

Systems that provide **version management** track changes to documents and provide features and functions to accommodate concurrent work. The means by which this is done depends on the particular system used. In this section, we consider three systems that you should consider for your team's work: wikis, Google Docs & Spreadsheets, and Microsoft Groove.

Wikis

The simplest version-management systems are wikis. A **wiki** (pronounced *we-key*) is a shared knowledge base in which the content is contributed and managed by the wiki's users. The most famous wiki is Wikipedia, a general encyclopedia available to the public (see Figure 2-6).

Collaborative teams can use wiki technology to create and maintain private wikis that serve as a repository of team knowledge. When a user contributes a wiki entry, the

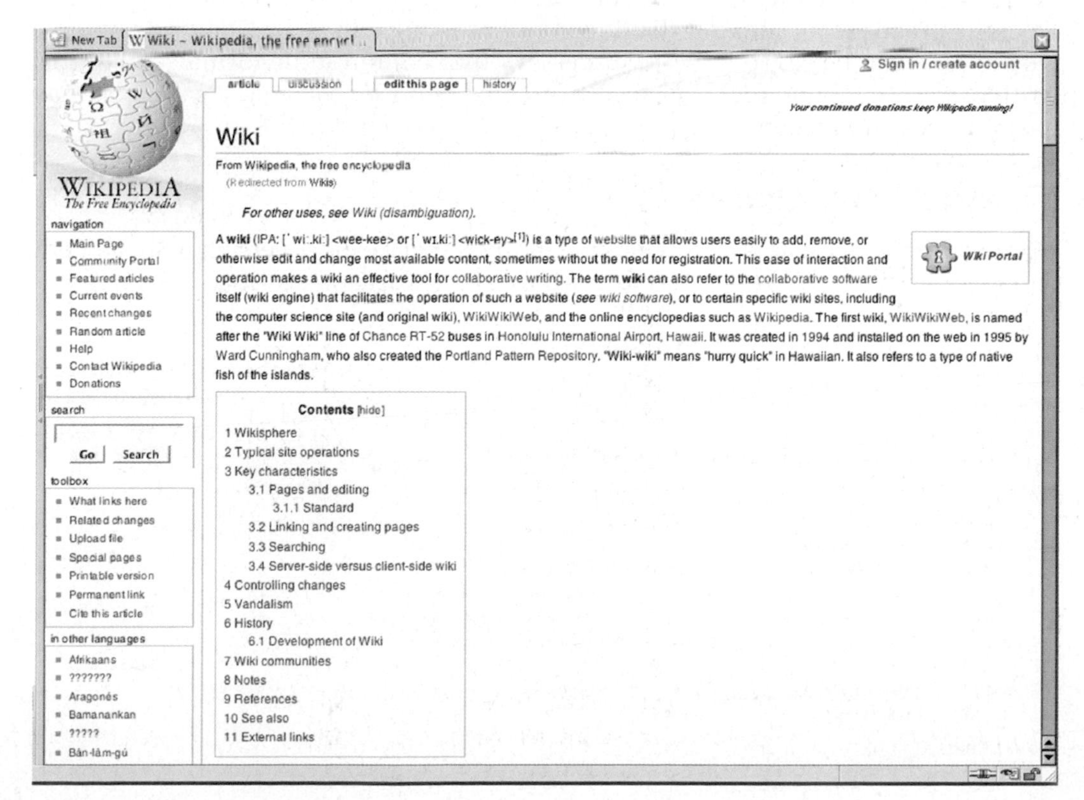

Figure 2-6
Wikipedia

system tracks who created the entry and the date of creation. As others modify the entry, the wiki software tracks the identity of the modifier, the date, and possibly other data. Some users are given permission to delete wiki entries.

Google Docs & Spreadsheets

Google Docs & Spreadsheets is a system for sharing documents and spreadsheet data. (This application is rapidly evolving; by the time you read this, Google may have added additional file types or changed the system from what is described here. Google the name *Google Docs & Spreadsheets* to obtain the latest information about it.)

With Google Docs & Spreadsheets, anyone who edits a document must have a Google account. (A Google account is not the same as a Gmail account.) You can establish a Google account with a Hotmail, a university, or any other email account. Your Google account will be affiliated with whatever email account you enter.

To create a Google document, go to *http://docs.google.com* (note there is no *www* in this address). Sign into (or create) your Google account. From that point on, you can upload documents and spreadsheets, share them with others, and download them to common file formats.

You can then make the document available to others by entering their email addresses (which need not be Google accounts). Those users are notified that the document exists and are given a link by which they can access it. If they have (or create) a Google account, they can edit the document.

With Google Docs & Spreadsheets, documents are stored on a Google server. Users can access the documents from Google and simultaneously see and edit documents. In the background, Google merges the users' activities into a single document. You are notified that another user is editing a document at the same time as you are, and you can refresh the document to see their latest changes. Google tracks document revisions, with brief summaries of changes made. Figure 2-7 shows a sample revision for a sample document that has been shared among three users.

Google Docs & Spreadsheets is free, but all documents must be processed by Google programs. A Microsoft Word or Excel document can be uploaded to a Google Docs & Spreadsheets site, but the document must be edited by Google programs. Documents can be saved in Word, Excel, or other common file formats. As of this writing, some common files, such as PowerPoint, cannot be shared. Again, that may change in the future, however.

Microsoft Office Groove

Microsoft Office Groove is a collaboration product that includes version management and other useful tools. Using Groove, a user creates a **workspace**, which is a collection

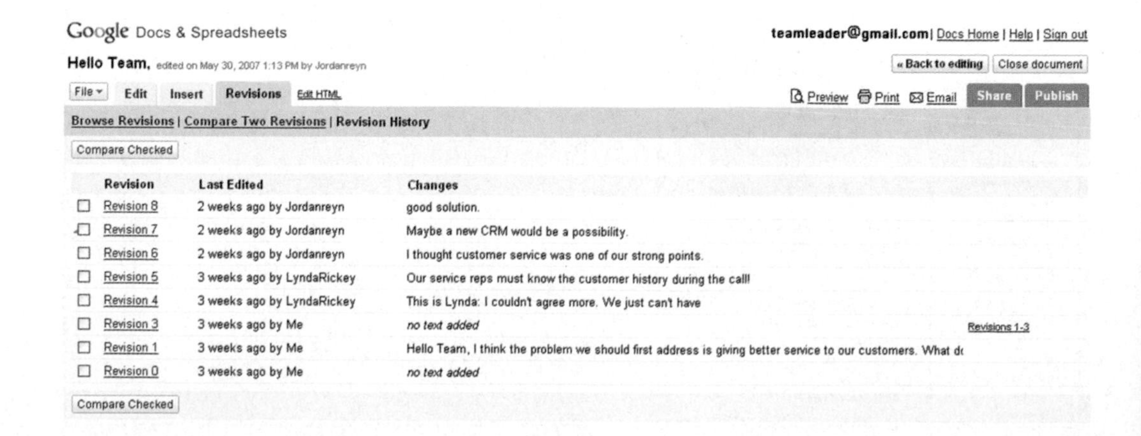

Figure 2-7
Sample Google Docs & Spreadsheets Document Versions

Source: GOOGLE Docs & Spreadsheets™. GOOGLE is a trademark of Google Inc.

of tools, documents, and users. The creator of the workspace invites others to join by sending them an email. The invitee accepts or declines the invitation. If the invitee accepts, he or she joins the workspace and can view all of the workspace content, including documents, schedules, drawings, announcements of meetings, and so forth.

When a user changes a document, Groove automatically propagates that change to workspaces on other users' computers. If two users attempt to change the same document at the same time, Groove disallows one of them until the other is finished. Groove provides a wide number of tools, including document repositories, discussion forums, to-do lists, meeting agendas, drawing spaces, calendars, and other features. Whenever a team member makes changes to the workspace—say, adding a calendar or a file of drawings or setting up a sequence of meetings—Groove propagates those changes to all team members' computers.

Collaboration tools provide useful capabilities, but also some potential security risks. The Security Guide on page 52 discusses these risks—and how to avoid them.

Groove can be used synchronously or asynchronously. For the former, Groove supports multiuser text chat. It also uses **Voice over IP (VoIP)** (discussed in Chapter 6) to enable meeting participants to conduct telephone conversations using the Internet connection. No separate phone line is necessary.

Team members can use Groove asynchronously. Working alone, they can modify documents, leave messages for one another, create new tasks, and so forth. As other team members rejoin the workspace, Groove will show them all work that was done while they were away. Groove can be hosted on any personal computer, and it can also be hosted on a server. If on a server, then the workspace is always available. If on a personal computer, then the workspace is available only when that computer is connected to the Internet.

Figure 2-8 shows a sample Groove workspace. Shared files are listed in the middle column. The users in the workspace are listed in the pane in the upper right-hand corner, a chat session appears in the middle pane on the right-hand side, and a list of tasks appear in the lower right-hand corner.

The downside to Groove is that to participate, all users must have purchased a license for Groove and have it installed on his or her computer. However, if your university participates in the Microsoft Developer Network Academic Alliance (and this is likely), you can obtain a license-free version of Groove through that program. Ask your instructor for more information.

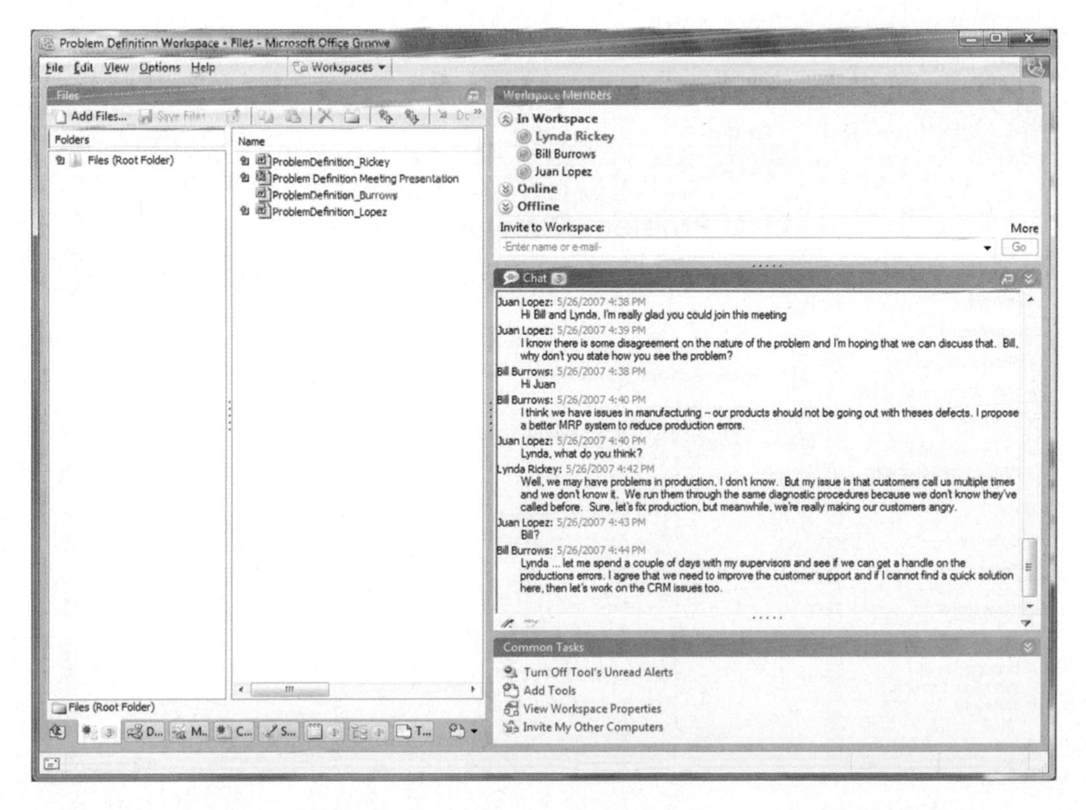

Figure 2-8
Example Groove Workspace

Source: Microsoft Office Groove Workspace. Reprinted with permission from Microsoft Corporation.

Both Google Docs & Spreadsheets and Microsoft Groove are easy to set up and learn. Both are incredibly useful products that can make your collaborative work easier and result in higher-quality output. Take a look at them!

Shared Content with Version Control

Version-management systems improve the tracking of shared content and potentially eliminate problems caused by concurrent document access. They do not, however, provide **version control**. They do not limit the actions that can be taken by any particular user, and they do not give control over the changes to documents to particular users.

With version-control systems, each team member is given an account with a set of permissions. Shared documents are placed into shared directories, sometimes called **libraries**. For example, on a shared site with four libraries, a particular user might be given read-only permission for library 1; read and edit permission for library 2; read, edit, and delete permission for library 3; and no permission even to see library 4.

Furthermore, document directories can be set up so that users are required to check out documents before they can modify them. When a document is checked out, no other user can obtain it for the purpose of editing it. Once the document has been checked in, other users can obtain it for editing. Figure 2-9 shows a user (Lori McGovern—see the welcome message in the top banner of the screen) checking out a document named Problem_Definition_Rickey. Of course, for the system to allow the checkout the user must have permission to edit that document.

Numerous version-control applications exist. **Microsoft SharePoint** is the most popular for general business use. Other document-control systems include Master Control (*www.mastercontrol.com*) and Document Locator (*www.documentlocator.com*). Software development teams use applications such as CVS (*www.CVS.com)* or Subversion *(www.subversion.com)* to control versions of software code, test plans, and product documentation.

By the way, SharePoint includes many collaboration features and functions besides document checkin/checkout. In addition to support for document libraries and lists, it

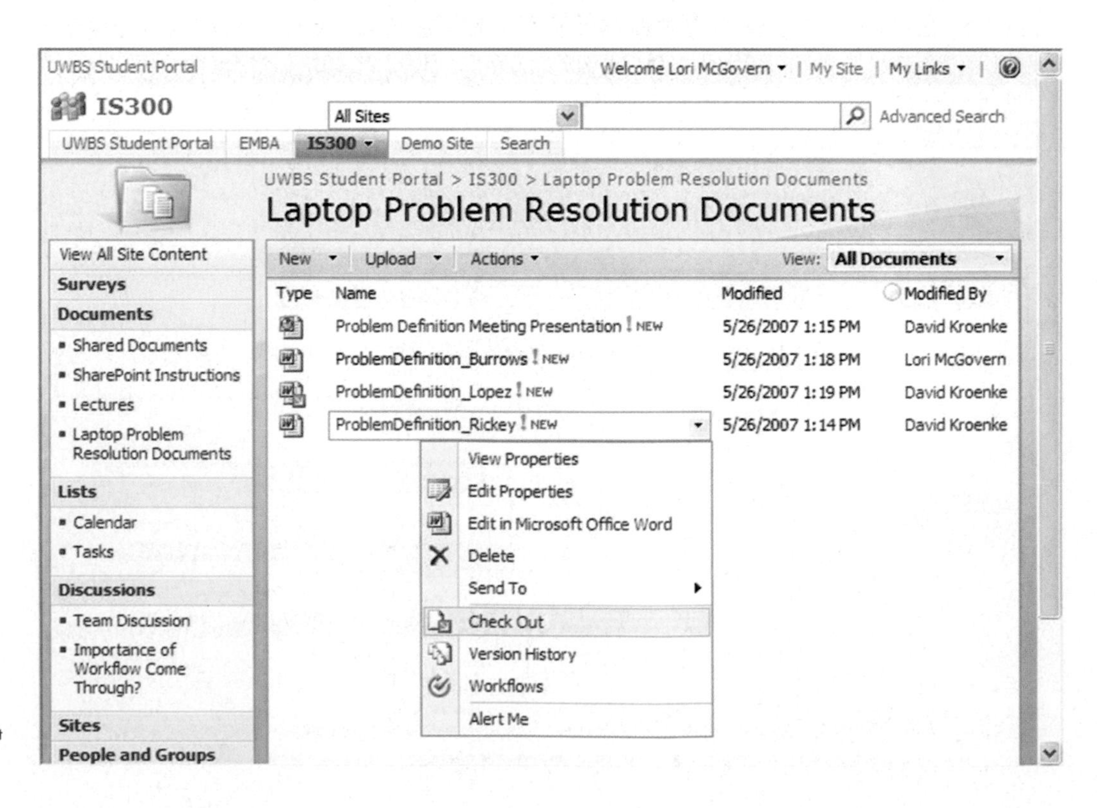

Figure 2-9
Example of Document Checkout

Source: Microsoft Office SharePoint Designer 2007. Reprinted with permission from Microsoft Corporation.

has features for creating and managing the following team work products: surveys, discussion forums, wikis, member blogs, member Web sites, and workflow (see next section).

For any but the most trivial team project, SharePoint is exceedingly useful. Unfortunately, installing SharePoint requires a publicly accessible server and more skill, experience, and knowledge than most college students are likely to have. Accordingly, Prentice Hall, this text's publisher, has set up SharePoint sites for you to use. See your instructor for information about how to create and use one of these SharePoint sites.

Q4 How Can You Use Collaboration Systems to Control Workflow?

So far you have learned how information systems can be used to facilitate team communication and manage content. It is possible to gain even more control by using information systems to manage workflow.

The Ethics Guide on page 42 addresses some of the ethical challenges that arise when teams hold virtual meetings.

Figure 2-10 shows a simple workflow example. This workflow is called a **sequential workflow** because activities occur in sequence. First, Burrows reviews the document, then McGovern, and finally Reynolds, one after the other in sequence. In a **parallel workflow**, the reviews would occur simultaneously. There are numerous other types of workflow that we will not consider here.[2]

You *can* manage a workflow such as that shown in Figure 2-10 manually. Someone, perhaps the group's manager, sends an email to Burrows requesting the review, possibly with the document as an attachment. After Burrows finishes the review, the manager sends the reviewed document to McGovern, and so forth. If Burrows forgets to do the review, the manager would send a follow-up email, and so forth. As you can imagine, manual enforcement of workflows is an administrative nightmare.

However, a number of collaboration tools are available that will manage workflows for you. Microsoft SharePoint is one. Look again at Figure 2-9. The user is about to click the *Check Out* command. However, from this same menu, the user could also click *Workflows* (two commands below *Check Out*) to define a workflow on this document.

If the user were to click *Workflow*, the screen shown in Figure 2-11 (on page 44) would appear. The user would fill out the entries in this form and in the one in Figure 2-12 (page 45) to define the workflow. Note in Figure 2-12 that the workflow is defined as sequential; the form is also used to identify the users who will review the document.

Once this workflow is defined, SharePoint will manage it. SharePoint will send an email to Burrows requesting the review and a copy of that email to the person who defined this workflow. SharePoint will also create a task in a new task list defined for this workflow. When Burrows completes his review, he will check the document back in, and SharePoint will mark the task as complete and send an email to McGovern, requesting her review. Copies of these emails will be sent to the workflow creator. If Burrows does not complete the task within five days (see the bottom of the form in Figure 2-12), SharePoint will send him a reminder as well as an advisory email to the creator of the workflow.

If you create a **SharePoint site**, you can define workflows just like this for your group. You can use this capability to ensure that all of your teammates perform the work they are requested to do.

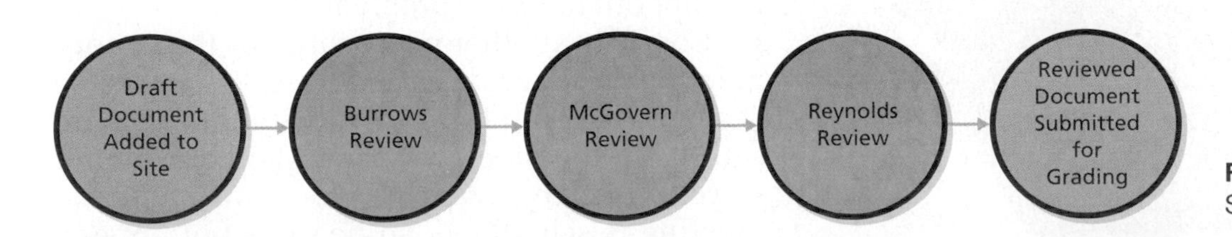

Figure 2-10
Sample Sequential Workflow

[2]For more information about workflows and the Windows Workflow Foundation, see David Mann, *Workflow in the 2007 Microsoft Office System* (Apress, 2007).

Ethics

GUIDE

Virtual Ethics?

The term *virtual* means something that appears to exist but does not exist in fact. A *virtual private network (VPN)* is an electronic network that appears to be private, but in fact operates on a public network (more on this in Chapter 6). The term *virtual meeting* describes a meeting in which everyone is present, but via an information system and not face-to-face.

However, and it is a big *however*, "Is everyone present?" Is the person who signed on as Lynda Rickey truly Lynda Rickey? Or is it someone else? Or is it Lynda Rickey with a staff of seven people, all of whom are anonymous to the rest of the group? Figure 2-8 shows a chat session among Lynda, Juan Lopez, and Bill Burrows. What if none of them was really there? What if, in fact, it was a chat session among Ashley, Haley, and Jordan, but none of them knew the others were *spoofing* (pretending to be someone they are not)? What if Jordan was actually Bill's son sitting in his organizational behavior class at college, giving noncommittal answers, while Bill played golf?

Suppose you run a consulting company and you want to send less experienced consultants out on jobs. During an initial meeting (held electronically, using text chat) with a potential client, you tell the client that he is meeting with Drew Suenas, a new and inexperienced employee. But, the meeting actually includes Drew and Eleanor Jackson, your most experienced and senior consultant. During the meeting, all of the remarks attributed to Drew were actually made by Eleanor. The client is most impressed with what it thinks are Drew's perceptive comments about its situation and agrees to hire Drew, even though he is inexperienced. You keep using Eleanor this way, spoofing several of your young associates to get jobs for them. You justify this by saying, "Well, if they get into trouble, we'll send Eleanor out to fix the problem."

Consider another possibility. For the Groove meeting in Figure 2-8, suppose you disagree strongly with Bill Burrows' position. If you are setting up the meeting, what if you decide not to send Bill an invite? He does not know the meeting is scheduled, so he does not appear. Much to your joy, issues on which you disagree with him go unaddressed. During the meeting, you remain silent when people ask, "I wonder why Bill isn't here?"

Or, suppose you have an archrival, Ashley. You and Ashley compete for a future promotion, and you just cannot stand the idea of her moving ahead of you. So you set up a sequence of virtual meetings, but you never invite Ashley. Then, just before a crucial meeting, one that involves senior members of your organization, you invite Ashley to be your silent helper. You tell her you do not have the authority to invite her, but you want her to have a chance to express her thoughts. So you attend the meeting and you incorporate Ashley's thinking into your chat comments. People think you are the sole author of those ideas and are impressed. Ashley's work is never attributed to her.

Or, let's bring it closer to home. Suppose you take online tests as part of your class. What keeps you from taking the test with your brother, who happens to work for Google as a product manager for Google Docs & Spreadsheets? Suppose you take the test by yourself, but you believe others are taking their tests with silent helpers. Given that belief, are you justified in finding your own helper?

What do you think? Are your ethics virtual? ■

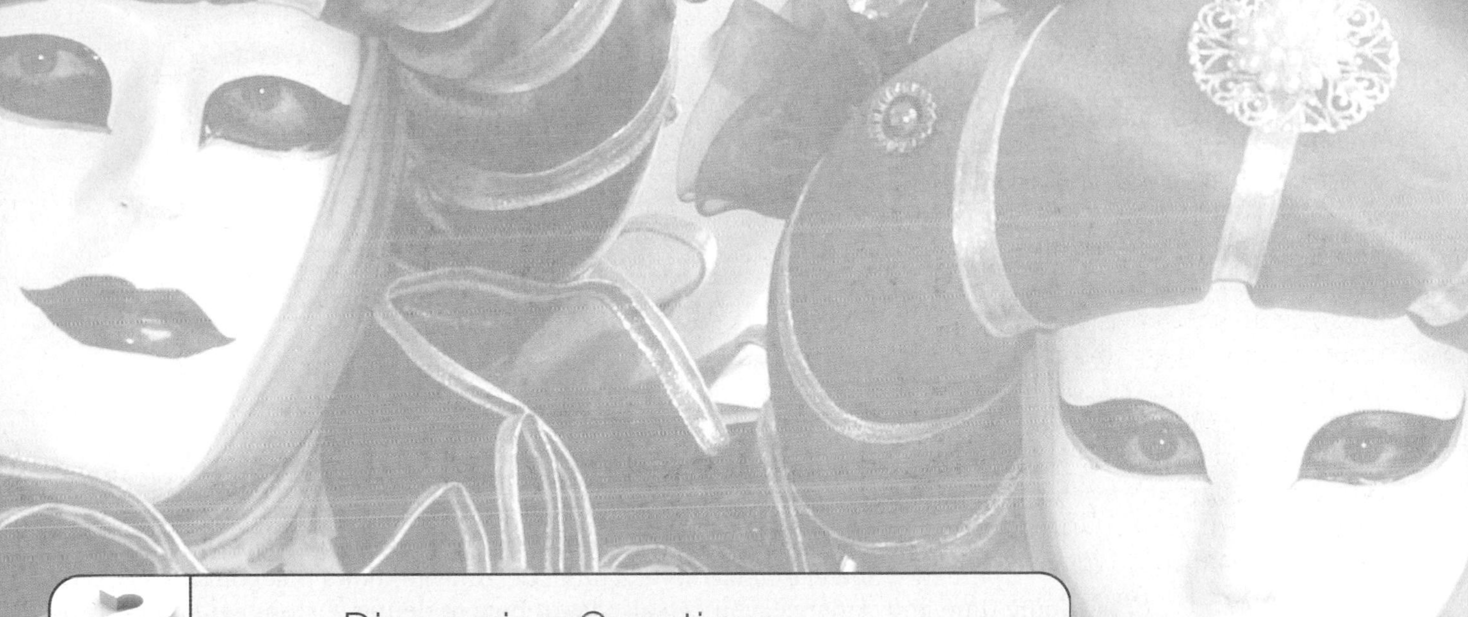

Discussion Questions

1. Is it *illegal* to spoof someone? Does it matter whether you have that person's permission to spoof them?
2. Is it *ethical* to spoof someone? Does it matter whether you have that person's permission?
3. Under what circumstances do you believe it is ethical to spoof someone?
4. Consider the meeting in which everyone was spoofing and no one knew it. What are the consequences to the organization of such a meeting? What happens when Bill meets Lynda in the hallway and Lynda asks, "What did you think of our meeting?" Who has the knowledge of the meeting? Who knows that they have that knowledge?
5. Considering Eleanor's spoofing of young associates, what is different between text chat and a speaker phone? Haven't we always had these problems, except Eleanor was passing notes and making comments while the phone was muted? What behavior should you follow when talking with someone who is on a speaker phone?
6. Is it ethical not to invite Bill to the meeting? Assume no one has asked you if you sent the invitation to him.
7. Is it cheating to have a helper on an online test? Are you justified if everyone else is doing it? What control is possible for online tests? Should such tests be used at all?

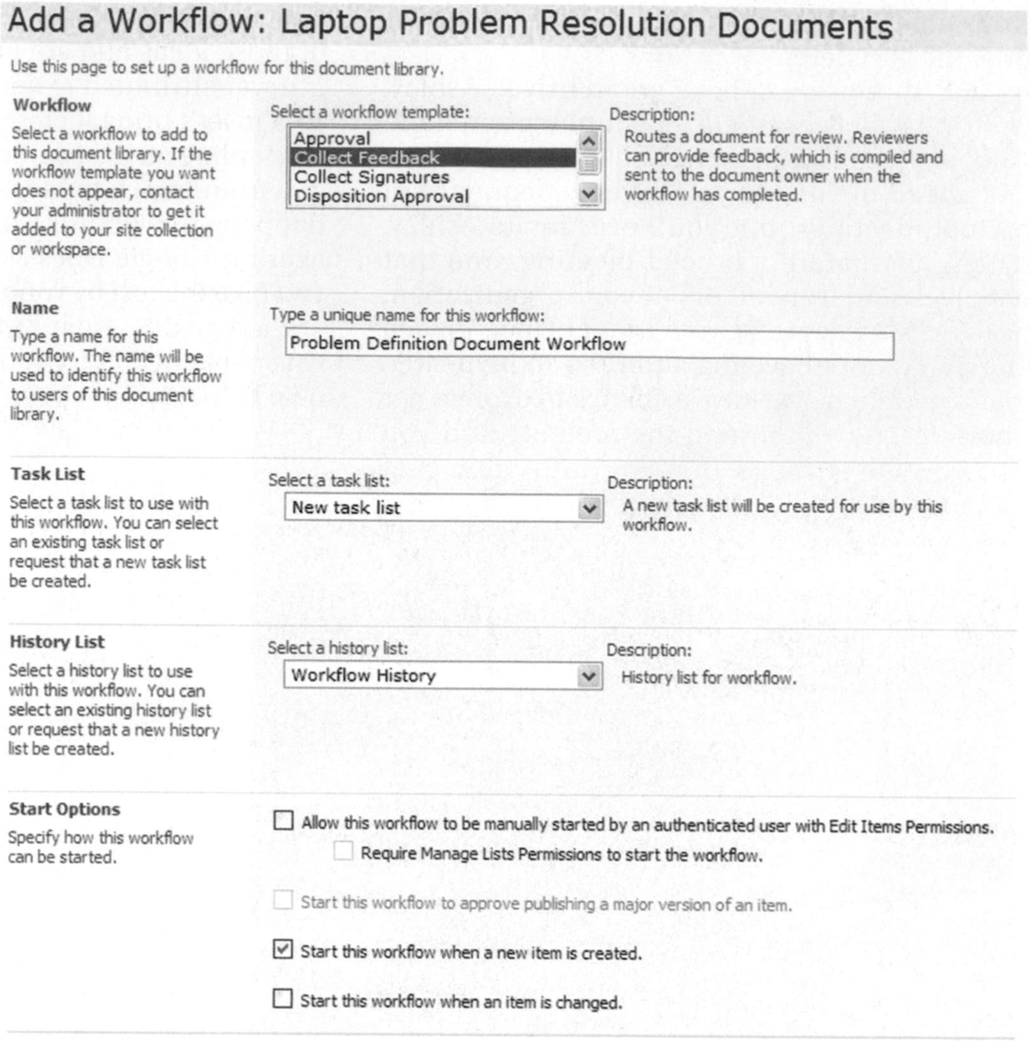

Figure 2-11
Defining a SharePoint Workflow, Part 1

Source: Microsoft Office SharePoint Designer 2007. Reprinted with permission from Microsoft Corporation.

Add a Workflow: Laptop Problem Resolution Documents

Use this page to set up a workflow for this document library.

Workflow
Select a workflow to add to this document library. If the workflow template you want does not appear, contact your administrator to get it added to your site collection or workspace.

Select a workflow template:
Approval
Collect Feedback
Collect Signatures
Disposition Approval

Description:
Routes a document for review. Reviewers can provide feedback, which is compiled and sent to the document owner when the workflow has completed.

Name
Type a name for this workflow. The name will be used to identify this workflow to users of this document library.

Type a unique name for this workflow:
Problem Definition Document Workflow

Task List
Select a task list to use with this workflow. You can select an existing task list or request that a new task list be created.

Select a task list:
New task list

Description:
A new task list will be created for use by this workflow.

History List
Select a history list to use with this workflow. You can select an existing history list or request that a new history list be created.

Select a history list:
Workflow History

Description:
History list for workflow.

Start Options
Specify how this workflow can be started.

☐ Allow this workflow to be manually started by an authenticated user with Edit Items Permissions.
☐ Require Manage Lists Permissions to start the workflow.
☐ Start this workflow to approve publishing a major version of an item.
☑ Start this workflow when a new item is created.
☐ Start this workflow when an item is changed.

By the way, SharePoint has several other default workflows that you can use. With some time and patience, you can also learn how to define custom workflows using Windows Office SharePoint Designer. And, if you are a programmer, you can use Visual Studio to create custom workflows that are limited only by your knowledge and programming skill.

Q5 How Do Businesses Use Collaboration Systems for Decision Making?

Innovation is a highly prized skill in business and, according to some, a key source of business competitiveness. See the Innovation in Practice box on page 46 for discussion of how existing companies can use technology to improve innovation.

So far you have learned how to use collaboration systems to manage team projects in school. This is interesting and useful, but such tools were not developed solely to benefit students. They were developed to help collaborative groups in businesses accomplish their goals and objectives. The balance of this chapter discusses how businesses use collaboration systems to improve decision making, to solve problems, and to manage projects. We begin with decision making.

Collaboration systems are not necessary for all types of decisions. So, to understand the role for collaboration we must first begin with an analysis of decision making. As Figure 2-13 shows, decisions occur at three levels in organizations: *operational, managerial,* and *strategic.* The types of decisions vary, depending on the level.

Operational decisions concern day-to-day activities. Typical operational decisions are: How many widgets should we order from vendor A? Should we extend credit

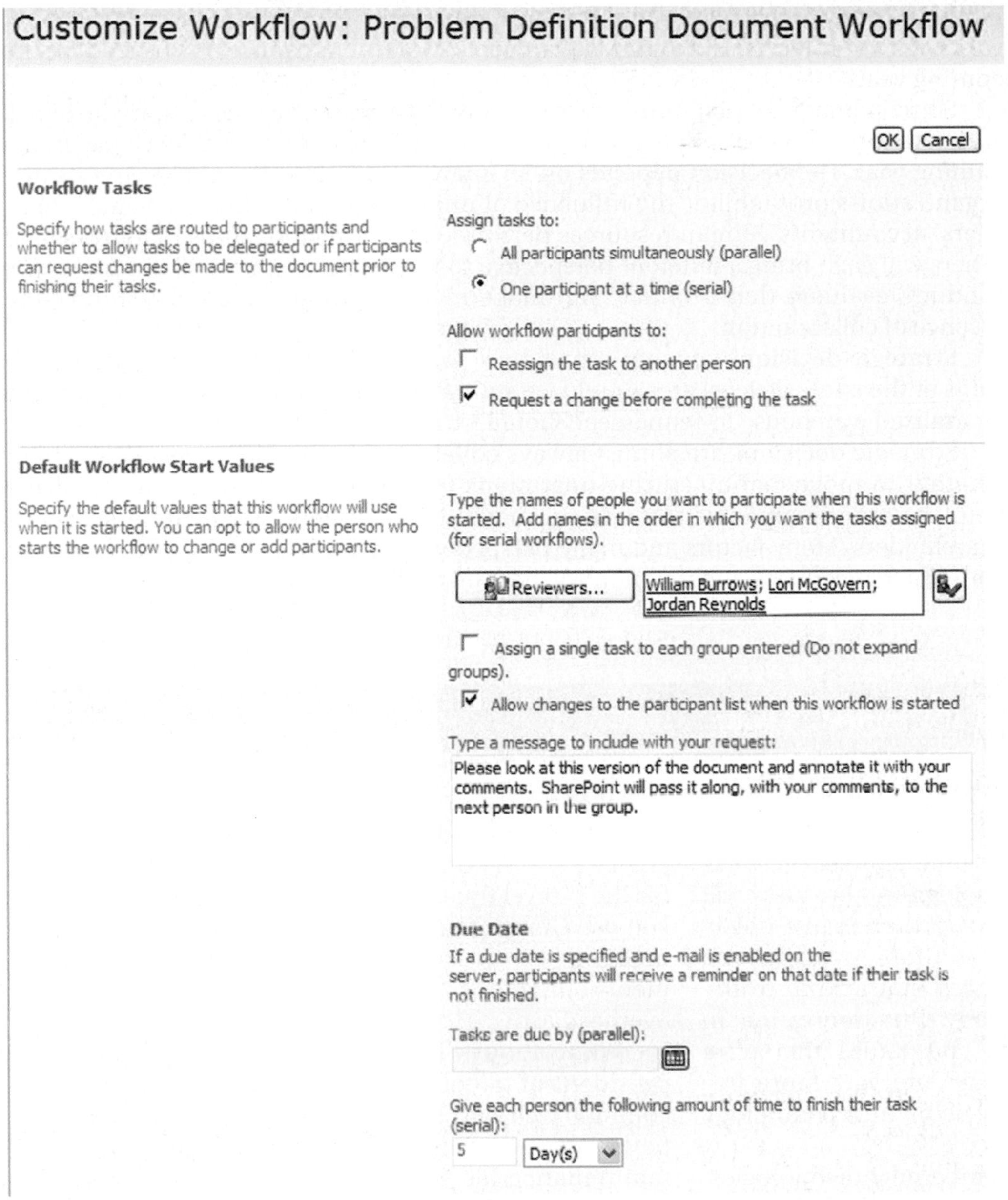

Customize Workflow: Problem Definition Document Workflow

OK Cancel

Workflow Tasks

Specify how tasks are routed to participants and whether to allow tasks to be delegated or if participants can request changes be made to the document prior to finishing their tasks.

Assign tasks to:
- All participants simultaneously (parallel)
- One participant at a time (serial)

Allow workflow participants to:
- Reassign the task to another person
- Request a change before completing the task

Default Workflow Start Values

Specify the default values that this workflow will use when it is started. You can opt to allow the person who starts the workflow to change or add participants.

Type the names of people you want to participate when this workflow is started. Add names in the order in which you want the tasks assigned (for serial workflows).

Reviewers... William Burrows; Lori McGovern; Jordan Reynolds

Assign a single task to each group entered (Do not expand groups).

Allow changes to the participant list when this workflow is started

Type a message to include with your request:

Please look at this version of the document and annotate it with your comments. SharePoint will pass it along, with your comments, to the next person in the group.

Due Date

If a due date is specified and e-mail is enabled on the server, participants will receive a reminder on that date if their task is not finished.

Tasks are due by (parallel):

Give each person the following amount of time to finish their task (serial):

5 Day(s)

Figure 2-12
Defining a SharePoint Workflow, Part 2

Source: Microsoft Office SharePoint Designer 2007. Reprinted with permission from Microsoft Corporation.

to vendor B? Which invoices should we pay today? Information systems that support operational decision making are called **transaction processing systems (TPS)**. In most cases, operational decisions require little in the way of collaboration.

Managerial decisions concern the allocation and utilization of resources. Typical managerial decisions are: How much should we budget for computer

- **Decision Level**
  - Operational
  - Managerial
  - Strategic
- **Decision Process**
  - Structured
  - Unstructured

Figure 2-13
Decision-Making Dimensions

hardware and programs for department A next year? How many engineers should we assign to project B? How many square feet of warehouse space do we need for the coming year?

Some managerial decisions are collaborative because they necessitate feedback and iteration. A good example is deciding how much to increase employee pay in the coming year. The decision depends on an analysis of inflation, industry trends, the organization's profitability, the influence of unions, and other factors. Senior managers, accountants, human resources personnel, labor relationships managers, and others will each bring a different perspective to the decision. They will produce work product, evaluate that product, and make revisions in an iterative fashion—the essence of collaboration.

Strategic decisions concern broader-scope, organizational issues. Typical decisions at the strategic level are: Should we start a new product line? Should we open a centralized warehouse in Tennessee? Should we acquire company A?

Strategic decisions are almost always collaborative. Consider a decision about whether to move manufacturing operations to China. This decision affects every employee in the organization, the organization's suppliers, its customers, and its shareholders. Many factors and many perspectives on each of those factors must be considered. Feedback and iteration will be crucial to this decision.

INNOVATION IN PRACTICE

BUSINESS ADVANTAGE THROUGH INNOVATION

As discussed in Chapter 1, according to a RAND Corporation study, the demand for highly skilled workers who can exploit new technologies in business will continue to explode. Look no further than Google, YouTube, or, for an earlier generation, Amazon.com, and you can see the advantages that accrue to the exploitation of new technology. But innovation in business is not confined to companies that were founded on the use of new technology; more frequently, innovation occurs by using new technology within existing companies.

This chapter introduces three new technologies: Google Docs & Spreadsheets, Groove, and SharePoint. How can these technologies be leveraged for advantage? If you can answer that question, you will add considerably to your value as an employee (or job candidate).

Innovation means doing something in a new way, but, as stated in Chapter 1, not just innovation for innovation's sake. The innovation must add value.

Take Google Docs & Spreadsheets. What is the essence of that product? It allows near-instantaneous editing of text and spreadsheet documents by geographically separated people. Who can use that capability? What about a small accounting firm? Could an accounting firm gain a competitive advantage by sharing spreadsheet documents with its clients via Google Docs & Spreadsheets? Would the clients want to do that? What are the security concerns?

Or, consider Groove. Suppose you are a shopping-center developer in Florida. During planning, you have many meetings with project architects and consulting engineers. Every time they come to your office, you pay for their travel time, and their time is expensive. Could you use Groove to conduct planning sessions without meeting face-to-face? Could you share design documents online? If so, you could eliminate considerable overhead expense.

What about SharePoint? Suppose you are the president of a local water association that shares a common well with 100 homes in a rural area. Members pay a cost per gallon of water used plus an annual maintenance fee. The association deals with many complex issues: Some members are concerned with water quality and want to see the county's water quality reports; some worry about the health of the well and water table and want to know what is being done to conserve water. Yet others believe the annual maintenance fee is too high and need to know where the money is going. In addition, the association bylaws require you to publish quarterly and annual reports, and postage costs are considerable. Can you use SharePoint to advantage in this situation? Would it be worth the time, trouble, and expense?

Innovation is exploiting new technologies in the production of goods and services. In this chapter, you have learned three new collaboration technologies. Don't sit on that knowledge!

This topic continues in Collaboration Exercise 2 on page 58.

The Decision Process

Figure 2-14 shows levels of information systems with two decision processes: *structured* and *unstructured*. These terms refer to the method or process by which the decision is to be made, not to the nature of the underlying problem. A **structured decision** process is one for which there is an understood and accepted method for making the decision. A formula for computing the reorder quantity of an item in inventory is an example of a structured decision process. A standard method for allocating furniture and equipment to employees is another structured decision process. Structured decisions seldom require collaboration.

An **unstructured decision** process is one for which there is no agreed-on decision-making method. Predicting the future direction of the economy or the stock market is a classic example. The prediction method varies from person to person; it is neither standardized nor broadly accepted. Another example of an unstructured decision process is assessing how well-suited an employee is for performing a particular job. Managers vary in the manner in which they make such assessments. Unstructured decisions are often collaborative.

Again, keep in mind that the terms *structured* and *unstructured* refer to the decision process, not the underlying subject. Weather forecasting is a structured decision because the *process* used to make the decision is standardized among forecasters. Weather itself, however, is a famously unstructured phenomenon, as tornadoes and hurricanes demonstrate every year.

The Relationship Between Decision Type and Decision Process

The decision type and decision process are loosely related. As Figure 2-14 shows, decisions at the operational level tend to be structured, and decisions at the strategic level tend to be unstructured. Managerial decisions tend to be both structured and unstructured.

We use the words *tend to be*, because there are exceptions to the relationship illustrated in Figure 2-14. Some operational decisions are unstructured (e.g., "How many taxicab drivers do we need on the night before the homecoming game?"), and some strategic decisions can be structured (e.g., "How should we assign sales quotas for a new product?"). In general, however, the relationship shown in Figure 2-14 holds.

Decision Making and Collaboration Systems

As stated, few structured decisions involve collaboration. Deciding, for example, how much of product A to order from vendor B does not require the feedback and iteration among members that typify collaboration. Although the process of generating the order

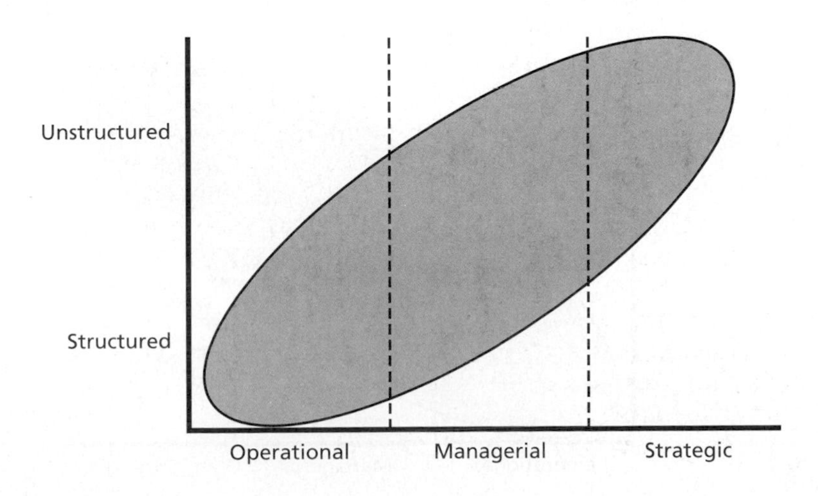

Figure 2-14
Decision Process and Decision Type

might require the coordinated work of people in purchasing, accounting, and manufacturing, there is seldom a need for one person to comment on someone else's work. In fact, involving collaboration in routine, structured decisions is expensive, wasteful, and frustrating. "Do we have to have a meeting about everything?" is a common lament.

The situation is different for unstructured decisions, because feedback and iteration are crucial. Members bring different ideas and perspectives about what is to be decided, how the decision will be reached, what criteria are important, and how decision alternatives score against those criteria. The group may make tentative conclusions, discuss potential outcomes of those conclusions, and members will often revise their positions. Figure 2-15 illustrates the change in the need for collaboration as decision processes become less structured.

Communications systems are the most important collaboration systems for unstructured decision processes. Because the process is unstructured, plans will evolve dynamically, and team members must be able to stay abreast of changes in tasks and direction. Content-management systems may also be important if elements of the decision are recorded in numerous versions of documents, designs, or data. Workflow systems are seldom of use, because work processes change frequently in an unstructured decision process.

Q6 How Do Businesses Use Collaboration Systems for Problem Solving?

You learned in Chapter 1 that problem solving is a critical skill for symbolic-analytic workers who compete in the global marketplace. You also learned three fundamental roles: problem-identifier, problem-solver, and solution-broker. Problem solving requires effective collaboration, because people in these three roles frequently provide feedback to each other as they iterate their work. To understand this better, consider the following example.

A Laptop Problem

Suppose you buy a new laptop computer and within a few days it fails. It locks up, and neither the mouse nor the keyboard will function until you turn the power off and then on. You call the manufacturer's customer support hotline, and the support representative leads you through a procedure to fix the problem by installing software from the manufacturer's Web site. After you follow the instructions, the laptop seems to work fine.

A day or so later, however, your computer locks up again. You call back to the support center, and this time you speak to a different representative, one who has no record of your prior call. She instructs you to repeat all the actions you performed before. This procedure takes time, but after you do it, the computer works again—for a while. Sure enough, several days later your laptop fails again.

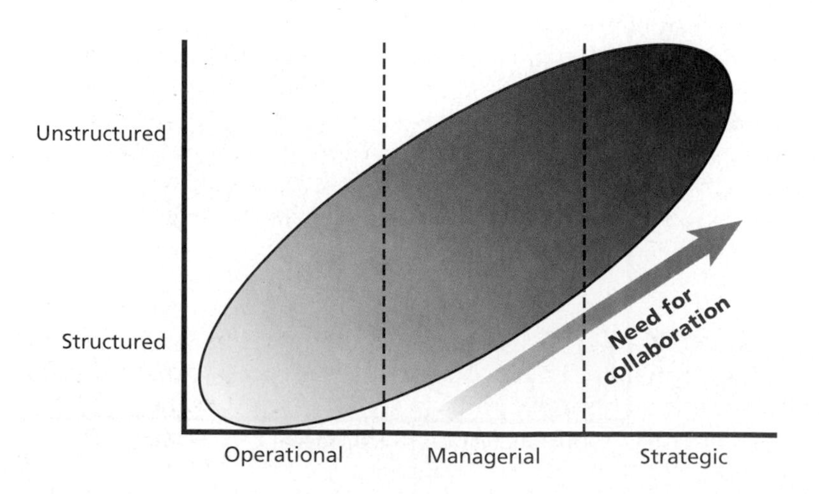

Figure 2-15
Collaboration Needs for Decision Types

Problem Definition

The first step in solving a problem is to define it. A **problem** is a *perceived difference between what is and what ought to be.* Notice that a problem is a *perception;* it is the view of a situation held by an individual or a group. Because a problem is a perception, different people or groups may have different problem definitions. For example, for the failing laptop computer, you might define the problem as, "The fix they gave me didn't work." The customer support representative, however, may define the problem as, "I have no record of the customer's prior contact with our company."

A good problem definition defines the difference between what is and what ought to be by describing both the current situation and the desired situation. You might define the problem as:

> *I spent 10 minutes on hold and then another 15 minutes following the instructions the support rep gave me. After almost a half hour of my time, my computer still wasn't fixed. I want to spend less than 5 minutes altogether, and I want the fix to work.*

This laptop problem helps demonstrate the important difference between egocentric thinking versus empathetic thinking, as discussed in the Problem-Solving Guide on page 54.

However, the support representative may define the problem as:

> *I had no data about the prior call. I wanted to know the customer's prior history with our company: the products he owns, previous problems reported, and contact data including the dates, the names of our representatives, and a summary of the situation for each prior call.*

A third person, someone in manufacturing, might define the problem as:

> *We are shipping too many faulty computers. We need to reduce our new-computer failure rate to less than one-half percent.*

All of these problem definitions are valid. None of them makes the others wrong, but before a work team can address potential solutions it must agree on a common problem definition. Obtaining that common definition will likely require feedback and iteration, hence the need for collaboration.

Problem Solutions and Solution Brokering

Identifying solution alternatives, choosing among those alternatives, and brokering the selected solution also involve feedback and iteration. The problem-solvers may need clarification on the problem definition, or they may seek a change in problem definition that will enable them to achieve a cheaper or more effective problem solution.

In the case of the laptop, suppose the team focuses on providing complete customer information to the support representative. Suppose the solution-providers obtain a solution that is too expensive for the solution-brokers to fund. Perhaps providing information about all of the customer's past interactions with the company is particularly difficult. In that case, the team will iterate back to the problem definition and redefine it, perhaps by eliminating the need for information about *all* past interactions. Instead, it may decide to store and report only information about current problems.

Such adjustment is typical. Often, the entire problem-solving team will work with the solution-broker to facilitate the acquisition of funds or organizational support or other resources needed to implement the solution. Problem-identifiers and solution-brokers will also provide feedback to the solution-broker about the best ways to sell the solution. They will also help the broker respond to objections from resource sources.

Problem Solving and Collaboration Systems

Both communication and content-management systems are highly important for problem solving. Problem-identifiers, solution-providers, and solution-brokers must be able to communicate regularly and reliably. They need readily available communication systems that meet their communication styles.

Content management is important to ensure that all team members are working on the same version of the issues. If there are three different problem definitions, and if two of them have been discarded in favor of the third, all team members should be working on that third definition. Or, if the problem has been redefined, all team members must be working on the modified definition.

This may seem obvious, but thousands of dollars can (and have) been wasted by creating solutions for out-of-date versions of problem definitions. In the laptop example, the problem was redefined to eliminate the need for providing data about all prior customer interactions. Without effective content management, however, some employees will continue to work against the original problem definition.

Although communications and content-management systems are both important to problem solving, workflow control is less so. Most problem-solving activities are unstructured, and the development of formal workflows and procedures is not feasible.

Q7 How Do Businesses Use Collaboration Systems for Project Management?

Project management is a broad and important topic. Here we will just touch on the fundamentals so that you can understand the need and role for collaboration systems in project management.

A **project** is a dynamic application of people and other resources for the creation of a product or the achievement of some aim. Examples of projects are the production of the first Boeing 787 or the election of Barack Obama (or any candidate) as President of the United States. A project is *dynamic* because the application of resources will be changed as events unfold and learning takes place. Projects normally have a limited duration; they start and are completed; they are not usually ongoing.

Project management is the application of tools and techniques to achieve the project's goals within time and budget constraints. Hundreds of different project management tools and techniques exist. The Project Management Institute (PMI) promulgates best practices for project management and publishes a summary of such practices in a document called the *PMBOK Guide*. Go to *www.PMI.org* for more information about this institute and document.

Project Management Stages and Tasks

Figure 2-16 lists the essential stages and tasks in project management.[3] In this list, the term **scope** refers to the requirements to be achieved by the project. For example, suppose a project has the goal of producing the design of a fast sailboat. Scope refers to the particulars of that goal: How fast? What kind of sailboat? How big a boat? For use in open ocean or protected waters? And so forth.

Because projects are dynamic, an organization must accordingly adjust scope changes and project tasks and activities. The management of scope changes is arguably the most important project-management task. The IRS case at the end of Chapter 1 (page 26) is an example of the costs of failure to manage scope.

Figure 2-16 uses the term **trade-off**. Because resources are scarce, project managers need to make choices among scope, time, cost, quality, risk, people, and other resources. It may be that producing the sailboat design by the specified date will result in unacceptable overhead costs and employee turnover. If so, the managers may need to trade off a delay in the project due date to reduce expenses and retain critical employees. Many other, similar trade-offs arise.

Notice feedback and iteration among these stages and tasks. As events unfold, as scope changes, and as problems develop, project managers continually revise, replan,

[3]For simplicity, Figure 2-16 mangles the management activities and knowledge areas of the PMBOK model. See the *PMBOK Guide* for a correct and complete version of this model.

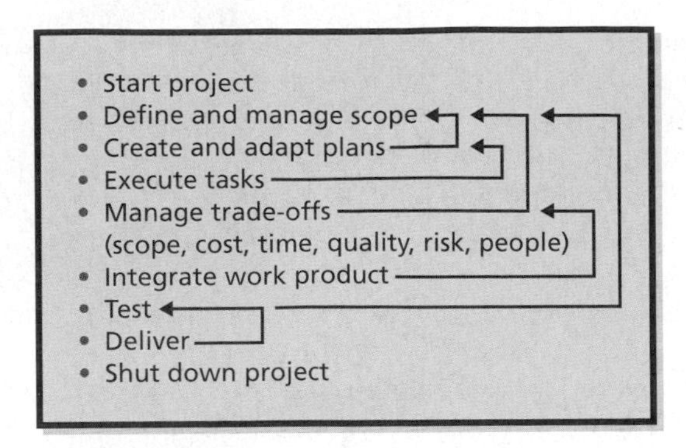

Figure 2-16
Summary of Project Management Activities and Common Feedback Paths

and reallocate. Because of feedback and iteration, project management is always a collaborative effort.

Collaboration Systems for Project Management

Before we consider the collaboration systems useful for project management, examine the relationships of decision making, problem solving, and project management shown in Figure 2-17. Decision making is the fundamental activity. It is important in its own right, and it is important because it supports problem solving and project management. Every problem solution and every project require effective decision making.

Similarly, problem solving is important in its own right, and it is also important because it supports project management. Projects are dynamic, and unexpected problems arise. For example, a change in sailboat racing rules may create scope changes and generate many problems to be solved in the design of the sailboat.

Because of the hierarchical nature of decision making, problem solving, and project management, collaboration systems that are important for lower-level activities are important for higher-level ones, too. Thus, because communication systems are vital to decision making, they are also vital to problem solving and project management. Because content-management systems are vital to problem solving, they are vital to project management as well.

Note, however, that in addition to communication and content management, project management also needs workflow-control systems. Project tasks have dependencies that constrain the points at which work can be initiated and completed. Considering the design of the Boeing 787, the team cannot start on the design of the landing gear until the weight of the plane is known. Similarly, the design of the wheels cannot be finalized until the design of the landing gear is complete.

Because of task dependencies, workflow control is critical to project management. For all but the simplest projects, workflows must be formally defined and compulsively enforced.

Before we conclude this chapter, understand that Figure 2-17 is a schematic of general tendencies. Many exceptions exist. For some decisions, coordination is as important as communication. Some projects do not require content management. However, in a general sense, the relationships in Figure 2-17 hold true and can be used as a guide.

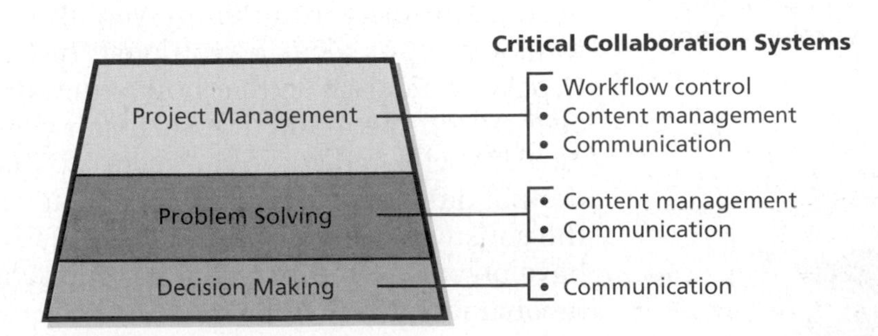

Figure 2-17
Collaboration Systems for Decision Making, Problem Solving, and Project Management

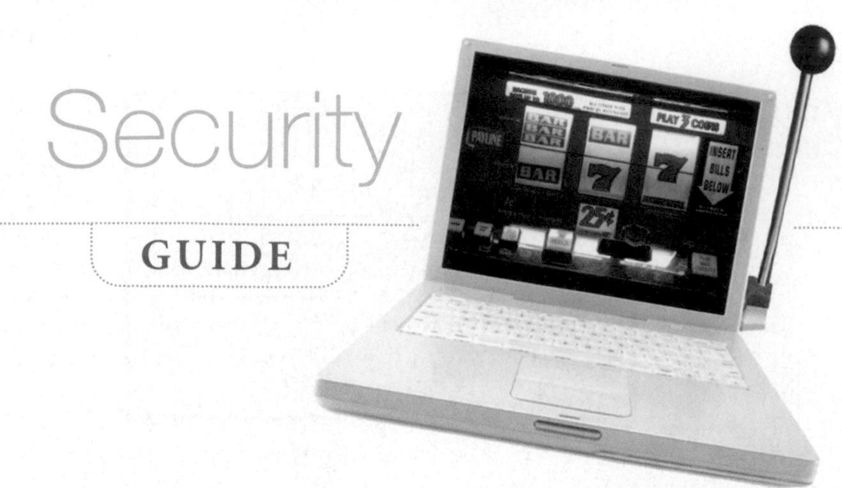

Security

GUIDE

Securing Collaboration

The collaboration tools described in this chapter do indeed facilitate collaboration: They help groups improve the quality of their work, while reducing travel and other logistical expenses, and they can enable people to participate in meetings asynchronously. However, they also pose security risks—possibly serious ones.

Consider Google Docs & Spreadsheets. All documents are stored on Google computers, which are located, well, who knows where? Does Google protect those computers appropriately? If those computers are located in, say, San Francisco, will they survive an earthquake? Google is a responsible, rich, and knowledgeable company that understands the need for disaster preparedness. But as outsiders, we do not know how they protect their sites. Natural disasters are not the only threat; computer crime, the actions of disgruntled employees, and computer viruses must be considered as well.

But, chances are... (even that phrase is revealing, do you really want to gamble with your data?)... chances are Google knows what it is doing, and your data is more than reasonably protected. However, how does the data get to a Google site? As you will learn in Chapter 6, most wireless traffic, including Google Docs & Spreadsheets, is unprotected from wireless snoopers. Are you processing that data at a local coffee shop? Do you care that anyone in that shop can copy your data?

Wireless snooping is not possible with Groove. All communications between your computer and the other Groove sites are automatically protected using up-to-date encryption technology (again, more to come in Chapter 6). No snooper can obtain your data. But Groove poses substantial security risks of a different kind.

Suppose you are the manager of a product line and you observe an odd pattern in sales for your products. That pattern might be related to differences in advertising among geographic regions, or it might have something to do with changes in consumer purchasing behavior. You decide to have a Groove meeting with some of your staff, employees of your advertising agency, and a marketing guru who specializes in contemporary consumer behavior.

To prepare for the meeting, you access your corporate computer systems and obtain all of the sales for your products over the past 12 months. That data is highly confidential and is protected by your IS department in many ways. You can access it only because you have access authority as an employee. But, without thinking about security, you post that data in a Groove workspace so that both your advertising agency and the marketing guru can view it. You have just violated corporate security. That confidential data is now available to the agency and the consultant. Either party can copy it, and you have no way of knowing that the copy was made or what was done with it.

Suppose the marketing guru makes a copy and uses it to improve her knowledge of consumer behavior. Unknown to you, she also consults for your chief rival. She has used your data to improve her knowledge and is now using that knowledge to benefit your competitor. (This sets aside the even uglier possibility that she gives or sells your data to that competitor.)

SharePoint has extensive security features, and as long as the administrator of your SharePoint site has implemented a proper security plan, it should be well protected. But, of course, SharePoint makes it easy to download data, and if you share that data with others via Google Docs & Spreadsheets or Groove... well, you get the picture.

Collaboration tools have many benefits, but they do open the door to loss of critical assets. Let the collaborator beware! ■

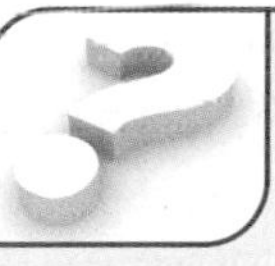

Discussion Questions

1. Any email or instant message that you send over a wireless device is open. Anyone with some free software and a bit of knowledge can snoop your communications. In class, your professor could read all of your email and instant messages, as could anyone else in the class. Does this knowledge change your behavior in class? Why or why not?
2. Unless you are so foolish as to reveal personal data, such as credit card numbers, Social Security number, or a driver's license number in an email or instant message, the loss of privacy to you as an individual is small. Someone might learn that you were gossiping about someone else and it might be embarrassing, but that loss is not critical. How does that situation change for business communications? Describe losses, other than those in this guide, that could occur when using email or Google Docs & Spreadsheets.
3. In addition to Google Docs & Spreadsheets, Google offers Gmail, a free email service with an easy-to-use interface and that famous Google search capability. Using Gmail, searching through past emails is very easy, fast, and accurate. In addition, because mail is stored on Google computers, it is easy to access one's email, contacts, and other data from any computer at any location. Many employees prefer using Gmail to their corporate email system. What are the consequences to the organization of some employees doing most of their email via Gmail? What are the risks?
4. Summarize the risks of using Groove in a business setting. How can organizations protect themselves from such risks? Is there any new risk here? After all, organizations have been sharing data in other formats with their business partners for years. Is this much ado about nothing? Why or why not?
5. Do you think the risks of using Groove can be so large that it makes sense for organizations to disallow its use? Why or why not? What are the costs of disallowing such use? How would the organization prevent an employee from purchasing a license for Groove and installing it on his own laptop computer at home? If the employee said that he needs it for work that does not involve corporate data, how should the organization respond?

Problem-Solving

GUIDE

Egocentric Versus Empathetic Thinking

As stated, a problem is a perceived difference between what is and what ought to be. When developing information systems, it is critical for the development team to have a common definition and understanding of the problem. This common understanding can be difficult to achieve, however.

Cognitive scientists distinguish between egocentric and empathetic thinking. Egocentric thinking centers on the self; someone who engages in egocentric thinking considers his or her view as "the real view" or "what really is." In contrast, those who engage in empathetic thinking consider their view as one possible interpretation of the situation and actively work to learn what other people are thinking.

Different experts recommend empathetic thinking for different reasons. Religious leaders say that such thinking is morally superior; psychologists say that empathetic thinking leads to richer, more fulfilling relationships. In business, empathetic thinking is recommended because it is smart. Business is a social endeavor, and those who can understand others' points of view are always more effective. Even if you do not agree with others' perspectives, you will be much better able to work with them if you understand their views.

Consider an example. Suppose you say to your MIS professor, "Professor Jones, I couldn't come to class last Monday. Did we do anything important?" Such a statement is a prime example of egocentric thinking. It takes no account of your professor's point of view and implies that your professor talked about nothing important. As a professor, it is tempting to say, "No, when I noticed you weren't there, I took out all the important material."

To engage in empathetic thinking, consider this situation from the professor's point of view. Students who do not come to class cause extra work for their professors. It does not matter how valid your reason for not attending class; you may actually have been contagious with a fever of 102. But, no matter what, your not coming to class is more work for your professor. He or she must do something extra to help you recover from the lost class time.

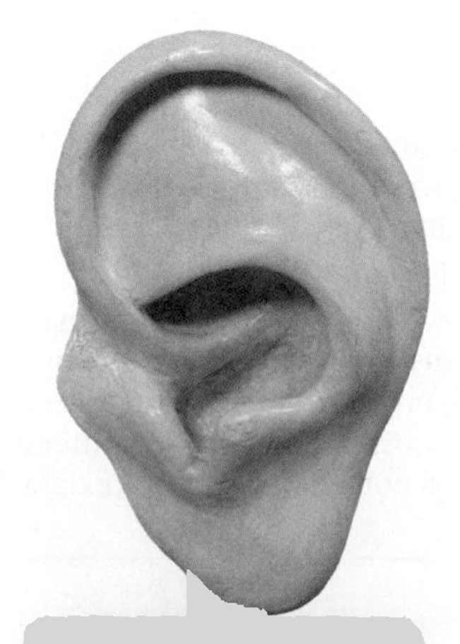

Using empathetic thinking, you would do all you can to minimize the impact of your absence on your professor. For example, you could say, "I couldn't come to class, but I got the class notes from Mary. I read through them, and I have a question about establishing alliances as competitive advantage.... Oh, by the way, I'm sorry to trouble you with my problem."

Before we go on, let's consider a corollary to this scenario: Never, ever, send an email to your boss that says, "I couldn't come to the staff meeting on Wednesday. Did we do anything important?" Avoid this for the same reasons as those for missing class. Instead, find a way to minimize the impact of your absence on your boss.

Now, what does all of this have to do with MIS? Consider the laptop problem introduced on page 48. In that scenario, there are three different views of the problem: (1) Customer support representatives do not have data about prior customer contacts; (2) the customer support representative recommended a solution that did not work; and (3) the company is shipping too many defective laptops. The solution to each of these different problem definitions requires a different information system.

Now imagine yourself in a Groove meeting about this situation and suppose that different people in the meeting hold the three problem views. If everyone engages in egocentric thinking, what will happen? The meeting will be argumentative and acrimonious and likely will end with nothing accomplished.

Suppose, instead, that the attendees think empathetically. In this case, people will make a concerted effort to understand the different points of view, and the outcome will be much more positive—possibly a definition of all three problems ranked in order of priority. In both scenarios, the attendees have the same information; the difference in outcomes results from the thinking style of the attendees.

Empathetic thinking is an important skill in all business activities. Skilled negotiators always know what the other side wants; effective salespeople understand their customers' needs. Buyers who understand the problems of their vendors get better service. And students who understand the perspective of their professors get better.... ■

Discussion Questions

1. In your own words, explain how egocentric and empathetic thinking differ.
2. Suppose you miss a staff meeting. Using empathetic thinking, explain how you can get needed information about what took place in the meeting.
3. How does empathetic thinking relate to problem definition?
4. Suppose you and another person differ substantially on a problem definition. Suppose she says to you, "No, the real problem is that..." followed by her definition of the problem. How do you respond?
5. Again, suppose you and another person differ substantially on a problem definition. Assume you understand his definition. How can you make that fact clear?
6. Explain the following statement: "In business, empathetic thinking is smart." Do you agree?

ACTIVE REVIEW

Use this Active Review to verify that you understand the ideas and concepts that answer the chapter's study questions.

Q1 What is collaboration?

Define *collaboration.* Explain how collaboration, communication, and coordination differ. Describe the role that feedback and iteration play in collaboration. Describe a team project that is cooperative but not collaborative. Name the three drivers of collaboration effectiveness and explain each.

Q2 How can you use collaboration systems to improve team communication?

Explain why communication is important to student collaborations. Define *synchronous* and *asynchronous* communication, and explain when each is used. Name two collaboration tools that can be used to help set up synchronous meetings. Describe collaboration tools that can be used for face-to-face meetings. Describe tools that can be used for virtual, synchronous meetings. Describe tools that can be used for virtual, asynchronous meetings. Compare and contrast the advantages of email, discussion forums, and team surveys.

Q3 How can you use collaboration systems to manage content?

Describe two ways that content is shared with no control, and explain the problems that can occur. Explain how control is provided by the following collaboration tools: wikis, Google Docs & Spreadsheets, and Microsoft Groove. Define *workspace,* and explain how Groove uses workspaces. Explain the difference between version management and version control. Describe how user accounts, passwords, and libraries are used to control user activity. Explain how checkin/checkout works. Identify major features in Microsoft SharePoint.

Q4 How can you use collaboration systems to control workflow?

Explain the difference between content management and workflow control. Give an example of a sequential workflow. Describe why manual enforcement of workflow is an administrative nightmare. Explain how Microsoft SharePoint can be used to enforce sequential workflow.

Q5 How do businesses use collaboration systems for decision making?

Name three levels of decision making, and give an example of each. Describe the difference between structured and unstructured decision making, and give an example of each. Explain how the need for collaboration changes among decision levels and decision processes.

Q6 How do businesses use collaboration systems for problem solving?

Define *problem.* Explain the importance of the fact that a problem is a perception; use the example of the laptop problem in your answer. Name and describe three problem-solving roles for symbolic-analytic workers. Explain how feedback and iteration apply to problem solving. Describe the ways that collaboration systems can be used for problem solving.

Q7 How do businesses use collaboration systems for project management?

Define *project* and *project management.* Define *scope* and explain its role in a project. Give an example of two trade-offs that might occur in the sailboat design project. Diagram the relationships among decision making, problem solving, and project management. Explain the role for collaboration systems for each activity in your diagram. Describe why and how workflow control can be used in project management.

KEY TERMS AND CONCEPTS

USING YOUR KNOWLEDGE

1. This exercise requires you to experiment with Google Docs & Spreadsheets. You will need two Google accounts to complete this exercise. If you have two different email addresses, then set up two Google accounts using those addresses. Otherwise, use your school email address and set up a Google Gmail account. A Gmail account will automatically give you a Google account.

   a. Using Microsoft Word, write a memo to yourself. In the memo, explain the nature of the communication collaboration driver. Go to *http://docs.google.com* and sign in with one of your Google accounts. Upload your memo using Google Docs & Spreadsheets. Save your uploaded document and share your document with the email in your second Google account. Sign out of your first Google account.

      (If you have access to two computers situated close to each other, use both of them for this exercise. You will see more of the Google Docs & Spreadsheets functionality by using two computers. If you have two computers, do not sign out of your Google account. Perform step b and all actions for the second account on that second computer. If you are using two computers, ignore the instructions to sign out of the Google accounts in the following steps.)

   b. Open a new window in your browser. Access *http://docs.google.com* from that second window and sign in using your second Google account. Open the document that you shared in step a.

   c. Change the memo by adding a brief description of the content-management driver. Save the document from your second account. If you are using just one computer, sign out from your second account.

   d. Sign in on your first account. Open the most recent version of the memo and add a description of the workflow control communication driver. Save the document. (If you are using two computers, notice how Google warns you that another user is editing the document at the same time. Click *Refresh* to see what happens.) If you are using just one computer, sign out from your first account.

   e. Sign in on your second account. Re-open the shared document. From the File menu, save the document as a Word document.

   f. Describe how Google processed the changes to your document.

2. This exercise requires you to experiment with Microsoft Office Groove. To perform it, you need to work with a classmate. Both you and your classmate must install a copy of Microsoft Office Groove. Check with your instructor to learn how to download a license-free version using the MSDN Academic Alliance. In the following steps, one of you should take the role of user A and the other should take the role of user B.

   a. User A should open the Groove launch bar and create a new workspace. Select *Standard*. In the lower right-hand section of the new workspace, invite user B to join the workspace by entering user B's email address. While you are waiting for user B to respond, use Word to write a memo briefly summarizing the need for version management. Save the memo using the file name *VersionManagement* and add it to the workspace by clicking *Add Files*.

   b. User B will receive an invitation to join the workspace. All user B needs to do is to click the link provided. The workspace will open. User B should write a memo summarizing the need for version control. Save that memo with the name *VersionControl* and add it to the workspace.

   c. User A should then open the chat window in the lower right-hand corner and enter a chat message asking user B to read *VersionManagement* and make comments.

   d. User B should respond to user A's chat and send a chat message to user A asking for a review of *VersionControl*. Make a few changes and save the document.

   e. User A should open and review *VersionManagement*. User B should open and review *VersionControl*. Make a few changes and save the document.

   f. Using chat, coordinate your efforts so that both users attempt to open the same document at the same time. Note what happens.

   g. Add a sketchpad tool to the workspace by clicking the icon (in the lower right-of-center section of the workspace) that shows a document and a green plus sign and selecting *Sketchpad*.

   h. Using chat, coordinate your efforts to modify the sketch at the same time. Note what happens.

   i. Using chat, describe your experiences. Both users should comment on what they have seen.

   j. Save your chat transcript as a file. Right-click in the chat window and select *Chat/Print transcript*. In the print window, select *print to file*. Submit your chat transcript as you answer to this exercise.

3. If your instructor has enabled a Microsoft SharePoint site for your class, you can perform exercises using SharePoint. Go to *www.prehall.com/kroenke* and find the file *Chapter 2 SharePoint Exercises*. Perform the exercises shown there.

COLLABORATION EXERCISES AND CASES

1. With a team of your fellow students, develop an answer to the following four questions. Use Google Docs & Spreadsheets, Groove, SharePoint, or some other collaboration system to conduct your meetings.
   a. What is collaboration?
   Reread Q1 in this chapter, but do not confine yourselves to that discussion. Consider your own experience working in collaborative teams, and search the Web to identify other ideas about collaboration. Dave Pollard, one of the authors of the survey on pages 32 and 33, is a font of ideas on collaboration.
   b. What characteristics make for an effective team member?
   The survey on pages 32 and 33 reports characteristics of an effective team member. Review those results as a group. Do you agree with them? What conclusions can you, as a team, take from this survey? Would you change the rankings? Are important characteristics missing?
   c. What would you do with an ineffective team member?
   Define an ineffective team member. Specify five or so characteristics of an ineffective team member. If your group has such a member, what action do you, as a group, believe should be taken?
   d. How do you know if you are collaborating well?
   When working with a group, how do you know whether you are working well or poorly? Specify five or so characteristics that indicate collaborative success. How can you measure those characteristics?
   Deliver your answers to these four questions to your instructor in the format required—on paper, as a Groove workspace, as a SharePoint site, or some other innovative format.
2. With a team of your fellow students, develop an answer to the following five questions. Use Google Docs & Spreadsheets, Groove, SharePoint, or some other collaboration system to conduct your meetings.
   a. Consider an innovative application of Google Docs & Spreadsheets.
      (1) Describe the innovative features of Google Docs & Spreadsheets.
      (2) Describe ways that Google Docs & Spreadsheets could be applied innovatively at three different organizations. Consider both for-profit and not-for-profit organizations. If you want, use the examples of the accounting firm, the shopping-center developer, and the community water association. Or, use examples based on your college campus.
      (3) Explain the benefits of each application in part 2.
      (4) Which of the three applications in your answer is most compelling? Why?
   b. Repeat part a, but use Groove instead. Does the application that is most compelling change? If so, why?
   c. Repeat part a, but use SharePoint instead. Does the application that is most compelling change from your answers in a and b when you are considering SharePoint? If so, why?
   d. Which of the three applications is most compelling? Why?
   e. Write a two-paragraph description of the application you selected in part d. Prepare the description so that you can use it in a job interview; write it to demonstrate your ability to think innovatively.

APPLICATION EXERCISES

1. Suppose that you have been asked to assist in the managerial decision about how much to increase pay in the next year. Assume you are given a list of the departments in your company, along with the average salary for employees in that department for major companies in your industry. Additionally, you are given the names and salaries of 10 people in each of three departments in your company.
   Assume you have been asked to create a spreadsheet that shows the names of the 10 employees in each department, their current salary, the difference between their current salary and the industry average salary for their department, and the percent their salary would need to be increased to meet the industry average. Your spreadsheet should also compute the average increase needed to meet the industry average for each department and the average increase, company-wide, to meet industry averages.
   a. Use the data in the file **Ch2Ex1.doc** and create the spreadsheet.
   b. How can you use this analysis to contribute to the employee salary decision? Based on this data, what conclusions can you make?
   c. Suppose other team members want to use your spreadsheet. Name three ways you can share it with them and describe the advantages and disadvantages of each.
2. Suppose that you have been asked to assist in the managerial decision about how much to increase pay in the next year. Specifically, you are

tasked to determine if there are significant salary differences among departments in your company.

You are given an Access database with a table of employee data with the following structure:

EMPLOYEE (Name, Department, Specialty, Salary)

where *Name* is the name of an employee who works in a department, *Department* is the department name, *Specialty* is the name of the employee's primary skill, and *Salary* is the employee's current salary. Assume that no two employees have the same name.

You have been asked to answer the following queries:

(1) List the names, department, and salary of all employees earning more than $100,000.

(2) List the names and specialties of all employees in the Marketing department.

(3) Compute the average, maximum, and minimum salary of employees in your company.

(4) Compute the average, minimum, and maximum salary of employees in the Marketing department.

(5) Compute the average, minimum, and maximum salary of employees in the Information Systems department.

(6) *Extra credit:* Compute the average salary for employees in every department. Use *Group By*.

a. Design and run Access queries to obtain the answers to these questions, using the data in the file **Ch2Ex2.mdb**.

b. Explain how the data in your answer contributes to the salary increase decision.

c. Suppose other team members want to use your Access application. Name three ways you can share it with them, and describe the advantages and disadvantages of each.

CASE STUDY 2

Customer Support and Knowledge Management at Microsoft

Many companies believe that "the best customer service is no service at all." In other words, the product works, the customer never calls, and there is never a need for service. The next-best customer service is that which someone else pays for. One such example occurs when users support one another. To this end, Microsoft and other software vendors create and administer "user communities" featuring newsgroups, user groups, and most valuable professionals (MVPs). See *microsoft.com/communities* for more examples.

In a *newsgroup*, users post questions about errors, problems, and product use. Other customers who have experience and expertise with the relevant product answer the posted questions. Microsoft employees can also post answers to questions. A side benefit for Microsoft is that it learns about product and documentation problems from the questions that are posted to the newsgroups.

A *user group* consists of product users who meet periodically in a particular geographic location. For example, a Microsoft Office user group in Washington, D.C., meets periodically to discuss best practices, new developments, problems, and other issues related to the use of Microsoft Office. User groups not only save Microsoft support dollars, but they also promulgate Microsoft products in a more intimate, local setting. Microsoft employees attend user groups as speakers, advisers, and observers.

Microsoft designates 1,900 individuals from its millions of users worldwide as MVPs, or Most Valuable Professionals. These people possess expert-level knowledge of Microsoft products that they share with peers and other Microsoft product users. Microsoft selects these people "for their outstanding efforts to help people around the world do amazing things with technology." These people, who are not Microsoft employees, serve as Microsoft product and technology ambassadors. Microsoft hosts them in an annual MVP Conference at which they meet senior executives such as Bill Gates and Steve Ballmer.

Source: Customer Support and Knowledge Management at Microsoft. Reprinted with permission from Microsoft Corporation.

Questions

1. Explain why the best customer support is none at all.
2. List the benefits and costs to Microsoft of support newsgroups.
3. Why do users bother to answer other users' questions? What's in it for them? Suppose you manage a group of technical personnel. How much time do you want them to spend each day solving other peoples' problems? How can you control such activities?
4. What are the dangers to Microsoft in supporting a newsgroup? How can a newsgroup backfire on Microsoft? Do you think Microsoft edits or censors the newsgroup postings? Should it be able to do so?
5. List the benefits and costs to Microsoft of supporting user groups. Consider both customer support and marketing benefits.
6. What are the dangers to Microsoft in supporting a user group? How can a user group backfire on Microsoft? What control can Microsoft exert over such groups?
7. How does an individual benefit from joining a user group?
8. List the benefits and costs to Microsoft in supporting the MVP program. Consider both support and marketing benefits.
9. Why, besides the chance to meet Bill Gates, would someone want to become an MVP? What benefits accrue with that status?
10. Summarize the information systems that Microsoft uses to support these programs.

3 Information Systems for Competitive Advantage

STUDY QUESTIONS

- **Q1** How does organizational strategy determine information systems structure?
- **Q2** What five forces determine industry structure?
- **Q3** What is competitive strategy?
- **Q4** What is a value chain?
- **Q5** How do business processes generate value?
- **Q6** How does competitive strategy determine business processes and the structure of information systems?
- **Q7** How do information systems provide competitive advantages?

Meet Neil Miyamoto

My favorite business books:
Selling to VITO (Very Important Top Officer) by Anthony Parinello; *Built to Last: Successful Habits of Visionary Companies* by Jim Collins and Jerry Porras; *Gocd to Great: Why Some Companies Make the Leap . . . Others Don't* by Jim Collins.

Don't do this to me in an interview:
Answer your cell phone.

My guiding principle:
Humility leads to wisdom; be slow to speak, slow to form opinion, quick to listen.

What I do when I'm not working:
Anything outside.

Neil Miyamoto graduated with a degree in finance from California State University, San Diego, in 1993. He spent a few months performing spreadsheet analyses for a commercial real estate company and decided finance wasn't the career for him. He had been successful in competitive sports (once ranked the top amateur surfer in Southern California) and decided to apply that competitive spirit to professional sales. In 1994, he joined Wall Data Corporation, working in telesales selling computer software solutions to *Fortune* 500 companies. He became a top performer and within a few years moved on to sell more sophisticated customer relationship management (CRM) software for Siebel Systems. After that, he joined Adaytum Corporation as its VP of sales. He left Adaytum when it was acquired by the Cognos Corporation.

At that time The Firm, the leading workout studio in Minneapolis (*TheFirmMpls.com*), was looking for someone to help transform its paper-record system into a modern CRM. Neil signed on for a 6-month contract to lead that project. He had so much fun and saw such great opportunity that he stayed on to manage the back-office systems, eventually becoming a partner in the business.

On the firm:

"This is a great place; just jammed with positive energy. People love the fast-paced environment, and the superb workouts they receive make them feel terrific. Over the years, the business has grown by leaps and bounds, and we've gradually taken more and more space until we now occupy the majority of the building. We host 15,000 visits per month and employ, either full or part time, more than 50 people. Some clients drive 45 minutes just to come to a workout, and they do that two or three times a week!

"We're a high-value organization. We provide the most effective and most personal workout experience, anywhere, period. Our key is *personalization*. Our trainers and employees get to know our clients and their needs. Our clients get to know each other . . . we practically have a networking business club in our early morning and late afternoon classes. And we personalize all of our contacts with the customer.

"That's where information systems come in. We track the purchases, the classes, and the activities of every customer, and then use that data to customize customer contacts. Say we decide to offer an early morning kickboxing class. Using our customer database, we know every customer who's ever taken an early morning class and every customer who's ever taken a kickboxing class. Using that data, we send an email announcing the class to that very select group. Our customers appreciate the personal solicitation.

My pet peeves:
Cell phones in restaurants.
Slow driving in the fast lane.
Obese adults feeding their kids honey buns at the airport.

My management style:
Actions speak louder than words.
Lead by example: Your example needs to be five times greater than what you expect from others.
Let people make mistakes; providing correction is an investment in those around you as well as yourself.

My very first job:
Age 7: pumpkin farmer
Age 13: paper route

My motto:
Humility leads to wisdom; underestimate nothing.

Neil Miyamoto

We don't send announcements for events in which they will never have an interest. It's all part of our business strategy: personalization.

"Our trainers and customers form strong relationships. When John S. (one of our popular trainers) offers a new spinning class, we send an announcement of that new offering to everyone who's ever taken a class with John. Everybody is grateful; John knows his customers will learn about his new class, our customers learn about an opportunity they want to know about, and we save money by promoting that class to the most likely prospects."

On the importance of information systems:

"Our database is our biggest asset. Take away anything else—the building, the equipment, the inventories, anything else—and we'd be back in business in 6 months or less. Take away our customer database however, and we'd have to start all over. It would take us another 8 years to get back to where we are.

"Technology is the key for any business owner. It's the key to decreasing expenses and the key to increasing revenue. Every business owner needs to determine the performance indicators that drive his or her business and then wrap technology around those indicators. For us, it's information about our customers."

On the need for knowledge of information systems:

"I'm lucky—my experience in software sales helps me make technology decisions every day. I constantly receive solicitations from IT vendors—upgrade your network, buy this hardware, license this software, etc. I'm sure every business manager does. My knowledge lets me separate what we need from what we don't. I don't know how someone without knowledge of IT can make it today. I imagine they waste money . . . or pass up technology and systems that actually could help them.

"Even new hires—just out of school—you see some that are comfortable with information systems, maybe it's nothing more than knowing how to run Excel, connect to their email, and generate a query against the database. But they come to work, dive in, and they're productive much sooner than others. I saw this especially in software sales. The people who could take advantage of our CRM, who could quickly figure out how to use IS to manage their contacts, those people put themselves on the fast track for success. Anyone who can't use technology is just making it hard, taking a longer road to wherever they want to go."

CHAPTER PREVIEW

Recall from Chapter 1 that MIS is the development and use of information systems that enable organizations to achieve their goals and objectives. In Chapter 2, you learned how information systems can help people collaborate. In this chapter, we will focus on how information systems relate to an organization's competitive strategy and how IS can create competitive advantages. As you will learn in your organizational behavior classes, there is a body of knowledge to help organizations analyze their industry, select a competitive strategy, and develop business processes. In the first part of this chapter, we will survey that knowledge and show how to use it, via several steps, to structure information systems. Then, in the last section, we will discuss how companies use information systems to gain a competitive advantage.

Q1 How Does Organizational Strategy Determine Information Systems Structure?

Recall from the definition of MIS that information systems exist to help organizations achieve their goals and objectives. As you will learn in your business strategy class, an organization's goals and objectives are determined by its *competitive strategy*. Thus, ultimately, competitive strategy determines the structure, features, and functions of every information system.

Figure 3-1 summarizes this situation. In short, organizations examine the structure of their industry and determine a competitive strategy. That strategy determines value chains, which in turn determine business processes. The nature of business processes determines the structure of an information system.

Michael Porter, one of the key researchers and thinkers in competitive analysis, developed three different models that can help you understand the elements of Figure 3-1. We begin with his five forces model.

Q2 What Five Forces Determine Industry Structure?

Organizational strategy begins with an assessment of the fundamental characteristics and structure of an industry. One model used to assess an industry structure is Porter's **five forces model**,[1] shown in Figure 3-2 (next page). According to this model, five competitive forces determine industry profitability: bargaining power of customers, threat of substitutions, bargaining power of suppliers, threat of new entrants, and rivalry among existing firms. The intensity of each of the five forces determines the characteristics of the industry, how profitable it is, and how sustainable that profitability will be.

To understand this model, consider the strong and weak examples for each of the forces in Figure 3-3 (next page). A good check on your understanding is to see if you can think of different forces of each category in Figure 3-3. Also, take a particular industry—say, auto repair—and consider how these five forces determine the competitive landscape of that industry.

Organizations examine these five forces and determine how they intend to respond to them. That examination leads to competitive strategy.

Q3 What Is Competitive Strategy?

An organization responds to the structure of its industry by choosing a **competitive strategy**. Porter followed his five forces model with the model of four competitive

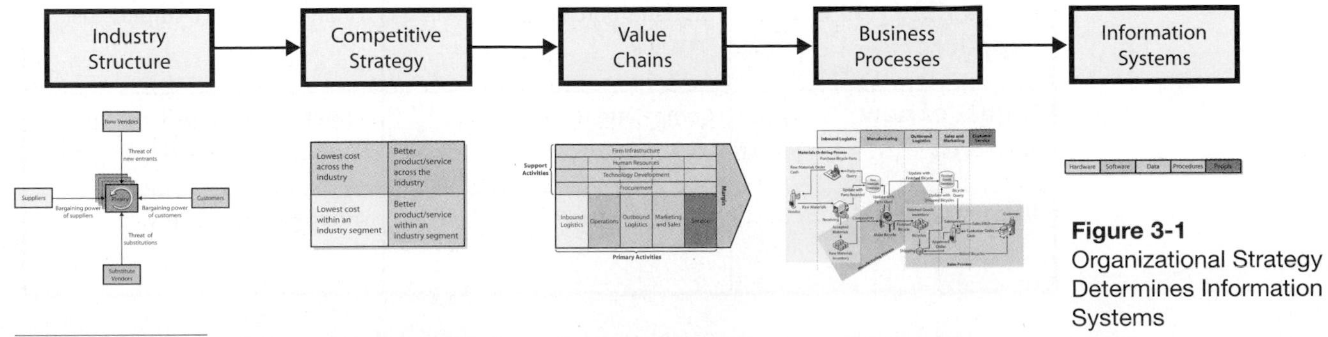

Figure 3-1
Organizational Strategy Determines Information Systems

[1]Michael Porter, *Competitive Strategy: Techniques for Analyzing Industries and Competitors* (New York: Free Press, 1980).

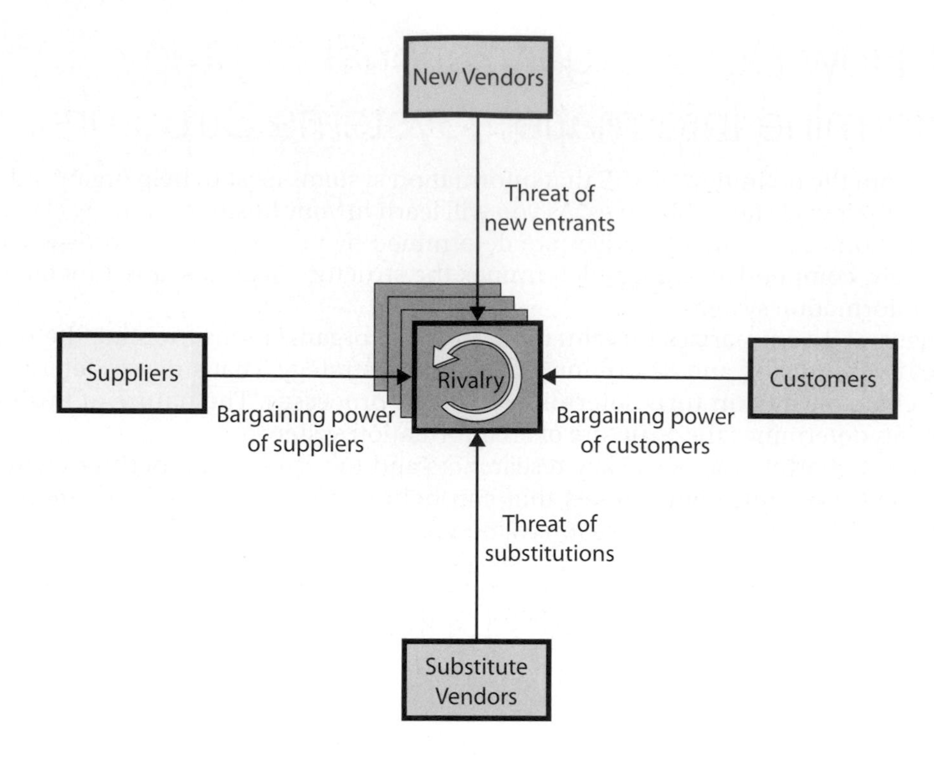

Figure 3-2
Porter's Five Forces Model of Industry Structure

Source: Adapted with the permission of The Free Press, a Division of Simon & Schuster Adult Publishing Group, from *Competitive Advantage: Creating and Sustaining Superior Performance* by Michael E. Porter.

strategies shown in Figure 3-4.[2] According to Porter, firms engage in one of these four strategies. An organization can focus on being the cost leader, or it can focus on differentiating its products from those of the competition. Further, the organization can employ the cost or differentiation strategy across an industry, or it can focus its strategy on a particular industry segment.

Consider the car rental industry, for example. According to the first column of Figure 3-4, a car rental company can strive to provide the lowest-cost car rentals across the industry, or it can seek to provide the lowest-cost car rentals to an industry segment—say, U.S. domestic business travelers.

As shown in the second column, a car rental company can seek to differentiate its products from the competition. It can do so in various ways—for example, by provid-

Force	Example of Strong Force	Example of Weak Force
Bargaining power of customers	Toyota's purchase of auto paint	Your power over the procedures and policies of your university
Threat of substitutions	Frequent-traveler's choice of auto rental	Patients using the only drug effective for their type of cancer
Bargaining power of suppliers	Students purchasing gasoline	Grain farmers in a surplus year
Threat of new entrants	Corner latte stand	Professional football team
Rivalry	Used car dealers	Internal Revenue Service

Figure 3-3
Examples of Five Forces

[2]Michael Porter, *Competitive Strategy* (New York: Free Press, 1985).

	Cost	Differentiation
Industry-wide	Lowest cost across the industry	Better product/service across the industry
Focus	Lowest cost within an industry segment	Better product/service within an industry segment

Figure 3-4
Porter's Four Competitive Strategies

ing a wide range of high-quality cars, by providing the best reservations system, by having the cleanest cars or the fastest check-in, or by some other means. The company can strive to provide product differentiation across the industry or within particular segments of the industry, such as U.S. domestic business travelers.

According to Porter, to be effective, the organization's goals, objectives, culture, and activities must be consistent with the organization's strategy. To those in the MIS field, this means that all information systems in the organization must reflect and facilitate the organization's competitive strategy.

Q4 What Is a Value Chain?

Organizations analyze the structure of their industry, and, using that analysis, they formulate a competitive strategy. They then need to organize and structure the organization to implement that strategy. If, for example, the competitive strategy is to be *cost leader*, then business activities need to be developed to provide essential functions at the lowest possible cost.

A business that selects a *differentiation* strategy would not necessarily structure itself around least-cost activities. Instead, such a business might choose to develop more costly systems, but it would do so only if those systems provided benefits that outweighed their risks. Porter defined **value** as the amount of money that a customer is willing to pay for a resource, product, or service. The difference between the value that an activity generates and the cost of the activity is called **margin**. A business with a differentiation strategy will add cost to an activity only as long as the activity has positive margin.

A **value chain** is a network of value-creating activities. Figure 3-5 (next page) shows the generic value chain model as developed by Porter. That generic chain consists of five **primary activities** and four **support activities**.

Primary Activities in the Value Chain

To understand the essence of the value chain, consider a small manufacturer—say, a bicycle maker. First, the manufacturer acquires raw materials using the inbound logistics activity. This activity concerns the receiving and handling of raw materials and other inputs. The accumulation of those materials adds value in the sense that even a pile of unassembled parts is worth something to some customer. A collection of the parts needed to build a bicycle is worth more than an empty space on a shelf. The value is not only the parts themselves, but also the time required to contact vendors for those parts, to maintain business relationships with those vendors, to order the parts, to receive the shipment, and so forth.

Identifying the activities that will create value is crucial but not always obvious, For an example, read the Innovation in Practice *box on page 67.*

In the operations activity, the bicycle maker transforms raw materials into a finished bicycle, a process that adds more value. Next, the company uses the outbound logistics activity to deliver the finished bicycle to a customer. Of course, there is no customer to send the bicycle to without the marketing and sales value activity. Finally, the service activity provides customer support to the bicycle users.

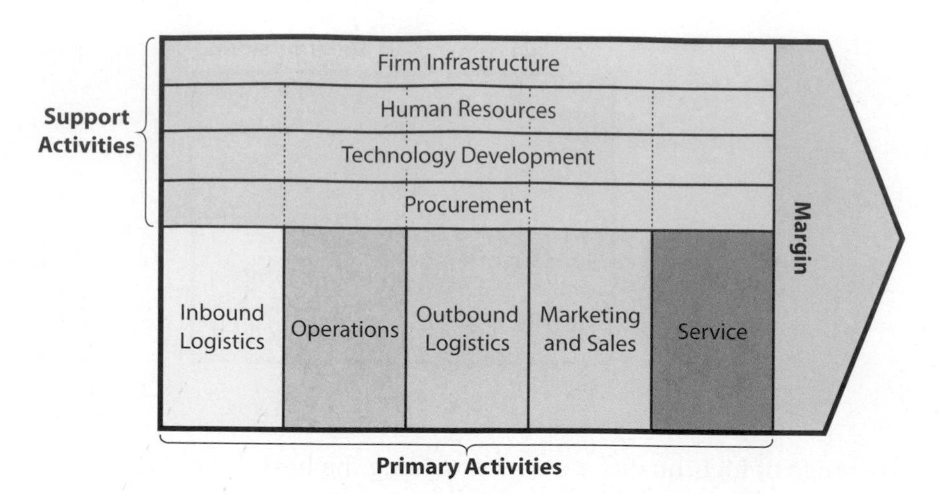

Figure 3-5
Porter's Value Chain Model

Source: Adapted with the permission of The Free Press, a Division of Simon & Schuster Adult Publishing Group, from *Competitive Advantage: Creating and Sustaining Superior Performance* by Michael E. Porter. Copyright © 1985, 1998 by Michael E. Porter. All rights reserved.

Each stage of this generic chain accumulates costs and adds value to the product. The net result is the total margin of the chain, which is the difference between the total value added and the total costs incurred. Figure 3-6 summarizes the primary activities of the value chain.

Support Activities in the Value Chain

The support activities in the generic value chain contribute indirectly to the production, sale, and service of the product. They include procurement, which consists of the processes of finding vendors, setting up contractual arrangements, and negotiating prices. (This differs from inbound logistics, which is concerned with ordering and receiving in accordance with agreements set up by procurement.)

Porter defined technology broadly. It includes research and development, but it also includes other activities within the firm for developing new techniques, methods, and procedures. He defined human resources as recruiting, compensation, evaluation, and training of full-time and part-time employees. Finally, firm infrastructure includes general management, finance, accounting, legal, and government affairs.

Supporting functions add value, albeit indirectly, and they also have costs. Hence, as shown in Figure 3-5, supporting activities contribute to a margin. In the case of supporting activities, it would be difficult to calculate the margin because the specific value added of, say, the manufacturer's lobbyists in Washington, D.C., is difficult to know. But there is a value added, there are costs, and there is a margin, even if it is only in concept.

Primary Activity	Description
Inbound logistics	Receiving, storing, and disseminating inputs to the product
Operations	Transforming inputs into the final product
Outbound logistics	Collecting, storing, and physically distributing the product to buyers
Marketing and sales	Inducing buyers to purchase the product and providing a means for them to do so
Service	Assisting customer's use of the product and thus maintaining and enhancing the product's value

Figure 3-6
Task Descriptions for Primary Activities of the Value Chain

Source: Adapted with the permission of The Free Press, a Division of Simon & Schuster Adult Publishing Group, from *Competitive Advantage: Creating and Sustaining Superior Performance* by Michael E. Porter. Copyright © 1985, 1998 by Michael E. Porter. All rights reserved.

INNOVATION IN PRACTICE

SELLING NEW SERVICES AT SINGING VALLEY

Singing Valley Resort is a top-end 50-unit resort located high in the Colorado mountains. Rooms rent for $400 to $4,500 per night, depending on the season and the type of accommodations. Singing Valley's clientele are well-to-do; many are famous entertainers, sports figures, and business executives. They are accustomed to, and demand, superior service.

Singing Valley resides in a gorgeous mountain valley and is situated a few hundred yards from a serene mountain lake. It prides itself on superior accommodations; tip-top service; delicious, healthful, organic meals; and exceptional wines. Because it has been so successful, Singing Valley is 90 percent occupied except during the "shoulder seasons" (November, after the leaves change and before the snow arrives, and late April, when winter sports are finished but the snow is still on the ground).

Singing Valley's owners want to increase revenue, but because the resort is nearly always full and because its rates are already at the top of the scale it cannot do so via occupancy revenue. Thus, over the past several years it has focused on up-selling to its clientele activities such as fly fishing, river rafting, cross-country skiing, snowshoeing, art lessons, yoga and other exercise classes, spa services, and the like.

To increase the sales of these optional activities, Singing Valley prepared in-room marketing materials to advertise their availability. Additionally, it trained all registration personnel on techniques of casually and appropriately suggesting such activities to guests on arrival.

The response to these promotions was only mediocre, so Singing Valley's management stepped up its promotions. The first step was to send email to its clientele advising them of the activities available during their stay. An automated system produced emails personalized with names and personal data.

Unfortunately, the automated email system backfired. Immediately upon its execution, Singing Valley management received numerous complaints. One long-term customer objected that she had been coming to Singing Valley for 7 years and asked if they had yet noticed that she was confined to a wheelchair. If they *had* noticed, she said, why did they send her a personalized invitation for a hiking trip? The agent of another famous client complained that the personalized email was sent to her client and her husband, when anyone who had turned on a TV in the past 6 months knew the two of them were involved in an exceedingly acrimonious divorce. Yet another customer complained that, indeed, he and his wife had vacationed at Singing Valley 3 years ago, but he had not been there since. To his knowledge, his wife had not been there, either, so he was puzzled as to why the email referred to their visit last winter. He wanted to know if, indeed, his wife had recently been to the resort, without him. Of course, Singing Valley had no way of knowing about customers it had insulted who never complained.

During the time the automated email system was operational sales of extra activities were up 15 percent. However, the strong customer complaints conflicted with its competitive strategy so, in spite of the extra revenue, Singing Valley stopped the automated email system, sacked the vendor who had developed it, and demoted the Singing Valley employee who had brokered the system. Singing Valley was left with the problem of how to increase its revenue.

You and a team of fellow students will be given an opportunity to solve Singing Valley's problem in Collaboration Exercise 1, which is located on page 86.

Linkages in the Value Chain

Porter's model of business activities includes **linkages**, which are interactions across value activities. For example, manufacturing systems use linkages to reduce inventory costs. Such a system uses sales forecasts to plan production; it then uses the production plan to determine raw materials needs and then uses the material needs to schedule purchases. The end result is just-in-time inventory, which reduces inventory sizes and costs.

By describing value chains and their linkages, Porter started a movement to create integrated, cross-departmental business systems. Over time, Porter's work led to the creation of a new discipline called *business process design*. The central idea is that organizations should not automate or improve existing functional systems. Rather, they should create new, more efficient business processes that integrate the activities of all departments involved in a value chain. You will see an example of a linkage in the next section.

Q5 How Do Business Processes Generate Value?

A **business process** is a network of activities that generate value by transforming inputs into outputs. The **cost** of the business process is the cost of the inputs plus the cost of the activities. The **margin** of the business process is the value of the outputs minus the cost.

A business process is a network of activities; each **activity** transforms **input resources** into **output resources**. Resources **flow** between or among activities. **Facilities** store resources; some facilities, such as inventories, store physical items. Other facilities, such as databases, hold data. (Recall Neil Miyamoto's comment in the opening interview that The Firm's database is its most important asset.) You can think of facilities as resources at rest. The organization's bank accounts are the facility of cash at rest.[3]

Consider the three business processes for a bicycle manufacturer shown in Figure 3-7. The materials ordering process transforms cash[4] into a raw materials inventory. The manufacturing process transforms raw materials into finished goods. The sales process transforms finished goods into cash. Notice that the business processes span the value chain activities. The sales process involves sales and mar-

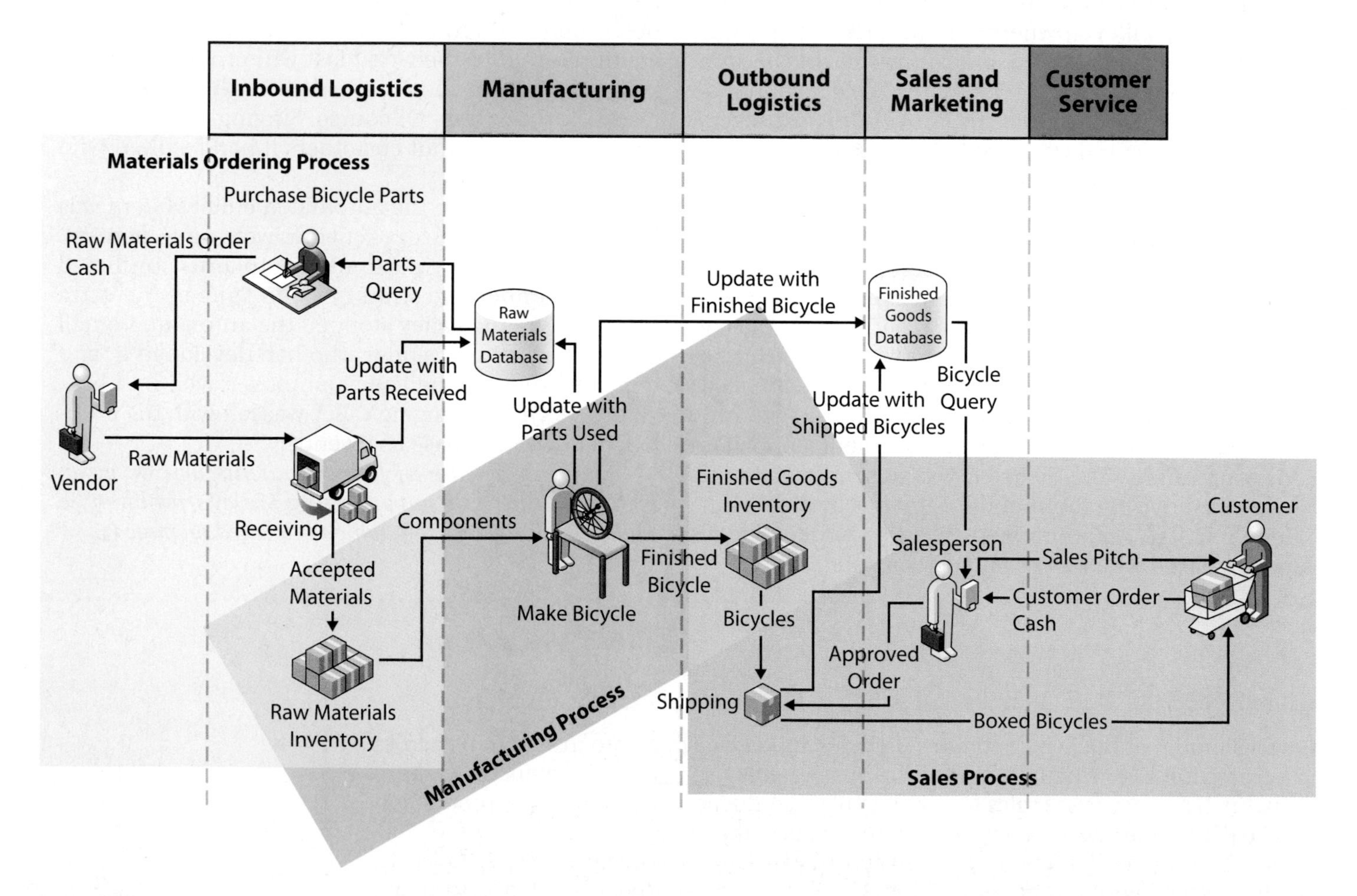

Figure 3-7
Three Examples of Business Processes

[3]OK, if you want to quibble, cash is earning interest, so it is not at rest. But that is another way of saying that we have not considered the interest-generating business process that transforms cash into more cash via investment activities.

[4]For simplicity, the flow of cash is abbreviated in this diagram. Business processes for authorizing, controlling, making payments, and receiving revenue are, of course, vital. You will learn more about such processes in Chapter 7.

keting as well as outbound logistics activities, as you would expect. Note, too, that while none of these three processes involve a customer-service activity, customer service plays a role in other business processes.

Also notice that activities get and put data resources from and to databases. For example, the purchase-bicycle-parts activity queries the raw materials database to determine the materials to order. The receiving activity updates the raw materials database to indicate the arrival of materials. The make-bicycle activity updates the raw materials database to indicate the consumption of materials. Similar actions are taken in the sales process against the finished goods database.

Business processes vary in cost and effectiveness. In fact, the streamlining of business processes to increase margin (add value, reduce costs, or both) is key to competitive advantage. You will learn about **business process redesign** in Chapter 7. To get a flavor of process redesign, however, consider Figure 3-8, which shows an alternate process for the bicycle manufacturer. Here, the purchase-bicycle-parts activity not only queries the raw materials inventory database, it also queries the finished goods inventory database. Querying both databases allows the purchasing department to make decisions not just on raw materials quantities, but also on customer demand. By using this data, purchasing can reduce the size of raw materials inventory, reducing production costs and thus adding margin to the value chain. This is an example of using a linkage across business processes to improve process margin.

As you will learn, however, changing business processes is not easy to do. Most process redesign requires people to work in new ways, to follow different procedures, and employees often resist such change. In Figure 3-8, the employees who perform the purchase-bicycle-parts activity need to learn to adjust their ordering processes to use customer purchase patterns. Another complication is that data stored in the

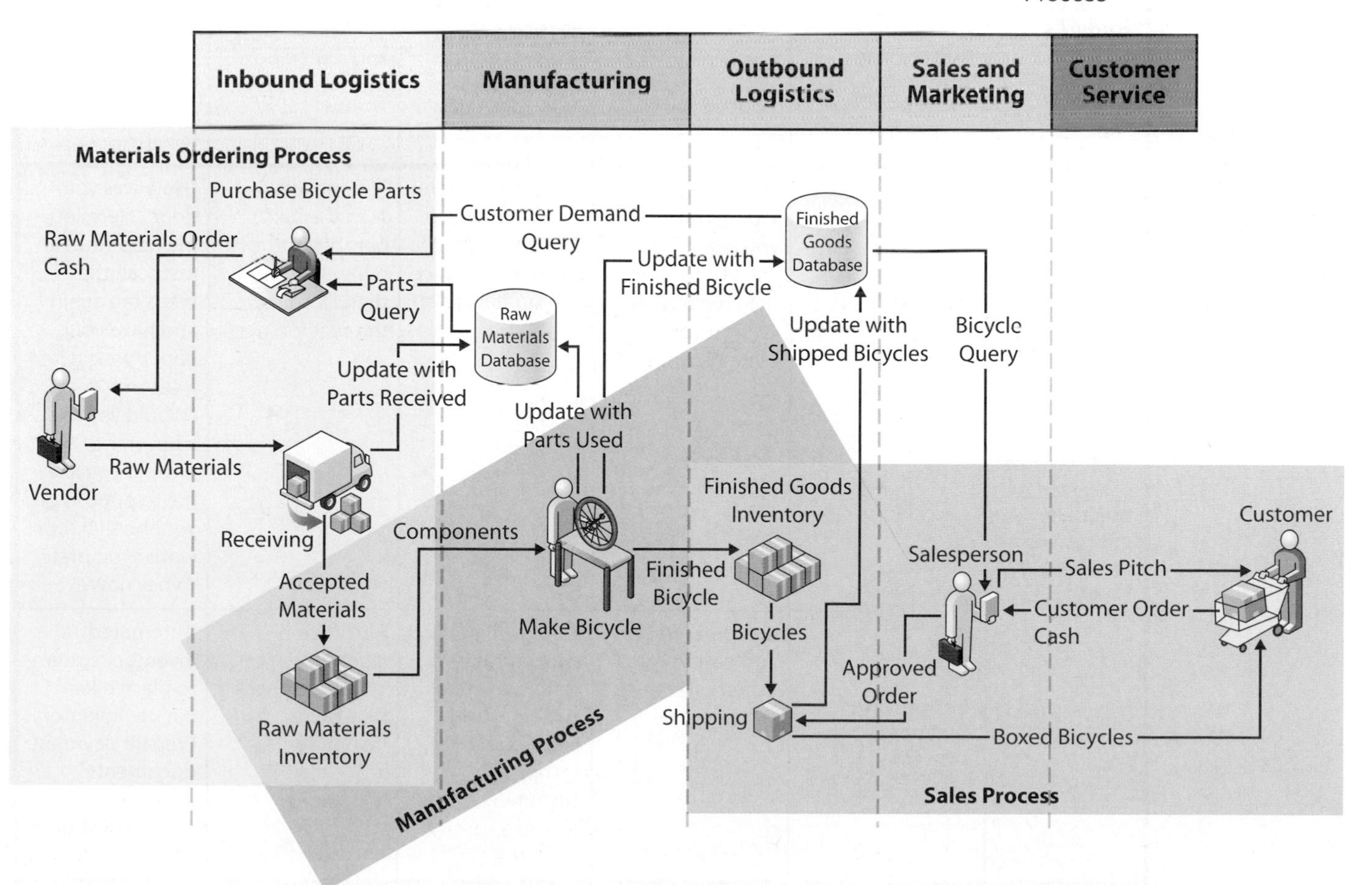

Figure 3-8
Improved Materials Ordering Process

The Business Process in Practice *box on page 73 demonstrates the need for business process redesign in a county-government permit office.*

finished goods database likely will need to be redesigned to keep track of customer demand data. As you will learn in Chapter 5, that redesign effort will require that some application programs be changed as well.

Q6 How Does Competitive Strategy Determine Business Processes and the Structure of Information Systems?

Figure 3-9 shows a business process for renting bicycles. The value-generating activities are shown in the top of the table, and the implementation of those activities for two companies with different competitive strategies is shown in the rows below.

The first company has chosen a competitive strategy of low-cost rentals to students. Accordingly, this business implements business processes to minimize costs. The second company has chosen a differentiation strategy. It provides "best-of-breed" rentals to executives at a high-end conference resort. Notice that this business has

Figure 3-9
Operations Value Chains for Bicycle Rental Companies

	Value-Generating Activity	**Greet Customer**	**Determine Needs**	**Rent Bike**	**Return Bike & Pay**
Low-cost rental to students	**Message that implements competitive strategy**	"You wanna bike?"	"Bikes are over there. Help yourself."	"Fill out this form, and bring it to me over here when you're done."	"Show me the bike." "OK, you owe $23.50. Pay up."
	Supporting business process	None.	Physical controls and procedures to prevent bike theft.	Printed forms and a shoe box to store them in.	Shoebox with rental form. Minimal credit card and cash receipt system.
High-service rental to business executives at conference resort	**Message that implements competitive strategy**	"Hello, Ms. Henry. Wonderful to see you again. Would you like to rent the WonderBike 4.5 that you rented last time?"	"You know, I think the WonderBike Supreme would be a better choice for you. It has..."	"Let me just scan the bike's number into our system, and then I'll adjust the seat for you."	"How was your ride?" "Here, let me help you. I'll just scan the bike's tag again and have your paperwork in just a second." "Would you like a beverage?" "Would you like me to put this on your hotel bill, or would you prefer to pay now?"
	Supporting business process	Customer tracking and past sales activity system.	Employee training and information system to match customer and bikes, biased to "up-sell" customer.	Automated inventory system to check bike out of inventory.	Automated inventory system to place bike back in inventory. Prepare payment documents. Integrate with resort's billing system.

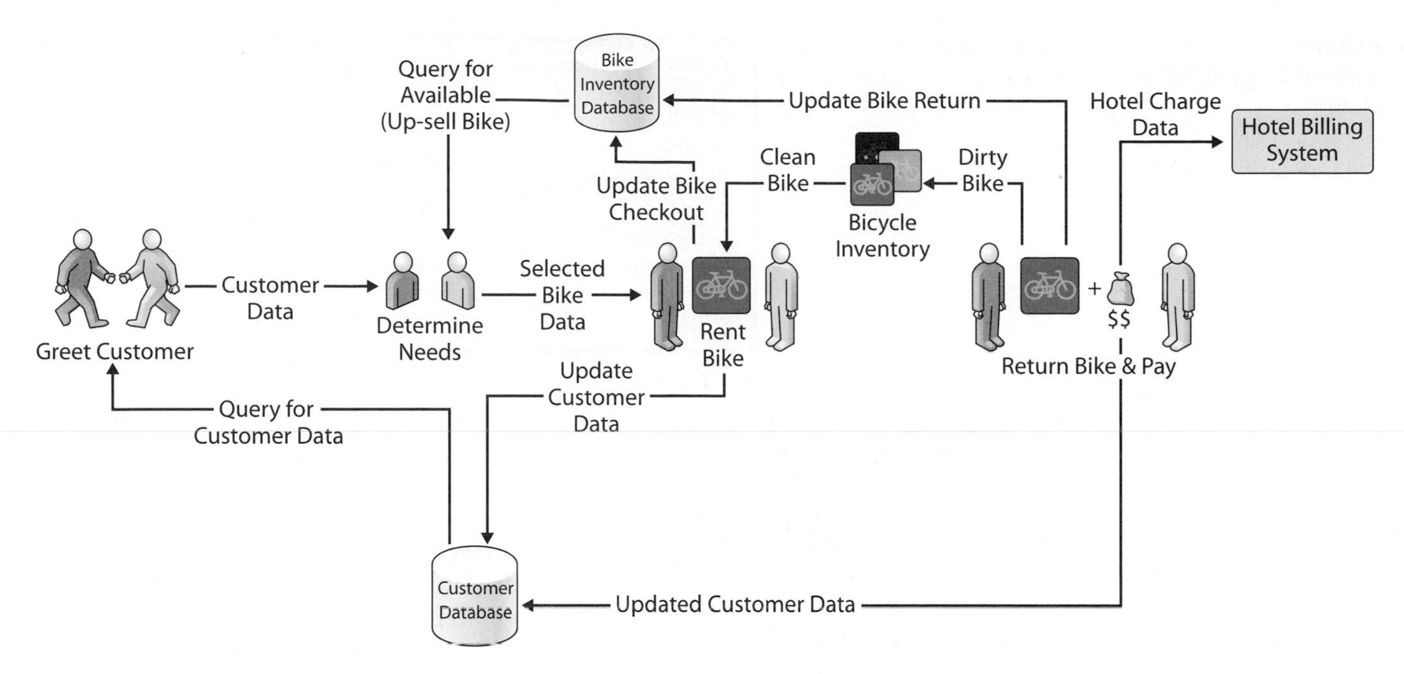

Figure 3-10
Business Process and Information Systems for High-Service Bike Rental

designed its business processes to ensure superb service. To achieve a positive margin, it must ensure that the value added will exceed the costs of providing the service.

Now, consider the information systems required for these business processes. The student rental business uses a shoebox for its data facility. The only computer/software/data component in its business is the machine provided by its bank for processing credit card transactions.

The high-service business, however, makes extensive use of information systems, as shown in Figure 3-10. It has a CRM database that tracks past customer rental activity, and an inventory database that is used to select and up-sell bicycle rentals as well as to control bicycle inventory with a minimum of fuss to its high-end customers.

So the bottom line is this: Organizations analyze their industry and choose a competitive strategy. Given that strategy, they design business processes that span value-generating activities. Those processes determine the scope and requirements of each organization's information systems. Given this background, we will now examine how information systems generate a competitive advantage.

Information systems like the resort's rental system contain valuable customer data, and this data must be protected by passwords and other means. You should learn how to create a strong password, for use in business and to protect your own data right now. See the Security Guide *on page 80.*

Q7 How Do Information Systems Provide Competitive Advantages?

In your business strategy class, you will study the Porter models in greater detail than we have discussed here. When you do so, you will learn numerous ways that organizations respond to the five competitive forces. For our purposes, we can distill those ways into the list of principles shown in Figure 3-11 (next page). Keep in mind that we are applying these principles in the context of the organization's competitive strategy.

Some of these competitive techniques are created via products and services, and some are created via the development of business processes. Consider each.

You can also apply these principles to a personal competitive advantage, as the Reflections Guide *on pages 82 discusses.*

Competitive Advantage via Products

The first three principles in Figure 3-11 concern products or services. Organizations gain a competitive advantage by creating *new* products or services, by *enhancing* existing products or services, and by *differentiating* their products and services from those of their competitors. For example, as Neil Miyamoto indicated in his interview, The Firm chose to differentiate itself on personalization of its services.

Figure 3-11
Principles of Competitive Advantage

Product Implementations
1. Create a new product or service
2. Enhance products or services
3. Differentiate products or services

System Implementations

4. Lock in customers and buyers
5. Lock in suppliers
6. Raise barriers to market entry
7. Establish alliances
8. Reduce costs

Information systems create competitive advantages either as part of a product or by providing support to a product. Consider, for example, a car rental agency like Hertz or Avis. An information system that produces information about the car's location and provides driving instructions to destinations is part of the car rental and thus is part of the product itself (see Figure 3-12a). In contrast, an information system that schedules car maintenance is not part of the product, but instead supports the product (see Figure 3-12b). Either way, information systems can help achieve the first three principles in Figure 3-11.

The remaining five principles in Figure 3-11 concern competitive advantage created by the implementation of business processes.

Competitive Advantage via Business Processes

Organizations can *lock in customers* by making it difficult or expensive for customers to switch to another product. This strategy is sometimes called establishing high **switching costs**. Organizations can *lock in suppliers* by making it difficult to switch to another organization, or, stated positively, by making it easy to connect to and work with the organization. Finally, competitive advantage can be gained by *creating entry barriers* that make it difficult and expensive for new competition to enter the market.

Another means to gain competitive advantage is to *establish alliances* with other organizations. Such alliances establish standards, promote product awareness and needs, develop market size, reduce purchasing costs, and provide other benefits. Finally,

a. Information System as Part of a Car Rental Product

b. Information System That Supports a Car Rental Product

Daily Service Schedule—November 17, 2005

StationID 22
StationName Lubrication

ServiceDate	ServiceTime	VehicleID	Make	Model	Mileage	ServiceDescription
11/17/2005	12:00 AM	155890	Ford	Explorer	2244	Std. Lube
11/17/2005	11:00 AM	12448	Toyota	Tacoma	7558	Std. Lube

StationID 26
StationName Alignment

ServiceDate	ServiceTime	VehicleID	Make	Model	Mileage	ServiceDescription
11/17/2005	9:00 AM	12448	Toyota	Tacoma	7558	Front end alignment inspect

StationID 28
StationName Transmission

ServiceDate	ServiceTime	VehicleID	Make	Model	Mileage	ServiceDescription
11/17/2005	11:00 AM	155890	Ford	Explorer	2244	Transmission oil change

Figure 3-12
Two Roles for Information Systems Regarding Products

BUSINESS PROCESSES IN PRACTICE

THE COUNTY PLANNING OFFICE

The county planning office issues building permits, septic system permits, and county road access permits for all building projects in a county in an eastern state. The planning office issues permits to homeowners and builders for the construction of new homes and buildings and for any remodeling projects that involve electrical, gas, plumbing, and other utilities as well as the conversion of unoccupied spaces, such as garages, into living or working space. The office also issues permits for new or upgraded septic systems and permits to provide driveway entrances to county roads.

Figure 1 (below) shows the permit process that the county used for many years. Contractors and homeowners found this process to be slow and very frustrating. For one, they did not like its sequential nature. Only after a permit had been approved or rejected by an engineering review process would applicants find out that a health or highway review was also needed. Because each of these reviews could take 3 or 4 weeks, applicants requesting permits wanted the review processes to be concurrent rather than serial. Also, both the permit applicants and county personnel were frustrated because they never knew where a particular application was in the permit process. A contractor would call to ask how much longer, and it might take an hour or more just to find which desk the permit was on.

Accordingly, the county changed the permit process to that shown in Figure 2 (next page). In this second process, the permit office made three copies of the permit and distributed one to each department. The departments would review the permits in parallel; a clerk would analyze the results and, if there were no rejections, approve the permit.

Unfortunately, this process had a number of problems, too. For one, some of the permit applications were lengthy; some included as many as 40 to 50 pages of large architectural drawings. The labor and copy expense to the county was considerable.

Second, in some cases departments reviewed documents unnecessarily. If, for example, the highway department rejected an application, then neither the engineering nor health departments needed to continue their reviews. At first, the county responded to this problem by having the clerk who analyzed results cancel the reviews of other departments when a rejection was received. However, that policy (not shown in Figure 2) was exceedingly unpopular with the permit applicants, because once an application was rejected and the problem corrected the permit had to go back through the

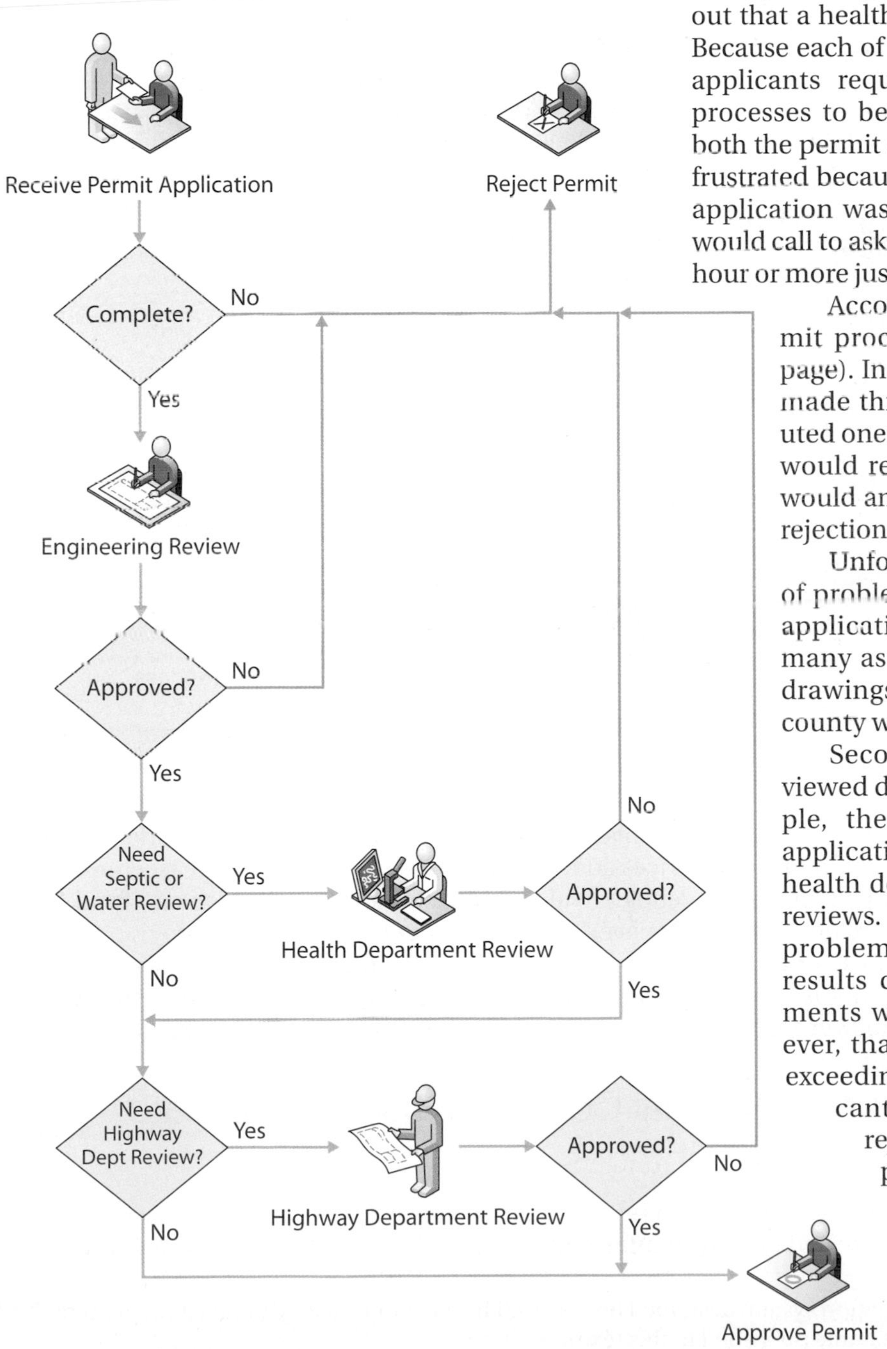

Figure 1
Sequential Permit-Review Process

other departments. The permit would go to the end of the line and work its way back into the departments from which it had been pulled. Sometimes this resulted in a delay of 5 or 6 weeks.

Canceling reviews was unpopular with the departments as well, because permit review work had to be repeated. An application might have been nearly completed when it was cancelled due to a rejection in another department. When the application came through again, the partial work results from the earlier review were lost.

Clearly, both of these processes have problems. *You and a team of your classmates will be given an opportunity to solve this problem in Collaboration Exercise 2, which is located on page 86.*

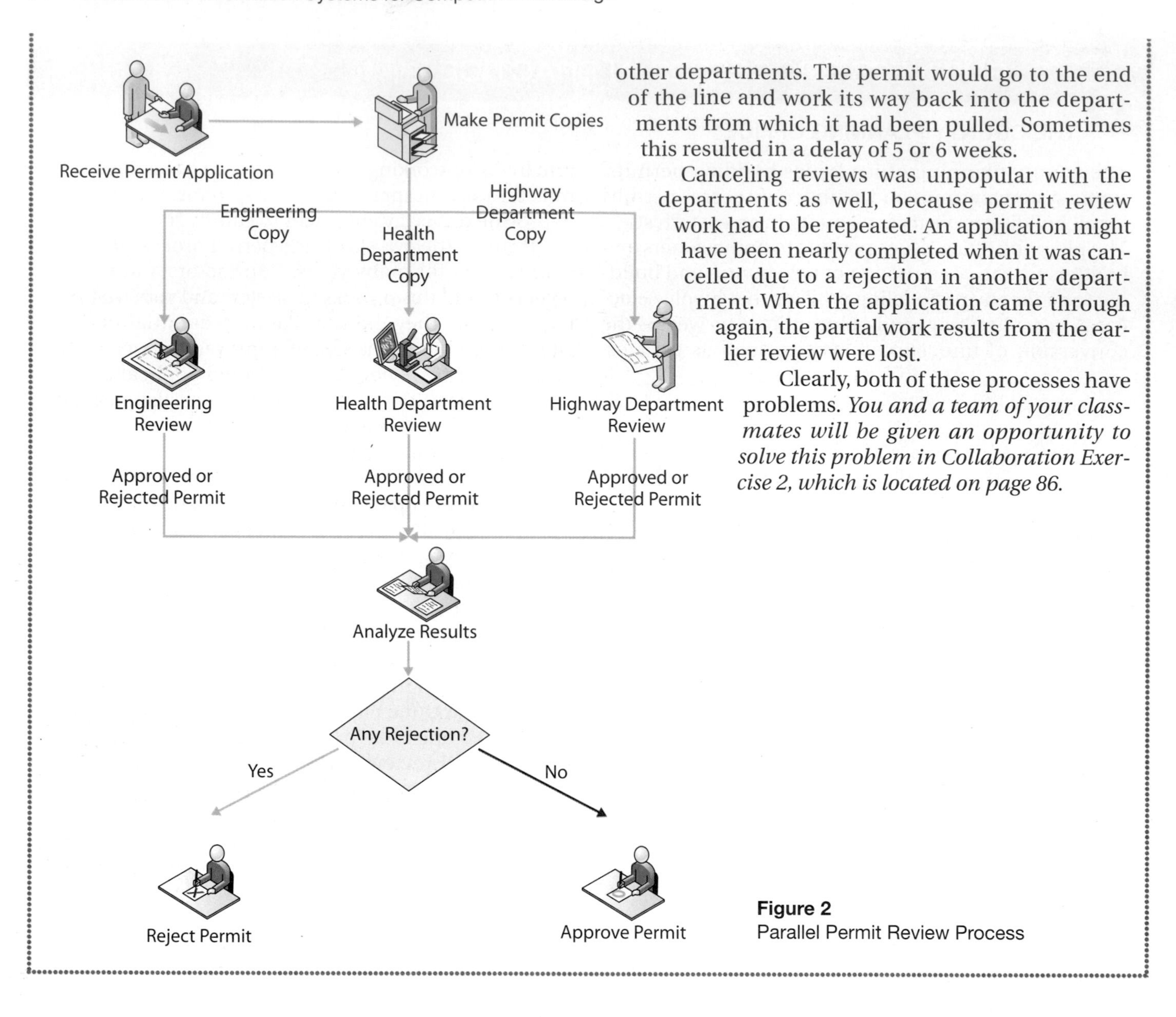

Figure 2
Parallel Permit Review Process

organizations can gain competitive advantage by *reducing costs*. Such reductions enable the organization to reduce prices and/or to increase profitability. Increased profitability means not just greater shareholder value, but also more cash, which can fund further infrastructure development for even greater competitive advantage.

All of these principles of competitive advantage make sense, but the question you may be asking is, "How do information systems help to create competitive advantage?" To answer that question, consider a sample information system.

How Does an Actual Company Use IS to Create Competitive Advantages?

ABC, Inc.[5] is a worldwide shipper with sales well in excess of $1 billion. From its inception, ABC invested heavily in information technology and led the shipping industry in

[5]The information system described here is used by a major transportation company that did not want its name published in this textbook.

the application of information systems for competitive advantage. Here we consider one example of an information system that illustrates how ABC successfully uses information technology to gain competitive advantage.

ABC maintains customer account data that include not only the customer's name, address, and billing information, but also data about the people, organizations, and locations to which the customer ships. Figure 3-13 shows a Web form that an ABC customer is using to schedule a shipment. When the ABC system creates the form, it fills the Company name drop-down list with the names of companies that the customer has shipped to in the past. Here, the user is selecting Prentice Hall.

When the user clicks on the Company name, the underlying ABC information system reads the customer's contact data from a database. The data consist of names, addresses, and phone numbers of recipients from past shipments. The user then selects a Contact name, and the system inserts that contact's address and other data into the form using data from the database, as shown in Figure 3-14 (next page). Thus, the system saves customers from having to reenter data for people to whom they have shipped in the past. Providing the data in this way also reduces data-entry errors.

Figure 3-15 (next page) shows another feature of this system. On the right-hand side of this form, the customer can request that ABC send email messages to the sender (the customer), the recipient, and others as well. The customer can choose for ABC to send an email when the shipment is created and when it has been delivered. In Figure 3-15, the user has provided three email addresses. The customer wants all three addresses to receive delivery notification, but only the sender will receive shipment notification. The customer can add a personal message as well. By adding this capability to the shipment scheduling system, ABC has extended its product from a package-delivery service to a package- *and* information-delivery service.

Figure 3-16 (on page 77) shows one other capability of this information system. It has generated a shipping label, complete with bar code, for the user to print. By doing this, the company not only reduces errors in the preparation of shipping labels, but it also causes the customer to provide the paper and ink for document printing! Millions of such documents are printed every day, resulting in a considerable savings to the company.

Only customers who have access to the Internet can use this shipping system. Do organizations have an ethical obligation to provide equivalent services to those who do not have access? The Ethics Guide *on page 78 explores this question.*

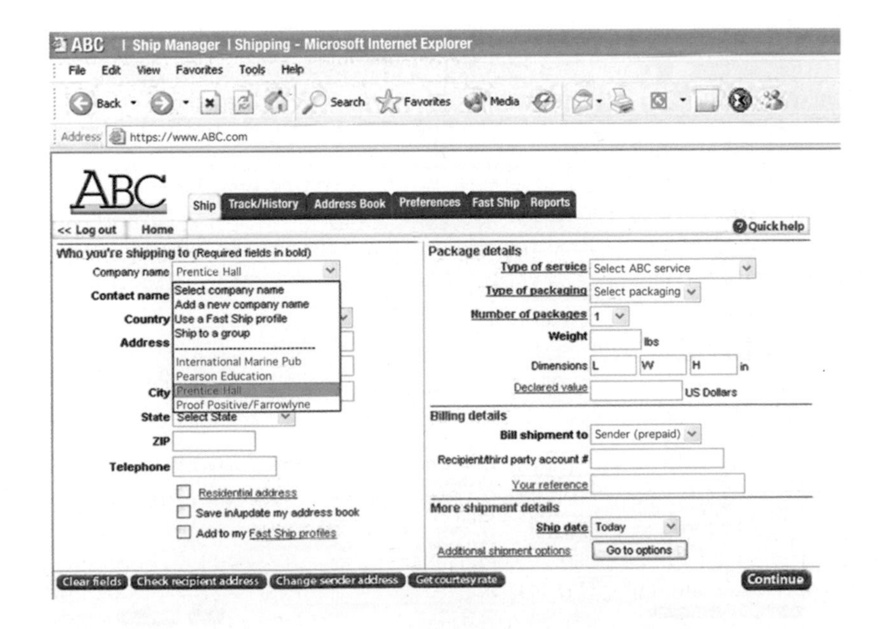

Figure 3-13
ABC, Inc. Web Page to Select a Recipient from the Customer's Records

Figure 3-14
ABC, Inc. Web Page to Select a Contact from the Customer's Records

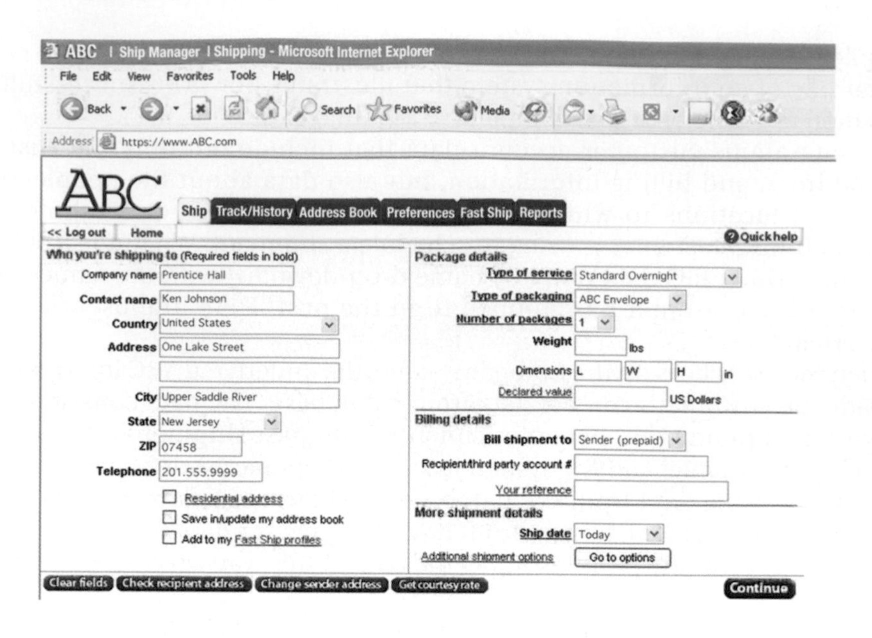

How Does This System Create a Competitive Advantage?

Now consider the ABC shipping information system in light of the competitive advantage factors in Figure 3-11. This information system *enhances* an existing service because it eases the effort of creating a shipment to the customer while reducing errors. The information system also helps to *differentiate* the ABC package delivery service from competitors that do not have a similar system. Further, the generation of email messages when ABC picks up and delivers a package could be considered to be a *new* service.

Because this information system captures and stores data about recipients, it reduces the amount of customer work when scheduling a shipment. Customers will be *locked in* by this system: If a customer wants to change to a different shipper, he or she will need to rekey recipient data for that new shipper. The disadvantage of rekeying data may well outweigh any advantage of switching to another shipper.

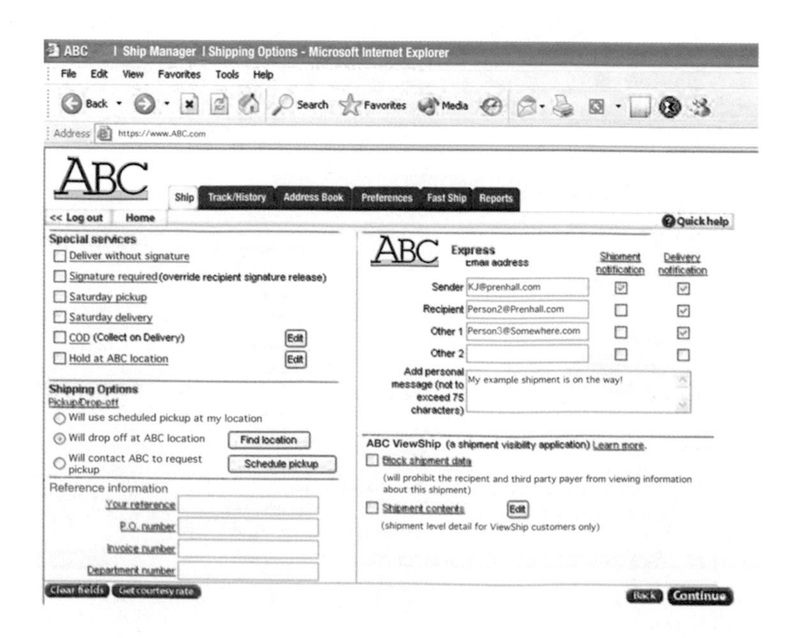

Figure 3-15
ABC, Inc. Web Page to Specify Email Notification

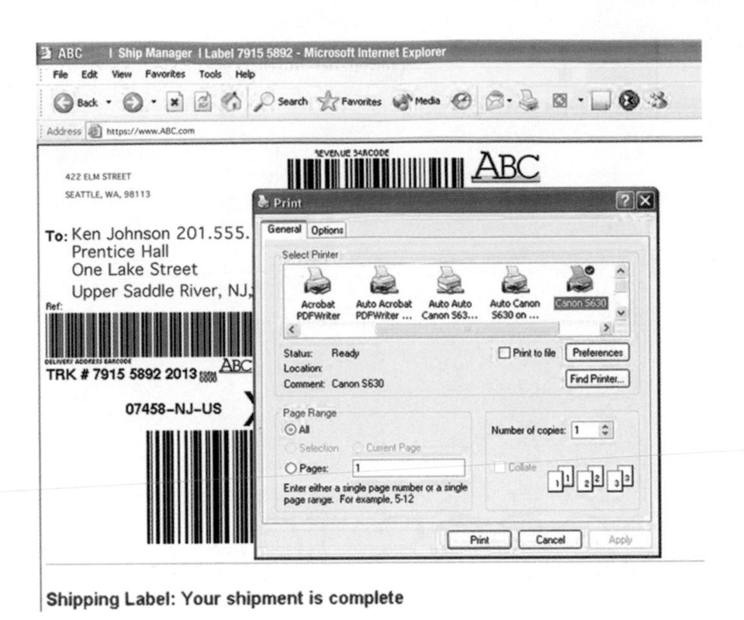

Figure 3-16
ABC, Inc. Web Page to Print a Shipping Label

This system achieves a competitive advantage in two other ways as well: First, it raises the barriers to market entry. If another company wants to develop a shipping service, it will not only have to be able to ship packages, but it will also need to have a similar information system. In addition, the system reduces costs. It reduces errors in shipping documents, and it saves ABC paper, ink, and printing costs.

Of course, to determine if this system delivers a *net savings* in costs, the cost of developing and operating the information system will need to be offset against the gains in reduced errors and paper, ink, and printing costs. It may be that the system costs more than the savings. Even still, it may be a sound investment if the value of intangible benefits, such as locking in customers and raising entry barriers, exceeds the net cost.

Before continuing, review Figure 3-11. Make sure that you understand each of the principles of competitive advantage and how information systems can help achieve them. In fact, the list in Figure 3-11 probably is important enough to memorize, because you can also use it for non-IS applications. You can consider any business project or initiative in light of competitive advantage.

Ethics

GUIDE

Limiting Access to Those Who Have Access

An adage of investing is that it's easier for the rich to get richer. Someone who has $10 million invested at 5 percent earns $500,000 per year. Another investor with $10,000 invested at that same 5 percent earns $500 per year. Every year, the disparity increases as the first investor pulls farther and farther ahead of the second.

This same adage applies to intellectual wealth as well. It's easier for those with considerable knowledge and expertise to gain even more knowledge and expertise. Someone who knows how to search the Internet can learn more readily than someone who does not. And every year, the person with greater knowledge pulls farther and farther ahead. Intellectual capital grows in just the same way that financial capital grows.

Searching the Internet is not just a matter of knowledge, however. It's also a matter of access. The increasing reliance on the Web for information and commerce has created a *digital divide* between those who have Internet access and those who do not. This divide continues to deepen as those who are connected pull farther ahead of those who are not.

Various groups have addressed this problem by making Internet access available in public places, such as libraries, community centers, and retirement homes. The Bill and Melinda Gates Foundation has given more than $262 million to public libraries for the purchase of personal computers and Internet access for them. Such gifts help, but not everyone can be served this way, and even with such access, there's a big convenience difference between going to the library and walking across your bedroom to access the Internet—and you don't have to stand in line.

The advantages accrue to everyone with access, every day. Do you want directions to your friend's house? Want to know when a movie is playing at a local theater? Want to buy music, books, or tools? Want convenient access to your checking account? Want to decide whether to refinance your condo? Want to know what TCP/IP means? Use the Internet.

All of this intellectual capital resides on the Internet because businesses benefit by putting it there. It's much cheaper to provide product support information over the Internet than on printed documents. The savings include not only the costs of printing, but also the costs of warehousing and mailing. Further, when product specifications change, the organization just changes the Web site. There is no obsolete material to dispose of and no costs for printing and distributing the revised material. Those who have Internet access gain current information faster than those who do not.

What happens to those who do not have Internet access? They fall farther and farther behind. The digital divide segregates the haves from the have-nots, creating new class structures.

Discussion Questions

1. Do you see evidence of a digital divide on your campus? In your hometown? Among your relatives? Describe personal experiences you've had regarding the digital divide.
2. Do organizations have a legal responsibility to provide the same information for nonconnected customers that they do for connected customers? If not, should laws be passed requiring organizations to do so?
3. Even if there is no current legal requirement for organizations to provide equal information to nonconnected customers, do they have an ethical responsibility to do so?
4. Are your answers to questions 2 and 3 different for government agencies than they are for commercial organizations?
5. Because it may be impossible to provide equal information, another approach for reducing the digital divide is for the government to enable nonconnected citizens to acquire Internet access via subsidies and tax incentives. Do you favor such a program? Why or why not?
6. Suppose that nothing is done to reduce the digital divide and that it is allowed to grow wider and wider. What are the consequences? How will society change? Are these consequences acceptable?

Such segregation is subtle, but it is segregation, nonetheless.

Do organizations have a responsibility to address this matter? If 98 percent of a company's market segment has Internet access, does the company have a responsibility to provide non-Internet materials to that other 2 percent? On what basis does that responsibility lie? Does a government agency have a responsibility to provide equal information to those who have Internet access and those who do not? When those who are connected can obtain information nearly instantaneously, 24/7, is it even possible to provide equal information to the connected and the unconnected?

It's a worldwide problem. Connected societies and countries pull farther and farther ahead. How can any economy that relies on traditional mail compete with an Internet-based economy?

If you're taking MIS, you're already connected; you're already one of the haves, and you're already pulling ahead of the have-nots. The more you learn about information systems and their use in commerce, the faster you'll pull ahead. The digital divide increases. ■

Passwords and Password Etiquette

All forms of computer security involve passwords. Most likely, you have a university account that you access with a user name and password. When you set up that account, you were probably advised to use a "strong password." That's good advice, but what is a strong password? Probably not "sesame," but what then? Microsoft, a company that has many reasons to promote effective security, provides a definition that is commonly used. Microsoft defines a **strong password** as one with the following characteristics:

- Has seven or more characters
- Does not contain your user name, real name, or company name
- Does not contain a complete dictionary word, in any language
- Is different from previous passwords you have used
- Contains both upper- and lowercase letters, numbers, and special characters (such as ~ ! @; # $ % ^ &; * ( ) _ +; - =; { } | [ ] \ : " ; ' <; >; ? , . /)

Examples of good passwords are:

- Qw37^T1bb?at
- 3B47qq<3>5!7b

The problem with such passwords is that they are nearly impossible to remember. And the last thing you want to do is write your password on a piece of paper and keep it near the workstation where you use it. Never do that!

One technique for creating memorable, strong passwords is to base them on the first letter of the words in a phrase. The phrase could be the title of a song or the first line of a poem or one based on some fact about your life. For example, you might take the phrase, "I was born in Rome, New York, before 1990." Using the first letters from that phrase and substituting the character < for the word *before*, you create the password IwbiR,NY<1990. That's an acceptable password, but it would be better if all of the numbers were not placed on the end. So, you might try the phrase, "I was born at 3:00 A.M. in Rome, New York." That phrase yields the password Iwba3:00AMiR,NY which is a strong password that is easily remembered.

Once you have created a strong password, you need to protect it with proper behavior. Proper password etiquette is one of the marks of a business professional. Never write down your password, and do not share it with others. Never ask

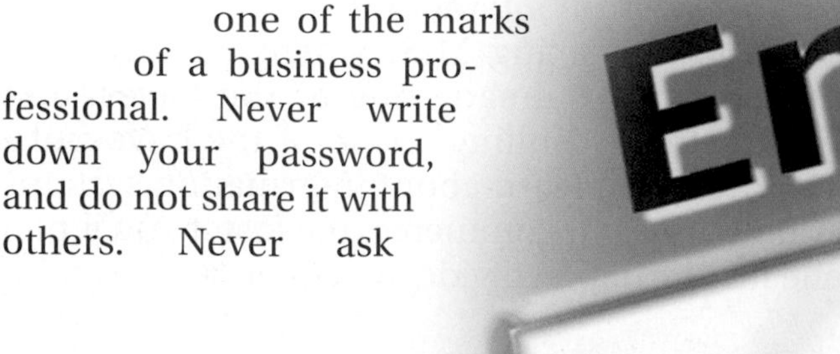

someone else for his password, and never give your password to someone else.

But, what if you need someone else's password? Suppose, for example, you ask someone to help you with a problem on your computer. You sign on to an information system, and for some reason, you need to enter that other person's password. In this case, say to the other person, "We need your password," and then get out of your chair, offer your keyboard to the other person, and look away while she enters the password. Among professionals working in organizations that take security seriously, this little "do-si-do" move—one person getting out of the way so that another person can enter her password—is common and accepted.

If someone asks for your password, do not give it out. Instead, get up, go over to that person's machine, and enter your own password, yourself. Stay present while your password is in use, and ensure that your account is logged out at the end of the activity. No one should mind or be offended in any way when you do this. It is the mark of a professional. ■

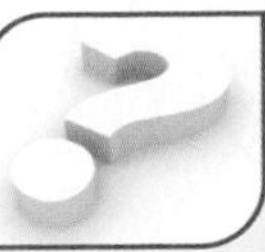

Discussion Questions

1. Here are the first two lines of a famous poem by T. S. Eliot, "Let us go then, you and I, When the evening is spread out against the sky." Explain how to use these lines to create a password. How could you add numbers and special characters to the password in a way that you will be able to remember?
2. List two different phrases that you can use to create a strong password. Show the password created by each.
3. One of the problems of life in the cyber-world is that we all are required to have multiple passwords—one for work or school, one for bank accounts, another for eBay or other auction sites, and so forth. Of course, it is better to use different passwords for each. But in that case you have to remember three or four different passwords. Think of different phrases you can use to create a memorable, strong password for each of these different accounts. Relate the phrase to the purpose of the account. Show the passwords for each.
4. Explain proper behavior when you are using your computer and you need to enter, for some valid reason, another person's password.
5. Explain proper behavior when someone else is using her computer and that person needs to enter, for some valid reason, your password.

Reflections Guide

GUIDE

Your Personal Competitive Advantage

Consider the following possibility: You work hard, earning your degree in business, and you graduate, only to discover that you cannot find a job in your area of study. You look for six weeks or so, but then you run out of money. In desperation, you take a job waiting tables at a local restaurant. Two years go by, the economy picks up, and the jobs you had been looking for become available. Unfortunately, your degree is now two years old; you are competing with students who have just graduated with fresh degrees (and fresh knowledge). Two years of waiting tables, good as you are at it, does not appear to be good experience for the job you want. You're stuck in a nightmare—one that will be hard to get out of, and one that you cannot allow to happen.

Examine Figure 3-11 again, but this time consider those elements of competitive advantage as they apply to you personally. As an employee, the skills and abilities you offer are your personal product. Examine the first three items in the list, and ask yourself, "How can I use my time in school—and in this MIS class, in particular—to create new skills, to enhance those I already have, and to differentiate my skills from the competition?" (By the way, you will enter a national/international market. Your competition is not just the students in your class; it's also students in classes in Ohio, California, British Columbia, Florida, New York, and every place else they're teaching MIS today.)

Suppose you are interested in a sales job. Perhaps you want to sell in the pharmaceutical industry. What skills can you learn from your MIS class that will make you more competitive as a future salesperson? Ask yourself, "How does the pharmaceutical industry use MIS to gain competitive advantage?" Get on the Internet and find examples of the use of information systems in the pharmaceutical industry. How does Parke-Davis, for example, use a customer information system to sell to doctors? How can your knowledge of such systems differentiate you from your competition for a job there? How does Parke-Davis use a knowledge management system? How does the firm keep track of drugs that have an adverse effect on each other?

The fourth and fifth items in Figure 3-11 concern locking in customers, buyers, and suppliers. How can you interpret those elements in terms of your personal competitive advantage? Well, to lock in, you first have to have a relationship to lock in. So do you have an internship? If not, can you get one? And once you have an internship, how can you use your knowledge of MIS to lock in your job so that you get a job offer? Does the company you are interning for have a CRM system (or any other information system that is important to the company)? If users are happy with the system, what characteristics make it worthwhile? Can you lock in a job by becoming an expert user of this system? Becoming an expert user not only locks you into your job, but it also raises barriers to entry for others who might be competing for the job. Also, can you suggest ways to improve the system, thus using your knowledge of the company and the system to lock in an extension of your job?

Human resources personnel say that networking is one of the most effective ways of finding a job. How can you use this class to establish alliances with other students? Does your class have a Web site? Is there an email list server for the students in your class? How can you use those facilities to develop job-seeking alliances with other students? Who in your class already has a job or an internship? Can any of those people provide hints or opportunities for finding a job?

Don't restrict your job search to your local area. Are there regions of your country where jobs are more plentiful? How can you find out about student organizations in those regions? Search the Web for MIS classes in other cities, and make contact with students there. Find out what the hot opportunities are in other cities.

Finally, as you study MIS, think about how the knowledge you gain can help you save costs for your employers. Even more, see if you can build a case that an employer would actually save money by hiring you. The line of reasoning might be that because of your knowledge of IS, you will be able to facilitate cost savings that more than compensate for your salary.

In truth, few of the ideas that you generate for a potential employer will be feasible or pragmatically useful. The fact that you are thinking creatively, however, will indicate to a potential employer that you have initiative and are grappling with the problems that real businesses have. As this course progresses, keep thinking about competitive advantage, and strive to understand how the topics you study can help you to accomplish, personally, one or more of the principles in Figure 3-11. ■

Discussion Questions

1. Summarize the efforts you have taken thus far to build an employment record that will lead to job offers after graduation.
2. Considering the first three principles in Figure 3-11, describe one way in which you have a competitive advantage over your classmates. If you do not have such competitive advantage, describe actions you can take to obtain one.
3. In order to build your network, you can use your status as a student to approach business professionals. Namely, you can contact them for help with an assignment or for career guidance. For example, suppose you want to work in banking and you know that your local bank has a customer information system. You could call the manager of that bank and ask him or her how that system creates a competitive advantage for the bank. You also could ask to interview other employees and go armed with the list in Figure 3-11. Describe two specific ways in which you can use your status as a student and the list in Figure 3-11 to build your network in this way.
4. Describe two ways that you can use student alliances to obtain a job. How can you use information systems to build, maintain, and operate such alliances?

ACTIVE REVIEW

Use this Active Review to verify that you understand the ideas and concepts that answer the chapter's study questions.

Q1 How does organizational strategy determine information systems structure?

Diagram and explain the relationship of industry structure, competitive strategy, value chains, business systems, and information systems. Working from industry structure to IS, explain how the knowledge you've gained in these first three chapters pertains to that diagram.

Q2 What five forces determine industry structure?

Name and briefly describe the five forces. Give your own examples of both strong and weak forces of each type similar to those in Figure 3-3.

Q3 What is competitive strategy?

Describe four different strategies as defined by Porter. Give an example of four different companies that have implemented each of the strategies.

Q4 What is a value chain?

Define the terms *value, margin,* and *value chain.* Explain why organizations that choose a differentiation strategy can use value to determine a limit on the amount of extra cost to pay for differentiation. Name the primary and support activities in the value chain and explain the purpose of each. Explain the concept of *linkages.*

Q5 How do business processes generate value?

Define *business process, cost,* and *margin* as they pertain to business processes. Explain the purpose of an activity and describe three types of facilities. Define *activity, resource, flow,* and *facility* and explain the role of each in Figure 3-8. Explain the importance of business process redesign and describe the difference between the business processes in Figure 3-8 and those in Figure 3-9.

Q6 How does competitive strategy determine business processes and the structure of information systems?

In your own words, explain how competitive strategy determines the structure of business processes. Use the examples of a clothing store that caters to struggling students and a clothing store that caters to professional business people in a high-end neighborhood. List the activities in the business process for the two companies and create a chart like that in Figure 3-9. Explain how the information systems requirements differ between the two stores.

Q7 How do information systems provide competitive advantages?

List and briefly describe eight principles of competitive advantage. Consider your college bookstore. List one application of each of the eight principles. Strive to include examples that involve information systems.

KEY TERMS AND CONCEPTS

Activity 68
Business process 68
Business process redesign 69
Competitive strategy 63
Cost [of a business process] 68
Facilities 68
Five forces model 63
Flow 68
Input resources 68

USING YOUR KNOWLEDGE

1. Apply the value chain model to a retailer such as Target (*http://target.com*). What is its competitive strategy? Describe the tasks Target must accomplish for each of the primary value chain activities. How does Target's competitive strategy and the nature of its business influence the general characteristics of Target's information systems?
2. Apply the value chain model to a mail-order company such as L.L Bean (*http://llbean.com*). What is its competitive strategy? Describe the tasks L.L. Bean must accomplish for each of the primary value chain activities. How does L.L. Bean's competitive strategy and the nature of its business influence the general characteristics of its information systems?
3. Suppose you decide to start a business that recruits students for summer jobs. You will match available students with available jobs. You need to learn what positions are available and what students are available for filling those positions. In starting your business, you know you will be competing with local newspapers, "Craig's List" (*www.craigslist.org*), and with your college. You will probably have other local competitors as well.

   a. Analyze the structure of this industry according to Porter's five forces model.
   b. Given your analysis in part a, recommend a competitive strategy.
   c. Describe the primary value chain activities as they apply to this business.
   d. Describe a business process for recruiting students.
   e. Describe information systems that could be used to support the business process in part d.
   f. Explain how the process you describe in part d and the system you describe in e reflect your competitive strategy.

4. Consider the two different bike rental companies in Figure 3-9. Think about the bikes that they rent. Clearly, the student bikes will be just about anything that can be ridden out of the shop. The bikes for the business executives, on the other hand, must be new, shiny, clean, and in tip-top shape.

   a. Compare and contrast the operations value chains of these two businesses as they pertain to the management of bicycles.
   b. Describe a business process for maintaining bicycles for both businesses.
   c. Describe a business process for acquiring bicycles for both businesses.
   d. Describe a business process for disposing of bicycles for both businesses.
   e. What roles do you see for information systems in your answers to the earlier questions? The information systems can be those you develop within your company or they can be those developed by others, such as "Craig's List."

5. Samantha Green owns and operates Twigs Tree Trimming Service. Samantha graduated from the forestry program of a nearby university and worked for a large landscape design firm, performing tree trimming and removal. After several years of experience, she bought her own truck, stump grinder, and other equipment and opened her own business in St. Louis, Missouri.

   Although many of her jobs are one-time operations to remove a tree or stump, others are recurring, such as trimming a tree or groups of trees every year or every other year. When business is slow, she calls former clients to remind them of her services and of the need to trim their trees on a regular basis.

   Samantha has never heard of Michael Porter nor any of his theories. She operates her business "by the seat of her pants."

   a. Explain how an analysis of the five competitive forces could help Samantha.
   b. Do you think Samantha has a competitive strategy? What competitive strategy would seem to make sense for her?

c. How would knowledge of her competitive strategy help her sales and marketing efforts?
d. Describe, in general terms, the kind of information system that she needs to support sales and marketing efforts.

6. FiredUp, Inc., is a small business owned by Curt and Julie Robards. Based in Brisbane, Australia, FiredUp manufactures and sells a lightweight camping stove called the FiredNow. Curt, who previously worked as an aerospace engineer, invented and patented a burning nozzle that enables the stove to stay lit in very high winds—up to 90 miles per hour. Julie, an industrial designer by training, developed an elegant folding design that is small, lightweight, easy to set up, and very stable. Curt and Julie manufacture the stove in their garage, and they sell it directly to their customers over the Internet and via phone.

a. Explain how an analysis of the five competitive forces could help FiredUp.
b. What does FiredUp's competitive strategy seem to be?
c. Briefly summarize how the primary value chain activities pertain to FiredUp. How should the company design these value chains to conform to its competitive strategy?
d. Describe business processes that FiredUp needs in order to implement its marketing and sales and also its service value chain activities.
e. Describe, in general terms, information systems to support your answer to question d.

COLLABORATION EXERCISES AND CASES

Collaborate with a group of students on the following exercises. Recall from Chapter 2 that collaboration is more than cooperation. Collaboration involves iteration and feedback. Post a document, a discussion item, a wiki item, or an idea and obtain feedback from your team members. Similarly, read the ideas of others and comment on them. Try to innovate in both the process by which you collaborate and the work product that you create. Avoid face-to-face meetings. Instead, use collaborative software such as Google Docs & Spreadsheets, Microsoft Groove, or Microsoft SharePoint to facilitate your ideas.

1. Consider the promotion problem at Singing Valley Resort (page 67). Develop two innovative ideas for solving that problem. Include the following in your response:

a. An analysis of the five forces of the Singing Valley market.
b. A statement of Singing Valley's competitive strategy.
c. A statement of the problem. Recall from Chapter 2 that a problem is a perceived difference between what is and what ought to be. If the members of your group have different perceptions of the problem, all the better. Use a collaborative process to obtain the best possible problem description to which all can agree.
d. Document in a general way (like the top row of Figure 3-9), the process of up-selling an activity.
e. Reread Neil Miyamoto's interview at the start of this chapter. State principles, if any, from The Firm's experience that you can apply to this problem.
f. Develop two innovative ideas for solving the Singing Valley problem. For each idea, provide:
   - A brief description of the idea
   - A process diagram (like Figure 3-7) of the idea
   - A description of the information system needed to implement the idea
g. Compare the advantages and disadvantages of your alternatives in part f and recommend one of them for implementation.

2. Consider the county permit review process in the *Business Processes in Practice* box on pages 73–74. Working with your team, do the following.

a. Analyze the sequential review process. What problems does it have? Consider problems other than those described on page 73.
b. Analyze the parallel review process. What problems does it have? Consider problems other than those described on pages 73–74.
c. Do you see a potential application for document versioning or workflow automation? If so, explain that application.

d. Develop a third process that solves the problems you identify in part a and b. Consider the use of databases, email, Google Docs & Spreadsheets, and Microsoft SharePoint. Document your solution in a process diagram like those shown on pages 73–74.

e. Describe how the process you identify in your answer to part d fixes the problems you identified in your answers to parts a and b.

f. Summarize the work that needs to be accomplished to implement your solution.

APPLICATION EXERCISES

1. Figure 3-17 shows an Excel spreadsheet that the resort bicycle rental business uses to value and analyze its bicycle inventory. Examine this figure to understand the meaning of the data. Now use Excel to create a similar spreadsheet. Note the following:

- The top heading is in 20-point Calibri font. It is centered in the spreadsheet. Cells A1through H1 have been merged.
- The second heading, Bicycle Inventory Valuation, is in 18-point Calibri, italics. It is centered in Cells A2 through H2, which have been merged.
- The column headings are set in 11-point Calibri, bold. They are centered in their cells, and the text wraps in the cells.

a. Make the first two rows of your spreadsheet similar to that in Figure 3-17. Choose your own colors for background and type, however.

b. Place the current date so that it is centered in cells C3, C4, and C5, which must be merged.

c. Outline the cells as shown in the figure.

d. Figure 3-17 uses the following formulas:

Cost of Current Inventory = Bike Cost × Number on Hand

Revenue per Bike = Total Rental Revenue / Number on Hand

Revenue as a Percent of Cost of Inventory = Total Rental Revenue / Cost of Current Inventory

Please use these formulas in your spreadsheet as shown in Figure 3-17.

e. Format the cells in the columns as shown.

f. Give three examples of decisions that management of the bike rental agency might make from this data.

g. What other calculation you could make from this data that would be useful to the bike rental management? Create a second version of this spreadsheet in your worksheet document that has this calculation.

	A	B	C	D	E	F	G	H
1	Resort Bicycle Rental							
2	*Bicycle Inventory Valuation*							
3			Monday, October 29, 2007					
4	**Make of Bike**	**Bike Cost**	**Number on Hand**	**Cost of Current Inventory**	**Number of Rentals**	**Total Rental Revenue**	**Revenue per Bike**	**Revenue as percent of Cost of Inventory**
5	Wonder Bike	$325	12	$3,900	85	$6,375	$531	163.5%
6	Wonder Bike II	$385	4	$1,540	34	$4,570	$1,143	296.8%
7	Wonder Bike Supreme	$475	8	$3,800	44	$5,200	$650	136.8%
8	LiteLift Pro	$655	8	$5,240	25	$2,480	$310	47.3%
9	LiteLift Ladies	$655	4	$2,620	40	$6,710	$1,678	256.1%
10	LiteLift Racer	$795	3	$2,385	37	$5,900	$1,967	247.4%

Figure 3-17

2. In this exercise, you will learn how to create to create a query based on data that a user enters and how to use that query to create a data entry form.

   a. Download the Microsoft Access file **Ch03Ex02**. Open the file and familiarize yourself with the data in the Customer table.
   b. Click *Create* in the Access ribbon. On the far right, select *Query Design*. Select the Customer table as the basis for the query. Drag CustomerName, Customer Email, Date Of Last Rental, Bike Last Rented, Total Number Of Rentals, and TotalRentalRevenue into the columns of the query results pane (the table at the bottom of the query design window).
   c. In the CustomerName column, in the row labeled Criteria, place the following text:

      [Enter Name of Customer:]

      Type this exactly as shown, including the square brackets. This notation tells Access to ask you for a customer name to query.
   d. In the ribbon, click the red exclamation mark labeled *Run*. Access will display a dialog box with the text "Enter Name of Customer:" (the text you entered in the query Criteria row). Enter the value *Scott, Rex* and click OK.
   e. Save your query with the name *Parameter Query.*
   f. Click the Home tab on the ribbon and click the Design View (upper left-hand button on the Home ribbon). Replace the text in the Criteria column of the CustomerName column with the following text. Type it exactly as shown:

      Like "*" & [Enter part of Customer Name to search by:] & "*"
   g. Run the query by clicking Run in the ribbon. Enter *Scott* when prompted *Enter part of Customer Name to search by.* Notice that the two customers who have the name Scott are displayed. If you have any problems, ensure that you have typed the phrase above *exactly* as shown into the Criteria row of the CustomerName column of your query.
   h. Save your query again under the name *Parameter Query*. Close the query window.
   i. Click *Create* in the Access ribbon. Under the Forms group, select the down arrow to the right of More Forms. Choose *Form Wizard*. In the dialog that opens, in the Tables/Queries box, click the down arrow. Select *Parameter Query*. Click the double chevron (>>) symbol and all of the columns in the query will move to the Selected Fields area.
   j. Click *Next* three times. In the box under *What title do you want for your form?* enter *Customer Query Form* and click *Finish.*
   k. Enter *Scott* in the dialog box that appears. Access will open a form with the values for Scott, Rex. At the bottom of the form, click the right-facing arrow and the data for Scott, Bryan will appear.
   l. Close the form. Select *Object Type* and *Forms* in the Access Navigation Pane. Double-click on Customer Query Form and enter the value *James*. Access will display data for all six customers having the value James in their name.

CASE STUDY 3

video

Bosu Balance Trainer

The Bosu balance trainer is a device for developing balance, strength, and aerobic conditioning. Invented in 1999, Bosu has become popular in leading health clubs, in athletic departments, and in homes. Bosu stands for "both sides up," because either side of the equipment can be used for training.

Bosu is not only a new training device, but it also reflects a new philosophy in athletic conditioning that focuses on balance. According to the Bosu inventor, David Weck, "The Bosu Balance Trainer was born of passion to improve my balance. In my lifelong pursuit of enhanced athleticism, I have come to understand that balance is the foundation on which all other performance components are built." Bosu devices are sold by *http://bosu.com.*

Bosu devices have been successful enough that copycat products are undoubtedly on the way. For Bosu to be successful over the long term, it must transform its early market lead into a sustainable and durable market share. This means that Bosu must be used and recommended by coaches, personal trainers, and other significant purchase influencers. Bosu must develop a reputation among these market leaders as delivering significant benefits without risk of injury.

Source: Bosu, *http://bosu.com* (accessed June 2007).

Questions

1. Review the principles of competitive advantage in Figure 3-11. What information systems can Bosu create to enhance its product or differentiate it from existing and emerging competition?
2. What information systems can Bosu develop to create barriers to entry to the competition and to lock in customers?
3. What information systems can Bosu develop to establish alliances?
4. Read Case Study 2, "Customer Support and Knowledge Management at Microsoft," on page 59. (You need not answer the questions in this case; just understand how Microsoft uses newsgroups, focus groups, and MVPs.) How can Bosu develop programs similar to those used by Microsoft to provide customer support and create a competitive advantage?
5. What information systems will Bosu need to develop to support the programs identified in your answer to question 4?

PART 1 THE INTERNATIONAL DIMENSION

The Global Economy

STUDY QUESTIONS

Q1 Why is the global economy important today?

Q2 How does the global economy change the competitive environment?

Q3 How does the global economy change competitive strategy?

Q4 How does the global economy change value chains and business processes?

Q5 How does the global economy change information systems?

Q1 Why Is the Global Economy Important Today?

Businesses compete today in a global market. International business has been sharply increasing since the middle of the twentieth century. After World War II, the Japanese and other Asian economies exploded when those countries began to manufacture and sell goods to the West. The rise of the Japanese auto industry and the rise of the semiconductor industry in southern Asia greatly expanded international trade. At the same time, the economies of North America and Europe became more closely integrated.

Since then, a number of other factors have caused international business to explode. The fall of the Soviet Union opened the economies of Russia and also Eastern Europe to the world market. Even more important, the telecommunications boom during the dot-com heyday caused the world to be encircled many times over by optical fiber that can be used for data and voice communications.

After the dot-com bust, this fiber was largely underutilized and could be purchased for pennies on the dollar. Plentiful, cheap telecommunications enabled people worldwide to participate in the global economy. Prior to the advent of the Internet, for a young Indian professional to participate in the western economy, he or she had to migrate to the West—a process that was politicized and limited. Today, that same young Indian professional can sell his or her goods or services over the Internet without leaving home. During this same period, the Chinese economy became more open to the world, and it too benefits from plentiful, cheap telecommunications.

Thomas Friedman estimates that from 1991 until now, some 3 billion people have been added to the world economy.[1] Not all of those people speak English, and not all are well enough educated (or equipped) to participate in the world economy. But even if just 10 percent are, then 300 million people have been added to the world economy in the last 15 years!

Q2 How Does the Global Economy Change the Competitive Environment?

To understand the impact of globalization, consider each of the elements in Figure 3-1 (page 63), starting with industry structure. The changes have been so dramatic that the structure of seemingly every industry has changed. The enlarged and Internet-equipped world economy has altered every one of the five competitive forces. Suppliers have to reach a wider range of customers, and customers have to consider a wider range of vendors. As you will learn when we address e-commerce in Chapter 8, suppliers and customers benefit not just from the greater size of the economy, but also by the ease with which businesses can learn of each other using infrastructure like Google.

Because of the information available on the Internet, customers can more easily learn of substitutions. The Internet has made it easier for new market entrants, although not in all cases. Amazon.com, Yahoo!, and Google, for example, have garnered such a large market share that it would be difficult for any new entrant to challenge them. Still, in other industries, the global economy facilitates new entrants. Finally, the global economy has intensified rivalry by increasing product and vendor choices and by accelerating the flow of information about price, product, availability, and service.

Q3 How Does the Global Economy Change Competitive Strategy?

Today's global economy changes competitive strategies analysis in two major ways. First, the sheer size and complexity of the global economy means that any organization that chooses a strategy to compete industry-wide is taking a very big bite! Competing in many different countries, with products localized to the language and culture of those countries, is an enormous and expensive task.

For example, to promote its Windows monopoly, Microsoft must produce a version of Windows in dozens of different languages. Even in English, there are U.K. versions, U.S. versions. Australian versions, and so forth. The problem for Microsoft is even greater because different countries use different character sets. In some languages, one writes left to right. In other languages, one writes right to left. When Microsoft set out to sell Windows worldwide, it embarked on an enormous project.

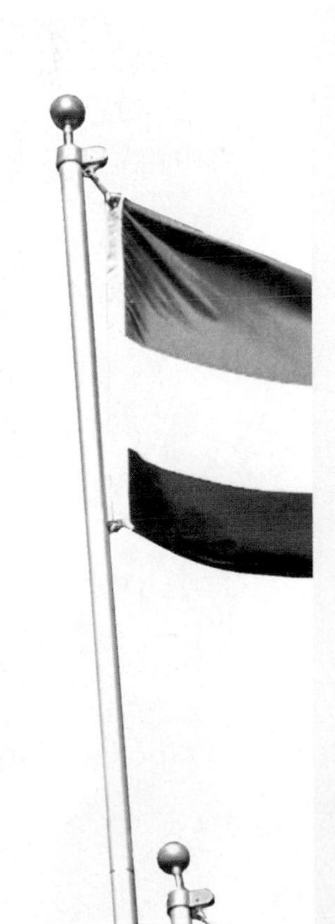

[1]Thomas L. Friedman, *The World is Flat* [Updated and Expanded]: *A Brief History of the Twenty-First Century* (New York: Farrar, Strauss, and Giroux, 2006).

The second major way today's world economy changes competitive strategies is that its size, combined with the Internet, enables unprecedented product differentiation. If you choose to produce the world's highest quality and most exotic oatmeal—and if your production costs require you to sell that oatmeal for $350 a pound—your target market may contain only 200 people worldwide. The Internet allows you to find them—and them to find you.

Decisions involving global competitive strategies involve the consideration of these two changing factors.

Q4 How Does the Global Economy Change Value Chains and Business Processes?

The growth in the world economy has major impacts on all activities in the value chain model. An excellent example concerns the manufacture of the Boeing 787. Every primary activity for this airplane has an international component. Companies all over the world produce its parts and subassemblies. Major components of the airplane are constructed in worldwide locations and shipped for final assembly to Boeing's plant in Everett, Washington. *Outbound logistics* for Boeing refers not just to the delivery of an airplane, but also to the delivery of spare parts and supporting maintenance equipment. All of those items are produced at factories worldwide and delivered to customers worldwide. The global sales also change the marketing, sales, and service activities for the 787.

As you learned in Chapter 3, each value chain activity is supported by one or more business processes. Those processes span the globe and need to address differences in language, culture, and economic environments. A process for servicing 787 customers in Egypt will be very different from the same service process in China, the United States, or India. For example, a business process organized around a central leader with strong authority may be expected in one culture and resisted in another. Global companies must design their business processes with these differences in mind.

Q5 How Does the Global Economy Change Information Systems?

To understand the impact of internationalization on information systems, consider the five components. Computer hardware is sold worldwide, and most vendors provide documentation in at least the major languages, so internationalization has little impact on that component. The remaining components of an information system, however, are markedly affected.

To begin, consider the user interface for an international information system. Does it include a localized version of Windows? What about the software application itself? Does an inventory system used worldwide by Boeing suppose that each user speaks English? If so, at what level of proficiency? If not, what languages must the user interface support? Most computer programs are written in computer languages that have an English base, but not all. Can an information system use a localized programming language?

Next, consider the data component. Suppose that the inventory database has a table for parts data and that table contains a column named *Remarks*. Suppose Boeing needs to integrate parts data from three different vendors: one in China, one in India, and one in Canada. What language is to be used for recording Remarks? Does someone need to translate all of the Remarks into one language? Into three languages?

The human components—procedures and people—are obviously affected by language and culture. As with business processes, information systems procedures need to reflect local cultural values and norms. For systems users, job descriptions and reporting relationships must be appropriate for the setting in which the system is used. We will say more about this in Part 4, when we discuss the development and management of information systems.

ACTIVE REVIEW

Use this Active Review to verify that you understand the ideas and concepts that answer the study questions in the International Dimension.

Q1 Why is the global economy important today?

Describe how the global economy has changed since the mid-twentieth century. Explain how the dot-com bust influenced the global economy and changed the number of workers worldwide.

Q2 How does the global economy change the competitive environment?

Summarize the ways in which today's global economy influences the five competitive forces. Explain how the global economy changes the way organizations analyze industry structure.

Q3 How does the global economy change competitive strategy?

Explain how size and complexity change the costs of a competitive strategy. Describe what the size of the global economy means to differentiation.

Q4 How does the global economy change value chains and business processes?

Describe, in general terms, how international business impacts value chains and business processes. Use the example of the Boeing 787 in your answer.

Q5 How does the global economy change information systems?

Describe how international business impacts each of the five components of an information system. Identify the components that are most impacted by the need to support multiple cultures and languages.

PART 1

CASE 1-1

Getty Images Serves Up Profit

Getty Images was founded in 1995 with the goal of consolidating the fragmented photography market by acquiring many small companies, applying business discipline to the merged entity, and developing modern information systems. The advent of the Web drove the company to e-commerce and in the process enabled Getty to change the workflow and business practices of the professional visual content industry. Getty Images has grown from a startup to become, by 2004, a global, $600 million plus, publicly traded (NYSE: GYI), very profitable company.

Getty Images obtains its imagery (both still and movie) from photographers under contract, and it owns the world's largest private archive of imagery. Getty also employs staff photographers to shoot the world's news, sport, and entertainment events. In the case of photography and film that it does not own, it provides a share of the revenue generated to the content owner. Getty Images is both a producer and a distributor of imagery, and all of its products are sold via e-commerce on the Web.

Getty Images employs three licensing models: The first is *subscription*, by which customers contract to use as many images as they want as often as they want (this applies to the news, sport, and entertainment imagery). The second model is *royalty-free*. In this model, customers pay a fee based on the file size of the image and can use the image any way they want and as many times as they want. However, under this model, customers have no exclusivity or ability to prevent a competitor from using the same image at the same time.

The third model, *rights managed*, also licenses creative imagery. In this model, which is the largest in revenue terms, users pay fees according to the rights that they wish to use—size, industry, geography, prominence, frequency, exclusivity, and so forth.

According to its Web site:

> Getty Images has been credited with the introduction of royalty-free photography and was the first company to license imagery via the Web, subsequently moving the entire industry online. The company was also the first to employ creative researchers to anticipate the visual content needs of the world's communicators, and Getty Images remains the first and only publicly traded imagery company in the world (*http://corporate.gettyimages.com/source/company.html*, accessed December 2004).

In 2003, Getty Images' Web site, *www.gettyimages.com*, received more than 51 million visits and served over 1.3 billion pages. Visitors to the site viewed more than 6.7 billion thumbnail-sized photos in the third quarter of 2004 alone.

Because Getty Images licenses photos in digital format, its variable cost of production is essentially zero. Once the company has obtained a photo and placed it in the commerce server database, the cost of sending it to a customer

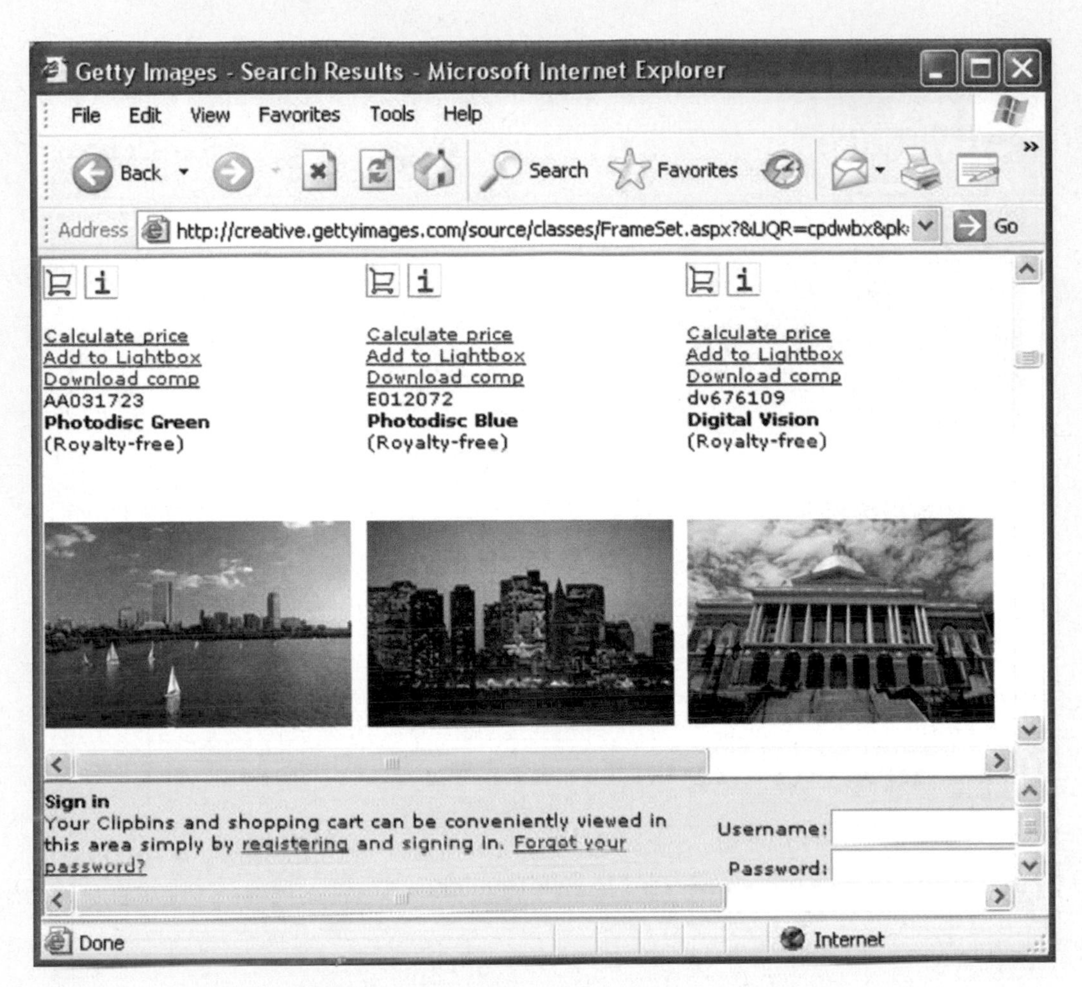

Figure 1
Getty Images' Search Results

Source: Used with permission from Getty Images, Inc. All Rights Reserved. © 2007 Getty Images, Inc.

is zero. Getty Images does have the overhead costs of setting up and operating the e-commerce site, and it does pay some costs for its images—either the costs of employing the photographer or the cost of setting up and maintaining the relationship with out-of-house photographers. For some images, it also pays a royalty to the owner. Once these costs are paid, however, the cost of producing a photo is nil. This means that Getty Images' profitability increases substantially with increased volume.

Figure 1 shows a page that the Getty Images commerce server produced when the user selected creative, royalty-free photography and searched on the term *Boston*.

When the user clicked "Calculate price" for the image named Photodisc Green, the commerce server produced the page shown in Figure 2. This Web page shows a default price. Users in different countries may have a different price depending on agreements, taxes, and local policies.

Source: www.gettyimages.com (accessed December 2004).

QUESTIONS

1. Visit *GettyImages.com,* and select "Creative/Search royalty-free." Search for an image of a city close to your campus. Select a photo and determine its default prices.

2. Explain how Getty Images' business model takes advantage of the opportunities created by IT as described in Chapter 1.

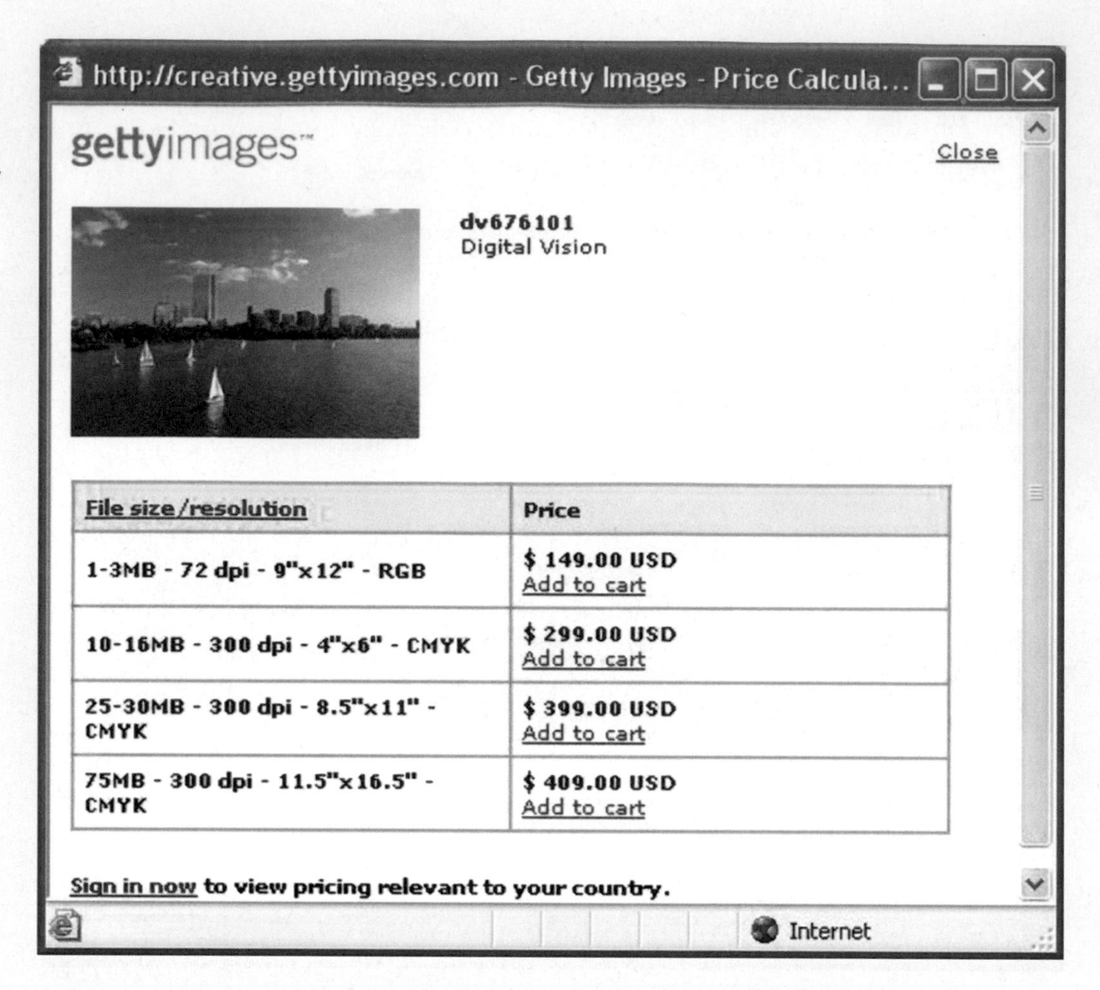

File size/resolution	Price
1-3MB - 72 dpi - 9"x12" - RGB	$ 149.00 USD Add to cart
10-16MB - 300 dpi - 4"x6" - CMYK	$ 299.00 USD Add to cart
25-30MB - 300 dpi - 8.5"x11" - CMYK	$ 399.00 USD Add to cart
75MB - 300 dpi - 11.5"x16.5" - CMYK	$ 409.00 USD Add to cart

Figure 2
Price Calculation for an Image of Boston

Source: Used with permission from Getty Images, Inc. All Rights Reserved. © 2007 Getty Images, Inc.

3. Evaluate the photography market using Porter's five forces. Do you think Getty Images' marginal cost is sustainable? Are its prices sustainable? What is the key to its continued success?

4. What seems to be Getty Images' competitive strategy?

5. Explain how Getty Images has used information systems to gain a competitive advantage.

6. Based on your answers to the previous questions, would you choose to buy Getty Images stock?

7. Getty Images has the enviable position of a near-zero variable cost of production. Describe two other businesses that could use emerging IT to attain the same advantage.

CASE 1-2

Knoll Inc.

Knoll, Inc. (*www.knoll.com*) is a leading manufacturer of office equipment. Founded in 1938, Knoll has always been known for its groundbreaking, innovative, and fashionable designs. Today, such innovation includes not only modern, contemporary designs, but also designs that recognize changes in the nature of the work environment. Knoll understood early on that new information systems would drive the redesign of value chains and business processes. Knoll realized that these changes would, in turn, impact the physical design of the workers' environments and alter the requirements for office furniture.

According to Christine Barber, who is Director of Workplace Research at Knoll:

> The explosion of information technology has caused a fundamental shift in company offices away from clerical and toward professional, managerial, and creative work . . . . Whereas white-collar labor in the nineteenth and most of the twentieth century involved an army of clerical workers performing rote tasks under the supervision of an elite corps of managers, most of the grunt work has now been turned over to computers . . . . Two-thirds [of office workers] describe themselves as "problem solvers," "information analyzers," and "idea generators". . . . Half of those working in midsize to large companies characterize their work as "collaborative" in nature (Barber and Yee, 2004).

Because of the importance of workplace changes to its market, Knoll commissioned a study involving 1,500 interviews of 350 office workers. Researchers asked those workers to rate the importance of office factors in terms of their contribution to productivity. The following are the top five factors, rated in decreasing order of productivity impact:

- State-of-the-art computer technology
- Ample storage space for work items
- Control over temperature
- Quiet workspace
- Space that can be personalized

In this study, Knoll also found a curious paradox in workers' attitudes toward privacy. Most workers want it both ways: They want their own office or private space in which to concentrate, perform uninterrupted work, and hold private meetings, but they also want open space for collaboration, a feeling of teamwork, and a sense of family. Modern workers, according to Knoll's study, "crave both privacy and intimacy." They want an open space design rather than a cubicle configuration. In fact, according to the research study, "the cubicle is the symbol of everything 'old economy' in workplace design, evoking images of 'prison,' conformity, being a number or stamped with a barcode" (Barber and DYG, Inc., 2004).

According to Barber, "As the workforce of the new economy performs increasingly cerebral, self-directed, and multidisciplinary tasks, the gap between managers and [those who are] managed narrows dramatically in terms of skills, experience, and responsibility. But the flattening of the organizational pyramid has not inspired any real change in office space" (Barber and DYG, Inc., 2004).

These are intriguing statements. We know that information systems improve communication and that they foster cross-departmental, process thinking. Do they also change the shape of the workplace? They should, at least according to Barber: "Businesses feel compelled to invest in cutting-edge information technology to stay competitive; but they persist in seeing offices as assembly lines, rather than as think tanks, for producing knowledge-based products and services" (Barber and Yee, 2004).

Sources: Christine Barber and DYG, Inc., "The 21st Century Workplace"; Christine Barber and Roger Yee, "Brave New Workplace" 2004, *www.knoll.com/research/index.htm* (accessed March 2005).

QUESTIONS

1. Given the fact that Knoll sponsored the research described here, is Knoll more likely to be engaging in a low cost or differentiation competitive strategy? Explain.

2. How will the change from hierarchical to cross-departmental process thinking affect the design of office furniture and equipment? Do you think there will be sufficient impact to justify Knoll's concern and research? What are the dangers to a company like Knoll of not considering these trends?

3. Describe two nontechnology-related industries, other than the office furniture industry, that are likely to be changed by cross-departmental, enterprise-wide information systems and related organizational changes. Explain the nature of the impact on those industries.

4. Suppose you are a product manager in Knoll's marketing group. Describe three ways you could use the five productivity factors listed in this case to design new products, product features, or product enhancements.

5. Suppose you manage a sales department with two types of salespeople: those who call on prospects to obtain new customers and those who sell to existing customers. Assume that each salesperson works in a personal cubicle and that salespeople are assigned to cubicles regardless of the type of sales they perform. Suppose your department is converting to a new sales support system, and you take that opportunity to propose an improvement to your sales team's workplace.

   a. Given the information in this case, what changes would you make?

   b. Suppose you ask the manager of the new sales support project for funds to purchase new office furniture and equipment. Suppose she rejects your request saying, "New furniture has absolutely nothing to do with the success of our new system." How do you respond?

   c. Rank the importance of the workspace arrangement for the users of a new information system. Is the environment as important as the system's features? More important? Less important? Explain.

Information Technology

The next three chapters address the information technology that underlies information systems. Chapter 4 discusses hardware and software and defines basic terms and fundamental computing concepts.

Chapter 5 addresses the data component of information technology by describing database processing. You will learn essential database terminology and be introduced to techniques for processing databases. We will also introduce data modeling, because you may be required to evaluate data models for databases that others develop for you.

Chapter 6 continues the discussion of computing devices begun in Chapter 4 and describes data communications and Internet technologies.

The purpose of these three chapters is to teach you technology sufficient for you to be an effective IT consumer. You will learn basic terms, fundamental ideas, and useful frameworks so that you will have the knowledge to ask good questions and make appropriate requests of the information systems professionals who will serve you.

4 Hardware and Software

STUDY QUESTIONS

Q1 What does a manager need to know about computer hardware?

Q2 How much does hardware cost?

Q3 What is the difference between a client and a server?

Q4 What does a manager need to know about software?

Q5 How much does software cost?

Q6 What are viruses, Trojan horses, and worms?

Q7 How can you use this knowledge?

Meet Cindy Lo

My guiding principle:
Be true to your words . . . and never promise someone something that you can't deliver.

My hero:
My husband. It definitely takes a special person to put up with my strong personality and dedication to work. Also, he's been very supportive since I started Red Velvet Events and has given me endless advice on how to grow and continue to build a strong team. And it doesn't hurt that he's a fellow techie, a computer science major with a lot of professional services and business experience.

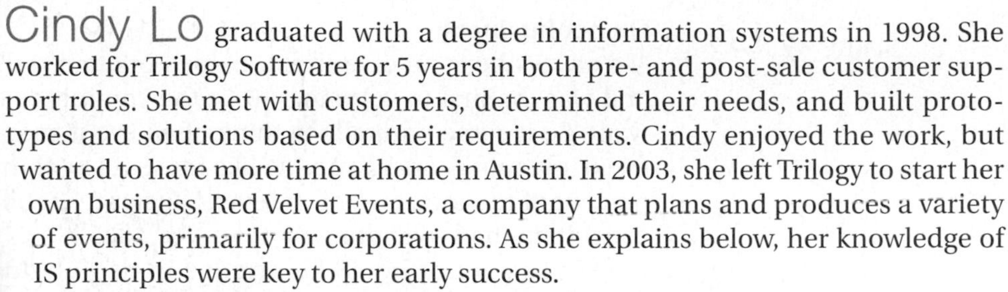

Cindy Lo graduated with a degree in information systems in 1998. She worked for Trilogy Software for 5 years in both pre- and post-sale customer support roles. She met with customers, determined their needs, and built prototypes and solutions based on their requirements. Cindy enjoyed the work, but wanted to have more time at home in Austin. In 2003, she left Trilogy to start her own business, Red Velvet Events, a company that plans and produces a variety of events, primarily for corporations. As she explains below, her knowledge of IS principles were key to her early success.

Cindy provides two perspectives on hardware and software: from sales support for software at Trilogy and from purchasing hardware and software for her own business.

On her major:

"I started as an accountant. Do you know the Asian stereotype—'If you're not going to be a doctor or a lawyer, then at least become an accountant'? So I majored in accounting for one year, and it just wasn't me. I didn't enjoy the classes, and I couldn't imagine an accounting career. I even had a summer internship at the now defunct Arthur Andersen.

"I'd taken some computer programming classes in high school, but I knew I didn't want to be a full-time programmer—sitting in a cubicle by myself all day writing programs. I talked to students who were IS majors, and they told me that IS combines business and technology, and that sounded interesting. I especially enjoyed the project-oriented classes when we had a real client and would develop a tangible system for them."

On her first job:

"Trilogy sells a wide variety of products. I had numerous assignments, but worked principally on systems for computing commission payments. I'd interview the client, determine their needs, and then build a prototype or a full system using our software. Some companies had really wild commission schemes: 'If you sell this amount of Products A and B in these regions, then your commission is X, but, of course, if the moon is out, it will be 10 percent less.' I'm kidding, but you get the idea.

"I enjoyed the combination of sales, project management, and technical work. I also liked producing tangible results. Interactions with the clients were fun, and I enjoyed learning about different industries. It was the travel and overtime that got to me. Trilogy treated us very well, but after seeing the world, I was ready to spend more time in Austin with family."

Don't do this to me in an interview:
Telling me that your biggest weakness is that you're a perfectionist. Never tell a perfectionist that you are a perfectionist—they can tell! And never tell a perfectionist that it's a weakness!

My career high:
Starting Red Velvet Events and seeing it grow the past 5 years.

My motto:
The same as the motto of my company: Outplan. Outplay. Outparty!

Today's hottest technology:
Continuous connectivity, no matter where you are, what you're doing, or what your choice of device is, you can stay connected to one another and to the Internet.

Cindy Lo

On her business:

"I'd always been an organizer, I helped organized the freshman orientation at school and was the first to volunteer to be the committee chair for events that others didn't want. So it came naturally to think of an event-management business. Actually, we're event-planning consultants. Unlike most of our competitors, we don't bill our fees as a percent of the total cost of the event. Instead, we bill hourly. That makes us more of a consultant than a vendor.

"I use a lot of my IS knowledge in my job. Just like with software, I sit down with my clients and determine their needs—the business objectives they want to accomplish with their event. Then I help them look at feasibility—can they accomplish their goals with the budget they have? This past week I spent 20 hours crunching numbers to help a client decide whether or not to cancel an event.

"When I first started the company, the event-planning industry was in the dark ages of technology. Actually, the industry is still far behind. But, given my IS background, that lag created opportunities for me, and still does.

"Early on, I built an Excel template so I could create event budgets quickly—people couldn't believe how fast I could put together a professional proposal using Word and Excel. I didn't even try to use Access—that would have been so far over their heads. Some of my clients would actually ignore my Excel formulas, get out their calculators, make the calculations, and type the numbers back into Excel on top of the formulas.

"I had to teach them not to do that. 'Look, just enter the number of people you want to attend your event, and the spreadsheet will recalculate the budget and make all the resulting calculations.' It's amazing how little some people know about Excel who claim they have expertise."

On the importance of hardware and software knowledge:

"You need to be an informed consumer. You can't just take what the salesperson offers. If you don't learn the basics in school, then you'll have to hire a consultant or find expertise from friends and family.

"When I buy laptops for my employees, I know we don't need the fastest CPU or largest main memory. We don't do that much—some Word, some Excel, and PowerPoint. We do, however, take a lot of photos and manage a lot of files for clients, so we need large hard drives. Knowing that, I buy only what I need.

"Regarding software, don't expect it to off-load all your pains and worries. If some salesperson says his or her software will do that, don't believe it. If you can find software that meets 90 percent of your needs, take it. And definitely ask around to see what others are using.

"One of my favorite software programs—one I couldn't run my business without—is a time-tracking program called AllNetic. We bill clients on an hourly basis, and it's important to capture all the time my team and I spend working on each account. It's really a rinky-dink little program, but it meets all of our needs; installs on the toolbar; and costs $40 per machine. That's peanuts. I think it might have been written by a college student. But, hey, I know what we need, and given my background, I'm confident in my knowledge, so I don't have to buy from Microsoft or Oracle just to be safe.

"After we've entered the data, I import it into Excel. Not only do we generate bills from the data, but I also use it as a management tool. If I see that someone took 16 hours to create a budget, I know something is wrong. Maybe they need more training. Whatever . . . but the data tells me I need to do something.

"Would I go back into software? I don't know. I'm having fun. But, I know a lot about sales and marketing, and well, never say never. . . ."

CHAPTER PREVIEW

As you learned in Chapter 1, hardware and software are the first two components of an information system. As a business professional, and possibly a future manager, you do not need to know details of hardware and software technology. You do need to know enough, however, to be an intelligent consumer. As Cindy Lo says about software, you need to be able to engage in an informed conversation with experts, and you need to know enough to express what you need and to assess vendors' and others' responses to your requirements.

The study questions in this chapter ask what hardware and software do and how much they cost. The goal is to prepare you to answer questions like the $80,000 question in the *Technology in Practice* box on page 104. In fact, you might want to read that box before proceeding with Q1—the $80,000 question sets the stage for what you need to know about hardware and software.

The $80,000 question in the Technology in Practice *box on page 104 sets the stage for what managers need to know about hardware and software.*

Q1 What Does a Manager Need to Know About Computer Hardware?

As discussed in the five-component framework, **hardware** consists of electronic components and related gadgetry that input, process, output, and store data according to instructions encoded in computer programs or software. Figure 4-1 shows the components of a generic computer. Notice that the basic hardware categories are input, process, output, and storage.

Basic Components

As shown in Figure 4-1, typical **input hardware** devices are the keyboard, mouse, document scanners, and bar-code (Universal Product Code) scanners like those used in grocery stores. Microphones also are input devices; with tablet PCs, human handwriting can be input as well. Older input devices include magnetic ink readers (used for reading the ink on the bottom of checks) and scanners such as the Scantron test scanner shown in Figure 4-2 (next page).

Processing devices include the **central processing unit (CPU)**, which is sometimes called "the brain" of the computer. Although the design of the CPU has nothing in common with the anatomy of animal brains, this description is helpful, because the

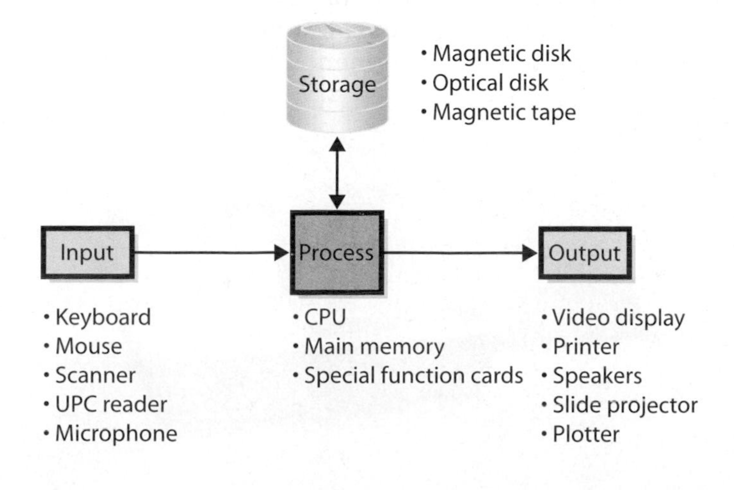

Figure 4-1
Input, Process, Output, and Storage Hardware

TECHNOLOGY IN PRACTICE

IS $80,000 ENOUGH?

Suppose you manage the sales and marketing department at a company that generates $100 million in sales—say, a manufacturer of fireplace inserts and related equipment. Assume you just started the job and that at the end of your second day the Corporate Operations Officer (COO) sticks her head into your office and announces, "I'm in a rush and have to go, but I wanted to let you know that I put $80,000 in the budget for computers for your department next year. Is that OK? Unfortunately, I've got to know by the day after tomorrow. Thanks."

How do you respond? You have 2 days to decide. If you agree to the $80,000 and it turns out to be insufficient, then sometime next year your department will lack computing resources and you'll have a management problem. If that happens, you may have to spend over your budget. You know that cost control is important to your new employer, so you dread overspending. However, if you ask for more than $80,000, you need to justify why you need it. You will need to document the computer equipment and software your department needs, explain why you need it, and estimate how much it will cost.

Given the short time frame, and given that as a new employee you probably have already scheduled the next 2 days full of meetings, you will need to delegate at least part of this problem to someone. You might delegate it to a computer salesperson, but that is akin to inviting the fox to babysit the chickens. Or, you could delegate it to some of your employees, but as a new employee you do not yet know who has the capability to answer this question. You could also ask the IS department at your organization to help you.

In any case, whether you find the time to answer this question yourself, or assign it to your employees, or ask for help from the IS department, you will need knowledge of computer hardware and software capabilities and costs in order to assess the quality of the answer you have.

You and a team of your fellow students will be given an opportunity to address this question in Collaboration Exercise 1, page 136.

CPU does have the "smarts" of the machine. The CPU selects instructions, processes them, performs arithmetic and logical comparisons, and stores results of operations in memory. Some computers have two or more CPUs. A computer with two CPUs is called a **dual-processor** computer. **Quad-processor** computers have four CPUs. Some high-end computers have 16 or more CPUs.

CPUs vary in speed, function, and cost. Hardware vendors such as Intel, Advanced Micro Devices, and National Semiconductor continually improve CPU speed and capabilities while reducing CPU costs (as discussed under Moore's Law in Chapter 1). Whether you or your department needs the latest, greatest CPU depends on the nature of your work, as you will learn.

The CPU works in conjunction with **main memory**. The CPU reads data and instructions from memory, and it stores results of computations in main memory. We will describe the relationship between the CPU and main memory later in the chapter. Main memory is sometimes called **RAM**, for random access memory.

Finally, computers also can have **special function cards** (see Figure 4-3) that can be added to the computer to augment its basic capabilities. A common

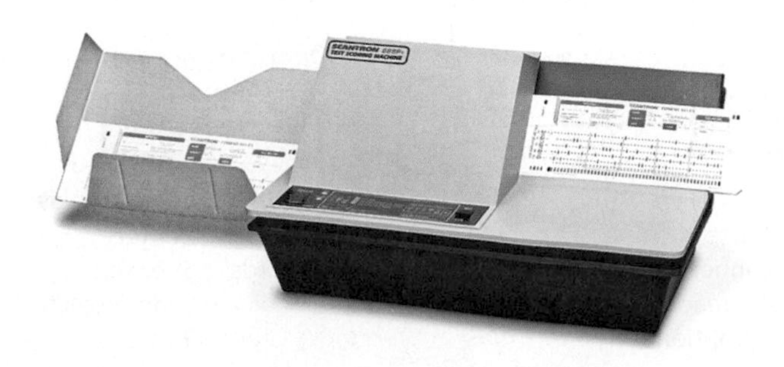

Figure 4-2
Scantron Scanner

Source: Courtesy of Harrison Public Relations Group, Scantron Corporation.

Figure 4-3
Special Function Card

Source: Photo courtesy of Creative Labs, Inc. Sound Blaster and Audigy are registered trademarks of CreativeTechnology Ltd. In the United States and other countries.

example is a card that provides enhanced clarity and refresh speed for the computer's video display.

Output hardware consists of video displays, printers, audio speakers, overhead projectors, and other special-purpose devices, such as large flatbed plotters.

Storage hardware saves data and programs. Magnetic disk is by far the most common storage device, although optical disks such as CDs and DVDs also are popular. In large corporate data centers, data is sometimes stored on magnetic tape.

Computer Data

Before we can further describe hardware, we need to define several important terms. We begin with binary digits.

Binary Digits

Computers represent data using **binary digits**, called **bits**. A bit is either a zero or a one. Bits are used for computer data because they are easy to represent physically, as illustrated in Figure 4-4. A switch can be either closed or open. A computer can be designed so that an open switch represents zero and a closed switch represents one. Or the orientation of a magnetic field can represent a bit; magnetism in one direction represents a zero, magnetism in the opposite direction represents a one. Or, for optical media, small pits are burned onto the surface of the disk so that they will reflect light. In a given spot, a reflection means a one; no reflection means a zero.

Sizing Computer Data

All computer data are represented by bits. The data can be numbers, characters, currency amounts, photos, recordings, or whatever. All are simply a string of bits.

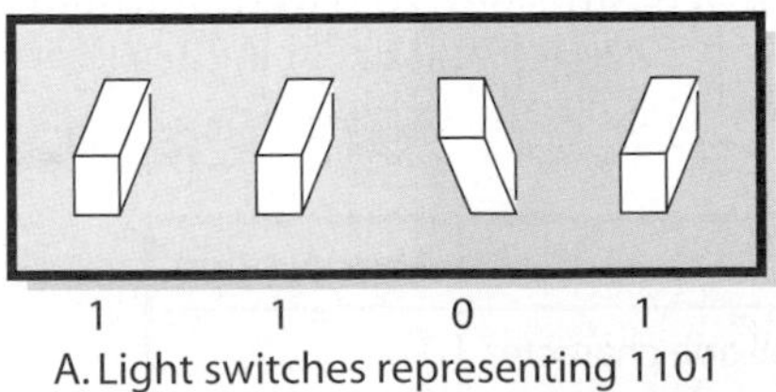

1 1 0 1
A. Light switches representing 1101

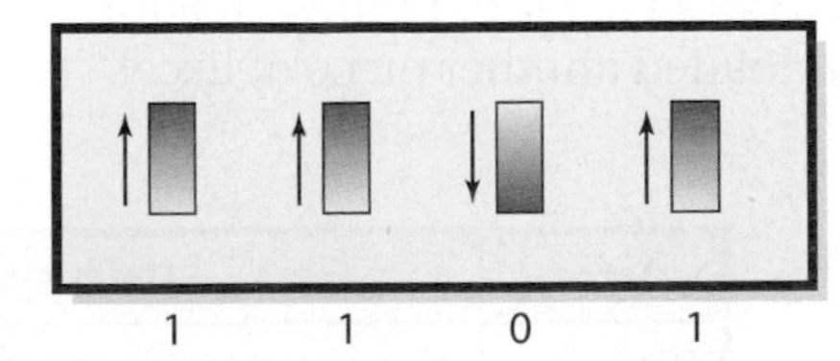

1 1 0 1
B. Direction of magnetism representing 1101

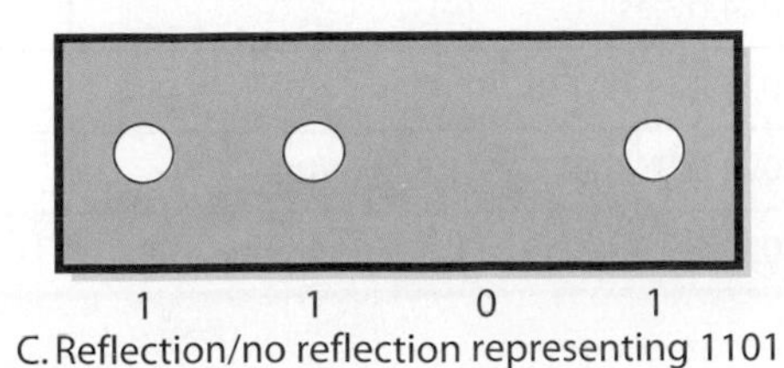

1 1 0 1
C. Reflection/no reflection representing 1101

Figure 4-4
Bits Are Easy to Represent Physically

For reasons that interest many but are irrelevant for future managers, bits are grouped into 8-bit chunks called **bytes**. For character data, such as the letters in a person's name, one character will fit into one byte. Thus, when you read a specification that a computing device has 100 million bytes of memory, you know that the device can hold up to 100 million characters.

Bytes are used to measure sizes of noncharacter data as well. Someone might say, for example, that a given picture is 100,000 bytes in size. This statement means the length of the bit string that represents the picture is 100,000 bytes or 800,000 bits (because there are 8 bits per byte). The specifications for the size of main memory, disk, and other computer devices are expressed in bytes. Figure 4-5 shows the set of abbreviations that are used to represent data-storage capacity. A **kilobyte**, abbreviated **K**, is a collection of 1,024 bytes. A **megabyte**, or **MB**, is 1,024 kilobytes. A **gigabyte**, or **GB**, is 1,024 megabytes, and a **terabyte**, or **TB**, is 1,024 gigabytes.

Sometimes you will see these definitions simplified as 1K equals 1,000 bytes and 1MB equals 1,000K. Such simplifications are incorrect, but they do ease the math. Also, disk and computer manufacturers have an incentive to propagate this misconception. If a disk maker defines 1MB to be 1 million bytes—and not the correct 1,024K—the manufacturer can use its own definition of MB when specifying drive capacities. A buyer may think that a disk advertised as 100MB has space for 100 × 1,024K bytes, but in truth the drive will have space for only 100× 1,000,000 bytes. Normally, the distinction is not too important, but be aware of the two possible interpretations of these abbreviations.

In Fewer Than 300 Words, How Does a Computer Work?

Figure 4-6 shows a snapshot of a computer in use. The CPU is the major actor. To run a program or process data, the computer must first transfer the program or data from disk to *main memory*. Then, to execute an instruction, it moves the instruction from main memory into the CPU via the **data channel** or **bus**. The CPU has a small amount of very fast memory called a **cache**. The CPU keeps frequently used instructions in the cache. Having a large cache makes the computer faster, but cache is expensive.

Main memory of the computer in Figure 4-6 contains program instructions for Microsoft Excel, Adobe Acrobat, and a browser (Microsoft Internet Explorer or Mozilla Firefox). It also contains a block of data and instructions for the **operating system (OS)**, which is a program that controls the computer's resources.

Main memory is too small to hold all of the programs and data that a user might want to process. For example, no personal computer has enough memory to hold all of the code in Microsoft Word, Excel, and Access. Consequently, the CPU loads programs into memory in chunks. In Figure 4-6, one portion of Excel was loaded into memory. When the user requested additional processing (say, to sort the spreadsheet), the CPU loaded another piece of Excel.

Term	Definition	Abbreviation
Byte	Number of bits to represent one character	
Kilobyte	1,024 bytes	K
Megabyte	1,024 K = 1,048,576 bytes	MB
Gigabyte	1,024 MB = 1,073,741,824 bytes	GB
Terabyte	1,024 GB = 1,099,511,627,776 bytes	TB

Figure 4-5
Important Storage-Capacity Terminology

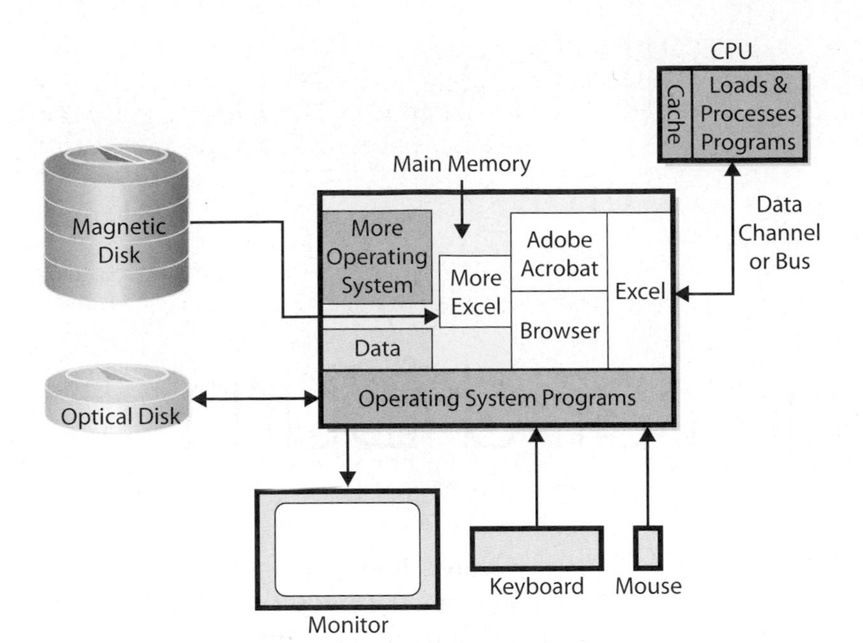

Figure 4-6
Computer Components, in Use

If the user opens another program (say, Word) or needs to load more data (say, a picture), the operating system will direct the CPU to attempt to place the new program or data into unused memory. If there is not enough memory, it will remove something, perhaps the block of memory labeled More Excel, and then it will place the just-requested program or data into the vacated space. This process is called **memory swapping**.

Why Does a Manager Care How a Computer Works?

You can order computers with varying sizes of main memory. An employee who runs only one program at a time and who processes small amounts of data requires very little memory—512MB would be just fine. However, an employee who processes many programs at the same time (say, Word, Excel, Firefox, Access, Acrobat, and other programs) or an employee who processes very large files (pictures, movies, or sound files) needs lots of main memory, perhaps 2GB or more. If that employee's computer has too little memory, then the computer will constantly be swapping memory, and it will be slow. (This means, by the way, that if your computer is slow and if you have many programs open, you likely can improve performance by closing one or more programs. Depending on your computer and the amount of memory it has, you might also be able to add more memory to it.)

You can also order computers with CPUs of different speeds. CPU speed is expressed in cycles called *hertz*. In 2007, a slow personal computer has a speed of 1 Gigahertz. A fast personal computer has a speed of 3 Gigahertz, with dual processing. As predicted by Moore's Law, CPU speeds continually increase.

An employee who does only simple tasks such as word processing does not need a fast CPU; 1 Gigahertz will be fine. However, an employee who processes large, complicated spreadsheets or who manipulates large database files or edits large picture, sound, or movie files needs a fast computer like a dual processor with 3 Gigahertz or more.

One last comment: The cache and main memory are **volatile**, meaning their contents are lost when power is off. Magnetic and optical disks are **nonvolatile**, meaning their contents survive when power is off. If you suddenly lose power, the contents of unsaved memory—say, documents that have been altered—will be lost. Therefore,

The Ethics Guide *on page 108 poses questions about computer hardware and software and how much we truly need.*

Ethics

GUIDE

Churn and Burn

An anonymous source, whom we'll call Mark, made the following statements about computing devices:

"I never upgrade my system. At least, I try not to. Look, I don't do anything at work but write memos and access email. I use Microsoft Word, but I don't use any features that weren't available in Word 3.0, 15 years ago. This whole industry is based on 'churn and burn': They churn their products so we'll burn our cash.

"All this hype about 3.0GHz processors and 350GB disks—who needs them? I'm sure I don't. And if Microsoft hadn't put so much junk into Windows, we could all be happy on an Intel 486 processor like the one I had in 1993. We're suckers for falling into the 'you gotta have this' trap.

"Frankly, I think there's a conspiracy between hardware and software vendors. They both want to sell new products, so the hardware people come up with these incredibly fast and huge computers. Then, given all that power, the software types develop monster products bloated with features and functions that nobody uses. It would take me months to learn all of the features in Word, only to find out that I don't need those features.

"To see what I mean, open Microsoft Word, click on View, then select Toolbars. In my version of Word, there are 19 toolbars to select, plus one more to customize my own toolbar. Now what in the world do I need with 19 toolbars? I write all the time, and I have two selected: Standard and Formatting. Two out of 19! Could I pay Microsoft 2/19 of the price of Word, because that's all I want or use?

"Here's how they get you, though. Because we live in a connected world, they don't have to get all of us to use those 19 toolbars, just one of us. Take Bridgette, over in Legal, for example. Bridgette likes to use the redlining features, and she likes me to use them when I change draft contracts she sends me. So if I want to work on her documents, I have to turn on the Reviewing toolbar. You get the idea; just get someone to use a feature and, because it is a connected world, then all of us have to have that feature.

"Viruses are one of their best ploys. They say you better buy the latest and greatest in software—and then apply all the patches that follow so that you'll be protected from the latest zinger from the computer 'bad guys.' Think about that for a minute. If vendors had built the products correctly the first time, then there would be no holes for the baddies to find, would there? So they have a defect in their products that they turn to a sales advantage. You see, they get us to focus on the virus and not on the hole in their product. In truth, they should be saying, 'Buy our latest product to protect yourself from the defective junk we sold you last year.' But truth in advertising hasn't come that far.

"Besides that, users are their own worst enemies as far as viruses are concerned. If I'm down on 17th Street at 4 in the morning, half drunk and with a bundle of cash hanging out of my pocket, what's likely to happen to me? I'm gonna get mugged. So if I'm out in some weirdo chat room—you know, out where you get pictures of weird sex acts and whatnot—and download and run a file, then of course I'm gonna get a virus. Viruses are brought on by user stupidity, that's all.

"One of these days, users are going to rise up and say, 'That's enough. I don't need any more. I'll stay with what I have, thank you very much.' In fact, maybe that's happening right now. Maybe that's why software sales aren't growing like they were. Maybe people have finally said, 'No more toolbars!'" ■

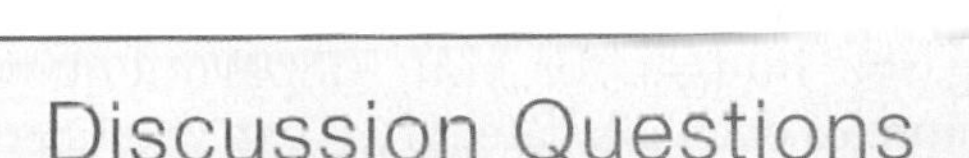

Discussion Questions

1. Summarize Mark's view of the computer industry. Is there merit to his argument? Why or why not?
2. What holes do you see in the logic of his argument?
3. Someone could take the position that these statements are just empty rantings—that Mark can say all he wants, but the computer industry is going to keep on doing as it has been. Is there any point in Mark sharing his criticisms?
4. Read the section on viruses, Trojan horses, and worms that appears later in this chapter (pages 125–126). Comment on Mark's statement—"Viruses are brought on by user stupidity, that's all."
5. All software products ship with known problems. Microsoft, Adobe, and Apple all ship software that they know has failures. Is it unethical for them to do so? Do software vendors have an ethical responsibility to openly publish the problems in their software? How do these organizations protect themselves from lawsuits for damages caused by known problems in software?
6. Suppose a vendor licenses and ships a software product that has both known and unknown failures. As the vendor learns of the unknown failures, does it have an ethical responsibility to inform the users about them? Does the vendor have an ethical responsibility to fix the problems? Is it ethical for the vendor to require users to pay an upgrade fee for a new version of software that fixes problems in an existing version?

get into the habit of frequently (every few minutes or so) saving documents or files that you are changing. Save your documents before your roommate trips over the power cord.

Q2 How Much Does Hardware Cost?

Read the *Technology in Practice* box if you have not already done so. To answer the $80,000 question, or to evaluate the quality of someone else's answer to that question, you need to understand hardware and software components, performance factors, benefits, applications, and costs. In this section, we will discuss each of those hardware factors.

Today, most computers are sold as packages to which the buyer can optionally upgrade and add equipment. You might choose a certain base package and add another gigabyte of memory or a larger disk. However, if you find that you are adding substantial equipment to a standard package, you usually are better off to back up and begin with a higher-grade standard package.

Laptop or Desktop?

To understand the computer buying process, visit *http://dell.com, http://HP.com, http://lenova.com,* or some other site. You first will be given a choice of computer type: laptop or desktop. In general, desktops are cheaper, so unless employees need to travel or take their computers to meetings, select a desktop. Also, desktops tend to be more reliable than laptops: They are neither bashed around at airport security check-ins nor dropped in the snow on the street. Furthermore, laptop designs force many components into a small shell and can have heat dissipation problems that lead to failure. Finally, as you will learn in Chapter 12, laptop theft is a serious problem.

When preparing the budget for your department, you need to make the laptop/desktop decision for each job category. Next, you need to select the CPU speed and size of main memory. We consider these components next. These and other essential knowledge that you need in order to be an effective consumer of computer hardware are outlined in Figure 4-7.

The CPU and Memory

As stated earlier, a fast CPU and data bus are most useful when processing data that already resides in main memory. Once you download a large spreadsheet, for example, a fast CPU will rapidly perform complicated, formula-based what-if analyses. A fast CPU also is useful for processing large graphics files. If, for example, you are manipulating the brightness of the elements of a large picture, a fast CPU will enable that manipulation to proceed quickly.

If the applications that you or your employees use do not involve millions of calculations or manipulations on data in main memory, then buying the fastest CPU is probably not worthwhile. In fact, a lot of the excitement about CPU speed is just industry "hype." Speed is an easily marketed and understood idea, but for most business processing having a very fast CPU is often not as important as other factors, such as main memory.

Main Memory

According to the second row of Figure 4-7, the two key performance factors for main memory are speed and size. Normally, a particular computer make and model is

Component	Performance Factors	Beneficial for:	Sample Application	Typical 2007 Price
CPU and data bus	• CPU speed • Cache memory • Data bus speed • Data bus width	Fast processing of data once the data reside in main memory	• Repetitive calculations of formulas in a complicated spreadsheet	*Laptop:* • $500 (1GHz) • $2,000 (3GHz) Dual *Desktop:* • $300 (1GHz) • $1,500 (3GHz) Dual
Main memory	• Size • Speed	• Holding multiple programs at one time • Processing very large amounts of data	• Running Excel, Word, Paint Shop Pro, Acrobat, several Web sites, and email while processing large files in memory and viewing video clips • 3D games	$100 per GB
Magnetic disk	• Size • Channel type and speed • Rotational speed • Seek time	• Storing many large programs • Storing many large files	• Store detailed maps of counties in the United States • Large data downloads from organizational servers • Store many audio or video files	$1 per GB
Optical disk—CD	• Up to 700MB • CD-ROM • CD-R (recordable) • CD-RW (rewritable)	• Process CDs • Writable media can be used to back up files	• Install new programs • Play and record music • Back up data • CD being replaced by DVD	Included with system
Optical disk—DVD	• Up to 4.7GB • DVD-ROM • DVD-R (recordable) • DVD-RW (rewritable)	• Process both DVDs and CDs • Writable media can be used to back up files	• Install new programs • Play and record music • Play and record movies • Back up data	Included to $150 for DVD-RW
Monitor—CRT	• Viewing size • Dot pitch • Optimal resolution • Video processor	• Superior color • Fast response	• Computer games • Specialized graphics • Rarely purchased today	$100–$500
Monitor—LCD	• Viewing size • Pixel pitch • Optimal resolution • Video processor • DVI or VGA	• Crowded workspaces • Brighter, sharper images • Large displays	• More than one monitor in use • Has become the standard	$100–$5,000+
Network access	• Wired • Wireless	Choose to fit organization's network	(See Chapter 6)	Included
Printers	• Shared • Personal	Reports		$100–$5,000+

Figure 4-7
Hardware Components, Performance Factors, and Prices

designed to use a given memory type, and the speed for that type is fixed. Once you buy the computer, there is nothing you can do to increase memory *speed*.

You can, however, increase the *amount* of main memory, up to the maximum size of memory that your computer brand and model can hold. In 2007, the maximum amount of memory for new personal computers ranged from 2.0 to 4.0GB.

By the way, if budget is a consideration, you can sometimes buy memory from third parties more economically than from the computer manufacturer. However, you must make sure that you buy the correct memory type. Installing more memory is easy; low-skill technicians can perform that task, or, if no vendor support is available, a technician in your IT department can do it.

As shown in Figure 4-7, installing more memory is beneficial for situations in which you run many different applications at the same time or if you process many large files (several megabytes or more, each). If your computer is constantly swapping files, installing more memory will dramatically improve performance. In truth, memory is cheap and is often the best way to get more performance out of a computer.

Your computer has tools and utilities that measure main memory utilization and file swapping. A computer technician can use these tools to determine, quite easily, whether more memory would be helpful.

Magnetic Disks

As stated earlier, magnetic and optical disks provide long-term, nonvolatile data storage. The types and sizes of such storage devices will affect computer performance. First, understand that data are recorded on magnetic disks in concentric circles (Figure 4-8). The disks spin inside the disk unit, and as they spin magnetic spots on the disk are read or written by the *read/write head.*

The time required to read data from a disk depends on two measures: The first measure, called the **rotational delay**, is the time it takes the data to rotate under the read/write head. The second, called **seek time**, is the time it takes the read/write arm to position the head over the correct circle. The faster the disk spins, the shorter the rotational delay. Seek time is determined by the make and model of the disk device.

Once the read/write head is positioned over the correct spot on the disk, data can flow over the channel to or from main memory. Like the data bus, the rate of data transfer depends on the width and speed of the channel. When you buy a disk, you may have several choices of disk-transfer rate. That rate will factor in rotational delay, seek time, and data bus width and speed.

In addition to transfer rate, you will be offered a number of choices in disk size. For most business users, 120GB is more than enough disk space. Large disks are cheap to manufacture, however, and you will be offered disks much larger than this (300GB or more). If you need to store a detailed map of every county in the United States, if you need to store huge downloads from your organization's server computers, or if you store many large audio or video files, then you may need such a large disk. Otherwise, don't fall prey to the hype; buy better monitors or something else for your employees, instead.

Optical Disks

There are two kinds of optical disks: compact discs (CDs) and digital versatile discs (DVDs). Both are made of plastic and are coated with a photosensitive material. As stated earlier, bits are recorded by burning a pit into the photosensitive material using a low-power laser. The presence of a pit causes light to reflect and signifies a one; the

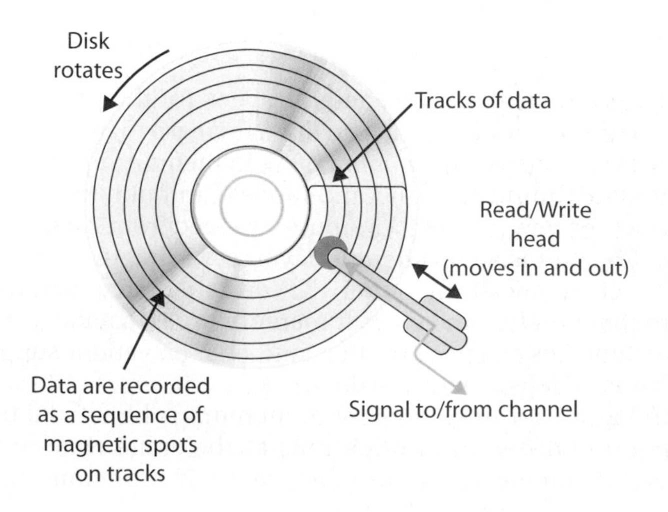

Figure 4-8
Magnetic Disk Components

absence of reflection signifies a zero. Like magnetic disks, optical disks are non-volatile; they maintain their contents even when not powered.

The major difference between CDs and DVDs is how they store data; that difference is unimportant to this discussion, however. The *practical* differences between CDs and DVDs are capacity and speed. A typical CD has a maximum capacity of 700MB, whereas a DVD disk can store up to 4.7GB. Additionally, DVD transfer rates are about 10 times faster than those for CDs.

As shown in Figure 4-7, some optical disks are *read only*; they cannot record data. These disks are abbreviated as **CD-ROM** and **DVD-ROM**. (*ROM* stands for *read-only memory*.) Other optical disks, denoted **CD-R** and **DVD-R**, can record data once. (The *R* stands for *recordable*.) A third group, denoted **CD-RW** and **DVD-RW**, can write data hundreds of times. (The *RW* stands for *rewritable*.)

CDs and DVDs see their greatest use in the entertainment industry for playing music and videos. Both are used widely in commerce for distributing programs and other large files. Operating systems and programs, such as Windows and Microsoft Office, are distributed and installed from CD, for example. Also, writable media can be used to back up magnetic disk files.

Today, every computer should have at least a CD-ROM for installing programs. Most computers should also have some version of a writable optical disk for backing up data. Beyond those purposes, the major reason for having a CD or DVD is entertainment, and that reason might not be the best use of your organization's resources.

Video Displays

There are two types of video display monitors: CRTs and LCDs. **CRT monitors** use *cathode-ray tubes*, the same devices used in traditional TV screens. Because they use a large tube, CRTs are big and bulky, about as deep as they are wide. **LCD monitors** use a different technology called *liquid crystal display* (LCD). With LCD monitors, no tube is required, so they are much slimmer, around 2 inches or so deep. CRTs are based on old technology and are becoming rare.

Both types of monitors display images by illuminating small spots on the screen called **pixels**. Pixels are arranged in a rectangular grid. An inexpensive monitor might display an image 800 pixels wide and 600 pixels high. A higher-quality monitor would display a grid of 1,024 × 768 pixels, and some display 1,680 × 1,050 pixels or more.

The number of pixels displayed depends not only on the size of the monitor, but also on the design of the mechanism that creates the image. For a CRT monitor, the **dot pitch** of the monitor is the distance between pixels. The smaller the dot pitch, the sharper and brighter the screen image will be. For an LCD monitor, the **pixel pitch** is the distance between pixels on the screen. As with CRT monitors, the smaller the pixel pitch, the sharper and brighter the image will be.

Each monitor has an **optimal resolution**, which is the size of the pixel grid (e.g., 1,024 × 768) that will give the best sharpness and clarity. This optimal resolution depends on the size of the screen, the dot or pixel pitch, and other factors. More expensive monitors have higher optimal resolution than others.

Each pixel on the monitor is represented in main memory. If the resolution of the monitor is 1,024 × 768, then there will be a table in memory with 1,024 rows and 768 columns. Each cell of this table has a numeric value that represents the color of the pixel that it represents. Programs change the display on the monitor by instructing the operating system to change values in this image table.

The amount of memory used for each cell in the pixel grid depends on the number of colors that each pixel is to display. For a black and white image, the cells can consist of a single bit: zero for white and one for black. To represent 16 colors, each pixel is represented by four bits. (Four bits can hold the numbers from 0 to 15—each number signifies a particular color.) Today, most monitors use a large color palette that necessitates 32 bits for each pixel and allows for 8,589,934,591 colors.

The Innovation in Practice *box on page 114 describes a new video display product whose innovative applications are just beginning to be imagined.*

INNOVATION IN PRACTICE

MICROSOFT SURFACE

In May 2007, Microsoft announced **Surface**, a new hardware-software product that enables people to interact with data on the surface of a table. Surface is a new product category, and the best way to understand it is to view one of Microsoft's promotional videos at *Microsoft.com/surface*.

Surface paints the surface of the 30-inch table with invisible, near-infrared light to detect the presence of objects. It can respond to up to 52 different touches at the same time. According to Microsoft, this means that each of four people sitting around the Surface could use all 10 fingers to manipulate up to 12 objects, all at the same time.

Surface uses wireless and other communications technologies to connect to devices that are placed on it, such as cameras or cell phones. When a camera is placed on Surface, pictures spill out of it, and users can manipulate those pictures with their hands. Products can be placed on Surface and product specifications displayed. Credit cards can be placed on Surface and items to be purchased dragged on dropped on the credit card.

Surface is scheduled to be shipped in the winter of 2007–2008. Its initial price is estimated to be between $5,000 and $10,000. If Surface becomes popular, that price will fall as volume increases.

The potential uses for Surface are staggering. Children can paint on the surface with virtual paintbrushes, maps can display local events, and consumers can purchase tickets to those events with their fingers. Surface can be used for new computer games and gambling devices. Myriads of other applications are possible. According to Steve Ballmer, CEO of Microsoft: "... We see this as a multibillion dollar category, and we envision a time when surface computing technologies will be pervasive, from tabletops and counters to the hallway mirror. Surface is the first step in realizing that vision."[1]

Initial customers include Harrah's Entertainment, which will use Surface at Caesars Palace and the Rio Casino to display dining, entertainment, nightlife, and gaming experiences at their casinos. Starwood Hotels and Resorts will use Surface at its Sheraton Hotels & Resorts to serve as an electronic concierge. T-Mobile will use it to enable customers to obtain information about cell phones and other products. International Game Technology (IGT) is developing new gaming and gambling devices using Surface.

This last possibility is disturbing to some. Imagine placing your credit card on a Surface gambling device and gambling the night away. Every time you lose, a charge is made against your credit card. Soon, you've run up $15,000 in debt, and the only way you know that is that you've reached the maximum credit limit on your card. Innovation creates exciting new products; whether companies and individuals put those innovations to responsible use is another issue entirely.

You and a team of your fellow students will be given an opportunity to innovate with Surface in Collaboration Exercise 2, page 137.

[1]Microsoft Press Release, May 29, 2007.

Substantial main memory is needed for this large palette. To represent an image in 1,024 × 768 resolution, a total of 3,145,728 bytes of memory (1,024 × 768 × 4 bytes) is needed. For reasons beyond the scope of this text, sometimes several versions of this pixel table are in memory. Most computers today dedicate a special CPU and memory, called a **video processor**, for the storing and processing of video images. When you buy a computer, you may have a choice of such video processors. For most business applications, an inexpensive video processor will be adequate.

LCD devices offer a choice of **VGA** (also called **D-sub**) or **DVI** signal interface. VGA is older technology, and DVI provides a better-quality image. DVI is more expensive, however, and to take advantage of it the video processor must support DVI.

For monitors of equivalent quality, the initial cost of CRT monitors is less than that for LCD monitors. LCD monitors have a longer life, however, so they may actually cost less over time. Because of the speed at which technology improvements take place, most people upgrade to a better computer before they ever wear out their monitor, so this extra life may not matter.

The big advantage of LCD monitors is, of course, their smaller footprint, which means they take up less desk space. They are especially desirable when work requires viewing more than one monitor at a time. Stock traders on Wall Street, for example, need three or four monitors, and these monitors are always LCDs.

Network Access

As you will learn in Chapter 6, every networked computer must have network interface capability. You can choose either wired or wireless connections, and the decision about which to choose will be dictated by the type of network your company has. Today, most computers ship with both types of network interface capability as standard equipment. If not, you will need to add the proper network interface capability to the computers you specify. Note, too, that wired computers can be readily upgraded to wireless by the installation of a wireless card.

Printers

Printers are available in many different types, sizes, and qualities. The discussion of those options is not within the scope of an MIS book. Visit *http://cnet.com/printers or* similar Web sites if you want to know more about printer options.

Here our only concern is whether you want to share a printer. If you do, there are two options: A printer can be attached to a computer and others can access the printer via that computer, or the printer can be equipped with its own network card and users can access it directly. For most purposes, the latter is preferred.

Mobile Devices

Before concluding the discussion of computer hardware, we should mention that mobile communications devices are also computers. A **BlackBerry** is a handheld computer that enables users to make cell phone calls, process emails, and access the Internet. An **iPhone** is a handheld computer from Apple that combines a cell phone, an Internet-connection device, and an iPod. Figure 4-9 shows the introductory menu for an iPhone.

Figure 4-9
iPhone, Showing Basic Menu

Source: Gene Blevins, *LA Daily News*, Corbis—NY. © Gene Blevins, *LA Daily News*, Corbis. All rights reserved.

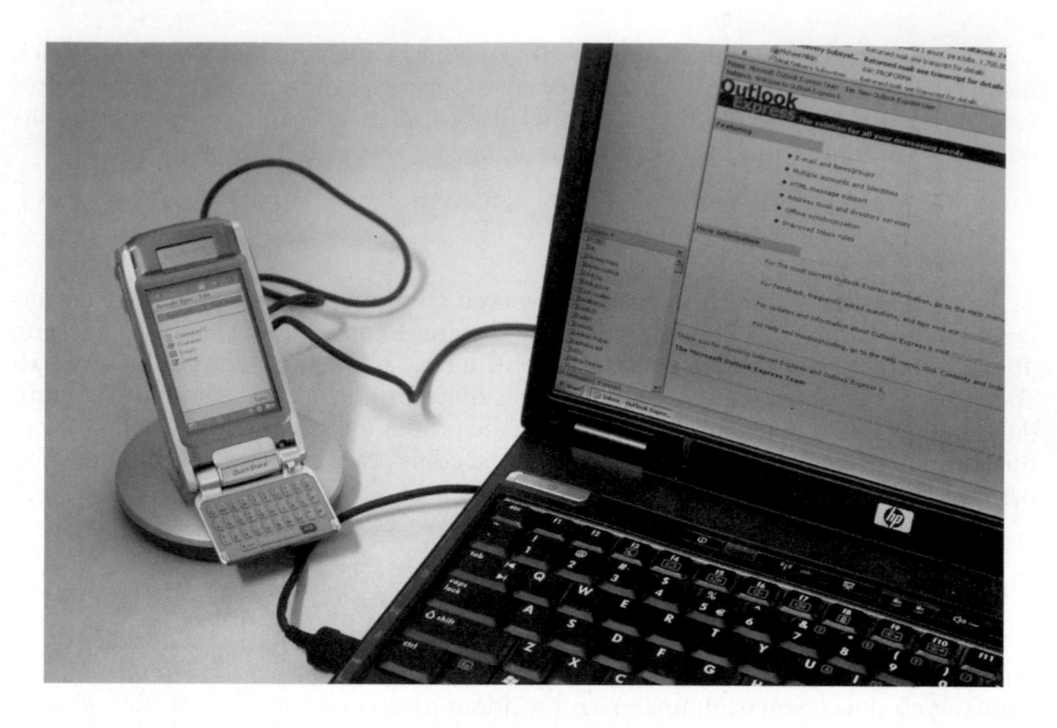

Figure 4-10
Synchronizing a BlackBerry with a Personal Computer

Source: Elena Ilise.

To maximize their effectiveness, mobile devices need to synchronize their data with personal computers. For example, when the user adds a new contact and phone number into a mobile device, that user needs to be able to readily transfer the new contact data into the contact file on his or her primary computer. Figure 4-10 shows a picture of the equipment used to synchronize a BlackBerry with a personal computer.

Mobile devices are becoming important part of information systems, particularly for users who do not work at a desk. Salespeople, production workers, and inventory clerks are typical examples.

Q3 What's the Difference Between a Client and a Server?

Before we can discuss computer software, you need to understand the difference between a client and a server. Figure 4-11 shows the environment of the typical computer user. Users employ **client** computers for word processing, spreadsheets, database access, and so forth. Most client computers also have software that enables them to connect to a network. It could be a private network at their company or school, or it could be the Internet, which is a public network. (We will discuss networks and related matter in Chapter 6. Just wait!)

Servers, as their name implies, provide some service. Some servers process email; others process Web sites; others process large, shared databases; and some provide all of these functions or other, similar functions.

A server is just a computer, but as you might expect, server computers must be fast and they usually have multiple CPUs. They need lots of main memory, at least 4GB, and they require very large disks—often a terabyte or more. Because servers are almost always accessed from another computer via a network, they have limited video displays, or even no display at all. For the same reason, many have no keyboard.

For sites with large numbers of users (e.g., Amazon.com), servers are organized into a collection of servers called a **server farm** like the one shown in

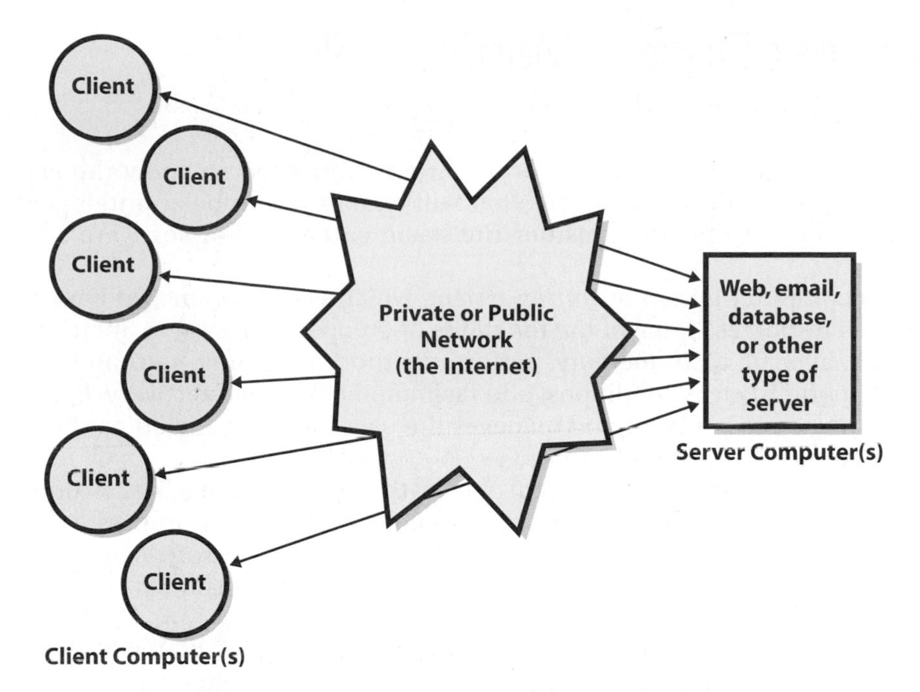

Figure 4-11
Client and Server Computers

Figure 4-12. Servers in a farm coordinate their activities in an incredibly sophisticated and fascinating technology dance. They receive and process hundreds, possibly thousands, of service requests per minute. For example, in December 2005, Amazon.com processed an average of 41 order items per second for 24 hours straight. In this dance, computers hand off partially processed requests to each other while keeping track of the current status of each request. They can pick up the pieces when a computer in the farm fails. All of this is done in an eyeblink, with the user never knowing any part of the miracle underway. It is absolutely gorgeous engineering!

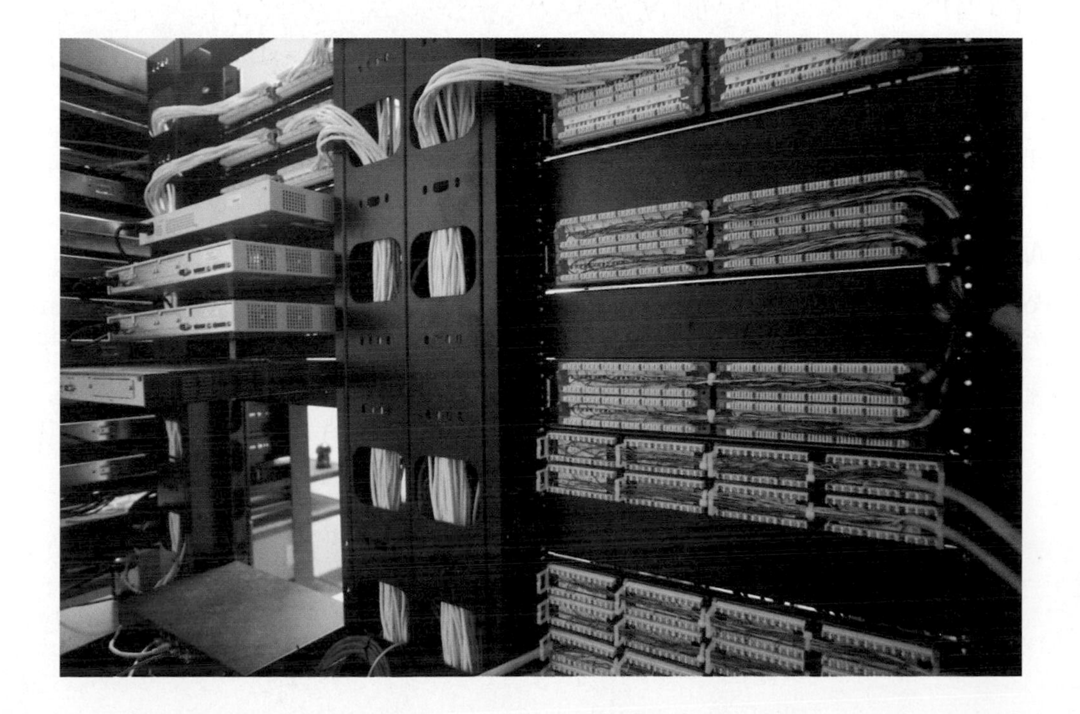

Figure 4-12
A Server Farm

Source: Lucidio Studios, Inc., The Stock Connection.

Q4 What Does a Manager Need to Know About Software?

As a future manager or business professional, you need to know the essential terminology and software concepts that will enable you to be an intelligent software consumer. To begin, consider the basic categories of software shown in Figure 4-13.

Every computer has an *operating system,* which is a program that controls that computer's resources. Some of the functions of an operating system are to read and write data, allocate main memory, perform memory swapping, start and stop programs, respond to error conditions, and facilitate backup and recovery. In addition, the operating system creates and manages the user interface, including the display, keyboard, mouse, and other devices.

Although the operating system makes the computer usable, it does little application-specific work. If you want to write a document or process a customer database, you need *application programs* such as Microsoft Word or Oracle Customer Relationship Management (CRM). These programs must be licensed in addition to the operating system.

Both client and server computers need an operating system, though they need not be the same. Further, both clients and servers can process application programs. The application's design determines the type of computer that processes it.

You need to understand two important software constraints. First, a particular version of an operating system is written for a particular type of hardware. In some cases, such as Windows, there is only one commercially important version. Windows works only on processors from Intel and companies that make processors that conform to the Intel **instruction set** (the commands that a CPU can process). In other cases, such as Linux, many versions exist for many different instructions sets.

Second, application programs are written to use a particular operating system. Microsoft Access, for example, will run only on the Windows operating system. Some applications come in multiple versions. There are, for example, Windows and Macintosh versions of Microsoft Word. But unless informed otherwise, assume that a particular application runs on just one operating system.

We will next consider the operating system and application program categories of software.

What Are the Four Major Operating Systems?

The four major operating systems are listed in Figure 4-14. Consider each.

Windows

For business users, the most important operating system is Microsoft **Windows**. Some version of Windows resides on more than 85 percent of the world's desktops, and,

	Operating System	Application Programs
Client	Programs that control the client computer's resources	Applications that are processed on client computers
Server	Programs that control the server computer's resources	Applications that are processed on server computers

Figure 4-13
Categories of Computer Software

Category	Operating System (OS)	Instruction Set	Common Applications	Typical User
Client	Windows	Intel	Microsoft Office: Word, Excel, Access, PowerPoint, many other applications	Business. Home.
	Mac OS (pre–2006)	Power PC	Macintosh applications plus Word and Excel	Graphic artists. Arts community.
	Mac OS (post–2006)	Intel	Macintosh applications plus Word and Excel. Can also run Windows on Macintosh hardware.	Graphic artists. Arts community.
	Unix	Sun and others	Engineering, computer-assisted design, architecture	Difficult for the typical client, but popular with some engineers and computer scientists.
	Linux	Just about anything	Open Office (Microsoft Office look-alike)	Rare—used where budget is very limited.
Server	Windows Server	Intel	Windows server-type applications	Business with commitment to Microsoft.
	Unix	Sun and others	Unix server applications	Fading...Linux taking its market.
	Linux	Just about anything	Linux & Unix server applications	Very popular—promulgated by IBM.

Figure 4-14
What a Manager Needs to Know About Software

considering just business users, the figure is more than 95 percent. Many different versions of Windows are available: Windows Vista and Windows XP run on user computers. Windows Server is a version of Windows designed for servers. Windows runs the Intel instruction set.[2]

Mac OS

Apple Computer, Inc. developed its own operating system for the Macintosh, **Mac OS**. The current version is Mac OS X. Macintosh computers are used primarily by graphic artists and workers in the arts community. Mac OS was designed originally to run the line of CPU processors from Motorola. In 1994, Mac OS switched to the PowerPC processor line from IBM. As of 2006, Macintosh computers are available for both PowerPC and Intel CPUs. A Macintosh with an Intel processor is able to run both Windows and the Mac OS.

Most people would agree that Apple has led the way in developing easy-to-use interfaces. Certainly, many innovative ideas have first appeared in a Macintosh and then later been added, in one form or another, to Windows.

Unix

Unix is an operating system that was developed at Bell Labs in the 1970s. It has been the workhorse of the scientific and engineering communities since then. Unix is

[2]Versions of Windows are available for other instruction sets, but they are rare and unimportant for our purposes.

generally regarded as being more difficult to use than either Windows or the Macintosh. Many Unix users know and employ an arcane language for manipulating files and data. However, once they surmount the rather steep learning curve, most Unix users become fanatic supporters of the system. Sun Microsystems and other vendors of computers for scientific and engineering applications are the major proponents of Unix. In general, Unix is not for the business user.

Linux

Linux is a version of Unix that was developed by the **open-source community**. This community is a loosely coupled group of programmers who mostly volunteer their time to contribute code to develop and maintain Linux. The open-source community owns Linux, and there is no fee to use it. Linux can run on client computers, but it is most frequently used for servers, particularly Web servers.

IBM is the primary proponent of Linux. Although IBM does not own Linux, IBM has developed many business systems solutions that use Linux. By using Linux, IBM does not have to pay a license fee to Microsoft or another vendor.

Own Versus License

When you buy a computer program, you are not actually buying that program. Instead, you are buying a **license** to use that program. For example, when you buy Windows, Microsoft is selling you the right to use Windows. Microsoft continues to own the Windows program.

In the case of Linux, no company can sell you a license to use it. It is owned by the open-source community, which states that Linux has no license fee (with certain reasonable restrictions). Large companies such as IBM and smaller companies such as RedHat can make money by supporting Linux, but no company makes money selling Linux licenses.

What Types of Applications Exist, and How Do Organizations Obtain Them?

Application software performs a service or function. Some application programs are general purpose, such as Microsoft Excel or Word. Other application programs provide specific functions. QuickBooks, for example, is an application program that provides general ledger and other accounting functions. We begin by describing categories of application programs and then describe sources for them.

What Categories of Application Programs Exist?

Horizontal-market application software provides capabilities common across all organizations and industries. Word processors, graphics programs, spreadsheets, and presentation programs are all horizontal-market application software.

Examples of such software are Microsoft Word, Excel, and PowerPoint. Examples from other vendors are Adobe Acrobat, Photoshop, and PageMaker and Jasc Corporation's Paint Shop Pro. These applications are used in a wide variety of businesses, across all industries. They are purchased off-the-shelf, and little customization of features is necessary (or possible).

Vertical-market application software serves the needs of a specific industry. Examples of such programs are those used by dental offices to schedule appointments and bill patients, those used by auto mechanics to keep track of customer data and customers' automobile repairs, and those used by parts warehouses to track inventory, purchases, and sales.

Vertical applications usually can be altered or customized. Typically, the company that sold the application software will provide such services or offer referrals to qualified consultants who can provide this service.

One-of-a-kind application software is developed for a specific, unique need. The IRS develops such software, for example, because it has needs that no other organization has.

Some application software does not neatly fit into the horizontal or vertical category. For example, CRM software is a horizontal application because every business has customers. But it usually needs to be customized to the requirements of businesses in a particular industry, and so it is also akin to vertical market software.

You will learn about other examples of such dual-category software in Chapter 7 when we discuss materials requirements planning (MRP), enterprise resource planning (ERP), and other such applications. In this text, we will consider such applications to be vertical market applications, even though they do not fit perfectly into this category.

How Do Organizations Acquire Application Software?

You can acquire application software in exactly the same ways that you can buy a new suit. The quickest and least risky option is to buy your suit off-the-rack. With this method, you get your suit immediately, and you know exactly what it will cost. You may not, however, get a good fit. Alternately, you can buy your suit off-the-rack and have it altered. This will take more time, it may cost more, and there's some possibility that the alteration will result in a poor fit. Most likely, however, an altered suit will fit better than an off-the-rack one.

Finally, you can hire a tailor to make a custom suit. In this case, you will have to describe what you want, be available for multiple fittings, and be willing to pay considerably more. Although there is an excellent chance of a great fit, there is also the possibility of a disaster. Still, if you want a yellow and orange polka-dot silk suit with a hissing rattlesnake on the back, tailor-made is the only way to go. You can buy computer software in exactly the same ways: **off-the-shelf-software**, **off-the-shelf with alterations software**, or tailor-made. Tailor-made software is called **custom-developed software**.

Organizations develop custom application software themselves or hire a development vendor. Like buying the yellow and orange polka-dot suit, such development is done in situations in which the needs of the organization are so unique that no horizontal or vertical applications are available. By developing custom software, the organization can tailor its application to fit its requirements.

Custom development is difficult and risky. Staffing and managing teams of software developers is challenging. Managing software projects can be daunting. Many organizations have embarked on application development projects only to find that the projects take twice as long—or longer—to finish as planned. Cost overruns of 200 and 300 percent are not uncommon. We will discuss such risks further in Chapter 10.

In addition, every application program needs to be adapted to changing needs and changing technologies. The adaptation costs of horizontal and vertical software are amortized over all of the users of that software, perhaps thousands or millions of customers. For custom software developed in-house, however, the developing company must pay all of the adaptation costs itself. Over time, this can be a heavy burden.

Because of the risk and expense, in-house development is the last-choice alternative and is used only when there is no other option. Figure 4-15 (next page) summarizes software sources and types.

Over the course of your career, application software, hardware, and firmware will change, sometimes rapidly. The Reflections Guide *on page 130 challenges you to choose a strategy for addressing this change.*

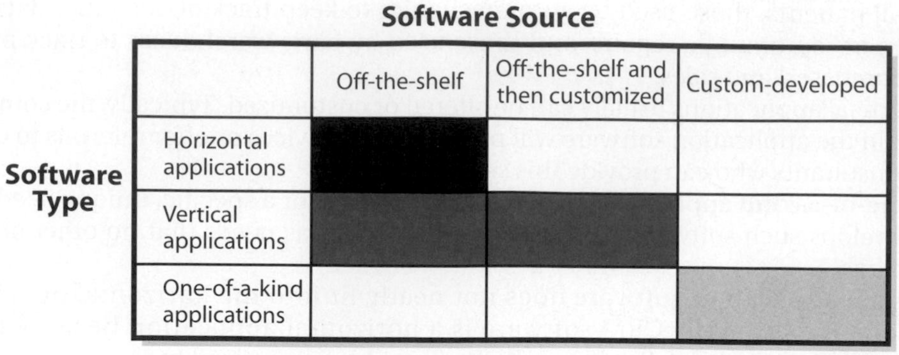

Figure 4-15
Software Sources and Types

Software Source

Software Type	Off-the-shelf	Off-the-shelf and then customized	Custom-developed
Horizontal applications			
Vertical applications			
One-of-a-kind applications			

What Is Firmware?

Firmware is computer software that is installed into devices such as printers, print servers, and various types of communication devices. The software is coded just like other software, but it is installed into special, read-only memory of the printer or other device. In this way, the program becomes part of the device's memory; it is as if the program's logic is designed into the device's circuitry. Users do not need to load firmware into the device's memory.

Firmware can be changed or upgraded, but this is normally a task for IS professionals. The task is easy, but it requires knowledge of special programs and techniques that most business users choose not to learn.

What Is the Difference Between a Thin and a Thick Client?

When you use client applications such as Word, Excel, or Acrobat, those programs run only on your computer. You need not be connected to the Internet or any other network for them to run.

Other applications, called **client-server applications**, require code on both the client and the server. Email is a good example. When you send email, you run a client program such as Microsoft Outlook on your computer, and it connects over the Internet or a private network to mail server software on a server. Similarly, when you access a Web site, you run a browser (client software) on your computer that connects over a network to Web server software on a server.

A client-server application that requires nothing more than a browser is called a **thin client**. An application such as Microsoft Outlook that requires programs other than a browser on the user's computer is called a **thick client**. The terms *thin* and *thick* refer to the amount of code that must run on the client computer. All other things being equal, thin-client applications are preferred to thick-client applications because they do not require the installation and administration of client software. However, the thick-client application may provide features and functions that more than compensate for the expense and administration of its installation.

As stated, client and server computers can run different operating systems. Many organizations have standardized on Windows for their clients but use Windows Server or Linux for their servers. Figure 4-16 shows an example. Two thin clients are connecting via browsers to a Web server that is running Windows Server. Two thick clients are connecting via an email client to an email server that is running Linux. Those two clients are thick because they have client email software installed.

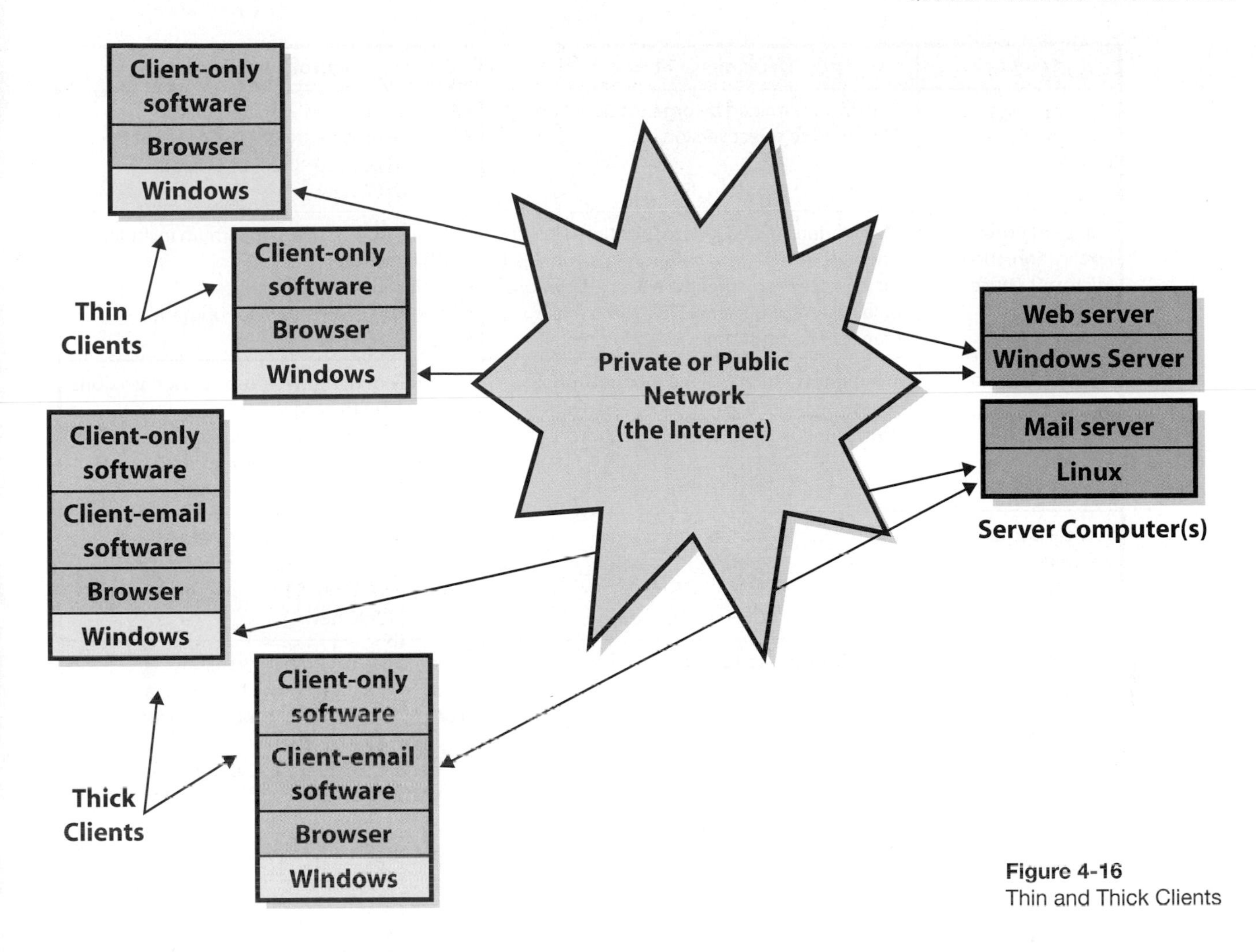

Figure 4-16
Thin and Thick Clients

Q5 How Much Does Software Cost?

To create a computer budget like that required in the $80,000 question in the *Technology in Practice* box, you need to understand how much software costs. Not surprisingly, the cost depends on the type of software and the function it provides. Figure 4-17 (next page) summarizes basic categories and 2007 costs.

You need to understand two terms used in this figure. **Site license** means that an organization has purchased a license to equip all of the computers on a site (or possibly across the company at many sites) with certain software. For example, Prentice Hall might negotiate with Microsoft to provide a version of Windows to all of its employees. The cost of a site license is high, but the per-unit cost is generally much less than the unit retail price. Also, purchasing a site license relieves the organization from tracking which computers have which software and ensuring that all licenses are paid appropriately.

The term **Upgrade** means just what it says: Vendors usually do not require their customers to pay the price of *new* software when upgrading from a previous version. For example, Microsoft offers a license to upgrade WindowsXP to Vista for less than the price of a new copy of Vista.

Operating Systems

Organizational policy usually determines the client operating system. Although some organizations permit users to run a mixture of operating systems, supporting two

Category	Decisions to Make	Typical 2006 Prices
Operating system (Windows, Mac OS, Linux)	• Usually determined by organizational policy • May need to select version	• Possibly included with hardware. • Possibly paid for by site license. • Otherwise, $100–$300 for upgrade. • $300–$500 new.
Standard horizontal application, such as Microsoft Office or OpenOffice	• May be determined by organizational policy. • Choose package with components you need: word processing, spreadsheet, presentation, email client, or personal DBMS (database management system).	• Usually only the very minimum included with hardware. • Possibly paid for by site license. • Otherwise, $100–$300 for upgrade. • $300–$500 new.
Other horizontal applications	Document creation (Adobe Acrobat), photo processing (Adobe Photoshop, Jasc Paint Shop Pro), illustration (Adobe Illustrator), etc.	• Possibly minimum feature "teaser" versions included with hardware. • Possibly paid for by site license. • Otherwise, $100–$300 for upgrade. • $300–$700 new.
Vertical package software (Goldmine, Act!, AutoCad)	Determined by job category needs.	• Seldom included with hardware. • Possibly paid for by site license. • Otherwise. $100–$300 for upgrade. • $300–$1,500 new.
Vertical applications (CRM, ERP, etc.)	Determined by job category needs.	• Not included with hardware. • Possibly paid for by site license, or a license for a certain number of seats (users). • Otherwise, $500–$1,000 per user or more.

Figure 4-17
Client-Software Prices

client operating systems is expensive, so most standardize on just one. As stated earlier, many organizations run a different operating system on servers than on user computers. We ignore servers here because you are unlikely to be involved in the decision of a server operating system.

Unless your organization is very small, it likely has an IT department. If so, that department will install the operating system on all new computers and will install upgrades on existing computers as well. In a small organization, you will likely buy a computer from a vendor such as Dell that has done the operating system installation for you.

Horizontal-Market Software

Most organizations today use Microsoft Office for their standard applications, such as word processing and spreadsheets. Microsoft Office licenses are sold in a number of different configurations. Some include just Word and Excel, whereas others include Word, Excel, PowerPoint, Access, Outlook, and possibly other applications. Your organization may have a site license for a particular version.

OpenOffice is an alternative to Office that is supported by the open-source community and is license-free in most cases. OpenOffice is gaining slowly in popularity, especially in organizations that are very cost-conscious. OpenOffice can process most documents prepared by Office, and the reverse. One exception to this is that OpenOffice does not have a personal database management system (DBMS) that is compatible with Access.

Your employees may require other types of horizontal software. Designers and other document preparers may need software for document preparation, photo processing, desktop publishing, or illustrations. Few organizations need multiple licenses of this type of software, so site licenses for this type are rare.

Oftentimes vendors of this software provide free teaser versions (products with limited functionality) of their products with new computers. Sometimes these limited versions provide sufficient capability for a given job. In the case of Adobe Acrobat, for example, Adobe makes the Acrobat Reader available license-free.

Vertical-Market Software

Examples of vertical-market software are contact managers such as Goldmine and Act! and engineering software such as AutoCad. Such products are almost never included in the price of a new computer. Your organization may have negotiated a site license for such software or purchased a restricted site license to provide it to the employees of certain departments.

Licenses for some of this software can be surprisingly expensive, and some small organizations elect to install the software without licenses. **This practice is both illegal and highly unethical.** Some small companies believe they are too small to be worth the cost of a lawsuit and they use the software anyway. Such practice is dishonest, disreputable, and entirely reprehensible.

As you will read in Chapter 7, CRM and ERP systems are used widely throughout an organization and can have hundreds or even thousands of users. The vendors of these products usually charge a license for each user or for a certain number of users (sometimes expressed in **seats**). Your organization might buy a license for, say, up to 500 seats of a particular application. If your department is using any of these systems, you need to check with your IT department to determine what costs apply to you.

Q6 What Are Viruses, Trojan Horses, and Worms?

A **virus** is a computer program that replicates itself. Unchecked replication is like computer cancer; ultimately, the virus consumes the computer's resources. Furthermore, many viruses also take unwanted and harmful actions.

The program code that causes unwanted activity is called the **payload**. The payload can delete programs or data—or, even worse, modify data in undetected ways. Imagine the impact of a virus that changed the credit rating of all customers. Some viruses publish data in harmful ways—for example, sending out files of credit card data to unauthorized sites.

There are many different virus types. **Trojan horses** are viruses that masquerade as useful programs or files. The name refers to the gigantic mock-up of a horse that was filled with soldiers and moved into Troy during the Trojan War. A typical Trojan horse appears to be a computer game, an MP3 music file, or some other useful, innocuous program.

Macro viruses attach themselves to Word, Excel, or other types of documents. When the infected document is opened, the virus places itself in the startup files of the application. After that, the virus infects every file that the application creates or processes.

A **worm** is a virus that propagates using the Internet or other computer network. Worms spread faster than other virus types because they are specifically programmed to spread. Unlike nonworm viruses, which must wait for the user to share a file with a second computer, worms actively use the network to spread. Sometimes, worms so choke a network that it becomes unusable.

In 2003, the Slammer worm clogged the Internet and caused Bank of America ATM machines and the information systems of hundreds of other organizations to fail. Slammer operated so fast that 90 percent of the vulnerable machines were infected within 10 minutes.

You can take several measures to prevent viruses. First, most viruses take advantage of security holes in computer programs. As vendors find these holes, they create program modifications, called **patches**, that fix the problem. To keep from getting a virus, check Microsoft and other vendor sites for patches, and apply them immediately. Or, you can configure your computer to automatically receive and install such patches. You should do this only for reputable vendors such as Microsoft and Adobe. A patch for the Slammer worm was available from Microsoft several months before Slammer occurred. The worm did not infect any site that had applied the patch.

When you think about it, it is not surprising that the problem occurred some time after the patch appeared. As soon as a vendor publishes the problem and the patch, every computer criminal in the world can learn about the hole. Virus developers can then write code to exploit the hole, and any machine that does not apply the patch is then doubly vulnerable. Therefore, the first rule in preventing viruses is to find and apply patches to the operating system and to applications.

Other prevention steps are:

- Never download files, programs, or attachments from unknown Web sites.
- Do not open attachments to emails from strangers.
- Do not open unexpected attachments to emails, even from known sources.
- Do not rely on file extensions. A file marked *MyPicture.jpg* is normally a picture (because of the *jpg* file extension). For a variety of reasons, however, this file may be something else—a virus.
- Companies such as Symantec, Sophos, McAfee, Norton, and others license products that detect and possibly eliminate viruses. Such products can operate in proactive mode by checking attachments as you receive them. They can also operate retroactively by checking memory and disk drives for the presence of viral code. You should run a retroactive antivirus program at regular intervals—at least once a week.

Such **antivirus programs** search the computer's memory and disk for known viruses. Obviously, if a virus is unknown to the antivirus software, then that virus will remain undetected. You should periodically obtain updates for the latest virus patterns from the vendor who produces the antivirus product. Additionally, realize that even though you use antivirus software, you are still vulnerable to viruses that are unknown to the virus detection company.

Now for the ugly news: What do you do if you have a virus? Most antivirus products include programs for removing viruses. If you have a virus, you can follow the instructions provided by that software to remove it. However, it is possible that the virus may have mutated into a different form. If so, the antivirus product will not see the mutated version, and it will remain on your computer.

Unfortunately, the only sure way to eliminate a virus is to delete everything on your magnetic disk by reformatting it. Then you must reinstall the operating system and all applications from known, clean sources (e.g., the original CD from the vendor). Finally, one by one, you must reload data files that you know are free of the virus. This is a laborious and time-consuming process, and it assumes that you have all of your data files backed up. Because of the time and expense involved, few organizations go through this process. However, reformatting the disk is the only sure way of removing a virus.

Viruses are expensive. CNET estimated that the Slammer worm caused between $950 million and $1.2 billion in lost productivity during its first 5 days. To protect your organization, you should ensure that procedures exist to install patches as soon as possible. Also, every computer should have and use a copy of an antivirus program. You and your organization cannot afford not to take these precautions. We will discuss other problematic programs, such as spyware, in more detail in Chapter 12.

Q7 How Can You Use This Knowledge?

As a future business professional, you will need basic knowledge of hardware and software for two major reasons. First, you will need it to make some decisions about which products you use. Second, as a manager, you will be involved in creating or approving hardware budgets. Consider each.

What Buying Decisions Do You Make?

In general, most business professionals have some role in the specification of the client hardware and software they use. Business managers also play a role in the specification of client hardware and software for employees whom they manage. The particular role depends on the policy of the manager's organization. Large organizations will have an IS department that is likely to set standards for client hardware and software. You will learn more about such standards in Chapter 11.

In medium to small organizations, policies are often less formal, and managers will need to take an active role in setting the specifications for their own and their employees' computers. Figure 4-18 lists the major criteria for selecting both hardware and software.

Except in rare circumstances, medium to small organizations will usually standardize on a single client operating system because the costs of supporting more than one are unjustifiable. Most organizations choose Microsoft Windows clients. Some arts and design businesses standardize on the Macintosh, and some engineering firms standardize on Unix. Organizations that have limited budgets might choose to use Linux on the clients, but this is rare.

Managers and their employees might have a role in specifying horizontal application software, such as Microsoft Office, or other software appropriate for their operating systems. They will also have an important role in specifying requirements for vertical market or custom applications. We will say more about this role in Chapter 10.

Concerning the server, a business manager typically has no role in the specification of server hardware, other than possibly approving the budget. Instead, technical personnel make such decisions. A business manager and those who will be the

Category	Hardware	Software
Client	Specify: • CPU speed • Size of main memory • Size of magnetic disk • CD or DVD and type • Monitor type and size	Specify: • Windows, Mac, or Linux OS. May be dictated by organizational standard. • PC applications such as Microsoft Office Adobe Acrobat, Photoshop, Paint Shop Pro. May be dictated by organizational standard. • Browser such as Internet Explorer, FireFox, or Netscape Navigator. • Requirements for the client side of client-server applications. • Need for thin or thick client.
Server	In most cases, a business manager has no role in the specification of server hardware (except possibly a budgetary one).	• Specify requirements for the server side of client-server applications. • Work with technical personnel to test and accept software.

Figure 4-18
A Business Manager's Role in Hardware and Software Specifications

Figure 4-19
A Process for Preparing a Departmental IT Budget

Determine base requirements:
- The types of workload your employees perform
- The hardware requirements for each type
- The software requirements for each type

Forecast requirement changes during the budget period:
- Changes in the number of employees
- Changes in workload—new job tasks or information systems
- Mandatory changes in hardware or software

Prepare the budget:
- Using guidance from the IT department and accounting, price the hardware and software
- Determine if your department will be charged for networks, servers, communications, or other overhead expenses
- Add overhead charges as necessary

Assess results:
- Consider budget in context of competitive strategy
- If substantial increases in budget size, prepare justification
- Consider budget in context of prior year's budgets
- Determine sources of significant difference and explain
- Modify budget as appropriate

Document results:
- Prepare for justification
- Save documents and notes for preparation of next year's IT budget

clients of a client-server application specify the requirements for vertical and custom-server software. They will also work with technical personnel to test and accept that software.

What Process Should I Use to Establish a Computer Budget?

The steps for preparing a departmental hardware budget are summarized in Figure 4-19. You need first to determine the base requirements. This involves assessing the work your employees perform, creating job categories, and determining the computer workload requirements for each category.

In accounts payable, for example, you might determine that you have three categories of workers: administrators, accounts payable specialists, and managers. You further determine that the administrators need hardware and software to access the company's Web portal, to email, and to perform minimal word processing. The accounts payable specialists need the same capabilities as the administrators, but they also need access to the organization's accounts payable system. Finally, you and other managers need to be able to perform the same work as the specialists, plus you need to process large spreadsheets for preparing budgets. You also need to access the company's payroll and human resources systems.

Once you have identified the job categories and the computer workload requirements for each, you can apply the knowledge from this chapter to determine hardware and software requirements for each type. You can also use past departmental experience as a guide. If employees complain about computer performance with the equipment they have, you can determine if more is needed. If there are no bottlenecks or performance problems, you know the current equipment will do.

Given the base requirements, the next step is to forecast changes. Will you be adding or losing employees during the year? Will the workload change? Will your department be given new tasks that will necessitate additional hardware or software? Finally, during the year will your organization mandate changes in hardware or software? Will you be required to upgrade your operating system or applications software? If so, will your budget be charged for those upgrades?

The process of establishing a computer budget involves knowing the right questions to ask. The Problem-Solving Guide *on page 132 discusses the importance of improving your ability to ask questions.*

Once you have the base requirements and your change forecasts, you can prepare the budget. The first task is to price the hardware and software. As you will learn in Chapter 11, your IT department will most likely have established standards for hardware and software from which you will select. They will probably have negotiated prices on your behalf. If not, the accounting department can probably help you estimate costs based on their prior experience. You can also learn from the past experience of your own department.

Your organization may have a policy of charging the department's overhead fees for networks, servers, and communications. If so, you will need to add those charges to the budget as well.

When you have finished the preparation of the budget, you should assess it for feasibility and reasonableness. First, consider your organization's competitive strategy. If your organization is a cost leader, any increases in your budget will be carefully scrutinized, and you should be prepared with strong justifications. If your organization uses a differentiation strategy, then be certain that any increases in your budget relate directly to the ways in which your company differentiates. Before submitting your budget, prepare justifications for any such increases.

You can expect that your budget will be reviewed in the context of prior years' budgets. If you are proposing substantial changes to your budget, anticipate that you will be asked to justify them. Reasons that you may need more equipment include:

- Substantial change in your departmental head count.
- Important new departmental functions or responsibilities.
- Upgrading to major new versions of operating system or other software.
- Implementation of new systems that require additional hardware.
- Change in the way overhead expenses are allocated to your department.

If you find it difficult to justify budgetary increases, you may need to review and revise your budget. Perhaps you can do with refurbished equipment, or maybe you can delay the upgrade of all of your computers to the new operating system, or maybe you can find ways of reallocating hardware among the employees in your department that will save costs. Even if none of these options are workable, you can document that you investigated them in your budget justification or mention them in any budgetary review meetings.

Finally, document your results. You can use such documentation not only to justify your budget this year but also to help you prepare next year's budget. Keep any spreadsheets (like the one in Figure 4-23 on page 138) as well as notes and documents used to prepare and justify your budget.

Reflections

GUIDE

Keeping Up to Speed

Have you ever been to a cafeteria where you put your lunch tray on a conveyor belt that carries the dirty dishes into the kitchen? That conveyor belt reminds me of technology. Like the conveyor, technology just moves along, and all of us run on top of the technology conveyor, trying to keep up. We hope to keep up with the relentless change of technology for an entire career without ending up in the techno-trash.

Technology change is a fact, and the only appropriate question is, "What am I going to do about it?" One strategy you can take is to bury your head in the sand: "Look, I'm not a technology person. I'll leave it to the pros. As long as I can send email and use the Internet, I'm happy. If I have a problem, I'll call someone to fix it."

That strategy is fine, as far as it goes, and many business people use it. Following that strategy won't give you a competitive advantage over anyone, and it will give someone else a competitive advantage over you, but as long as you develop your advantage elsewhere, you'll be OK—at least for yourself.

What about your department, though? If an expert says, "Every computer needs a 250GB disk," are you going to nod your head and say, "Great. Sell 'em to me!" Or are you going to know enough to realize that's a big disk (by 2007 standards, anyway) and ask why everyone needs such a large amount of storage? Maybe then you'll be told, "Well, it's only another $150 per machine from the 80GB disk." At that point, you can make a decision, using your own decision-making skills, and not rely solely on the IS expert. Thus, the prudent business professional in the twenty-first century has a number of reasons not to bury his or her head in the technology sand.

At the other end of the spectrum are those who love technology. You'll find them everywhere—they may be accountants, marketing professionals, or production-line supervisors who not only know their field, but also enjoy information technology. Maybe they were IS majors or had double majors that combined IS with another area of expertise (e.g., IS with accounting). These people read CNET News and ZDNet most days, and they can tell you the latest on IPv6 addresses (Chapter 6—just wait!). Those people are sprinting along the technology conveyor belt; they will never end up in the techno-trash, and they will use their knowledge of IT to gain competitive advantage throughout their careers.

Many business professionals fall in between these extremes. They don't want to bury their heads, but they don't have the desire or interest to become technophiles (lovers of technology) either. What to do? There are a couple of strategies. For one, don't allow yourself to ignore technology. When you see a technology article in the *Wall Street Journal*, read it. Don't just skip it because it's about technology. Read the technology ads, too. Many vendors invest heavily in ads that instruct without seeming to. Another option is to take a seminar or pay attention to professional events that combine your specialty with technology. For example, when you go to the banker's convention, attend a session or two on "Technology Trends for Bankers." There are always sessions like that, and you might make a

contact with similar problems and concerns in another company.

Probably the best option, if you have the time for it, is to get involved as a user representative in technology committees in your organization. If your company is doing a review of its CRM system, for instance, see if you can get on the review committee. When there's a need for a representative from your department to discuss needs for the next-generation help-line system, sign up. Or later in your career, become a member of the business practice technology committee, or whatever they call it at your organization.

Just working with such groups will add to your knowledge of technology. Presentations made to such groups, discussions about uses of technology, and ideas about using IT for competitive advantage will all add to your IT knowledge. You'll gain important contacts and exposure to leaders in your organization as well.

It's up to you. You get to choose how you relate to technology. But be sure you choose; don't let your head fall into the sand without thinking about it. ■

Discussion Questions

1. Do you agree that the change of technology is relentless? What do you think that means to most business professionals? To most organizations?
2. Think about the three postures toward technology presented here. Which camp will you join? Why?
3. Write a two-paragraph memo to yourself justifying your choice in question 2. If you chose to ignore technology, explain how you will compensate for the loss of competitive advantage. If you're going to join one of the other two groups, explain why, and describe how you're going to accomplish your goal.
4. Given your answer to question 2, assume that you're in a job interview and the interviewer asks about your knowledge of technology. Write a three-sentence response to the interviewer's question.

Problem-Solving

GUIDE

Questioning Your Questions

Many school experiences mislead you to believe that answering a question is the important part of learning. In fact, answering a question is the easy part. For most problems in the business world, the difficult and creative acts are generating the questions—and formulating a strategy for getting the answers. Once the questions and strategy are set, the rest is simply legwork.

As a future consumer of information technology and services, you will benefit from being able to ask good questions and effectively obtain answers to them. It is probably the single most important behavior you can learn. Because of the rapid change of technology, you will constantly be required to learn about new IS alternatives and how you can apply them in your business.

"It is not possible to become a good thinker and be a poor questioner. Thinking is not driven by answers, but rather, by questions."*

Perhaps you've heard that "there is no such thing as a bad question." This statement is nonsense. There are billions of bad questions, and you will be better off if you learn not to ask them.

Questions can be bad in three ways: They can be irrelevant, dead, or asked of the wrong source. Consider the first way. If you know the subject and if you're paying attention, you can avoid asking irrelevant questions. One of the goals of this text is to teach you about IT and IS so that you can avoid asking irrelevant technology questions.

A dead question is one that leads to nowhere—it provides no insight into the subject. Here's an example of a dead question: "Is the material on How a Computer Works going to be on the test?" The answer will tell you whether or not you need to study that topic for the exam, but it won't tell you why. The answer will help you in school, but it won't help you use MIS on the job.

Instead, ask questions like, "What is the purpose of the section on how a computer works?" "Why are we studying it?" or "How will it help me use MIS in my career?" These are good questions because they go somewhere. Your professor may respond, "From that discussion you'll learn how to save money because you'll know whether to buy your staff more memory or a faster CPU." Possibly, you won't understand that answer; in that case, you can ask more questions that will lead you to understand how it pertains to your use of MIS.

*Richard Paul and Linda Elder, *Critical Thinking* (Upper Saddle River, NJ: Prentice Hall, 2001), p. 113.

Or, your professor may say, "Well, I think that section is a waste of time, and I told the author that in a recent email." From there, you can ask your professor why she thinks it's a waste of time, and you can wonder why the author would write something that is a waste of time. Maybe the author and your professor have different points of view. Such musings are excellent because they lead you to more learning.

The third way questions can be bad is that they are asked of the wrong source. Information technology questions fall into three types: "What is it?" "How can I use it?" and "Is it the best choice?" The first type asks for a simple definition. You can easily look up the answers to such questions in a book or at Internet sites like *whatis.com*. You ought not to ask "What is it?" questions of valuable or expensive sources; you are wasting your money and their time if you do. Also, when you ask such a question, you appear unprepared because you didn't take the time to find the easy answer.

The next type of question, "How can I use it?" is harder. Answering that question requires knowledge of both technology and your business. Although you can research that question over the Internet, you need knowledge to relate it to your present circumstance. In a few years, this is the sort of question that you will be expected to answer for your organization. It's also the type of question you might ask an expert.

Finally, the most difficult type of question is, "Is it the best choice?" Answering this type of question requires the ability to judge among alternatives according to appropriate criteria. These are the kinds of questions you probably do want to ask an expensive source.

Notice, too, that only "What is it?" questions have a verifiably correct answer. The next two types are questions of judgment. No answer can be shown to be correct, but some answers are better than others. As you progress in your educational career, you should be learning how to discern the quality of judgment and evaluative answers. Learn to question your questions. ■

Discussion Questions

1. Using your own words, distinguish between a good question and a bad one.
2. What types of questions waste time?
3. What types of questions are appropriate to ask your professor?
4. Under what circumstances would you ask a question to which you already know the answer?
5. Suppose you have 15 minutes with your boss's boss's boss. What kinds of questions are appropriate in such an interview? Even though you don't pay money to meet with this person, explain how this is an expensive source.
6. How do you know when you have a good answer to a question? Consider the three types of questions described here in your answer.
7. Evaluate the quality of questions 1 through 5. Which are the best questions? What makes one better than the other? If you can, think of better ways of asking these questions, or even better questions.

ACTIVE REVIEW

Use this Active Review to verify that you understand the ideas and concepts that answer the chapter's study questions.

Q1 What does a manager need to know about computer hardware?

List categories of hardware and explain the purpose of each. Define *bit* and *byte*. Explain why bits are used to represent computer data. Define the units of bytes used to size memory. In general terms, explain how a computer works. Explain how a manager can use this knowledge. Explain why you should save your work from time to time while you are using your computer.

Q2 How much does hardware cost?

Review Figure 4-7 and explain the meaning of each cell of this table. Describe the circumstances under which laptops are preferred over desktops. Describe a workload that requires a fast CPU. Describe a workload that requires considerable main memory. Explain the advantages of an LCD monitor over a CRT monitor. Name and describe two mobile computing devices.

Q3 What's the difference between a client and a server?

Explain the functions of client and server computers. Describe how the hardware requirements vary between the two types. Define *server farm* and describe the technology dance that occurs on a server farm.

Q4 What does a manager need to know about software?

Review Figure 4-14 and explain the meaning of each cell in this table. Explain the difference between software ownership and software licenses. Explain the differences among horizontal-market, vertical-market, and one-of-a-kind applications. Describe the three ways that organizations can acquire software. Explain the difference between thin and thick clients and describe one advantage of each.

Q5 How much does software cost?

Review Figure 4-17 and explain the meaning of each cell in this table. Explain the term *site license* and describe the advantage of a software upgrade. Describe how the term *seat* pertains to software license costs.

Q6 What are viruses, Trojan horses, and worms?

Define *virus* and *payload*. Explain the differences among Trojan horses, macro viruses, and worms. Explain the importance of applying patches promptly. Describe other prevention steps. Describe the use of antivirus software and explain what must be done to eradicate a virus from an infected computer.

Q7 How can you use this knowledge?

Describe the two major reasons you need the knowledge of this chapter. Review Figure 4-18 and explain each cell of this table. Summarize the process you should use to develop a computer budget.

KEY TERMS AND CONCEPTS

USING YOUR KNOWLEDGE

1. Figure 4-20 shows a portion of an ad for desktop computers. Four computers are presented, from left to right, in decreasing order of cost. Interpret this ad to answer the following questions.
   a. What is the difference in processor capability for the four computers?
   b. What is the difference in main memory capability for the four computers?
   c. Explain the specifications for the magnetic disks, called *hard drives*, in the ad. (SATA is a disk drive data bus standard.) What differences exist for hard drives in these four computers?
   d. What is the difference in optical drives for these four computers?
   e. Comment on the operating system that is loaded on these computers.
   f. Compare the offer for the computer in the first column with an offer for an equivalent computer from *Dell.com*. Which offer is better? Why?
2. Suppose that your roommate, a political science major, asks you to help her purchase a new laptop computer. She wants to use the computer for email, Internet access, and for note-taking in class. She wants to spend less than $1,000.

	Price: $989	**Price: $900**	**Price: $900**	**Price: $729**
Operating System	Genuine Windows Vista Business	Genuine Windows Vista Business	Genuine Windows Vista Business	Genuine Windows Vista Home
Processor(s)	Dual processor, 1.86 GHz, 2MB L2 Cache 1066 MHz front side bus	Dual processor, 2.00 GHz, 2MB L2 Cache 800 MHz front side bus	Dual processor, 2.00 GHz, 2MB L2 Cache 800 MHz front side bus	Dual processor, 3.0 GHz, 4MB L2 Cache 800 MHz front side bus, 64 bit
Memory	1 GB SDRAM	1 GB SDRAM	1 GB SDRAM	512 MB SDRAM
Hard drives	160 GB 7200 rpm SATA 3.0 Gb/s	80 GB 7200 rpm SATA 3.0 Gb/s	80 GB 7200 rpm SATA 3.0 Gb/s	80 GB 7200 rpm SATA 3.0 Gb/s
Optical drives	8X DVD-RW	48X DVD/CD-RW	48X DVD/CD-RW	48X CD-RW

Figure 4-20
Desktop-Computer Specifications

a. What CPU, memory, and disk specifications would you recommend?
b. What software does she need?
c. Shop Dell, HP, and Lenova for the best computer deal.
d. Which computer would you recommend, and why?

3. Suppose that your father asks you to help him purchase a new computer. He wants to use his computer for email, Internet access, downloading pictures from his digital camera, uploading those pictures to a shared photo service, and writing documents to members of his antique auto club.

a. What CPU, memory, and disk specifications would you recommend?
b. What software does he need?
c. Shop Dell, HP, and Lenova for the best computer deal.
d. Which computer would you recommend, and why?

4. Microsoft offers free licenses of certain software products to students at colleges and universities that participate in the Microsoft Developer Network (MSDN) Academic Alliance (AA). If your college or university participates in this program, you have the opportunity to obtain hundreds of dollars of software, for free. Here is a partial list of the software you can obtain:

- Microsoft Access 2007
- One Note
- Vista business edition
- SharePoint Designer
- Web Expressions
- Windows 2003 Server
- Microsoft Project 2007
- Visual Studio Developer
- SQL Server 2005
- Visio

a. Access *http://Microsoft.com* or *http://Google.com* and determine the function of each of these software products.
b. Which of these software products are operating systems and which are application programs?
c. Which of these programs are DBMS products (the subject of the next chapter)?
d. Which of these programs should you download and install tonight?
e. Either (1) download and install the programs in your answer to part d, or (2) explain why you would not choose to do so.
f. Does the MSDN AA provide an unfair advantage to Microsoft? Why or why not?

COLLABORATION EXERCISES AND CASES

Collaborate with a group of students on the following exercises. Recall from Chapter 2 that collaboration is more than cooperation. Collaboration involves iteration and feedback. Post a document, a discussion item, a wiki item, or an idea and obtain feedback from your team members. Similarly, read the ideas of others and comment on them. Try to innovate in both the process by which you collaborate and the work product that you create. Avoid face-to-face meetings. Instead, use collaborative software such as Google Docs & Spreadsheets, Microsoft Groove, or Microsoft SharePoint to facilitate your ideas.

1. Consider the $80,000 question from the *Technology in Practice* box on page 104. Suppose you have been given the following list of data about the department and its information needs:

   - You will upgrade all of your department's computers to Windows Vista and Office 2007 in the next year. Your company has negotiated a site license for these products, and the IS department allocates that license cost to each computer. For your department, you will pay $100 for each computer that uses Office 2007 and another $75 for each computer that uses Vista. You are not required nor allowed to buy any software for new computers. If the computer comes with software, that software will be destroyed by the IS department's standard installation process.
   - You have identified three classes of computer users in your department. The main memory, RAM, and disk storage requirements for each class of user are shown in Figure 4-21. This figure shows the specifications of existing computers as well as the hardware requirements for each class after the upgrade.
   - Figure 4-22 shows the job titles of employees in your department, the number of employees of each type, the class of computer they require, and whether they use a desktop or a laptop. (You are a new employee, do not yet have a computer, and can specify your own requirements.)

Class of Computer	Current Hardware Specification (Main Memory, Processor, Disk)	Hardware Required after Upgrade (Main Memory, Processor, Disk)
A	256MB, 0.5 GHz, 30GB	1GB, 1GHz, 80GB
B	512MB, 1GHz, 80GB	2GB, 2GHz, 150GB
C	1GB, 2GHz, 2 x 125GB	4GB, 2GHz—dual, 2 x 250GB

Figure 4-21
Hardware Specifications for Three Classes of Computers

- A computer can be reassigned to other employees as long as the computer meets the minimum processing requirements. A laptop can substitute for a desktop if a display, keyboard, and mouse is purchased to go with it.
- The IS department assesses each computer an annual $1,200 fee for network, server, and other overhead costs.
- Assume that telesales personnel will grow by 10 percent in the next year but there will be no other changes in the number of personnel in your department.
- Ten of the existing class B computers have a maximum main memory of 1GB. The rest of the class B computers have a maximum main memory of 512MB. All of the existing class C computers have a maximum main memory of 4GB.

a. Given this data, is $80,000 enough? If not, how much money should be allocated in your department?

b. Explain how you will meet the computer needs of the employees in your department. Assume you are required to buy new computers and equipment from Dell, HP, or Lenova.

c. Describe the modification and reallocation of existing computers (e.g., upgrading an existing class B computer and assigning it to an employee who next year needs a class A computer). You may wish to develop the spreadsheet in Application Exercise 1 (Excel) on page 138 to facilitate your analysis.

2. Reread the *Innovation in Practice* box on page 114 and view the Surface promotional video at *http://Microsoft.com/surface*. Recall the RAND study cited in Chapter 1 that stated there will be increased demand, worldwide, for workers who can apply new technology to solve business problems in innovative ways. Surface is an excellent example of a new technology that will be applied innovatively.

   a. Consider uses for Surface at your university. How might Surface be used in architecture, chemistry, law, medicine, business, geography, political science, art, music, or any other discipline in which

Job Title	Number of Employees	Computer System Required	Computer Type
Product manager	8	B	Laptop
Telesales	12	A	Desktop
Department administrator	2	A	Desktop
Marketing communications manager	4	B	Laptop
Marketing analyst	4	C (desktop) B (laptop)	Both, a desktop and laptop for each analyst
Marketing programs manager	6	B	Desktop
You	1	???	???

Figure 4-22
Department Employees and Computer Requirements

your team has interest? Describe a potential application for Surface in five different disciplines.

b. List specific features and benefits for each of the five applications you selected in part a.

c. Describe, in general terms, the work that need to be accomplished to create the applications you identified in part a.

d. Using the five-component framework, describe the tools, documentation, and facilities that Microsoft or one of its partners must provide to enable widespread development of Surface applications.

e. Suppose you and your teammates want to start a consulting firm. Describe the opportunity for your firm that exists either in your answer to question d. Describe specific services that you could provide to help others create Surface applications.

f. Suppose you and your teammates want to start a consulting firm. Describe the opportunity that exists as a developer of complete and finished Surface applications.

g. You will sometimes hear the expression, "Emerging technology is constantly leveling the playing field," meaning that technology eliminates competitive advantages of existing companies and enables opportunities for new companies. How does this statement pertain to your answers to parts e and f?

APPLICATION EXERCISES

1. Reread the *Technology in Practice* box on page 104 and also Collaboration Exercise 1 on pages 136 and 137.

Create an Excel spreadsheet to compute the cost of new computers for the $80,000 problem. Use the spreadsheet in Figure 4-23 as an example.

Construct your spreadsheet so that you can change prices, charges, and job title employee count and Excel will update the Total Cost for Category as well as Total Cost. As stated in the note in the spreadsheet, the costs shown here are only examples, as is the choice of computer for the manager (you).

2. Sometimes you will have data in one Office application and want to move it to another Office application without rekeying it. Often this occurs when data was created for one purpose but then is used for a second purpose. For example, Figure 4-24 presents a portion of an Excel spreadsheet that shows the assignment of computers to employees.

	A	B	C	D	E	F	G
2				New-Hardware Cost Calculator			
3							
4		Laptop	Desktop				
5	Price of Class A Computer	$1,500	$1,000		Note for teams answering the $80,000 collaboration project: Prices shown are just examples. Actual prices will likely be different. Also, the choice of Laptop B for the manager is only for example. Another choice may make more sense.		
6	Price of Class B Computer	$2,000	$1,500				
7	Price of Class C Computer	$2,500	$2,000				
8							
9	Vista Software Charge	$75	$75				
10	Office 2007 Software Charge	$100	$100				
11	Network and Server Charge	$1,200	$1,200				
12							
13							
14							
15	Job Title	Number of Employees	Computer System Required	Computer Type	Hardware and Software Cost	Total Cost for Category	
16	Product manager	8	B	Laptop	$3,375	$27,000	
17	Telesales	12	A	Desktop	$2,375	$28,500	
18	Department Admin	2	A	Desktop	$2,375	$4,750	
19	Marketing Communications Manager	4	B	Laptop	$3,375	$13,500	
20	Marketing Analyst	4	C (desktop)	Both, a desktop and	$3,375	$13,500	
21			B (laptop)	laptop for each analyst	$2,575	$10,300	
22	Marketing Programs Manager	6	B	Desktop	$1,375	$8,250	
23	Manager (You)	1	B	Laptop	$3,375	$3,375	
24							
25					Total Cost	$109,175	

Figure 4-23
New-Hardware Cost Calculator

Source: Microsoft product screen shot reprinted with permission from Microsoft Corporation.

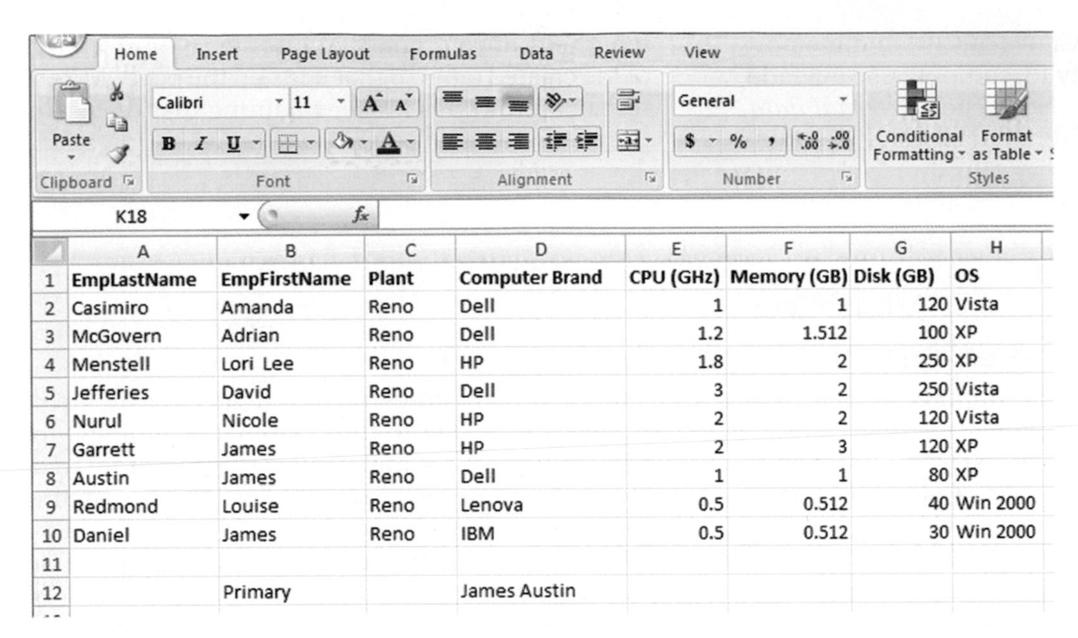

	A	B	C	D	E	F	G	H
1	EmplastName	EmpFirstName	Plant	Computer Brand	CPU (GHz)	Memory (GB)	Disk (GB)	OS
2	Casimiro	Amanda	Reno	Dell	1	1	120	Vista
3	McGovern	Adrian	Reno	Dell	1.2	1.512	100	XP
4	Menstell	Lori Lee	Reno	HP	1.8	2	250	XP
5	Jefferies	David	Reno	Dell	3	2	250	Vista
6	Nurul	Nicole	Reno	HP	2	2	120	Vista
7	Garrett	James	Reno	HP	2	3	120	XP
8	Austin	James	Reno	Dell	1	1	80	XP
9	Redmond	Louise	Reno	Lenova	0.5	0.512	40	Win 2000
10	Daniel	James	Reno	IBM	0.5	0.512	30	Win 2000
11								
12		Primary		James Austin				

Figure 4-24
Sample Excel Data for Import

Source: Microsoft product screen shot reprinted with permission from Microsoft Corporation.

Suppose that you want to use this data to help you assess how to upgrade computers. Let's say, for example, that you want to upgrade all of the computers' operating systems to Vista. Furthermore, you want to first upgrade the computers that most need upgrading, but suppose you have a limited budget. To address this situation, you would like to query the data in Figure 4-24, find all computers that do not have Vista, and then select those with slower CPUs or smaller memory as candidates for upgrading. To do this, you need to move the data from Excel and into Access.

Once you have analyzed the data and determined the computers to upgrade, you want to produce a report. In that case, you may want to move the data from Access and back to Excel, or perhaps into Word. In this exercise, you will learn how to perform these tasks.

a. To begin, download the Excel file **Ch04Ex02** from this text's Web site into one of your directories. We will import the data in this file into Access, but before we do so, familiarize yourself with the data by opening it in Excel. Notice that there are three worksheets in this workbook. Close the Excel file.

b. Create a blank Access database. Name the database Ch04Ex02_Answer. Place it in some directory; it may be the same directory into which you have placed the Excel file, but it need not be. Close the default table that Access creates and delete it.

c. Now, we will import the data from the three worksheets in the Excel file **Ch04Ex02** into a single table in your Access database. In the ribbon, select *External Data* and *Import from Excel.* Start the import. For the first worksheet (Denver), you should select *Import the source data into a new table in the current database.* Be sure to click *First Row Contains Column Headings* when Access presents your data. You can use the default Field types and let Access add the primary key. Name your table *Employees* and click *Finish.* There is no need to save your import script.

For the second and third worksheets, again click *External Data, Import Excel,* but this time select *Append a copy of the records to the table Employees.* Import all data.

d. Open the *Employee* table and examine the data. Notice that Access has erroneously imported a blank line and the *Primary Contact* data into rows at the end of each data set. This data is not part of the employee records, and you should delete it (in three places—once for each worksheet). The *Employee* table should have a total of 40 records.

e. Now, create a parameterized query on this data. Place all of the columns except *ID* into the query. In the *OS* column, set the criteria to select rows for which the value is not *Vista.* In the *CPU* (GHz) column, enter the criterion: *<=[Enter cutoff value for CPU]* and in the *Memory* (GB) column, enter the criterion: *<=[Enter cutoff value for Memory].* Test your query. For example, run your query and enter a value of *2* for both CPU and memory. Verify that the correct rows are produced.

f. Use your query to find values of CPU and memory that give you as close to a maximum of 15 computers to upgrade as possible.

g. When you have found values of CPU and memory that give you 15, or nearly 15, computers to upgrade, leave your query open. Now, click *External data, Word*, and create a Word document that contains the results of your query. Adjust the column widths of the created table so that it fits on the page. Write a memo around this table explaining that these are the computers that you believe should be upgraded.

CASE STUDY 4

Dell Leverages the Internet, Directly

When Michael Dell started Dell Computer in 1984, personal computers were sold only in retail stores. Manufacturers shipped to wholesalers, who shipped to retail stores, which sold to end users. Companies maintained expensive inventories at each stage of this supply chain. Dell thought that if he could eliminate the retail channel by selling computers directly to consumers, he could dramatically reduce the machines' prices. In 2004, while speaking to a group of students in New York City, he recalled,

> I was inspired by how I saw computers being sold. It seemed to me that it was very expensive and it was inefficient. A computer cost at the time about $3,000 but there were only about $600 worth of parts inside the computer. And so I figured, hey, what if you sold the computer for $800? You don't need to sell it for $3,000. And so we changed the whole way computers were being sold by lowering the cost of distribution and sales and taking out this extra cost that was inefficient.
>
> Now, what I didn't know was that the Internet would come along and now people can go on the Internet and they can go to *Dell.com* and buy a computer and that makes it a lot easier.
>
> I'd say the most important thing we did was listen very carefully to our customers. We asked, what do they want, what do they need and how can we meet their needs and provide something that's really valuable to them? Because if we could take care of our customers, they'll want to buy more products from us, and they have.[3]

Indeed they have. In 2006, Dell's revenue topped $56 billion, representing over 18 percent of the computer hardware market. Dell employs over 50,000 people worldwide, and its investors have benefited as well. A share of Dell purchased for $8.50 in the initial public offering would be worth over $2,400 in 2006 (allowing for multiple stock splits over the years).

Eliminating retail stores not only reduced costs, but it also brought Dell closer to the customer, enabling it to listen better than the competition. It also eliminated sales channel inventories, which allowed Dell to rapidly bring new computers with new technology to the customer. This eliminates the need to recycle or sell off existing pipeline inventory whenever a new model is announced. In fact, today Dell builds every computer system to customer order. Every computer in Dell's finished goods inventory has already been sold!

Additionally, Dell focused on its suppliers and now has one of the most efficient supply chains in the industry. Dell pays close attention to its suppliers and shares information with them on product quality, inventory, and related subjects via its secure Web site *http://valuechain.dell.com.* According to its Web site, the first two qualities Dell looks for in suppliers are (1) cost competitiveness and (2) an understanding of Dell's business. Dell listens to its customers, and it expects its suppliers to do the same in return.

In addition to computer hardware, Dell provides a variety of services. It provides basic technical support with every computer, and customers can upgrade this basic support by purchasing one of four higher levels of support. Additionally, Dell offers deployment services to organizations to configure and deploy Dell systems, both hardware and preinstalled software, into customers' user environments. Dell offers additional services to maintain and manage Dell systems once they have been deployed.

Source: © 2005 Dell Inc. All Rights Reserved.

Questions

1. Explain how selling direct has given Dell a competitive advantage. Use the factors listed in Figure 3-11 (page 72) in your answer.
2. What information systems does Dell need to have to sell directly to the consumer? Visit *http://dell.com* for inspiration and ideas.

[3]Michael Dell, speech before the Miami Springs Middle School, September 1, 2004. Retrieved from *http://dell.com*, under Michael/Speeches (accessed January 2005).

3. Besides selling direct, what other programs has Dell created that give it a competitive advantage?
4. HP, Toshiba, Sony, and other computer manufacturers sell both directly and through Internet stores. Visit *http://cnet.com* and search for the term notebook. The site will return laptop computers from several manufacturers. If you look at notebooks from HP, Toshiba, or Sony, you will see that they must be purchased from Internet vendors. (Click Check Prices to see vendor sources.) In contrast, Dell computers can be purchased only from Dell, as you will see when you check for prices for one of its computers.

   In order to use an intermediary, HP and others must sell their computers to the supplier at a price below the consumer's price; otherwise the supplier has no incentive to sell the product. But those vendors cannot offer the supplier's price to the public without losing its suppliers. Does this situation mean that Dell computers will be cheaper than HP and other computers? Why or why not?
5. Assume that because of the need to sell through a channel, HP's computers will always be more expensive than Dell's. How can HP successfully compete with Dell?
6. What information systems can HP set up that will better enable it to compete with Dell? Visit *http://hp.com* for inspiration and ideas.
7. Do you think Dell would have been successful if the Internet had not been invented? Why or why not?

5 Database Processing

STUDY QUESTIONS

- Q1 What is the purpose of a database?
- Q2 What is a database?
- Q3 What are the components of a database application system?
- Q4 How do database applications make databases more useful?
- Q5 How are data models used for database development?
- Q6 How is a data model transformed into a database design?
- Q7 What is the users' role in the development of databases?
- Q8 What are the responsibilities for database administration?

Meet Rick Torbert

My motto:
Less is more.

My guiding principle:
Make designs elegant and workable. Databases should be like fine wine or great poetry: They should be richly textured, resonate on many levels, and be totally accessible and understandable.

One thing you must know about information systems:
They are a means to end, not an end in themselves.

Rick Torbert has more than 20 years experience developing databases for a number of Fortune 500 companies, and even more experience working with information systems of all types. Rick majored in English literature in college but had always enjoyed technical subjects. A summer job at New Jersey Bell working with early report generators convinced him that he wanted to work with information technology. During his career, he has been both a manager and a technical developer and often worked as a project lead with a foot in both camps. Currently, he is a database architect for a major financial-services provider in the Midwest, where he works on database solutions involving large amounts of corporate, or enterprise, data.

On database development:

"The purpose of a database is to give people access to the information they need so that they can do their jobs more easily or more quickly. Of course, no database designer knows the users' needs ahead of time, so finding out what they need is the essential first step. The only way to do that is to ask the users, and we need to do so using their own vocabulary.

"Database development is a collaborative process. We ask the users what they want and then we respond, maybe by building a prototype. The users will say, 'No, that's not quite it,' or 'Yes, that's a start, but I also need to know…,' and the process goes back and forth for a while. We work together in an iterative manner to learn what we need to build and how to best present it.

"Often the users can't describe exactly what they want. They need to see something, relate it to their work, and then they respond with changes. That's OK; that's how it happens, and we all need patience as we work together to uncover the true requirements.

"This iterative process is essential; users need to commit to it and to fully engage with the developers. Database developers are not mind readers, and users should not expect to get what they need the first time. By the same token, database developers should not be surprised when users change their minds or extend what they said they wanted. Revision and iteration is the nature of database design."

On the single biggest challenge:

"Not having the time to do the job right. Too often, people are in a hurry to get something out the door. As consultants, we are sometimes accused of 'analysis paralysis,' or worse, of making up work to increase billable hours. While

My heroes:
Inspiring people who perform difficult tasks with grace:
In sports: Bill Russell, Roberto Clemente, Michael Jordan.
In politics: Winston Churchill, John Lindsey (mayor of NYC in the 1960's).

Career highs:
My first database development job cut the time of a capital budgeting process from 2 days to a few hours. I've had a few other highs like that.

My favorite business books:
Rapid Development by Steve McConnell; *The Peter Principle* by Laurence J. Peter and Raymond Hull; and Alvin Toffler's *The Third Wave.*

clients need to be aware that this could happen, it is not usually the case. However, it *should* set off warning bells if someone promises to deliver a solution without first demonstrating an understanding of what is required. If someone says, 'Oh, I can build your database in four weeks,' I wouldn't believe it. No developer can know what needs to be done, or how long it will take, until he or she knows what the client wants.

"So how do users protect themselves? Well, they should ensure that the results they're getting relate to what they've said. Not perfectly, but at least strongly relate. Early prototypes, for example, should demonstrate that the developers understand, or are at least beginning to understand, the users' problem. An iterative process that shows small successes early in the process and builds from there is often the best approach. Finding and fixing problems in the early stages of a project is far less expensive than having to deal with them after the system has been installed.

"If the developers demonstrate they understand the requirements and if they have a quality reputation, then take the time to collaborate with them to craft a solution. Don't be slaves to a schedule that was set at the beginning, when you knew the least about the problem. Don't let schedules force omissions and compromises that will hurt later."

On database project management:
"Project management lets me do both technical and managerial work. I've held jobs that were 100% management, and I didn't find them as satisfying. It isn't that I dislike management, but more, technology keeps pulling me back. (It probably has something to do with my enjoyment of puzzle solving.)

"By the same token, I don't want to work just on technical problems. I like having some control over the scope of what we do, and I enjoy the interaction with users and management. Project management is a good combination of the two directions."

On technology:
"Technology is important. It's what enables us to do our jobs. But, don't let it get in the way. You have to rise above the noise of technology, the latest trend or system or capability, and focus instead on producing useful results that users want.

"Databases are about organization. They bring data together in ways, in structures, that enable and encourage the creation of information. The tools we use are just that: tools. Knowing how to use the latest tools is important, but ultimately it's about communicating with users, finding out the information they need, and designing databases to create that information."

On database development as a career:
"Would I advise someone to do this work? Yes—principally because you have a chance to make a big difference in people's lives. You listen to what people want and what information they need, help them clarify their requirements, and then deconstruct, dissect, and recombine using database principles, technology, and tools. Ultimately, the information you produce helps them do their jobs faster and better."

The bottom line:
"Databases should make it easy for people to find the data or information they are looking for."

CHAPTER PREVIEW

Businesses of every size organize data records into collections called *databases*. At one extreme, small businesses use databases to keep track of customers; at the other extreme, huge corporations such as Dell and Amazon.com use databases to support complex sales, marketing, and operations activities.

This chapter discusses the why, what, and how of database processing. We begin by describing the purpose of databases and then explain the important components of database systems. We then overview the process of creating a database system and summarize your role as a future user of such systems.

Users have a crucial role in the development of database applications. Specifically, the structure and content of the database depends entirely on how users view their business activity. To build the database, the developers will create a model of that view using a tool called the entity-relationship model. You need to understand how to interpret such models, because the development team might ask you to validate the correctness of such a model when building a system for your use. Finally, we describe the various database administration tasks.

This chapter focuses on database technology. Here we consider the basic components of a database and their functions. You will learn about the use of databases reporting and data mining in Chapter 9.

Q1 What Is the Purpose of a Database?

The purpose of a database is to keep track of things. When most students learn that, they wonder why we need a special technology for such a simple task. Why not just use a list? If the list is long, put it into a spreadsheet.

In fact, many professionals do keep track of things using spreadsheets. If the structure of the list is simple enough, there is no need to use database technology. The list of student grades in Figure 5-1, for example, works perfectly well in a spreadsheet.

Suppose, however, that the professor wants to track more than just grades. Say that the professor wants to record email messages as well. Or, perhaps the professor wants to record both email messages and office visits. There is no place in Figure 5-1 to record that additional data. Of course, the professor could set up a separate spreadsheet for email messages and another one for office visits, but that awkward solution would be difficult to use because it does not provide all of the data in one place.

Instead, the professor wants a form like that in Figure 5-2 (next page). With it, the professor can record student grades, emails, and office visits all in one place. A form like the one in Figure 5-2 is difficult, if not impossible, to produce from a spreadsheet. Such a form is easily produced, however, from a database.

The key distinction between Figures 5-1 and 5-2 is that the list in Figure 5-1 is about a single theme or concept. It is about student grades only. The list in Figure 5-2

	A	B	C	D	E
1	Student Name	Student Number	HW1	HW2	MidTerm
2					
3	BAKER, ANDREA	1325	88	100	78
4	FISCHER, MAYAN	3007	95	100	74
5	LAU, SWEE	1644	75	90	90
6	NELSON, STUART	2881	100	90	98
7	ROGERS, SHELLY	8009	95	100	98
8	TAM, JEFFREY	3559		100	88
9	VALDEZ, MARIE	5265	80	90	85
10	VERBERRA, ADAM	4867	70	90	92

Figure 5-1
A List of Student Grades, Presented in a Spreadsheet

Figure 5-2
Student Data Shown in a Form, from a Database

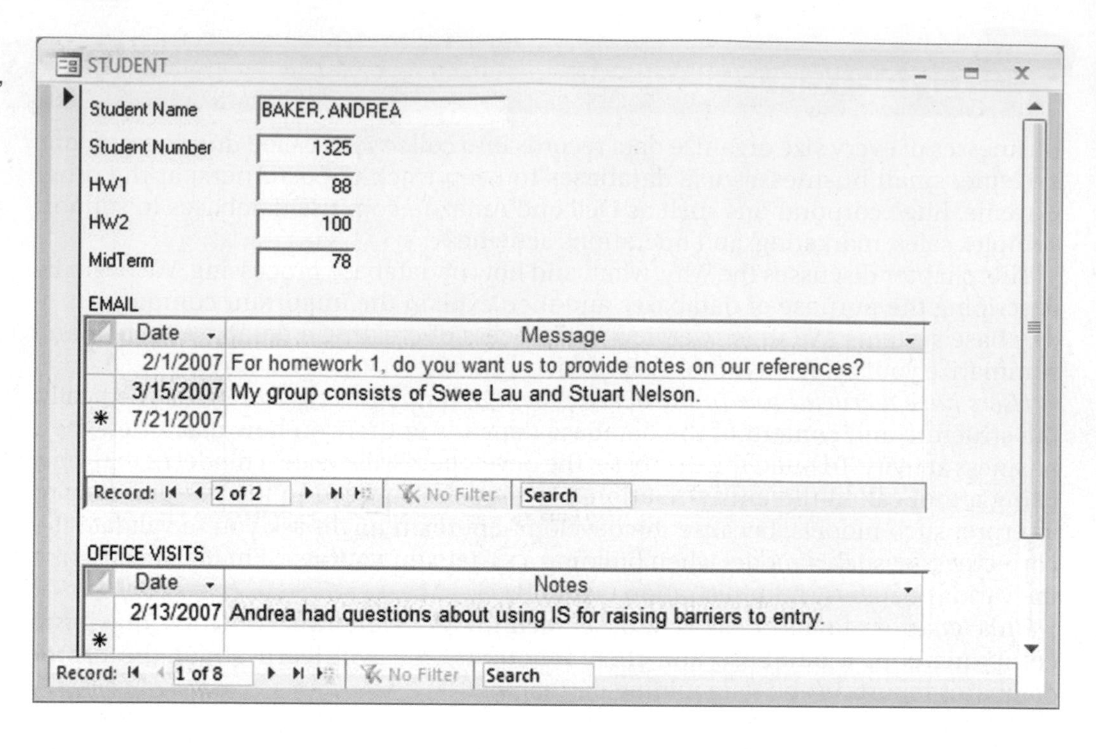

As you will see, databases can be more difficult to develop than spreadsheets; this difficulty causes some people to resist the idea of using a database, as discussed in the Opposing Forces Guide *on page 172.*

has multiple themes; it shows student grades, student emails, and student office visits. We can make a general rule from these examples: Lists that involve a single theme can be stored in a spreadsheet; lists that involve multiple themes require a database. We will say more about this general rule as this chapter proceeds.

To summarize, the purpose of a database is to keep track of things that involve more than one theme.

Q2 What Is a Database?

A **database** is a self-describing collection of integrated records. To understand this definition, you first need to understand the terms illustrated in Figure 5-3. As you learned in Chapter 4, a **byte** is a character of data. In databases, bytes are grouped into

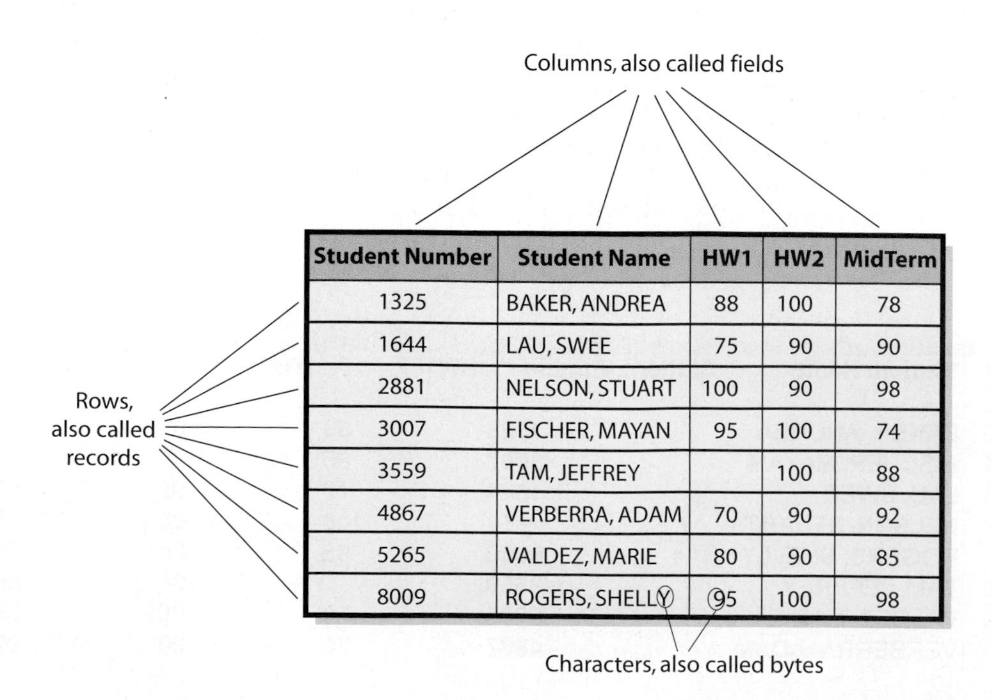

Student Number	Student Name	HW1	HW2	MidTerm
1325	BAKER, ANDREA	88	100	78
1644	LAU, SWEE	75	90	90
2881	NELSON, STUART	100	90	98
3007	FISCHER, MAYAN	95	100	74
3559	TAM, JEFFREY		100	88
4867	VERBERRA, ADAM	70	90	92
5265	VALDEZ, MARIE	80	90	85
8009	ROGERS, SHELLY	95	100	98

Figure 5-3
Student Table (also called a file)

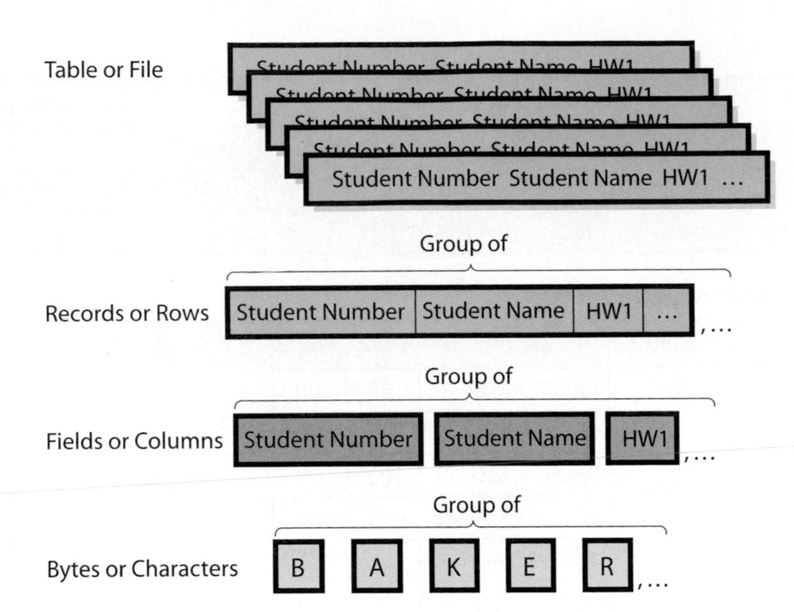

Figure 5-4
Hierarchy of Data Elements

columns, such as *Student Number* and *Student Name*. Columns are also called **fields**. Columns or fields, in turn, are grouped into **rows**, which are also called **records**. In Figure 5-3, the collection of data for all columns (*Student Number*, *Student Name*, *HW1*, *HW2*, and *MidTerm*) is called a *row* or a *record*. Finally, a group of similar rows or records is called a **table** or a **file**. From these definitions, you can see that there is a hierarchy of data elements, as shown in Figure 5-4.

It is tempting to continue this grouping process by saying that a database is a group of tables or files. This statement, although true, does not go far enough. As shown in Figure 5-5, a database is a collection of tables *plus* relationships among the rows in those tables, *plus* special data, called *metadata*, that describes the structure of the database. By the way, the cylindrical symbol represents a computer disk drive. It is used in diagrams like that in Figure 5-5 because databases are normally stored on magnetic disks.

What Are Relationships Among Rows?

Consider the terms on the left-hand side of Figure 5-5. You know what tables are. To understand what is meant by *relationships among rows in tables*, examine Figure 5-6 (next page). It shows sample data from the three tables *Email*, *Student*, and *Office_Visit*. Notice the column named *Student Number* in the *Email* table. That column indicates the row in *Student* to which a row of *Email* is connected. In the first row of *Email*, the *Student Number* value is 1325. This indicates that this particular email was received from the student whose *Student Number* is 1325. If you examine the *Student* table, you will see that the row for Andrea Baker has this value. Thus, the first row of the *Email* table is related to Andrea Baker.

Now consider the last row of the *Office_Visit* table at the bottom of the figure. The value of *Student Number* in that row is 4867. This value indicates that the last row in *Office_Visit* belongs to Adam Verberra.

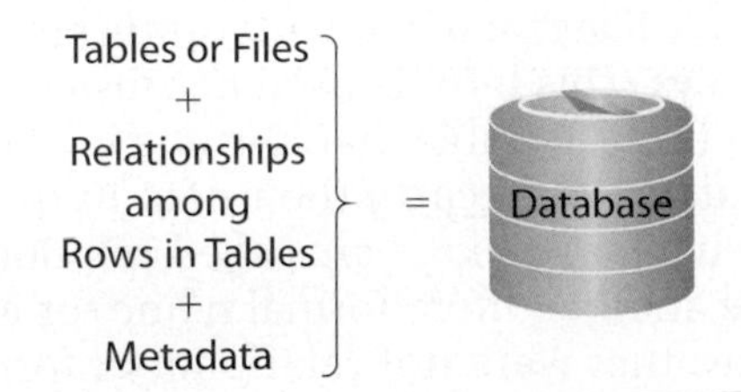

Figure 5-5
Components of a Database

Figure 5-6
Example of Relationships Among Rows

Email Table

EmailNum	Date	Message	Student Number
1	2/1/2004	For homework 1, do you want us to provide notes on our references?	1325
2	3/15/2004	My group consists of Swee Lau and Stuart Nelson.	1325
3	3/15/2004	Could you please assign me to a group?	1644

Student Table

Student Number	Student Name	HW1	HW2	MidTerm
1325	BAKER, ANDREA	88	100	78
1644	LAU, SWEE	75	90	90
2881	NELSON, STUART	100	90	98
3007	FISCHER, MAYAN	95	100	74
3559	TAM, JEFFREY		100	88
4867	VERBERRA, ADAM	70	90	92
5265	VALDEZ, MARIE	80	90	85
8009	ROGERS, SHELLY	95	100	98

Office_Visit Table

VisitID	Date	Notes	Student Number
2	2/13/2004	Andrea had questions about using IS for raising barriers to entry.	1325
3	2/17/2004	Jeffrey is considering an IS major. Wanted to talk about career opportunities.	3559
4	2/17/2004	Will miss class Friday due to job conflict.	4867

From these examples, you can see that values in one table relate rows of that table to rows in a second table. Several special terms are used to express these ideas. A **key** is a column or group of columns that identifies a unique row in a table. *Student Number* is the key of the *Student* table. Given a value of *Student Number,* you can determine one and only one row in *Student.* Only one student has the number 1325, for example.

Every table must have a key. The key of the *Email* table is *EmailNum,* and the key of the *Student_Visit* table is *VisitID.* Sometimes more than one column is needed to form a unique identifier. In a table called *City,* for example, the key would consist of the combination of columns (*City, State*), because a given city name can appear in more than one state.

Student Number is not the key of the *Email* or the *Office_Visit* tables. We know that about *Email* because there are two rows in *Email* that have the *Student Number* value 1325. The value 1325 does not identify a unique row, therefore *Student Number* is not the key of *Email.*

Nor is *Student Number* a key of *Office_Visit,* although you cannot tell that from the data in Figure 5-6. If you think about it, however, there is nothing to prevent a student from visiting a professor more than once. If that were to happen, there would be two rows in *Office_Visit* with the same value of *Student Number.* It just happens that no student has visited twice in the limited data in Figure 5-6.

Columns that fulfill a role like that of *Student Number* in the *Email* and *Office_Visit* tables are called **foreign keys**. This term is used because such columns are keys, but they are keys of a different (foreign) table than the one in which they reside.

Before we go on, databases that carry their data in the form of tables and that represent relationships using foreign keys are called **relational databases**. (The term *relational* is used because another, more formal name for a table is **relation**.) In the past, there were databases that were not relational in format, but such databases have nearly disappeared. Chances are you will never encounter one, and we will not consider them further.[1]

Metadata

Recall the definition of database: A database is a self-describing collection of integrated records. The records are integrated because, as you just learned, relationships among rows are represented in the database. But what does *self-describing* mean?

It means that a database contains, within itself, a description of its contents. Think of a library. A library is a self-describing collection of books and other materials. It is self-describing because the library contains a catalog that describes the library's contents. The same idea also pertains to a database. Databases are self-describing because they contain not only data, but also data about the data in the database.

Metadata are data that describe data. Figure 5-7 shows metadata for the *Email* table. The format of metadata depends on the software product that is processing the database. Figure 5-7 shows the metadata as they appear in Microsoft Access. Each row of the top part of this form describes a column of the *Email* table. The columns of these descriptions are *Field Name, Data Type*, and *Description. Field Name* contains the name of the column, *Data Type* shows the type of data the column may hold, and *Description* contains notes that explain the source or use of the column. As you can see, there is one row of metadata for each of the four columns of the *Email* table: *EmailNum, Date, Message*, and *Student Number.*

The bottom part of this form provides more metadata, which Access calls *Field Properties*, for each column. In Figure 5-7, the focus is on the *Date* column (note the light rectangle drawn around the *Date* row). Because the focus is on *Date* in the top pane, the details in the bottom pane pertain to the *Date* column. The Field Properties describe formats, a default value for Access to supply when a new row is created, and the constraint that a value is required for this column. It is not important for you to remember these details. Instead, just understand that metadata are data about data and that such metadata are always a part of a database.

Metadata make databases easy to use—for both authorized and unauthorized purposes, as described in the Ethics Guide *on page 150.*

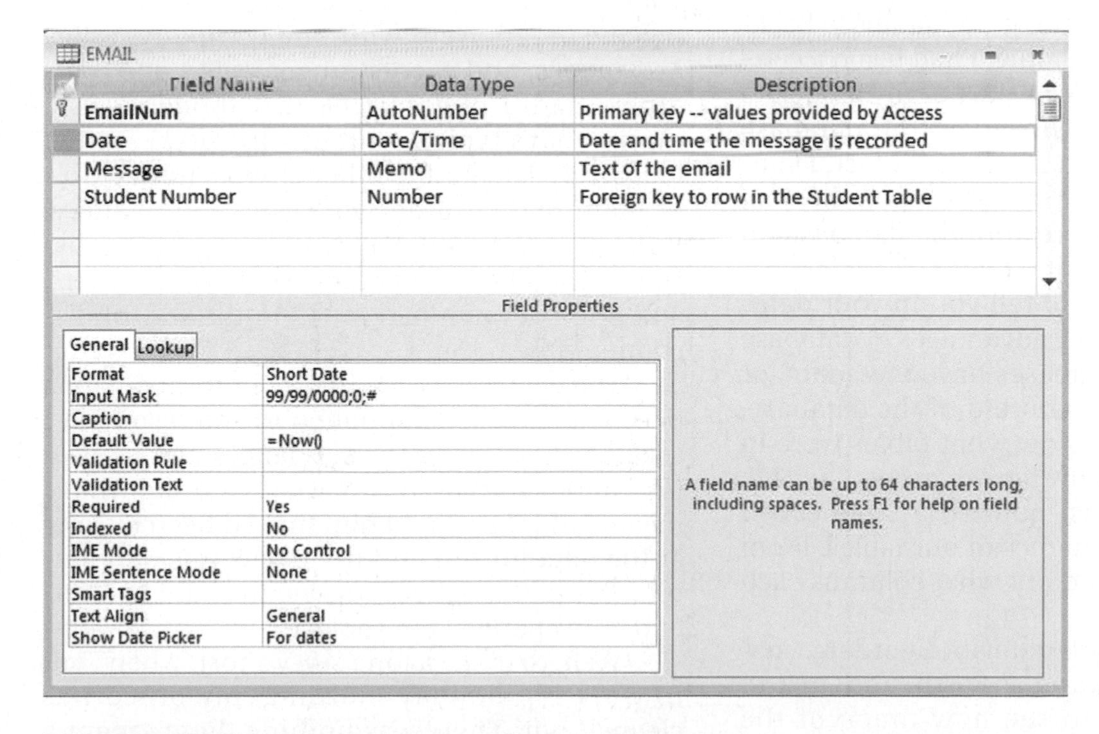

Figure 5-7
Sample Metadata (in Access)

[1]Another type of database, the **object-relational database**, is rarely used in commercial applications. Search the Web if you are interested in learning more about object-relational databases. In this book, we will describe only relational databases.

Ethics

GUIDE

Nobody Said I Shouldn't

My name is Kelly and I do systems support for our group. I configure the new computers, set up the network, make sure the servers are operating, and so forth. I also do all of the database backups. I've always liked computers. After high school, I worked odd jobs to make some money, then I got an associate degree in information technology from our local community college.

"Anyway, as I said, I make backup copies of our databases. One weekend, I didn't have much going on, so I copied one of the database backups to a CD and took it home. I had taken a class on database processing as part of my associate degree, and we used SQL Server (our database management system) in my class. In fact, I suppose that's part of the reason I got the job. Anyway, it was easy to restore the database on my computer at home, and I did.

"Of course, as they'll tell you in your database class, one of the big advantages of database processing is that databases have metadata, or data that describe the content of the database. So, although I didn't know what tables were in our database, I did know how to access the SQL Server metadata. I just queried a table called *sysTables* to learn the names of our tables. From there it was easy to find out what columns each table had.

"I found tables with data about orders, customers, salespeople, and so forth, and, just to amuse myself, and to see how much of the query language SQL that I could remember, I started playing around with the data. I was curious to know which order entry clerk was the best, so I started querying each clerk's order data, the total number of orders, total order amounts, things like that. It was easy to do and fun.

"I know one of the order entry clerks, Jason, pretty well, so I started looking at the data for his orders. I was just curious, and it was very simple SQL. I was just playing around with the data when I noticed something odd. All of his biggest orders were with one company, Valley Appliances, and even stranger, every one of its orders had a huge discount. I thought, well, maybe that's typical. Out of curiosity, I started looking at data for the other clerks, and very few of them had an order with Valley Appliances. But, when they did, Valley didn't get a big discount. Then I looked at the rest of Jason's orders, and none of them had much in the way of discounts, either.

"The next Friday, a bunch of us went out for a beer after work. I happened to see Jason, so I asked him about Valley Appliances and made a joke about the discounts. He asked me what I meant, and then I told him that I'd been looking at the data for fun and that I saw this odd pattern. He just laughed, said he just 'did his job,' and then changed the subject.

"Well, to make a long story short, when I got to work on Monday morning, my office was cleaned out. There was nothing there except a note telling me to go see my boss. The bottom line was, I was fired. The company also threatened that if I didn't return all of its data, I'd be in court for the next five years... things like that. I was so mad I didn't even tell them about Jason. Now my problem is that I'm out of a job, and I can't exactly use my last company for a reference." ■

Discussion Questions

1. Where did Kelly go wrong?
2. Do you think it was illegal, unethical, or neither for Kelly to take the database home and query the data?
3. Does the company share culpability with Kelly?
4. What do you think Kelly should have done upon discovering the odd pattern in Jason's orders?
5. What should the company have done before firing Kelly?
6. Is it possible that someone other than Jason is involved in the arrangement with Valley Appliances? What should Kelly have done in light of that possibility?
7. What should Kelly do now?
8. "Metadata make databases easy to use—for both authorized and unauthorized purposes." Explain what organizations should do in light of this fact.

The presence of metadata makes databases much more useful. Because of metadata, no one needs to guess, remember, or even record what is in the database. To find out what a database contains, we just look at the metadata inside the database.

Q3 What Are the Components of a Database Application System?

A database, all by itself, is not very useful. The tables in Figure 5-6 have all of the data the professor wants, but the format is unwieldy. The professor wants to see the data in a form like that in Figure 5-2 and also as a formatted report. Pure database data are correct, but in raw form they are not pertinent or useful.

Figure 5-8 shows the components of a **database application system**. Such applications make database data more accessible and useful. Users employ a database application that consists of forms (like that in Figure 5-2), formatted reports, queries, and application programs. Each of these, in turn, calls on the database management system (DBMS) to process the database tables. We will first describe DBMSs and then discuss database application components.

What Is a Database Management System?

A **database management system (DBMS)** is a program used to create, process, and administer a database. As with operating systems, almost no organization develops its own DBMS. Instead, companies license DBMS products from vendors such as IBM, Microsoft, Oracle, and others. Popular DBMS products are **DB2** from IBM, **Access** and **SQL Server** from Microsoft, and **Oracle** from the Oracle Corporation. Another popular DBMS is **MySQL**, an open-source DBMS product that is license-free for most applications. Other DBMS products are available, but these five process the great bulk of databases today.

Note that a DBMS and a database are two different things. For some reason, the trade press and even some books confuse the two. A DBMS is a software program; a database is a collection of tables, relationships, and metadata. The two are very different concepts.

Creating the Database and Its Structures

Database developers use the DBMS to create tables, relationships, and other structures in the database. The form in Figure 5-7 can be used to define a new table or to modify an existing one. To create a new table, the developer just fills the new table's metadata into the form.

To modify an existing table—say, to add a new column—the developer opens the metadata form for that table and adds a new row of metadata. For example, in Figure 5-9 the developer has added a new column called *Response?*. This new column has the data type *Yes/No*, which means that the column can contain only one value—*Yes* or *No*. The professor will use this column to indicate whether he has responded to the student's email. A column can be removed by deleting its row in this table, though doing so will lose any existing data.

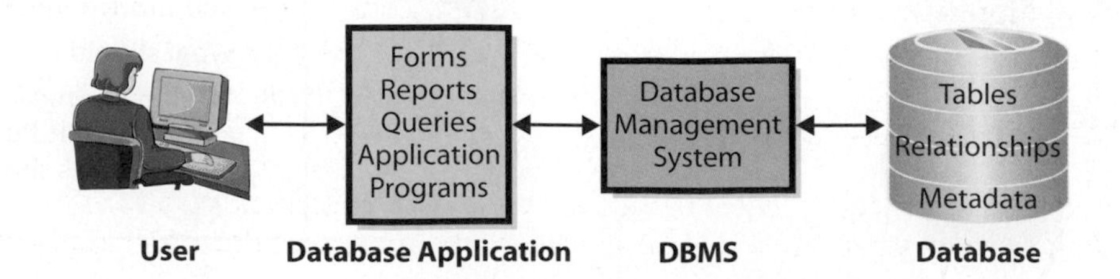

Figure 5-8
Components of a Database Application System

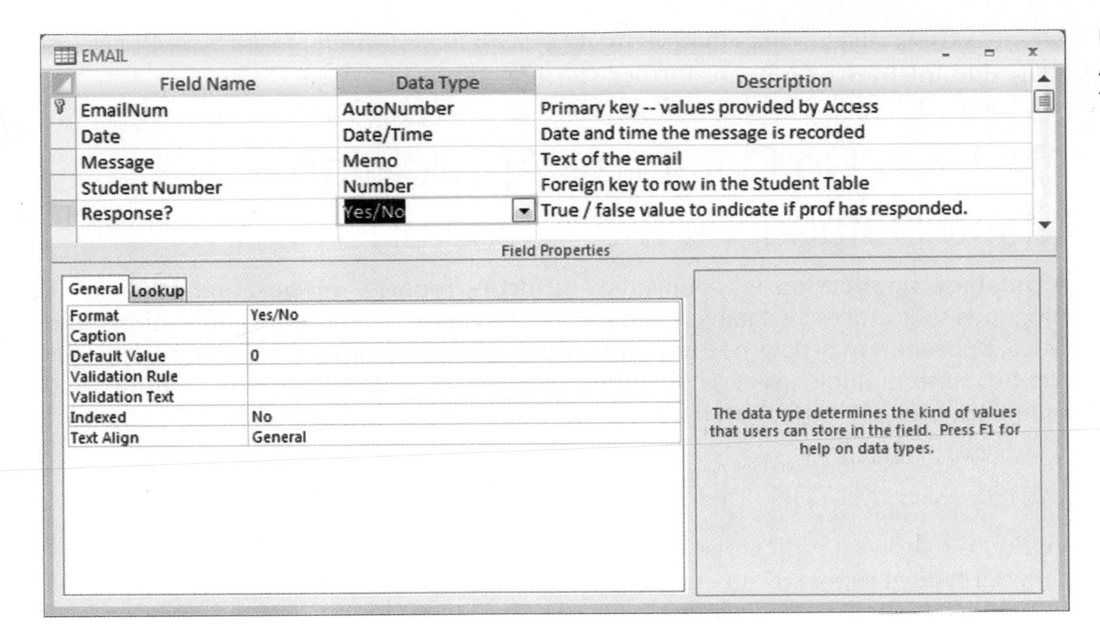

Figure 5-9
Adding a New Column to a Table (in Access)

Processing the Database

The second function of the DBMS is to process the database. Applications use the DBMS for four operations: to *read, insert, modify,* or *delete* data. The applications call upon the DBMS in different ways. From a form, when the user enters new or changed data, a computer program behind the form calls the DBMS to make the necessary database changes. From an application program, the program calls the DBMS directly to make the change.

Structured Query Language (SQL) is an international standard language for processing a database. All five of the DBMS products mentioned earlier accept and process SQL (pronounced "see-quell") statements. As an example, the following SQL statement inserts a new row into the *Student* table:

```
INSERT INTO Student
([Student Number], [Student Name], HW1, HW2, MidTerm)
VALUES
(1000, 'Franklin, Benjamin', 90, 95, 100);
```

As stated, statements like this one are issued "behind the scenes" by programs that process forms. Alternatively, they can be issued directly to the DBMS by an application program.

You do not need to understand or remember SQL language syntax. Instead, just realize that SQL is an international standard for processing a database. SQL can also be used to create databases and database structures. You will learn more about SQL if you take a database management class.

Administering the Database

A third DBMS function is to provide tools to assist in the administration of the database. Database administration involves a wide variety of activities. For example, the DBMS can be used to set up a security system involving user accounts, passwords, permissions, and limits for processing the database. To provide database security, a user must sign on using a valid user account before she can process the database.

Permissions can be limited in very specific ways. In the Student database example, it is possible to limit a particular user to reading only *Student Name* from the *Student* table. A different user could be given permission to read all of the *Student* table, but limited to update only the *HW1, HW2,* and *MidTerm* columns. Other users can be given still other permissions.

In addition to security, DBMS administrative functions include backing up database data, adding structures to improve the performance of database applications, removing data that are no longer wanted or needed, and similar tasks. We will discuss these administrative functions further, starting on page 169.

Q4 How Do Database Applications Make Databases More Useful?

A **database application** is a collection of forms, reports, queries, and application programs that process a database. A database may have one or more applications, and each application may have one or more users. Figure 5-10 shows three applications; the top two have multiple users. These applications have different purposes, features, and functions, but they all process the same inventory data stored in a common database.

What Are Forms, Reports, and Queries?

Figure 5-2 shows a typical database application data entry **form**, and Figure 5-11 shows a typical **report**. Data entry forms are used to read, insert, modify, and delete data. Reports show data in a structured context.

Recall from Chapter 1 that one of the definitions of information is "data presented in a meaningful context." The structure of this report creates information because it shows the student data in a context that will be meaningful to the professor. Some reports, like the one in Figure 5-11, also compute values as they present the data. An example is the computation of *Total weighted points* in Figure 5-11.

DBMS programs provide comprehensive and robust features for querying database data. For example, suppose the professor who uses the Student database remembers that one of the students referred to the topic *barriers to entry* in an office visit, but cannot remember which student or when. If there are hundreds of students and visits recorded in the database, it will take some effort and time for the professor to search through all office visit records to find that event. The DBMS, however, can find any such record quickly. Figure 5-12(a) shows a **query** form in which the professor types in the keyword for which she is looking. Figure 5-12(b) (page 156) shows the results of the query.

Why Are Database Application Programs Needed?

Forms, reports, and queries work well for standard functions. However, most applications have unique requirements that a simple form, report, or query cannot meet. For example, in the order-entry application in Figure 5-10, what should be done if only a

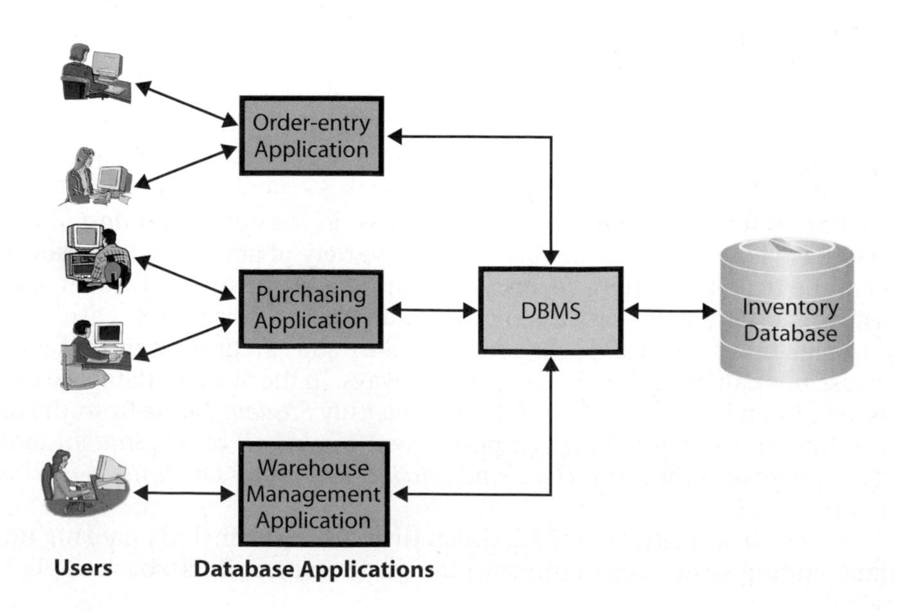

Figure 5-10
Use of Multiple Database Applications

Student Report with Emails

Student Name	BAKER, ANDREA	HW1	88
		HW2	100
Student Number	1325	MidTerm	78 (= 3 homeworks)
		Total weighted points:	422

Emails Received

Date	Message
2/1/2007	For homework 1, do you want us to provide notes on our references?
3/15/2007	My group consists of Swee Lau and Stuart Nelson.

Student Name	LAU, SWEE	HW1	75
		HW2	90
		MidTerm	90 (= 3 homeworks)
Student Number	1644		
		Total weighted points:	435

Emails Received

Date	Message
3/15/2007	Could you please assign me to a group?

Figure 5-11
Example of a Student Report

portion of a customer's request can be met? If someone wants 10 widgets and we only have 3 in stock, should a backorder for 7 more be generated automatically? Or, should some other action be taken?

Application programs process logic that is specific to a given business need. In the Student database, an example application is one that assigns grades at the end of the term. If the professor grades on a curve, the application reads the breakpoints for each grade from a form, and then processes each row in the *Student* table, allocating a grade based on the break points and the total number of points earned.

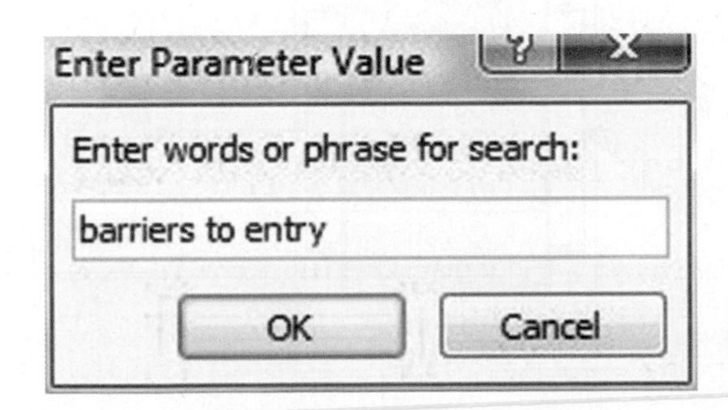

Figure 5-12(a)
Sample Query—Form used to enter phrase for search

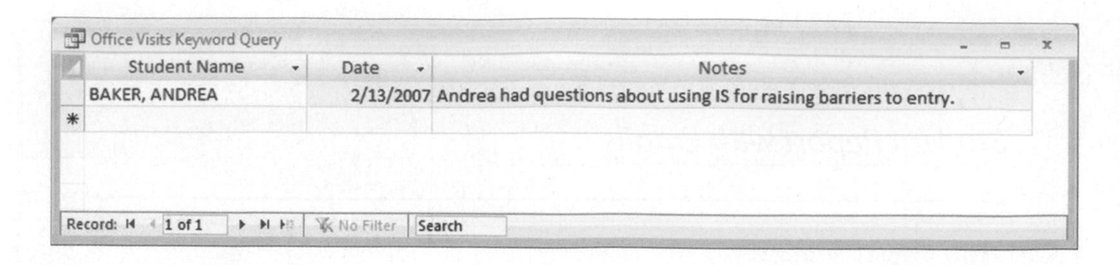

Office Visits Keyword Query

Student Name	Date	Notes
BAKER, ANDREA	2/13/2007	Andrea had questions about using IS for raising barriers to entry.

Record: 1 of 1 No Filter Search

Figure 5-12(b)
Sample Query—Results of query operation

Another important use of application programs is to enable database processing over the Internet. For this use, the application program serves as an intermediary between the Web server and the database. The application program responds to events, such as when a user presses a submit button; it also reads, inserts, modifies, and deletes database data.

For example, Figure 5-13 shows four different database application programs running on a Web server computer. Users with browsers connect to the Web server via the Internet. The Web server directs user requests to the appropriate application program. Each program then processes the database as necessary. You will learn more about Web-enabled databases in the discussion of e-commerce in Chapter 8.

Multi-User Processing

Figures 5-10 and 5-13 show multiple users processing the database. Such **multi-user processing** is common, but it does pose unique problems that you, as a future manager, should know about. To understand the nature of those problems, consider the following scenario.

Two users, Andrea and Jeffrey, are clerks using the order entry application in Figure 5-10. Andrea is on the phone with her customer, who wants to purchase 5 widgets. At the same time, Jeffrey is talking with his customer, who wants to purchase 3 widgets. Andrea reads the database to determine how many widgets are in inventory. (She unknowingly invokes the order-entry application when she types in her data entry form.) The DBMS returns a row showing 10 widgets in inventory.

Meanwhile, just after Andrea accesses the database, Jeffrey's customer says she wants widgets, and so he also reads the database (via the order entry application program) to determine how many widgets are in inventory. The DBMS returns the same row to him, indicating that 10 widgets are available.

Andrea's customer now says that he will take 5 units, and Andrea records this fact in her form. The application rewrites the widget row back to the database, indicating that there are 5 widgets in inventory.

Meanwhile, Jeffrey's customer says that he will take 3 units. Jeffrey records this fact in his form, and the application rewrites the widget row back to the database.

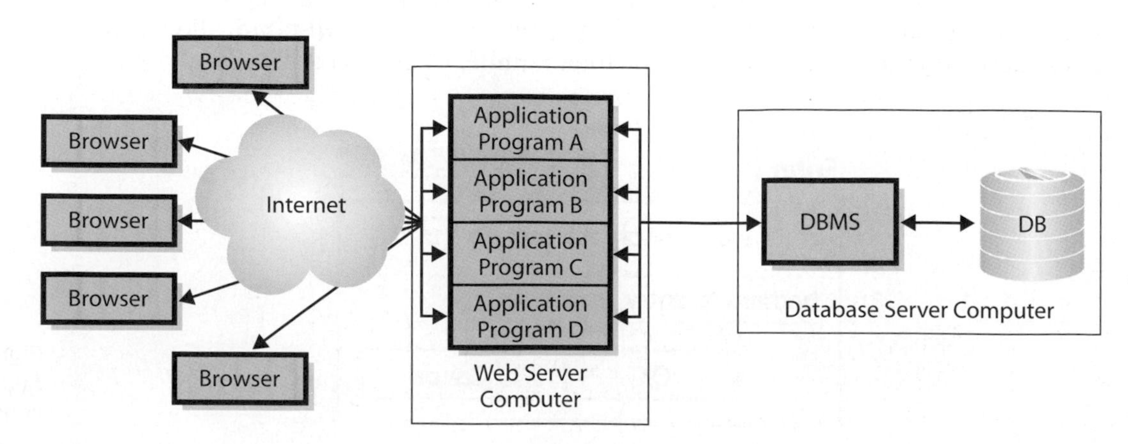

Figure 5-13
Four Application Programs on a Web Server Computer

However, Jeffrey's application knows nothing about Andrea's work and subtracts 3 from the original count of 10, thus storing an incorrect count of 7 widgets in inventory.

Clearly, there is a problem. We began with 10 widgets, Andrea took 5 and Jeffrey took 3, but the database says there are 7 widgets in inventory. It should show 2, not 7.

This problem, known as the **lost-update problem**, exemplifies one of the special characteristics of multi-user database processing. To prevent this problem, some type of locking must be used to coordinate the activities of users who know nothing about one another. Locking brings its own set of problems, however, and those problems must be addressed as well. We will not delve further into this topic here, however.

Realize from this example that converting a single-user database to a multi-user database requires more than simply connecting another computer. The logic of the underlying application processing needs to be adjusted as well.

Be aware of possible data conflicts when you manage business activities that involve multi-user processing. If you find inaccurate results that seem not to have a cause, you may be experiencing multi-user data conflicts. Contact your IS department for assistance.

Enterprise DBMS Versus Personal DBMS

DBMS products fall into two broad categories. **Enterprise DBMS** products process large organizational and workgroup databases. These products support many, possibly thousands, of users and many different database applications. Such DBMS products support 24/7 operations and can manage databases that span dozens of different magnetic disks with hundreds of gigabytes or more of data. IBM's DB2, Microsoft's SQL Server, and Oracle's Oracle are examples of enterprise DBMS products.

Personal DBMS products are designed for smaller, simpler database applications. Such products are used for personal or small workgroup applications that involve fewer than 100 users, and normally fewer than 15. In fact, the great bulk of databases in this category have only a single user. The professor's Student database is an example of a database that is processed by a personal DBMS product.

In the past, there were many personal DBMS products—Paradox, dBase, R:base, and FoxPro. Microsoft put these products out of business when they developed Access and included it in the Microsoft Office suite. Today, about the only remaining personal DBMS is Microsoft Access.

To avoid one point of confusion for you in the future, the separation of application programs and the DBMS shown in Figure 5-10 is true only for enterprise DBMS products. Microsoft Access includes features and functions for application processing along with the DBMS itself. For example, Access has a form generator and a report generator. Thus, as shown in Figure 5-14, Access is both a DBMS *and* an application development product.

If one is to find innovative applications of database technology today, the best opportunity lies with inventing new applications, as discussed in the Innovation in Practice *box* *on page 158.*

Q5 How Are Data Models Used for Database Development?

In Chapter 10, we will describe the process for developing information systems in detail. However, business professionals have such a critical role in the development of database applications that we need to anticipate part of that discussion here by introducing two topics—data modeling and database design.

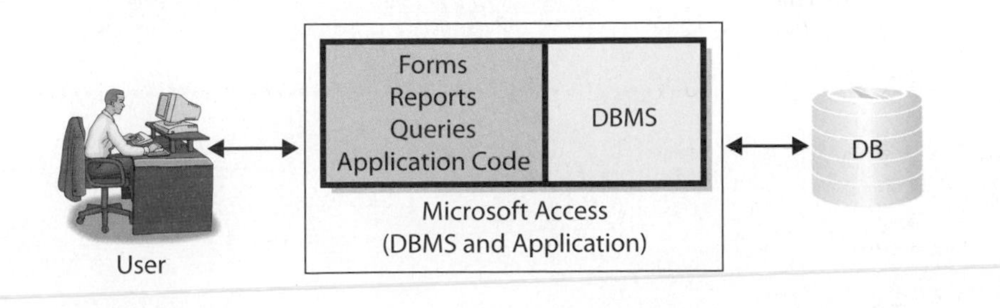

Figure 5-14
Personal Database System

INNOVATION IN PRACTICE

CHOIR INNOVATION

The RAND study cited in Chapter 1 indentified two types of innovation: inventing new technology and inventing new uses for existing technology. Relational database technology is more than 30 years old, and in the realm of information technology, that is ancient. Although there have been innovations, such as object-relational databases, semantic data models, form-oriented storage, and others, none have gained commercial prominence. Relational technology is a workhorse that works.

So, if one is to find innovative applications of database technology today, the best opportunity lies with inventing new applications, and one good source of such opportunities is spreadsheets that are misused for tasks better suited for databases.

For example, consider the spreadsheet in Figure 1, below, which is used to track the assignment of sheet music to a choir—it could be a church choir or school or community choir. The type of choir does not matter, because the problem is universal. Sheet music is expensive, choir members need to be able to take sheet music away for practice at home, and not all of the music gets back to the inventory. (Sheet music can be purchased or rented, but either way, lost music is an expense.)

Look closely at this data and you will see some data integrity problems—or at least some possible data integrity problems. For one, do Sandra Corning and Linda Duong really have the same copy of music checked out? Second, did Mozart and J. S. Bach both write a Requiem, or in row 15 should J. S. Bach actually be Mozart? Also, there is a problem with Eleanor Dixon's phone number; several phone numbers are the same as well, which seems suspicious.

Additionally, this spreadsheet is confusing and hard to use. The column labeled *First Name* includes both people names and the names of choruses. *Email* has both email addresses and composer names, and *Phone* has both phone numbers and copy identifiers. Furthermore, to record a checkout of music the user must first add a new row and then reenter the name of the work, the composer's name, and the copy to be checked out. Finally, consider what happens when the user wants to find all copies of a particular work: The user will have to examine the rows in each of four spreadsheets for the four voice parts.

In fact, a spreadsheet is ill-suited for this application. A database would be a far better tool, and situations like this are obvious candidates for innovation.

This example is continued as Collaboration Exercise 1 on page 178.

	A	B	C	D	E
1	**Last Name**	**First Name**	**Email**	**Phone**	**Part**
2	Ashley	Jane	JA@somewhere.com	703.555.1234	Soprano
3	Davidson	Kaye	KD@somewhere.com	703.555.2236	Soprano
4	Ching	Kam Hoong	KHC@overhere.com	703.555.2236	Soprano
5	Menstell	Lori Lee	LLM@somewhere.com	703.555.1237	Soprano
6	Corning	Sandra	SC2@overhere.com	703.555.1234	Soprano
7		B-minor mass	J.S. Bach	Soprano Copy 7	
8		Requiem	Mozart	Soprano Copy 17	
9		9th Symphony Chorus	Beethoven	Soprano Copy 9	
10	Wei	Guang	GW1@somewhere.com	703.555.9936	Soprano
11	Dixon	Eleanor	ED@thisplace.com	703.555.12379	Soprano
12		B-minor mass	J.S. Bach	Soprano Copy 11	
13	Duong	Linda	LD2@overhere.com	703.555.8736	Soprano
14		B-minor mass	J.S. Bach	Soprano Copy 7	
15		Requiem	J.S. Bach	Soprano Copy 19	
16	Lunden	Haley	HL@somewhere.com	703.555.0836	Soprano
17	Utran	Diem Thi	DTU@somewhere.com	703.555.1089	Soprano

Figure 1
Spreadsheet Used for Assignment of Sheet Music

As Rick Torbert says in this chapter's opening interview, user involvement is critical for database development because the design of the database depends entirely on how users view their business environment. Think about the Student database. What data should it contain? Possibilities are: *Students, Classes, Grades, Emails, Office_Visits, Majors, Advisers, Student_Organizations*—the list could go on and on. Further, how much detail should be included in each? Should the database include campus addresses? Home addresses? Billing addresses?

In fact, there are dozens of possibilities, and the database developers do not and cannot know what to include. They do know, however, that a database must include all the data necessary for the users to perform their jobs. Ideally, it contains that amount of data and no more. So, during database development the developers must rely on the users to tell them what to include in the database.

Database structures can be complex, in some cases very complex. So, before building the database the developers construct a logical representation of database data called a **data model**. It describes the data and relationships that will be stored in the database. It is akin to a blueprint. Just as building architects create a blueprint before they start building, so, too, database developers create a data model before they start designing the database.

To understand the underlying nature of the problem, see the Problem-Solving Guide *on page 174.*

Figure 5-15 summarizes the database development process. Interviews with users lead to database requirements, which are summarized in a data model. Once the users have approved (validated) the data model, it is transformed into a database design. That design is then implemented into database structures. We will consider data modeling and database design briefly in the next two sections. Again, your goal should be to learn the process so that you can be an effective user representative for a development effort.

What Is the Entity-Relationship Data Model?

The **entity-relationship (E-R) data model** is a tool for constructing data models. Developers use it to describe the content of a data model by defining the things (*entities*) that will be stored in the database and the *relationships* among those entities. A second, less popular, tool for data modeling is the **Unified Modeling Language (UML)**. We will not describe that tool here. However, if you learn how to interpret E-R models, with a bit of study you will be able to understand UML models as well.

Entities

An **entity** is some thing that the users want to track. Examples of entities are *Order, Customer, Salesperson,* and *Item.* Some entities represent a physical object, such as *Item* or *Salesperson;* others represent a logical construct or transaction, such as *Order* or *Contract.* For reasons beyond this discussion, entity names are always singular. We use *Order,* not *Orders; Salesperson,* not *Salespersons.*

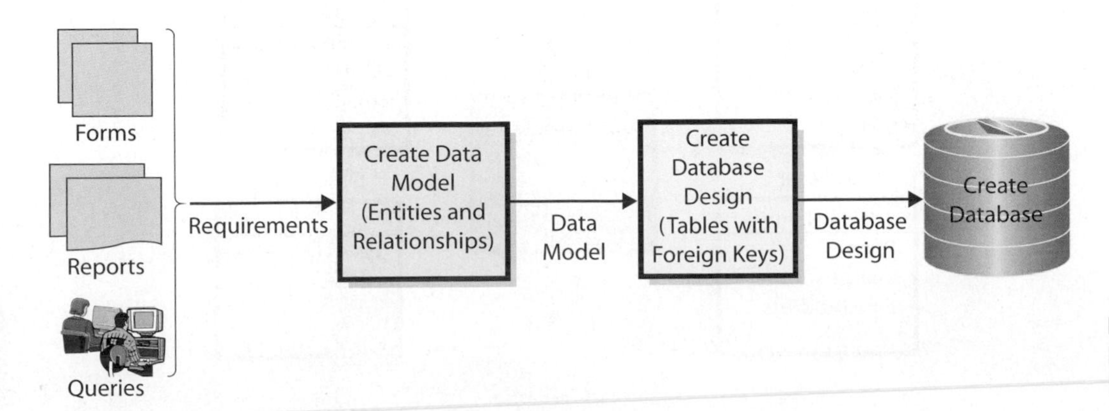

Figure 5-15
Database Development Process

Entities have **attributes** that describe characteristics of the entity. Example attributes of *Order* are *OrderNumber, OrderDate, SubTotal, Tax, Total,* and so forth. Example attributes of *Salesperson* are *SalespersonName, Email, Phone,* and so forth.

Entities have an **identifier**, which is an attribute (or group of attributes) whose value is associated with one and only one entity instance. For example, *OrderNumber* is an identifier of *Order,* because only one *Order* instance has a given value of *OrderNumber.* For the same reason, *CustomerNumber* is an identifier of *Customer.* If each member of the sales staff has a unique name, then *SalespersonName* is an identifier of *Salesperson.*

Before we continue, consider that last sentence. Is the salesperson's name unique among the sales staff? Both now and in the future? Who decides the answer to such a question? Only the users know whether this is true; the database developers cannot know. This example underlines why it is important for you to be able to interpret data models, because only users like you will know for sure.

Figure 5-16 shows examples of entities for the Student database. Each entity is shown in a rectangle. The name of the entity is just above the rectangle, and the identifier is shown in a section at the top of the entity. Entity attributes are shown in the remainder of the rectangle. In Figure 5-16, the *Adviser* entity has an identifier called *AdviserName* and the attributes *Phone, CampusAddress,* and *EmailAddress.*

Observe that the entities *Email* and *Office_Visit* do not have an identifier. Unlike *Student* or *Adviser*, the users do not have an attribute that identifies a particular email. We *could* make one up. For example, we could say that the identifier of *Email* is *EmailNumber*, but if we do so we are not modeling how the users view their world. Instead, we are forcing something onto the users. Be aware of this possibility when you review data models about your business. Do not allow the database developers to create something in the data model that is not part of your business world.

Relationships

Entities have **relationships** to each other. An *Order,* for example, has a relationship to a *Customer* entity and also to a *Salesperson* entity. In the Student database, a *Student* has a relationship to an *Adviser*, and an *Adviser* has a relationship to a *Department.*

Figure 5-17 shows sample *Department, Adviser,* and *Student* entities and their relationships. For simplicity, this figure shows just the identifier of the entities and not the other attributes. For this sample data, *Accounting* has three professors—Jones, Wu, and Lopez—and *Finance* has two professors—Smith and Greene.

The relationship between *Advisers* and *Students* is a bit more complicated, because in this example an adviser is allowed to advise many students, and a student

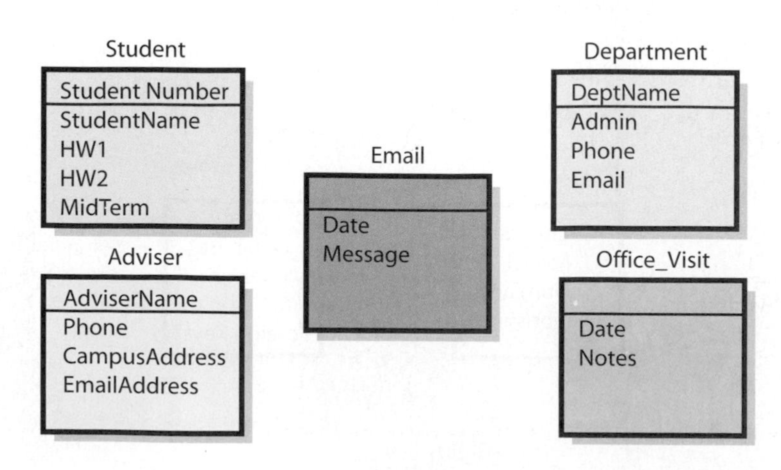

Figure 5-16
Student Data Model Entities

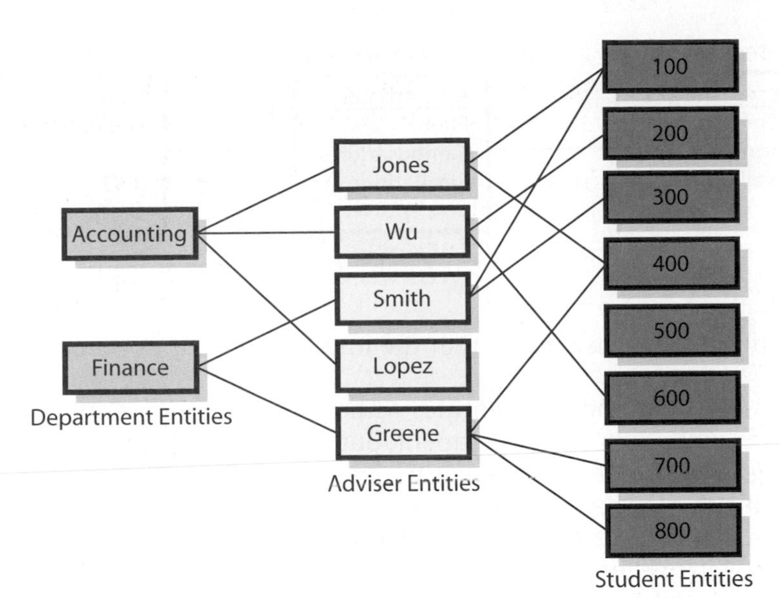

Figure 5-17
Example of Department, Adviser, and Student Entities and Relationships

is allowed to have many advisers. Perhaps this happens because students can have multiple majors. In any case, note that Professor Jones advises students 100 and 400 and that student 100 is advised by both Professors Jones and Smith.

Diagrams like the one in Figure 5-17 are too cumbersome for use in database design discussions. Instead, database designers use diagrams called **entity-relationship (E-R) diagrams**. Figure 5-18 shows an E-R diagram for the data in Figure 5-17. In this figure, all of the entities of one type are represented by a single rectangle. Thus, there are rectangles for the *Department, Adviser,* and *Student* entities. Attributes are shown as before in Figure 5-16.

Additionally, a line is used to represent a relationship between two entities. Notice the line between *Department* and *Adviser,* for example. The forked lines on the right side of that line signify that a department may have more than one adviser. The little lines, which are referred to as **crow's feet**, are shorthand for the multiple lines between *Department* and *Adviser* in Figure 5-17. Relationships like this one are called **1:N**, or **one-to-many**, relationships because one department can have many advisers.

Now examine the line between *Adviser* and *Student.* Here, a crow's foot appears at each end of the line. This notation signifies that an adviser can be related to many students and that a student can be related to many advisers, which is the situation in Figure 5-17. Relationships like this one are called **N:M**, or **many-to-many**, relationships because one adviser can have many students and one student can have many advisers.

Students sometimes find the notation N:M confusing. Interpret the *N* and *M* to mean that a variable number, greater than one, is allowed on each side of the relationship. Such a relationship is not written *N:N,* because that notation would imply that there are the same number of entities on each side of the relationship, which is not necessarily true. *N:M* means that more than one entity is allowed on

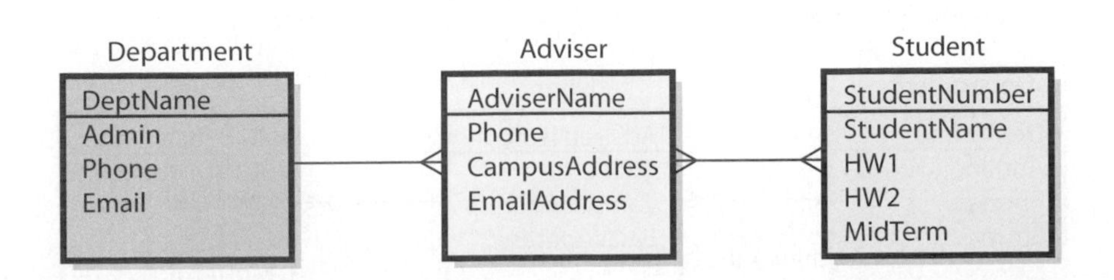

Figure 5-18
Sample Relationships—Version 1

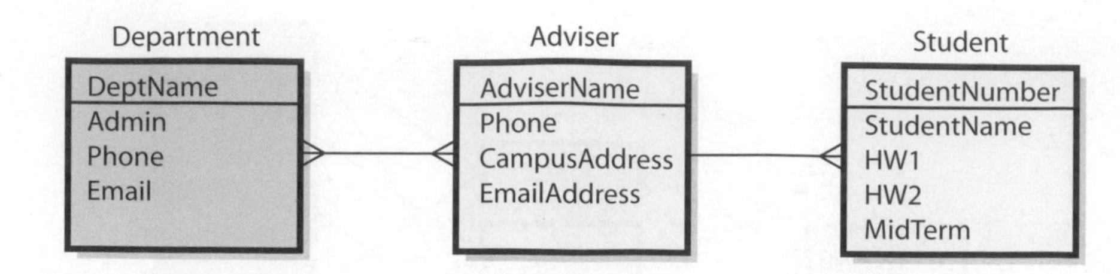

Figure 5-19
Sample Relationships—Version 2

each side of the relationship and that the number of entities on each side can be different.

Figure 5-19 shows the same entities with different assumptions. Here, advisers may advise in more than one department, but a student may have only one adviser, representing a policy that students may not have multiple majors.

Which, if either, of these versions is correct? Only the users know. These alternatives illustrate the kinds of questions you will need to answer when a database designer asks you to check a data model for correctness.

Figure 5-18 and 5-19 are typical examples of an entity-relationship diagram. Unfortunately, there are several different styles of entity-relationship diagrams. This one is called, not surprisingly, a **crow's-foot diagram version**. You may learn other versions if you take a database management class.

The crow's-foot notation shows the maximum number of entities that can be involved in a relationship. Accordingly, they are called the relationship's **maximum cardinality**. Common examples of maximum cardinality are 1:N, N:M, and 1:1 (not shown).

Another important question is, "What is the minimum number of entities required in the relationship?" Must an adviser have a student to advise, and must a student have an adviser? Constraints on minimum requirements are called **minimum cardinalities**.

Figure 5-20 presents a third version of this E-R diagram that shows both maximum and minimum cardinalities. The vertical bar on a line means that at least one entity of that type is required. The small oval means that the entity is optional; the relationship *need not* have an entity of that type.

Thus, in Figure 5-20 a department is not required to have a relationship to any adviser, but an adviser is required to belong to a department. Similarly, an adviser is not required to have a relationship to a student, but a student is required to have a relationship to an adviser. Note, also, that the maximum cardinalities in Figure 5-20 have been changed so that both are 1:N.

The Database Processing in Practice *box on page 163 demonstrates the importance of having a data model that reflects the way the users think about their activities.*

Is the model in Figure 5-20 a good one? It depends on the policy of the university. Again, only the users know for sure.

Q6 How Is a Data Model Transformed Into a Database Design?

Database design is the process of converting a data model into tables, relationships, and data constraints. The database design team transforms entities into tables and expresses relationships by defining foreign keys. Database design is a

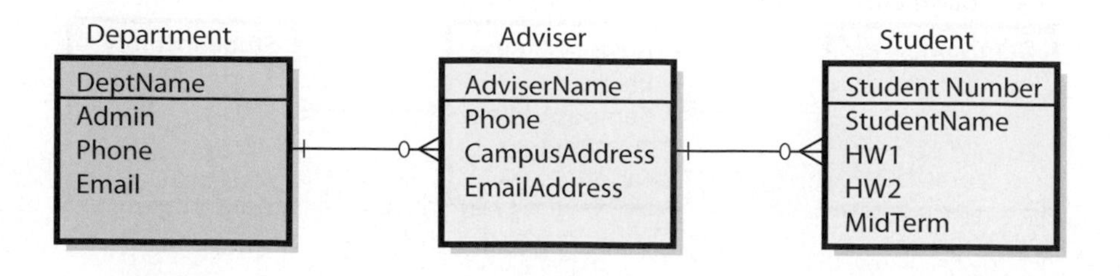

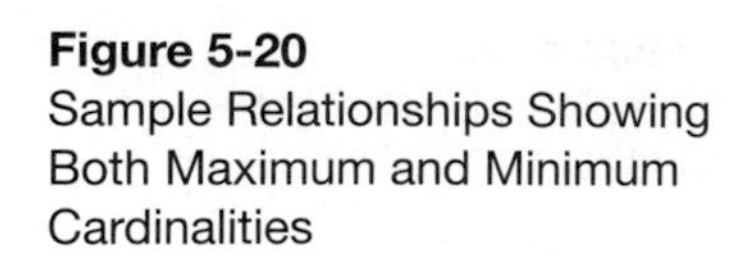
Figure 5-20
Sample Relationships Showing Both Maximum and Minimum Cardinalities

DATABASE PROCESSING IN PRACTICE

THANKS FOR VOLUNTEERING

Suppose you are the manager of fund-raising for a local public television station. Twice a year you conduct fund drives during which the station runs commercials that ask viewers to donate. These drives are important; they provide nearly 40 percent of the station's operating budget.

One of your job functions is to find volunteers to staff the phones during these drives. You need 10 volunteers per night for 6 nights, or 60 people, twice per year. The volunteers' job is exhausting, and normally a volunteer will work only one night during a drive.

Finding volunteers for each drive is a perpetual headache. Two months before a drive begins, you and your staff start calling to find volunteers. You first call volunteers from prior drives, using a roster that your administrative assistant prepares for each drive. Some volunteers have been helping for years; you'd like to know that information before you call them so that you can tell them how much you appreciate their continuing support. Unfortunately, the roster does not have that data.

Additionally, some volunteers are more effective than others. Some have a particular knack for increasing the callers' donations. Although those data are available, the information is not in a format that you can use when calling for volunteers. You think you could better staff the fund-raising drives if you had that missing information.

You know that you can use a computer database to keep better track of prior volunteers' service and performance. You are not quite sure how to proceed until you learn that one of your volunteers is a database consultant, and you ask her to help. Unfortunately, she has very little time, and in fact is about to move overseas for an extended consulting agreement. She does, however, have time to interview key members of your staff.

Before she leaves, she creates the prototype (a sample) of a data entry form, which is shown in Figure 1, below. She says she thinks the form represents the way that employees view their data, but she isn't sure. Normally, she would create a data model of this form and review that data model with your employees. Unfortunately, she does not have time to do that before she leaves.

You and a team of your fellow students will be given an opportunity, in Collaboration Exercise 2, page 179, to develop and review the data model that underlies this prototype. You will also have a chance to design the database for the data model you create.

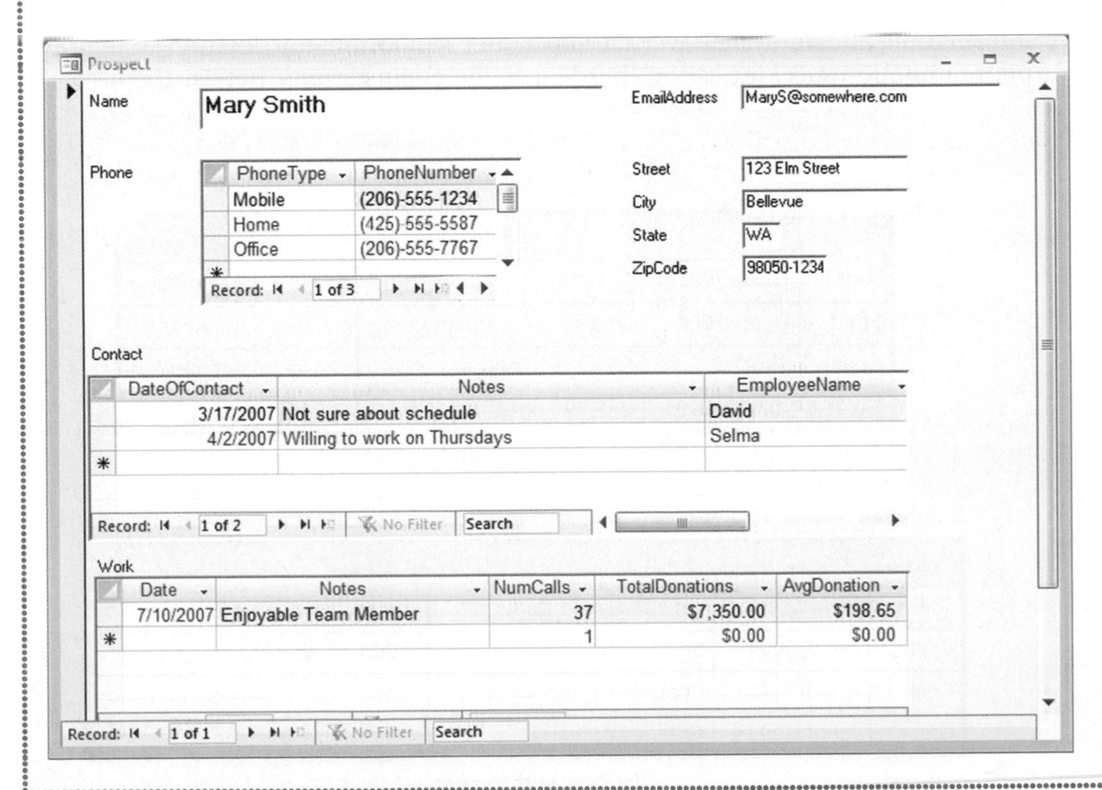

Figure 1
Prototype Data-Entry Form for Volunteer Prospects

complicated subject; as with data modeling, it occupies weeks in a database management class. In this section, however, we will introduce two important database design concepts: normalization and the representation of two kinds of relationships. The first concept is a foundation of database design, and the second will help you understand important design considerations.

Normalization

Normalization is the process of converting a poorly structured table into two or more well-structured tables. A table is such a simple construct that you may wonder how one could possibly be poorly structured. In truth, there are many ways that tables can be malformed—so many, in fact, that researchers have published hundreds of papers on this topic alone.

Consider the *Employee* table in Figure 5-21(a). It lists employee names, hire dates, email addresses, and the name and number of the department in which the employee works. This table seems innocent enough. But consider what happens when the Accounting department changes its name to Accounting and Finance. Because department names are duplicated in this table, every row that has a value of "Accounting" must be changed to "Accounting and Finance."

Data Integrity Problems

Suppose the Accounting name change is correctly made in two rows, but not in the third. The result is shown in Figure 5-21(b). This table has what is called a **data integrity problem**: Some rows indicate that the name of Department 100 is "Accounting and Finance," and another row indicates that the name of Department 100 is "Accounting."

This problem is easy to spot in this small table. But consider a table like the *Customer* table in the Amazon.com database or the Verizon database. Those databases may have millions of rows. Once a table that large develops serious data integrity problems, months of labor will be required to remove them.

Data integrity problems are serious. A table that has data integrity problems will produce incorrect and inconsistent information. Users will lose confidence in the information, and the system will develop a poor reputation. Information systems with poor reputations become serious burdens to the organizations that use them.

Employee

Name	HireDate	Email	DeptNo	DeptName
Jones	Feb 1, 2002	Jones@ourcompany.com	100	Accounting
Smith	Dec 3, 2004	Smith@ourcompany.com	200	Marketing
Chau	March 7, 2004	Chau@ourcompany.com	100	Accounting
Greene	July 17, 2003	Greene@ourcompany.com	100	Accounting

(a) Table Before Update

Employee

Name	HireDate	Email	DeptNo	DeptName
Jones	Feb 1, 2002	Jones@ourcompany.com	100	Accounting and Finance
Smith	Dec 3, 2004	Smith@ourcompany.com	200	Marketing
Chau	March 7, 2004	Chau@ourcompany.com	100	Accounting and Finance
Greene	July 17, 2003	Greene@ourcompany.com	100	Accounting

(b) Table with Incomplete Update

Figure 5-21
A Poorly Designed Employee Table

Normalizing for Data Integrity

The data integrity problem can occur only if data are duplicated. Because of this, one easy way to eliminate the problem is to eliminate the duplicated data. We can do this by transforming the table in Figure 5-21 into two tables, as shown in Figure 5-22. Here, the name of the department is stored just once, therefore no data inconsistencies can occur.

Of course, to produce an employee report that includes the department name, the two tables in Figure 5-22 will need to be joined back together. Because such joining of tables is common, DBMS products have been programmed to perform it efficiently, but it still requires work. From this example, you can see a trade-off in database design: Normalized tables eliminate data duplication, but they can be slower to process. Dealing with such trade-offs is an important consideration in database design.

The general goal of normalization is to construct tables such that every table has a *single* topic or theme. In good writing, every paragraph should have a single theme. This is true of databases as well; every table should have a single theme. The problem with the table in Figure 5-21 is that it has two independent themes: employees and departments. The way to correct the problem is to split the table into two tables, each with its own theme. In this case, we create an *Employee* table and a *Department* table, as shown in Figure 5-22.

As mentioned, there are dozens of ways that tables can be poorly formed. Database practitioners classify tables into various **normal forms** according to the kinds of problems they have. Transforming a table into a normal form to remove duplicated data and other problems is called *normalizing* the table.[2] Thus, when you hear a database designer say, "Those tables are not normalized," she does not mean that the tables have irregular, not-normal data. Instead, she means that the tables have a format that could cause data integrity problems.

Summary of Normalization

As a future user of databases, you do not need to know the details of normalization. Instead, understand the general principle that every normalized (well-formed) table has one and only one theme. Further, tables that are not normalized are subject to data integrity problems.

Be aware, too, that normalization is just one criterion for evaluating database designs. Because normalized designs can be slower to process, database designers

Employee

Name	HireDate	Email	DeptNo
Jones	Feb 1, 2002	Jones@ourcompany.com	100
Smith	Dec 3, 2004	Smith@ourcompany.com	200
Chau	March 7, 2004	Chau@ourcompany.com	100
Greene	July 17, 2003	Greene@ourcompany.com	100

Department

DeptNo	DeptName
100	Accounting
200	Marketing
300	Information Systems

Figure 5-22
Two Normalized Tables

[2]See David Kroenke, *Database Processing*, 10th ed. (Upper Saddle River, NJ: Prentice Hall, 2006) for more information.

sometimes choose to accept non-normalized tables. The best design depends on the users' requirements.

Representing Relationships

Figure 5-23 shows the steps involved in transforming a data model into a relational database design. First, the database designer creates a table for each entity. The identifier of the entity becomes the key of the table. Each attribute of the entity becomes a column of the table. Next, the resulting tables are normalized so that each table has a single theme. Once that has been done, the next step is to represent relationship among those tables.

For example, consider the E-R diagram in Figure 5-24(a). The *Adviser* entity has a 1:N relationship to the *Student* entity. To create the database design, we construct a table for *Adviser* and a second table for *Student,* as shown in Figure 5-24(b). The key of the *Adviser* table is *AdviserName,* and the key of the *Student* table is *StudentNumber*.

Further, the *EmailAddress* attribute of the *Adviser* entity becomes the *EmailAddress* column of the *Adviser* table, and the *StudentName* and *MidTerm* attributes of the *Student* entity become the *StudentName* and *MidTerm* columns of the *Student* table.

The next task is to represent the relationship. Because we are using the relational model, we know that we must add a foreign key to one of the two tables. The possibilities are: (1) place the foreign key *StudentNumber* in the *Adviser* table or (2) place the foreign key *AdviserName* in the *Student* table.

The correct choice is to place *AdviserName* in the *Student* table, as shown in Figure 5-24(c). To determine a student's adviser, we just look into the *AdviserName* column of that student's row. To determine the adviser's students, we search the *AdviserName* column in the *Student* table to determine which rows have that adviser's name. If a student changes advisers, we simply change the value in the *AdviserName* column. Changing *Jackson* to *Jones* in the first row, for example, will assign student 100 to Professor Jones.

For this data model, placing *StudentNumber* in *Adviser* would be incorrect. If we were to do that, we could assign only one student to an adviser. There is no place to assign a second adviser.

This strategy for placing foreign keys will not work for all relationships, however. Consider the data model in Figure 5-25(a) (page 168); here advisers and students have a many-to-many relationship. An adviser may have many students, and a student may have multiple advisers (for multiple majors).

The foreign key strategy we used for the 1:N data model will not work here. To see why, examine Figure 5-25(b). If student 100 has more than one adviser, there is no place to record second or subsequent advisers.

To represent an N:M relationship, we need to create a third table as shown in Figure 5-25(c). The third table has two columns, *AdviserName* and *StudentNumber*. Each row of the table means that the given adviser advises the student with the given number.

As you can imagine, there is a great deal more to database design than we have presented here. Still, this section should give you an idea of the tasks that need to be accomplished to create a database. You should also realize that the database design is a direct consequence of decisions made in the data model. If the data model is wrong, the database design will be wrong as well.

- Represent each entity with a table
  - Entity identifier becomes table key
  - Entity attributes become table columns
- Normalize tables as necessary
- Represent relationships
  - Use foreign keys
  - Add additional tables for N:M relationships

Figure 5-23
Transforming a Data Model into a Database Design

Figure 5-24
Representing a 1:N Relationship

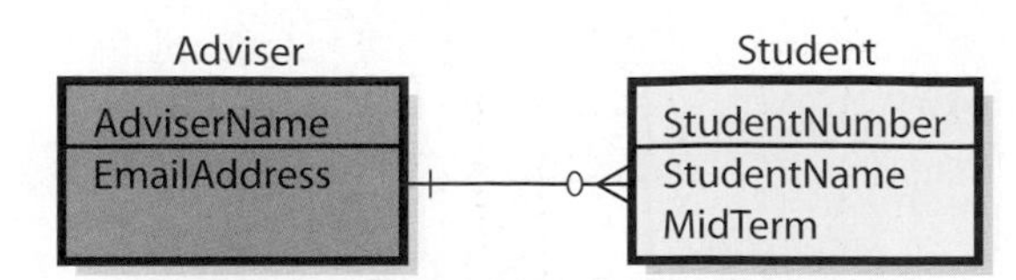

(a) 1:N Relationship Between Adviser and Student Entities

Adviser Table—Key is AdviserName

AdviserName	EmailAddress
Jones	Jones@myuniv.edu
Choi	Choi@myuniv.edu
Jackson	Jackson@myuniv.edu

Student Table—Key is StudentNumber

StudentNumber	StudentName	MidTerm
100	Lisa	90
200	Jennie	85
300	Jason	82
400	Terry	95

(b) Creating a Table for Each Entity

Adviser Table—Key is AdviserName

AdviserName	Email
Jones	Jones@myuniv.edu
Choi	Choi@myuniv.edu
Jackson	Jackson@myuniv.edu

Student—Key is StudentNumber

Foreign Key Column Represents Relationship

StudentNumber	StudentName	MidTerm	AdviserName
100	Lisa	90	Jackson
200	Jennie	85	Jackson
300	Jason	82	Choi
400	Terry	95	Jackson

(c) Using the *AdviserName* Foreign Key to Represent the 1:N Relationship

Q7 What Is the Users' Role in the Development of Databases?

As stated, a database is a model of how the users view their business world. This means that the users are the final judges as to what data the database should contain and how the records in that database should be related to one another.

The easiest time to change the database structure is during the data modeling stage. Changing a relationship from one-to-many to many-to-many in a data model is simply a matter of changing the 1:N notation to N:M. However, once the database has been constructed, loaded with data, and application forms, reports, queries, and application programs have been created, changing a one-to-many relationship to many-to-many means weeks of work.

Figure 5-25
Representing an N:M Relationship

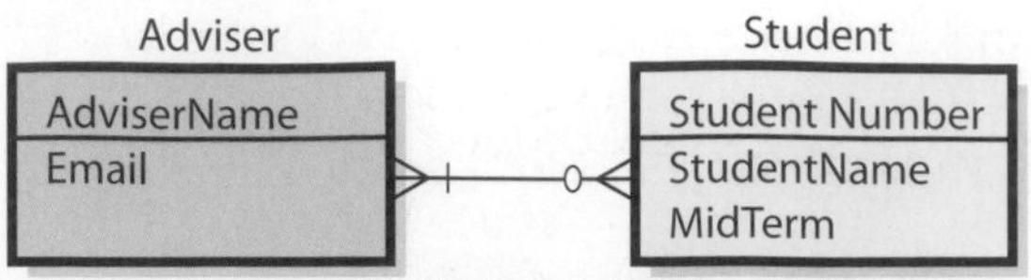

(a) N:M Relationship Between Adviser and Student

Adviser—Key is AdviserName

AdviserName	Email
Jones	Jones@myuniv.edu
Choi	Choi@myuniv.edu
Jackson	Jackson@myuniv.edu

No room to place second or third AdviserName

Student—Key is StudentNumber

StudentNumber	StudentName	MidTerm	AdviserName
100	Lisa	90	Jackson
200	Jennie	85	Jackson
300	Jason	82	Choi
400	Terry	95	Jackson

(b) Incorrect Representation of N:M Relationship

Adviser—Key is AdviserName

AdviserName	Email
Jones	Jones@myuniv.edu
Choi	Choi@myuniv.edu
Jackson	Jackson@myuniv.edu

Student—Key is StudentNumber

StudentNumber	StudentName	MidTerm
100	Lisa	90
200	Jennie	85
300	Jason	82
400	Terry	95

Adviser_Student_Intersection

AdviserName	StudentNumber
Jackson	100
Jackson	200
Choi	300
Jackson	400
Choi	100
Jones	100

Student 100 has three advisers.

(c) Adviser_Student_Intersection Table Represents the N:M Relationship

You can glean some idea of why this might be true by contrasting Figure 5-24(c) with Figure 5-25(c). Suppose that instead of having just a few rows, each table has thousands of rows; in that case, transforming the database from one format to the other involves considerable work. Even worse, however, is that someone must change application components as well. For example, if students have at most one adviser, then a single text box can be used to enter *AdviserName*. If students can have multiple advisers, then a multiple-row table will need to be used to enter *AdviserName* and a program will need to be written to store the values of *AdviserName* into the *Adviser_Student_Intersection* table. There are dozens of other consequences, consequences that will translate into wasted labor and wasted expense.

Thus, ***user review of the data model is crucial***. When a database is developed for your use, you must carefully review the data model. If you do not understand any aspect of it, you should ask for clarification until you do. *Entities must contain all of the data you and your employees need to do your jobs, and relationships must accurately reflect your view of the business.* If the data model is wrong, the database will be designed incorrectly, and the applications will be difficult to use, if not worthless. Do not proceed unless the data model is accurate.

As a corollary, when asked to review a data model, take that review seriously. Devote the time necessary to perform a thorough review. Any mistakes you miss will come back to haunt you, and by then the cost of correction may be very high with regard to both time and expense. This brief introduction to data modeling shows why databases can be more difficult to develop than spreadsheets.

Q8 What Are the Responsibilities for Database Administration?

Databases are valuable and often critical resources. Recall from the Chapter 3 interview that the COO of The Firm said the one asset they could not afford to lose is their customer database. In other companies, hundreds or even thousands of users depend on database applications to perform their jobs. Some databases are critical components of operational systems, and the failure of the database can mean stopping the production line. Smaller databases, even personal databases, can contain critical data, and their failure can mean lost opportunities and wasted labor.

In general, the more encompassing the database—the more systems and business functions it touches—the greater the utility of the database. At the same time, the more encompassing the database, the greater the potential for problems. For example, those who work in production and those who work in sales have very different goals and objectives. Long-term planning in production is 3 to 5 years from now; long-term planning in sales is, "What are we doing after lunch?" For a database being designed to serve both groups, a development pace that seems timely to one group can seem glacial to another.

In light of both the importance and the management challenges of databases, most organizations have created a staff function called **database administration.** In smaller organizations, this function usually is served by a single person, sometimes even on a part-time basis. Larger organizations assign several people to an office of database administration. Depending on context, the letters **DBA** either stand for the *database administrator* or for the *office of database administration.*

The purpose of database administration is to manage the development, operation, and maintenance of the database so as to achieve the organization's objectives. This function requires balancing two conflicting goals: protecting the database while maximizing its availability for authorized use. It is a staff function; DBAs seldom have direct management authority over either developers or users. Yet to be successful, the DBA must often influence and control the actions of each group.

Figure 5-26 (next page) summarizes database administration tasks. In the next section, we will describe these tasks as they would be performed by an office of database administration that is supporting a major enterprise database. Database administration for smaller workgroup and personal databases is similar, except that the work is reduced in scale and scope.

DBA Development Responsibilities

Generally, the DBA function is staffed sometime during the first systems development project that requires the database. The earlier in the systems development process the DBA is created the better. We will say more about project management for systems development in Chapter 10; here we will focus on those aspects that pertain to the DBA.

The DBA is not a user of the database or of any of its applications. Instead, the DBA is an auditor, a consultant, sometimes a policeman, and a diplomat who works as

Figure 5-26
Summary of Database Administration Tasks

Category	Database Administration Task	Description
Development	Create and staff DBA function	Size of DBA group depends on size and complexity of database. Groups range from one part-time person to small group.
	Form steering committee	Consists of representatives of all user groups. Forum for community-wide discussions and decisions.
	Specify requirements	Ensure that all appropriate user input is considered.
	Validate data model	Check data model for accuracy and completeness.
	Evaluate application design	Verify that all necessary forms, reports, queries, and applications are developed. Validate design and usability of application components.
Operation	Manage processing rights and responsibilities	Determine processing rights/restrictions on each table and column.
	Manage security	Add and delete users and user groups as necessary; ensure that security system works.
	Track problems and manage resolution	Develop system to record and manage resolution of problems.
	Monitor database performance	Provide expertise/solutions for performance improvements.
	Manage DBMS	Evaluate new features and functions.
Backup and Recovery	Monitor backup procedures	Verify that database backup procedures are followed.
	Conduct training	Ensure that users and operations personnel know and understand recovery procedures.
	Manage recovery	Manage recovery process.
Adaptation	Set up request tracking system	Develop system to record and prioritize requests for change.
	Manage configuration change	Manage impact of database structure changes on applications and users.

a liaison between the users and professional developers. Accordingly, one of the first tasks for the DBA is to create a steering committee that consists of key users. The DBA uses this committee as a forum for community-wide decisions regarding the development, use, and maintenance of the database.

From the start, the DBA needs to ensure that users are appropriately involved in the development process. The requirements specifications must include the needs of all appropriate users. Representatives from all key user groups need to verify and validate the data model during the development process. Also, the DBA needs to ensure that user representatives verify and validate application component designs and implementations.

DBA Operations Responsibilities

Humans struggle to share. We see that played out with toys in the sandbox in preschool, and we see it with databases in organizations at work. People want to process the database to meet their own needs, first. Conflict is inevitable.

For example, suppose an employee leaves the firm. When should that employee's records be deleted from the database? From the point of view of those who write the company's paychecks, they should be deleted at the end of the next pay period. From the point of view of those who prepare the end-of-quarter financial statements, they should be deleted at the end of the quarter. From the point of view of those who write out W-2 tax forms, they should be deleted at the end of the year. From the point of view of those who respond to an IRS audit of the company, they should be deleted after 3, 7, or more years.

Without someone to help users manage these different views, chaos results. The user with the loudest voice wins. Thus, an important DBA function is to establish community-wide policies for the processing of the database. The DBA uses the steering committee to determine processing rights for each column of each table. These rights include what data users are authorized to read, create, modify, and delete. The DBA also works with development personnel to ensure that a security system is in place to enforce these processing rights.

Finally, the DBA needs to track problems and manage problem solutions. Sometimes the solutions involve new user procedures and training; other times they require changes in application programs or the database. Sometimes solutions involve installing new features of the DBMS. Enterprise DBMS products such as Oracle or DB2 provide many different DBMS features and functions. In some cases, the DBA and development personnel can resolve problems by installing and using additional DBMS functions.

DBA Backup and Recovery Responsibilities

Failures occur. Hardware malfunctions, software has errors, users make mistakes, hurricanes and earthquakes happen. The time to think about these possibilities is long before they occur.

As the protector of the database, the DBA has the responsibility to ensure that appropriate procedures and policies exist for backing up the database and that those procedures are followed. Additionally, the DBA needs to ensure that users and operations personnel are appropriately trained with regard to backup and recovery procedures.

Finally, when failures occur, in many organizations the DBA is responsible for managing the recovery process. Even if the DBA does not have the ultimate responsibility for recovery (it may lie with the operations staff), the DBA has a key role during these times. We will discuss the development of such procedures in Chapter 11.

DBA Responsibilities for Adaptation

Adaptation is the last category of responsibilities in Figure 5-26. Over time, requirements for the database will change. In fact, the database and the systems that process it are often a major cause of the need for change. Changes that benefit one group in the organization may not benefit other groups. For example, a new feature for one group may mean slower performance for another group. Accordingly, the DBA needs to set up a system for recording and tracking requests for changes.

The steering committee meets periodically to discuss and prioritize the implementation of new features of the database and new functions for database applications. Again, these decisions must be made with a community-wide view. The responsibility of the DBA is to provide the forum and to ensure that requests are considered and acted upon in a responsible manner.

Is the DBA a Technical Person?

The DBA function has broad managerial responsibilities for the database. Part of that function is technical: Monitoring performance, managing the DBMS, and developing backup and recovery procedures all require strong technical DBMS skills. But, for larger organizations, and for databases that touch many different departments and business functions, the DBA's job is more diplomatic than technical. It is a mistake to staff the DBA function only with technical personnel. The DBA is a staff function with little authority. It can only request changes; it cannot order them. Therefore, for the person in this role, much of the time, diplomacy matters more than technical skill.

Opposing Forces

GUIDE

No, Thanks, I'll Use a Spreadsheet

I'm not buying all this stuff about databases. I've tried them and they're a pain—way too complicated to set up, and most of the time, a spreadsheet works just as well. We had one project at the car dealership that seemed pretty simple to me: We wanted to keep track of customers and the models of used cars they were interested in. Then, when we got a car on the lot, we could query the database to see who wanted a car of that type and generate a letter to them.

"It took forever to build that system, and it never did work right. We hired three different consultants, and the last one finally did get it to work. But it was so complicated to produce the letters. You had to query the data in Access to generate some kind of file, then open Word, then go through some mumbo jumbo using mail/merge to cause Word to find the letter and put all the Access data in the right spot. I once printed over two hundred letters and had the name in the address spot and the address in the name spot and no date. And it took me over an hour to do even that. I just wanted to do the query and push a button to get my letters generated. I gave up. Some of the salespeople are still trying to use it, but not me.

"No, unless you are General Motors or Toyota, I wouldn't mess with a database. You have to have professional IS people to create it and keep it running. Besides, I don't really want to share my data with anyone. I work pretty hard to develop my client list. Why would I want to give it away?

"My motto is, 'Keep it simple.' I use an Excel spreadsheet with four columns: Name, Phone Number, Car Interests, and Notes. When I get a new customer, I enter the name and phone number, and then I put the make and model of cars they like in the Car Interests column. Anything else that I think is important I put in the Notes column—extra phone numbers, address data if I have it, email addresses, spouse names, last time I called them, etc. The system isn't fancy, but it works fine.

"When I want to find something, I use Excel's Data Filter. I can usually get what I need. Of course, I still can't send form letters, but it really doesn't matter. I get most of my sales using the phone, anyway." ■

Discussion Questions

1. To what extent do you agree with the opinions presented here? To what extent are the concerns expressed here justified? To what extent might they be due to other factors?
2. What problems do you see with the way that the car salesperson stores address data? What will he have to do if he ever does want to send a letter or an email to all of his customers?
3. From his comments, how many different themes are there in his data? What does this imply about his ability to keep his data in a spreadsheet?
4. Does the concern about not sharing data relate to whether or not he uses a database?
5. Apparently, management at the car dealership allows the salespeople to keep their contact data in whatever format they want. If you were management, how would you justify this policy? What disadvantages are there to this policy?
6. Suppose you manage the sales representatives, and you decide to require all of them to use a database to keep track of customers and customer car interest data. How would you sell your decision to this salesperson?
7. Given the limited information in this scenario, do you think a database or a spreadsheet is a better solution?

Problem-Solving

GUIDE

Immanuel Kant, Data Modeler

Only the users can say whether a data model accurately reflects their business environment. What happens when the users disagree among themselves? What if one user says orders have a single salesperson but another says that sales teams produce some orders? Who is correct?

It's tempting to say, "The correct model is the one that better represents the real world." The problem with this statement is that data models do not model "the real world." A data model is simply a model of what the data modeler perceives. This very important point can be difficult to understand; but if you do understand it, you will save many hours in data model validation meetings and be a much better data modeling team member.

The German philosopher Immanuel Kant reasoned that what we perceive as reality is based on our perceptive apparatus. That which we perceive he called phenomena. Our perceptions, such as of light and sound, are processed by our brains and made meaningful. But we do not and cannot know whether the images we create from the perceptions have anything to do with what might or might not really be.

Kant used the term *noumenal world* to refer to the essence of "things in themselves"—to whatever it is out there that gives rise to our perceptions and images. He used the term *phenomenal world* to refer to what we humans perceive and construct.

It is easy to confuse the noumenal world with the phenomenal world, because we share the phenomenal world with other humans. All of us have the same mental apparatus, and we all make the same constructions. If you ask your roommate to hand you the toothpaste, she hands you the toothpaste, not a hairbrush. But the fact that we share this mutual view does not mean that the mutual view describes in any way what is truly out there. Dogs construct a world based on smells, and orca whales construct a world based on sounds. What the "real world" is to a dog, a whale, and a human are completely different. All of this means that we cannot ever justify a data model as a "better representation of the real world." Nothing that humans can do represents the real, noumenal world. A data model, therefore, is a model of a human's model of what appears to be "out there." For example, a model of a salesperson is a model of the model that humans make of salespeople.

To return to the question that we started with, what do we do when people disagree about what should be in a data model? First, realize that anyone attempting to justify her data model as a better representation of the real world is saying, quite arrogantly, "The way I think of the world is the way that counts." Second, in times of disagreement we must ask the question, "How well does the data model fit the mental models of the people who are going to use the system?" The person who is constructing the data model may think the model under construction is a weird way of viewing the world, but that is not the point. The only valid point is whether it reflects how the users view their world. Will it enable the users to do their jobs? ■

Discussion Questions

1. What does a data model represent?
2. Explain why it is easy for humans to confuse the phenomenal world with the noumenal world.
3. If someone were to say to you, "My model is a better model of the real world," how would you respond?
4. In your own words, how should you proceed when two people disagree on what is to be included in a data model?

ACTIVE REVIEW

Use this Active Review to verify that you understand the ideas and concepts that answer the chapter's study questions.

Q1 What is the purpose of a database?

State the purpose of a database. Explain the circumstances in which a database is preferred to a spreadsheet. Describe the key difference between Figures 5-1 and 5-2.

Q2 What is a database?

Define the term *database.* Explain the hierarchy of data and the name three elements of a database. Define *metadata.* Using the example of *Student* and *Office_Visit* tables, show how relationships among rows are represented in a database. Define the terms *key, foreign key,* and *relational database.*

Q3 What are the components of a database application system?

Explain why a database, by itself, is not very useful to business users. Name the components of a database application system and sketch their relationship. Explain the acronym DBMS and name its functions. List five popular DBMS products. Explain the difference between a DBMS and a database. Summarize the functions of a DBMS. Define *SQL.*

Q4 How do database applications make databases more useful?

Name and describe the components of a database application. Explain the need for application programs. For multi-user processing, describe one way in which one user's work can interfere with another's. Explain why multi-user database processing involves more than just connecting another computer to the network. Define two broad categories of DBMS and explain their differences.

Q5 How are data models used for database development?

Explain why user involvement is critical during database development. Describe the function of a data model. Sketch the database development process. Define *entity-relationship model, entity, relationship, attribute,* and *identifier.* Give an example, other than one in this text, of an *entity-relationship diagram.* Define *maximum cardinality* and *minimum cardinality.* Give an example of three maximum cardinalities and two minimum cardinalities. Explain the notation in Figures 5-17 and 5-18.

Q6 How is a data model transformed into a database design?

Name the three components of a database design. Define *normalization* and explain why it is important. Define *data integrity problem* and describe its consequences. Give an example of a table with possible data integrity problems and show how it can be normalized into two or more tables that do not have such problems. Describe two steps in transforming a data model into a database design. Using an example not in this chapter, show how 1:N and N:M relationships are represented in a relational database.

Q7 What is the users' role in the development of databases?

Describe the users' role in the development of a database. Explain why it is easier and cheaper to change a data model than to change an existing database. Use the examples of Figures 5-24(c) and Figures 5-25(c) in your answer. Describe two criteria for judging a data model. Explain why it is important to devote necessary time to understanding a data model.

Q8 What are the responsibilities for database administration?

Explain why a database is a critical resource and why the more encompassing it is, the greater the potential for problems. Explain two meanings for *DBA* and define the purpose of database administration. Summarize the DBA's responsibilities for database development, operations, backup and recovery, and adaptation. Describe the authority problem that most DBAs have and explain how that problem influences the choice of DBA personnel.

KEY TERMS AND CONCEPTS

Access 152
Attribute 160
Byte 146
Column 147
Crow's foot 161
Crow's-foot diagram version 162
Data integrity problem 164
Data model 159
Database 146
Database administration 169
Database application 154
Database application system 152

USING YOUR KNOWLEDGE

1. Draw an entity-relationship diagram that shows the relationships among a database, database applications, and users.
2. Consider the relationship between *Adviser* and *Student* in Figure 5-19. Explain what it means if the maximum cardinality of this relationship is:
   a. N:1
   b. 1:1
   c. 5:1
   d. 1:5
3. Identify two entities in the data entry form in Figure 5-27. What attributes are shown for each? What do you think are the identifiers?
4. Using your answer to question 3, draw an E-R diagram for the data entry form in Figure 5-27. Specify cardinalities. State your assumptions.
5. The partial E-R diagram in Figure 5-28 (next page) is for a sales order. Assume there is only one *Salesperson* per *SalesOrder*.
   a. Specify the maximum cardinalities for each relationship. State your assumptions, if necessary.
   b. Specify the minimum cardinalities for each relationship. State your assumptions, if necessary.
6. Refer to Figure 5-2 on page 150.
   a. Construct a data model for the data in Figure 5-2.
   b. The database in Figure 5-2 contains data for a single class. Suppose the professor who uses this database wants to keep data for several classes. Further suppose that some students enroll in more than one of a professor's classes. Revise your data model to show this changed assumption.
   c. Is your first or second data model better?

Employee Class Attendance

EmployeeNumber: 1299393
FirstName: Mary
LastName: Lopez
Email: Mlopez@somewhere.com

Class

CourseName	CourseDate	Instructor	Remarks
Presentation Skills I	3/17/2005	Johnson	Excellent presenter!
CRM Administrator	5/19/2006	Wu	Needs work on security administration
*			

Figure 5-27
Sample Data Entry Form

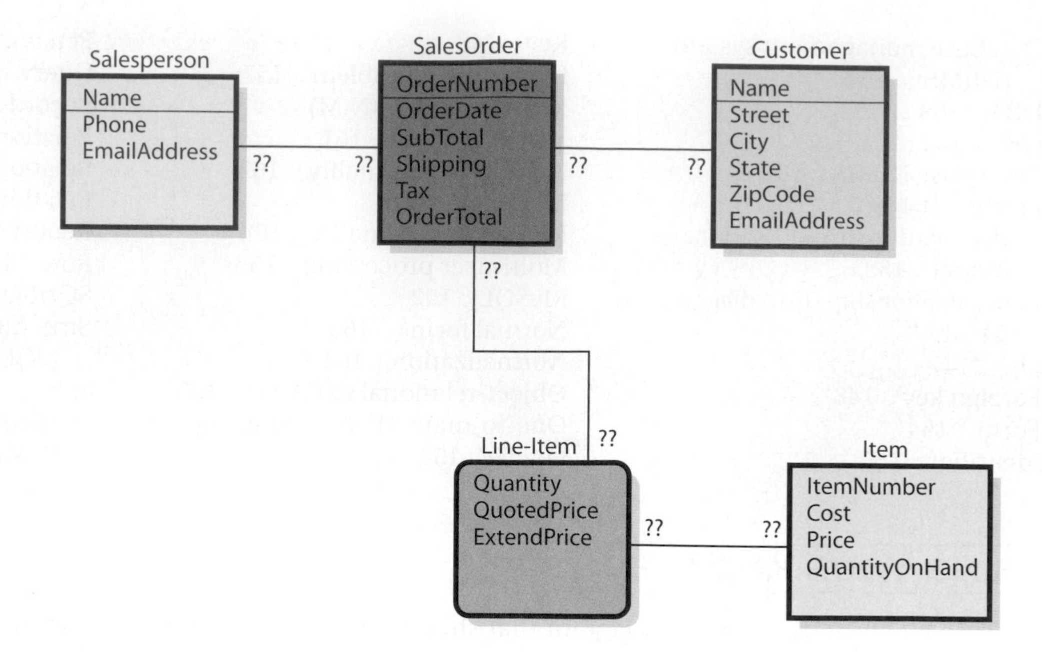

Figure 5-28
Partial E-R Diagram for *SalesOrder*

COLLABORATION EXERCISES AND CASES

Collaborate with a group of students on the following exercises. Recall from Chapter 2 that collaboration is more than cooperation because it involves iteration and feedback. Post a document, a discussion item, a wiki item, or an idea and obtain feedback from your team members. Similarly, read the ideas of others and comment on them. Try to innovate in both the process by which you collaborate and the work product that you create. Avoid face-to-face meetings. Instead, use collaborative software such as Google Docs & Spreadsheets, Microsoft Groove, or Microsoft SharePoint to facilitate your ideas.

1. In this exercise, you will evaluate alternative data models for the sheet-music-tracking problem described in the *Innovation in Practice* box on page 158. Work collaboratively with your team to answer the following questions.

   a. Analyze the spreadsheet shown on page 158 and list all of the problems that occur when trying to track the assignment of sheet music using this spreadsheet.

   b. Figure 5-29(a) shows a two-entity data model for the sheet-music-tracking problem.

      (1) Select identifiers for the *ChoirMember* and *Work* entities. Justify your selection.

      (2) This design does not eliminate the potential for data integrity problems that occur in the spreadsheet. Explain why not.

      (3) Design a database for this data model. Specify key and foreign key columns.

   c. Figure 5-29(b) shows a second alternative data model for the sheet-music-tracking problem. This alternative shows two variations on the *Work* entity. In the second variation, an attribute named *WorkID* has been added to *Work_Version3*. This attribute is a unique identifier for the work; the DBMS will assign a unique value to *WorkID* when a new row is added to the *Work* table.

      (1) Select identifiers for *ChoirMember*, *Work_Version2*, *Work_Version3*, and *Copy_Assignment*. Justify your selection.

      (2) Does this design eliminate the potential for data integrity problems that occur in the spreadsheet? Why or why not?

      (3) Design a database for the data model that uses *Work_Version2*. Specify key and foreign key columns.

      (4) Design a database for the data models that uses *Work_Version3*. Specify key and foreign key columns.

      (5) Is the design with *Work_Version2* better than the design for *Work_Version3*? Why or why not?

   d. Figure 5-29(c) shows a third alternative data model for the sheet-music-tracking problem. In this data model, use either *Work_Version2* or *Work_Version3*, whichever you think is better.

(1) Select identifiers for each entity in your data model. Justify your selection.

(2) Summarize the differences between this data model and that in Figure 5-29(b). Which data model is better? Why?

(3) Design a database for this data model. Specify key and foreign key columns.

e. Which of the three data models is the best? Justify your answer.

2. In this exercise, you will create a data model for the prototype form shown in Figure 1 on page 163. You will then need to review the form with your team, and once you agree on the appropriateness of your model, design the database. You should begin by rereading the volunteer problem described in the *Database Processing in Practice* box on page 163.

a. There are at least four entities represented in the form in Figure 1: *Prospect, Phone, Contact,* and

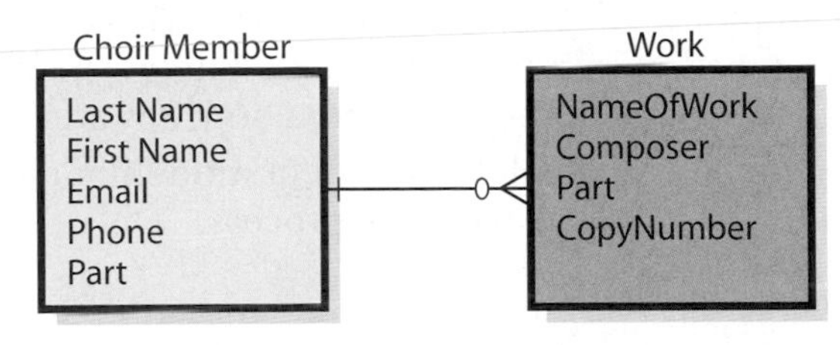

(a) Data-Model Alternative 1

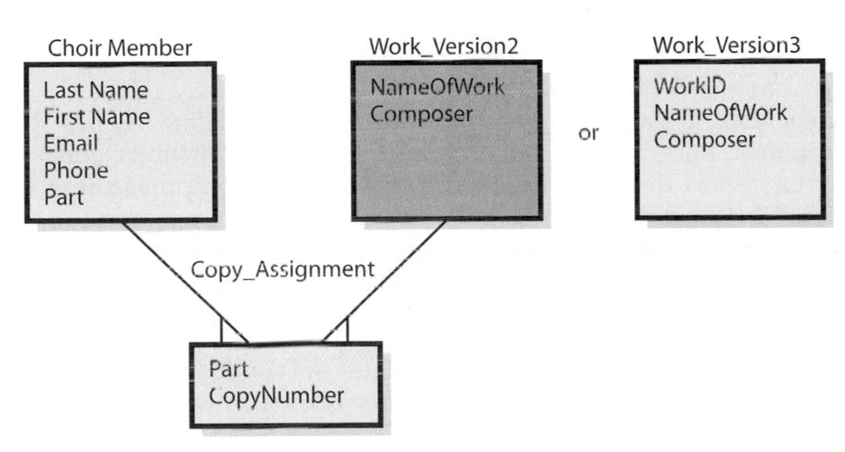

(b) Data-Model Alternative 2

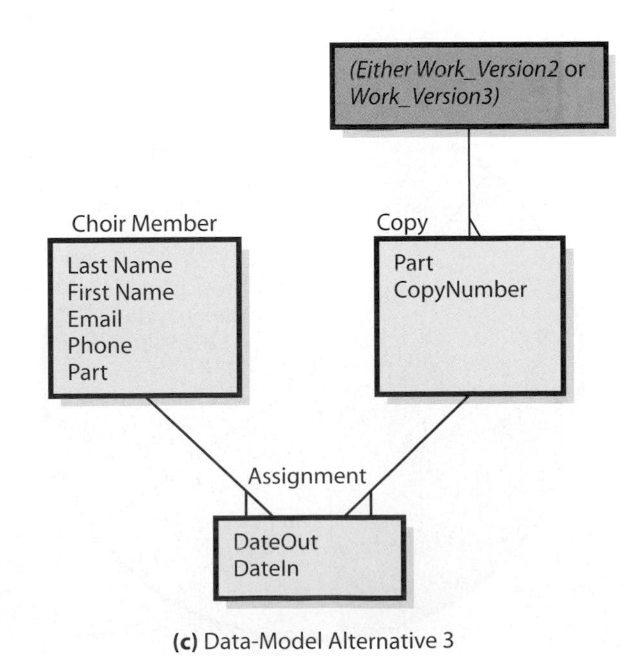

(c) Data-Model Alternative 3

Figure 5-29
Three Data-Model Alternatives
(a) Data-Model Alternative 1
(b) Data-Model Alternative 2
(c) Data-Model Alternative 3

Work. Using the example of the form, document the attributes of each of these entities. As an example, according to form's data, *Phone* has two attributes: *PhoneType* and *PhoneNumber*.

b. Select one of the attributes of *Prospect* to be the *Prospect* identifier. Justify your decision.

c. Determine the relationships that exist among *Prospect, Phone, Contact,* and *Work*. Create an entity-relationship diagram and show the maximum cardinality using the crow's-foot notation. Justify your maximum cardinality decisions. Pay particular attention to the relationship between *Prospect* and *Phone*: Is it a 1:N or N:M relationship? Why or why not? Is there a difference between what *could be* and what *needs to be* represented in the database? Is that distinction important? Why or why not? Decide these issues as a group.

d. Specify the minimum cardinality for each relationship. You cannot determine the minimum cardinality from Figure 1 so you will have to make your own assumptions. Justify your cardinality decisions.

e. Specify the identifiers for *Phone, Contact,* and *Work*.

f. Explain how the data in Figure 1 might suggest the need for *Home, Office,* or *Employee* entities. Under what circumstances would it be important to include those entities? If you disagree as a group, even better. Explain your answers or, if you disagree, your different answers.

g. Assume there are only the four entities: *Prospect, Phone, Contact,* and *Work*. Design the database from your model. Show which columns are keys, foreign keys, and both key and foreign key.

h. Explain why data modeling and review must be a collaborative process.

APPLICATION EXERCISES

1. Excel and Access can often be used advantageously together. A common scenario is to use Access to process relational data, import that data into Excel, and then use Excel's tools for creating professional looking charts and graphs. You will do exactly that in this exercise.

   Download the Access file **Ch05Ex01** from *www.prenhall.com/kroenke*. Open the database, select *Database Tools/Relationships*. As you can see, there are three tables: *Product, VendorProductInventory,* and *Vendor*. Open each table individually to familiarize yourself with the data.

   For this problem, we will define *InventoryCost* as the product of *IndustryStandardCost* and *QuantityOnHand*. The query *InventoryCost* computes these values for every item in inventory for every vendor. Open that query and view the data to be certain you understand this computation. Open the other queries as well so that you understand the data they produce.

   a. Sum this data by vendor and display it a pie chart like that shown in Figure 5-30. Proceed as follows:

      (1) Open Excel and create a new spreadsheet.

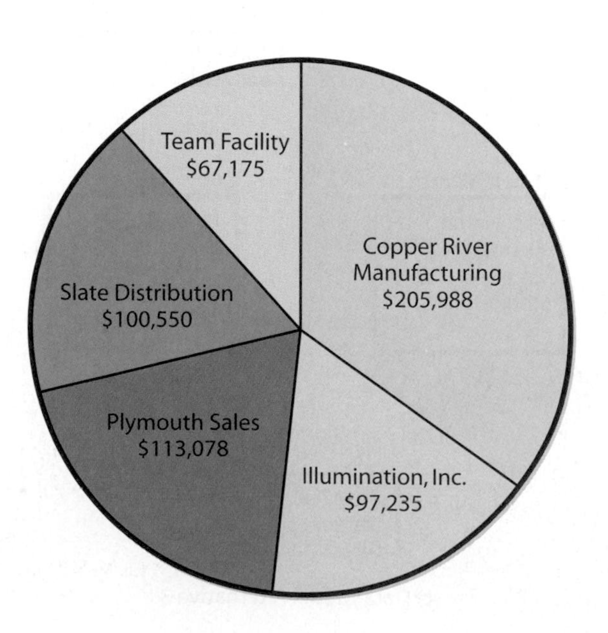

Figure 5-30
Data Displayed in Pie-Chart Format

(2) Click *Data* on the ribbon and select *Access* in the *Get External Data* ribbon category.
(3) Navigate to the location in which you have stored the Access file **Ch05Ex01**.
(4) Select the query that contains the data you need for this pie chart.
(5) Import the data into a table.
(6) Format the appropriate data as currency.
(7) Select the range that contains the data, press the function key and proceed from there to create the pie chart. Name the data and pie chart worksheets appropriately.

b. Follow a similar procedure to create the bar chart shown in Figure 5-31. Place the data and the chart in separate worksheets and name them appropriately.

2. Read the *Opposing Forces Guide* on page 172. Suppose you are given the task of converting the salesperson's data into a database. Because his data is so poorly structured, it will be a challenge, as you will see.

a. Download the Excel file named **Ch05Ex02** from www.prenhall.com/kroenke. This spreadsheet contains data that fits the salesperson's description in the *Opposing Forces Guide.* Open the spreadsheet and view the data.
b. Download the Access file with the same name, **Ch05Ex02**. Open the database, select *Database Tools,* and click *Relationships.* Examine the four tables and their relationships.
c. Somehow, you have to transform the data in the spreadsheet into the table structure in the database. Because so little discipline was shown when creating the spreadsheet, this will be a labor-intensive task. To begin, import the spreadsheet data into a new table in the database; call that table *Sheet1* or some other name.
d. Copy the *Name* data in *Sheet1* onto the clipboard. Then, open the *Customer* table and paste the column of name data into that table.
e. Unfortunately, the task becomes messy at this point. You can copy the *Car Interests* column into *Make or Model of Auto*, but then you will need to straighten out the values by hand. Phone numbers will need to be copied one at a time.
f. Open the *Customer* form and manually add any remaining data from the spreadsheet into each customer record. Connect the customer to his or her auto interests.
g. The data in the finished database has much more structure than that in the spreadsheet. Explain why that is both an advantage and a disadvantage. Under what circumstances is the database more appropriate? Less appropriate?

3. In this exercise, you will create a two-table database, define relationships, create a form and a report, and use them to enter data and view results.

a. Download the Excel file **Ch05Ex03** from *www.prenhall.com/kroenke.* Open the spreadsheet and review the data in the *Employee* and *Computer* worksheets.
b. Create a new Access database with the name *Ch05Ex03_Solution.* Close the table that Access automatically creates and delete it.

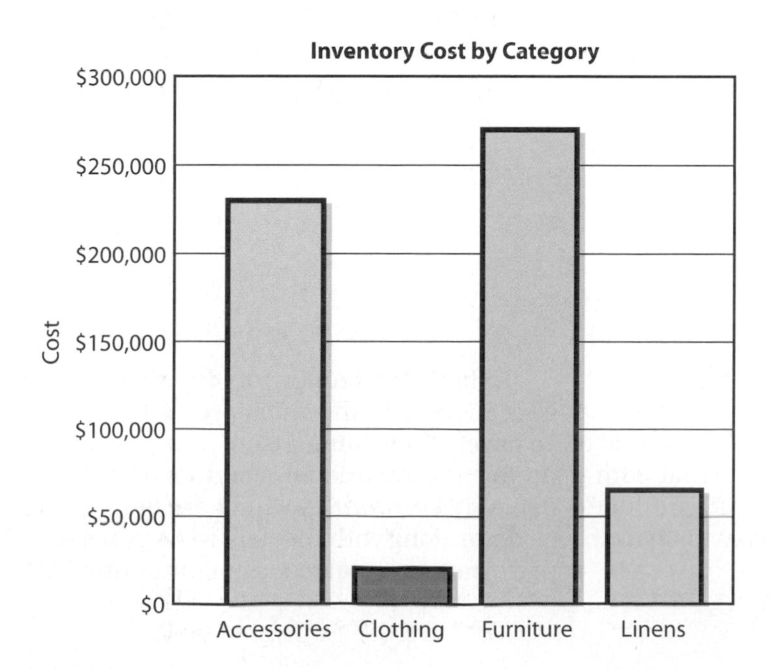

Figure 5-31
Data Displayed in Bar-Chart Format

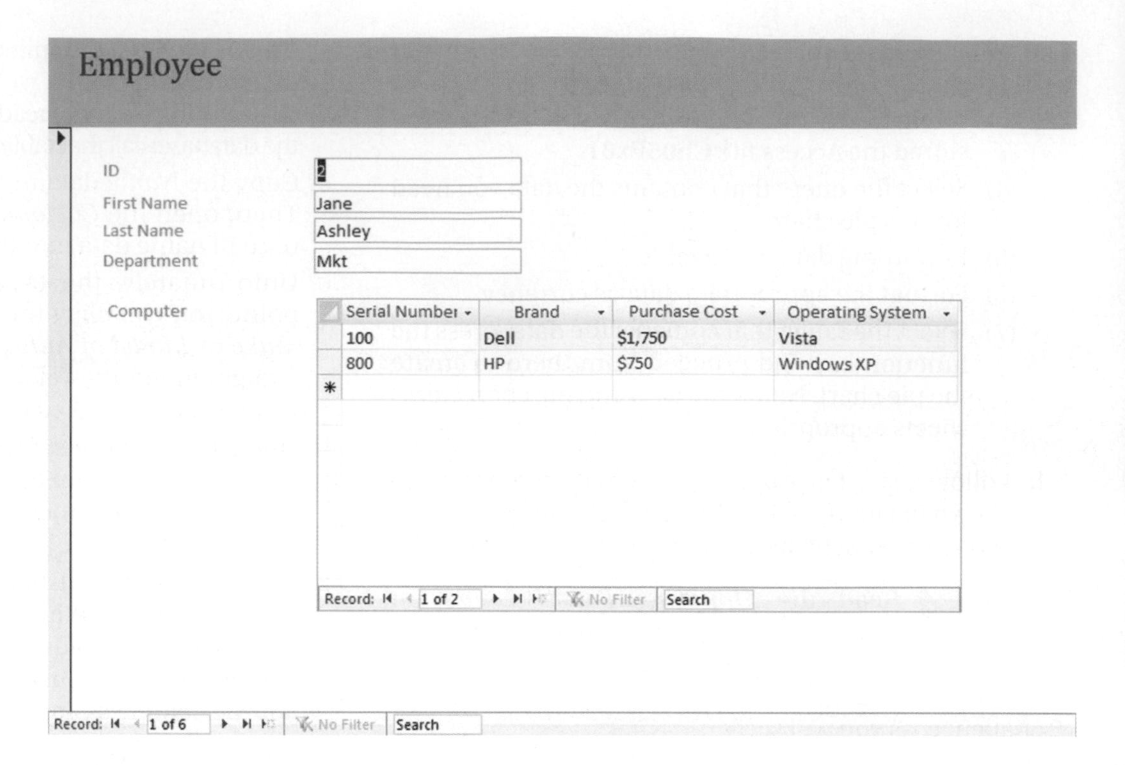

Figure 5-32
Employee Computer Assignment Form

c. Import the data from the Excel spreadsheet into your database. Import the *Employee* worksheet into a table named *Employee*. Be sure to check *First Row Contains Column Headings*. Select *Choose my own primary key* and use the ID field as that key.

d. Import the *Computer* worksheet into a table named *Computer*. Check *First Row Contains Column Headings*, but let Access create the primary key.

e. Open the relationships window and add both *Employee* and *Computer* to the design space. Drag ID from *Employee* and drop it on *EmployeeID* in *Computer*. Check *Enforce Referential Integrity* and the two checkmarks below. Ensure you know what these actions mean.

f. Open the Form Wizard dialog box (under *Create, More Forms*) and add all of the columns for each of your tables to your form. Select *View your data by Customer*. Title your form *Employee* and your subform *Computer*.

g. Open the *Computer* subform and delete *EmployeeID* and *ComputerID*. These values are maintained by Access, and it is just a distraction to keep them. Your form should appear like the one shown in Figure 5-32.

h. Use your form to add two new computers to *Jane Ashley*. Both computers are Dells, and both use Vista; one costs $750, and the second costs $1,400.

i. Delete the Lenovo computer for Rex Scott.

j. Use the Report Wizard (under *Create*) to create a report having all data from both the *Employee* and *Computer* tables. Play with the report design until you find a design you like. Correct label alignment if you need to.

CASE STUDY 5

Benchmarking, Bench Marketing, or Bench Baloney?

Which DBMS product is the fastest? Which product yields the lowest price/performance ratio? What computer equipment works best for each DBMS product? These reasonable questions should be easy to answer. They are not.

In fact, the deeper you dig, the more problems you find. To begin with, which product is fastest doing *what*? To have a valid comparison, all compared products must do the same work. So, vendors and third parties have defined *benchmarks*, which are descriptions of work to be done along with the data to be processed. To compare performance, analysts run competing DBMS products on the same benchmark and measure the results. Typical measures are number of transactions processed per second, number of Web pages served per second, and average response time per user.

At first, DBMS vendors set up their own benchmark tests and published those results. Of course, when vendor A used its own benchmark to claim that its product was superior to all others, no one believed the results. Clearly, vendor A had an incentive to set up the benchmark to play to its product strengths. So, third parties defined standard benchmarks. Even that led to problems, however. According to *The Benchmark Handbook* (at *http://benchmarkresources.com/handbook*):

> When comparative numbers were published by third parties or competitors, the losers generally cried foul and tried to discredit the benchmark. Such events often caused benchmark wars. Benchmark wars start if someone loses an important or visible benchmark evaluation. The loser reruns it using regional specialists and gets new and winning numbers. Then the opponent reruns it using his regional specialists, and of course gets even better numbers. The loser then reruns it using some one-star gurus. This progression can continue all the way to five-star gurus.

For example, in July 2002 *PC Magazine* ran a benchmark using a standard benchmark called the *Nile benchmark*. This particular test has a mixture of database tasks that are processed via Web pages. The faster the DBMS, the more pages that can be served. The results of the test were as shown in Figure 5-33.

The test compared five DBMS products: DB2 (from IBM), MySQL (a license-free, open-source DBMS product from MySQL.com), Oracle (from Oracle Corporation), SQL Server (from Microsoft), and ASE (from Sybase Corporation). The vertical axis in the graph shows the number of pages processed per second; as the label says, higher is better.

From this graph, you can see that SQL Server's performance was the worst. In the magazine review, the authors stated that they believed SQL Server scored poorly because the test used a new version of a non–Microsoft driver (a program that sends requests and returns results to and from the DBMS).

As you might imagine, no sooner was this test published than the phones and email server at *PC Magazine* were inundated by objections from Microsoft. *PC Magazine* reran the tests, replacing the suspect driver

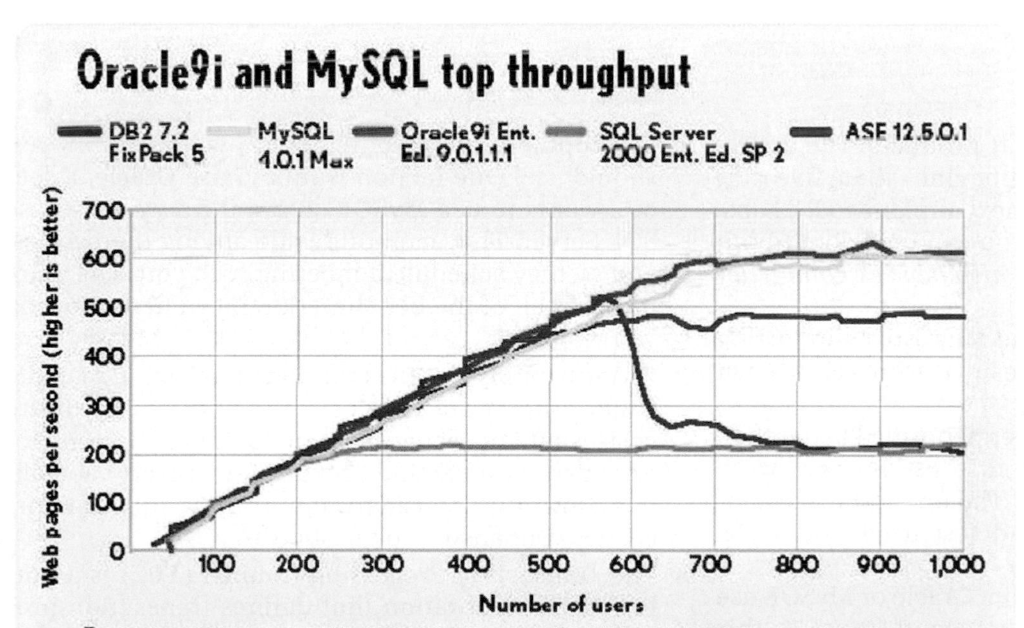
Oracle9i and MySQL top throughput
DB2 7.2 FixPack 5
MySQL 4.0.1 Max
Oracle9i Ent. Ed. 9.0.1.1.1
SQL Server 2000 Ent. Ed. SP 2
ASE 12.5.0.1
Web pages per second (higher is better)
700
600
500
400
300
200
100
0
100
200
300
400
500
600
700
800
900
1,000
Number of users
Throughput is in returned Web pages per second from the application server. Number of users is number of concurrent Web clients driving the load. Response time is the time to complete the six bookstore user action sequences, weighted by frequency of each sequence in the mix. All tests were conducted on an HP NetServer LT 6000r with four 700MHz Xeon CPUs, 2GB of RAM, a Gigabit Ethernet Intel Corp. Pro/1000 F Server Adapter and 24 9.1GB Ultra3 SCSI hard drives used for database storage.

Figure 5-33
Results of First Nile Benchmark Test

Source: Reprinted from www.eWEEK.com, 2007, with permission.

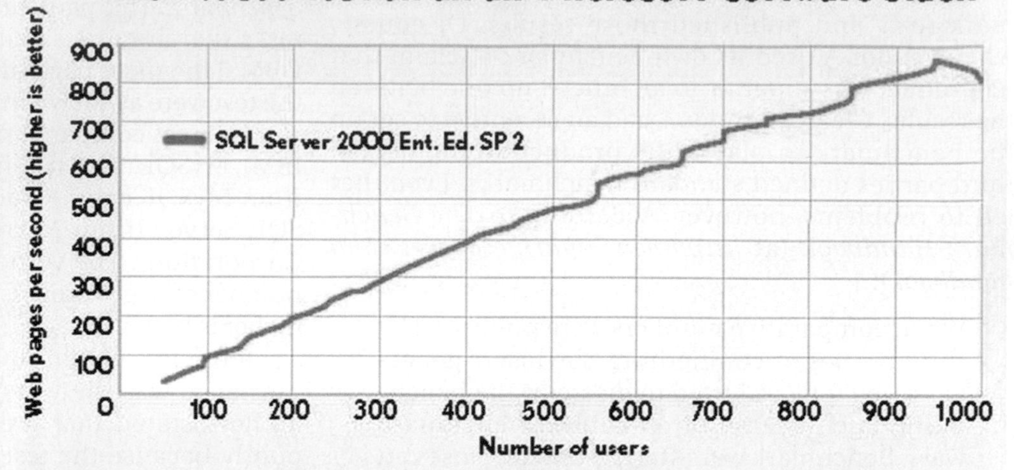
SQL Server 2000 performed very well in ASP .Net-based test on an all-Microsoft software stack
Web pages per second (higher is better)
900
800
700
600
500
400
300
200
100
0
SQL Server 2000 Ent. Ed. SP 2
100
200
300
400
500
600
700
800
900
1,000
Number of users
Throughput is in returned Web pages per second from the application server. Number of users is number of concurrent Web clients driving the load. Response time is the time to complete the six bookstore user action sequences, weighted by frequency of each sequence in the mix. All tests were conducted on an HP NetServer LT 6000r with four 700MHz Xeon CPUs, 2 GB of RAM, a Gigabit Ethernet Intel Pro/1000 F Server Adapter and 24 9.1GB Ultra3 SCSI hard drives used for database storage.

Figure 5-34
Results of Second Nile Benchmark Test

Source: Reprinted from www.eWEEK.com, 2007, with permission.

with a full panoply of Microsoft products. The article doesn't say, but one can imagine that five-star Microsoft gurus chartered the next airplane to PC Labs, where the testing was done. (You can read about both phases of the benchmark at *http://eweek.com/article2/0,4149,293,00.asp.*)

Rerunning the test with the Microsoft-supporting software, the SQL Server results were as shown in Figure 5-34.

In the second test, SQL Server performed better than all of the other products in the first test. But now we're comparing apples and oranges. The first test used standard software, and the second test used Microsoft-specific software.

When the five-star gurus from Oracle or MySQL use *their* favorite supporting products and "tune" to this particular benchmark, their re-rerun results will be superior to those for SQL Server. And round and round it will go.

Questions

1. Suppose you manage a business activity that needs a new information system with a database. The development team is divided on which DBMS you should use. One faction wants to use Oracle, a second wants to use MySQL, and a third wants to use SQL Server. They cannot decide among themselves, and so they schedule a meeting with you. The team presents all of the benchmarks shown here. How do you respond?
2. Performance is just one criterion for selecting a DBMS. Other criteria are the cost of the DBMS, hardware costs, staff knowledge, ease of use, ability to tune for extra performance, and backup and recovery capabilities. How does consideration of these other factors change your answer to question 1?
3. The Transaction Processing Council (TPC) is a not-for-profit corporation that defines transaction processing and database benchmarks and publishes vendor-neutral, verifiable performance data. Visit its Web site at *http://tpc.org.*
   a. What are TPC-C, TPC-R, and TPC-W?
   b. Suppose you work in the marketing department at Oracle Corporation. How would you use the TPC results in the TPC-C benchmark?

c. What are the dangers to Oracle in your answer to part b?

d. Suppose you work in the marketing department for DB2 at IBM. How would you use the TPC results in the TPC-C benchmark?

e. Do the results for TPC-C change your answer to question 1?

f. If you are a DBMS vendor, can you ignore benchmarks?

4. Reflect on your answers to questions 1 through 3. On balance, what good are benchmarks? Are they just footballs to be kicked around by vendors? Are advertisers and publishers the only true beneficiaries? Do DBMS customers benefit from the efforts of TPC and like groups? How should customers use benchmarks?

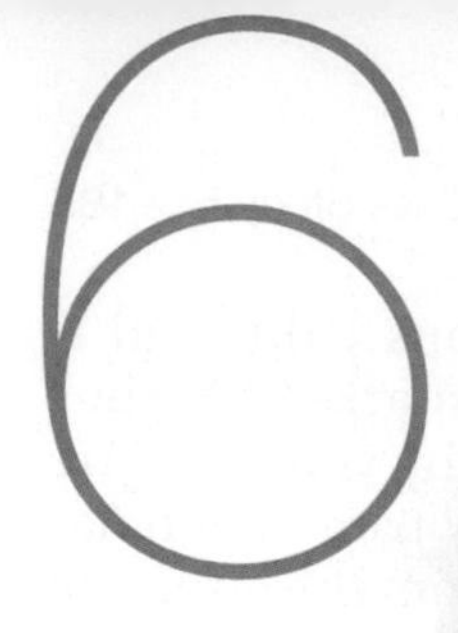

6 Data Communication

STUDY QUESTIONS

- Q1 What is a computer network?
- Q2 What are the components of a LAN?
- Q3 What are the alternatives for a WAN?
- Q4 What criteria can you use for comparing WANs?
- Q5 How does encryption work?
- Q6 What is the purpose of a firewall?

Meet Posy Gering

My favorite business book:
The Art of the Long View: Planning for the Future in an Uncertain World by Peter Schwartz.

My career high:
My current job—it combines so many aspects that are truly me: creativity, strategy, bossing other people around.

My pet peeve:
People who talk on speaker-phones when there's no one else in the room.

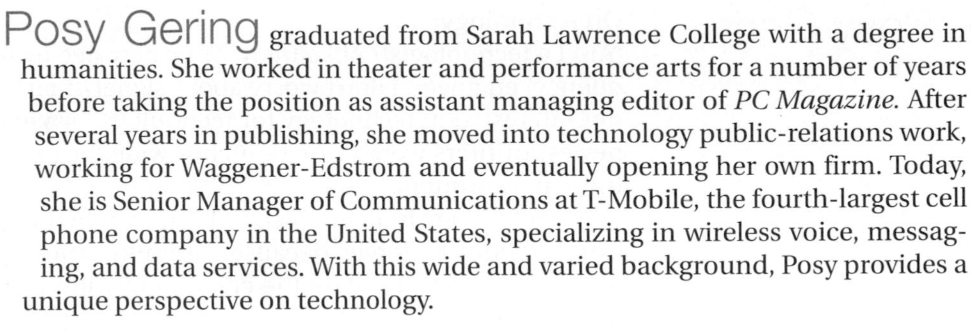

Posy Gering graduated from Sarah Lawrence College with a degree in humanities. She worked in theater and performance arts for a number of years before taking the position as assistant managing editor of *PC Magazine*. After several years in publishing, she moved into technology public-relations work, working for Waggener-Edstrom and eventually opening her own firm. Today, she is Senior Manager of Communications at T-Mobile, the fourth-largest cell phone company in the United States, specializing in wireless voice, messaging, and data services. With this wide and varied background, Posy provides a unique perspective on technology.

On her career:

"I was a penniless, itinerant storyteller living in Green Valley, California, when a friend called from *PC Magazine*. Ziff-Davis had purchased the magazine; my friend needed an assistant managing editor, and I talked him into hiring me. I knew nothing about publishing, but I figured if I could put together a play, I could put together a magazine. I also knew nothing about technology, but I figured it out—like learning a foreign language. This was back in 1984—the personal computer was just gaining popularity, and lots of people, like me, knew nothing about computers but wanted to learn.

"After four years at the magazine, MicroRim, a little database company based in Seattle, hired me to do public relations for them. I knew all the editors and writers in the business, so that job was a natural. Eventually, I owned my own firm and served lots of infrastructure companies, as well as dot-coms. In 2000, after the dot-com bust, I had no clients and was tired of public relations—dealing with the big egos on both sides. Also, the joy was gone. Unlike the early days of the PC when we looked for the best products and technology, it had become a money game—who had the deepest pockets and the best parties."

On her job at T-Mobile:

"Today, I'm still doing employee-focused communications, but as an employee working for T-Mobile. I facilitate the communications between engineering and the rest of the company. I help the company know what we're doing in engineering, the successes we're having, how best to work with our engineering teams. Also, I help engineering work with the rest of the company. I get involved in how all the parts of our business contribute to the customers' experience.

"A big part of my job is offering different perspectives. People get stuck viewing a problem from a single vantage point. I try to help them turn the problem upside down, reframe it, consider it in new ways. Often, it is your perspective that makes a problem seem difficult."

My management style:
Hire great people, give them the vision, and get out of their way.

What I want to learn next:
How to enable change.

My motto:
Treat the impossible like the lower limit, not the ceiling.

Posy Gering

On technology:
"Am I a technologist? Absolutely! I'm a new-age technologist. I'm not an RF (radio frequency) engineer. I don't worry about signal quality, though that's important. And I'm not interested in technology for technology's sake. At *PC Magazine* I didn't care if the newest printers were 11 or 12 inches wide, I cared about what people could do with those new printers.

"Technology is an enabler. With it, people do new things, relate in new ways. I'm excited about T-Mobile, because communications products are key to organizations of the future. We facilitate the creation of widely disbursed, distributed, even virtual organizations.

"I guess you could call me an applied technologist. I help our organization use its incredible engineering talent to develop products that enable new behaviors and capabilities for people and organizations."

On the difference between technology and products:
"There's a huge difference between a technology and a product. Suppose one of our engineers develops a breakthrough signal-processing algorithm. At that point, it's just an idea. How do we turn that idea into a product that someone can buy? How do we make a sustainable business out of it? How do we integrate it into our existing systems so the customer has one seamless, unified experience of the service and we don't crash our network? How do we make sure we can get paid for the new product?

"These questions represent a huge opportunity for business students: Help make a business out of technology *and* help make business understand the implications, possibilities, and limitations of technology. To do that, you need to learn enough technology, data communications, or whatever so you can engage in the conversation and play in that problem-space. You need to be able to talk to the engineers and to understand the practical import of the development. Then, use your business knowledge and skills to turn that technology into products and sustainable businesses. If you can do that, you'll always be on the leading edge."

On the future of data communications:
"Just look at your own life; it's all about communication. How do you stay in touch with friends? Family? The world? What holds businesses together? Communication is at the core of everything people do.

"This industry is constantly emerging, always on the edge. Who knows how this technology will evolve? No one. The future of this business is in your hands. You're used to the always-on, always-available, always-in-your-hand communications devices. We, in the industry, study what you and the next generations do—how you communicate, what habits you have—and we use that knowledge to shape our technology into products.

"I don't know where we're going, but I do know that communications will play a huge role."

On a career in IS:
"Would I advise someone on a career in IS? Yes, absolutely. For one, the possibilities are endless. Information systems are the circulatory system of business. They're the lifeblood of the organization, and no business can operate today without effective IS. Work in IS and you can work in every aspect of the business. And, notice that the boundaries have blurred so the focus is not only business innovation, it's innovation for life problems.

"Finally, it's always interesting. Technology continues to emerge and to create new possibilities and new business opportunities."

Advice to business students:
"Get out and talk to people. Ask your relatives, friends, and friends of your parents to give you a half hour. You'll be amazed and inspired."

Discussion Questions

1. Is it ethical for you to send the email and picture to your friend at work?
2. Does your answer to question 1 change depending on the size of the picture?
3. Does your answer to question 1 change if your email concerns an injury to yourself? If it concerns your need for a ride from the airport?
4. Does your answer change if you send 10 pictures? If you send 100 pictures? If you send 1,000 pictures? If your answer does change, where do you draw the line?
5. Is it more ethical for you to send one picture to 100 friends in 100 different companies or 100 pictures to one friend in one company? Explain your answer.
6. Once the picture is stored on OhioCompany's email server, who owns the picture? Who controls the picture? Does OhioCompany have the right to inspect the contents of its employees' mailboxes? If so, what should managers do when they find your picture that has absolutely nothing to do with the company's business?
7. What company resources will be involved if your friend downloads your email from his private account at work? Is it more ethical to send your picture to your friend's private Yahoo! email account?
8. What do you think is the greater cost to OhioCompany: the cost of the infrastructure to transmit and store the email or the cost of the time your friend takes at work to read and view your picture? Does this consideration change any of your answers above?
9. Although not defined in this sidebar, what do you think the term *email nuisance* might mean?

Instead, the company contracts with a communications vendor that is licensed by the government and that already has lines or has the authority to run new lines between the two cities.

An **internet** is a network of networks. Internets connect LANs, WANs, and other internets. The most famous internet is **"the Internet"** (with an uppercase letter *I*), the collection of networks that you use when you send email or access a Web site. In addition to the Internet, private networks of networks, called *internets*, also exist.

The networks that comprise an internet use a large variety of communication methods and conventions, and data must flow seamlessly across them. To provide seamless flow, an elaborate scheme called a *layered protocol* is used. You can learn more about the various protocols in the appendix that follows this chapter. For now, understand that a **protocol** is a set of rules that two communicating devices follow. There are many different protocols; some are used for LANs, some are used for WANs, some are used for internets and the Internet, and some are used for all of these. The important point is that for two devices to communicate, they must both use the same protocol.

Q2 What Are the Components of a LAN?

A LAN is a group of computers connected together on a single company site. Usually the computers are located within a half mile or so of each other. The key distinction, however, is that all of the computers are located on property controlled by the company that operates the LAN. This means that the company can run cables wherever needed to connect the computers.

Consider the LAN in Figure 6-2. Here, five computers and two printers connect via a **switch**, which is a special-purpose computer that receives and transmits messages on the LAN. In Figure 6-2, when computer 1 accesses printer 1, it does so by sending the print job to the switch, which then redirects that data to printer 1.

Each device on a LAN (computer, printer, etc.) has a hardware component called a **network interface card (NIC)** that connects the device's circuitry to the cable. The NIC works with programs in each device to implement the protocols necessary for communication. On older machines, the NIC is a card that fits into an expansion slot. Almost every new computer today, however, has an **onboard NIC**, which is an NIC built into the computer's circuitry.

Each NIC has a unique identifier, which is called the **MAC (media access control) address**. The computers, printers, switches, and other devices on a LAN are

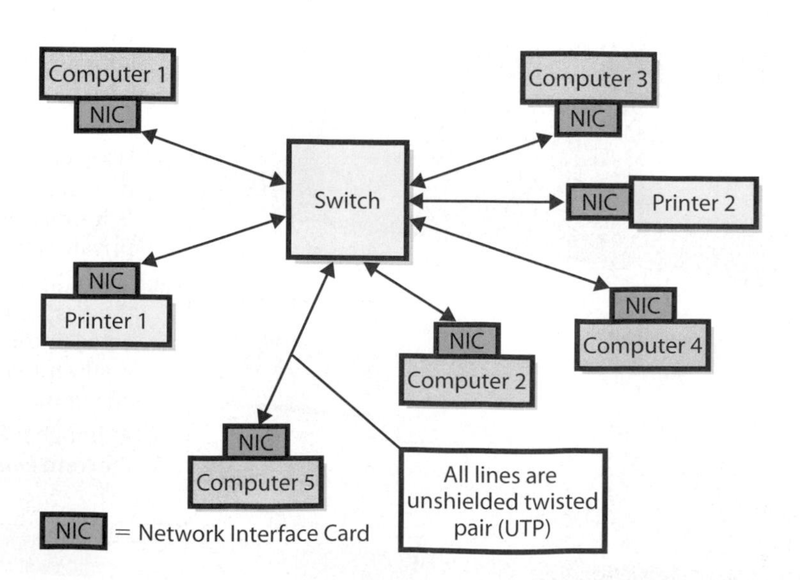

Figure 6-2
Local Area Network (LAN)

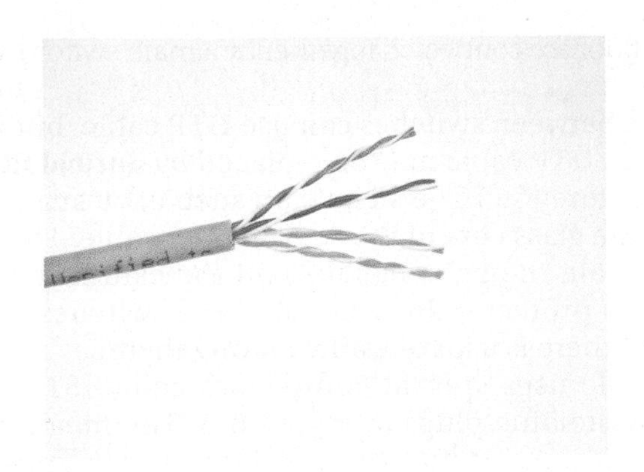

Figure 6-3
Unshielded Twisted Pair (UTP) Cable

Source: Belkin Components. Courtesy of Belkin Corporation.

connected using one of two media. Most connections are made using **unshielded twisted pair (UTP) cable**. Figure 6-3 shows a section of UTP cable that contains four pairs of twisted wire. A device called an RJ-45 connector is used to connect the UTP cable into NIC devices on the LAN.

By the way, wires are twisted for reasons beyond aesthetics and style. Twisting the wires substantially reduces the cross-wire signal interference that occurs when wires run parallel for long distances.

Some LANs, usually those larger than the one in Figure 6-2, use more than one switch. Typically, in a building with several floors a switch is placed on each floor, and the computers on that floor are connected to the switch with UTP cable. As shown in Figure 6-4,

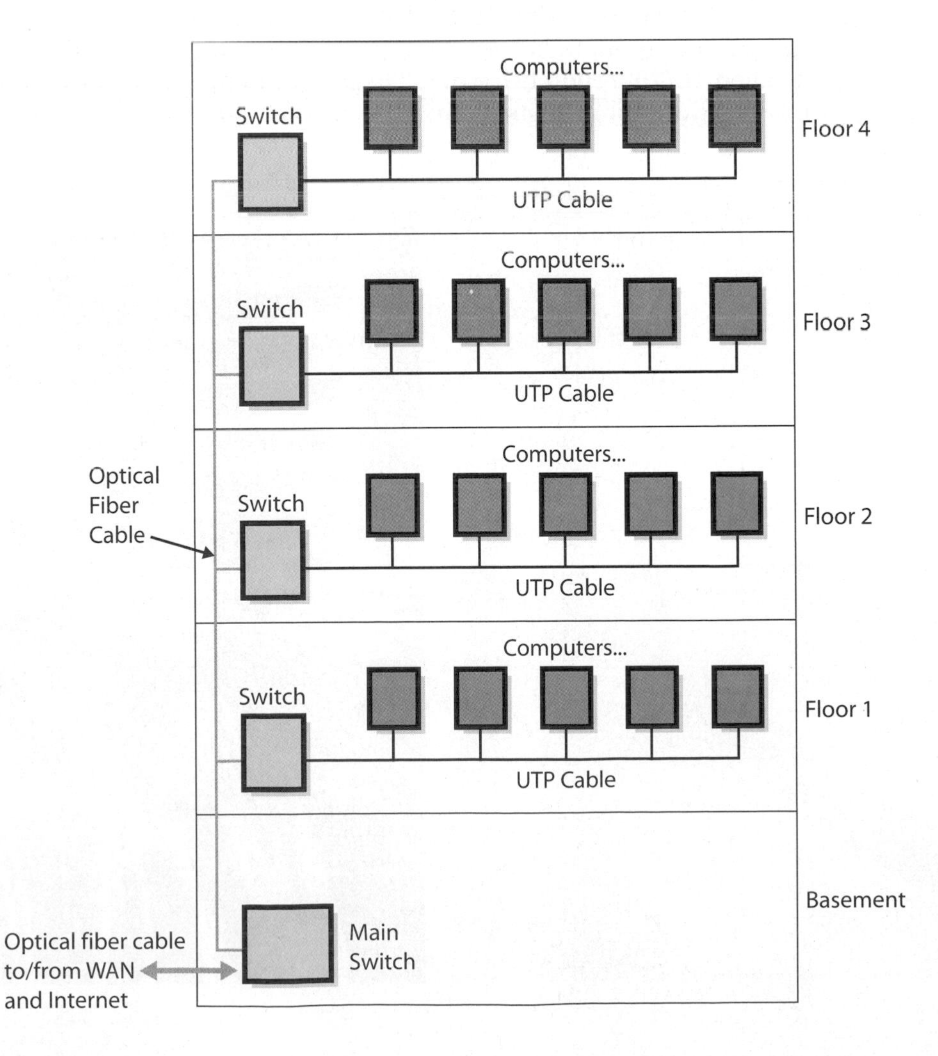

Figure 6-4
Typical Arrangement of Switches in a Multistory Building

the switches on each floor are connected together by a main switch, which is often located in the basement.

The connections between switches can use UTP cable, but if they carry a lot of traffic or are far apart, UTP cable may be replaced by **optical fiber cables**. (See the left-hand photo in Figure 6-5.) The signals on such cables are light rays, and they are reflected inside the glass core of the optical fiber cable. The core is surrounded by a *cladding* to contain the light signals, and the cladding, in turn, is wrapped with an outer layer to protect it. In Figure 6-4, the switches are connected using optical fiber because there is a lot of traffic among them.

Optical fiber cable uses special connectors called ST and SC connectors, which are shown as the blue plugs in Figure 6-5. The meaning of the abbreviations ST and SC are unimportant; they are just the two most common optical connectors.

The IEEE 802.3, or Ethernet, Protocol

For a LAN to work, all devices on the LAN must use the same protocol. The Institute for Electrical and Electronics Engineers (IEEE, pronounced "I triple E") sponsors committees that create and publish protocols and other standards. The committee that addresses LAN standards is called the *IEEE 802 Committee*. Thus, IEEE LAN protocols always start with the numbers 802.

Today, the world's most popular protocol for LANs is the **IEEE 802.3 protocol**. This protocol standard, also called **Ethernet**, specifies hardware characteristics, such as which wire carries which signals. It also describes how messages are to be packaged and processed for transmission over the LAN.

Most personal computers today are equipped with an onboard NIC that supports what is called **10/100/1000 Ethernet**. These products conform to the 802.3 specification and allow for transmission at a rate of 10, 100, or 1,000 Mbps

Figure 6-5
Optical Fiber Cable

Source: Getty Images, Inc.–Photodisc and Michael Smith, Getty Images, Inc.

(megabits per second). Switches detect the speed that a given device can handle and communicate with it at that speed. If you check computer listings at Dell, HP, Toshiba, and other manufacturers, you will see PCs advertised as having 10/100/1000 Ethernet.

By the way, the abbreviations used for communications speeds differ from those used for computer memory. For communications equipment, *k* stands for 1,000, not 1,024 as it does for memory. Similarly, *M* stands for 1,000,000, not 1,024 × 1,024; *G* stands for 1,000,000,000, not 1,024 × 1,024 × 1,024. Thus, 100 Mbps is 100,000,000 bits per second. Also, communications speeds are expressed in *bits*, whereas memory sizes are expressed in *bytes*.

IEEE 802.11 Wireless Protocol

In recent years, wireless connections have become popular for LANs. Figure 6-6 shows a LAN in which two of the computers and one printer have wireless connections. Notice that the NIC for the wireless devices have been replaced by a **wireless NIC (WNIC)**. Today, almost all personal computers are equipped with onboard WNIC.

The technology that enables wireless connections is the **IEEE 802.11 protocol**. Several versions of 802.11 exist. As of 2007, the most popular is IEEE 802.11g. The differences among the variations are beyond the scope of this discussion. Just note that the current standard, 802.11g, allows speeds of up to 54 Mbps.

Observe that the LAN in Figure 6-6 uses both the 802.3 and 802.11 protocols. The NICs operate according to the 802.3 protocol and connect directly to the switch, which also operates on the 802.3 standard. The WNICs operate according to the 802.11 protocol and connect to an **access point (AP)**. The AP must be able to process messages according to both the 802.3 and 802.11 standards, because it sends and receives wireless traffic using the 802.11 protocol and then communicates with the switch using the 802.3 protocol. Characteristics of LANs are summarized in the top part of Figure 6-7 (next page).

Knowledge of LANs and wireless technology enabled one student to start a successful and profitable business, while still in college. Read the Innovation in Practice *box on page 197 to see how.*

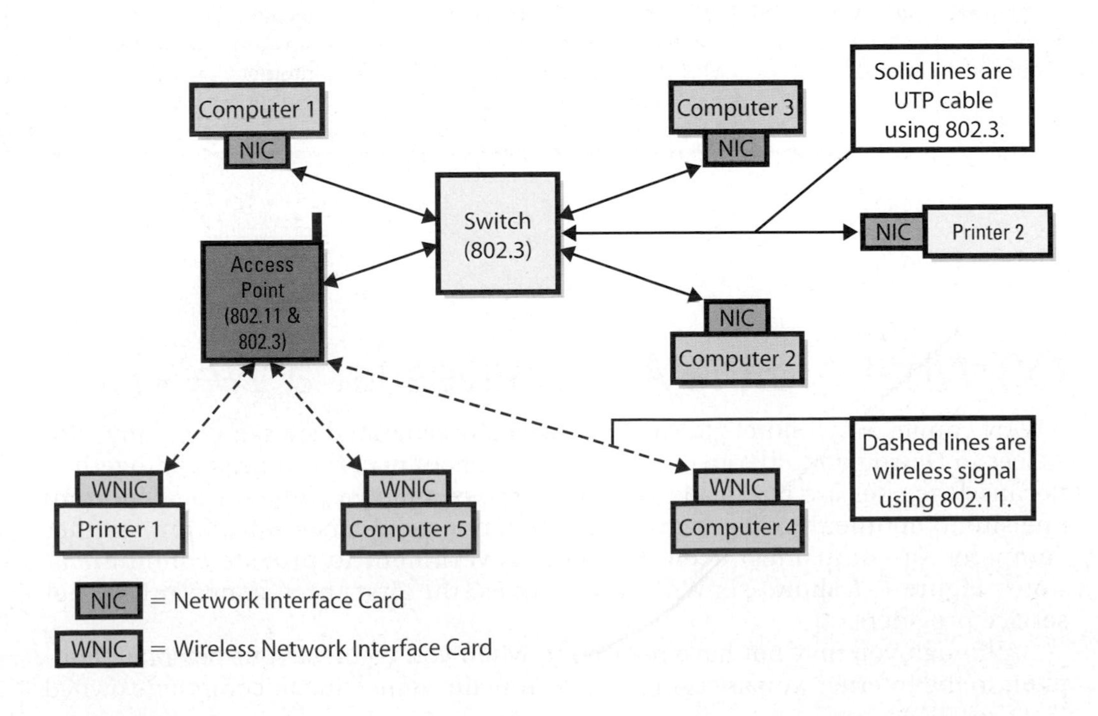

Figure 6-6
LAN with Wireless

Type	Topology	Transmission Line	Transmission Speed	Equipment Used	Protocol Commonly Used	Remarks
Local area network	Local area network	UTP or optical fiber	10,100, or 1,000 Mbps	Switch NIC UTP or optical	IEEE 802.3 (Ethernet)	Switches connect devices, multiple switches on all but small LANs.
	Local area network with wireless	UTP or optical for non-wireless connections	Up to 54 Mbps	Wireless access point Wireless NIC	IEEE 802.11g	Access point transforms wired LAN (802.3) to wireless LAN (802.11).
Wide area network	Dial-up modem to Internet service provider (ISP)	Regular telephone	Up to 55 kbps	Modem Telephone line	Modulation standards (V.32, V90, V92), PPP	Modulation required for first part of telephone line. Computer use blocks telephone use.
	DSL modem to ISP	DSL telephone	Personal: Upstream to 256 kbps, downstream to 1.544 Mbps	DSL modem DSL-capable telephone line	DSL	Can have computer and phone use simultaneously. Always connected.
	Cable modem to ISP	Cable TV lines to optical cable	Upstream to 256 kbps Downstream 300–600 kbps (10 Mbps in theory)	Cable modem Cable TV cable	Cable	Capacity is shared with other sites; performance varies depending on others' use.
	Point to point lines	Network of leased lines	T1–1.5 Mbps T3– 44.7Mbps OC48–2.5Gbps OC768–40 Gbps	Access devices Optical cable Satellite	PPP	Span geographically distributed sites using lines provided by licensed communications vendors. Expensive to set up and manage.
	PSDN	Lease usage of private network	56 Kbps–40 Mbps+	Leased line to PSDN POP	Frame relay ATM 10 Gbps and 40 Gbps Ethernet	Lease time on a public switched data network–operated by independent party. Ineffective for intercompany communication.
	Virtual private network (VPN)	Use the Internet to provide private network	Varies with speed of connection to Internet	VPN client software VPN server hardware and software	PPTP IPSec	Secure, private connection provides a tunnel through the Internet. Can support intercompany communication.

Figure 6-7
Summary of LAN and WAN Networks

Q3 What Are the Alternatives for a WAN?

A WAN connects computers located at physically separated sites. A company with offices in Detroit and Atlanta must use a WAN to connect the computers together. Because the sites are physically separated, the company cannot string wire from one site to another. Rather, it must obtain connection capabilities from another company (or companies) licensed by the government to provide communications. Figure 6-7 shows six WAN alternatives, the first three concern Internet service providers.

Although you may not have realized it, when you connect your personal computer to the Internet, you are using a WAN. You are connecting to computers owned

INNOVATION IN PRACTICE

LARRY JONES (STUDENT) NETWORK SERVICES

Several years ago, Larry Jones was an entering freshman at Big State University. (This case is real; however, to protect privacy, the student and university names are fictional.) Larry had always been interested in technology and as a high school student had won a scholarship from Cisco Corporation (a maker of communications hardware). As part of his scholarship, Larry had attended several Cisco training classes on setting up LANs, switches, and other devices.

Larry pledged a fraternity at Big State, and when the fraternity leadership learned of his expertise, they asked him to set up a LAN with an Internet connection for the fraternity house. It was a simple job for Larry, and his fraternity brothers were quite satisfied with his solution. He did it for free, as a volunteer, and appreciated the introductions the project gave him to senior leaders of the fraternity. The project enabled him to build his network of personal contacts.

Over the summer, however, it dawned on Larry that his fraternity was not the only one on the Big State campus that had the need for a LAN with access to the Internet. Accordingly, that summer he developed marketing materials describing the need and the services he could provide. That fall he called on fraternities and sororities and made presentations of his skills and of the network he had built for the fraternity. Within a year, he had a dozen or so fraternities and sororities as customers.

Larry quickly realized that he couldn't just set up a LAN and Internet connection, charge his fee, and walk away. His customers had continuing problems that required him to return to resolve problems, add new computers, add printer servers, and so forth. At first, he provided such support as part of his installation package price. He soon learned that he could charge a support fee for regular support, and even add extra charges for support beyond normal wear and tear. By the end of his sophomore year, support fees were meeting all of Larry's college expenses, and then some.

When I last saw him, Larry had formed a partnership with several other students to expand his services to local apartment houses and condominiums.

Perhaps, you, too, can set up a communications consulting business as a student. Although it might be too late to do so for wireless LANs, other opportunities are in the offing. See Collaboration Exercise 1 on page 213 to develop that possibility.

and operated by your **Internet service provider (ISP)** that are not located physically at your site.

An ISP has three important functions. First, it provides you with a legitimate Internet address. Second, it serves as your gateway to the Internet. The ISP receives the communications from your computer and passes them on to the Internet, and it receives communications from the Internet and passes them on to you. Finally, ISPs pay for the Internet. They collect money from their customers and pay access fees and other charges on your behalf.

We begin our discussion of WANs by considering modem connections to ISPs.

Connecting the Personal Computer to an ISP: Modems

Home computers and those of small businesses are commonly connected to an ISP in one of three ways: using a regular telephone line, using a special telephone line called a DSL line, or using a cable TV line.

All three of these alternatives require that the *digital data* in the computer be converted to an **analog**, or wavy, signal. A device called a **modem**, or modulator/demodulator, performs this conversion. Figure 6-8 (next page) shows one way of converting the digital byte 01000001 to an analog signal.

As shown in Figure 6-9 (next page), once the modem converts your computer's digital data to analog, that analog signal is then sent over the telephone line or TV cable. If sent by telephone line, the first telephone switch that your signal reaches converts the signal into the form used by the international telephone system.

Figure 6-8
Analog Versus Digital Signals

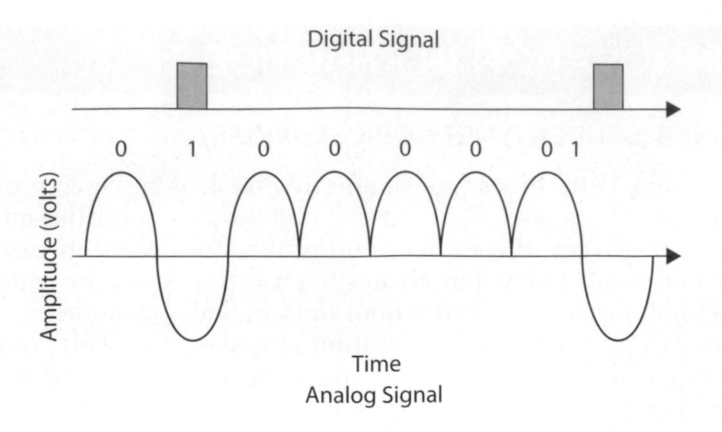

Dial-Up Modems

A **dial-up modem** performs the conversion between analog and digital in such a way that the signal can be carried on a regular telephone line. As the name implies, you dial the phone number for your ISP and connect. The maximum transmission speed for a switch is 56 kbps (in practice, the limit is 53 kbps). By the way, when two devices connected by modems use different speeds, the slower speed is the one at which they operate.

Modulation is governed by one of three standards: V.34, V.90, and V.92. These standards specify how digital signals will be transformed into analog. The way in which messages are packaged and handled between your modem and the ISP is governed by a protocol known as the **Point-to-Point Protocol (PPP)**.

Once the workhorse of Internet access, dial-up modems today are rare. Although you might encounter one in a remote location or foreign country with limited infrastructure, dial-up modems have been largely replaced by DSL and cable modems.

DSL Modems

A **DSL modem** is the second modem type. DSL stands for **digital subscriber line**. DSL modems operate on the same lines as voice telephones and dial-up modems, but they operate so that their signals do not interfere with voice telephone service. DSL modems provide much faster data transmission speeds than dial-up modems. Additionally, DSL modems always maintain a connection, so there is no need to dial up; the Internet connection is available immediately.

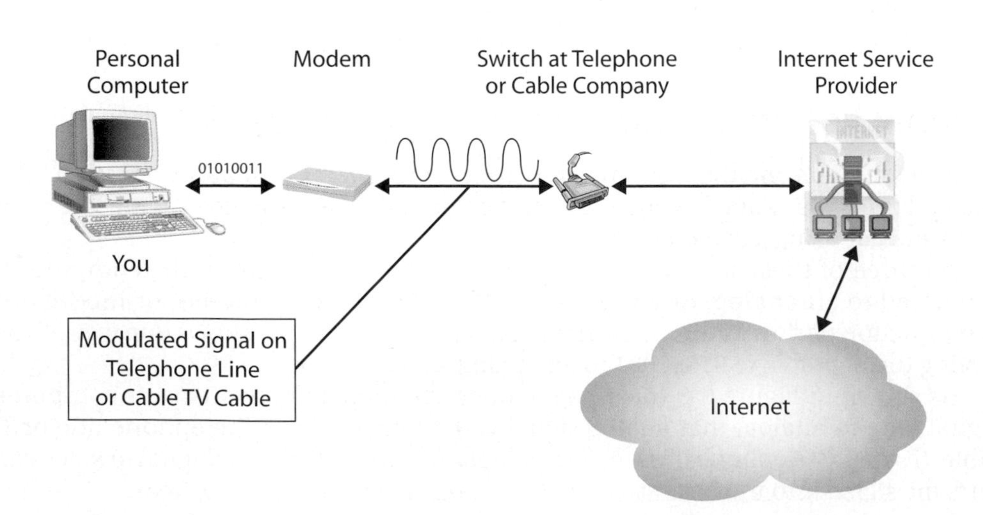

Figure 6-9
Personal Computer (PC) Internet Access

Because DSL signals do not interfere with telephone signals, DSL data transmission and telephone conversations can occur simultaneously. A device at the telephone company separates the phone signals from the computer signals and sends the latter signal to the ISP. DSL modems use their own protocols for data transmission.

There are gradations of DSL service and speed. Most home DSL lines can download data at speeds ranging from 256 kbps to 1.544 Mbps and can upload data at slower speeds—for example, 256 kbps. DSL lines that have different upload and download speeds are called **asymmetric digital subscriber lines (ADSL)**. Most homes and small businesses can use ADSL because they receive more data than they transmit (e.g., pictures in news stories), and hence they do not need to transmit as fast as they receive.

Some users and larger businesses, however, need DSL lines that have the same receiving and transmitting speeds. They also need performance-level guarantees. **Symmetrical digital subscriber lines (SDSL)** meet this need by offering the same fast speed in both directions. As much as 1.544 Mbps can be guaranteed.

Cable Modems

A **cable modem** is the third modem type. Cable modems provide high-speed data transmission using cable television lines. The cable company installs a fast, high-capacity optical fiber cable to a distribution center in each neighborhood that it serves. At the distribution center, the optical fiber cable connects to regular cable-television cables that run to subscribers' homes or businesses. Cable modems modulate in such a way that their signals do not interfere with TV signals. Like DSL lines, they are always on.

Because up to 500 user sites can share these facilities, performance varies depending on how many other users are sending and receiving data. At the maximum, users can download data up to 10 Mbps and can upload data at 256 kbps. Typically, performance is much lower than this. In most cases, the speed of cable modems and DSL modems is about the same. Cable modems use their own protocols. Figure 6-7 (page 196) summarizes these alternatives.

You will sometimes hear the terms *narrowband* and *broadband* with regard to communications speeds. **Narrowband** lines typically have transmissions speeds less than 56 kbps. **Broadband** lines have speeds in excess of 256 kbps. Thus, a dial-up modem provides narrowband access, and DSL and cable modems provide broadband access.

The variety of LAN and WAN connections have resulted in the almost unbelievable growth of personal and business computing in the past 10 years. The Problem-Solving Guide *on page 208 discusses possible responses to such exponential growth.*

Networks of Leased Lines

The fourth WAN alternative shown in Figure 6-7 is to create a **network of leased lines** between company sites. Figure 6-10 shows a WAN that connects computers located at three geographically distributed company sites. The lines that connect these sites are leased from telecommunications companies that are licensed to provide them.

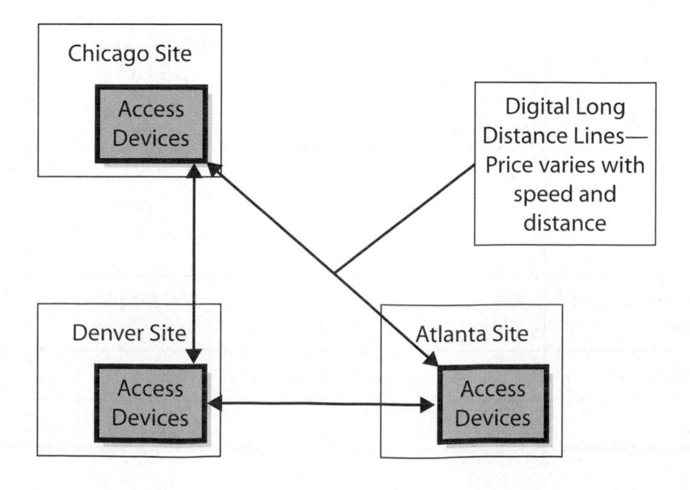

Figure 6-10
WAN Using Leased Lines

A variety of **access devices** connect each site to the transmission lines. These devices are typically special-purpose computers; the particular devices required depend on the line used and other factors. Sometimes switches are used, and in other cases, a device called a *router* is used. A **router** is a special-purpose computer that moves network traffic from one node on a network to another. See the appendix (page 216) for more information.

Several leased-line alternatives exist. As shown in Figure 6-11, lines are classified by their use and speed. A T1 line can support up to 1.544 Mbps; a T3 line can support up to 44.736 Mbps. Using optical fiber cable, even faster lines are possible; an OC-768 line supports 40 Gbps. Except for T1 speeds, faster lines require either optical fiber cable or satellite communication. T1 speeds can be supported by regular telephone wires, as well as by optical fiber cable and satellite communication.

Setting up a point-to-point line, once it has been leased, requires considerable work by highly trained, expensive specialists. Connecting the company's LANs and other facilities is a challenging task, and maintaining those connections is expensive. In some cases, organizations contract with third parties to set up and support the lines they have leased.

Notice, too, that with point-to-point lines, as the number of sites increases, the number of lines required increases dramatically. If another site is added to the network in Figure 6-10, up to three new leased lines will be needed. In general, if a network has *n* sites, as many as *n* additional lines need to be leased, set up, and supported to connect a new site to all the other sites.

Furthermore, only predefined sites can use the leased lines. It is not possible for an employee working at a temporary, remote location, such as a hotel, to use this network. Similarly, customers or vendors cannot use such a network, either.

However, if an organization has substantial traffic between fixed sites, leased lines can provide a low cost per bit transmitted. A company such as Boeing, for example, with major facilities in Seattle, St. Louis, and Los Angeles, could benefit by using leased lines to connect these sites. The operations of such a company require transmitting huge amounts of data between those fixed sites. Further, such a company knows how to hire and manage the technical personnel required to support this infrastructure.

Public Switched Data Network

Yet another WAN alternative is a **public switched data network (PSDN)**, a network of computers and leased lines that is developed and maintained by a vendor that leases time on the network to other organizations. A PSDN is a utility that supplies

Line Type	Use	Maximum Speed
Telephone line (twisted pair copper lines)	Dial-up modem	56 Kbps
	DSL modem	1.544 Mbps
	WAN—T1—using a pair of telephone lines	1.544 Mbps
Coaxial cable	Cable modem	Upstream to 256 Kbps Downstream to 10 Mbps (usually much less, however)
Unshielded twisted pair (UTP)	LAN	100 Mbps
Optical fiber cable	LAN and WAN—T3, OC-768, etc.	40 Gbps or more
Satellite	WAN—OC-768, etc.	40 Gbps or more

Figure 6-11
Transmission Line Types, Uses, and Speeds

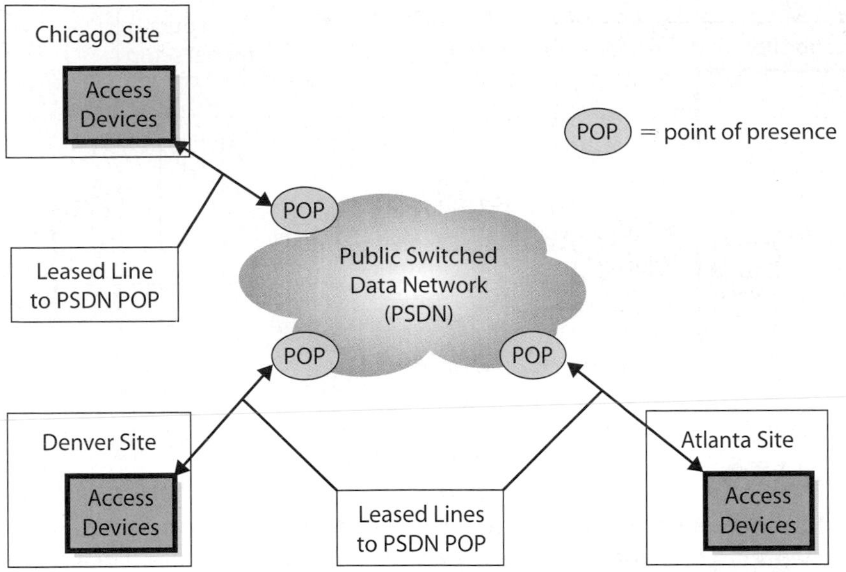

Chicago Site
Access Devices
POP = point of presence
POP
Leased Line to PSDN POP
Public Switched Data Network (PSDN)
POP
POP
Denver Site
Access Devices
Leased Lines to PSDN POP
Atlanta Site
Access Devices

Figure 6-12
WAN Using PSDN

a network for other companies to lease. Figure 6-12 shows the PSDN as a cloud of capability. What happens within that cloud is of no concern to the lessees. As long as they get the availability and speed they expect, the PSDN could consist of strings of spaghetti connected by meatballs. (This is not likely to be the case, however.)

When using a PSDN, each site must lease a line to connect to the PSDN network. The location at which this occurs is called a **point of presence (POP)**; it is the access point into the PSDN. Think of the POP as the phone number that one dials to connect to the PSDN. Once a site has connected to the PSDN POP, the site obtains access to all other sites connected to the PSDN.

PSDNs save the setup and maintenance activities required when using leased lines. They also save costs, because a company does not have to pay for the entire network; the company can pay just for the traffic that it sends. Further, using a PSDN requires much less management involvement than using leased lines. Another advantage of PSDNs is that only one line is required to connect a new site to all other sites.

Three protocols are used with PSDNs: Frame Relay, ATM (asynchronous transfer mode), and Ethernet. **Frame Relay** can process traffic in the range of 56 kbps to 40 Mbps. **Asynchronous transfer mode (ATM)** can process speeds from 1 to 156 Mbps. Frame Relay, although slower, is simpler and easier to support than ATM, and PSDNs can offer it at lower cost than ATM. However, some organizations need ATM's faster speed. Also, ATM can support both voice and data communications.

Often, PSDNs offer both Frame Relay and ATM on their network. Customers can choose whichever technique better fits their needs. Some companies use a PSDN network in lieu of a long-distance telephone carrier.

Ethernet, the protocol developed for LANs, also is used as a PSDN protocol. Newer versions of Ethernet can operate at speeds of 10 and 40 Gpbs.

Virtual Private Network

The last WAN alternative shown in Figure 6-7 is the **virtual private network (VPN)**. A VPN uses the Internet or a private internet to create the appearance of private point-to-point connections. In the IT world, the term *virtual* means something that appears to exist that does not in fact exist. Here, a VPN uses the public Internet to create the appearance of a private connection.

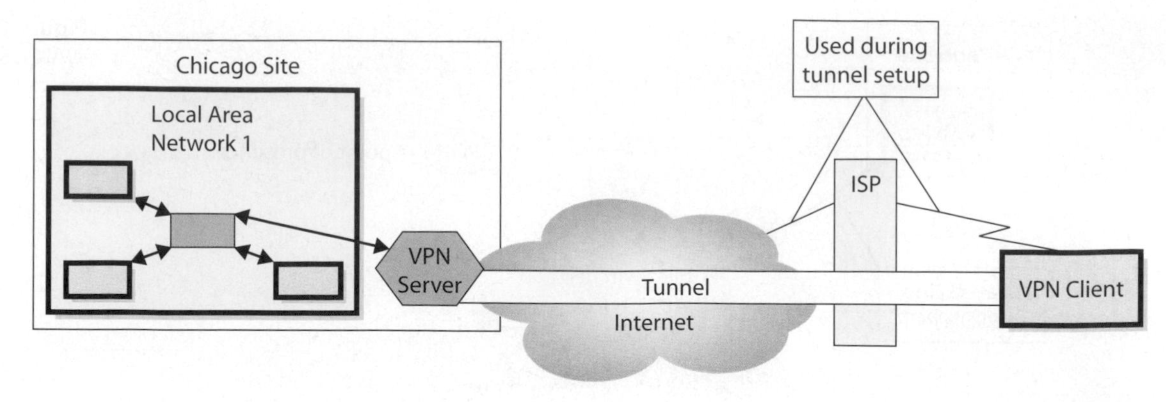

Figure 6-13
Remote Access Using VPN: Actual Connections

A Typical VPN

Figure 6-13 shows one way to create a VPN to connect a remote computer, perhaps an employee working at a hotel in Miami, to a LAN at a Chicago site. The remote user is the VPN client. That client first establishes a connection to the Internet. The connection can be obtained by accessing a local ISP, as shown in the figure; or, in some hotels, the hotel itself provides a direct Internet connection.

In either case, once the Internet connection is made, VPN software on the remote user's computer establishes a connection with the VPN server in Chicago. The VPN client and VPN server then have a point-to-point connection. That connection, called a **tunnel**, is a virtual, private pathway over a public or shared network from the VPN client to the VPN server. Figure 6-14 illustrates the connection as it appears to the remote user.

VPN communications are secure, even though they are transmitted over the public Internet. To ensure security, VPN client software *encrypts*, or codes (see the Q5 discussion, page 206), the original message so that its contents are protected from snooping. Then the VPN client appends the Internet address of the VPN server to the message and sends that package over the Internet to the VPN server. When the VPN server receives the message, it strips its address off the front of the message, *decrypts* the coded message, and sends the plain text message to the original address on the LAN. In this way, secure private messages are delivered over the public Internet.

VPNs offer the benefit of point-to-point leased lines, and they enable remote access, both by employees and by any others who have been registered with the VPN server. For example, if customers or vendors are registered with the VPN server, they can use the VPN from their own sites. Figure 6-15 shows three tunnels: one supports a point-to-point connection between the Atlanta and Chicago sites and the other two support remote connections.

Wireless technologies are expanding data communications possibilities. For more on how one company is addressing the "problem of the last mile," read the Data Communications in Practice *box on page 203.*

Microsoft has fostered the popularity of VPNs by including VPN support in Windows. All versions of Microsoft Windows have the capability of working as VPN clients. Computers running Windows Server can operate as VPN servers.

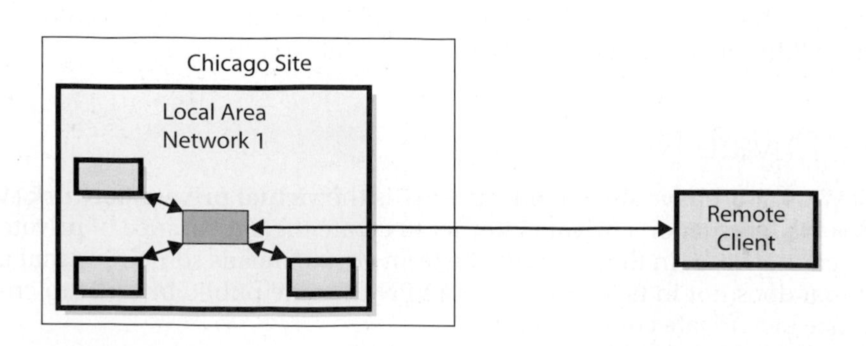

Figure 6-14
Remote Access Using VPN: Apparent Connection

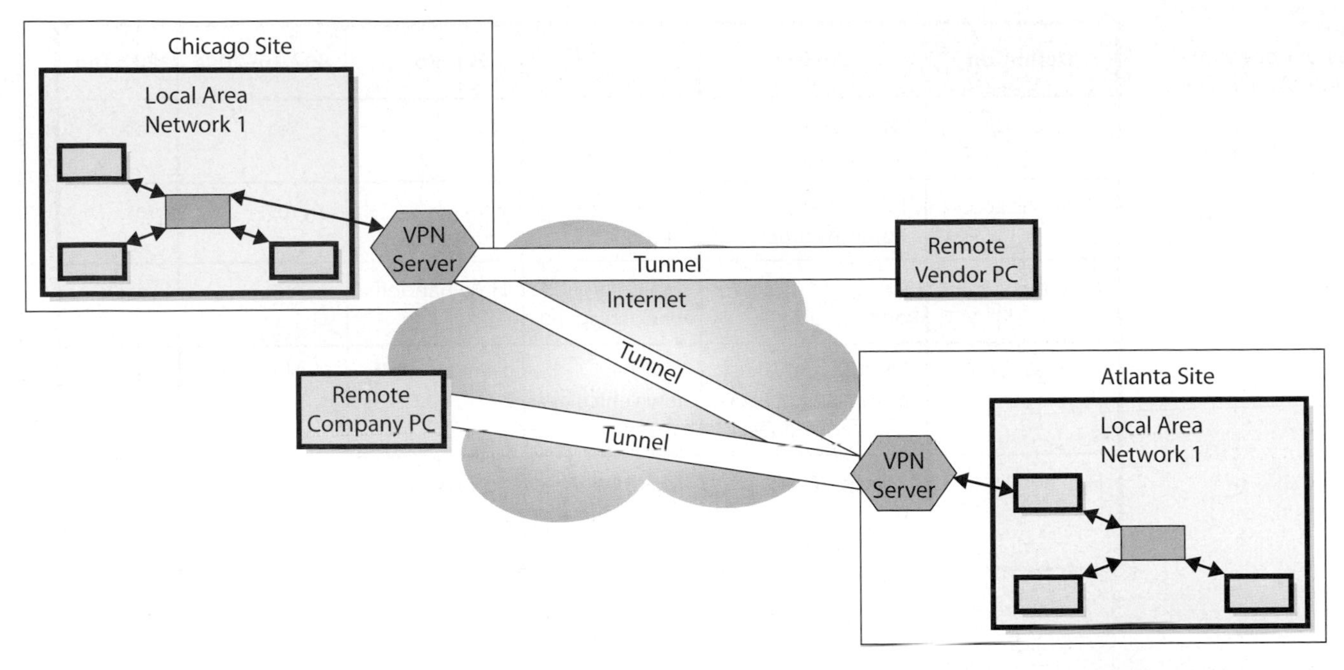

Figure 6-15
WAN Using VPN

DATA COMMUNICATIONS IN PRACTICE

KEEPING UP WITH WIRELESS

Data communications technology is one of the fastest-changing technologies, if not *the* fastest changing, in all of IT. Substantial portions of the knowledge you gain from this chapter will be obsolete within the first 5 years of your career. Unfortunately, we do not know which portion that will be.

Consider the example of wireless technology. Craig McCaw built one of the world's first cellular networks in the early 1980s and brought cells phones to the masses. In the 1990s, he sold his company to AT&T for $11.5 billion. In 2003, McCaw started a new venture, Clearwire, that uses an emerging technology called **WiMax** to address what is called the "problem of the last mile." Will WiMax replace existing wireless technology? We do not know. But, when someone with McCaw's knowledge, experience, and wealth starts a new venture based on that new technology, we all should pay attention.

To begin, what is the **problem of the last mile**? The bottleneck on data communications into homes, and into smaller businesses, is the last mile. Fast optical-fiber transmission lines lie in the street in front of your apartment or office; the problem is getting that capacity into the building and to your computer or TV. Digging up the street and backyard of every residence and small business to install optical fiber is not an affordable proposition. Even if that could be done, such infrastructure cannot be used by mobile devices. You cannot watch a downloaded movie on a commuter train using an optical fiber line.

Existing wireless technology does not solve the problem. Cell phones do not have the capacity to transmit video, and wireless technology based on the IEEE 802.11 standard is limited to devices within a few hundred feet. WiMax, the technology chosen by Clearwire, solves both of these problems: It is fast, and its range is measured in miles.

According to the WiMax Forum:

> WiMAX is a standards-based technology enabling the delivery of last-mile wireless broadband access as an alternative to wired broadband like cable and DSL. WiMAX provides fixed, nomadic, portable and, soon, mobile wireless broadband connectivity without the need for direct line-of-sight with a base station. In a typical cell radius deployment of three to ten kilometers, WiMAX Forum Certified™ systems can be expected to deliver capacity of up to 40 Mbps per channel, for fixed and portable access applications.[1]

[1] *www.wimaxforum.org/technology*, accessed August 2007.

Figure 1
Types of Access to a WiMAX Network

Source: "Types of Access to a WiMAX Network," Table 1 from *Fixed, Nomadic, Portable, and Mobile Applications for 802.16–2004 and 802.16e WiMAX Networks* prepared by Senza Fili Consulting on behalf the WIMAX Forum. © 2005 WiMAX Forum. www.wimaxforum.org.

Definition	Devices	Locations/ Speed	Handoffs	802.16–2004	802.16e
Fixed access	Outdoor and indoor CPEs	Single/ stationary	No	Yes	Yes
Nomadic access	Indoor CPEs, PCMCIA cards	Multiple/ stationary	No	Yes	Yes
Portability	Laptop PCMCIA or mini cards	Multiple/ walking speed	Hard handoffs	No	Yes
Simple mobility	Laptop PCMCIA or mini cards, PDAs or smartphones	Multiple/ low vehicular speed	Hard handoffs	No	Yes
Full mobility	Laptop PCMCIA or mini cards, PDAs or smartphones	Multiple/ high vehicular speed	Soft handoffs	No	Yes

What do the terms *fixed, nomadic, portable,* and *mobile* mean? The WiMax Forum published a white paper with the table shown above in Figure 1.

Using knowledge from this chapter, you can guess the meaning of the last two columns. They must refer to IEEE standards: 802.3 is Ethernet and 802.11 is standard wireless, so the **802.16 protocol** must be a new IEEE WiMax standard. CPE stands for *customer premises equipment* (meaning a device, such as a computer chip or an access device, that Intel, Clearwire, or another vendor will sell to the customer). PCMCIA cards are older technology; think instead of onboard devices that Intel will make for new-generation laptops.

With these definitions, you can interpret this table. *Nomadic use* allows a user to sign in, for example, from sites at home and at work, but not to be connected in transit. *Portable use* would allow the user to walk to work while connected; *simple mobility* supports connections while driving on city streets, and *full mobility* allows access on the freeway or a fast train.

Now, bring this back to Craig McCaw. He made cell phones accessible to the public in the 1980s, and he intends to make portable, wireless, broadband accessible with WiMax today. Although we can wonder what he'll do with another $11 billion, a better question to ask is, "What opportunities will this create for you?" That's the upside of all this change; it continually creates new opportunities for those who look for them.

See Collaboration Exercise 2 on page 214 to explore WiMax opportunities.

Q4 What Criteria Can You Use for Comparing WANS?

As you have learned, many different computer networking alternatives are available, each with different characteristics. Choosing among them can be a complicated task. Figure 6-16 lists three categories of criteria you can use to compare alternatives.

As shown, managers need to consider three types of costs. *Setup costs* include the costs of acquiring transmission lines and equipment, such as switches, routers, and access devices. If lines or equipment are leased, setup fees also may be involved. Additionally, if your company is performing some of the setup work itself, labor costs need to be included. Finally, there are training costs. *Operational costs* include lease fees for lines and equipment, charges of the ISP, and the cost of ongoing training. *Maintenance costs* include those for periodic maintenance, for problem diagnosis and repair, and for mandatory upgrades.

Criteria Category	Criteria	Description
Cost	Initial setup	Transmission line; equipment setup fees, including labor and training costs
	Operational	Fees for leases of lines and equipment; ISP and other service fees; ongoing training
	Maintenance	Periodic maintenance costs; problem diagnosis and repair costs; mandatory upgrade costs
Performance	Speed	Line and equipment speed
	Latency	Delays during busy periods
	Availability	Frequency of service outage
	Loss rate	Frequency retransmission required
	Transparency	User involvement in operation
	Performance guarantees?	Vendors agree to cost penalties if levels of service not met
Other	Growth potential	How difficult to upgrade when service needs or capacity increase?
	Commitment periods	Length of leases and other agreements
	Management time	How much management activity is required?
	Risk, financial	How much is at stake if system not effective?
	Technical	If using new technology, what is the likelihood of failure?

Figure 6-16
Criteria for Comparing Network Alternatives

Figure 6-16 shows six considerations with regard to performance: Line and equipment *speed* are self-explanatory. **Latency** is the transmission delay that occurs due to network congestion during busy periods. **Availability** refers to the frequency and length of service outages. **Loss rate** is the frequency of problems in the communications network that necessitate data retransmission. **Transparency** is the degree to which the user is unaware of the underlying communications system. For example, a DSL modem that is always connected is more transparent than a dial-up modem, which must find a phone line that is not in use and then dial the ISP number. The greater the transparency, the greater the ease of network use. Finally, many vendors of communications equipment and services are willing to make **performance guarantees** that commit them to levels of service quality. When a performance guarantee is in place, the vendor agrees to cost penalties if agreed-upon levels are not met.

Other criteria to consider when comparing network alternatives include the growth potential (greater capacity) and the length of contract commitment periods. Shorter periods allow for greater flexibility and usually are preferred. Also, how much management time is required? An alternative that requires in-house technical staff will require more management time than one that does not. The final two criteria consider financial and technical risk.

In this chapter, you've learned (a lot we hope) about computer networks. Read the Reflections Guide *on page 210 for insights into the importance of your human networks as well.*

Q5 How Does Encryption Work?

Encryption is the process of transforming clear text into coded, unintelligible text for secure storage or communication. Encryption is used for VPNs, for secure Web sites, and for other purposes as well. Considerable research has gone into developing **encryption algorithms** that are difficult to break. Commonly used methods are DES, 3DES, and AES; search the Internet for these terms if you want to know more about them.

A **key** is a number used to encrypt the data. The encryption algorithm applies the key to the original message to produce the coded message. Decoding (decrypting) a message is similar; a key is applied to the coded message to recover the original text. In **symmetric encryption**, the same key is used to encode and to decode. With **asymmetric encryption**, different keys are used; one key encodes the message, and the other key decodes the message. Symmetric encryption is simpler and much faster than asymmetric encryption.

A special version of asymmetric encryption, **public key/private key**, is popular on the Internet. With this method, each site has a public key for encoding messages and a private key for decoding them. (For now, suppose we have two generic computers, A and B.) To exchange secure messages, A and B send each other their public keys as plain, or uncoded, text. Thus, A receives B's public key and B receives A's public key, all as plain text. Now, when A sends a message to B, it encrypts the message using B's public key and sends the encrypted message to B. Computer B receives the encrypted message from A and decodes it using its private key. Similarly, when B wants to send an encrypted message to A, it encodes its message with A's public key and sends the encrypted message to A. Computer A then decodes B's message with its own private key. The private keys are never communicated.

Most secure communication over the Internet uses a protocol called **HTTPS**. With HTTPS, data are encrypted using a protocol called the **Secure Socket Layer (SSL)**, also known as **Transport Layer Security (TLS)**. SSL/TLS uses a combination of public key/private key and symmetric encryption. It works as follows: First, your computer obtains the public key of the Web server to which it will connect. Your computer then generates a key for symmetric encryption and encodes that key using the Web site's public key. It sends the encrypted symmetric key to the Web site. The Web site then decodes the symmetric key using its private key.

From that point forward, your computer and the Web site communicate using symmetric encryption. At the end of the session, your computer and the secure site discard the keys. Using this strategy, the bulk of the secure communication occurs using the faster symmetric encryption. Also, because keys are used for short intervals, there is less likelihood they can be discovered.

Use of SSL/TLS makes it safe to send sensitive data such as credit card numbers and bank balances. Just be certain that you see *https//:* in your browser and not just *http://.* You will learn more about SSL/TLS, HTTPS, and public/private keys in Chapter 12, Information Security Management.

Warning: Under normal circumstances, neither email nor instant messaging (IM) uses encryption. It would be quite easy for one of your classmates or your professor to read any email or IM that you send over a wireless network in your classroom, in the student lounge, at a coffee shop, or in any other wireless setting. Let the sender beware!

Q6 What Is the Purpose of a Firewall?

A **firewall** is a computing device that prevents unauthorized network access. A firewall can be a special-purpose computer, or it can be a program on a general-purpose computer or on a router.

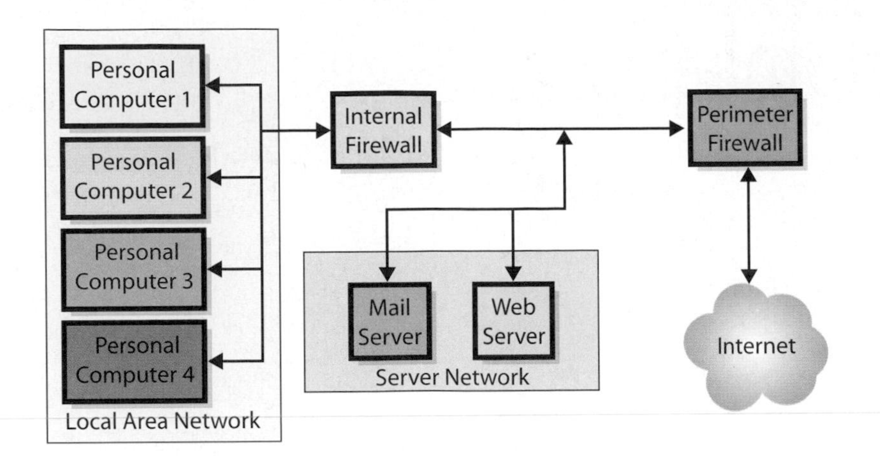

Figure 6-17
Use of Multiple Firewalls

Organizations normally use multiple firewalls. A **perimeter firewall** sits outside the organizational network; it is the first device that Internet traffic encounters. In addition to perimeter firewalls, some organizations employ **internal firewalls** inside the organizational network. Figure 6-17 shows the use of a perimeter firewall that protects all of an organization's computers and a second internal firewall that protects a LAN.

A **packet-filtering firewall** examines each part of a message and determines whether to let that part pass. To make this decision, it examines the source address, the destination address(es), and other data.

Packet-filtering firewalls can prohibit outsiders from starting a session with any user behind the firewall. They can also disallow traffic from particular sites, such as known hacker addresses. They also can prohibit traffic from legitimate, but unwanted, addresses, such as competitors' computers. Firewalls can filter outbound traffic as well. They can keep employees from accessing specific sites, such as competitors' sites, sites with pornographic material, or popular news sites.

A firewall has an **access control list (ACL)**, which encodes the rules stating which addresses are to be allowed and which are to be prohibited. As a future manager, if you have particular sites with which you do not want your employees to communicate, you can ask your IS department to enforce that limit via the ACL in one or more routers. Most likely, your IS organization has a procedure for making such requests.

Packet-filtering firewalls are the simplest type of firewall. Other firewalls filter on a more sophisticated basis. If you take a data communications class, you will learn about them. For now, just understand that firewalls help to protect organizational computers from unauthorized network access.

No computer should connect to the Internet without firewall protection. Many ISPs provide firewalls for their customers. By nature, these firewalls are generic. Large organizations supplement such generic firewalls with their own. Most home routers include firewalls, and Windows XP and Vista have built-in firewalls as well. Third parties such as Norton and Symantec also license firewall products.

Problem-Solving

GUIDE

Thinking Exponentially Is Not Possible, but…

Nathan Myhrvold, the chief scientist at Microsoft Corporation during the 1990s, once said that humans are incapable of thinking exponentially. Instead, when something changes exponentially, we think of the fastest linear change we can imagine and extrapolate from there, as illustrated in the figure on the next page. Myhrvold was writing about the exponential growth of magnetic storage. His point was that no one could then imagine how much growth there would be in magnetic storage and what we would do with it.

This limitation pertains equally well to the growth of computer network phenomena. We have witnessed exponential growth in a number of areas: the number of Internet connections, the number of Web pages, and the amount of data accessible on the Internet. And, all signs are that this exponential growth isn't over.

What, you might ask, does this have to do with me? Well, suppose you are a product manager for home appliances. When most homes have a wireless network, it will be cheap and easy for appliances to talk to one another. When that day arrives, what happens to your existing product line? Will the competition's talking appliances take away your market share? On the other hand, talking appliances may not satisfy a real need. If a toaster and a coffee pot have nothing to say to each other, you'll be wasting money to create them.

Every business, every organization, needs to be thinking about the ubiquitous and cheap connectivity that is growing exponentially. What are the new opportunities? What are the new threats? How will our competition react? How should we position ourselves? How should we respond? As you consider these questions, keep in mind that because humans cannot think exponentially, we're all just guessing.

So what can we do to better anticipate changes brought by exponential phenomena? For one, understand that technology does not drive people to do things they've never done before, no matter how much the technologists suggest it might. (Just because we *can do* something does not mean anyone will *want to do* that something.)

Social progress occurs in small, evolutionary, adaptive steps. Right now, for example, thousands of people are driving to stores to rent a movie. When they get there, they may not find the movie they want, they may wait in a long line, or they may never find a parking spot. Is it likely that someone would want to view a movie online, over the Internet, if they could? Probably so; online viewing is an extension of what people are already doing. It solves a problem that people already have. So, when network capacities support online movie viewing, it's likely to be a success.

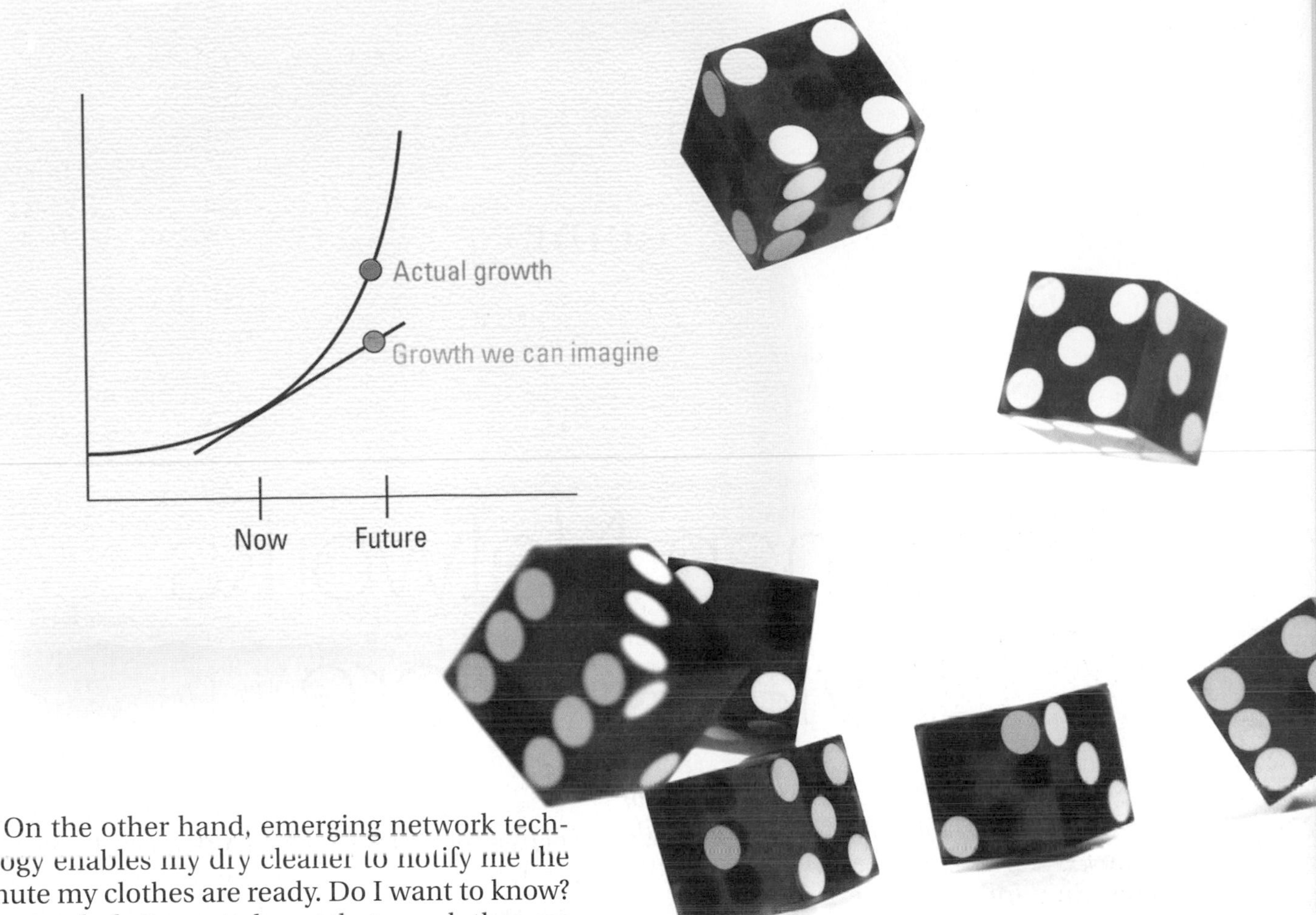

On the other hand, emerging network technology enables my dry cleaner to notify me the minute my clothes are ready. Do I want to know? How much do I care to know that my clothes are ready Monday at 1:45 rather than sometime after 4:00 on Tuesday? In truth, I don't care. Such technology does not solve a problem that I have.

So, even if technology enables a capability, that possibility doesn't mean anyone wants that capability. People want to do what they're already doing, but more easily; they want to solve problems that they already have.

Another response to exponential growth is to hedge your bets. If you can't know the outcome of an exponential phenomenon, don't commit to one direction. Position yourself to move as soon as the direction is clear. Develop a few talking appliances, position your organization to develop more, but wait for a clear sign of market acceptance before going all out.

Finally, notice in the exponential curve that the larger the distance between Now and the Future, the larger the error. In fact, the error increases exponentially with the length of the prediction. So, if you read in this textbook that IPv6 will replace IPv4 in one year, assign that statement a certain level of doubt. On the other hand, if you read in this text that it will replace IPv4 in 5 years, assign that statement an exponentially greater level of doubt. ■

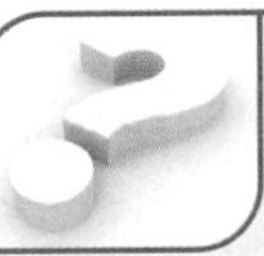

Discussion Questions

1. In your own words, explain the meaning of the claim that no one can think exponentially. Do you agree with this claim?
2. Describe a phenomenon besides connectivity or magnetic memory that you believe is increasing exponentially. Explain why it is difficult to predict the consequences of this phenomenon in 3 years.
3. To what extent do you think technology is responsible for the growth in the number of news sources? On balance, do you think having many news sources of varying quality is better than having a few with high quality control?
4. List three products or services, such as online movie viewing, that could dramatically change because of increased connectivity. Do not include movie viewing.
5. Rate your answers to question 3 in terms of how closely they fit with problems that people have today.

Reflections

GUIDE

Human Networks Matter More

In case you missed it, *Six Degrees of Separation* is a play by John Guare that was made into a movie starring Stockard Channing and Donald Sutherland. The title is related to the idea, originated by the Hungarian writer Frigyes Karinthy, that everyone on earth is connected to everyone else by five (Karinthy) or six (Guare) people.* For example, according to the theory, you are connected to Eminem by no more than five or six people, because you know someone who knows someone, who knows someone, etc. By the same theory, you are also connected to a Siberian seal hunter. Today, in fact, with the Internet, the number may be closer to three people than to five or six, but in any case, the theory points out the importance of human networks.

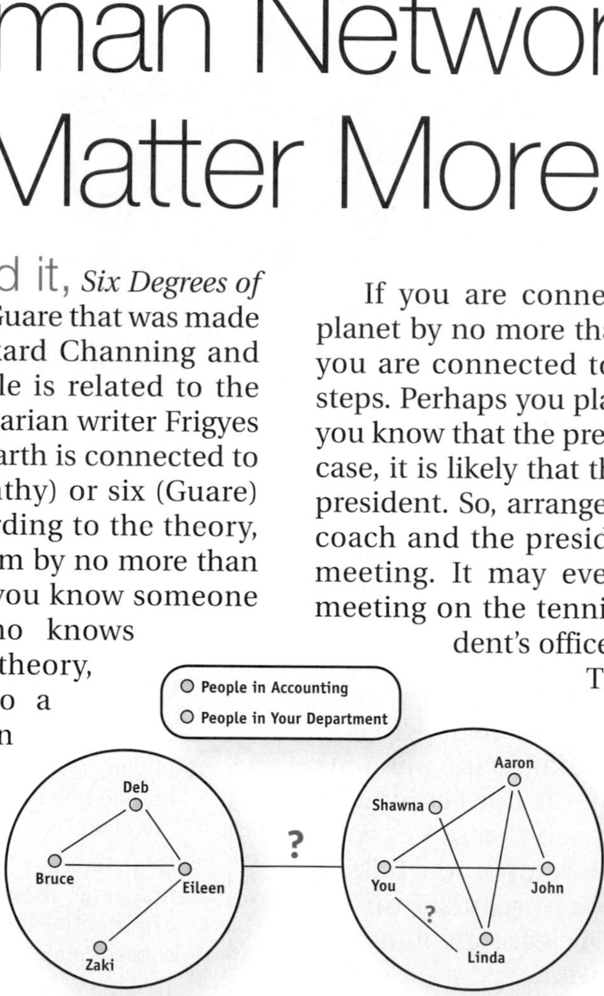

Suppose you want to meet your university's president. The president has a secretary who acts as a gatekeeper. If you walk up to that secretary and say, "I'd like a half an hour with President Jones," you're likely to be palmed off to some other university administrator. What else can you do?

If you are connected to everyone on the planet by no more than six degrees, then surely you are connected to your president in fewer steps. Perhaps you play on the tennis team, and you know that the president plays tennis. In that case, it is likely that the tennis coach knows the president. So, arrange a tennis match with your coach and the president. Voilà! You have your meeting. It may even be better to have the meeting on the tennis court than in the president's office.

The problem with the six-degree theory, as Stockard Channing said so eloquently, is that even though those six people do exist, we don't know who they are. Even worse, we often don't know who the person is with whom we want to connect. For example, there is someone, right now who knows someone who has a job for which you are perfectly suited. Unfortunately, you don't know the name of that person.

It doesn't stop when you get your job, either. When you have a problem at work, like the

*See "The Third Link" in Albert Laszlo Barabasi's book *Linked* (New York: Perseus Publishing, 2002) for background on this theory.

$80,000 question in Chapter 4, there is someone who knows exactly how to help you. You, however, don't know who that is.

Accordingly, most successful professionals consistently build personal human networks. They keep building them because they know that somewhere there is someone whom they need to know or will need to know. They meet people at professional and social situations, collect and pass out cards, and engage in pleasant conversation (all part of a social protocol) to expand their networks.

You can apply some of the ideas about computer networks to make this process more efficient. Consider the network diagram on page 210. Assume that each line represents a relationship between two people. Notice that the people in your department tend to know each other, and the people in the accounting department also tend to know each other. That's typical.

Now suppose you are at the weekly employee after-hours party and you have an opportunity to introduce yourself either to Linda or Eileen. Setting aside personal considerations, thinking just about network building, which person should you meet?

If you introduce yourself to Linda, you shorten your pathway to her from two steps to one and your pathway to Shawna from three to two. You do not open up any new channels because you already have them to the people in your floor.

However, if you introduce yourself to Eileen, you open up an entirely new network of acquaintances. So, considering just network building, you use your time better by meeting Eileen and other people who are not part of your current circle. It opens up many more possibilities.

The connection from you to Eileen is called a weak tie in social network theory,** and such links are crucial in connecting you to everyone in six degrees. *In general, the people you know the least contribute the most to your network.*

This concept is simple, but you'd be surprised by how few people pay attention to it. At most company events, everyone talks with the people they know, and if the purpose of the function is to have fun, then that behavior makes sense. In truth, however, no business social function exists for having fun, regardless of what people say. Business functions exist for business reasons, and you can use them to create and expand networks. Given that time is always limited, you may as well use such functions efficiently. ■

Discussion Questions

1. Determine the shortest path from you to your university's president. How many links does it have?
2. Give an example of a network to which you belong that is like your department in the figure on the preceding page. Sketch a diagram of who knows whom for six or so members of that group.
3. Recall a recent social situation and identify two people, one of whom could have played the role of Linda (someone in your group whom you do not know) and one of whom could have played the role of Eileen (someone in a different group whom you do not know). How could you have introduced yourself to either person?
4. Does it seem too contrived and calculating to think about your social relationships in this way? Even if you do not approach relationships like this, are you surprised to think that others do? Under what circumstances does this kind of analysis seem appropriate, and when does it seem inappropriate?
5. Consider the phrase, "It's not what you know, it's whom you know that matters." Relate this phrase to the diagram. Under what circumstances is this likely to be true? When is it false?
6. Describe how you can apply the principle, "The people you know the least contribute the most to your network" to the process of a job search.

**See Terry Granovetter, "The Strength of Weak Ties," *American Journal of Sociology*, May 1973.

Use this Active Review to verify that you understand the ideas and concepts that answer the chapter's study questions.

Q1 What is a computer network?

Define *computer network*. Explain the differences among LANs, WANs, internets, and the Internet. Describe the purpose of a protocol.

Q2 What are the components of a LAN?

Explain the key distinction of a LAN. Describe the purpose of each component in Figure 6-2. Define *MAC* and *UTP*. Describe the placement of switches in a multi-floor building. Explain when optical fiber cables are used for a LAN. Explain Ethernet. Describe the purpose of each of the wireless components in Figure 6-6.

Q3 What are the alternatives for a WAN?

Explain why your connection to an ISP is a WAN and not a LAN. Name three functions of an ISP. Describe the purpose of a modem. Explain three ways you can connect to the Internet. Describe the difference between DSL and cable modems. Explain the advantages and disadvantages of leased lines. Explain each cell of Figure 6-7. Explain each cell of Figure 6-11.

Describe the problem that a VPN solves. Use Figure 6-15 to explain one way that a VPN is set up and used. Define *tunnel*. Describe how encryption is used in a VPN. Explain why a Windows user does not need to license or install other software to use a VPN.

Q4 What criteria can you use for comparing WANs?

Explain the differences among three types of costs in Figure 6-16. Describe factors to consider for network performance. Summarize the "Other" criteria in Figure 6-16. Using these criteria, explain what you think are the major differences between a network of leased lines and a VPN. In your answer, be guided by the definitions of leased lines and VPN as well as your own intuition.

Q5 How does encryption work?

Define the terms *encryption* and *key*. Explain the difference between an encryption key and a key of a database table (Chapter 5). Explain the difference between symmetric and asymmetric encryption. Describe the advantages of each. Explain how public key/private key encryption works. Explain why SSL/TLS is important. Explain why you should be careful with what you write in emails and instant messages.

Q6 What is the purpose of a firewall?

Define *firewall*. Explain the role for each firewall in Figure 6-17. Describe how a manager might ask to shut off access to or from a particular site.

KEY TERMS AND CONCEPTS

USING YOUR KNOWLEDGE

1. Suppose you manage a group of seven employees in a small business. Each of your employees wants to be connected to the Internet. Consider two alternatives:

   - Alternative A: Each employee has his or her own modem and connects individually to the Internet
   - Alternative B: The employees' computers are connected using a LAN, and the network uses a single modem to connect.

   a. Sketch the equipment and lines required for each alternative.
   b. Explain the actions you need to take to create each alternative.
   c. Compare the alternatives using the criteria in Figure 6-16.
   d. Which of these two alternatives do you recommend?

2. Consider the situation of a company that has two offices at physically separated sites. Suppose each office has a group of 15 computers.

   a. If the two offices are retail art galleries, what is likely to be the most common type of interoffice communication? Given your answer, what type of WAN do you think is most appropriate?
   b. Suppose the two offices are manufacturing sites that communicate via email and that regularly exchange large drawings and plans. What are the advantages and disadvantages of each of the four WAN types for these offices? Under what circumstances would you recommend a leased-line WAN?
   c. Suppose the two offices are the same as described in part b, but that in addition each has salespeople on the road who need to connect to the office computers. How would your answer to part b change?
   d. Would you change your answer to part c if both offices are located in the same building? Why or why not?
   e. What additional factors would you need to consider if one of the offices in part c was in Los Angeles and the other was located in Singapore?

3. Reread the Larry Jones (Student) Network Services case in the *Innovation in Practice* box on page 197.

   a. Consider the first fraternity house that Larry equipped. Explain how a LAN could be used to connect all of the computers in the house. Would you recommend an Ethernet LAN, an 802.11 LAN, or a combination? Justify your answer.
   b. This chapter did not provide enough information for you to determine how many switches the fraternity house might need. However, in general terms, describe how the fraternity could use a multiple-switch system.
   c. Considering the connection to the Internet, would you recommend that the fraternity house use a dial-up, a DSL, or a cable modem? Although you can rule out at least one of these alternatives with the knowledge you already have, what additional information do you need in order to make a specific recommendation?
   d. Should Larry develop a standard package solution for each of his customers? What advantages accrue from a standard solution? What are the disadvantages?

COLLABORATION EXERCISES AND CASES

Collaborate with a group of students on the following exercises. Recall from Chapter 2 that collaboration is more than cooperation because it involves iteration and feedback. Post a document, a discussion item, a wiki item, or an idea and obtain feedback from your team members. Similarly, read the ideas of others and comment on them. Try to innovate in both the process by which you collaborate and the work product that you create. Avoid face-to-face meetings. Instead, use collaborative software such as Google Docs & Spreadsheets, Microsoft Groove, or Microsoft SharePoint to facilitate your ideas.

1. Reread the Larry Jones (Student) Network Services case in the *Innovation in Practice* box on page 197. Larry Jones based his consulting services on the installation of wireless services and SOHO networks for fraternity and sorority houses. It is probably too late for you to do the same using wireless, but you do have expertise that you might sell.

a. Consider the information technology skills and needs of your parents, relatives, family friends, and others in the Baby Boomer generation. Though you may not know it, you possess many skills that generation wants but does not have. You know how to text chat, how to download music from iTunes, how to buy and sell items on eBay, how to use Craigslist, and how to use a PDA, an iPhone, and so forth. You probably can even run the navigation system in your parents' car.

Thinking about Baby Boomers whom you know, brainstorm with your team the skills that you possess that they do not. Consider all of the items just described and others that come to mind. Make a common team list of all those skills.

b. Interview, survey, or informally discuss the items on your list in part a with your parents and other Baby Boomers. As a team, determine the five most frustrating and important skills that these people do not possess.

c. The Baby Boomer market has both money and time, but not as much information technology capability as they need, and they do not like it.

With your team, brainstorm products that you could sell to this market that would address the Baby Boomers' techno-ignorance. For example, you might create a video of necessary skills, or you might provide a consulting service setting up Microsoft Home Server computers. Consider other ideas and describe them as specifically as you can. You should consider at least five different product concepts.

d. Develop sales material that describes your services, the benefits they provide, and why your target market should buy those products. Try your sales pitch on friends and family.

e. How viable is your concept? Do you think you can make money with these products? If so, summarize an implementation plan. If not, explain why not.

2. Reread the *Data Communications in Practice* box on page 203. Clearwire has implemented the 802.16–2004 standard, which provides fixed and nomadic WiMax. In May 2007, Clearwire conducted a successful test in Portland, Oregon of limited portability using the 802.16e standard (*http://clearwire.com/company/news/05_21_07.php*).

Without portability, think of Clearwire as a very large wireless hotspot. Instead of wireless in a coffee shop, it is wireless over a several mile or larger region. When portability is available, think of it as a cell phone with very high speed communications access.

It is easy to understand why Clearwire can be a success to its shareholders, and how it will benefit chip manufacturers, who will sell additional hardware. However, how might it benefit you? What could you, a future business professional, do with it?

On its Web site, Clearwire publishes some of the innovative applications of its network that may jog your creativity:

> Clearwire . . . customers use the Internet in unexpected places and ways:
>
> - Oregon Wildfire Fighters: Firefighters battling the 2005 Wasson fire used Clearwire to download maps, stay in contact with the forestry service, and provide up-to-date information to citizens via their Web site.
> - Hurricane Katrina Victims: After the devastation of Hurricane Katrina, Clearwire set up towers quickly along the Gulf Coast so relief agencies could receive Internet access. Clearwire provided VoIP and Internet service to shelters that had none, and provided residents of "tent cities" with the means to communicate their health and well-being to loved ones.
> - Realtors: In several Clearwire markets, realtors use Clearwire service to check MLS listings for clients, show newly listed homes to clients, fill out paperwork and communicate with their offices from the field. In some cases, realtors are powering up their modems via their car's cigarette lighter and creating mobile hot spots.
> - Homebuilders: Working in new home construction often means conducting business out of temporary office trailers located on remote construction sites. Homebuilders rely on Clearwire's service because of its portability. Without the need for cable or phone lines, homebuilders can maintain Internet access and stay connected to important information as they move their operations from job site to job site.
> - Classroom on Wheels: Mobile classrooms in Reno are using Clearwire service to connect to the Internet and provide free, quality preschool services to children ages 3 to 5, who have no other opportunity for a preschool education. The five buses are "unwired" and are able to have Internet access wherever they travel around the community.
> - Hawaiian Virtual Weddings: Two men in Hawaii are in the business of sharing wedding memories, and they use Clearwire to broadcast weddings over the Internet for those who cannot travel to Hawaii to witness the big event.[2]

[2] *http://www.clearwire.com/company/press/kits/Innovativeproductuses.swf.* © Clearwater Corporation (accessed June 2007).

Think about these applications as you address the following questions.

a. Review the discussion of collaboration and decision making in Chapter 2 (page 44). Working with your team, develop a list of the advantages of Clearwire for decision making. Consider both structured and unstructured decision processes and both collaborative and noncollaborative decisions.

b. Using your list from part a, describe three opportunities for Clearwire capability. Consider both present capability and future portable capability.

c. Review the discussion of collaboration and problem solving in Chapter 2 (page 48). Working with your team, develop a list of the advantages of Clearwire for problem solving. Consider the problem-identifier, solution provider, and solution broker roles.

d. Using your list in your answer to part c, describe three opportunities for Clearwire capability. Consider both the present capability as well as the future portable capability.

e. Review the discussion of collaboration and project management in Chapter 2 (page 50). Working with your team, develop a list of the advantages of Clearwire for project management. Describe how its capability would be useful for workflow control.

f. Using your list in your answer to part e, describe three opportunities for Clearwire capability. Consider both its present capability as well as the future portable capability.

g. As a team, evaluate the nine opportunities you have developed. Select the three best and explain why you believe they are the best.

h. Clearwire is not the only company implementing WiMax. Search the Internet for other companies that provide WiMax capability. Do they appear to be stronger than Clearwire? Why or why not?

i. Clearwire is publicly traded. What else do you need to know before deciding to invest?

APPLICATION EXERCISES

1. Numerous Web sites are available that will test your Internet data communications speed. You can find one good at *www.speakeasy.net/speedtest/*. (If that site is no longer active, Google "What is my Internet speed?" to find another speed-testing site. Use it.)

   a. While connected to your university's network, go to Speakeasy and test your speed against servers in Seattle, New York City, and Atlanta. Compute your average upload and download speeds. Compare your speed to the speeds listed in Figure 6-11.

   b. Go home, or to a public wireless site, and run the Speakeasy test again. Compute your average upload and download speeds. Compare your speed to those listed in Figure 6-11. If you are performing this test at home, are you getting the performance you are paying for?

   c. Contact a friend or relative in another state. Ask him or her to run the Speakeasy test against those same three cities.

   d. Compare the results in parts a, b, and c. What conclusion, if any, can you make from these tests?

2. Suppose you work for a company that installs computer networks. Assume that you have been given the task of creating spreadsheets to generate cost estimates.

   a. Create a spreadsheet to estimate hardware costs. Assume that the user of the spreadsheet will enter the number of pieces of equipment and the standard cost for each type of equipment. Assume that the networks can include the following components: NIC cards; WNIC cards; wireless access points; switches of two types, one faster, one slower, at two different prices; and routers. Also assume that the company will use both UTP and optical fiber cable and that prices for cable are stated as per foot. Use the network in Figure 6-6 as an example.

   b. Modify your spreadsheet to include labor costs. Assume there is a fixed cost for the installation of each type of equipment and a per foot cost for the installation of cable.

   c. Give an example of how you might use this spreadsheet for planning network installations. Explain how you could adapt this spreadsheet for project tracking and billing purposes.

Chapter 6 Appendix

How the Internet Works

STUDY QUESTIONS

Q1 How does email travel?

Q2 What is a communications protocol?

Q3 What are the functions of the five TCP/IP–OSI layers?

Q4 How does the Internet work?

Q5 How does *www.prenhall.com* become 165.193.123.253?

When you send something as simple as an email with an attachment, a true techno-miracle occurs. You are about to learn how. In the process, you will learn important terms such as *router, IP address*, and *TCP/IP*, and you will see how they relate to make the Internet work.

Q1 How Does Email Travel?

Suppose you are on vacation in Hawaii and you want to send a photo of your amazing surfing skills to a friend in snowbound Cincinnati, Ohio. You plug your portable computer into your hotel's network, fire up your email program, write the email, attach the photo, and press Send. That's it. In a matter of minutes, your friend will be admiring your surfing antics. Even though you may not know it, a techno-miracle occurred.

Figure 6A-1 shows the networks involved in sending your email message and picture. There is a LAN at your hotel, a LAN at your friend's company, and the Internet connects the two. Assume that you sent your message from computer 3 (C3) at the hotel and that your friend is sitting at computer 10 (C10) in the company in Ohio.

You know that your email and picture traveled over the Internet, which is a network of networks. But how? A host of problems had to be overcome: Your friend has an Apple computer, and you have a Dell. The two of you use different operating systems and two different email programs. As shown, both you and your friend are connected to LANs, but your hotel's LAN uses wires, and your friend's company's LAN is wireless. Thus, the LANs are of different types and process messages differently.

Furthermore, your message and picture were sent over an optical fiber cable underneath the sea and received by a computer in San Francisco. But, your picture was too big to send in one big chunk, so it was broken into pieces, and the pieces traveled separately. When the pieces (called *packets*) arrived in San Francisco, a device (called a *router*) determined that the best way to get them to your friend was to send them to a router in Los Angeles, which sent the pieces to a router in Denver, which sent them to a router in Cincinnati, which sent them to a company that contracts with your friend's employer to provide Internet access, which sent them to the email server at your friend's company. Meanwhile, your computer determined that one of the pieces got lost along the way, and it automatically resent that piece.

When all of the pieces have been assembled, your friend gets the "You've got mail" indicator on his computer. He looks at your picture and asks, "How does she do that?" What he should be asking is, "How does the Internet do that?"

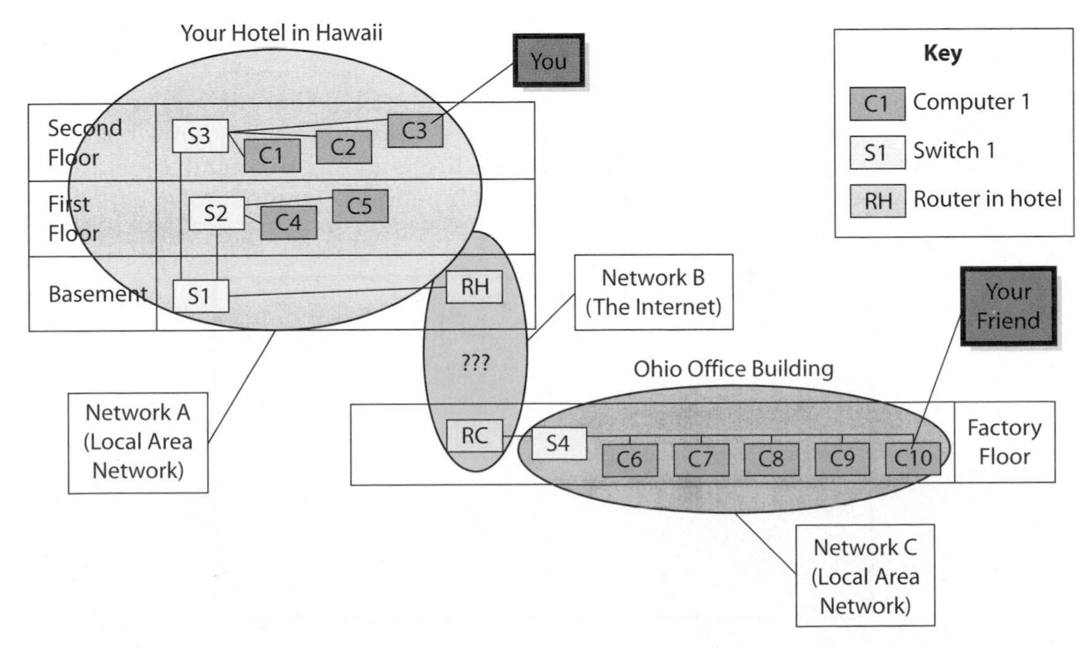

Figure 6A-1
Sample Networks

The key concept is *divide and conquer*. All of the work is divided into categories, and the categories of work are arranged into layers. To understand this further, we must first explain communications protocols.

Q2 What Is a Communications Protocol?

A **protocol** is a standardized means for coordinating an activity between two or more entities. Humans use social protocols. For example, a protocol exists for introducing two people to one another. Another human protocol, illustrated in Figure 6A-2, occurs at the grocery store. This protocol, like all protocols, proceeds through a sequence of ordered steps. If, in response to the clerk's query "Debit or credit," you enter your PIN, you are skipping steps and violating the protocol. The clerk will correct you and ask her question again. Notice, too, that the protocol has a decision branch. If you say, "credit," then the clerk will not ask the question about cash back or ask you to enter your PIN.

A **communications protocol** is a means for coordinating activity between two or more communicating computers. Two machines must agree on the protocol to use, and they must follow that protocol as they send messages back and forth. Because there is so much to do, communications protocols are broken up into levels or layers.

Q3 What Are the Functions of the Five TCP/IP—OSI Layers?

Several different **layered protocol** schemes, or **protocol architectures**, have been proposed. The **International Organization for Standardization (ISO)** developed the **Reference Model for Open Systems Interconnection (OSI)**, an architecture that has seven layers. Another group, the **Internet Engineering Task Force (IETF)**, developed a four-layer scheme called the **Transmission Control Program/Internet Protocol (TCP/IP) architecture**. For reasons that are beyond our discussion, the Internet uses a five-layer blend of these two architectures called the **TCP/IP—OSI architecture**.

Figure 6A-3 shows the five layers of this hybrid architecture. As shown in the right-most column, the bottom two layers concern the transmission of data within a single network. The next two layers are used for data transmission across an internet (a network of networks, including the Internet). The top layer provides protocols that enable applications to interact.

Layer 5

Examine the networks in Figure 6A-1 between your hotel in Hawaii and your friend. Unknown to you or your friend, each of your computers contains programs that operate at all five layers of the TCP/IP—OSI architecture. Your email program operates at Layer 5. It generates and receives email (and attachments like your photo) according to

Clerk:	Your total is $57.55.
You:	[You slide your credit/debit card through the machine.]
Clerk:	Debit or credit?
You:	Debit.
Clerk:	OK, any cash back?
You:	Yup, $50, please.
Clerk:	Enter your PIN.
You:	[You enter PIN.] OK?
Clerk:	OK, sign here.
You:	[You sign.]
Clerk:	Here's your $50.

Figure 6A-2
Example of a Grocery Store Protocol

Layer	Name	Specific Function	Broad Function
5	Application	The application layer governs how two applications work with each other, even if they are from different vendors.	Interoperability of application programs
4	Transport	Transport layer standards govern aspects of end-to-end communication between two end hosts that are not handled by the internet layer. These standards also allow hosts to work together even if the two computers are from different vendors and have different internal designs.	Transmission across an internet
3	Internet	Internet layer standards govern the transmission of packets across an internet—typically by sending them through several routers along the route. Internet layer standards also govern packet organization, timing constraints, and reliability.	
2	Data Link	Data link layer standards govern the transmission of frames across a single network—typically by sending them through several switches along the data link. Data link layer standards also govern frame organization, timing constraints, and reliability.	Transmission across a single network
1	Physical	Physical layer standards govern transmission between adjacent devices connected by a transmission medium.	

Figure 6A-3
TCP/IP—OSI Architecture

Source: Panko, Ray, *Business Data Networks and Telecommunications*, 5th, © 2005. Electronically reproduced by permission of Pearson Education, Inc., Upper Saddle River, New Jersey.

one of the standard email protocols defined for Layer 5. Most likely, it uses a protocol called **Simple Mail Transfer Protocol (SMTP)**.

There are many other Layer-5 protocols. **Hypertext Transfer Protocol (HTTP)** is used for the processing of Web pages. When you type the address *www.ibm.com* into your browser, notice that your browser adds the notation *http://.* (Try this, if you've never noticed that it happens.) By filling in these characters, your browser is indicating that it will use the HTTP protocol to communicate with the IBM site.

By the way, the Web and the Internet are not the same thing. The Web, which is a subset of the Internet, consists of sites and users that process the HTTP protocol. The Internet is the communications structure that supports all application-layer protocols, including HTTP, SMTP, and other protocols.

File Transfer Protocol (FTP) is another application-layer protocol. You can use FTP to copy files from one computer to another. In Figure 6A-1, if computer 1 wants to copy a file from computer 9, it would use FTP.

Three important terms lurk in this discussion:

1. **Architecture**. An *architecture* is an arrangement of protocol layers in which each layer is given specific tasks to accomplish.
2. **Protocol**. At each layer of the architecture, there are one or more *protocols*. Each protocol is a set of rules that accomplish the tasks assigned to its layer.
3. **Program**. A *program* is a specific computer product that implements a protocol.

So, for example, the TCP/IP—OSI architecture has five layers. At the top level are numerous protocols, including HTTP, SMTP, and FTP. For each of those protocols, there are program products that implement the protocol. Some of the programs that implement the HTTP protocol of the TCP/IP—OSI architecture are called *browsers*. Two common browsers are Mozilla Firefox and Microsoft Internet Explorer.

Layer 4

As Figure 6A-4 shows, your email program (which uses SMTP) interacts with another protocol called **Transmission Control Program (TCP)**. TCP operates at Layer 4 of the TCP/IP—OSI architecture. Note that we are using the acronym TCP in two ways: as the name of a Layer-4 *protocol* and as part of the name of the TCP/IP—OSI protocol architecture. In fact, the architecture gets its name because it usually includes the TCP protocol.

TCP performs many important tasks. Your Dell and your friend's Apple have different operating systems that represent data in different ways. Programs in those operating systems that implement the TCP protocol make conversions from one data representation to the other. Also, a TCP program examines your email and picture and breaks lengthy messages (like your picture) into pieces called **segments**. When it does this, it places identifying data at the front of each segment that are akin to the To and From addresses that you would put on a letter for the postal mail.

TCP programs also provide reliability. It was the TCP program on your computer that noticed that one of the pieces did not arrive at your friend's computer, and so it resent that piece.

Your friend's Apple computer also has a program that runs the TCP protocol. It receives the segments from your computer and sends acknowledgments back to your computer when it receives each segment. The TCP program also translates the segments from Windows (Dell) to Macintosh (Apple) format, reassembles the segments into a coherent whole, and makes that assembly available to your friend's email program.

Layer 3

TCP interacts with protocols that operate at Level 3, the next layer down. For the TCP/IP architecture, the Layer-3 protocol is the **Internet Protocol (IP)**. The chief purpose of IP is to route messages across an internet. In the case of your email, the IP program on your computer does not know how to reach your friend's computer, but it does know how to start. Namely, it knows to send all of the pieces of your email and picture to a device in your hotel's network called a *router*. In Figure 6A-1, that router is labeled RH. (This is not a brand of router, it is just the label we will put on the hotel's router in this figure.)

To send a segment to RH, the IP layer program on your computer first packages each segment into a **packet**. As shown in Figure 6A-4, it also places IP data in front of the

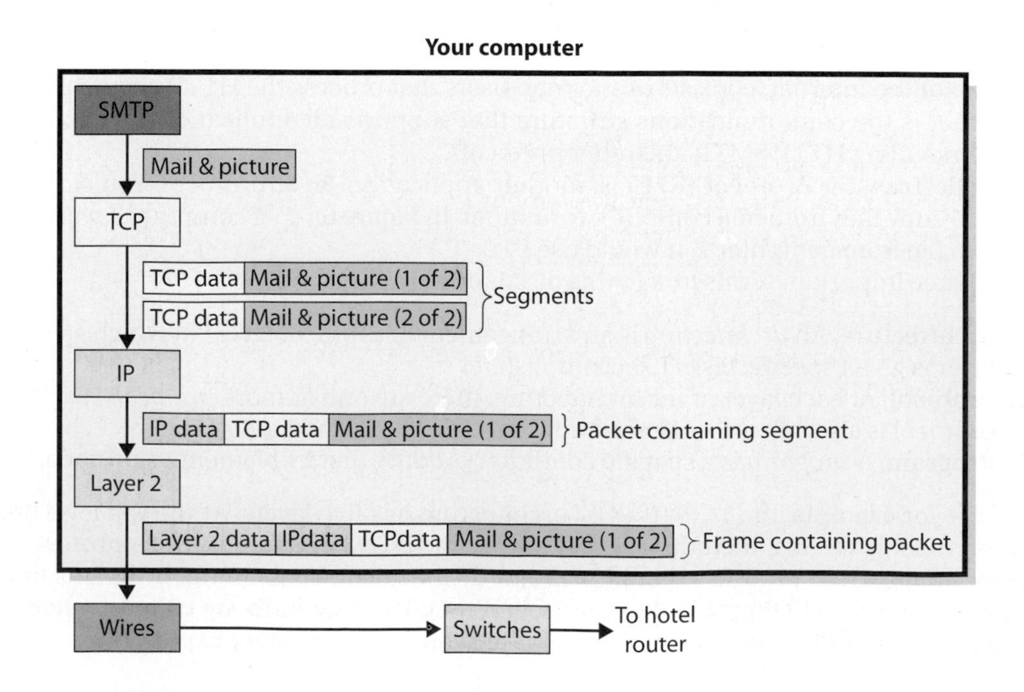

Figure 6A-4
TCP/IP—OSI on Your Computer

packet, in front of the TCP data. This action is akin to wrapping a letter inside another envelope and placing additional To/From data in the header of the outer envelope.

Routers are special-purpose computers that implement the IP protocol. The router labeled RH examines the destination of your packets and uses the rules of the IP protocol to decide where to send them. RH does not know how to get them all the way to Ohio, but it does know how to get them started on their way. In this case, it decides to send them to another router located in San Francisco. Dozens of other routers on the Internet will eventually cause the packets containing your message and picture to arrive at a router at your friend's employer. We will explain more about this process later in this appendix.

Layers 1 and 2

As shown in Figure 6A-1, your hotel uses a LAN to connect the computers in its hotel rooms. (Lucky you—you're staying at such an exclusive hotel that it has just two floors and five rooms!) Basic computer connectivity is accomplished using Layers 1 and 2 of the TCP/IP—OSI architecture. As you learned in Chapter 6, computing devices called **switches** facilitate that data communications. (See Figure 6A-4.)

A program implementing a Layer-2 protocol will package each of your packets into **frames**, which are the containers used at Layers 1 and 2. (Segments go into packets, and packets go into frames.) Then, programs, switches, and other devices cause the pieces of your email and picture to pass from your computer to switch 3, from switch 3 to switch 1, and from switch 1 to router RH. (See Figure 6A-1.)

Q4 How Does the Internet Work?

Given this background, we can now explain how your email travels over the networks to reach your friend. This is the most complicated section in this textbook. To understand this material, we will break the discussion into four sections. First, we will consider the addressing of computers and other devices. As you will learn, each computer and device has two addresses, a physical address and a logical one. Next, we will consider how protocols at all five layers of the TCP/IP—OSI model operate to send a request to a Web server within a LAN. Third, we will consider how those same protocols work to send messages across the Internet. Finally, we will wrap up with some details about IP addresses and the domain name system. Be patient, and take your time; you may need to read this section more than once. We begin with addresses.

Network Addresses: MAC and IP

On most networks, and on every internet, two address schemes identify computers and other devices. Programs that implement Layer 2 protocols use *physical addresses*, or *MAC addresses*. Programs that implement Layer 3, 4, and 5 protocols use *logical addresses*, or *IP addresses*. We will consider each type.

Physical Addresses (MAC Addresses)

As stated in Chapter 6, every network device, including your computer, has a NIC for accessing the network. Each NIC is given an address at the factory. That address is the device's **physical address**, or **MAC address**. By agreement among computer manufacturers, such addresses are assigned so that no two NICs will ever have the same MAC address.

MAC addresses are used within networks at Layer 2 of the TCP/IP—OSI model. Physical addresses are only known, shared, and used within a particular network or network segment. For internets, including the Internet, another scheme of addresses must be used. That scheme turned out to be so useful that it is also used within LANs, in addition to MAC addressing.

Logical Addresses (IP Addresses)

Internets, including the Internet, and many private networks use **logical addresses**, which are also called **IP addresses**. You have probably seen IP addresses; they are written as a series of dotted decimals, for example, 192.168.2.28.

IP addresses are not permanently associated with a given hardware device. They can be reassigned to another computer, router, or other device when necessary. To understand one advantage of logical addresses, consider what happens when an organization like IBM changes the device (a router) that receives requests when users type *www.ibm.com*. That name is associated with a particular IP address (as we will explain later in this appendix). If IP addresses were permanent, like MAC addresses, then when IBM upgrades its entry router, all of the users in the world would have to change the IP address associated with *www.ibm.com* to the new address. Instead, with logical IP addresses, a network administrator need only reassign IBM's IP address to the new router.

Public Versus Private IP Addresses

In practice, two kinds of IP addresses exist. **Public IP addresses** are used on the Internet. Such IP addresses are assigned to major institutions in blocks by the **Internet Corporation for Assigned Names and Numbers (ICANN)**. (We'll talk more about ICANN later.) Each IP address is unique across all computers on the Internet. In contrast, **private IP addresses** are used within private networks and internets. They are controlled only by the company that operates the private network or internet.

Dynamic Host Configuration Protocol

Today, in most cases, when you plug your computer into a network (or sign on to a wireless network), a program in Windows or other operating system will search that network for a DHCP server, which is a computer or router that hosts a program called **Dynamic Host Configuration Protocol (DHCP)**. When the program finds such a device, your computer will request a temporary IP address from the DHCP server. That IP address is loaned to you while you are connected to the LAN. When you disconnect, that IP address becomes available, and the DHCP server will reuse it when needed.

Of course, within a private network, administrators can assign private IP addresses manually as well. Often, the strategy within a private network is to manually assign IP addresses to computers that operate Web servers or other shared devices for which it is desirable to have a fixed IP address. Today, most users, however, are assigned IP addresses using DHCP.

Private IP Addresses at the Hawaii Hotel

To make sense of the discussion so far, consider Figure 6A-5, which shows the LAN operated by your hotel in Hawaii. Let's suppose that you occupy the penthouse suite (more good luck!) and that you plug your computer into the network as computer C3 in Figure 6A-5. When you do so, a program in your operating system searches the network for a DHCP server. It turns out that the router labeled RH is such a server. Your computer asks RH for an IP address, and RH assigns one. It will be a number like 192.168.2.28, but for simplicity let's denote your IP address by the symbol IP3.

Using TCP/IP—OSI Protocols within the Hotel

Once you have an IP address, protocol programs on your computer at Layers 3, 4, and 5 can communicate with any other computer in your network. Suppose, for example, that the computer labeled HS is running a Web server that provides information to hotel guests. This Web server is private; the hotel wants only guests and others within the hotel to be able to access it. Hence, the server operates only within the LAN.

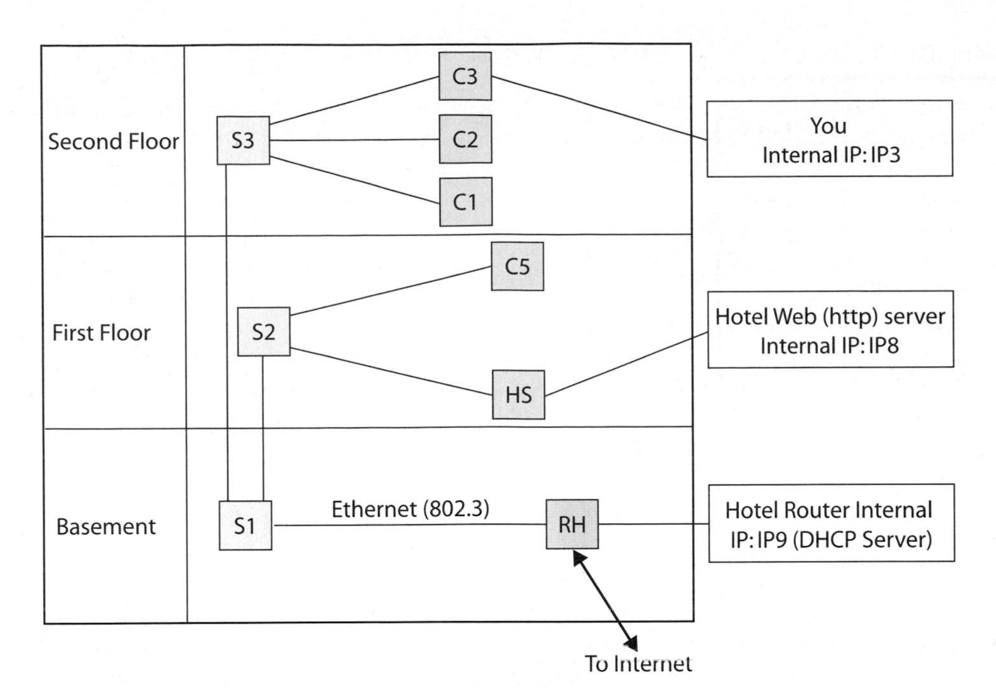

Figure 6A-5
Hotel LAN in Hawaii

Suppose the IP address of the server has been assigned by a network administrator; let's denote that address as IP8. The router, RH in Figure 6A-5, also has an IP address. Denote that address as IP9. Now, let's see how all of these addresses are used within the hotel's LAN.

Communications Processing on Your Computer

The hotel provides a brochure in your room that tells you how to sign on to the local Web server by entering a name into your browser. When you follow those instructions, your browser constructs a request for the server and uses the HTTP protocol to send it to HS.

We can follow the action in Figure 6A-6 (next page). Your browser sends its service request for HS to a program that implements TCP. One function of TCP is to break requests into segments, when necessary. In this case, suppose it breaks the request into two segments. The TCP program adds additional data to the segments. Here we show a header with *IP3 To: IP8*, but other data, and possibly a trailer, are added as well. We will ignore the real headers and trailers to focus on basic concepts.

The TCP program hands the segment(s) to a program that implements IP. As stated, the major function of that IP program is routing. It determines that the only route to IP8 is through the router at RH, whose IP address is IP9. So, the IP program adds the IP9 header and passes the wrapped packet down to a program that implements Ethernet.

The Ethernet program translates the IP address into a MAC address. Ethernet determines that the device at IP9 has a particular MAC address, which will be a long number. Here, for simplicity, we denote that address as RH. Ethernet will wrap the packet into a frame that is addressed to device RH.

When you signed onto the LAN, your Ethernet program learned that the only way it can connect to other computers is via switch S3 (see Figure 6A-5). Accordingly, it sends the frame to S3.

Communications Processing on the Switches

All switches have a table of data called a **switch table**. This table tells the switch where to send traffic to get it to its destination. The table on switch S3 has entries for every other device on the LAN. It knows, for example, that to get a frame to RH, it must send it to switch S1. Accordingly, it sends the frame to S1.

S1 also has a switch table. S1 consults that table and determines that it has a direct connection to RH. Therefore, it sends the frame to RH.

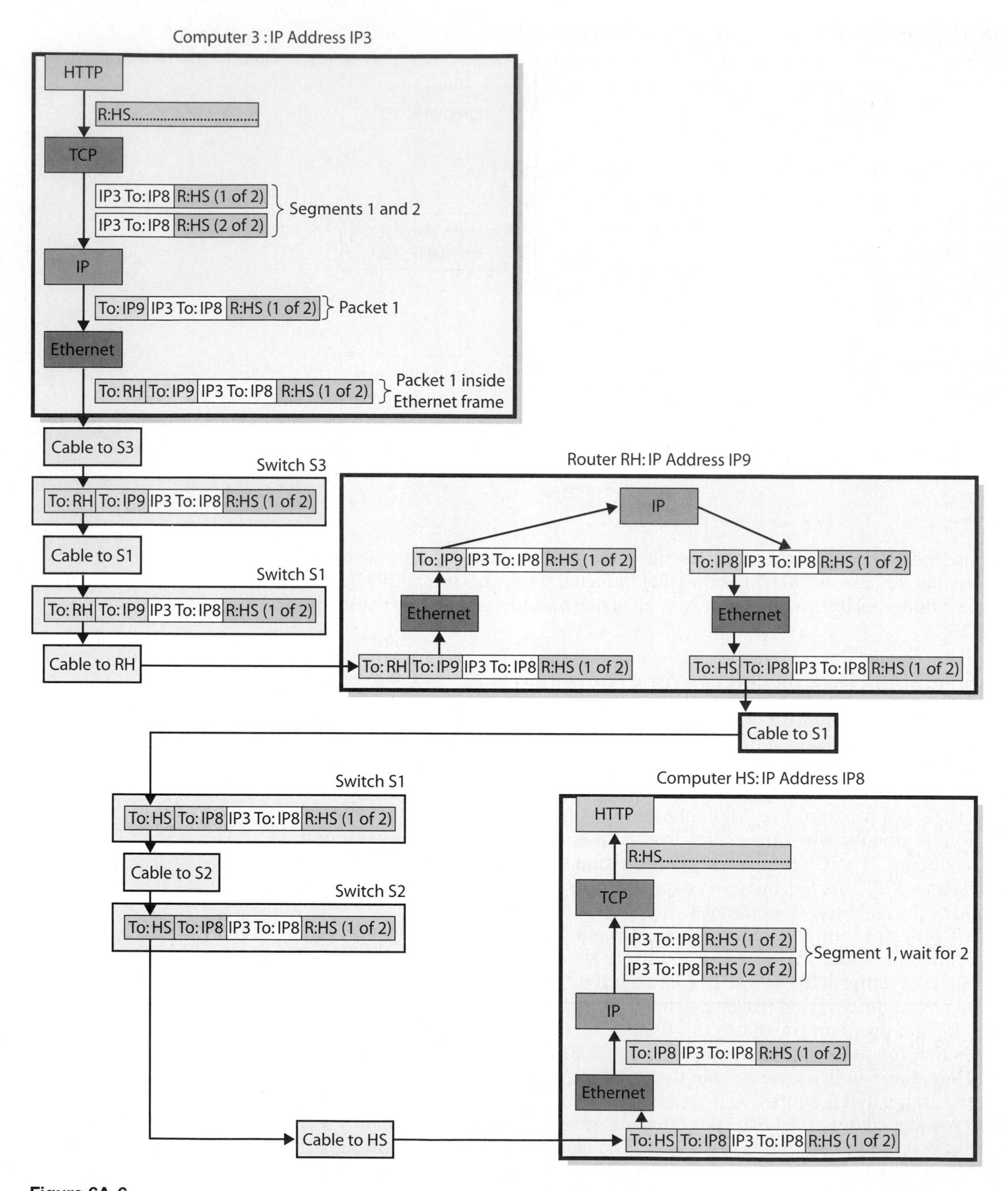

Figure 6A-6
Accessing the (Private) Hotel Web Server

Communications Processing on the Router

When the frame arrives at RH, it has arrived at its destination, and so Ethernet unpacks the frame and sends the contained packet up to IP. IP examines the packet and determines that the packet's destination is IP8. RH, which is a router, has a **routing table** that tells it where to send traffic for IP8. This routing table indicates that IP8 is just one hop away. So, IP changes the destination of the packet to IP8 and passes it back down to Ethernet.

Ethernet determines that the device at IP8 has the MAC address HS. So, it packages the packet into a frame and gives that frame the address HS. It then sends the frame to its switch S1. S1 consults its switch table and sends the frame to S2; S2 sends the frame to HS.

Communications Processing on the Web Server

The Ethernet program at HS unpacks the frame and sends the contained packet to the IP program. IP8 is the destination for the packet, so the IP program strips off the IP header and sends the contained segment up to a program that implements TCP. That program examines the segment and determines that it is the first of two. TCP sends an acknowledgment back to your computer to indicate that it received the first segment. (Of course, the acknowledgment must be routed and switched as well.) TCP waits for the second segment to arrive.

Once both segments have arrived, the TCP program sends the complete request up to the Web server program that processes the HTTP protocol. (Whew!)

To summarize:

- *Switches* work with *frames* at *Layer 2*. They send frames from switch to switch until they arrive at their destination. They use *switch tables* and *MAC addresses*.
- *Routers* work with *packets* at *Layer 3*. They send packets from router to router until they arrive at their destination. They use *router tables* and *IP addresses*.

Using TCP/IP—OSI Protocols over the Internet

Finally, we are in position to describe how your email gets from you at the hotel in Hawaii to your friend in the company in Ohio. In fact, you need to know just one more topic to understand the techno-miracle that occurs: how private and public IP addresses are converted.

Network Address Translation

All of the IP addresses described in the prior section were private IP addresses. They are used within the LAN at your hotel. For Internet traffic, however, only public IP addresses can be used. These addresses are assigned in blocks to large companies and organizations such as ISPs.

Your hotel has an ISP that it uses to connect to the Internet. That ISP assigned one of its public IP addresses to the router in your hotel. We will denote that IP address as IPx. (Again, it will be a four-part, dotted-decimal number, but ignore that right now.)

Therefore, as shown in Figure 6A-7 (next page), router RH has two IP addresses: a private one, *IP9*, and a public one, *IPx*. All Internet traffic aimed at any computer within the hotel LAN will be sent over the Internet using IP address IPx. The router will receive all packets for all computers at the hotel. When it receives a packet, it determines the internal IP address within the LAN for that computer. It then changes the address in the packet from IPx (the router's IP address) to the internal IP address of a computer in the hotel—the packet's true destination. Thus, if the router receives some traffic intended for you, it will change the packet's address from IPx to IP3 and send it to you.[1]

The process of changing public IP addresses into private IP addresses, and the reverse, is called **Network Address Translation (NAT)**. NAT uses a concept called ports. . . . But, let's stop there. We've had enough. If you take a data communications class, you can learn about NAT. Let's just move on and trust that NAT works.

[1]Believe it or not, we are simplifying. This description is typical for a SOHO network (see page 232). A real hotel and company would use devices in addition to the router for DHCP and NAT.

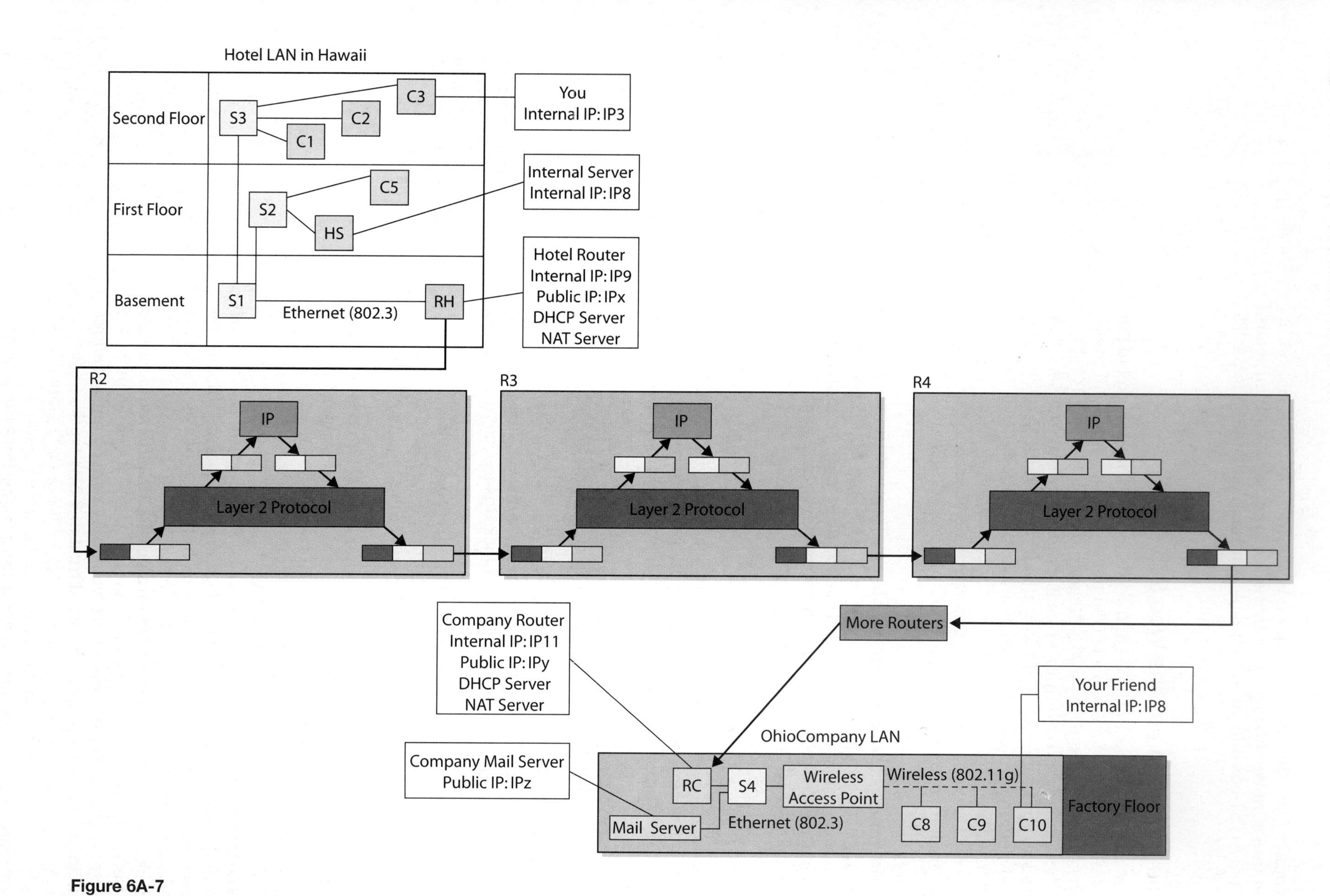

Figure 6A-7
Hawaii Hotel to OhioCompany via Internet

Your Email (!)

Finally, we can describe how your email gets to your friend in Ohio. You start your email program, and you enter your friend's email address. Suppose that your friend's name is Carter, and his email address is CarterK@OhioCompany.com. Your email program works at the application layer, and it implements SMTP. According to this protocol, your email will be sent to a mail server at the Internet address *OhioCompany.com.*

Your email program will use the domain name system (described later) to obtain the public IP address for the mail server at *OhioCompany.com*. Let's denote that address as *IPz.*

The message to IPz is then sent to the router RH as follows: Your email program implements SMTP, which sends the message to TCP. There it is broken into segments, and each segment is sent to IP, where they are placed into packets and routed to RH. Then, each packet is sent to your Ethernet program, where it is placed in a frame and sent to switch S3, and then S1, and then the router.

When one of the packets from your email and picture arrives at the router, it implements NAT and replaces your private IP address, IP3, with its public IP address, IPx. Router RH consults its routing table and determines how best to get the packet to IPz. Suppose that it determines that it should send the packet to Internet router R2.

The processing of the packet over the Internet is just the same as that described for the hotel in Figure 6A-1. Packets are sent from router to router until they reach the router RC, the gateway router at your friend's company, which sends them to the mail server.

At that server, segments will be unpacked from packets and sent to a TCP program on the mail server that will send an acknowledgment back to your computer. Then TCP will wait for all of the segments in your mail (and picture) to arrive. TCP will then send the entire message and photo attachment to the program that implements SMTP. That program, which operates at Layer 5, will place the message and photo in the mailbox for CarterK.

When your friend checks his mail, the mail program on his computer will use all five layers of the TCP/IP OSI architecture to send his mail check request to the mail server. His computer, which is also operating behind a router that provides NAT, has the internal IP address IP8. Notice that he has the same IP address as the server HS at your hotel. This duplication will not cause a problem, because these IP addresses are used only in local, private networks. Neither address is used on the public Internet.

Carter's computer connects to the mail server using a wireless protocol, 802.11g, but the essence of his communications to the mail server is the same as that on your hotel LAN. The mail server will send your email and picture to a TCP program on the mail server, from there to an IP program for routing to IP8, and from there to a program that processes Ethernet. Switch S4 will then convert the Ethernet frames into 802.11g frames and send them to your friend's computer.

That's how it works!

TCP/IP architecture can carry voice communications as well as data, as the Innovation in Practice *box on page 228 describes.*

Q5 How Does *www.prenhall.com* Become 165.193.123.253?

IP addresses are useful for computer-to-computer communication, but they are not well suited for human use. I want to be able to enter a name like *www.icann.org* into my browser and not have to remember and enter its public IP address, which is 208.77.188.103. The purpose of the **domain name system (DNS)** is to convert user-friendly names into their IP addresses. Any registered, valid name is called a **domain name**. The process of changing a name into its IP address is called *resolving the domain name.*

This process requires the solution of two problems. First, to be useful, every domain name must be unique, worldwide. To ensure that duplicates do not occur, an agency registers names and records the corresponding IP addresses in a global directory. Second, when the user enters a domain name into his or her browser or other Layer 5 application, there needs to be some way for the application to resolve the domain name. We will consider each problem in turn.

INNOVATION IN PRACTICE

VOIP AND IPTV

The TCP/IP—OSI architecture was originally designed to support text messages among computers on a network of networks. Nothing in this architecture required that it only carry text, however; as the email example shows, IP packets can carry photos or music just as well. In fact, packets can carry anything represented by bits.

Voice over IP (VoIP, pronounced "voyp") uses the TCP/IP—OSI architecture to carry telephone voice conversations. With VoIP, voice conversations are stored as bits, broken into IP packets, and routed over the Internet. No separate telephone line is required; the same connection that routes email, HTTP, and other data also carries the voice conversation. In Chapter 2, you saw that Microsoft Groove uses VoIP to transmit voice communications.

A problem occurs when a user who is connected to the Internet wants to dial someone who has only regular telephone access, or, equivalently, when someone who has a regular telephone wants to call someone who has a VoIP connection. Companies such as **Skype** (now owned by Yahoo!) have solved this problem and offer their subscribers unrestricted telephone access using VoIP. Skype is particularly economical for those who make frequent international calls. Some users complain that the quality of transmission is not as high as for the regular telephone, but they use Skype anyway because the cost savings are worth it.

IPTV (Internet Protocol television) uses TCP/IP—OSI to transmit television and other video signals. Because of the amount of data, a broadband connection is required. A device called a **set-top box** receives the IPTV signal and distributes it to multiple televisions or home entertainment centers. Some set-top devices provide VoIP, text chat, and other services as well. (For an example, Google the *Tornado M10 Media Center*.)

You can expect to see increased use of both VoIP and IPTV in the years to come.

Domain Name Registration

ICANN is a nonprofit organization that is responsible for administering the registration of domain names. ICANN does not register domain names itself; instead, it licenses other organizations to register names. ICANN is also responsible for managing the *domain name resolution system*.

The last letters in any domain name are referred to as the **top-level domain (TLD)**. For example, in the domain name *www.icann.org,* the TLD is *.org*. Similarly, in the domain name *www.ibm.com, .com* is the TLD. For non–U.S. domain names, the TLD is often a two-letter abbreviation for the country in which the service resides. For example, a name like *www.somewhere.cn* would be a domain name in China, and *www.somewhere.uk* would be a domain name in the United Kingdom.

Figure 6A-8 shows the U.S. top-level domains as of 2007. Some of these TLDs are restricted to particular industries, purposes, or organizations. The TLD *.aero,* for example, is restricted for use by organizations in the air transport industry. Similarly, *.name* is intended for use by individuals, and *.mil* is reserved for use by the U.S. military.

If you want to register a domain name, the first step is to determine the appropriate TLD. You must then visit *icann.org* and determine which agencies ICANN has licensed to register domains for that TLD. Finally, you need to follow the registration process required by one of those agencies. If the domain name you want is already in use, your registration will be disallowed, and you will need to select another domain name.

Domain Name Resolution

A **uniform resource locator (URL)**, pronounced either by saying the three letters or as "Earl," is a document's address on the Web. URLs begin with a domain name and then are followed by optional data that locates a document within that domain. Thus, in the URL *www.prenhall.com/kroenke,* the domain name is *www.prenhall.com, and /kroenke* is a directory within that domain.

Domain name resolution is the process of converting a domain name into a public IP address. The process starts from the TLD and works to the left across the URL. As of 2007, ICANN manages 13 special computers called **root servers** that are distributed around the world. Each root server maintains a list of IP addresses of servers that resolve each type of TLD.

For example, to resolve the address *www.somewhere.biz,* you would first go to a root server and obtain the IP address of a server that resolves *.biz* domain names. To resolve the address *www.somewhere.com,* you would go to a root server and obtain the IP address of a server that resolves *.com* domain names. In the first case, given the address of the server that resolves *.biz,* you would query that server to determine the IP address of the server that resolves the particular name *somewhere.biz.* Then you would go to that server to determine the IP address of the server that manages *www.somewhere.biz.*

In practice, domain name resolution proceeds more quickly because there are thousands of computers called **domain name resolvers** that store the correspondence of domain names and IP addresses. These resolvers reside at ISPs, at academic institutions, at large companies, at governmental organizations, and so forth. A domain name resolver may even be located on your campus. If so, whenever anyone on your campus resolves a domain name, that resolver will store, or **cache**, the domain name and IP address on a local file. Then, when someone else on campus needs to resolve that same domain name, there is no need to go through the entire resolution process. Instead, the resolver can supply the IP address from the local file.

TLD	Introduced	Purpose	Sponsor/Operator
.aero	2001	Air-transport industry	Societe Internationale de Telecommunications Aeronautiques SC (SITA)
.biz	2001	Businesses	
.com	1995	Unrestricted (but intended for commercial registrants)	VeriSign, Inc.
.coop	2001	Cooperatives	DotCooperation, LLC
.edu	1995	U.S. educational institutions	EDUCAUSE
.gov	1995	U.S. government	U.S. General Services Administration
.info	2001	Unrestricted use	Afilias, LLC
.int	1998	Organizations established by international treaties between governments	Internet Assigned Numbers Authority
.mil	1995	U.S. military	U.S. DoD Network Information Center
.museum	2001	Museums	Museum Domain Management Association (MuseDoma)
.name	2001	For registration by individuals	Global Name Registry, LTD
.net	1995	Unrestricted (but intended for network providers, etc.)	VeriSign, Inc.
.org	1995	Unrestricted (but intended for organizations that do not fit elsewhere)	Public Interest Registry; Global Registry Services
.pro	2002	Accountants, lawyers, physicians, and other professionals	RegistryPro, LTD

Figure 6A-8
U.S. Top-Level Domains, 2007

Of course, domain names and their IP addresses can change. Therefore, from time to time, the domain name resolvers delete old addresses from their lists or refresh old addresses by checking their correctness.

By the way, if you're curious to know your current IP address, go to *www.WhatIs MyIPAddress.com*. That site will tell you not only your own address, but you can also obtain the IP address of any URL. Similarly, you can do a reverse lookup, enter an IP address, and it will give you the registered URL at that address, if any.

ACTIVE REVIEW

Use this Active Review to verify that you understand the ideas and concepts that answer the appendix's study questions.

Q1 How does email travel?

Identify the LANs and the Internet network in Figure 6A-1. Describe some of the problems that must be overcome in sending your email and picture to your friend. Explain why some of your message was broken into sections. Describe the route your message took. Explain what happened when one of the sections was lost.

Q2 What is a communications protocol?

Give an example of a social protocol other than paying at the grocery store. In your own words, describe what a protocol does. Define *communications protocol.*

Q3 What are the functions of the five TCP/IP—OSI layers?

Compare and contrast the terms *communications protocol architecture, communications protocol,* and *program.* Using the example of Firefox (a browser) processing a Web site on the Internet, give an example of each of these. Using Figure 6A-3 as a guide, explain the purpose of each layer of the TCP/IP architecture in layperson's terms. Name the layers used for an internet and the layers used for a LAN. Explain how Figure 6A-4 shows a message being wrapped in packages, packages within packages, and so forth.

Q4 How does the Internet work?

Define the terms *MAC address* and *IP address*. Define the terms *physical address* and *logical address*, and relate them to MAC and IP addresses. Explain which layers of the TCP/IP—OSI architecture use MAC addresses. Explain which use IP addresses. Explain the advantage of being able to transfer an IP address from one device or computer to another.

Compare and contrast a public IP address and a private IP address. State who assigns each type of address. Explain the meaning of the statement, "Most user computers obtain IP addresses from DHCP servers." Explain the process by which you were granted an IP address at your hotel. Identify the computer that provided that address to you.

Using the network structure in Figure 6A-5, explain the message processing shown in Figure 6A-6. Explain how switches use MAC addresses and switch tables, whereas the router and the Web server use IP addresses and routing tables. Ensure you understand the differences in each of the rectangles in Figure 6A-6.

Explain why the router in your hotel needs two IP addresses. Explain how it uses IP9 and how it uses IPx. Show an example value for either IP address. Explain why your internal, private IP address must be transformed. Explain why all traffic directed to you from outside of the hotel will be sent to address IPx. Identify the device that translates your IP address into IPx and the reverse. Explain, at a high level, the purpose of network address translation.

Trace the flow of one email from you to your friend in Figure 6A-7. On each line that connects two devices, state whether a MAC or an IP address is used. If it is an IP address, state whether it is an internal or an external IP address. Explain why it is possible that your computer and the computer of your friend can have the same IP address. Compare and contrast segment, packet, and frame.

Q5 How does *www.prenhall.com* become 165.193.123.253?

Explain the meaning of the phrase *resolving a domain name*. Define the term *top-level domain*, and indicate the top-level domains of *www.prenhall.com, www.irs.gov,* and *www.myvalleyInn.uk*. Define *uniform resource locator*. Explain the role of ICANN with regard to domain registration. Summarize the process for registering the domain *www.mydogspot.info*. Explain ICANN's role with regard to domain name resolution, and describe the purpose of a root server. Summarize the process of resolving the URL *www.mydogspot.info*. Explain why it is likely that the first person to access *www.mydogspot.info* at a major university is likely to wait longer for a response than will subsequent people who access that same site.

KEY TERMS AND CONCEPTS

Architecture 219
Cache 229
Communications protocol 218
Domain name 227
Domain name resolution 229
Domain name resolver 229
Domain name system (DNS) 227
Dynamic Host Configuration Protocol (DHCP) 222
File Transfer Protocol (FTP) 219
Frame 221
Hypertext Transfer Protocol (HTTP) 210
International Organization for Standardization (ISO) 218
Internet Corporation for Assigned Names and Numbers (ICANN) 222
Internet Engineering Task Force (IETF) 218
Internet Protocol (IP) 220
IP address 222
IPTV 228
Layered protocols 218
Logical address 222
MAC address 221
Network Address Translation (NAT) 225
Packet 220
Physical address 221
Private IP address 222
Program (that implements a protocol) 219
Protocol 218
Protocol architecture 218
Public IP address 222
Reference Model for Open Systems Interconnection (OSI) 218
Root server 229
Routing table 224
Segment 220
Set-top box 228
Simple Mail Transfer Protocol (SMTP) 219
Skype 228
Switch 221
Switch table 223
TCP/IP—OSI (protocol) architecture 218
Top-level domain (TLD) 228
Transmission Control Program (TCP) 220
Transmission Control Program/Internet Protocol (TCP/IP) architecture 218
Uniform resource locator (URL) 228
Voice over IP (VoIP) 228

USING YOUR KNOWLEDGE

1. Assume you teach your MIS class and that a student comes to your office one day and asks, "Why do I have to learn how the Internet works? Give me three practical applications of this knowledge." How would you respond? Before you answer this question, read and think about the questions that follow.
2. How important do you think the existence of the TCP/IP—OSI protocols and architecture are to the success of the Internet? How did they contribute to the growth of the Internet? In what ways do protocols decrease competition? In what ways do they increase competition? In what ways do protocols stifle innovation? In what ways do they facilitate innovation? Explain how protocol architectures enable many different vendors to create interoperable products. In 2007 and beyond, what other industries might benefit from a similar standard?
3. Search the Internet for four companies that make products for one or more of the five layers of the TCP/IP—OSI architecture. Search for terms introduced in Chapter 6 and in this appendix, such as *802.3, 802.11, optical cable, VPN, firewall, switch, FTP,* and others. For each company, name one of their products, explain its function, and describe how that product relates to the TCP/IP—OSI architecture.
4. At one time, it was believed that the world would soon run out of IP addresses. Accordingly, a new protocol called IPv6 was proposed with longer IP addresses that provide many more unique IP addresses. During that same time, however, DHCP and NAT began to see widespread use, and their use dramatically reduced the growth in need for unique IP addresses. Explain why this is so. Suppose you are the director of product planning for a high-tech company, and 5 years ago you had been the initiator and principal proponent for the development of a new line of products based on IPv6. Your product sales have been substantially below your estimates. What do you do now? What product development principle(s) can you extract from this situation? How can you protect your organization from such situations in the future?
5. The biggest bottleneck in the Internet is the last mile from the ISP to the home. Numerous cities are developing plans and proposals to provide optical fiber cable to the doors of small businesses and homes. When this occurs, applications that require high bandwidth, such as home movies, will become feasible. Explain how companies such as Netflix are positioning themselves to pounce on that high bandwidth when it becomes available. Name three other products or services that become feasible when most homes have optical fiber cable at the door. What companies or industries stand to lose from the development of high-bandwidth capability? If you worked in one of those companies, how would you respond to this threat? How can you use the knowledge you gained from this question to guide your search for your first job?

CASE STUDY 6

SOHO Network Administration

The photo in Figure 1, below, shows LAN and Internet hardware used in a *SOHO (small office, home office)* company. This messy set of wires, devices, and office paraphernalia illustrates the use of many of the concepts in Chapter 6 and its appendix.

The small, flat, black box is a DSL modem that is connected to a telephone line. The DSL modem also connects to the silver, upright box with the small dark gray antenna. That silver box is a Microsoft Wireless Base Station. Wireless Base Station is a marketing term that Microsoft uses to soften the complexity of what's actually in that gray box. Amazingly, that little box contains an Ethernet LAN switch, an 802.11g wireless access point, and a router. Notice the several UTP cables that connect the Wireless Base Station to computers and other devices on the LAN. A generic term for Microsoft's Wireless Base Station is *device access router*, the term you should use when you go shopping for one.

In addition to the switch, access point, and router, the Wireless Base Station also contains a small special-purpose computer that has firmware programs installed. These programs provide DHCP service as well as NAT (described in the chapter appendix). The Wireless Base Station also has programs for administration and for setting up wireless security.

Notice the printer (behind the tape dispenser). The printer has a small black box with a gray UTP cable and a small black power line going into it. The black box is an NIC that connects the printer to the LAN. This NIC is called a *printer server*, and it, too, has a special-purpose computer with firmware that allows for setting up and administering the printer server and printer. Using the printer server, the printer is not directly connected to any computer. Any of the users on the LAN can use the printer without turning on a computer to serve the printer.

Figure 2 (next page) illustrates the structure of the SOHO network.

Both of these offices are in the same building. As shown, the base station includes an Ethernet switch, a wireless access point, a router, a DHCP server, and a NAT server. The base station, which is more generally called a *device access router*, has room for up to four physical connections from computers and servers.

Questions

1. Using the concepts from this chapter and its appendix, answer the following questions:

    a. What hardware is needed to add an additional computer to the LAN using Ethernet?
    b. Describe the advantages of using DHCP for the new computer.
    c. The line between the base station and the modem is not a telephone line. Which line(s) will be telephone line(s)?
    d. Which lines will be UTP cables?
    e. What hardware is needed to add another wireless computer?
    f. The computer user in office 2 must enter office 1 to access the printer. This is a problem to the occupants of both offices. What must be done to move the printer to a neutral location between the two offices?
    g. With regard to part f, suppose the users of this LAN decide to use a wireless printer server. Go to *http://cnet.com* or another site that lists computer

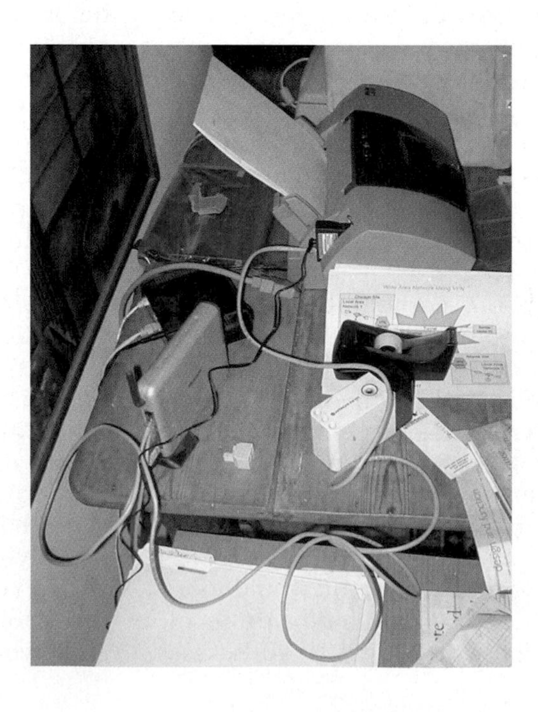

Figure 1
A SOHO Network

Source: David M. Kroenke.

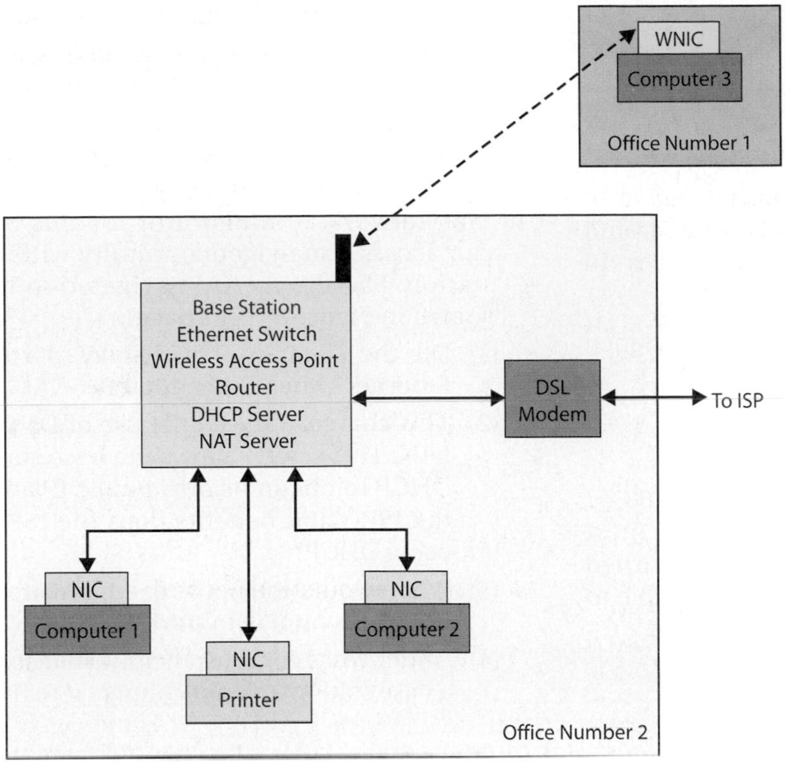

Figure 2
Structure of a SOHO Network

hardware and determine the approximate cost of a wireless printer server. Under what conditions is it better to buy a wireless printer server? Under what conditions is it better to buy a second printer for office 2 instead of a printer server?

h. The base station has room to connect only four Ethernet devices. If three computers and the printer are already connected using Ethernet, what options are available for adding yet another computer to the LAN?

i. All of the computers in this LAN run Microsoft Windows. A user at computer 1 clicked the LAN icon at the bottom of his screen and the screen shown in Figure 3 appeared.

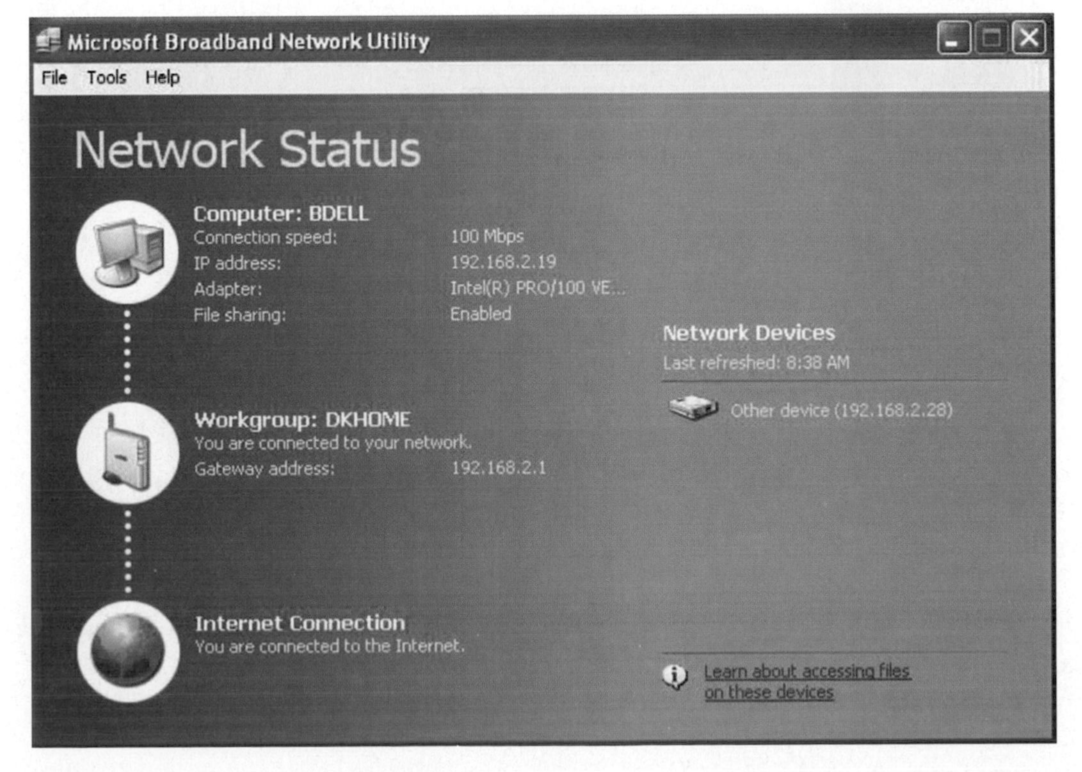

Figure 3

Source: Microsoft product screen shot reprinted with permission from Microsoft Corporation.

(1) Are the IP addresses in this screen internal or public IP addresses?

(2) What computer is located at IP address 192.168.2.19?

(3) What device is located at IP address 192.168.2.1?

2. The user did not know what device was located at IP address 192.168.2.28, so he opened his browser and typed: *http://192.168.2.28.* The screen shown in Figure 4, below, appeared.

   a. Which device on the SOHO LAN has been assigned this IP address?
   b. Which device created this display?
   c. What is the purpose of this display?

3. Out of curiosity, the user then entered *http://192.168.2.1* into his browser. The display shown in Figure 5 (next page) resulted. In this chapter, you have not learned what a *subnet mask* is. However, you should be able to figure out the meanings of the data in this display.

   a. Which device produced this display?
   b. What does "DHCP server: enabled" mean?
   c. Explain the entries in the DHCP section.
   d. The base station has two MAC addresses. What two devices inside the base station do you think they refer to?
   e. What is the MAC address of the printer server? (Use data from the last two displays.)
   f. The network administrator for this SOHO LAN can access a management utility within the base station. She did so and navigated to the display shown in Figure 6 (next page).

      (1) Do the data in this display pertain to the Ethernet switch or the router?

      (2) This chapter showed the use of DHCP within a LAN. This screen allows the base station to use DHCP to obtain its own public IP address from the ISP. What benefits does the ISP accrue by using DHCP?

      (3) When would the network administrator *not* use DHCP to connect to the ISP?

      (4) Under what circumstances would someone use a base station and not connect it to the Internet?

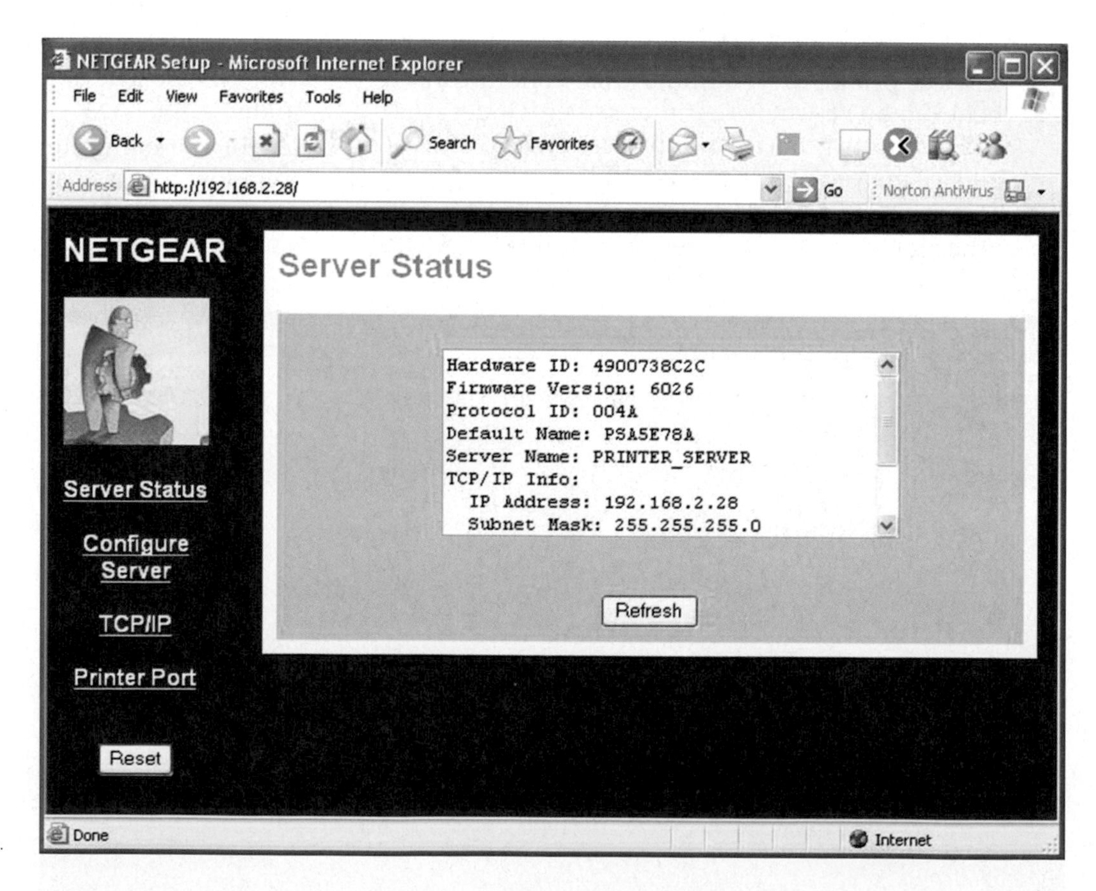

Figure 4

Source: Used with permission of NETGEAR, Inc.

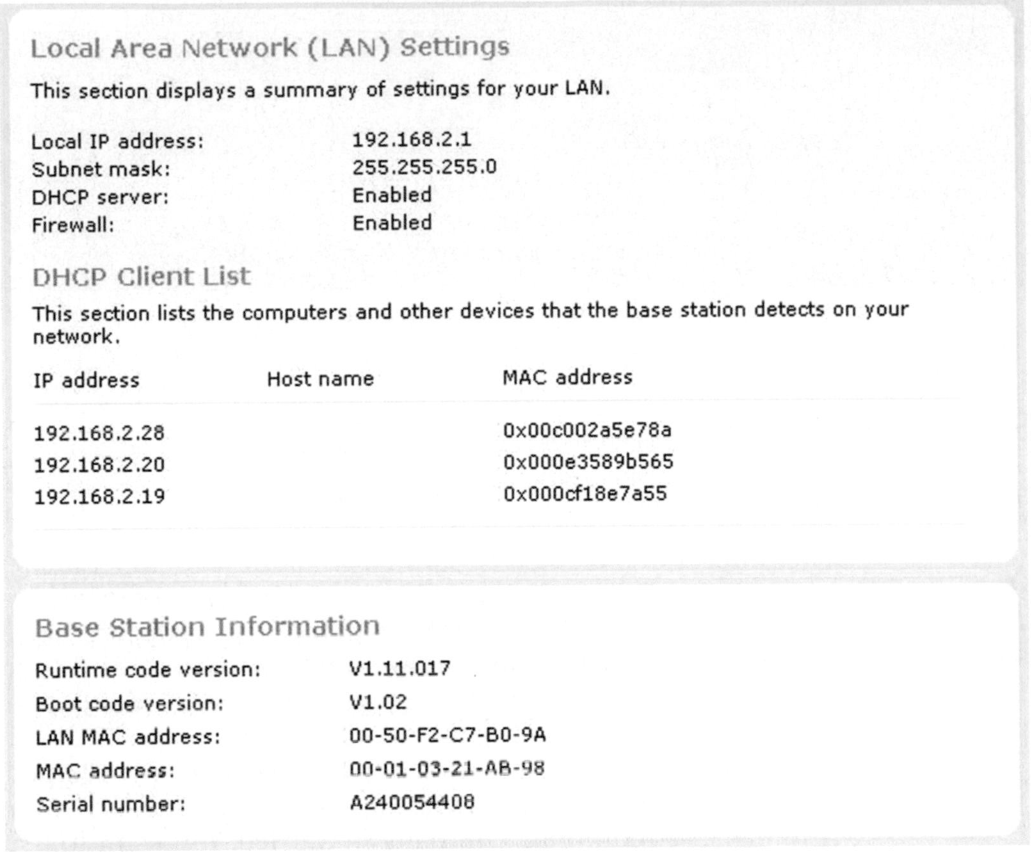

Figure 5

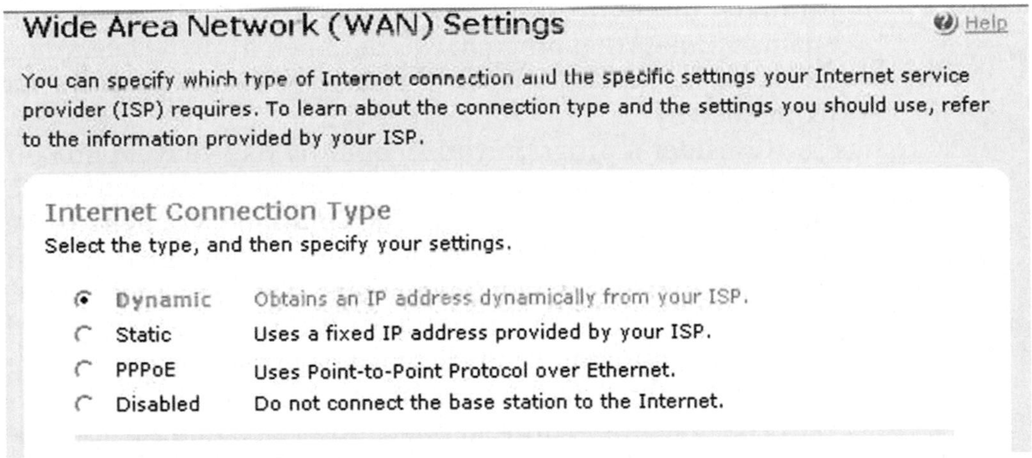

Local Area Network (LAN) Settings

This section displays a summary of settings for your LAN.

Local IP address:	192.168.2.1
Subnet mask:	255.255.255.0
DHCP server:	Enabled
Firewall:	Enabled

DHCP Client List

This section lists the computers and other devices that the base station detects on your network.

IP address	Host name	MAC address
192.168.2.28		0x00c002a5e78a
192.168.2.20		0x000e3589b565
192.168.2.19		0x000cf18e7a55

Base Station Information

Runtime code version:	V1.11.017
Boot code version:	V1.02
LAN MAC address:	00-50-F2-C7-B0-9A
MAC address:	00-01-03-21-AB-98
Serial number:	A240054408

Wide Area Network (WAN) Settings

Help

You can specify which type of Internet connection and the specific settings your Internet service provider (ISP) requires. To learn about the connection type and the settings you should use, refer to the information provided by your ISP.

Internet Connection Type

Select the type, and then specify your settings.

(•)	Dynamic	Obtains an IP address dynamically from your ISP.
( )	Static	Uses a fixed IP address provided by your ISP.
( )	PPPoE	Uses Point-to-Point Protocol over Ethernet.
( )	Disabled	Do not connect the base station to the Internet.

Figure 6

PART 2 THE INTERNATIONAL DIMENSION

Global Communication

STUDY QUESTIONS

- Q1 What does it mean to localize software?
- Q2 What are the problems and issues of localizing and distributing databases worldwide?
- Q3 What are the consequences of global data communication?

Q1 What Does It Mean to Localize Software?

The process of making a computer program work in a second language is called **localizing** that software. It turns out to be surprisingly hard to do. If you think about localizing a document or a Web page, all you need to do is hire a translator to convert your document or page from one language to another. The situation is more difficult for a computer program, however.

Suppose, for example, that your company has developed its own inventory-control database application and that your firm has just acquired a company in Mexico. You want to use that same inventory- control program for your Mexican operations. As a new manager, suppose you haven't even considered this matter during the acquisition process. After the acquisition is done, you ask your technical people to give you a time estimate for converting your inventory application into Spanish. Unless that program was designed from the beginning to be localized, you will be shocked at the effort and cost required. Why?

Consider a program you frequently use—say, Microsoft Word—and ask what would need to be done to translate it to a different language. The entire user interface will need to be translated. The menu bar and the commands on the menu bar will need to be translated. It is possible that some of the icons (the small graphics on a menu bar) will need to be changed because some graphic symbols that are harmless in one culture are confusing or offensive in another.

The inventory-control application is a database application, so it will have forms, reports, and queries. The labels on each of these will need to be translated. Of course, not all labels translate into words of the same length, and so the forms and reports may need to be redesigned. The questions and prompts for queries, such as "Enter part number for back order," must also be translated.

All of the documentation will need to be translated. That should be just a matter of hiring a translator, except that all of the illustrations in the documentation will need to be redrawn in the second language.

Think, too, about error messages. When someone attempts to order more items than there are in inventory, your application produces an error message. All of those messages will need to be translated. There are other issues as well. Sorting order is one. Spanish uses accents on certain letters, and it turns out that an accented *ó* will sort after *z* when you use the computer's default sort ordering. Your programmers will have to deal with that issue as well.

Figure 1 presents a short list of issues that emerge when localizing a computer program.

Programming techniques can be used to simplify and reduce the cost of localization. However, those techniques must be used in the beginning. For example, suppose that when a certain condition occurs the program is to display

- Translate the user interface, including menu bars and commands.
- Translate, and possibly redesign, labels in forms, reports, and query prompts.
- Translate all documentation and help text.
- Redraw and translate diagrams and examples in help text.
- Translate all error messages.
- Translate text in all message boxes.
- Adjust sorting order for different character set.
- Fix special problems in Asian character sets and in languages that read and write from right to left.

Figure 1
Issues to Address When Localizing a Computer Program

the message, "Insufficient quantity in stock." If the programmer codes all such messages into the computer program, then, to localize that program, the programmer will have to find every such message in the code and then ask a translator to change that code. A preferred technique is to give every error message a number and to place the number and text of the error message into a separate file. Then, the code is written to display a particular error number from that file. During localization, translators simply translate the file of error messages into the second language.

The bottom line for you as a future manager is to understand two points: (1) Localizing computer programs is much more difficult, expensive, and time-consuming than translating documents. (2) If a computer program is likely to be localized, then plan for that localization from the beginning. In addition, when considering the acquisition of a company in a foreign country, be sure to budget time and expense for the localization of information systems.

Q2 What Are the Problems and Issues of Localizing and Distributing Databases Worldwide?

Consider the acquisition of the Mexican company just described. You have decided to localize your inventory-control application. The next question is, "Do you want to localize your inventory database?"

Assume that you have a centralized inventory database in the United States. Do you want the inventory-control programs that will run in Mexico to access that same database? With modern data communications, that is entirely possible.

However, your business requirements may dictate that you need to create a second database in Mexico. In that case, there are two issues. First, you will need to localize it. Second, you will need to determine the relationship between the two databases. Do the contents of those two databases refer to a single centralized inventory, or do they refer to two different inventories? If, for example, the two databases both indicate that there are 10 widgets in inventory, is that a single centralized inventory, or are there two separate inventories, one in the United States and one in Mexico, and do they both happen to have 10 widgets in stock?

Consider database localization first. In most cases, when companies localize databases they choose to translate the data, but not the metadata. Thus, the contents of the *Remarks* field or the *Description* files are translated. However, the names of tables, the names of fields, the description of the meaning of the fields, and other such metadata are left in English (or whatever the original language was). As stated in the previous section, forms, reports, queries, and database application programs will also need to be localized.

Now consider the relationship between the two databases. If they refer to two separate inventories, then there is no problem. Each database can be processed and administered as an independent entity. If the two databases refer to the *same* inventory, however, then they contain duplicated records. Such databases are said to be **replicated**. In this case, if it is possible to partition the workload so that the inventory application running on a server in Mexico updates different records than the inventory application running on a server in the United States, then the situation can be managed.

If, however, the two inventory applications running on the two servers can update the *same items at the same time*, serious problems occur. Considerable time, expense, and sophisticated programming are necessary to develop and support such databases. Because of the expense, difficulty, and risk, most organizations define their business processes to avoid this situation.

This problem, by the way, is not strictly an international problem. The two separate servers could be running in the same country, and the problem will be the same. The situation arises more frequently, however, in international situations.

Q3 What Are Consequences of Global Data Communication?

We discussed the impact of modern data communications on the development of the global economy in the previous part (page 90). In brief, data communications have tremendously expanded the size of the global economy and the global workforce.

In this section, consider the impact of data communications on less-developed countries. One of the most positive aspects of IT is that technology users can skip generations. People can benefit from the most modern technology without having to use the earlier technology. When Microsoft introduces a new version of Word, you can receive the benefit of that new version without having to learn Word 1.0, then Word 2.0, then Word 3.0, and so forth. Similarly, you can buy a cell phone and use it without ever having used a wired phone. You can do instant messaging with your friends without ever having sent an email.

What are the consequences? In many developing countries, cell or satellite phones are the first phones that most people use. Some parts of the world do not have telephone wires and never will. In some countries, the first weather forecast someone sees will be presented on a Web page that is delivered via a cell phone.

The economic, social, and political consequences of this phenomenon are staggering. A coffee farmer in Kenya, someone who has never sold his or her beans to anyone but a local trader, can suddenly sell them to Starbucks in Seattle. A basket weaver in Cameroon, who has sold her wares only at the local market, can suddenly sell her baskets to collectors in Tokyo. People whose world horizon has been restricted to rural villages or streets in their city suddenly find themselves connected to the rest of the world. Local laws and customs become outmoded, even irrelevant.

Furthermore, existing companies, organizations, and governments are seriously challenged. The public telephone utility in many countries has been a profitable monopoly and medium of control. Cell and satellite phones threaten this monopoly and reduce the power of individuals and cartels. In some countries, there has been a backlash and restriction of the spread of technology. Such measures only delay the inevitable. How can a country with serious penalties for using a copy machine for political purposes maintain control in the face of email, instant messaging, and the Web?

During your career, these countries will see unprecedented change. This change will create many opportunities for interesting jobs, careers, and new businesses.

ACTIVE REVIEW

Use this Active Review to verify that you understand the ideas and concepts that answer the study questions in the International Dimension.

Q1 What does it mean to localize software?

Explain why information systems, and in particular, software, should be a consideration during the merger and acquisition process. Summarize the work required to localize a computer program. In your own words, explain why it is better to design a program to be localized rather than attempt to adapt an existing single-language program to a second language.

Q2 What are the problems and issues of distributing databases worldwide?

Explain what is required to localize a database. Explain possible relationships of two databases. Define *replicated databases*. Explain the conditions under which replicated databases are not a problem. Explain the conditions under which replicated databases are a problem. How do most organizations deal with this problem?

Q3 What are the consequences of global data communication?

Explain the statement, "technology users can skip generations." Illustrate this principle with an example from your own life. Describe the economic consequences of this principle on developing countries. Describe the social and political consequences of this principle. Give an example of a job, career, or business opportunity that these changes will present.

KEY TERMS AND CONCEPTS

CASE 2-1

PART 2

Aviation Safety Network

The mission of the Aviation Safety Network (ASN) is to provide up-to-date, complete, and reliable information on airliner accidents and safety issues to those with a professional interest in aviation. ASN defines an *airliner* as an aircraft capable of carrying 14 or more passengers. ASN data include information on commercial, military, and corporate airplanes.

ASN Aviation Safety Database results

24 occurrences in the ASN safety database:

date	type	registration	operator	fat.	location	pic	cat
26-JUN-1988	Airbus A.320	F-GFKC	Air France	3	France		A1
14-FEB-1990	Airbus A.320	VT-EPN	Indian Airlines	92	India		A1
20-JAN-1992	Airbus A.320	F-GGED	Air Inter	87	France		A1
27-MAR-1993	Airbus A.320	VT-E..	Indian Airlines	0	India		H2
26-AUG-1993	Airbus A.320	G-KMAM	Excalibur Airways	0	U.K.		I2
14-SEP-1993	Airbus A.320	D-AIPN	Lufthansa	2	Poland		A1
22-OCT-1993	Airbus A.320	F-....	Air Inter	0	France		I2
10-DEC-1993	Airbus A.320	F-GF..	Air France	0	France		H2
19-DEC-1996	Airbus A.320	F-OHMK	Mexicana	0	Mexico		A2
10-MAR-1997	Airbus A.320	A4O-EM	Gulf Air	0	U.A.E.		A1
22-MAR-1998	Airbus A.320	RP-C3222	Philippine Air Lines	0	Philippines		A1
12-MAY-1998	Airbus A.320	SU-GB?	EgyptAir	0	Egypt		A2
21-MAY-1998	Airbus A.320	G-UKLL	Air UK Leisure	0	Spain		I2
12-FEB-1999	Airbus A.320	F-GJVG	Air France	0	France		U2
02-MAR-1999	Airbus A.320	F-G...	Air France	0	France		H2
26-OCT-1999	Airbus A.320	VT-ESL	Indian Airlines	0	Myanmar		A2
11-APR-2000	Airbus A.320	F-OHMD	Mexicana	0	Mexico		O1
05-JUL-2000	Airbus A.320		Royal Jordanian	1	Jordan		H2
23-AUG-2000	Airbus A.320	A4O-EK	Gulf Air	143	Bahrain		A1
07-FEB-2001	Airbus A.320	EC-HKJ	Iberia	0	Spain		A1
17-MAR-2001	Airbus A.320	N357NW	Northwest Airlines	0	USA		A2
20-MAR-2001	Airbus A.320	D-AIP.	Lufthansa	0	Germany		I2
24-JUL-2001	Airbus A.320	4R-ABA	SriLankan Airlines	0	Sri Lanka		O1
28-AUG-2002	Airbus A.320	N635AW	America West	0	USA		A1

Figure 1
Incidents and Accidents Involving the Airbus 320 from the ASN Aviation Safety Database

Source: Reprinted by permission of Aviation Safety Network, © 2007 ASN. www.aviation-safety.net.

ASN gathers data from a variety of sources, including the International Civil Aviation Board, the National Transportation Safety Board, and the Civil Aviation Authority. Data are also taken from magazines, such as *Air Safety Week* and *Aviation Week and Space Technology*; from a variety of books; and from prominent individuals in the aviation safety industry.

ASN compiles the source data into a Microsoft Access database. The core table contains over 10,000 rows of data concerning incident and accident descriptions. This table is linked to several other tables that store data about airports, airlines, aircraft types, countries, and so forth. Periodically, the Access data are reformatted and exported to a MySQL database, which is used by programs that support queries on ASN's Web site (*http://aviation-safety.net*).

On that site, incident and accident data can be accessed by year, by airline, by aircraft, by nation, and in other ways. For example, Figure 1 (page 241) shows a list of incidents and accidents that involved the Airbus 320. When the user clicks on a particular accident, such as the one on March 20, 2001, a summary of the incident is presented, as shown in Figure 2.

In addition to descriptions of incidents and accidents, ASN also summarizes the data to help its users determine airliner accident trends. For example,

Incident Description Status: **Final** [legenda]

Date: **20 MAR 2001**
Time: 12:00
Type: Airbus A.320-211
Operator: Lufthansa
Registration: D-AIP.
Year built: 1990
Engines: 2 CFMI CFM56-5A1
Crew: 0 fatalities / 6 on board
Passengers: 0 fatalities / 115 on board
Total: 0 fatalities / 121 on board
Airplane damage: None
Location: Frankfurt International Airport (FRA) (Germany)
Phase: Take-off
Nature: International Scheduled Passenger
Departure airport: Frankfurt International Airport (FRA)
Destination airport: Paris

Narrative:
The Airbus 320 hit turbulence just after rotation from runway 18 and the left wing dipped. The captain responded with a slight sidestick input to the right but the aircraft banked further left. Another attempt to correct the attitude of the plane resulted in a left bank reaching ca 22deg. The first officer then said "I have control", and switched his sidestick to priority and recovered the aircraft. The left wingtip was reportedly just 0.5m off the ground. The aircraft climbed to FL120 where the crew tried to troubleshoot the problem. When they found out that the captain's sidestick was reversed in roll, they returned to Frankfurt. Investigation revealed that maintenance had been performed on the Elevator Aileron Computer no. 1 (ELAC). Two pairs of pins inside the connector had accidentally been crossed during the repair.

Figure 2
Incidents Description Summary from the ASN Aviation Safety Database

Source: Reprinted by permission of Aviation Safety Network, © 2007 ASN. www.aviation-safety.net.

Figure 3 shows the safest location on the aircraft for a selection of airliner accidents. (A value of *ER* in the *Phase* column means the accident occurred while the aircraft was en route; *LA* means the accident occurred during landing; and *TO* means that accident occurred during takeoff.) According to ASN, "there is no significant difference regarding survival for passengers seated in the front or the rear of the plane."

Hugo Ranter of the Netherlands started the ASN Web site in 1995. Fabian I. Lujan of Argentina has maintained the site since 1998. ASN has more than 10,000 email subscribers in 150 countries, and the site receives over 50,000 visits per week.

Date	Type	Occupants	Survivors	Phase [1]	Safest location
02 MAY 1970	DC-9	63	40	ER	rear
04 APR 1977	DC-9	85	22	ER	rear
12 AUG 1985	Boeing 747	524	4	ER	rear
11 NOV 1965	Boeing 727	91	48	LA	rear
20 NOV 1967	Convair CV-880	82	12	LA	rear
13 JAN 1969	DC-8	45	30	LA	front
08 DEC 1972	Boeing 737	61	18	LA	rear
29 DEC 1972	Lockheed L-1011	176	77	LA	front & rear
30 JAN 1974	Boeing 707	101	4	LA	center
11 SEP 1974	DC-9	82	12	LA	rear
24 JUN 1975	Boeing 727	124	9	LA	rear
27 APR 1976	Boeing 727	88	51	LA	front
11 FEB 1978	Boeing 737	49	7	LA	rear
28 DEC 1978	DC-8	189	179	LA	rear
02 JUN 1983	DC-9	46	23	LA	center
02 AUG 1985	Lockheed L-1011	163	29	LA	rear
15 SEP 1988	Boeing 737	104	69	LA	rear
08 JAN 1989	Boeing 737	126	79	LA	front
19 JUL 1989	DC-10	296	185	LA	center
01 FEB 1991	Boeing 737	89	67	LA	rear
20 JAN 1992	Airbus A.320	96	9	LA	rear
26 APR 1994	Airbus A.300	271	7	LA	center
01 JUN 1999	DC-9	145	134	LA	front & rear
03 DEC 1990	DC-9	44	36	TA	front
27 NOV 1970	DC-8	229	182	TO	front
13 JAN 1982	Boeing 737	79	5	TO	rear
22 AUG 1985	Boeing 737	137	82	TO	front
15 NOV 1987	DC-9	82	54	TO	rear
31 AUG 1988	Boeing 727	108	94	TO	front & center
22 MAR 1992	Fokker F-28	51	24	TO	front & rear
02 JUL 1994	DC-9	57	20	TO	rear
31 OCT 2000	Boeing 747	179	96	TO	front & rear

Figure 3
Safest Location on Aircraft from the ASN Aviation Safety Database

Source: Reprinted by permission of Aviation Safety Network, © 2007 ASN. www.aviation-safety.net.

QUESTIONS

1. All of the data included in this database are available in public documents. Because this is the case, what is the value of the Aviation Safety Network? Why don't users just consult the online version of the underlying references? In your answer, consider the difference between data and information.

2. What was the cause of the incident shown in Figure 2? That incident, in which no one was injured, occurred in an Airbus 320 airplane that was flown by Lufthansa Airlines out of an airport in Germany. It would be illogical to conclude from this one incident that it is dangerous to fly Airbus 320s, Lufthansa, or out of Germany. Suppose, however, that you wanted to determine whether there is a systematic pattern of maintenance problems with the A320, Lufthansa, or airports in Germany. How would you proceed? How would you use the resources of *aviation-safety.net* to make this determination?

3. The ASN database and Web site were created and are maintained by two individuals. The database might be complete and accurate, or it might not be. To what extent should you rely on these data? What can you do to decide whether you should rely on the data at this site?

4. Consider the data in Figure 3. Do you agree that there appears to be no significant difference between passengers in the front and the rear of the airplane? Why or why not? There does seem to be a difference between the number of accidents and the phase of the flight. What is that difference, and how can you use it to limit your exposure to aircraft accidents?

5. Suppose you work in the marketing department for an airline. Can you use these data in your marketing efforts? If so, how? What are the dangers of basing a marketing campaign on safety?

6. Suppose you are a maintenance manager for a major airline. How can you use these data? Would it be wise to develop your own, similar database? Why or why not?

CASE 2-2

Computerizing the Ministry of Foreign Affairs

In 1994, the Ministry of Foreign Affairs of a West African country embarked on an ambitious program to computerize its internal services and communications. The project began slowly, with limited funding, and it relied on donated hardware and software. In 1999, the goals of the project were revised to include the development of Web-based applications, and at that point the project received internal budget allocations. Between 1999 and 2002, a total of $650,000 was allocated.

The system's purpose was to make the organization dynamic and modern via the use of information technology. For example, the United Nations provides data and documents electronically, and the Foreign Affairs Ministry wanted to participate in the use of this new technology.

Another project goal was to facilitate communication between the Ministry of Foreign Affairs home office and its diplomatic missions abroad. In particular, the new system would use an external Web site and email to distribute information and facilitate discussions and decision making between geographically separated participants. A specific objective was to reduce travel costs by half.

Unfortunately, by 2002 the project had delivered few benefits. Data continued to be stored on paper, a local computer network within the Ministry of Foreign Affairs was inoperative, and the diplomatic correspondence bag remained the primary means of exchanging paper-based information. Diplomats continued to travel, and travel expenses were not reduced by the new system. In short, the project was a failure.

In his case study of this application, Kenhago Olivier identified three factors behind the failure of this system:

1. Vendor contracts were awarded not on the basis of competence, but rather on personal relations between Ministry of Foreign Affairs officials and vendor personnel.
2. The major application threatened the perquisites ("perks") of diplomats. Travel is an important source of revenue for headquarters personnel; they compensate for their low salaries by travel compensation and by the opportunity to trade goods.
3. The computing infrastructure was limited; there were a maximum of two personal computers per department at headquarters and only 35 computers in a building housing more than 300 officials.

Source: K. T. Olivier, "Problems in Computerising the Ministry of Foreign Affairs," *Success/Failure Case Study No. 23, eGovernment for Development, http://egov4dev.org/mofa.htm* (accessed October 2004).

QUESTIONS

1. The purpose of this system was for the Ministry of Foreign Affairs "to become a more dynamic, modern organization via the use of information technology." What are the dangers of stating the purpose of a system in this way? How could this statement be improved?

2. Why was the goal of reducing travel costs not achieved? What steps would need to be taken before this goal could ever be achieved? What is the likely outcome in any system in which the goals of the system conflict with the interests of important users? Which is stronger—the momentum of the new system or the resistance of the users?

3. When the features of new information systems conflict with the needs and desires of important user groups, what should be done? Should system development be stopped? If not, should the features be changed? What can be done to reduce the users' resistance? Who is in a position to resolve the conflict—the development team? The business users? Someone else?

4. This case description implies that the project was severely underfunded. Attempting to modernize a department with donated equipment sounds desperate, and trying to change communication patterns using email when 300 officials share 35 personal computers is probably impossible. The desire to use the U.N.'s computer-based systems to reduce travel and to enable email communication are appropriate goals for a governmental organization

today. But the limited funding is a reality. If you were placed in charge of a project that was underfunded like this one, what would you do?

5. In most cases, the costs of an information system are not known at the beginning of a project. It is only after specifying requirements and identifying alternative solutions that costs can be approximated. Knowing this, how would you proceed if you were given the responsibility for managing a new development project? What would you do if you found that the funding available is not nearly enough? What would you do if you found that the funding is 10 to 20 percent too low? What would you do if the funding appeared to be adequate, but you sensed that the cost estimates were optimistically low? In each of these cases, what is the best strategy for your organization? For your career?

Information Systems

The three chapters in this part describe the principal information systems used in organizations today. Each of these systems applies the information technology that you learned in Chapters 4 through 6 to help businesses and organizations gain competitive advantage and otherwise accomplish their goals and objectives.

Chapter 7 considers information systems within organizations. It describes both functional applications that benefit a single business activity as well as integrated applications that support cross-departmental processes. Chapter 8 addresses information systems among firms. It discusses e-commerce and supply chains and describes how information systems are used to solve problems and integrate the activities of multiple organizations. Chapter 9 describes business intelligence and knowledge management systems. You will learn about reporting systems, data warehouses, data mining applications, and knowledge management systems.

7 Information Systems Within Organizations

STUDY QUESTIONS

Q1 What are the differences between functional and cross-functional systems?

Q2 How do functional systems relate to the value chain?

Q3 What are the functions of the five basic functional systems?

Q4 What are the problems of functional systems?

Q5 What is business process design?

Q6 What are the functions and characteristics of the three major cross-functional systems?

Meet Brian Street

Your favorite business book:
Who Moved My Cheese? by Spencer Johnson and Kenneth Blanchard.

My hero:
My mom. Single parent of two. Gave up everything to raise her two children.

A mistake I wish I hadn't made:
Being so optimistic on the new ERP software and the timeframe in which the implementation would be completed.

Brian Street is Vice President and COO of Rhon Ernest-Jones Consulting Engineers in Coral Springs, Florida. He graduated with a Civil Engineering degree from Clemson University and started his career as a design engineer. Within a few years, Brian realized he was interested in the business aspects of running a company, but as an engineering student, he'd never taken any business courses. Accordingly (with the advice of Professor Bob Grauer), Brian enrolled in the University of Miami's MBA program for working professionals.

As he attended classes, Brian continued to work as a design engineer and project manager. Just before he finished his MBA, the firm's business manager left the firm. Brian applied for and got that position. He soon realized that the firm had outgrown its information systems and that it needed new technology and information systems to become more efficient and profitable. Further, with the Florida real estate boom, the demand for civil engineering consulting services was growing, and the business expanded rapidly. He knew the existing systems had to be replaced.

On the need for new systems:

"When I started as business manager, we had outgrown our existing information systems. A consulting engineering firm lives or dies by its ability to bill clients. We were using a timesheet program that worked well when the firm had 15 people, but with 50 employees and rapidly growing, the system couldn't keep up. For accounting we used QuickBooks, a completely different program, and while that product is fine for small businesses with modest needs, it has virtually no controls.

"Even worse, the project data were processed in Excel and Word with absolutely no integration to the timesheet or accounting data, meaning that our bookkeeper had to enter some data three times. As a result, project managers did not have the information they needed to manage their projects and were unable to bill in a timely or efficient manner. It is critical for our organization to know the status of each project: how much money has been spent, and how much more work remains to be done. With our patchwork of systems, that information was difficult to obtain."

On the ERP project:

"I talked with friends and associates in other firms and with some of our clients about the systems they were using. Many of them had chosen an ERP system from Deltek, a company with 9,000 architectural and engineering customers, similar to us. After some investigation, I put together a business plan, including a justification for the capital expense, the anticipated rate of return, etc., and the owners and managers of the firm agreed to proceed.

My career high:
Becoming VP at age 31.

My motto:
Help everyone and get the job done.

My very first job:
Pizza maker.

My pet peeve:
People who just don't try. Something new will always be "scary" at first, but just give it a chance. If you don't, you are doomed to fail every time.

Brian Street

"Like so many organizations that convert to ERP, we had more than a few surprises: the system cost more than I had estimated, and the project was 6 months late. But, eventually we got there, and we're beginning to see the benefits. We can now produce reports that were simply not possible with our multiple disparate systems.

"As the costs mounted and delays occurred my management team was (naturally) concerned. They wondered what I'd gotten them into and whether we'd ever finish the project. Meanwhile, we had a cash-flow problem because the conversion delayed our ability to send bills, and when clients don't get a bill, they don't . . . well, you get the picture. But, we made it."

On the challenges:
"Data conversion was our biggest challenge. It turns out that QuickBooks is a black hole. You can put data in, but you can't get it out. We talked frequently with their customer support, and they said they just didn't provide for the data export we needed. Eventually, we found a way to generate QuickBook reports, force those reports into Excel, and then import that data from Excel into Deltek. But, to do all that, I had to hire a SQL programmer and, of course, they aren't cheap.

"Hardware expenses turned out to be higher than we expected, too. And all of these expenses are overhead. Unlike AutoCAD or other systems that directly support our revenue stream, the ERP expenses were strictly overhead, which made it harder for management to accept.

"For any organization thinking about an ERP project, I'd say that no matter how much you prepare and plan, something will go wrong and the system will cost more and take longer than you expect. Plan on it. Depending on the size of the project and the organization, put in an extra $100,000 to $200,000 and plan for 6 months or a year longer than you anticipate. Or more. There will be surprises that you just can't anticipate. Think of 'good, quick, and cheap' as characteristics of a new system; you can achieve one or two, but never all three. In our case, the new system was good (actually very good), but the implementation wasn't quick, and it wasn't cheap."

On the need for knowledge of IS:
"Technology is the wave of the future. You need to understand what technology can do and how it can help your business. You don't need to know the details, but as a business professional, you do need a core understanding of the basic technology. You don't want to be sitting in a management meeting when someone asks you your opinion about an ERP system and have to say, 'What's that?' And technology won't stand still. It keeps changing. We're implementing VoIP, and 2 years ago I'd never heard of it. You need to keep learning."

CHAPTER PREVIEW

If you walk into any organization today (say, for example, your first employer), you will find a confusing maze of information systems. Some of those systems support processes within that organization, and some support processes across organizations. The goal of this chapter is to give you a framework for understanding information systems that operate within organizations.

Information systems within the organization can be divided into two major categories: functional and cross-functional. This chapter begins by explaining the difference between those two categories. After that, we will consider how functional systems relate to Porter's value chain, what such systems do, and, finally, what problems they present. Then, we will consider cross-functional systems: how they solve the problems of functional systems, why they require business process design, and, finally, what they do.

Q1 What Are the Differences Between Functional and Cross-Functional Systems?

It will be easier for you to understand IS within organizations if we begin with a short history. Figure 7-1 shows three categories of IS that have evolved since the computer was first applied to business problems.

Calculation Systems

The very first information systems, **calculation systems**, are now antiquated, but they were used not long ago, possibly by your grandfather. The purpose of those early systems was to relieve workers of tedious, repetitive calculations. They computed payroll and wrote paychecks; they applied debits and credits to the general ledger and balanced the company's accounting records. They also kept track of inventory quantities. As calculating machines, they were more accurate than humans—as long as the systems actually worked. (Computer failure rates were high.) Those systems were labor-saving devices, but in truth, they produced little information. None of them survive today, and we will not consider them further.

Functional Systems

The **functional systems** of the second era facilitated the work of a single department or function. They grew as a natural expansion of the capabilities of calculation systems. For example, payroll expanded to become human resources, general ledger became financial reporting, and inventory was merged into operations or manufacturing. The changes were more than just in name. In each functional area, companies added features and capabilities to information systems to support more functional-area activity.

The problem with functional applications is their isolation. In fact, functional applications are sometimes called **islands of automation** because they work independently of one another. Unfortunately, independent, isolated systems cannot produce the productivity and efficiency necessary for modern businesses. Purchasing influences inventory, which influences production, which influences customer satisfaction, which influences future sales. Decisions that are appropriate when

Figure 7-1
History of IS Within Organizations

Name	Era	Scope	Perspective	Example	Technology Symbols
Calculation systems	1950–1980 (Your grandfather)	Single purpose	Eliminate tedious human calculations. "Just make it work!"	Payroll General ledger Inventory	Mainframe Punch card
Functional systems	1975–20?? (Your mother)	Business function	Use computer to improve operation and management of individual departments.	Human resources Financial reporting Order entry Manufacturing (MRP and MRP II)	Mainframe Stand-alone PCs Networks and LANs
Integrated systems (also cross-functional or process-based systems)	2000— (You)	Business process	Develop IS to integrate separate departments into organization-wide business processes.	Customer relationship management (CRM) Enterprise resource planning (ERP)	Networked PCs Client-servers The Internet Intranets

considering only a single function, such as purchasing, might create inefficiencies in the context of an entire process.

Integrated, Cross-Functional Systems

The isolation problems of functional systems led to the third era of information systems, in which systems were designed to integrate the activities of an entire business process. Because those activities cross departmental boundaries, such systems are sometimes called **cross-functional** or **cross-departmental systems**. Because they support complete business processes, they are sometimes also called **process-based systems**.

Transitioning from single-purpose to functional applications was easy. The newer systems provided increased functionality, and system users were grateful for the additional help. However, the transition from functional systems to integrated systems often is problematic. Integrated processing requires many departments to coordinate their activities. Users must change the way they work. There is no clear line of authority, peer competition can be fierce, and interdepartmental rivalries can subvert the development of the new system.

Most organizations today are a mixture of functional and integrated systems. To successfully compete globally, however, organizations must achieve the efficiencies of integrated, cross-departmental, process-based systems. Thus, during your career, you can expect to see an increasing number of integrated systems and fewer functional systems. In fact, you will likely be one of the business leaders asked to implement new integrated systems.

By the way, do not assume that the systems and processes discussed in the remainder of the chapter apply only to commercial, profit-making organizations. Not-for-profit and government organizations have most of these same processes, but with a different orientation. Your state's Department of Labor, for example, has both employees and customers. The Girl Scouts of America (a not-for-profit organization) has a general ledger and financial statements, as well as operational systems. Information systems for not-for-profit and for government organizations are oriented toward quality of service and efficiency rather than toward profit, but those systems still exist.

Q2 How Do Functional Systems Relate to the Value Chain?

We can use Porter's value chain model (Chapter 3) to explain the scope of different types of information systems within the organization. For our purposes, the value chain model will be more useful if we redraw it as shown in Figure 7-2.

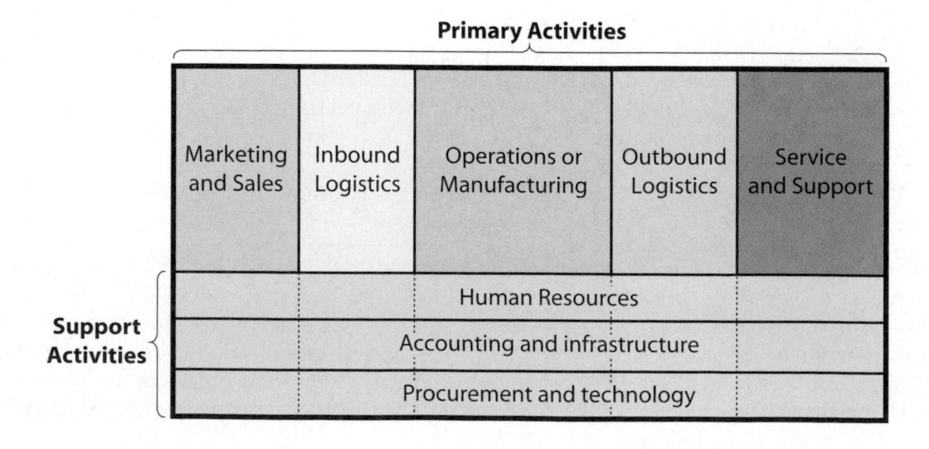

Figure 7-2
Reorganized Porter Value Chain Model

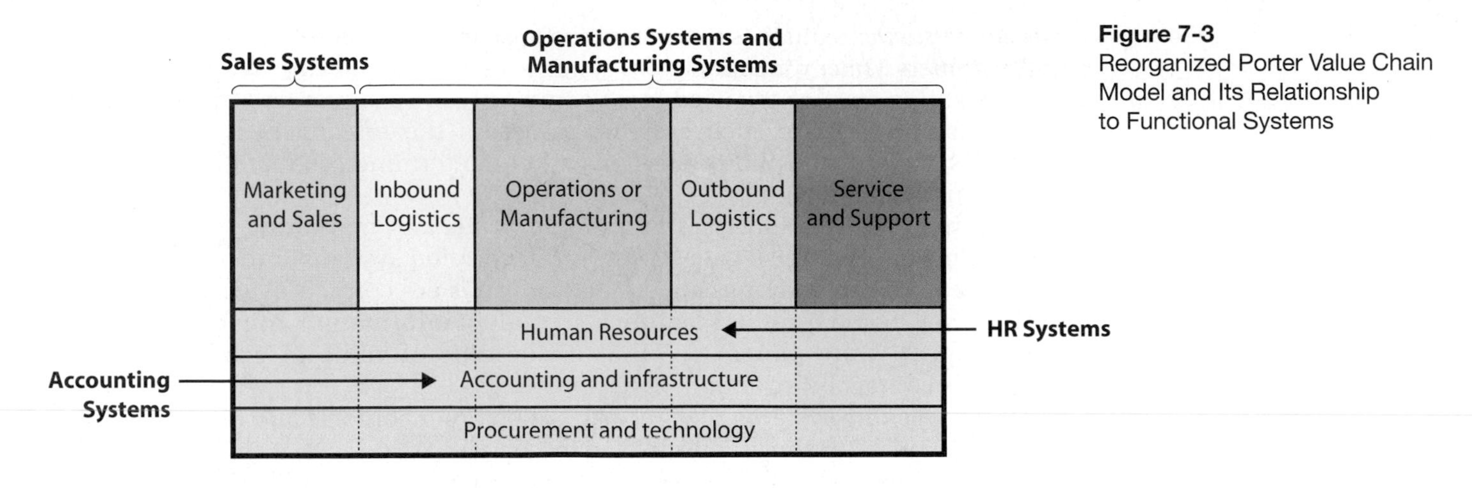

Figure 7-3
Reorganized Porter Value Chain Model and Its Relationship to Functional Systems

From a customer perspective, the value chain starts with marketing and sales. Sales and order activities are followed by inbound logistics, operations and manufacturing, outbound logistics, and finally, service and support. Porter termed each of these activities *primary activities* because they relate directly to the organization's customers and products.

The primary activities are facilitated by various organizational activities—human resources, accounting and infrastructure, procurement, and technology. Porter termed these latter functions *support activities*. As we have redrawn the value chain in Figure 7-2, the primary activities occur in the order shown: They are supported first by the humans that perform work in the primary activities; the primary activities and human resources are supported, in turn, by accounting and other infrastructure.

Figure 7-3 shows five functional systems and their relationship to the value chain. As you would expect, each functional system is closely allied with the activities it supports; there is no crossover among activities.

Q3 What Are the Functions of the Five Basic Functional Systems?

Before we address specific functional systems, understand the difference between a functional application and a functional system. A **functional application** is a computer program that provides features and functions necessary to support a particular business activity. A *functional system* is an information system having the five components of all information systems: hardware, software, data, procedures, and people. You can buy hardware, and you can license a functional application. You cannot, however, buy or license procedures, nor can you buy people who are trained for an organization's specific system(s). Those components of a functional system must be developed in-house. Similarly, although the functional application will have built-in database designs and built-in features for processing and storing data, the data itself must come from you and your organization.

As a manager, it will be your job to ensure that procedures are developed and that your employees are trained on the use of those procedures. The licensing of the software and the buying of the hardware are the easy parts. Integrating those components into an effective system in your organization is more challenging.

Sales and Marketing Information Systems

Sales and marketing information systems support the basic sales and marketing functions. The purpose of *sales systems* is to find prospects and to transform those prospects into customers by selling them something. Sales systems also are used to *manage customers*, which is a euphemism for selling more goods or services to existing customers. Other functional sales systems are used to forecast future sales.

Marketing systems are used most commonly for product and brand management. Companies use such systems to assess the effectiveness of marketing messages, advertising, and promotions and to determine product demand among various market segments.

Figure 7-4 shows specific functions for sales and marketing systems. **Lead-generation systems** (also called *prospect-generation* systems) include those used to send both postal mailings and email. Web sites are commonly used to generate leads as well. Some Web sites feature just product information; others offer to send the prospect white papers or other documents of value in exchange for the prospect's contact information.

Lead-tracking systems keep records of customer contacts and record customer interests. Figure 7-5 shows a form used by a small company that sells classic 1960s muscle cars (fast cars with large engines and underdesigned brakes). The company uses this form for both lead tracking and customer management. (Note that the company uses the term *customer* rather than *lead* or *prospect*.) As you can see, the system maintains customer name and contact data, the customer's product interests, past purchases, and a history of all contacts with the customer.

It is not clear from this form whether *Autos Currently Owned* represents autos purchased just from Bainbridge or autos the customer has purchased from any source. This ambiguity illustrates the need for a system, including procedures and employee training. If Bainbridge has five salespeople, and if two salespeople record only autos purchased from Bainbridge while the three other salespeople record autos purchased

Figure 7-4
Functions of Sales and Marketing Systems

- **Prospect (or lead) generation**
  - Mailings
  - Emailings
  - Web site

- **Lead tracking**
  - Record leads
  - Track product interests
  - Maintain history of contacts

- **Customer management**
  - Maintain customer contact and order history
  - Track product interests
  - Report credit status

- **Sales forecasting**
  - Record individual sales projections
  - Roll up sales projections into district, region, national, and international
  - Track variances over time

- **Product and brand management**
  - Obtain sales results from order processing or receivables systems
  - Compare results to projections
  - Assess promotions, advertising, and sales channels
  - Asses product success in market segments
  - Manage product life cycle

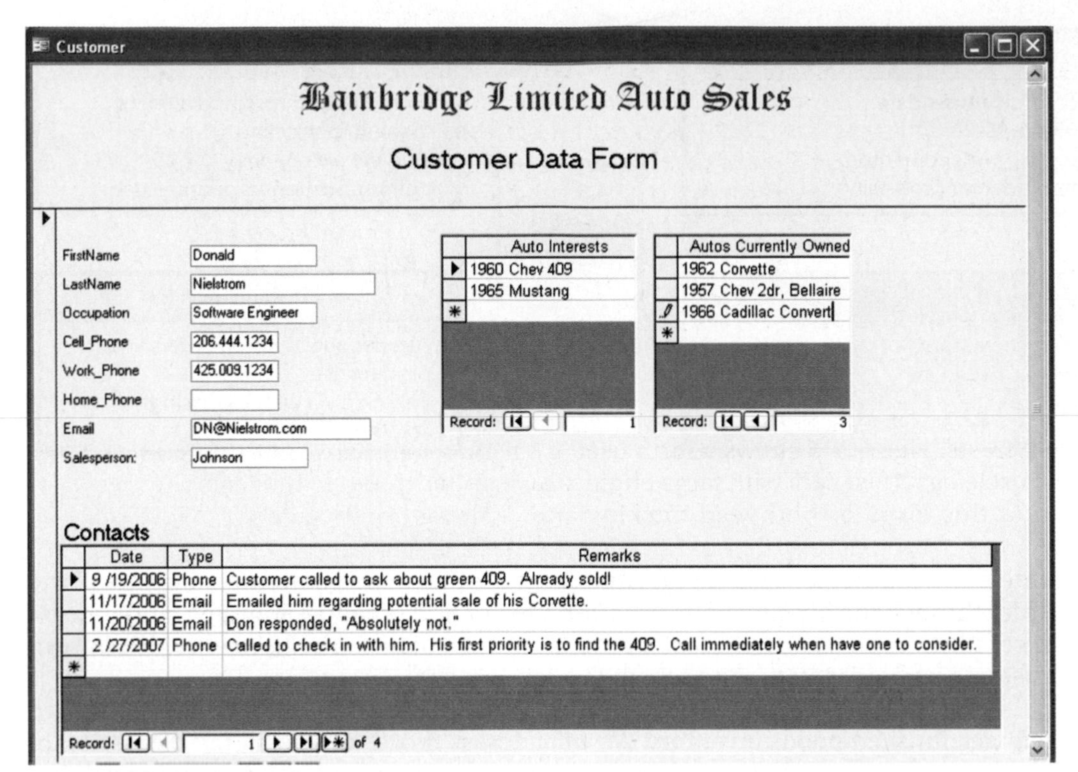
Customer

Bainbridge Limited Auto Sales

Customer Data Form

FirstName: Donald
LastName: Nielstrom
Occupation: Software Engineer
Cell_Phone: 206.444.1234
Work_Phone: 425.009.1234
Home_Phone:
Email: DN@Nielstrom.com
Salesperson: Johnson

Auto Interests
1960 Chev 409
1965 Mustang

Record: 1

Autos Currently Owned
1962 Corvette
1957 Chev 2dr, Bellaire
1966 Cadillac Convert

Record: 3

Contacts

Date	Type	Remarks
9 /19/2006	Phone	Customer called to ask about green 409. Already sold!
11/17/2006	Email	Emailed him regarding potential sale of his Corvette.
11/20/2006	Email	Don responded, "Absolutely not."
2 /27/2007	Phone	Called to check in with him. His first priority is to find the 409. Call immediately when have one to consider.

Record: 1 of 4

Figure 7-5
Form Used for Lead Tracking and Customer Management

from any source, the data will be inconsistent. Subsequent reports or analyses based on this data will be hampered by this discrepancy. Again, applications (programs) are not information systems!

Companies use **customer-management systems** to obtain additional sales from existing customers. As shown in Figure 7-4, such systems maintain customer contact and order-history data and track product interests; some include information about the customer's credit status with the organization (not shown in Figure 7-5). Credit data is used to prevent salespeople from generating orders that the accounts receivable department will later refuse due to poor customer credit.

The most common functional systems in marketing are **product and brand management systems**. With these, records of past sales are imported from order processing or accounts receivable systems and compared to projections and other sales estimates. The company uses the comparisons to assess the effectiveness of promotions and advertising as well as sales channels. It also can use such systems to assess the desirability of the product to different market segments. Finally, the company uses such systems to manage the product through its life cycle. Sales trends might indicate the need for new versions or help to determine when it is time to remove a product from the market. OLAP systems, discussed in Chapter 9, are frequently used for product management.

In truth, it is impossible to manage a product or a brand without these kinds of information. Without the data, there is no feedback, and anyone's guess is as good as any other's with regard to the effectiveness of the marketing messaging, promotions, advertising, and other marketing activities.

Operations Information Systems

Operations activities concern the management of finished-goods inventory and the movement of goods from that inventory to the customer. **Operations information systems** functions are summarized in Figure 7-6 (next page). Order-entry systems record customer purchases. Typically, an order-entry system obtains customer contact and shipping data, verifies customer credit, validates the payment method, and

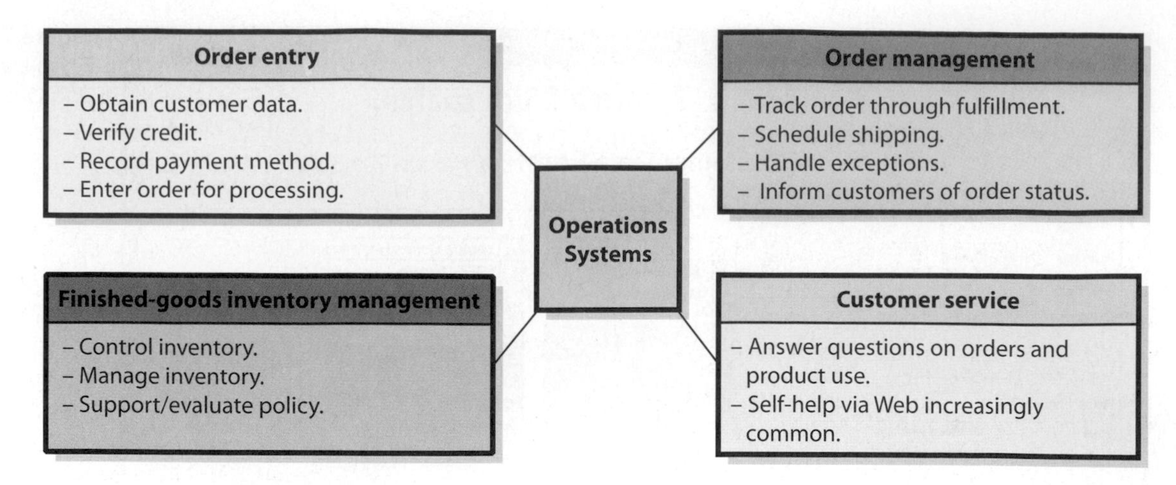

Figure 7-6
Functions of Operations Information Systems

enters the order into a queue for processing. Order-management systems track the order through the fulfillment process, arrange for and schedule shipping, and process exceptions, such as out-of-stock products. Order-management systems also inform customers of order status and scheduled delivery dates.

In nonmanufacturing organizations, operations systems include systems to manage finished-goods inventory. We will address those systems in the discussion of inventory processing for manufacturing systems in the next section. As you read that discussion, keep in mind that nonmanufacturers have only finished-goods inventories; they do not have raw materials or goods-in-process inventories.

Customer service is the last operations system in Figure 7-6. Customers call customer service to ask questions about products, order status, and problems and to make complaints. Today, many organizations are placing as much of the customer service function on Web pages as they can. Many organizations allow customers direct access to order status and delivery information. Also, organizations are increasingly providing product-use support via Web systems.

Manufacturing Information Systems

Manufacturing information systems facilitate the production of goods. As shown in Figure 7-7, manufacturing systems include inventory, planning, scheduling, and manufacturing operations. Consider inventory first.

Inventory Information Systems

Manufacturing activities concern three types of inventory: raw materials, goods-in-process, and finished goods. **Inventory information systems** support inventory control, management, and policy for all three types. In terms of inventory control, inventory applications track goods and materials into, out of, and between inventories. Inventory tracking requires that items be identified by a number. In the least-sophisticated systems, employees enter inventory numbers manually, though most systems use at least UPC bar codes (codes like those on items you buy at the grocery store).

Today, both operations and manufacturing activities are beginning to track inventory using **radio-frequency identification tags (RFIDs)**. Major retailers, such as Wal-Mart, stipulate that their suppliers place RFIDs on products they supply. An RFID is a computer chip that transmits data about the container, product, or equipment to which it is attached (see Figure 7-8). RFID data include not just product numbers, but also data about where the product was made, the product's components, special handling requirements, and, for perishable products, when the contents will expire. RFIDs can record and transmit custom, application-specific data as well. Sensors connected to inventory and other functional systems receive RFID signals and automatically

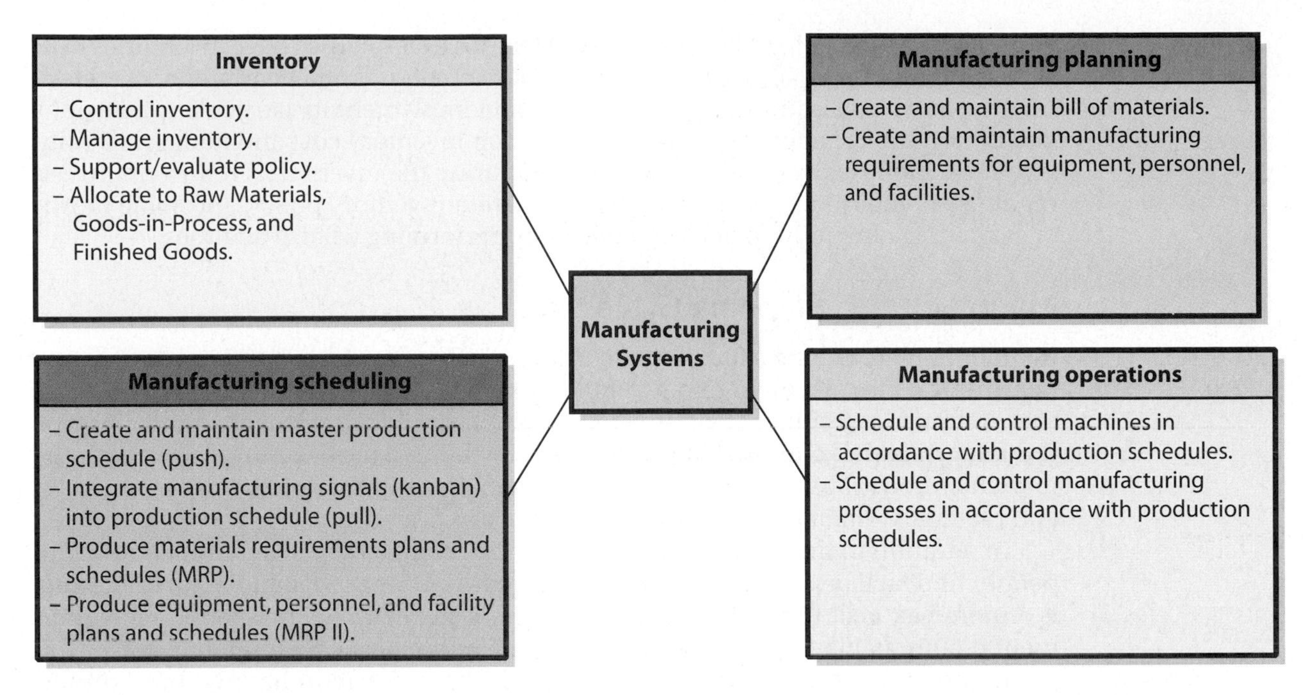

Figure 7-7
Functions of Manufacturing Information Systems

record the arrival, departure, or movement of the item. Many innovative applications of RFIDs are being developed today, even as you read this sentence.

Inventory-management applications use past data to compute stocking levels, reorder levels, and reorder quantities in accordance with inventory policy. They also have features for assisting inventory counts and for computing inventory losses from those counts and from inventory-processing data.

Concerning inventory policy, there are two schools of thought in modern operations management. Some companies view inventories primarily as assets. In this view, large inventories are beneficial. Their cost is justified because large inventories minimize disruptions in operations or sales due to outages. Large finished-goods inventories increase sales by offering greater product selection and availability to the customer.

Other companies, such as Dell, view inventories primarily as liabilities. In this view, companies seek to keep inventories as small as possible and to eliminate them completely if possible. The ultimate expression of this view is demonstrated in the **just-in-time (JIT) inventory policy**. This policy seeks to have production inputs (both raw materials and work-in-process) delivered to the manufacturing site just as they are needed. By scheduling delivery of inputs in this way, companies are able to minimize inventory costs.

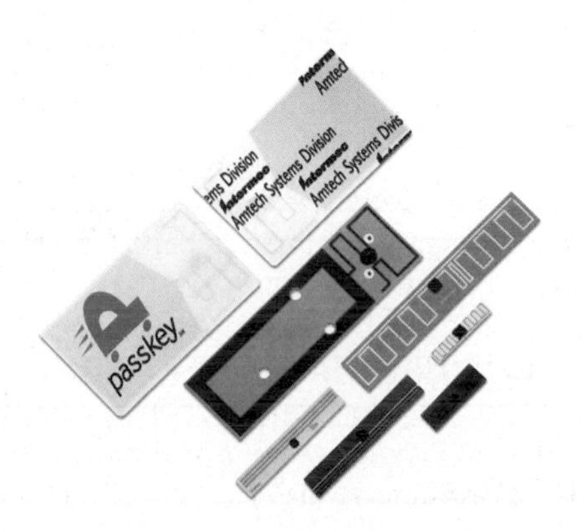

Figure 7-8
Examples of Radio-Frequency Identification (RFID) Tags

Still others use both philosophies: Wal-Mart, for example, has large inventories in its stores, but minimizes all other inventories in its warehouses and distribution centers.

Inventory applications help an organization implement its particular philosophy and determine the appropriate balance between inventory cost and item availability, given that philosophy. Features include computing the inventory's return on investment (ROI), reports on the effectiveness of current inventory policy, and some means of evaluating alternative inventory policies by performing what-if analyses.

Manufacturing Planning Systems

In order to plan materials for manufacturing, it is first necessary to record the components of the manufactured items. A **bill of materials (BOM)** is a list of the materials that comprise a product. This list is more complicated than it might sound, because the materials that comprise a product can be subassemblies that also need to be manufactured. Thus, the BOM is a list of materials, and materials within materials, and materials within materials within materials, and so forth.

In addition to the BOM, if the manufacturing application schedules equipment, people, and facilities, then a record of those resources for each manufactured product is required as well. The company might augment the BOM to show labor and equipment requirements or it might create a separate nonmaterial requirements file.

Figure 7-9 shows a sample BOM for a child's red wagon having four components: handlebar, wagon body, front-wheel assembly, and rear-wheel assembly. Three of these have the subcomponent parts shown. Of course, each of these subcomponents could have sub-subcomponents, and so forth, but these are not shown. Altogether, the BOM shows all of the parts needed to make the wagon and the relationships of those parts to each other.

Manufacturing-Scheduling Systems

Companies use three philosophies to create a manufacturing schedule. One is to generate a **master production schedule (MPS)**, which is a plan for producing products.

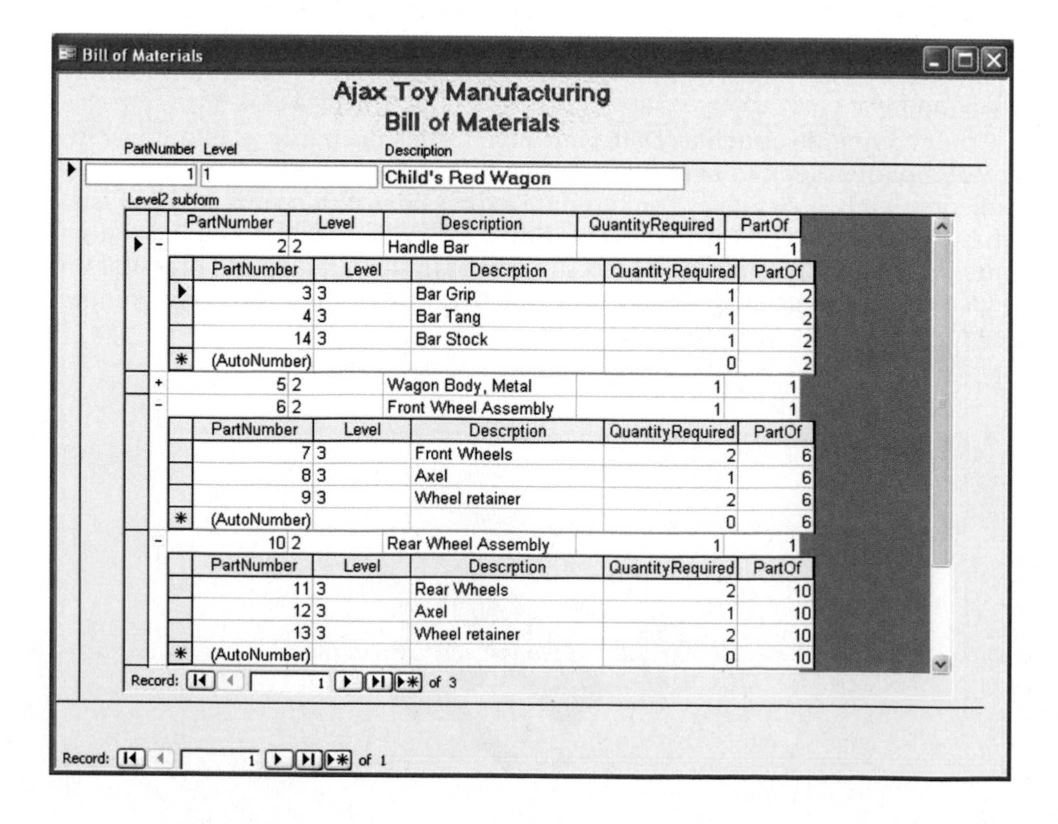
Bill of Materials

Ajax Toy Manufacturing
Bill of Materials

PartNumber	Level	Description
1	1	Child's Red Wagon

Level2 subform

PartNumber	Level	Description	QuantityRequired	PartOf
2	2	Handle Bar	1	1

PartNumber	Level	Descrption	QuantityRequired	PartOf
3	3	Bar Grip	1	2
4	3	Bar Tang	1	2
14	3	Bar Stock	1	2
(AutoNumber)			0	2

PartNumber	Level	Description	QuantityRequired	PartOf
5	2	Wagon Body, Metal	1	1
6	2	Front Wheel Assembly	1	1

PartNumber	Level	Descrption	QuantityRequired	PartOf
7	3	Front Wheels	2	6
8	3	Axel	1	6
9	3	Wheel retainer	2	6
(AutoNumber)			0	6

PartNumber	Level	Description	QuantityRequired	PartOf
10	2	Rear Wheel Assembly	1	1

PartNumber	Level	Descrption	QuantityRequired	PartOf
11	3	Rear Wheels	2	10
12	3	Axel	1	10
13	3	Wheel retainer	2	10
(AutoNumber)			0	10

Record: 1 of 3

Record: 1 of 1

Figure 7-9
Bill of Materials Example

To create the MPS, the company analyzes past sales levels and estimates future sales. This process is called **push production planning**, because the company pushes the products into sales (and customers) according to the MPS.

Use of master production schedules can greatly streamline manufacturing operations. However, read the Ethics Guide *on page 260 for discussion of some possible dangers.*

Figure 7-10 shows a manufacturing schedule for wagon production at a toy company. This plan includes three colors of wagons and shows subtle production increases prior to the summer months and prior to the holiday season. Again, the company obtains these production levels by analyzing past sales. The MPS for an actual manufacturer would, of course, be more complicated.

A second philosophy is not to use a preplanned, forecasted schedule, but rather to plan manufacturing in response to signals from customers or downstream production processes that products or components are currently needed. The Japanese word *kanban*, which means "card," is sometimes used to refer to the signal to build something. Manufacturing processes that respond to kanbans must be more flexible than those that are MPS based. A process based on such signals is sometimes called **pull production planning**, because the products are pulled through manufacturing by demand.

Finally, a third philosophy is a combination of the two. The company creates an MPS and plans manufacturing according to the MPS, but it uses kanban-like signals to modify the schedule. For example, if the company receives signals that indicate increased customer demand, it might add an extra production shift for a while in order to build inventory to meet the increased demand. This combination approach requires sophisticated information systems for implementation.

Two acronyms are common in the manufacturing domain: **Materials requirements planning (MRP)** is an information system that plans the need for materials and inventories of materials used in the manufacturing process. MRP does not include the planning of personnel, equipment, or facilities requirements.

Manufacturing resource planning (MRP II) is a follow-on to MRP that includes the planning of materials, personnel, and machinery. MRP II supports many linkages across the organization, including linkages with sales and marketing via the development of a master production schedule. MRP II also includes the capability to perform what-if analyses on variances in schedules, raw materials availabilities, personnel, and other resources.[1]

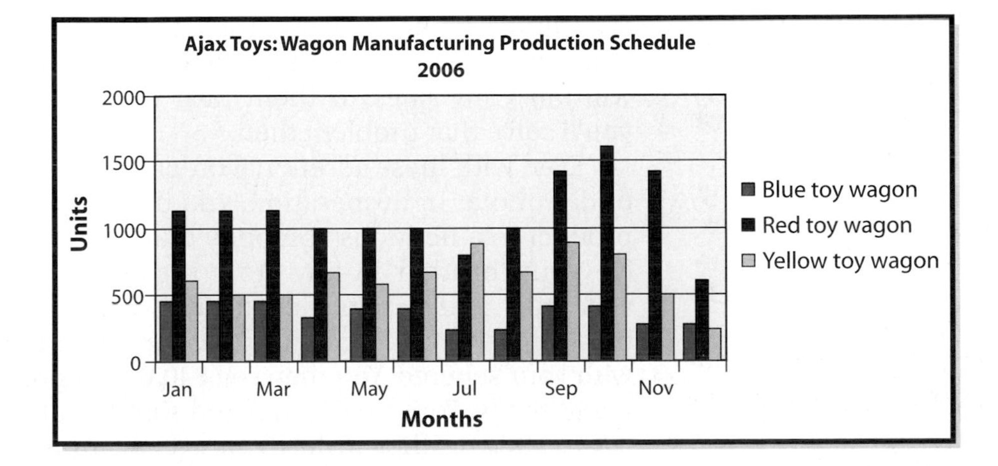

Figure 7-10
Sample Manufacturing Plan

[1]To add even more complication to this subject, some in the operations management field use the terms *MRP Type I* and *MRP Type II* instead of *MRP* and *MRPII*. **MRP Type I** refers to material requirements planning; **MRP Type II** refers to manufacturing resource planning. When used in this way, the different interpretations of the letters *MRP* are ignored, as if *MRP* were not an acronym.

Ethics

GUIDE

Dialing for Dollars

Suppose you are a salesperson and your company's sales forecasting system predicts that your quarterly sales will be substantially under quota. You call your best customers to increase sales, but no one is willing to buy more.

Your boss says that it has been a bad quarter for all of the salespeople. It's so bad, in fact, that the VP of Sales has authorized a 20 percent discount on new orders. The only stipulation is that customers must take delivery prior to the end of the quarter so that accounting can book the order. "Start dialing for dollars," she says, "and get what you can. Be creative."

Using your customer management system, you identify your top customers and present the discount offer to them. The first customer balks at increasing her inventory, "I just don't think we can sell that much."

"Well," you respond, "how about if we agree to take back any inventory you don't sell next quarter?" (By doing this, you increase your current sales and commission, and you also help your company make its quarterly sales projections. The additional product is likely to come back next quarter, but you think, "Hey, that's then and this is now.")

"OK," she says, "but I want you to stipulate the return option on the purchase order."

You know that you cannot write that on the purchase order because accounting won't book all of the order if you do. So you tell her that you'll send her an email with that stipulation. She increases her order, and accounting books the full amount.

With another customer, you try a second strategy. Instead of offering the discount, you offer the product at full price, but agree to pay a 20 percent credit in the next quarter. That way you can book the full price now. You pitch this offer as follows: "Our marketing department analyzed past sales using our fancy new CRM computer system, and we know that increasing advertising will cause additional sales. So, if you order more product now, next quarter we'll give you 20 percent of the order back to pay for advertising."

In truth, you doubt the customer will spend the money on advertising. Instead, they'll just take the credit and sit on a bigger inventory. That will kill your sales to them next quarter, but you'll solve that problem then.

Even with these additional orders, you're still under quota. In desperation, you decide to sell product to a fictitious company that is "owned" by your brother-in-law. You set up a new account, and when accounting calls your brother-in-law for a credit check, he cooperates with your scheme. You then sell $40,000 of product to the fictitious company and ship the product to your brother-in-law's garage. Accounting books the revenue in the quarter, and you have finally made quota. A week into the next quarter, your brother-in-law returns the merchandise.

Meanwhile, unknown to you, your company's MRP II system is scheduling production. The program that creates the MPS reads the sales from your activities (and those of the other salespeople) and finds a sharp increase in product demand. Accordingly, it generates an MPS that calls for substantial production increases and schedules workers for the production runs. The MRP system, in turn, schedules the material requirements with the inventory application, which increases raw materials purchases to meet the increased production schedule. ■

Discussion Questions

1. Is it ethical for you to write the email agreeing to take the product back? If that email comes to light later, what do you think your boss will say?
2. Is it ethical for you to offer the "advertising" discount? What effect does that discount have on your company's balance sheet?
3. Is it ethical for you to ship to the fictitious company? Is it legal?
4. Describe the impact of your activities on next quarter's inventories.
5. If you were the COO of this company, would you instruct manufacturing to ignore the sales increases?
6. What would you do if you were the salesperson in this situation?
7. What, in your opinion, should this company do?

Manufacturing Operations

A fourth category of IS in manufacturing is the control of machinery and production processes. Computer programs operate lathes, mills, robots, and even entire production lines. In a modern facility, these programs have linkages to the manufacturing-scheduling systems. Because they are not information systems in the sense we consider in this text, we will not consider them further.

Human Resources Information Systems

Human resources information systems support recruiting, compensation, assessment, development and training, and planning. The first-era human resources (HR) applications did little more than compute payroll. Modern HR applications concern all dimensions of HR activity, as shown in Figure 7-11.

Depending on the size and sophistication of the company, recruiting methods can be simple or very complex. In a small company, posting a job might be a simple task requiring one or two approvals. In a larger, more formal organization, posting a new job might involve multiple levels of approval requiring use of tightly controlled and standardized procedures.

Compensation includes payroll for both salaried employees and hourly employees. It may also include pay to consultants and permanent, but nonemployee, workers, such as contractors and full-time consultants. Compensation means not only pay, but also the processing and tracking of vacation, sick leave, and health care and other benefits. Compensation activities also support retirement plans, company stock purchases, and stock options and grants. They can also include transferring employee contribution payments to organizations such as the United Way and others.

Employee assessment includes the publication of standard job and skill descriptions as well as support for employee performance evaluations. Such support may include systems that allow employees to create self-evaluations as well as evaluations of peers and subordinates. Employee assessment is used for the basis of compensation increases as well as promotion.

Development and training activities vary widely from firm to firm. Some organizations define career paths formally, with specific jobs, skills, experience, and training

Figure 7-11
Functions of Human Resources Information Systems

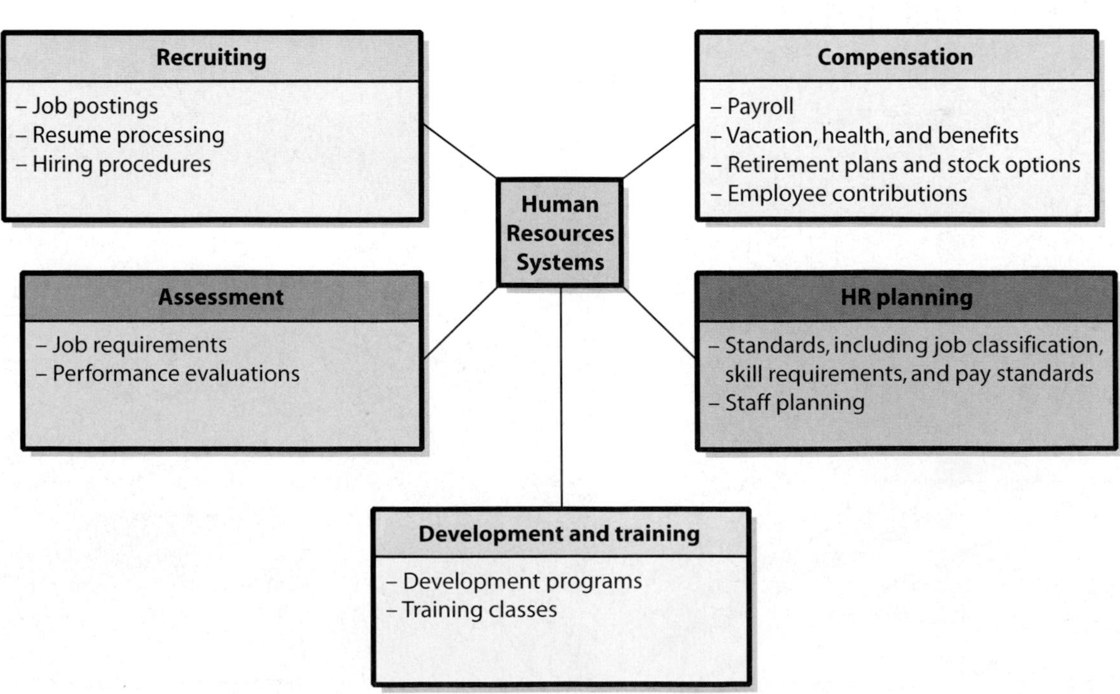

requirements. HR systems have features and functions to support the publication of these paths. Some HR applications track training classes, instructors, and students.

Finally, HR applications must support planning functions. These include the creation and publication of organizational standards job classifications and compensation ranges for those classifications. Planning also includes determining future requirements for employees by level, experience, skill, and other factors.

Accounting Information Systems

In some companies, accounting functions are performed entirely by accounting personnel; in other companies (typically, larger ones), the functions are divided between accounting and finance departments. Figure 7-12 ignores this possibility and groups both accounting and finance systems under one heading.

You know from your accounting classes what a general ledger is. Financial reporting applications use the general ledger data to produce financial statement and other reports for management, investors, and federal agencies such as the SEC.

Cost-accounting applications determine the marginal cost and relative profitability of products and product families. Budgeting applications allocate and schedule revenues and expenses and compare actual financial results to the plan.

Accounts receivable includes not just recording receivables and the payments against receivables, but also account aging and collections management. Accounts payable systems include features to reconcile payments against purchases and to schedule payments according to the organization's payment policy.

Cash management is the process of scheduling payments and receivables and planning the use of cash so as to balance the organization's cash needs against cash availability. Other financial-management applications concern checking and other account reconciliation as well as managing electronic funds transfer throughout the organization. Finally, treasury applications concern the management and investment of the organization's cash, as well as the payment of cash dividends.

Since its passage in 2002, the Sarbanes-Oxley Act has had a significant impact on accounting information systems. For more about "Sarbox," read the Information Systems in Practice *box* *on page 264.*

Figure 7-12
Functions of Accounting Information Systems

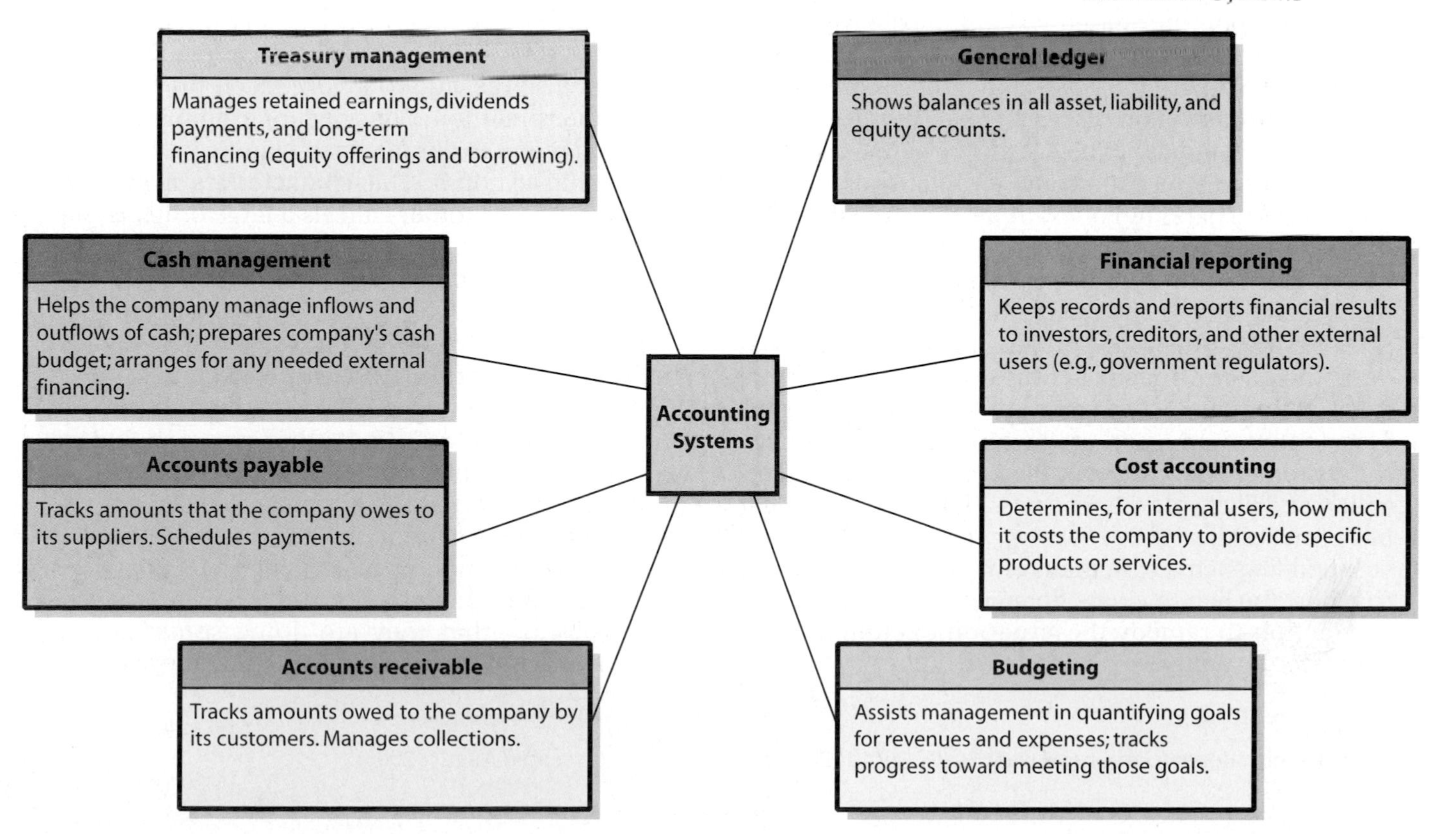

Treasury management
Manages retained earnings, dividends payments, and long-term financing (equity offerings and borrowing).
General ledger
Shows balances in all asset, liability, and equity accounts.
Cash management
Helps the company manage inflows and outflows of cash; prepares company's cash budget; arranges for any needed external financing.
Financial reporting
Keeps records and reports financial results to investors, creditors, and other external users (e.g., government regulators).
Accounting Systems
Accounts payable
Tracks amounts that the company owes to its suppliers. Schedules payments.
Cost accounting
Determines, for internal users, how much it costs the company to provide specific products or services.
Accounts receivable
Tracks amounts owed to the company by its customers. Manages collections.
Budgeting
Assists management in quantifying goals for revenues and expenses; tracks progress toward meeting those goals.

INFORMATION SYSTEMS IN PRACTICE

THE SARBANES-OXLEY ACT

The **Sarbanes-Oxley Act of 2002** is a revision of the Securities Exchange Act of 1934 that governs the reporting requirements of publicly held companies. Sarbanes-Oxley was enacted to prevent future corporate frauds like those perpetrated by WorldCom, Enron, and others. It requires management to create internal controls sufficient to produce reliable financial statements and to protect the organization's assets. Management is further required to issue a statement indicating it has done so. The organization's external auditor must also issue an opinion on the quality of the internal controls and the credibility of management's statement. Sarbanes-Oxley exposes both management and the external auditor to financial and potential criminal liability if subsequent events should show that internal controls were defective.

An example of an internal control is **separation of duties and authorities**. In an accounts payable system, for example, three separate individuals are required: one to authorize the expense, a second to issue the check, and a third to account for the transaction. No one person should perform two or more of these actions. You will learn about other such controls in your accounting classes.

If management is relying on computer-based accounting information systems for the preparation of financial statements—and all large organizations do—then those computer-based systems must have appropriate controls, and according to the rules of Sarbanes-Oxley, management must assert that those controls are reliable. This assertion places a greater burden on the development and use of IS.

Additionally, IS can produce valuable assets that are subject to liability. For example, the database of an order-processing information system that stores customer identities and credit card data contains an organizational asset. If the design of the IS ineffectively prevents unauthorized persons from accessing that data, then a **contingent liability** (a possible liability) exists. Without effective controls, someone could steal a customer's name and credit card data and damage the customer. The customer then could sue the organization and likely prevail. The possibility that this might occur makes the liability *contingent*. Even if no one has yet sued, in such a case management is required both to report the liability in its financial statements and to take action to remedy the situation to eliminate the contingent liability.

CIO Magazine publishes articles of interest and importance to chief information officers (CIOs, discussed in Chapter 11). If you search for topics on Sarbanes-Oxley at *http://CIO.com*, you will find a revealing sequence of articles. Initial articles reported confusion and concern among CIOs. Then articles appeared that explained how to comply. Most recently, *CIO Magazine*'s editor, Gary Beach, published an editorial entitled, "Repeal Sarbanes-Oxley." What happened? According to Mr. Beach, ". . . while foreign companies are free to grab market share, U.S. executives are instead grabbing their Sarbanes-Oxley manuals" to learn how to comply with the act.[2]

According to a poll conducted by *CIO Magazine*, large companies expect to divert more than 15 percent of their IS budgets to Sarbanes-Oxley compliance. That represents a huge investment, and given the importance of a favorable audit report it is an expense that organizations view as mandatory, whether or not it is sensible.

Part of the problem is that, even in 2008, no one knows what exactly is necessary to comply with Sarbanes-Oxley. The act requires external auditors to become even more independent than they had been in the past, and thus many will not issue opinions on the specific controls that IS needs. The attitude seems to be, "Show us what you have, and we'll tell you if it's enough." IS managers are understandably frustrated.

Further, the wording of the act is so vague that, to protect themselves, auditors have taken the broadest possible interpretation. Consider, for example, Section 409, which requires disclosure of significant financial events within 48 hours. What characterizes an event as *significant*? If a customer cancels a large order, is that significant? If so, how large must an order be to be considered large? If a supplier is devastated by a hurricane, is that significant? "How," many CIOs ask, "can we determine from our information systems that a significant event has occurred? And within 48 hours? Are we supposed to reprogram our applications to include alerts on all such events? What other events should we look for? And who's paying for all of this?"

One thing is certain: The Sarbanes-Oxley Act will provide full employment for internal auditors in general and for IT auditors in particular. Organizations will have to sponsor a flurry of activity, however uneconomic, to show that they are doing something to comply. No company can afford to ignore the act.

[2] Gary Beach, "Repeal Sarbanes-Oxley," *CIO*, April 1, 2005, *http://CIO.com* (accessed August 2006).

Senators Sarbanes and Oxley are both attorneys, and neither has ever worked in a publicly traded company. In the light of the financial disasters at Enron and WorldCom, their law was highly praised by the public. But, is it worth its cost? Will millions, perhaps billions, be wasted in unnecessary compliance? In the long run, will it hamper U.S. corporations that must compete internationally against corporations that are not burdened by this act? Will it ultimately work to reduce investor choices? And, given the requirements of the Sarbanes-Oxley Act, why would privately owned companies ever choose to go public?

To assess the wisdom of the Sarbanes-Oxley Act, see Collaboration Exercise 1, on page 284.

Q4 What Are the Problems of Functional Systems?

Functional systems are a big improvement over calculation systems, but, as stated, they operate in isolation, as islands of automation. The result is the problems summarized in Figure 7-13. First, each functional system processes its own data. Customer, product, employee, and other kinds of data are duplicated in each functional application. As you learned in Chapter 5, the problem with data duplication is the potential for a lack of data integrity. For example, a change to a customer address in a lead-tracking system may not reach manufacturing or customer support for days or weeks. During that interval, products might be shipped to the wrong address or mailings might be wrongly addressed.

Second, when systems are isolated, business processes are disjointed. There is no easy way for the sales/marketing system, for example, to integrate activity with the accounting system. As Brian Street said in the chapter opening interview, just sending the data from one system to the other can be problematic.

Consider the simple example in Figure 7-14 (next page). Suppose the order entry and inventory systems define a product number as three characters, a dash, and four numeric digits. Yet, suppose the manufacturing system in the same company defines a product as four digits followed by characters. Every time parts data are exported from order entry and imported into manufacturing (or the reverse), the data must be

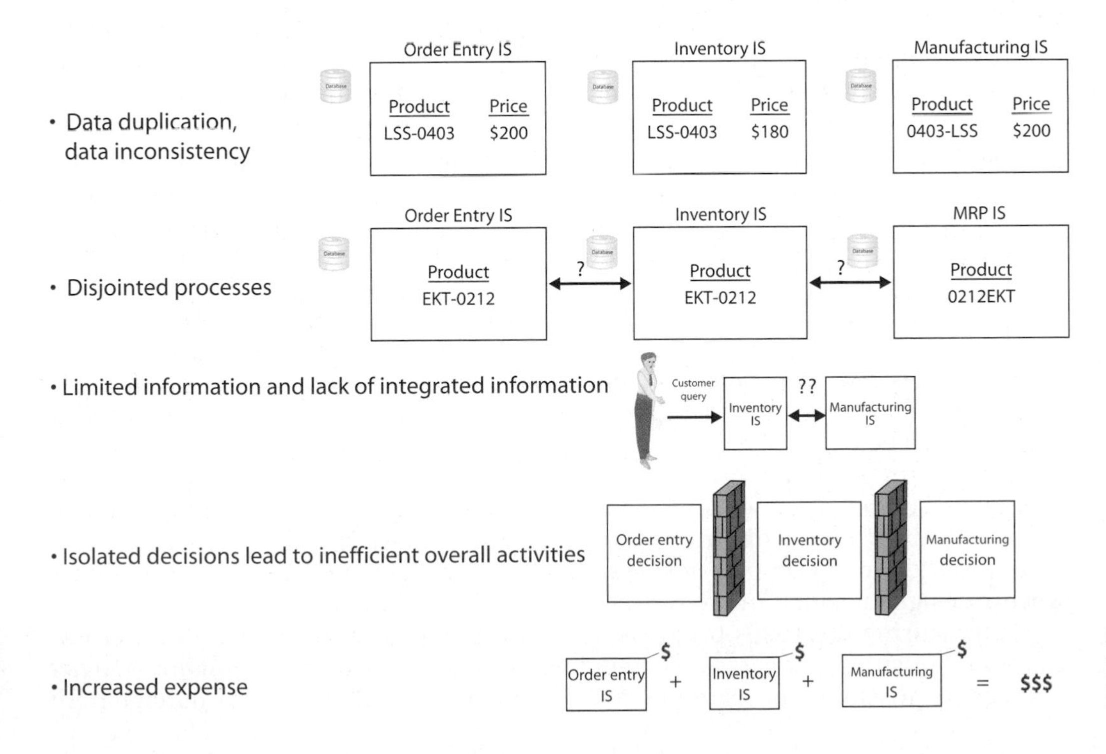

Figure 7-13
Major Problems of Isolated Functional Systems

Figure 7-14
Example of System Integration Problem

- Order Entry System Product Number:
  Format: ccc–nnnn
  Example: COMP–3344
- Manufacturing System Product Number:
  Format: nnnnccc
  Example: 3344COMP

converted from one scheme to the other. Multiply this conversion process by several hundred data items, and possibly dozens of other systems, and you can see why processing is disjointed across functional applications.

Third, isolated systems cannot provide integrated enterprise information. When a customer inquires about an order, information about that order will exist in several different systems. Some order information is in the order-entry system, some is in the finished-goods inventory system, and some is in the manufacturing system. Obtaining a consolidated statement about the customer's order will require processing each of these systems, with possibly inconsistent data.

A fourth consequence of isolated systems is inefficiency. When using isolated functional systems, a department can make decisions based only on the isolated data that it has. So, for example, raw materials inventory systems will make inventory replenishment decisions based only on costs and benefits in that single inventory. However, it might be that the overall efficiency of the sales, order entry, and manufacturing activities, considered together across the enterprise, will be improved by carrying a less than optimal number of products in raw materials inventory.

Finally, isolated functional systems can result in increased cost for the organization. Duplicated data, disjointed systems, limited information, and inefficiencies all mean higher costs.

Q5 What Is Business Process Design?

In essence, the problem of system isolation is that the left hand of the organization does not know what the right hand is doing. Organizations with isolated systems find themselves providing $1,000 of customer support to a customer whose lifetime order total is $150. Or, they may accelerate production on an order to meet a customer's schedule requirements, only to learn the customer has $100,000 in overdue payments and the credit department refuses to release the order for shipment.

Although the problem of isolation is obvious, the solution, unfortunately, is not. What is the best way to integrate the activities of the sales, operations, support, and credit departments? What specific problem needs to be solved? As you learned in Chapter 2, a problem is a perception, and employees in each department will each have their own perceptions. Further, once the problem is agreed on, what is the best solution? Who should send what data or documents to whom and when and on what schedule? And what happens when they do not comply? Understandably, each department will have its own answers.

These questions came to a head in the 1990s, when computer networks and database technology made it possible to develop integrated information systems that could support activities across an entire business process. Unlike functional systems, which automated or otherwise improved existing processes, cross-functional systems necessitated answers to questions like those just discussed. The new technology could not be effectively used without the design of more efficient business processes. This need led to the creation of a new systems development specialty called **business process design**, or sometimes *business process redesign*.

Thus, during the 1990s progressive organizations began to create new cross-functional business processes. The goal was to take advantage of as many activity linkages as possible. For example, a cross-departmental customer-management process would integrate all interactions with the customer, from prospect, through initial order, through repeat orders, including customer support, credit, and accounts receivable.

Challenges of Business Process Design

Unfortunately, process design projects are expensive and difficult. Highly trained systems analysts interview key personnel from many departments and document the existing system as well as one or more system alternatives. Key personnel review the results of the analysts' activity, usually many times, and attempt to develop new, improved processes. Then new information systems are developed to implement those new business processes. All of this takes time, and meanwhile, the underlying processes are changing, which means the process design may need to be redesigned before the project is completed.

Once these difficulties have been overcome and the new integrated systems designed, an even greater challenge arises during implementation: Employees resist change. People do not want to work in new ways, they do not want to lose authority, they do not want to see their department reorganized or abolished, and they do not want to work for someone new. Even if the system can be implemented over this resistance, some people will continue to resist by sabotaging the system. All of these difficulties translate into labor hours, which translate into costs. Thus, business process design is very expensive.

The Problem-Solving Guide *on page 278 discusses in more detail the effects of organizational change.*

Even worse, the ultimate outcome is uncertain. Some businesses are successful in their process design activities, but many others fail. In some cases, millions of dollars are spent on projects that ultimately are abandoned. The idea of designing business processes for greater integration was floundering when it received a boost from an unexpected source: integrated application vendors.

Benefits of Inherent Processes

Many early business process design projects failed because they were tailor-made. They were custom-fit to a particular organization, and so just one company bore the cost of the design effort. In the mid-1990s, a number of successful software vendors began to market premade integrated applications, with built-in processes. Such processes saved hundreds of hours of design work.

When an organization acquires a business application from, say, Oracle or SAP, the processes for using the software are built-in, **inherent processes**. In most cases, to use the software, the organization must conform its activities to those processes. If the software is designed well, the inherent processes will effectively integrate activities across departments. These prebuilt processes will save the organization the substantial, sometimes staggering, costs of designing new processes itself.

Figure 7-15 (next page) shows an example of an inherent process in a software product called *SAP R/3*, a product licensed by SAP AG Corp. (a German company). When an organization licenses this product, SAP provides hundreds of diagrams just like this one. These diagrams show the business processes that must be created in order to effectively use the software.

This diagram shows the flow and logic of one set of inherent processes. In the top lines, if the purchase requisition does not exist and if the request for quotation (RFQ) is to be created, then the purchasing department creates an RFQ and sends it to potential vendors. You can read through the rest of this sample diagram to obtain the gist of this process snippet.

To some, when an organization licenses cross-departmental software, the primary benefit is not the software, but the inherent processes for using the software. Licensing an integrated application not only saves the organization the time, expense, and agony of process design, it also enables the organization to benefit immediately from tried and tested cross-departmental processes.

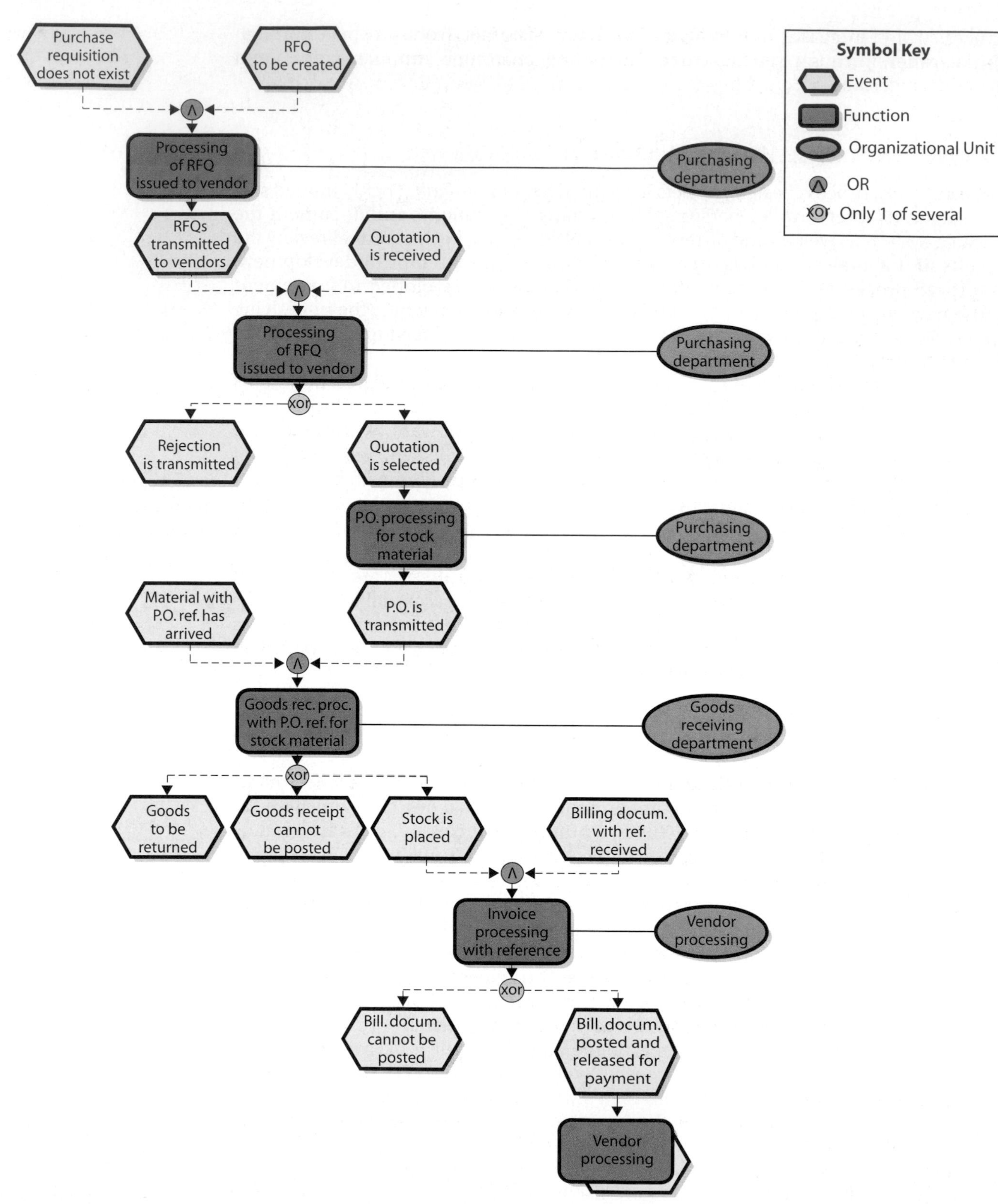

Figure 7-15
Example of SAP R/3 Ordering Process

Source: Adapted from Curran, Thomas A.; Ladd, Andrew; Ladd, Dennis, *SAP R/3 Reporting and E-Business Intelligence*, 1st ed., © 2000. Reprinted by permission of Pearson Education, Inc., Upper Saddle River, NJ.

Of course, there is a disadvantage. The inherent processes may be very different from existing processes and thus require the organization to change dramatically. Such change will be disruptive to ongoing operations and very disturbing to employees.

In spite of these challenges, many organizations have converted to cross-functional systems. In the interview that opened this chapter, Brian Street described such a conversion. And, because the benefits of such systems can be huge, many other organizations are starting to convert to such systems. We consider the three major types of cross-functional systems next.

Employees react in a variety of ways to process changes, especially to dramatic ones. See the Opposing Forces Guide *on page 280 for one disgruntled employee's view of business process change.*

Q6 What Are the Functions and Characteristics of the Three Major Cross-Functional Systems?

Three cross-functional application categories have emerged: CRM, ERP, and EAI. We consider these categories next.

Customer Relationship Management (CRM) Systems

As you can see in Figure 7-16, **customer relationship management (CRM) systems** integrate all of the primary business activities. They track all interactions with the customer from prospect through follow-up service and support. Vendors of CRM applications claim that using their products makes the organization *customer-centric*. Though that term reeks of sales hyperbole, it does indicate the nature and intent of CRM systems.

A key element of CRM is that all customer data is stored in a single database. This characteristic eliminates the possibility of inconsistent customer data. It also enables employees in every department to see and know the customer's complete history. For example, when a salesperson calls a customer for follow-up business, he or she will know not only how much the customer has ordered in the past, but also the complaints or issues the customer has had, any existing open orders, the customer's credit status, and other relevant customer data.

By the way, some CRM applications include software installed at customer sites. Such systems support linkages between two organizations and are discussed in the next chapter in the context of supply chain management.

Figure 7-17 (next page) shows four phases of the **customer life cycle**: marketing, customer acquisition, relationship management, and loss/churn. Marketing sends messages to the target market to attract customer prospects. When prospects order, they become customers who need to be supported. Additionally, resell processes increase the value of existing customers. Inevitably, over time the organization loses

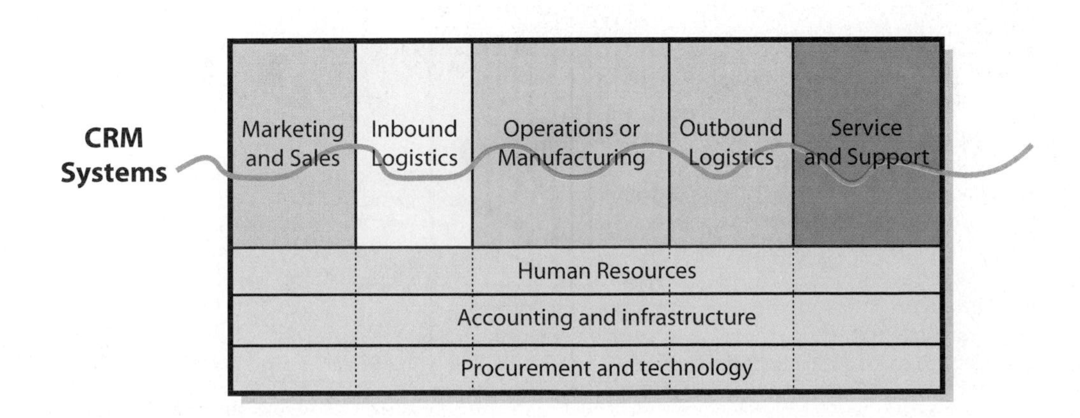

Figure 7-16
CRM and the Value Chain Model

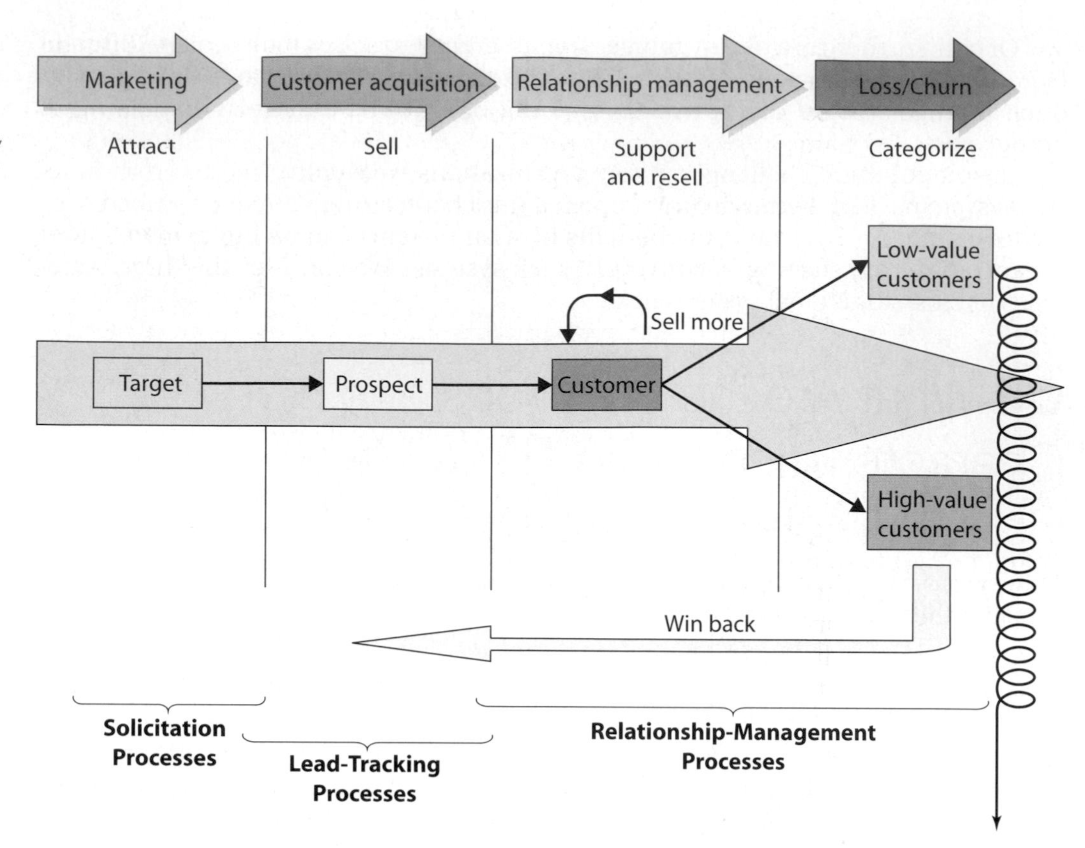

Figure 7-17
The Customer Life Cycle

Source: The Customer Life Cycle. Used with permission from Douglas Maclachlan, Professor, UW Business School, University of Washington, Seattle, WA.

customers. When this occurs, win-back processes categorize customers according to value and attempt to win back high-value customers.

Figure 7-18 shows the major components of a CRM system. Notice there are components for each stage of the customer life cycle. Information systems that support solicitation include email applications and organizational Web sites. Additionally, some information systems support traditional direct mail, catalog, and other solicitations.

The organizational Web site is an increasingly important solicitation tool. Web addresses are easy to promote (and remember), and once a target prospect is on the site

Figure 7-18
CRM Components

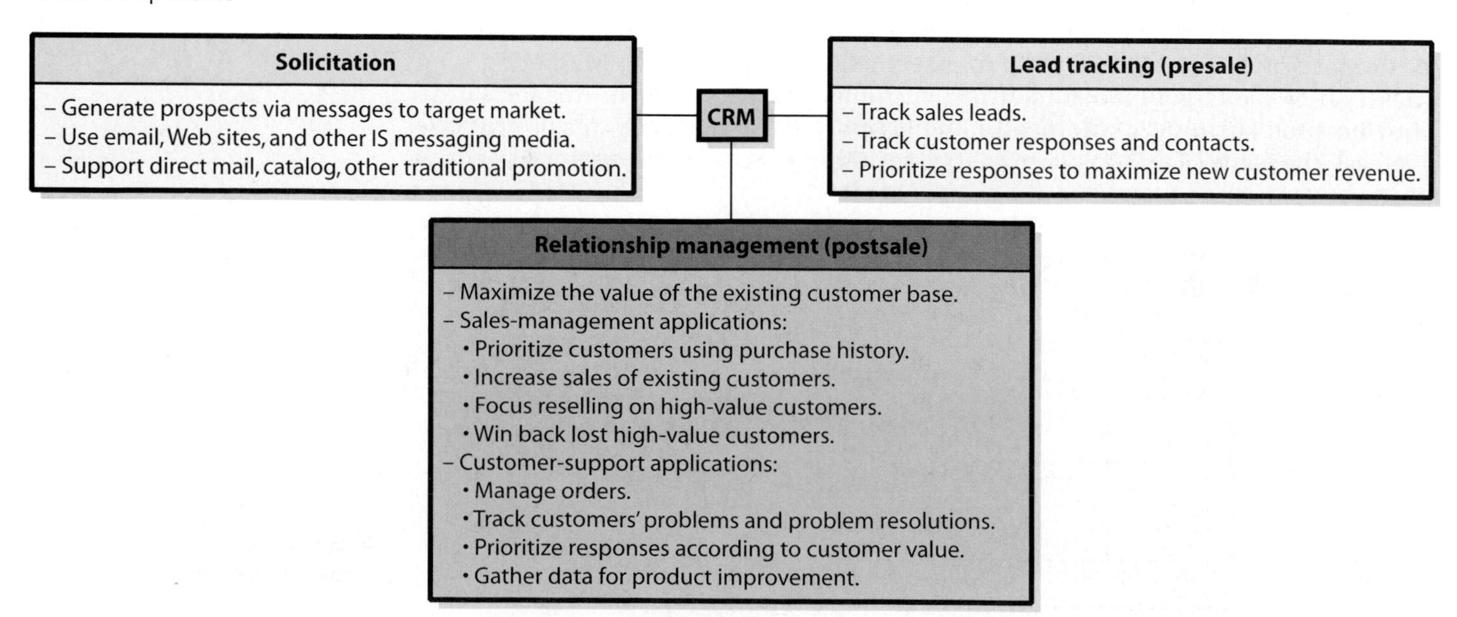

product descriptions, use cases, success stories, and other solicitation materials can be provided easily. Further, the cost of distributing these materials via the Web is substantially less than the cost of creating and distributing printed materials. Many Web sites require customer name and contact information before releasing high-value promotional materials. That contact information then feeds lead-tracking applications.

The purpose of lead-tracking, or presale, applications is to turn prospects into customers. Such applications track sales leads and record customer responses and contacts. Most of these applications enable the sales department to prioritize contacts so as to focus on high-potential prospects.

Lead-tracking systems are particularly important when multiple salespeople call on the same customer. Often salespeople may join forces to work out a strategy for sales calls and follow-ups. If nothing else, consolidated lead tracking can keep sales personnel from duplicating efforts and from interfering with one another.

With the first order, a prospect becomes a customer and is a candidate for relationship-management applications. The purpose of relationship-management applications is to maximize the value of the existing customer base. As Figure 7-18 shows, two types of applications are used. Sales-management applications support sales to existing customers. They have features to prioritize customers according to their purchase history. Salespeople can increase sales to existing customers by focusing on customers who have already made large purchases, by focusing on large organizations that have the potential to make large purchases, or both. The goal of such applications is to ensure that sales management has sufficient information to prioritize and allocate sales time and effort.

Sales-management applications also have features to prioritize lost customers, to determine which of those are high-value lost customers, and to help the sales team to develop a strategy to win those customers back. Surprisingly, it can be difficult for a company to know when it has lost a customer. A telephone company will know it has lost a customer when the customer cancels the service, but an online retailer may not know when it has lost a customer. In such a case, only an analysis of past purchase history can indicate that the customer is gone.

Of course, it is cheaper to keep an existing customer than to acquire a new customer or to win back a lost one. Accordingly, another important component to relationship management is customer support. Order-management applications help the customer to determine the status of an order, how and when it was shipped, the status of returns, and so forth. Additionally, other customer-support applications track customer problems and resolutions and ensure that customers need not repeat their problem history to each new support representative.

Integrated CRM applications store data in a single database, as shown in Figure 7-19. Because all customer data reside in one location, CRM processes can be linked to one another. For example, customer-service activities can be linked to customer-purchase records. In this way, both sales and marketing know the status of customer satisfaction, both on an individual customer basis for future sales calls and also collectively for analyzing customers' overall satisfaction. Also, many customer-support applications prioritize

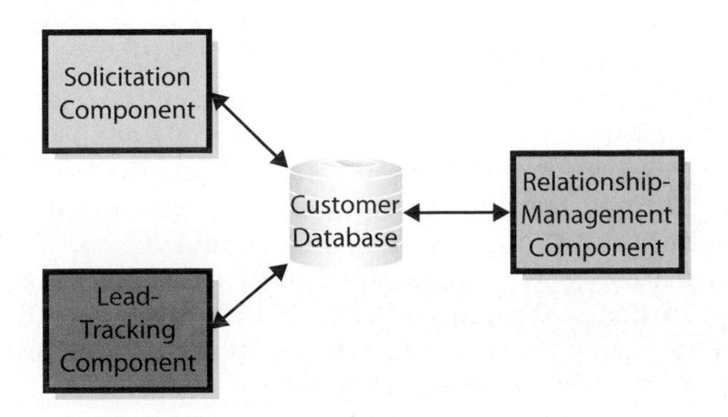

Figure 7-19
CRM Centered on Integrated Customer Database

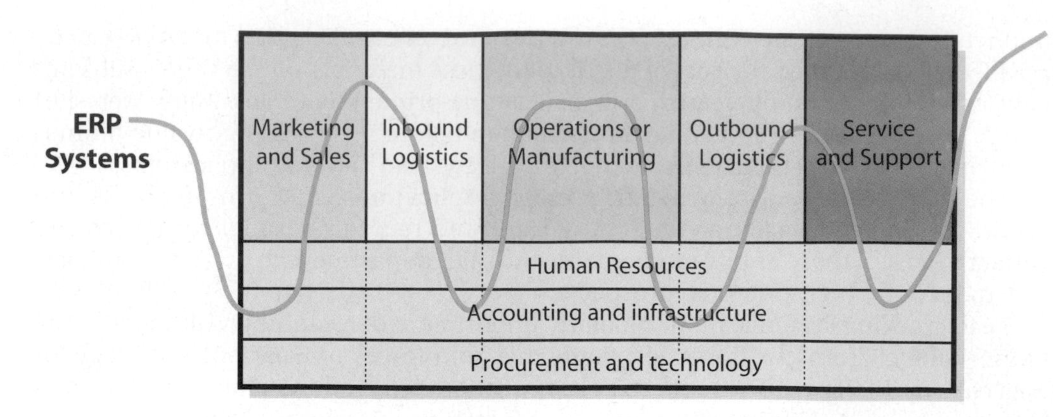

Figure 7-20
ERP Systems and the Value Chain

customers in order to avoid the problem of giving $1,000 worth of support to a customer with a lifetime value of $150. Finally, customer support has an important linkage to product marketing and development; it knows more than any other group what customers are doing with the product and what problems they are having with it.

Enterprise Resource Planning (ERP) Systems

Enterprise resource planning (ERP) systems provide even more integration than CRM. As Figure 7-20 shows, ERP integrates the primary value chain activities with human resources and accounting. ERP systems are truly enterprise-wide. They track customers, process orders, manage inventory, pay employees, and provide general ledger, payable, receivables, and other necessary accounting functions. Thus far, ERP represents the ultimate in cross-functional systems.

ERP is an outgrowth of MRP II, and the primary ERP users are manufacturing companies. The first and most successful vendor of ERP software is SAP (from SAP AG Corp.). According to the company, more than 12 million people use SAP in over 100,000 SAP installations worldwide. Oracle is a second major ERP vendor. These vendors provide not only software, but also predesigned databases, inherent procedures, and job descriptions for organization-wide process integration.

The benefits of inherent processes and procedures are clear, but they raise a related issue—the effect of these processes on innovation. The Innovation in Practice *box below addresses that issue.*

Before continuing, be aware that some companies misapply the term *ERP* to their systems. It is a hot topic, and there is no truth-in-ERP-advertising group to ensure that all of the vendors that claim ERP capability have anything remotely close to it. Let the buyer beware.

INNOVATION IN PRACTICE

ERP AND THE STANDARD, STANDARD BLUEPRINT

ERP vendors such as SAP have invested millions of labor hours into the business blueprints that underlie their ERP solutions. These blueprints consist of hundreds or thousands of different business processes. Examples are processes for hiring employees, processes for acquiring fixed assets, processes for acquiring consumable goods, and processes for custom "one-off" (a unique product with a unique design) manufacturing, to name just a few.

Additionally, ERP vendors have implemented their business processes in hundreds of organizations. In so doing, they have been forced to customize their standard blueprint for use in particular industries. For example, SAP has a distribution-business blueprint that is customized for the auto parts industry, for the electronics industry, and for the aircraft industry. Hundreds of other customized solutions exist as well.

Even better, the ERP vendors have developed software solutions that fit their business-process blueprints. In theory, no software development is required at all if the organization can adapt to the standard blueprint of the ERP vendor.

As described in this chapter, when an organization implements an ERP solution, it first determines any differences that exist between its business processes and the standard blueprint. Then, the organization must remove that difference, which can be done in one of two ways: It changes business processes to fit the standard blueprint. Or, the ERP vendor or a consultant modifies the standard blueprint (and software solution that matches that blueprint) to fit the unique requirements.

In practice, such variations from the standard blueprint are rare. They are difficult and expensive to implement, and they require the using organization to maintain the variations from the standard as new versions of the ERP software are developed. Consequently, most organizations choose to modify their processes to meet the blueprint, rather than the other way around. Although such process changes also are difficult to implement, once the organization has converted to the standard blueprint it no longer needs to support a "variation." So, from a standpoint of cost, effort, risk, and avoidance of future problems, there is a huge incentive for organizations to adapt to the standard ERP blueprint.

Initially, SAP was the only true ERP vendor, but other companies, such as Oracle, have developed and acquired ERP solutions as well. Because of competitive pressure across the software industry, all of these products are beginning to have the same sets of features and functions. ERP solutions are becoming a commodity.

All of this is fine as far as it goes, but it introduces a nagging question: If, over time, every organization tends to implement the standard ERP blueprint, and if, over time, every software company develops essentially the same ERP features and functions, then won't every business come to look just like every other business? How will organizations gain a competitive advantage if they all use the same business processes?

If every auto parts distributor uses the same business processes, based on the same software, are they not all clones of one another? How will a company distinguish itself? How will innovation occur? Even if one parts distributor does successfully innovate a business process that gives it a competitive advantage, will the ERP vendors be conduits to transfer that innovation to competitors? Does the use of "commoditized" standard blueprints mean that no company can sustain a competitive advantage? And, does it doom the idea of process innovation?

To address these questions, see Collaboration Exercise 2, on page 284.

ERP Characteristics

Of the major ERP characteristics listed in Figure 7-21, the first is that ERP takes a cross-functional, process view of the entire organization. With ERP, the entire organization is considered a collection of interrelated activities.

• Provides cross-functional, process view of organization

Acctg Sales OPS Mfg

• Has a formal approach based on formal business models

• Maintains data in centralized database

Data Data Data Data

• Offers large benefits but is difficult, fraught with challenges, and can be slow to implement

• Often VERY expensive

$ $ $ Separate functional applications

$ ERP

Figure 7-21
Characteristics of ERP

Second, true ERP is a formal approach that is based on documented, tested business models. ERP applications include a comprehensive set of inherent processes for all organizational activities. SAP defines this set as the **process blueprint** and documents each process with diagrams that use a set of standardized symbols. The process diagram in Figure 7-15 is a SAP process diagram.

As stated, ERP applications are based on formally defined procedures, and organizations must adapt their processing to the ERP blueprint. If they do not, the system cannot operate effectively, or even correctly. In some cases, it is possible to adapt ERP software to procedures that are different from the blueprint, but such adaptation is expensive and often problematic.

With ERP systems, organizational data are processed in a centralized database. Such centralization makes it easy for authorized users to obtain needed information from a single source.

Once an organization has implemented an ERP system, it can achieve large benefits. However, as shown in Figure 7-21, the process of moving from separated, functional applications to an ERP system is difficult, fraught with challenge, and can be slow. In particular, changing organizational procedures has proved to be a great challenge for many organizations, and in some cases was even a pitfall that prevented successful ERP implementation. Finally, the switch to an ERP system is very costly—not only because of the need for new hardware and software, but also due to the costs of developing new procedures, training employees, converting data, and other developmental expenses.

Benefits of ERP

Figure 7-22 summarizes the potential benefits of ERP. First, the processes in the business blueprint have been tried and tested over hundreds of organizations. The processes are effective and often very efficient. Organizations that convert to ERP do not need to reinvent business processes. Rather, they gain the benefit of processes that have already been proved successful.

By taking an organization-wide view, many organizations find they can reduce their inventories, sometimes dramatically. With better planning, it is not necessary to maintain large buffer stocks. Additionally, items remain in inventory for shorter periods of time, sometimes no longer than a few hours or a day.

Another advantage is that ERP helps organizations reduce lead times. Because of the more efficient processes and better information, organizations can respond more quickly to process new orders or changes in existing orders. This means they can deliver goods to customers faster. In some cases, ERP-based companies can receive payments on orders shipped before they pay for the raw materials used in the parts on the order.

As discussed earlier, data inconsistency problems are not an issue because all ERP data are stored in an integrated database. Further, because all data about a customer, order, part, or other entity reside in one place, the data are readily accessible. This means that organizations can provide better information about orders, products, and customer status to their customers. All of this results not only in better, but also less costly, customer service. Integrated databases also make company-wide data readily accessible and result in greater, real-time visibility, thus allowing timely insights into the status of the organization.

- Efficient business processes
- Inventory reduction
- Lead-time reduction
- Improved customer service
- Greater, real-time insight into organization
- Higher profitability

Figure 7-22
Potential Benefits of ERP

Finally, ERP-based organizations often find that they can produce and sell the same products at lower costs due to smaller inventories, reduced lead times, and cheaper customer support. The bottom-line result is higher profitability. The trick, however, is getting there.

How Is an ERP System Implemented?

Figure 7-23 summarizes the major tasks in the implementation of an ERP system. The first task is to model the current business processes. Managers and analysts then compare these processes to the ERP blueprint processes and note the differences. The company then must find ways to eliminate the differences, either by changing the existing business process to match the ERP process or by altering the ERP system.

Modeling the current business processes is a difficult and time-consuming task. Trained and skilled analysts are needed to observe, investigate, and document current practices. Often, existing procedures are not documented and are known only by those who perform them. Many meetings, interviews, and observations can be necessary to tease out and document these procedures. This activity is crucial because the organization must understand what procedural changes will be necessary before converting to the new system.

To appreciate the magnitude of these tasks, consider that the SAP blueprint contains over a thousand process models. Organizations that are adopting ERP must review those models and determine which ones are appropriate to them. Then, they compare the ERP models to the models developed based on their current practices. Inevitably, some current-practice models are incomplete, vague, or inaccurate, so the team must repeat the existing process models. In some cases, it is impossible to reconcile any existing system against the blueprint model. If so, the team must adapt, cope, and define new procedures, often to the confusion of current employees.

Once the differences between as-is processes and the blueprint have been reconciled, the next step is to implement the system. Before implementation starts, however, users must be trained on the new processes, procedures, and use of the ERP system's features and function. Additionally, the company needs to conduct a simulation test of the new system to identify problems. Then, the organization must convert its data, procedures, and personnel to the new ERP system. All of this happens while the business continues to run on the old system.

As will be explained in Chapter 10, plunging the organization into the new system is an invitation to disaster. Instead, a thorough and well-planned test of the new system is necessary, followed by a careful rollout of the new system in stages. Realize, too, that while the new ERP system is being installed normal business activity continues. Somehow the employees of the organization must continue to run the company while the rollout is underway. It is a difficult and challenging time for any organization that undergoes this process.

Figure 7-23
ERP Implementation

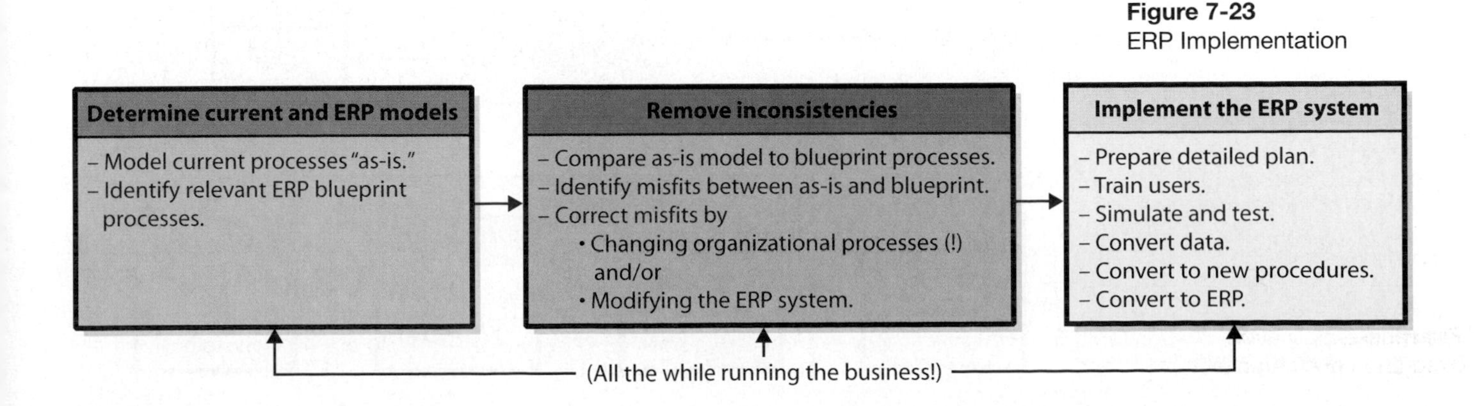

Implementing an ERP system is not for the faint of heart. Because so much organizational change is required, all ERP projects must have the full support of the CEO and executive staff. Because ERP processes cross departmental boundaries, no single departmental manager has the authority to force an ERP implementation. Instead, full support for the task must come from the top of the organization. Even with such support, as implied by Brian Street, there is bound to be concern and second-guessing.

Enterprise Application Integration (EAI) Systems

ERP systems are not for every organization. For example, some nonmanufacturing companies find the manufacturing orientation of ERP inappropriate. Even for manufacturing companies, some find the process of converting from their current system to an ERP system too daunting. Others are quite satisfied with their MRP systems and do not wish to change them.

Companies for which ERP is inappropriate still have the problems of isolated systems, however, and some choose to use **enterprise application integration (EAI)** to solve those problems. EAI integrates existing systems by providing layers of software that connect applications together. EAI does the following:

- It connects system "islands" via a new layer of software/system.
- It enables existing applications to communicate and share data.
- It provides integrated information.
- It leverages existing systems—leaving legacy/functional applications as is, but providing an integration layer over the top.
- It enables a gradual move to ERP.

The layers of EAI software shown in Figure 7-24 enable existing applications to communicate with each other and to share data. For example, EAI software can be configured to automatically make the data conversion required in Figure 7-14 (page 266). When the CRM applications send data to the MRP system, for example, the CRM system sends its data to an EAI software program. That EAI program makes the conversion and then sends the converted data to the ERP system. The reverse action is taken to send data back from the ERP to the CRM.

Although there is no centralized EAI database, the EAI software keeps files of metadata that describe where data are located. Users can access the EAI system to find the data they need. In some cases, the EAI system provides services that provide a "virtual integrated database" for users to query and process.

Benefits of EAI

Compared to ERP, EAI offers a lower-cost and less disruptive way to eliminate at least some of the problems of isolated functional systems. Unlike ERP, which by its nature

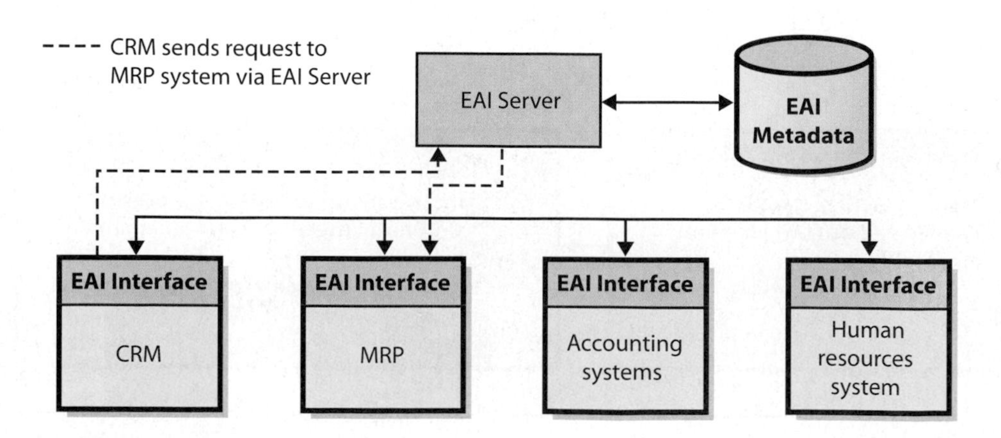

Figure 7-24
Enterprise Application Integration (EAI) Architecture

influences many, if not all, parts of the organization, an EAI system can be designed to integrate just selected parts of the organization. Further, if planned correctly, EAI will disrupt only those parts that will receive the greatest benefit—those that endure the greatest inefficiencies due to their isolation from one another.

EAI also allows a step-wise implementation process. An organization can develop EAI to integrate two or three departments, enjoy the benefits of that integration, and then decide whether to integrate even more departments. If so, another step can be taken down the path toward full integration.

Some organizations find that partial-departmental integration is sufficient and maintain their EAI systems indefinitely. Others continue down the integration path and use EAI as a stepping stone to full ERP integration. Thus, EAI becomes a years-long process of converting to ERP. While the process takes longer, the organization enjoys benefits of partial integration, reduces disruption, and eventually achieves the full benefits of ERP.

How Is an EAI System Implemented?

The steps for implementing an EAI project are as follows:

- Identify sources of major isolation problems.
- Specify the scope of the EAI implementation.
- Develop and implement selected EAI systems.
- Assess the benefits of EAI.
- Stop further EAI development, expand EAI efforts, or switch to ERP.

First the organization needs to determine sources of major isolation problems. Is the problem a lack of integrated customer information? Or is the problem a lack of integrated inventory or manufacturing? Or is there a need to integrate customer-service data with manufacturing-quality data?

After defining specific isolation problems, the next step is to define the scope of the EAI implementation. Will the EAI attempt to solve all of the identified problems, or just some of the most significant ones? Given the scope, the next step is to develop and implement the selected system(s). After those systems have been in operation, the organization then assesses the benefits received and any remaining isolation problems. The next steps can be to do nothing further regarding EAI development, to implement additional EAI capability, or to switch to a full ERP system.

As you can see, EAI offers numerous possibilities for integrating disparate information systems and allows the organization the potential of moving toward ERP in smaller steps. In general, it is not possible to say whether moving from isolated functional systems to EAI and then from EAI to ERP is more or less advisable than going from functional systems directly to ERP. Organizations should evaluate both possibilities.

Problem-Solving

GUIDE

Thinking About Change

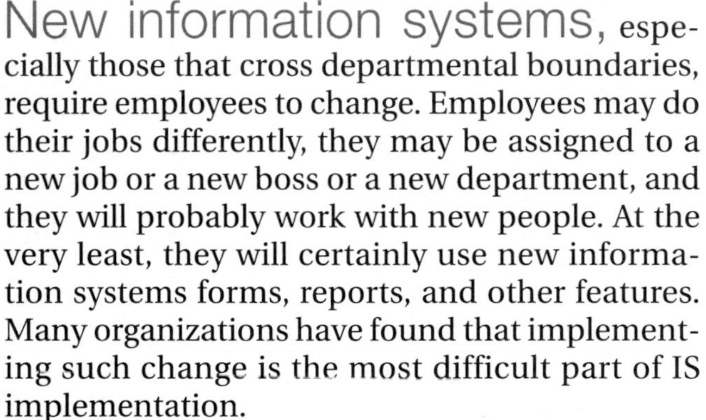

New information systems, especially those that cross departmental boundaries, require employees to change. Employees may do their jobs differently, they may be assigned to a new job or a new boss or a new department, and they will probably work with new people. At the very least, they will certainly use new information systems forms, reports, and other features. Many organizations have found that implementing such change is the most difficult part of IS implementation.

Because organizational change is a common problem, a change management industry has emerged to help organizations deal with it. Change management is a blend of business, engineering, sociology, and psychology that strives to understand the dynamics of organizational change and to develop and communicate theories, methods, and techniques that enable successful organizational change.

According to Adel Aladwani (2001), the top obstacle to successful change is employee resistance. Employees resist change for several reasons. For one, change requires adapting to a new situation or system, and, for a while, all changes make work harder, not easier. Unless employees understand the need for change, they will be unwilling to devote the extra energy and work required.

To be willing to change, employees need to understand the importance of and need for the new system or project. The CEO or other senior manager needs to sponsor the new system. The sponsor should explain the rationale for the system at the onset and throughout the project. Many managers, when reviewing their projects after implementation, say that they did not communicate the need for the new system frequently enough. Experience shows that employees want to hear about the necessity for change from two people: the CEO and their immediate boss.

Another reason that employees resist change is fear of the unknown. Recent motivational research focuses on the concept of self-efficacy. Self-efficacy means that people believe they have the knowledge and skills necessary to be successful at their jobs. When employees feel that way, they not only are happier, but they also work better. Self-efficacy breeds success: When employees feel confident, they bring more and more of their natural abilities to the problems they face.

Change, however, threatens self-efficacy. When change is underway, people ask questions like, "Will I understand how to use the new system?" "Will I be as successful with it as I was in the past?" "Will I be asked to do things I don't know how to do?" Just having such questions impairs one's ability to work.

Because change is threatening, organizations need to take steps to increase employees' sense of self-efficacy. These steps must go beyond explaining the need for the system. Employees need to be shown how the new system will improve their work situation. They need to be trained on new procedures. If possible, employees should be given opportunities to gain confidence in the new system and in their ability to use it. They also need to see others, either employees in their own organization or other organizations, achieve positive outcomes from the new system. Some organizations find that creating networks or alliances of employees helps to reduce the stress of the change.

In a recent study, Siebel Systems identified a number of key factors in successful change management. Of those factors, two emerged as most important: bosses' behavior and communication. Employees respond to how the boss responds. If their boss supports the change, not just with words, but also with his attitude and actions, then employees are more likely to accept the change. Also, frequent two-way communication is important. Management frequently needs to explain the rationale and importance of the change, and employees need frequent opportunities to express their thoughts and feelings about the change.

Employees tend to support what they create. When employees are given an opportunity to participate in the change and to express their thoughts about the change (how it could be improved and so forth), they have a stake in the change and are more likely to support it. ■

Sources: Adel Aladwani, "Change Management Strategies for Successful ERP Implementation," *Business Process Management Journal*, vol. 7, no. 3, 2001, page 266; Siebel Systems, "Applied Change Management: A Key Ingredient for CRM Success," Siebel eBusiness, June 2003, *http://siebel.com/resource-library/reg-resource.shtm* (accessed June 2005); Tom Werner, "Change Management and E-Learning," *http://brandon-hall.com* (accessed September 2004).

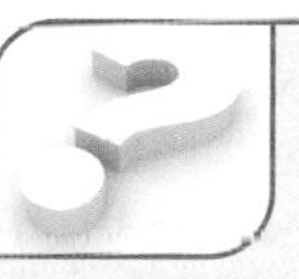

Discussion Questions

Imagine that your university announces that next semester students will be required to use a new information system to enroll in classes.

1. What is your first feeling (not thought) on hearing that news?
2. What would you like the university administration to communicate to you about the change?
3. Explain the term *self-efficacy* in relation to this change. What could the university do to increase your sense of self-efficacy?
4. Suppose a good friend tries the new system and says, "Hey, it's much better than the old one. Very easy to use." How does that affect your feelings about the change? What if your friend says, "It's terrible, such a hassle." How does that affect your feelings?
5. Given your answer to question 4, what programs could the university develop to reduce resistance to the change?
6. What might your professors say about the change that would cause you to feel better about it? What might your professors say that would cause you to feel worse about it?
7. In this situation, which is more powerful, the opinions of your good friend or the opinions of your professor? Explain your response. In business, which would be more important, your coworkers' opinions or those of your boss?

TQM

Opposing Forces

GUIDE

KNOWLEDGE MANAGEMENT

The Flavor of the Month Club

Oh, come on. I've been here 30 years and I've heard it all. All these management programs. . . . Years ago, we had Zero Defects. Then came Total Quality Management, and after that, Six Sigma. We've had all the pet theories from every consultant in the Western Hemisphere. No, wait, we had consultants from Asia, too.

"Do you know what flavor we're having now? We're redesigning ourselves to be 'customer centric.' We are going to integrate our CRM system into an ERP system to transform the entire company to be 'customer focused.'

"You know how these programs go? First, we have a pronouncement at a 'kick-off meeting' where the CEO tells us what the new flavor is going to be and why it's so important. Then a swarm of consultants and 'change management' experts tell us how they're going to 'empower' us. Then HR adds some new item to our annual review, such as, 'Measures taken to achieve customer-centric company.'

"So, we all figure out some lame thing to do so that we have something to put in that category of our annual review. Then we forget about it because we know the next new flavor of the month will be along soon. Or worse, if they actually force us to use the new system, we comply, but viciously. You know, go out of our way to show that the new system can't work, that it really screws things up.

"You think I sound bitter, but I've seen this so many times before. The consultants and rising stars in our company get together and dream up one of these programs. Then they present it to the senior managers. That's when they make their first mistake: They think that if they can sell it to management, then it must be a good idea. They treat senior management as the customer. They should have to sell the idea to those of us who actually sell, support, or make things. Senior management is just the banker; the managers should let us decide if it's a good idea.

"If someone really wanted to empower me, she would listen rather than talk. Those of us who do the work have hundreds of ideas of how to do it better. Now it's customer centric? As if we haven't been trying to do that for years!

"Anyway, after the CEO issues the pronouncements about the new system, he gets busy with other things and forgets about it for a while. Six months might go by, and then we're either told we're not doing enough to become customer centric (or whatever the flavor is) or the company announces another new flavor.

"In manufacturing they talk about push versus pull. You know, with push style, you make things and push them onto the sales force and the customers. With pull style, you let the customers'

demand pull the product out of manufacturing. You build when you have holes in inventory. Well, they should adapt those ideas to what they call 'change management.' I mean, does anybody need to manage real change? Did somebody have a 'Use the cell phone' program'? Did some CEO announce, 'This year, we're all going to use the cell phone'? Did the HR department put a line into our annual evaluation form that asked how many times we'd used a cell phone? No, no, no, and no. Customers pulled the cell phone through. We wanted it, so we bought and used cell phones. Same with color printers and iPhones and wireless networks.

"That's pull. You get a group of workers to form a network, and you get things going among the people who do the work. Then you build on that to obtain true organizational change. Why don't they figure it out?

"Anyway, I've got to run. We've got the kick-off meeting of our new initiative—something about supply chain management. Now they're going to empower me to buy things from our suppliers. Like I haven't been doing that all these years. Oh, well, I plan to retire soon.

"Oh, wait. Here, take my t-shirt from the knowledge management program 2 years ago. I never wore it. It says, 'Empowering You through Knowledge Management.' That one didn't last long." ■

Discussion Questions

1. Clearly, this person is bitter about new programs and new ideas. What do you think might have been the cause of his antagonism? What seems to be his principal concern?
2. What does he mean by "vicious" compliance? Give an example of an experience you've had that exemplifies such compliance.
3. Consider his point that the proponents of new programs treat senior managers as the customer. What does he mean? To a consultant, is senior management the customer? What do you think he's trying to say?
4. What does he mean when he says, "If someone wants to empower me, she would listen rather than talk"? How does listening to someone empower that person?
5. His examples of "pull change" all involve the use of new products. To what extent do you think pull works for new management programs?
6. How do you think management could introduce new programs in a way that would cause them to be pulled through the organization? Consider the suggestion he makes, as well as your own ideas.
7. If you managed an employee who had an attitude like this, what could you do to make him more positive about organizational change and new programs and initiatives?

ACTIVE REVIEW

Use this Active Review to verify that you understand the ideas and concepts that answer the chapter's study questions.

Q1 What are the differences between functional and cross-functional systems?

Using Figure 7-1, explain the three categories of IS. Give an example of each. Describe how each type overcomes problems in the earlier type. Explain which of these systems you are likely to encounter in your career. Describe a problem that is likely to concern you. Explain how the systems and processes in this chapter pertain to not-for-profit organizations.

Q2 How do functional systems relate to the value chain?

Draw the Porter value chain model as shown in this chapter. Explain the nature of the work performed at each value chain activity. Show how the fundamental types of functional information systems relate to value chain activities. Explain the difference between a functional application and a functional system and what that difference means to you.

Q3 What are the functions of the five basic functional systems?

Name five categories of functional systems. List primary functions for each. Explain the differences among manufacturing, operations, scheduling, inventory, and planning systems. Explain how inventory system requirements differ between manufacturing and non-manufacturing organizations. Describe two different inventory philosophies. Explain the difference between a UPC code and an RFID tag. Define *MPS* and explain how it is used. Differentiate between push and pull production planning. Explain how MRP and MRP II differ.

Q4 What are the problems of functional systems?

Name five problems of functional systems and describe each. Give an example of a data integration problem. Describe the consequences of a lack of data integrity.

Q5 What is business process design?

Explain the statement, "While the problem of isolation is obvious, the solution is not." Summarize challenges that arise when creating cross-functional systems. Define *business process design*. Describe factors that make business process design difficult. Explain how inherent processes reduce process design risks. Summarize the advantages and disadvantages of inherent processes.

Q6 What are the functions and characteristics of the three major cross-functional systems?

Describe the meaning and purpose of CRM, ERP, and EAI. Using the Porter model, explain how the scope of CRM and ERP differ. Summarize the features of CRM and describe the major advantage of CRM over functional sales and marketing applications. Summarize ERP characteristics and benefits. Explain, at a high level, how ERP systems are implemented. Explain how EAI differs from ERP. Describe conditions under which an organization might choose EAI over ERP.

KEY TERMS AND CONCEPTS

USING YOUR KNOWLEDGE

1. Choose one of the following basic business processes: inventory management, operations, manufacturing, HR management, or accounting/financial management. Use the Internet to identify three vendors that license a product to support that process. Compare offerings from the three vendors as follows.
   a. Determine differences in terminology, especially differences in the ways that the vendors use the same terms.
   b. Compare features and functions of each of the product offerings.
   c. For each vendor, specify the characteristics of a company for which that vendor's offering would be ideal.
2. Reread the Brian Street interview at the start of this chapter.
   a. Google *Deltek ERP*. Go to one or more of the references shown and determine the major features of this ERP system. Briefly list or describe those features.
   b. Search the Web for case histories about the use of Deltek's ERP system. What seems to be the principal benefits of this application? Compare those benefits to the benefits described by Mr. Street.
   c. Search the Web for products that compete with Deltek's ERP. Find what seems to you to be the most promising of those two products. Compare features and functions of the product you found with those of Deltek.
   d. Suppose you were asked to recommend either the Deltek ERP system or the one you found in part c. How would you proceed?
3. The text claims that there is no truth-in-ERP advertising. Google ERP and find three products that call themselves ERP products but that seem to lack the ERP features described in this chapter. Choose the grossest violators that you can find.
   a. Name the products and describe the features they lack. Use the Porter value chain model in your answer.
   b. Is it ethical for businesses to call their products *ERP products* when they lack so many ERP features?
   c. Why do you think companies mislabel their products? What advantage accrues to them by doing so?
   d. Do you think a group of legitimate ERP vendors should form an industry group and attempt to eliminate gross violations of the use of the term *ERP*? Why or why not?
4. Briefly summarize the Sarbanes-Oxley Act. Explain how this act creates job opportunities for internal auditors and IS professionals. How does the Sarbanes-Oxley Act influence what you, a future business professional, need to learn in this class?

COLLABORATION EXERCISES AND CASES

Collaborate with a group of students on the following exercises. Recall from Chapter 2 that collaboration is more than cooperation because it involves iteration and feedback. Post a document, a discussion item, a wiki item, or an idea and obtain feedback from your team members. Similarly, read the ideas of others and comment on them. Try to innovate in both the process by which you collaborate and the work product that you create. Avoid face-to-face meetings. Instead, use collaborative software such as Google Docs & Spreadsheets, Microsoft Groove, or Microsoft SharePoint to facilitate your ideas.

1. In this exercise, you and your team will assess the wisdom and efficacy of the Sarbanes-Oxley Act and issue an opinion as to whether it should be kept as-is, abolished altogether, or kept but modified in some way. Begin by rereading the *Information Systems in Practice* box on page 264.

   a. Summarize the provisions of the act. Explain how the act came into being and describe the companies to which it pertains.

   b. Using the Web, find five articles that support the Sarbanes-Oxley Act. Summarize the arguments in those five articles.

   c. Using the Web, find five articles that are critical of the Sarbanes-Oxley Act. Summarize the arguments in those five articles.

   d. In what ways are the provisions of the act ambiguous? Should the language of the act be tightened to remove that ambiguity? Why or why not?

   e. Using your answers to the questions above, discuss the wisdom of the Sarbanes-Oxley Act. Do you think it should exist? Is it likely to be effective? Do you think it imposes so much expense that it will make U.S. corporations noncompetitive on the world market?

   f. What changes could be made to the act to make it less onerous or more effective?

   g. Construct a team opinion on the Sarbanes-Oxley Act. State whether you believe it should be kept as-is, eliminated, or modified in some way. Justify your opinion. A survey is one good way to gather team opinions for answering this question.

2. In this exercise, you will consider the possible disadvantages of standard business processes and seek innovative ways to gain competitive advantages in the presence of such processes. Begin by rereading the *Innovation in Practice* box on page 272.

   a. Explain how processes are inherent in application software. Are processes inherent only in ERP software, such as SAP, or are they inherent in other products as well? Does Microsoft Word, for example, have inherent processes? What characteristics and classifications of inherent processes does the comparison of SAP and Word suggest?

   b. Summarize the advantages and disadvantages of inherent processes.

   c. The contention of the *Innovation in Practice* box on page 272 is that ERP applications are becoming commodities. Define *commodity* and explain how the term pertains to ERP systems and processes. How does a vendor gain a competitive advantage when producing a commodity? Specifically, how could Oracle, for example, gain a competitive advantage over SAP?

   d. Suppose that two companies using the same ERP system have the exact same business processes. Does it necessarily follow that neither company can gain a competitive advantage over the other? Is there some way that one company can gain an advantage by better executing the identical process? How? Is such a competitive advantage sustainable? Would you rather have a competitive advantage by having better processes or a competitive advantage by having the same processes, but executing them better? Explain your reasoning.

   e. Suppose that an ERP system maintains customer order data in the following three tables:

      CUSTOMER (<u>CustNum</u>, Name, IndustryCode, Annual Sales)

      ORDER (<u>OrderNumber</u>, OrderDate, SalesPerson Name, Amount, *CustNum*)

      PAYMENT (<u>*OrderNumber*</u>, <u>PaymentDate</u>, Payment Amount)

      (1) Explain the relationships that are defined for these three tables.

      (2) Suppose that a company extracts this data from its ERP system and uses it to inform sales activities. What information could be obtained from this data?

      (3) How can the information obtained from this data provide a competitive advantage?

   f. What does your answer to part e suggest about a way that one company can gain a competitive advantage over another, even though both are using the same ERP system and processes?

APPLICATION EXERCISES

1. Suppose your manager asks you to create a spreadsheet to compute a production schedule. Your schedule should stipulate a production quantity for seven products that is based on sales projections made by three regional managers at your company's three sales regions.

   a. Create a separate worksheet for each sales region. Use the data in the Word file **Ch07Ex01**, which you can download from the text's Web site. This file contains each manager's monthly sales projections for the past year, actual sales results for those same months, and projections for sales for each month in the coming quarter.
   b. Create a separate worksheet for each manager's data. Import the data from Word into Excel.
   c. On each of the worksheets, use the data from the prior four quarters to compute the discrepancy between the actual sales and the sale projections. This discrepancy can be computed in several ways: You could calculate an overall average, or you could calculate an average per quarter or per month. You could also weight recent discrepancies more heavily than earlier ones. Choose a method that you think is most appropriate. Explain why you chose the method you did.
   d. Modify your worksheets to use the discrepancy factors to compute an adjusted forecast for the coming quarter. Thus, each of your spreadsheets will show the raw forecast and the adjusted forecast for each month in the coming quarter.
   e. Create a fourth worksheet that totals sales projections for all of the regions. Show both the unadjusted forecast and the adjusted forecast for each region and for the company overall. Show month and quarter totals.
   f. Create a bar graph showing total monthly production. Display the unadjusted and adjusted forecasts using different colored bars.

2. Figure 7-9, the sample bill of materials, is a form produced using Microsoft Access. Producing such a form is a bit tricky, so this exercise will guide you through the steps required. You can then apply what you learn to produce a similar report. You can also use Access to experiment on extensions of this form.

   a. Create a table named *PART* with columns *PartNumber, Level, Description, QuantityRequired,* and *PartOf. Description* and *Level* should be text, *PartNumber* should be AutoNumber, and *QuantityRequired* and *PartOf* should be numeric, long integer. Add the *PART* data shown in Figure 7-9 to your table.
   b. Create a query that has all columns of *PART*. Restrict the view to rows having a value of 1 for *Level*. Name your query *Level1*.
   c. Create two more queries that are restricted to rows having values of 2 or 3 for *Level*. Name your queries *Level2* and *Level3*, respectively.
   d. Create a form that contains *PartNumber, Level,* and *Description* from *Level1*. You can use a wizard for this if you want. Name the form *Bill of Materials*.
   e. Using the subform tool in the Toolbox, create a subform in your form in part d. Set the data on this form to be all of the columns of *Level2*. After you have created the subform, ensure that the Link Child Fields property is set to *PartOf* and that the Link Master Fields property is set to *PartNumber*. Close the *Bill of Materials* form.
   f. Open the subform created in part e and create a subform on it. Set the data on this subform to be all of the columns of *Level3*. After you have created the subform, ensure that the Link Child Fields property is set to *PartOf* and that the Link Master Fields property is set to *PartNumber*. Close the *Bill of Materials* form.
   g. Open the *Bill of Materials* form. It should appear as in Figure 7-9. Open and close the form and add new data. Using this form, add sample BOM data for a product of your own choosing.
   h. Following the process similar to that just described, create a *Bill of Materials Report* that lists the data for all of your products.
   i. **(Optional, challenging extension)** Each part in the BOM in Figure 7-9 can be used in at most one assembly (there is space to show just one *PartOf* value). You can change your design to allow a part to be used in more than one assembly as follows: First, remove *PartOf* from PART. Next, create a second table that has two columns: *AssemblyPartNumber* and *ComponentPart Number*. The first contains a part number of an assembly and the second a part number of a component. Every component of a part will have a row in this table. Extend the views described above to use this second table and to produce a display similar to Figure 7-9.

CASE STUDY 7

The Brose Group Implements SAP—One Site at a Time

The Brose Group supplies windows, doors, seat adjusters, and related products for more than 40 auto brands. Major customers include General Motors, Ford, DaimlerChrysler, BMW, Porsche, Volkswagen, Toyota, and Honda. Founded as an auto and aircraft parts manufacturer in Berlin in 1908, the company today has facilities at more than 30 locations in 20 different countries. Revenue for 2004 exceeded 2 billion euros.

In the 1990s, Brose enjoyed rapid growth but found that existing information systems were unable to support the company's emerging needs. Too many different information systems meant a lack of standardization and hampered communication among suppliers, plants, and customers. Brose decided to standardize operations on R/3, an ERP application licensed by SAP that supports more than a thousand different business processes. Rather than attempt to implement those processes on its own, Brose hired SAP Consulting to lead the project.

The SAP team provided process consulting and implementation support, and it trained end users. According to Christof Lutz, SAP project manager, "Our consultants and the Brose experts worked openly, flexibly, and constructively together. In this atmosphere of trust, we created an implementation module that the customer can use as a basis for the long term."

The Brose/SAP consulting team decided on a pilot approach. The first installation was conducted at a new plant in Curitiba, Brazil. The team constructed the implementation to be used as a prototype for installations at additional plants. Developing the first implementation was no small feat, because it involved information systems for sales and distribution, materials management, production planning, quality management, and financial accounting and control.

Once the initial system was operational at the Curitiba plant, the prototype was rolled out to additional facilities. The second implementation, in Puebla, Mexico, required just 6 months for first operational capability, and the next implementation in Meerane, Germany, was operational in just 19 weeks.

The conversion to the ERP system has contributed to dramatically increased productivity. In 1994, Brose achieved sales of 541 million euros with 2,900 employees, or 186,000 euros per employee. Ten years later, in 2004, Brose attained sales of 2 billion euros with 8,200 employees, or 240,000 euros per employee. Modern manufacturing seeks to improve productivity by reducing waste, which means eliminating:

- Overproduction that leads to excess inventories
- Unavailable needed parts, which idle workers and facilities
- Wasted motion and processing due to poorly planned materials handling and operations activities

Manufacturing that eliminates these wastes is called *lean manufacturing*.

To accomplish lean manufacturing, SAP has invented a business process it calls *just-in-sequence (JIS)* manufacturing. JIS is an extension of just-in-time (JIT), the pull manufacturing philosophy described in this chapter. JIS extends JIT so that parts not only arrive just in time, but also arrive in just the correct sequence.

For example, the Brose Group factory in Brazil manufactures doors for General Motors. When General Motors starts the construction of a new auto, it sends a signal of the need for doors to the Brose Group. That signal starts the construction of the four doors on four separate production lines in Brazil. Brose schedules the work on each of these lines so as to produce the four doors and their related equipment and deliver them at the correct time and in the correct sequence at General Motors. Thus, if General Motors needs the rear-door frames, then the front-door frames, then the front doors, and finally the rear doors, Brose will schedule manufacturing and delivery accordingly.

To achieve JIS, Brose used SAP R/3 combined with a supplementary SAP module called SAP for Automotive with JIS. Like all ERP software, these applications include inherent (i.e, built-in) processes that the organization does not need to design separately. In this case, those business processes include manufacturing planning methods and procedures for JIS performance.

Sources: http://brose.de/en/pub/company (accessed November 2007); *http://sap.com/industries/automotive/pdf/CS_Brose_Group.pdf,* 2003 (accessed March 2007).

Questions

1. Reflect on the nature of JIS planning. In general terms, what kinds of data must Brose have in order to provide JIS to its customers? What does Brose need to know? It certainly needs a bill of materials for the items it produces. What other categories of information will Brose need?
2. According to the description on page xx, the SAP system included applications for sales and distribution, materials management, production planning, quality management, and financial accounting and control. Describe, in general terms, features and functions of these applications that are necessary to provide JIS.
3. The Brose factory in Brazil produces more than doors for General Motors. The factory must coordinate the

door orders with orders for other products and orders from other manufacturers. What kinds of IS are necessary to provide such coordinated manufacturing planning?

4. Brazilians speak Portuguese, workers in the United States speak English and Spanish, and personnel at the Brose headquarters speak German. Summarize challenges to Brose and SAP Consulting when implementing a system for users who speak four different languages and live in four (at least) different cultures.
5. Visit *http://sap.com/industries/automotive* and investigate SAP for Automotive with JIS. What features and functions does this product have that standard SAP R/3 does not have? What advantages does SAP obtain by creating and licensing this product? What advantages do SAP's customers obtain from this product? In your response, consider both R/3 customers who are and who are not automotive manufacturers.
6. Brose seeks to provide JIS service to its customers. Does this goal necessitate that Brose suppliers also provide JIS service to Brose? What can Brose do if its suppliers do not provide such service? Is there any reason why Brose would not want them to provide such service? Do you think that before one company in a supply chain can offer JIS, all companies in the supply chain must offer the service?

8 E-Commerce and Supply Chain Systems

STUDY QUESTIONS

Q1 How do companies use e-commerce?

Q2 What technology is needed for e-commerce?

Q3 Why is Web 2.0 important to business?

Q4 How can information systems enhance supply chain performance?

Q5 How can information systems support supplier relationship management?

Q6 How do organizations exchange data?

Q7 How can organizations connect computer programs?

Meet Caprice Leinonen

Your favorite business book:
The Instant Economist by John Charles Pool and Ross M. La Roe, because of its simplicity on a complex subject.

My hero:
Alexander Hamilton—a great thinker who accomplished much for our country even though he was discriminated against because of his heritage.

My very first job:
McDonald's, of course!

Caprice Leinonen began her career as a medical technologist working in a hospital medical laboratory. She enjoyed lab work for several years, but it became routine and repetitive, and eventually boring. In the medical laboratory, she had experience using computer systems, and while thinking about where to go after the lab, a friend suggested that she approach Shared Medical Systems about a new job. She did, and Shared Medical hired her to help install new information systems. Because of her knowledge of lab technology, she could serve as an intermediary between the customer's lab personnel and Shared Medical's systems analysts. Lab systems use complex terminology, some of which is unique to each hospital. So, her job was to customize forms and reports into the particular terms and format needed by each customer's physicians, nurses, and lab technicians.

After several installations, she once again wanted a career change and asked the Shared Medical sales manager to consider her for a sales position. He suggested she attend Toastmasters public-speaking courses and, on her own, read business books to learn business terminology, concepts, and principles. She must have been a good student: In 2006 alone, she sold $67 million of health-care information systems! In 2007, she left software sales to write a book, *Transforming Health Care in America*.

On her career in sales:

"Installing systems was fascinating for a while, but after I'd done several of them, I wanted a change. I saw the salespeople doing business while having lunch and playing golf, and I thought, 'That looks pretty good.'

"Selling medical systems was great. I helped my clients give better patient service, reduce expenses, and, bottom line, improve health care. That felt good. Also, I advanced to the point that I was selling big, strategic solutions to senior management. These are highly intelligent customers working to solve complex, important problems. Some of my solutions had 10 or 15 different information systems that required 3 to 5 years to implement.

"Our industry has done a great job of providing systems solutions within hospitals. ERP might be new in some industries, but it's old news to hospitals. They know how to manage their inventory and facilities. Hospitals have gone past ERP to information systems that manage workflows.

"Hospitals have dozens of different workflows. Take the patient discharge process, for example. There are 20 or more steps in discharging a patient.

One thing you must know about information systems:
Critique the accuracy of information you get—Garbage In / Garbage Out.

One characteristic of a superior employee:
Ethical interpersonal transactions.

Guiding principle:
Maintain optimism and courage to follow your own path—despite how it appears to others.

It begins with the discharge order, which triggers a notice to nursing to get the patient ready, an order to the pharmacy for medication to take home, an advice to nutrition to cancel the patient's food preparation, a call to the family to pick up the patient, and so forth.

"Our software managed the entire workflow, generating alerts when something wasn't done on time, and escalating alerts to higher management when necessary. Workflow management leads not only to better experience for the patient and staff, it saves the hospital money, which ultimately reduces total health-care costs.

On interorganizational health-care systems:
"They're a mess. We've done an exceedingly poor job of integrating information systems across hospitals, clinics, and doctors. We have limited—and underline *limited*—interconnectivity among organizations. You could go into any one of a number of large, special-purpose hospitals and find patients standing in line with shopping carts full of their medical records. I kid you not. A patient who has a serious medical problem here in Seattle might go to a specialist hospital at the University of Washington, or in California, or back East, and has to take his or her medical records along. There is some limited point-to-point interconnectivity using EDI. But it's just that: *point-to-point*. There is no interorganizational health-care system.

What health care needs:
"I can go to an ATM in New York City and withdraw $250, and my bank here in Washington knows about it within minutes. My bank and the ATM's bank may not have heard of one another, but the financial information systems of the world handle the transaction with no problem, at very low cost. Why can't we do that in health care?

"We need to get away from proprietary systems. Hospital A has its own patient records management system, and hospital B has another such system. If they work together a lot, they may have figured out some proprietary way of connecting those two systems. But there is no general-purpose way of connecting all the health-care providers.

"We need to move toward technology and architectures that allow information systems in hospitals and other medical agencies to interoperate. The particulars of that are complex and are evolving. It will probably proceed in a series of steps and involve the use of service-oriented architectures (SOA). The goal will be to minimize the amount of change required to existing systems, while allowing for standardized interoperability among care providers. It will not be easy because health-care data is far more complex than account transfers in the banking system.

"Like all complex and important problems, this will be a great opportunity for tomorrow's business professionals!"

Advice for someone interested in software sales:
"In heath care, you need to believe and remember that you're helping to improve health care, and selling software is just the way you do that. Next, you need to have a good understanding of the technology, but equally important—maybe more important—you need to understand the business of health care or whatever industry in which you are selling. Specifically, you need to be able to talk ROI, cost-benefit, payback, and so forth.

"Then you need to work hard. You work on your own time, you figure out what you need to do or know, and then you do it or learn it. In business, at least at this level, there is no faking it. Pay attention, work hard, do what needs to be done, and you'll be rewarded. Business needs intelligent, high-integrity professionals, and never more so than now."

CHAPTER PREVIEW

Chapter 7 surveyed information systems within organizations. This chapter builds on that discussion and describes information systems across and among organizations. Such interorganizational information systems have increased in importance in recent years because of the increased availability of computer networks—the Internet, as well as private and proprietary networks

We begin by defining e-commerce and related terms and assessing economic factors that favor and that hamper e-commerce. Then we consider the basic technology that supports e-commerce systems. Next, we discuss why the phenomenon known as Web 2.0 is important to business.

We then turn to information systems that facilitate supply chain management. We describe the structure and characteristics of supply chains and explain two important supply chain problems. Then we consider EDI and XML, two technologies used for exchanging messages and data on supply chains. We conclude with a brief discussion of distributed computing with proprietary and service-oriented architectures using XML Web services.

Q1 How Do Companies Use E-Commerce?

E-commerce is the buying and selling of goods and services over public and private computer networks. Notice that this definition restricts e-commerce to buying and selling transactions. Checking the weather at *http://yahoo.com* is not e-commerce, but buying a weather-service subscription that is paid for and delivered over the Internet is.

Figure 8-1 lists categories of e-commerce companies. The U.S. Census Bureau, which publishes statistics on e-commerce activity, defines **merchant companies** as those that take title to the goods they sell. They buy goods and resell them. It defines **nonmerchant companies** as those that arrange for the purchase and sale of goods without ever owning or taking title to those goods. Regarding services, merchant companies sell services that they provide; nonmerchant companies sell services provided by others. We will consider merchants and nonmerchants separately in the following sections.

E-Commerce Merchant Companies

The three main types of merchant companies are those that sell directly to consumers, those that sell to companies, and those that sell to government. Each uses slightly different information systems in the course of doing business. **B2C**, or **business-to-consumer**, e-commerce concerns sales between a supplier and a retail customer (the consumer). A typical information system for B2C provides a Web-based application or **Web storefront** by which customers enter and manage their orders. Amazon.com, REI.com, and LLBean.com are examples of companies that use B2C information systems.[1]

The term **B2B**, or **business-to-business**, e-commerce or refers to sales between companies. As Figure 8-2 (next page) shows, raw materials suppliers use B2B systems

Merchant companies	Nonmerchant companies
- Business-to-consumer (B2C) - Business-to-business (B2B) - Business-to-government (B2G)	- Auctions - Clearinghouses - Exchanges

Figure 8-1
E-Commerce Categories

[1]Strictly speaking, B2C is not commerce between two organizations. However, because it is commerce between two independently owned entities (the retailer and the consumer), we include it in this chapter.

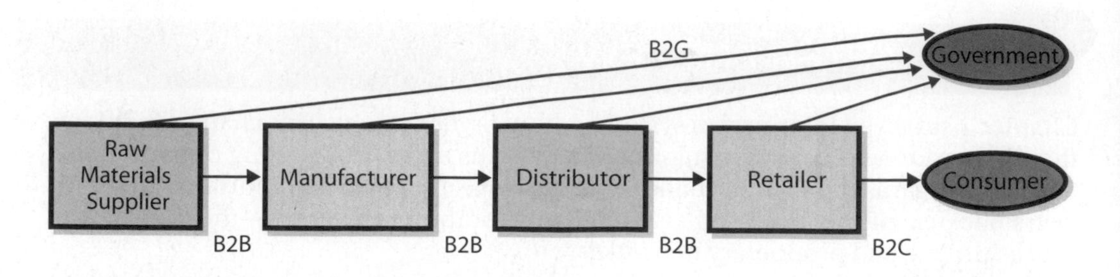

Figure 8-2
Example of Use of B2B, B2G, and B2C

to sell to manufacturers, manufacturers use B2B systems to sell to distributors, and distributors uses B2B systems to sell to retailers.

B2G, or **business-to-government**, refers to sales between companies and governmental organizations. In Figure 8-2, the manufacturer that uses an e-commerce site to sell computer hardware to the U.S. Department of State is engaging in B2G commerce. Suppliers, distributors, and retailers sell to the government as well.

B2C applications first captured the attention of mail-order and related businesses. However, companies in all sectors of the economy soon realized the enormous potential of B2B and B2G. The number of companies engaged in B2B and B2G commerce now far exceeds those engaging in B2C commerce.

Furthermore, today's B2B and B2G applications implement just a small portion of their potential capability. Their full utilization is some years away. Although most experts agree that these applications will involve some sort of integration of CRM and SRM (supplier relationship management) systems, the nature of that integration is not well understood and is still being developed. Consequently, you can expect further progress and development in B2B and B2G applications during your career. Later in this chapter, we will discuss some of the problems of B2B and the technology that is used to solve those problems.

Nonmerchant E-Commerce

The most common nonmerchant e-commerce companies are auctions and clearinghouses. E-commerce **auctions** match buyers and sellers by using an e-commerce version of a standard auction. This e-commerce application enables the auction company to offer goods for sale and to support a competitive-bidding process. The best-known auction company is eBay, but many other auction companies exist; many serve particular industries.

Clearinghouses provide goods and services at a stated price and arrange for the delivery of the goods, but they never take title. One division of Amazon.com, for example, operates as a nonmerchant clearinghouse and sells books owned by others. As a clearinghouse, Amazon.com matches the seller and the buyer and then takes payment from the buyer and transfers the payment to the seller, minus a commission. Figure 8-3 shows a typical Amazon.com listing for selling books that it does not own.

Another type of clearinghouse is an **electronic exchange** that matches buyers and sellers; the business process is similar to that of a stock exchange. Sellers offer goods at a given price through the electronic exchange, and buyers make offers to purchase over the same exchange. Price matches result in transactions from which the exchange takes a commission. Priceline.com is an example of an exchange used by consumers.

How Does E-Commerce Improve Market Efficiency?

The debate continues among business observers as to whether e-commerce is something new or if it is just a technology extension to existing business practice. During the dot-com heyday of 1999–2000, some claimed that e-commerce was ushering in a new era and a "new economy." Although experts differ as to whether a "new economy" was created, all agree that e-commerce does lead to greater market efficiency.

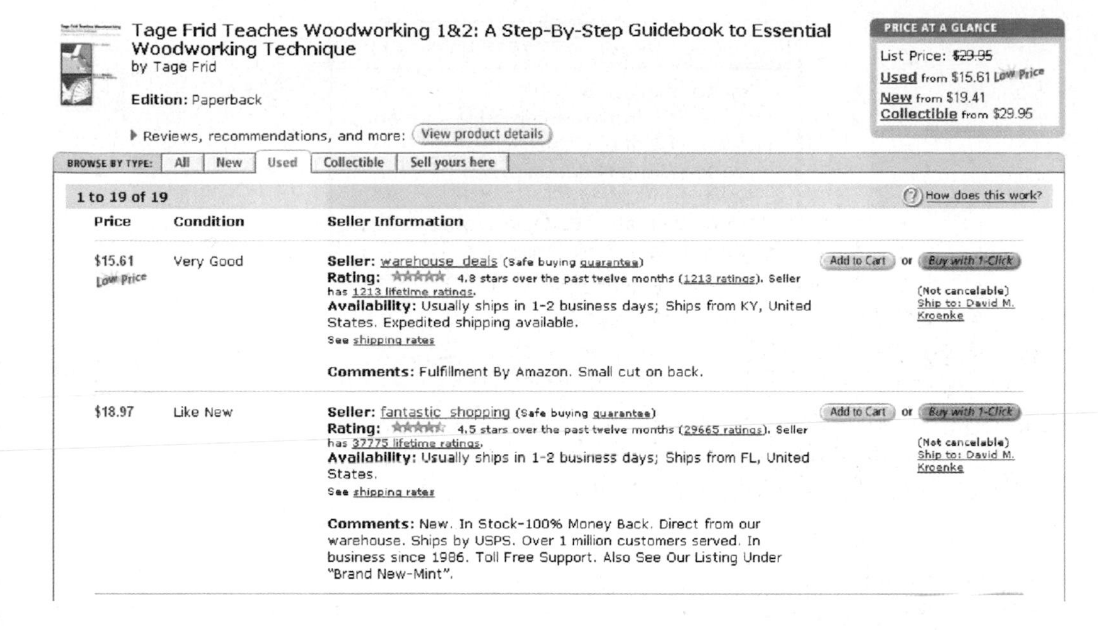

Figure 8-3
Amazon Clearinghouse Sales

Source: © 2006 Amazon.com, Inc. or its affiliates. All Rights Reserved.

For one, e-commerce leads to **disintermediation**, which is the elimination of middle layers in the supply chain. You can buy a flat-screen LCD HDTV from a typical "bricks-and-mortar" electronics store, or you can use e-commerce to buy it from the manufacturer. If you take the latter route, you eliminate the distributor, the retailer, and possibly more. The product is shipped directly from the manufacturer's finished goods inventory to you. You eliminate the distributor's and retailer's inventory carrying costs, and you eliminate shipping overhead and handling activity. Because the distributor and associated inventories have become unnecessary waste, disintermediation increases market efficiency.

E-commerce also improves the flow of price information. As a consumer, you can go to any number of Web sites that offer product price comparisons. You can search for the HDTV you want and sort the results by price and vendor reputation. You can find vendors that avoid your state sales tax or that omit or reduce shipping charges. The improved distribution of information about price and terms enables you to pay the lowest possible cost and serves ultimately to remove inefficient vendors. The market as a whole becomes more efficient.

From the seller's side, e-commerce produces information about **price elasticity** that has not been available before. Price elasticity measures the amount that demand rises or falls with changes in price. Using an auction, a company can learn not just what the top price for an item is, but also the second, third, and other prices from the losing bids. In this way, the company can determine the shape of the price elasticity curve.

Similarly, e-commerce companies can learn price elasticity directly from experiments on customers. For example, in one experiment, Amazon.com created three groups of similar books. It raised the price of one group 10 percent, lowered the price of the second group 10 percent, and left the price of the third group unchanged. Customers provided feedback to these changes by deciding whether to buy books at the offered prices. Amazon.com measured the total revenue (quantity times price) of each group and took the action (raise, lower, or maintain prices) on all books that maximized revenue. Amazon.com repeated the process until it reached the point at which the indicated action was to maintain current prices.

Managing prices by direct interaction with the customer yields better information than managing prices by watching competitors' pricing. By experimenting with customers, companies learn how customers have internalized competitors' pricing, advertising, and messaging. It might be that customers do not know about a competitor's lower prices, in which case there is no need for a price reduction. Or, it may be that the competitor is using a price that, if lowered, would increase demand sufficiently to increase total revenue. Figure 8-4 summarizes the ways e-commerce generates market efficiencies.

Figure 8-4
E-Commerce Market Efficiencies

Market Efficiencies

- Disintermediation
- Increased information on price and terms
- Knowledge of price elasticity
  - Losing-bidder auction prices
  - Price experimentation
  - More accurate information obtained directly from customer

What Economic Factors Disfavor E-Commerce?

Although there are tremendous advantages and opportunities for many organizations to engage in e-commerce, the economics of some industries may disfavor e-commerce activity. Companies need to consider the following economic factors:

- Channel conflict
- Price conflict
- Logistics expense
- Customer-service expense

Consider the example of the manufacturer selling directly to a government agency shown in Figure 8-2 (page 292). Before engaging in such e-commerce, the manufacturer must consider the unfavorable economic factors just listed. First, what **channel conflict** will develop? Suppose the manufacturer is a computer maker that is selling directly, B2G, to the State Department. When the manufacturer begins to sell goods B2G that State Department employees used to purchase from a retailer down the street, that retailer will resent the competition and might drop the manufacturer. If the value of the lost sales is greater than the value of the B2G sales, e-commerce is not a good solution, at least not on that basis.

Furthermore, when a business engages in e-commerce it may also cause **price conflict** with its traditional channels. Because of disintermediation, the manufacturer may be able to offer a lower price and still make a profit. However, as soon as the manufacturer offers the lower price, existing channels will object. Even if the manufacturer and the retailer are not competing for the same customers, the retailer still will not want a lower price to be readily known via the Web.

Also, the existing distribution and retailing partners do provide value; they are not just a cost. Without them, the manufacturer will have the increased *logistics expense* of entering and processing orders in small quantities. If the expense of processing a 1-unit order is the same as that for processing a 12-unit order (which it might be), the average logistics expense per item will be much higher for goods sold via e-commerce.

Similarly, *customer-service* expenses are likely to increase for manufacturers that use e-commerce to sell directly to consumers. The manufacturer will be required to provide service to less sophisticated users and on a one-by-one basis. For example, instead of explaining to a single sales professional that the recent shipment of 100 Gizmo 3.0s requires a new bracket, the manufacturer will need to explain that 100 times to less knowledgeable, frustrated customers. Such service requires more training and more expense.

All four economic factors are important for organizations to consider when they contemplate e-commerce sales.

Q2 What Technology Is Needed for E-Commerce?

Consider what happens when you buy something over the Internet. You go to the Web site—say, *http://REI.com*—and you navigate to the product(s) that you want to buy. When you find something you want, you add it to your shopping cart and keep shopping. At some point you check out by supplying credit card data.

While you're shopping, do you ever wonder what is happening behind the scenes? What systems and technology does the vendor use to support its Web storefront? Or, from another perspective, if you want to set up a Web storefront for your company, what facilities do you need?

Three-Tier Architecture

Almost all e-commerce applications use the **three-tier architecture** shown in Figure 8-5. The tiers refer to three different classes of computers. The **user tier** consists of computers that have browsers that request and process Web pages. The **server tier** consists of computers that run Web servers and process application programs. The **database tier** consists of computers that run a DBMS that processes SQL requests to retrieve and store data. Figure 8-5 shows only one computer at the database tier. Some sites have multicomputer database tiers as well.

Communication between the user and server computers is governed by a protocol called **hypertext transfer protocol (HTTP)**. This protocol is a set of rules for transferring documents and data over the Internet. (For more on the HTTP protocol, see the Appendix to Chapter 6, starting on page 216.) A **Web page** is a document, coded in one of the standard page markup languages, that is transmitted using HTTP. The most popular page markup language is the *Hypertext Markup Language (HTML)*, which is described later in this section.

Web servers are programs that run on a server tier computer and that manage HTTP traffic by sending and receiving Web pages to and from clients. A **browser** is a computer program on the client computer that processes Web pages. When you type *http://ibm.com*, your browser issues a request via HTTP for the Web server at the domain name *ibm.com* to send you its default Web page. The two most popular Web server programs are Apache, commonly used on Linux, and IIS (Internet Information Server), a component of Windows XP Professional, Windows Server, and Windows Vista. Common browsers are Microsoft's Internet Explorer and Mozilla's Firefox.

A **commerce server** is an application program that runs on a server tier computer. A commerce server receives requests from users via the Web server, takes some action, and returns a response to the users via the Web server. Typical commerce server functions are to obtain product data from a database, manage the items in a shopping cart, and coordinate the checkout process. In Figure 8-5, the server tier computers are

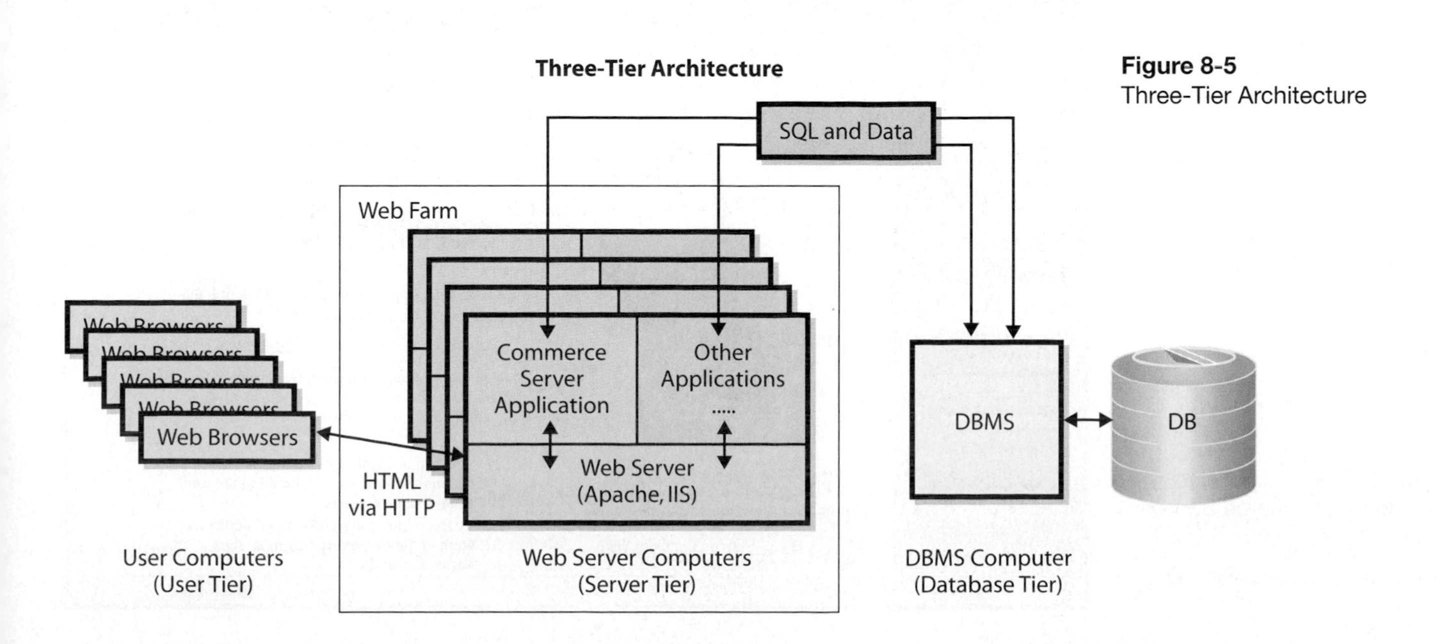

Figure 8-5
Three-Tier Architecture

running a Web server program, a commerce server application, and other applications having an unspecified purpose.

To ensure acceptable performance, commercial Web sites usually are supported by several or even many Web server computers in a facility called a **Web farm**. Work is distributed among the computers in a Web farm so as to minimize customer delays. The coordination among multiple Web server computers is a fantastic dance, but, alas, we do not have space to tell that story here. Just imagine the coordination that must occur as you add items to an online order when, to improve performance, different Web server computers receive and process each addition to your order.

Watch the Three Tiers in Action!

To see a three-tier example in action, go to your favorite Web storefront site, place something in a shopping cart, and consider Figure 8-5 as you do so. As stated earlier, when you enter an address into your browser, the browser sends a request for the default page to a server computer at that address. A Web server and possibly a commerce server process your request and send back the default page.

As you click Web pages to find products you want, the commerce server accesses the database to retrieve data about those products. It creates pages according to your selections and sends the results back to your browser via the Web server. Again, different computers on the server tier may process your series of requests and must constantly communicate about your activities. You can follow this process in Figure 8-6.

In Figure 8-6(a), the user has navigated through climbing equipment at REI.com to find a particular item. To produce this page, the commerce server accessed a database to obtain the product picture, price, special terms (a 5 percent discount for buying six or more), product information, and related products.

Figure 8-6(a)
Sample of Commerce Server Pages: Product-Offer Page

Source: Used with permission of REI & Black Diamond.

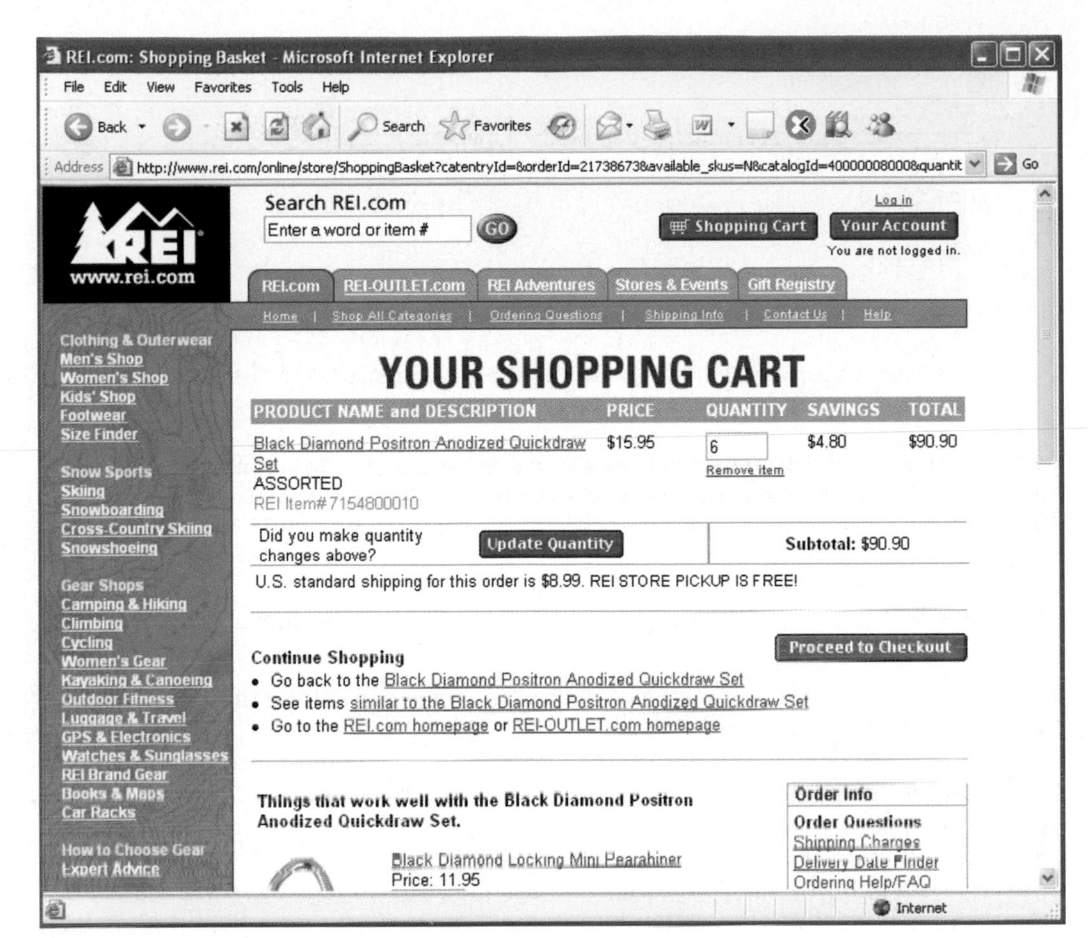

Figure 8-6(b)
Shopping-Cart Page

Source: Used with permission of REI.

The user placed six items in her basket, and you can see the response in Figure 8-6(b). Again, trace the action in Figure 8-5 and imagine what occurred to produce the second page. Notice that the discount was applied correctly.

When the customer checks out, the commerce server program will be called to process payment, schedule inventory processing, and arrange for shipping. Most likely the commerce server interfaces with CRM applications for processing the order. Truly this is an amazing capability!

What Is Hypertext Markup Language (HTML)?

Hypertext Markup Language (HTML) is the most common language for defining the structure and layout of Web pages. An HTML **tag** is a notation used to define a data element for display or other purposes. The following HTML is a typical heading tag:

```
<h2>Price of Item</h2>
```

Notice that tags are enclosed in < > (called *angle brackets*) and that they occur in pairs. The start of this tag is indicated by <h2>, and the end of the tag is indicated by </h2>. The words between the tags are the value of the tag. This HTML tag means to place the words "Price of Item" on a Web page in the style of a level-two heading. The creator of the Web page will define the style (font size, color, and so forth) for h2 headings and the other tags to be used.

Web pages include **hyperlinks**, which are pointers to other Web pages. A hyperlink contains the URL (the Uniform Resource Locator, described in Chapter 6, page 228) of the Web page to find when the user clicks the hyperlink. The URL can

Figure 8-7(a)
Sample HTML Document

```
<html>

<head>
<meta http-equiv="Content-Language" content="en-us">
<title>Using MIS</title>
</head>

<body>

<h1 align="center"><font color="#800080">Using MIS</font></h1>
<p> </p>
<h2><font color="#000080">Example HTML Document</font></h2>

<p> </p>
<p>Click here for textbook web site at Prentice-Hall: 
<a href="http://www.prenhall.com/kroenke">Web Site Link</a></p>

</body>

</html>
```

reference a page on the server that generated the page containing the hyperlink or it can reference a page on another server.

Figure 8-7(a) shows a sample HTML document. The document has a heading that provides metadata about the page and a body that contains the content. The tag <h1> means to format the indicated text as a level-one heading; <h2> means a level-two heading. The tag <a> defines a hyperlink. This tag has an **attribute**, which is a variable used to provide properties about a tag. Not all tags have attributes, but many do. Each attribute has a standard name. The attribute for a hyperlink is *href*, and its value indicates which Web page is to be displayed when the user clicks the link. Here, the page *http://prenhall.com/kroenke* is to be returned when the user clicks the hyperlink. Figure 8-7(b) shows this page as rendered by Internet Explorer.

We've discussed the technology needed in e-commerce. Read the E-Commerce in Practice *box on page 299 for an example of how two magazines have used e-commerce technology for different strategic purposes.*

By the way, some HTML documents contain snippets of program code. That code is sent from the Web server to the user's browser and is processed by the browser on the user's computer.

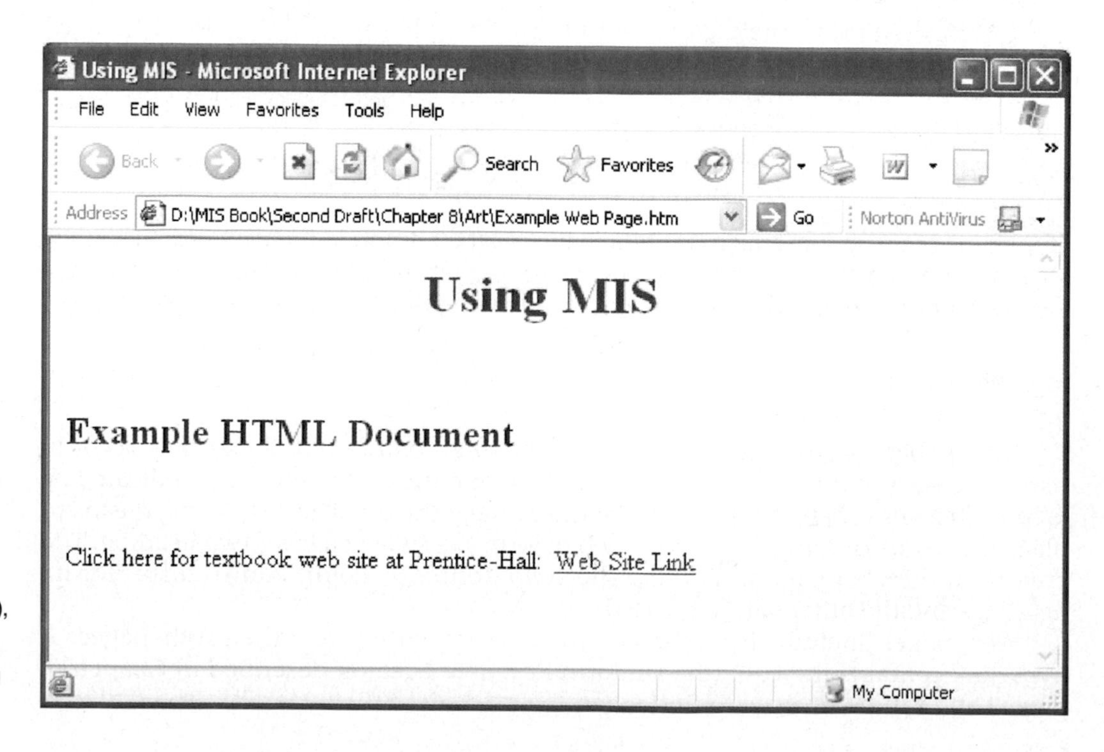

Figure 8-7(b)
HTML Document in Figure 8-7(a), rendered using Internet Explorer

Source: Microsoft product screen shot reprinted with permission from Microsoft Corporation.

E-COMMERCE IN PRACTICE

FINE WOODWORKING VERSUS WOODEN BOATS

Fine Woodworking is a high-quality, bimonthly publication that addresses topics of interest to serious woodworking enthusiasts. Issues include woodworking techniques, project descriptions, tool reviews, classified ads, and considerable advertising. *Fine Woodworking* has been published for about 30 years.

Wooden Boat is also a high-quality, bimonthly publication; it focuses on the design and construction of wooden boats. Issues include boat-building techniques; project descriptions; reviews of tools, books, and boats; classified ads; and considerable advertising. It, too, has been published for about 30 years.

These two publications, which are very similar, are owned and published by different companies. In recent years, both publications have sought to use e-commerce and the Web to leverage the value of their past issues, but they have done so in two different ways.

Wooden Boat provides an online index to past issues at *http://woodenboat.com*. Subscribers who have kept past issues frequently access this site to locate an article about some topic. While readers are at the site, *Wooden Boat* offers to sell them a number of products, as you can see when you visit the site. One of the products for sale is past issues of the magazine. Thus, using the online index, if you locate an article you want, and if you do not have that issue, you can buy it from the Web site.

Fine Woodworking has taken a different approach. It offers an online subscription to the magazine and its archives for an annual fee. Go to *http://finewoodworking.com* to see its current offer. Anyone who has paid that fee can access the site, search for topics of interest, and download articles about that topic in pdf format. If you want to know how, for example, to sharpen a hand plane, you can search for that topic and download quite a number of articles from the magazine's archive.

You and a team of your classmates will have an opportunity to compare and evaluate these uses of e-commerce in Collaboration Exercise 1 on page 323.

Q3 Why Is Web 2.0 Important to Business?

The first e-commerce sites duplicated the experience of shopping in a grocery store or other retail shop. The customer moved around the store, placed items in a shopping cart, and then checked out. It was a familiar scenario, but it did not take advantage of the Web's potential.

Amazon.com was one of the first to recognize other possibilities when it added the "Customers Who Bought This Book Also Bought" feature to its Web site. With that feature, e-commerce broke new ground. No grocery store could or would have a sign that announced, "Customers who bought this tomato soup, also bought. . . ." That idea was the first step toward what has come to be known as Web 2.0.

What Is Web 2.0?

The term *Web 2.0* originated at a 2001 conference brainstorming session between O'Reilly Publications and MediaLive International.[2] Although the specific meaning of **Web 2.0** is hard to pin down, it generally refers to a loose cloud of capabilities, technologies, business models, and philosophies. Figure 8-8 (next page) compares Web 2.0 to traditional processing. (For some reason, the term *Web 1.0* is not used.)

Software as a Service

Google, Amazon.com, and eBay exemplify Web 2.0. These companies do not sell software licenses, because software is not their product. Instead, they provide **software**

[2] *http://oreillynet.com/pub/a/oreilly/tim/news/2005/09/30/what-is-web-20.html.*

Figure 8-8
Comparison of Web 2.0 with Traditional Processing

Web 2.0 Processing	Traditional Processing
Major winners: Google, Amazon.com, eBay	Major winners: Microsoft, Oracle, SAP
Software as service	Software as product
Frequent releases of perpetual betas	Infrequent, controlled releases
Business model relies on advertising or other revenue-from-use	Business model relies on sale of software licenses
Viral marketing	Extensive advertising
Product value increases with use and users	Product value fixed
Organic interfaces, mashups encouraged	Controlled, fixed interface
Participation	Publishing
Some rights reserved	All rights reserved

as a service. You can search Google, run Google Docs & Spreadsheets, use Google Earth, process Gmail, and access Google maps—all from a thin-client program in your browser, with the bulk of the processing occurring on a Google server, somewhere on the Internet. Google releases new versions of its programs, like all of those in Web 2.0, frequently. Instead of software license fees, the Web 2.0 business model relies on advertising or other revenue that results as users employ the software as a service.

Many Web 2.0 programs are perpetually classified as "beta." Traditionally, a **beta program** is a prerelease version of software that is used for testing; it becomes obsolete when the final version is released. In the Web 2.0 world, many programs are always beta. Figure 8-9 shows Gmail as a beta program. I have been using this "beta" program for more than 2 years. Features and functions are constantly changing; none of the functions listed in the *More* menu item existed 2 years ago. But, because the program remains classified as beta, with no license fee, no user can complain about the changing user interface.

Software as a service clashes with the software model used by traditional software vendors such as Microsoft, Oracle, and SAP. For such companies, software is their product. They release new versions and new products infrequently. For example, 4 years separated the release of Microsoft Office 2007 from 2003. Releases are made in a very controlled fashion, and extensive testing and true beta programs precede every release.

Traditional software vendors depend on software license fees. If many Office users switched to word processors and spreadsheets provided as software as a service, the hit on Microsoft revenue would be catastrophic. Because of the importance of software license revenue, substantial marketing efforts are made to convert users to new releases.

In the Web 2.0 world, no such marketing is done; new features are released and vendors wait for users to spread the news to one another, in what is called **viral marketing**. Google has never announced, in a formal marketing campaign, any software. Users carry the message to one another. In fact, if a product requires advertising to be successful, then it is not a Web 2.0 product.

Use Increases Value

Another characteristic of Web 2.0 is that the value of the site increases with users and use. Amazon.com gains more value as more users write more reviews. Amazon.com

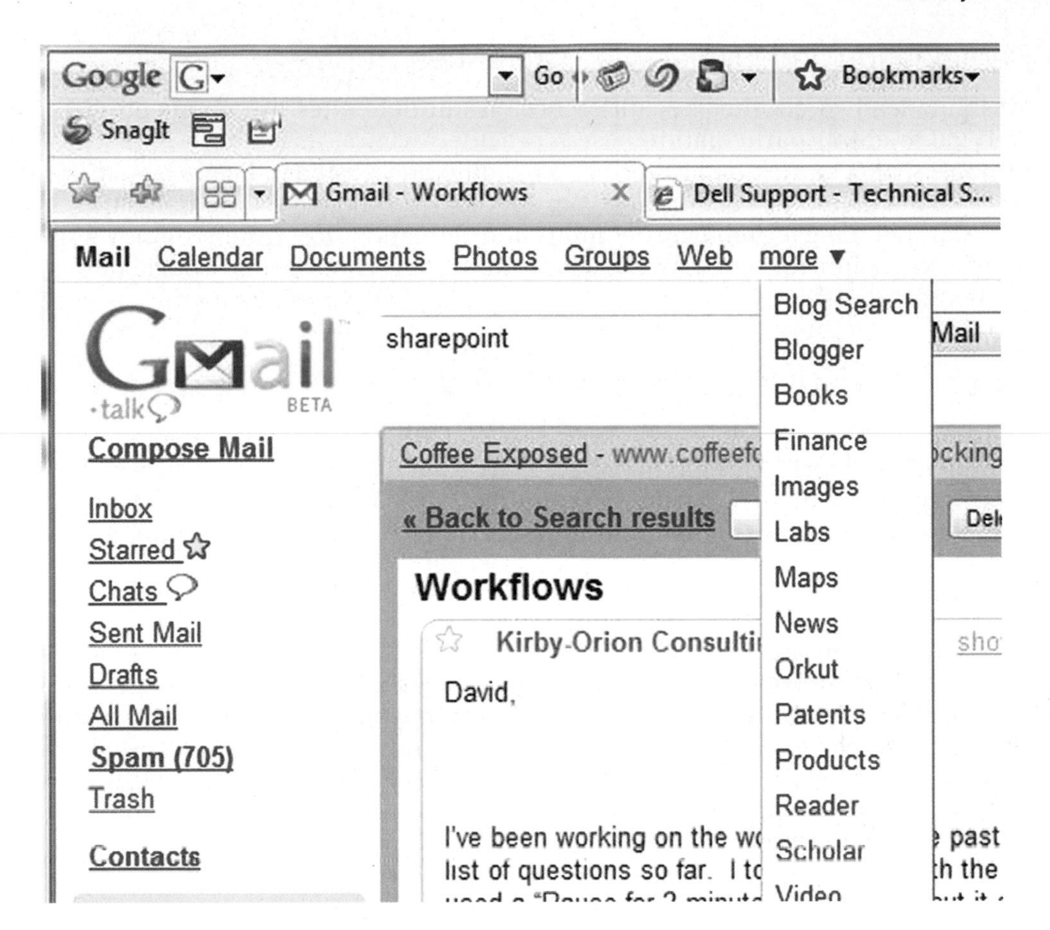

Figure 8-9
Sample Gmail Screen

Source: gMail™. GOOGLE is a trademark of Google Inc.

becomes *the* place to go for information about books or other products. Similarly, the more people who buy or sell on eBay, the more eBay gains value as a site.

Contrast this with traditional products where the value is fixed. Millions upon millions of Microsoft Word users may have created templates of potential use to others, but because Microsoft does not serve as a clearinghouse for sharing those templates the value of Word does not grow with the number of Word users.

Organic User Interface and Mashups

The traditional software model carefully controls the users' experience. All Office programs share a common user interface; the ribbon (toolbar) in Word is similar to the ribbon in PowerPoint and in Excel. In contrast, Web 2.0 interfaces are organic. Users find their way around eBay and PayPal, and if the user interface changes from day to day, well, that is just the nature of Web 2.0. Further, Web 2.0 encourages **mashups**, which occur when the output from two or more Web sites is combined into a single user experience.

Google's My Maps is an excellent mashup example. Google publishes Google Maps (created, incidentally, by a vendor other than Google) and provides tools for users to make custom modifications to those maps. Thus, users mash the Google map product with their own knowledge. One user demonstrated the growth of gang activity to the local police by mapping new graffiti sites on Google maps. Other users share their experiences or photos of hiking trips or other travel.

In Web 2.0 fashion, Google provides users a means for sharing their mashed-up map over the Internet and then indexes that map for Google search. If you publish a mashup of a Google map with your knowledge of a hiking trip on Mt. Pugh, anyone who googles Mt. Pugh will find your map. Again, the more users who create "My Maps," the greater the value of the My Maps site.

Participation and Ownership Differences

Mashups lead to another key difference. Traditional sites are about publishing; Web 2.0 is about participation. Users provide reviews, map content, discussion responses, blog entries, and so forth. A final difference, listed in Figure 8-8, concerns *ownership*. Traditional vendors and Web sites lock down all the legal rights they can. For example, Oracle publishes content and demands that others obtain written permission before reusing it. Web 2.0 locks down only some rights. Google publishes maps and says, "Do what you want with them. We'll help you share them."

How Can Businesses Benefit from Web 2.0?

Amazon.com, Google, eBay and other Web 2.0 companies have pioneered Web 2.0 technology and techniques to their benefit. A good question today, however, is how these techniques might be used by non-Internet companies. How might 3M, or Alaska Airlines, or Procter and Gamble, or the bicycle shop down the street use Web 2.0?

Advertising

When Oracle runs an ad in the *Wall Street Journal*, it has no control over who reads that ad, nor does it know much about the people who do (just that they fit the general demographic of *Wall Street Journal* readers). On any particular day, 10,000 qualified buyers for Oracle products might happen to read the ad, or then again perhaps only 1,000 qualified buyers read it. Neither Oracle nor the *Wall Street Journal* knows the number, but Oracle pays the same amount for the ad, regardless of the number of readers or who they are.

In the Web 2.0 world, advertising is specific to user interests. Someone who Googles *enterprise database management* is likely an IT person (or a student) who has at least a strong interest in Oracle and its competing products. Oracle would like to advertise to that person.

Google pioneered Web 2.0 advertising. With software called **Ad Words**, vendors agree to pay a certain amount for particular search words. The Firm, the workout studio featured in the interview at the start of Chapter 3, might agree to pay $2 for the word *workout*. When someone Googles that term, Google will display a link to The Firm's Web site. If the user clicks that link (and *only* if the user clicks that link), Google charges The Firm's account $2. The Firm pays nothing if the user does not click. If it chooses, The Firm can agree to pay for clicks on the word only by users in certain geographic areas.

The amount that a company pays per word can be changed from day to day and even hour to hour. If The Firm is about to start a new spinning class, it will pay more for the word *spinning* just before the class starts than it will afterwards. The value of a click on *spinning* is low when the start of the next spinning class is a month away.

Ad Sense is another advertising alternative. Google searches an organization's Web site and inserts ads that match content on that site. When users click on those ads, Google pays the organization a fee. Other Web 2.0 vendors offer services similar to Ad Words and Ad Sense.

With Web 2.0, the cost of reaching a particular, qualified person is much smaller than in the traditional advertising model. As a consequence, many companies are switching to the new lower-cost medium, and newspapers and magazines are struggling with a sharp reduction in advertising revenue.

Social Networking

The term **social networking** refers to connections of people with similar interests. Although sociologists used the term prior to Web 2.0, most people today use it to refer to connections between people that are supported by Web 2.0 technology.

For example, Zillow.com offers free appraisals of homes and condominiums. The site is supported by advertising by lenders and other companies. In addition to appraisals, Zillow provides comprehensive resources about the buying process and about neighborhoods. Zillow includes a discussion site in which users can discuss matters important to a given neighborhood or city. Zillow adds value to its site by enabling people with an interest in real estate in the same area to share knowledge and experience.

Mashups

How can two non-Internet companies mash the content of their products? Suppose you're watching a hit movie and you would like to buy the jewelry, dress, or watch worn by the leading actress. Suppose that Nordstrom's sells all those items. With Web 2.0 technology, the movie's producer and Nordstrom's can mash their content together so that you, watching the movie at home, can click on the watch and be directed to a Nordstrom's e-commerce site that will sell it to you. Or, perhaps Nordstrom's is disintermediated out of the transaction, and you are taken to the e-commerce site of the watch's manufacturer. Such possibilities are on the leading edge of e-commerce today. Many will be developed during your business career.

See the Innovation in Practice *box below for ideas on how to creatively think of new Web 2.0 possibilities.*

Who Is in Control?

Before we get too carried away with the potential for Web 2.0, note that not all business information systems benefit from flexibility and organic growth. Any information system that deals with assets, whether financial or material, requires, some level of control. You probably do not want to mash up your credit card transactions on My Map and share that mashup with the world. As CFO, you probably do not want your

INNOVATION IN PRACTICE

WEB 2.0 AND COMPETITIVE ADVANTAGE

Clearly, many opportunities exist for the innovative application of Web 2.0 technologies. One way to imagine those opportunities is to examine Web 2.0 in the context of the eight competitive advantage principles in Figure 3-11 (page 72). For example, here is one application of Web 2.0 for each principle:

1. *New product or service.* Use a mashup to combine your company's product with Google Maps.
2. *Enhance product or service.* Use social networking to connect your customers to each other.
3. *Differentiate product or service.* Add a marketplace in which your customers can sell innovative applications of your products to each other.
4. *Lock in customers and buyers.* Provide an information system by which your customers can mash up their product documentation with documentation of components that you sell them. For example, when one of your customer's customers seeks product maintenance instructions, a mashup automatically provides your instructions for the components you supply in your customer's product.
5. *Lock in suppliers.* For a company with part-time contractors, such as a workout studio, use social networking to connect your instructors to their customers, but only in the context of your studio. (But be careful! Many Web 2.0 services that you might develop for your suppliers could benefit your competition as much as yourself.)
6. *Raise barriers to entry.* Increase customer loyalty by developing a social network of customers who obtain value from each other via your network.
7. *Establish alliances.* If your organization provides face-to-face services (e.g., a workout studio), organize a consortium of similar companies in different regions to buy Ad Words. Your consortium will be better able to compete with national firms that are buying the same words.
8. *Reduce costs.* Reduce sales costs by creating a social network for your sales staff to share knowledge, experience, and sales opportunities. For example, when your electronics salesperson to Ford learns there's also a fabric sales opportunity, use social networking to distribute that knowledge to the fabric sales team.

You and a team of your classmates will have an opportunity to apply these ideas to a company in Collaboration Exercise 2 on page 324.

accounts payable or general ledger system to have an organic user interface; in fact, Sarbanes-Oxley prohibits that possibility.

Web 2.0 is great technology for Internet companies, and aspects of Web 2.0 will be important for other organizations as well. However, Web 2.0 is just one tool in the IS toolbox. If you seek the right opportunities, you may have the chance to help your organization determine which parts of Web 2.0 technology are appropriate for which parts of your business. It will be fascinating!

Q4 How Can Information Systems Enhance Supply Chain Performance?

A **supply chain** is a network of organizations and facilities that transforms raw materials into products delivered to customers. Figure 8-10 shows a generic supply chain. Customers order from retailers, who in turn order from distributors, who in turn order from manufacturers, who in turn order from suppliers. In addition to the organizations shown here, the supply chain also includes transportation companies, warehouses, and inventories and some means for transmitting messages and information among the organizations involved.

Because of disintermediation, not every supply chain has all of these organizations. Dell, for example, sells directly to the customer. Both the distributor and retailer organizations are omitted from its supply chain. In other supply chains, manufacturers sell directly to retailers and omit the distribution level.

The term *chain* is misleading. *Chain* implies that each organization is connected to just one company up the chain (toward the supplier) and down the chain (toward the customer). That is not the case. Instead, at each level an organization can work with many organizations both up and down the supply chain. Thus, a supply chain is a *network*.

To understand the operation of a supply chain, consider Figure 8-11. Suppose you decide to take up cross-country skiing. You go to REI (either by visiting one of its stores or its Web site) and purchase skis, bindings, boots, and poles. To fill your order, REI removes those items from its inventory of goods. Those goods have been purchased, in turn, from distributors. According to Figure 8-11, REI purchases the skis, bindings, and poles from one distributor and boots from a second. The distributors in turn purchase the required items from the manufacturers, which in turn buy raw materials from their suppliers.

The only source of revenue in a supply chain is the customer. In the REI example, you spend your money on the ski equipment. From that point all the way back up the supply chain to the raw material suppliers, there is no further injection of cash. The money you spend on the ski equipment is passed back up the supply chain as payments for goods or raw materials. Again, the customer is the only source of revenue.

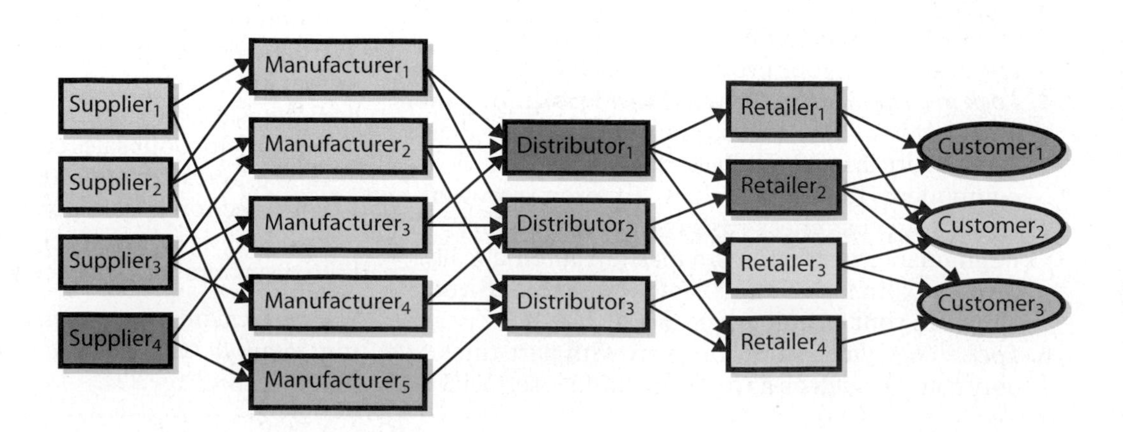

Figure 8-10
Supply Chain Relationships

Figure 8-11
Supply Chain Example

What Factors Drive Supply Chain Performance?

As shown in Figure 8-12, four factors drive supply chain performance: facilities, inventory, transportation, and information.[3] *Facilities* concern the location, size, and operations methodology of the places where products are fabricated, assembled, or stored. *Inventory* includes all of the materials in the supply chain, including raw materials, in-process work, and finished goods. *Transportation*, the third driver in Figure 8-12, concerns the movement of materials in the supply chain. These three factors are important drivers, but they do not concern IS directly. It is the fourth driver, *information*, that most concerns us.

Information influences supply chain performance by affecting the ways that organizations in the supply chain request, respond, and inform one another. Figure 8-12 lists three factors of information: purpose, availability, and means. The *purpose* of the information can be transactional, such as orders and order returns, or it can be informational, such as the sharing of inventory and customer order data. *Availability*

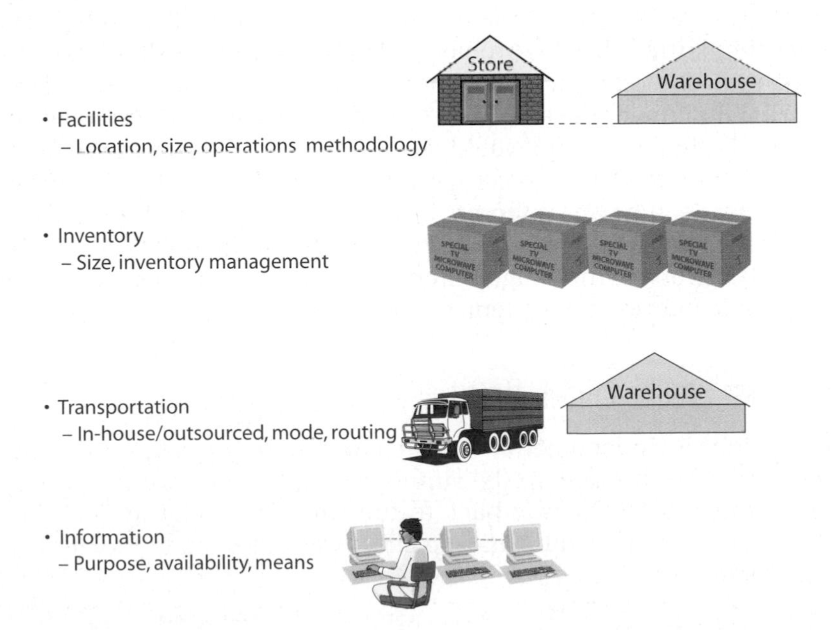

Store
Warehouse
• Facilities
– Location, size, operations methodology
• Inventory
– Size, inventory management
• Transportation
– In-house/outsourced, mode, routing
Warehouse
• Information
– Purpose, availability, means

Figure 8-12
Drivers of Supply Chain Performance

[3]Sunil Chopra and Peter Meindl, *Supply Chain Management* (Upper Saddle River, NJ: Prentice Hall, 2004), pp. 51–53.

refers to the ways in which organizations share their information—that is, which organizations have access to which information and when. Finally, *means* refers to the methods by which the information is transmitted. EDI and XML are two types of means discussed later in this chapter.

We will expand on the role of information in the supply chain later in this chapter. For now, however, consider two of the ways that information can affect supply chain performance: supply chain profitability and the bullwhip effect.

How Does Supply Chain Profitability Differ from Organizational Profitability?

Each of the organizations in Figures 8-10 and 8-11 is an independent company, with its own goals and objectives. Each has a competitive strategy that may differ from the competitive strategies of the other organizations in the supply chain. Left alone, each organization will maximize its own profit, regardless of the consequences of its actions on the profitability of the others.

Supply chain profitability is the difference between the sum of the revenue generated by the supply chain and the sum of the costs that all organizations in the supply chain incur to obtain that revenue. In general, the maximum profit to the supply chain *will not* occur if each organization in the supply chain maximizes its own profits in isolation. Usually, the profitability of the supply chain increases if one or more of the organizations operates at less than its own maximum profitability.

To see why this is so, consider your purchase of the ski equipment from REI. Assume that you purchase either the complete package of skis, bindings, boots, and poles or you purchase nothing. If you cannot obtain boots, for example, the utility of skis, bindings, and poles is nil. In this situation, an outage of boots causes a loss of revenue not just for the boots, but also for the entire ski package.

According to Figure 8-11, REI buys boots from distributor 2 and the rest of the package from distributor 1. If boots are unavailable, distributor 2 loses the revenue of selling boots, but does not suffer any of the revenue loss from the nonsale of skis, bindings, and poles. Thus, distributor 2 will carry an inventory of boots that is optimized considering only the loss of boot revenue—not considering the loss of revenue for the entire package. In this case, the profitability to the supply chain will increase if distributor 2 carries an inventory of boots larger than is optimal for its business alone.

In theory, the way to solve this problem is to use some form of transfer payment to induce distributor 2 to carry a larger boot inventory. For example, REI could pay distributor 2 a premium for the sale of boots in packages and recover a portion of this premium from distributor 1, who would recover a portion of it from the manufacturers, and so forth, up the supply chain. For higher-priced items or for items with very high volume, there can be an economic benefit for creating an information system to identify such a situation. If the dynamic is long-lasting, it will be worthwhile to negotiate the transfer-payment agreements. All of this requires a comprehensive supply-chain-wide information system, as you will see.

In truth, the transfer-payment solution is difficult to implement, as illustrated in the Opposing Forces Guide *on page 318.*

What Is the Bullwhip Effect?

The **bullwhip effect** is a phenomenon in which the variability in the size and timing of orders increases at each stage up the supply chain, from customer to supplier (in Figure 8-11, from *You* all the way back to the suppliers). Figure 8-13 depicts the situation. In a famous study,[4] the bullwhip effect was observed in Procter & Gamble's supply chain for diapers.

[4]Hau L. Lee, V. Padmanabhan, and S. Whang, "The Bullwhip Effect in Supply Chains," *Sloan Management Review*, Spring 1997, pp. 93–102.

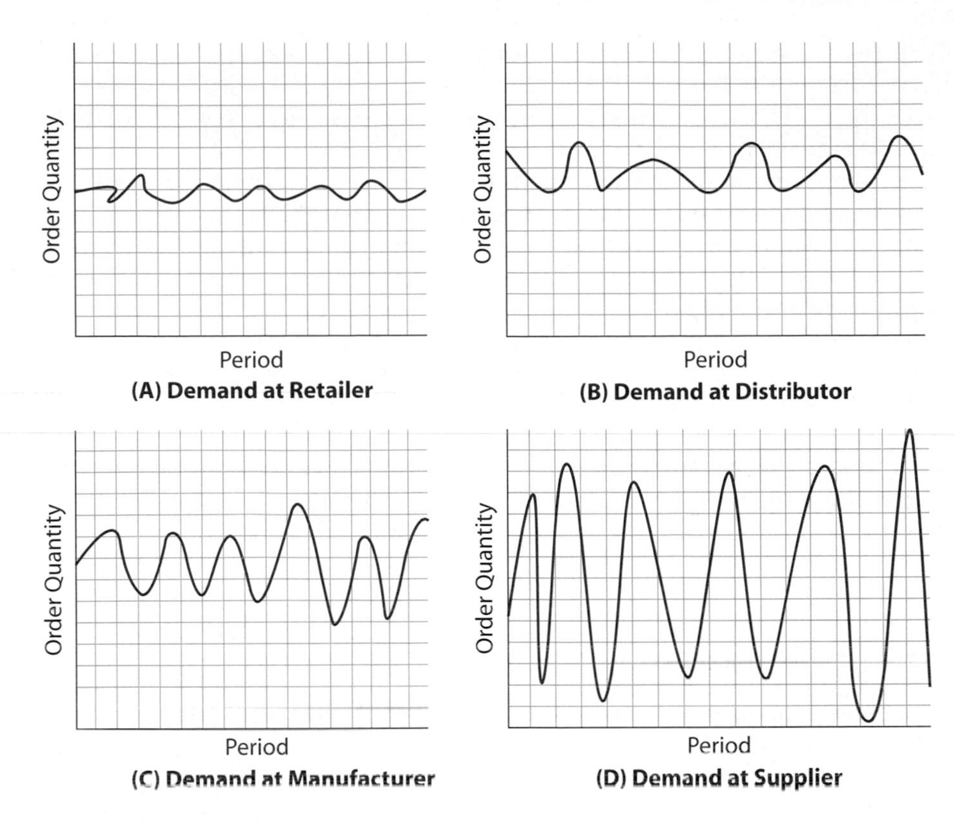

Figure 8-13
The Bullwhip Effect

Except for random variation, diaper demand is constant. Diaper use is not seasonal; the requirement for diapers does not change with fashion or anything else. The number of babies determines diaper demand, and that number is constant or possibly slowly changing.

Retailers do not order from the distributor with the sale of every diaper package. The retailer waits until the diaper inventory falls below a certain level, called the *reorder quantity*. Then the retailer orders a supply of diapers, perhaps ordering a few more than it expects to sell to ensure that it does not have an outage.

The distributor receives the retailer's orders and follows the same process. It waits until its supply falls below the reorder quantity, and then it reorders from the manufacturer, with perhaps an increased amount to prevent outages. The manufacturer, in turn, uses a similar process with the raw-materials suppliers.

Because of the nature of this process, small changes in demand at the retailer are amplified at each stage of the supply chain. As shown in Figure 8-13, those small changes become quite large variations on the supplier end.

The bullwhip effect is a natural dynamic that occurs because of the multistage nature of the supply chain. It is not related to erratic consumer demand, as the study of diapers indicated. You may have seen a similar effect while driving on the freeway. One car slows down, the car just behind it slows down a bit more abruptly, which causes the third card in line to slow down even more abruptly, and so forth, until the 30th car or so is slamming on its brakes.

The large fluctuations of the bullwhip effect force distributors, manufacturers, and suppliers to carry larger inventories than should be necessary to meet the real consumer demand. Thus, the bullwhip effect reduces the overall profitability of the supply chain.

One way to eliminate the bullwhip effect is to give all participants in the supply chain access to consumer-demand information from the retailer. Each organization can thus plan its inventory or manufacturing based on the true demand (the demand from the only party that introduces money into the system) and not on the observed demand from the next organization up the supply chain. Of course, an *interorganizational information system* is necessary to share such data.

Q5 How Can Information Systems Support Supplier Relationship Management?

Figure 8-14 shows the three fundamental information systems involved in supply chain management: supplier relationship management (SRM), inventory, and CRM. Note that a manufacturer may also have manufacturing applications such as MRP, MRP II, or ERP systems. We discussed all of these applications except SRM in Chapter 7.

Supplier relationship management (SRM) is a business process for managing all contacts between an organization and its suppliers. Note: The term *supplier* in *supplier relationship management* is broader than the use of the term *supplier* in Figures 8-10 and 8-11. In those figures, the term refers to the supplier of raw materials and assemblies to a manufacturer. *Supplier* in SRM is used generically: It refers to *any organization* that sells something to the organization that operates the SRM application. Thus, in this generic sense, a manufacturer is a supplier to a distributor.

What SRM Processes Do Information Systems Support?

SRM is a cross-functional system in the same sense of CRM, ERP, and EAI, which were described in Chapter 7. With regard to Porter's model, an SRM supports both the inbound logistics primary activity and the procurement support activity. Considering business processes, SRM information systems need features to support three SRM processes: source, purchase, and settle, as summarized in Figure 8-15.

Considering sourcing, the organization needs to find possible vendors of needed supplies, materials, or services; to assess the vendors that it does find; to negotiate terms and conditions; and to formalize those terms and conditions in a procurement contract. SRM software is especially relevant to finding and assessing vendors. Some SRM applications have features to search for product sources and to find evaluations of vendors and products. You see something akin to this functionality when you search for electronics products on a site such as *http://cnet.com.* There you can readily determine which vendors provide which products, and you can also obtain evaluations of products and vendors. Similar capabilities are built into SRM packages.

Once the company has identified vendors and has procurement contracts in place, the next stage is to procure the goods. The SRM application requests information, quotations, and proposals from would-be suppliers. The company then can use the SRM to manage the approval workflow in order to approve the purchase and issue the order.

Figure 8-14
B2B in One Section of the Supply Chain

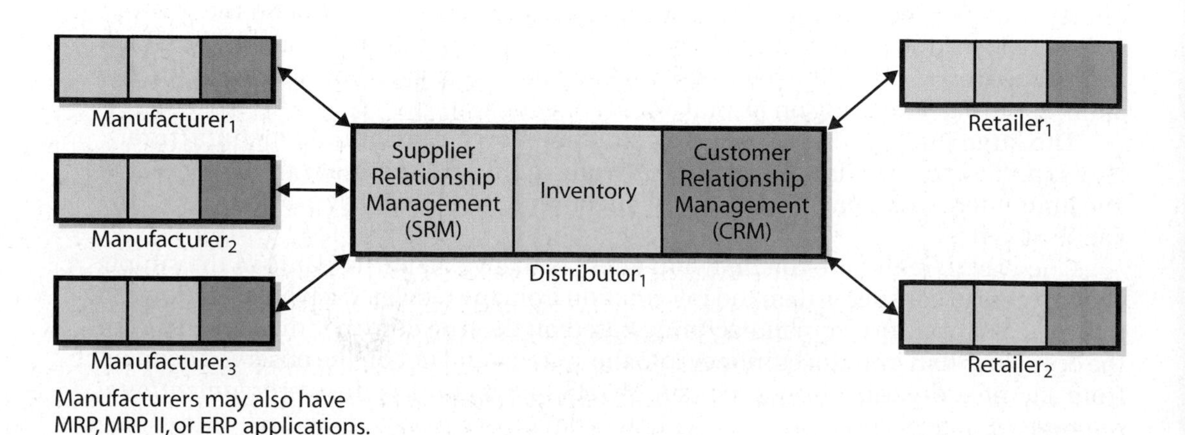

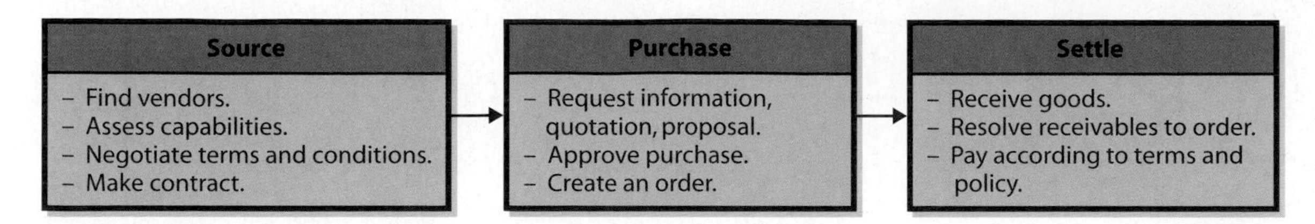

Figure 8-15
Summary of SRM Processes

The third major SRM activity is to settle. Here, the accounting department reconciles the receipt of the goods or services against the purchase documents and schedules the vendor payment. The payment portion of the SRM typically connects to the cash management subsystem in the financial management application.

Some SRM packages include features to support procurement auctions. Generally, companies use auctions to obtain large amounts of materials, energy, or other consumables. In these procurement auctions, an organization indicates its desire to purchase a product or service and invites would-be sellers to submit bids. Typically, the low bid wins the auction. Organizational auctions can attract a large number of vendors and often result in substantial cost savings.

How Does SRM Integrate with CRM?

According to Figure 8-16, the supplier's CRM application interfaces with the purchaser's SRM application. In fact, from a process standpoint, these two systems are two sides of the same coin and share the same process goals. Both the supplier and the customer want to perform the ordering process as cheaply and efficiently as possible. To do this, the CRM and SRM applications need to be integrated.

Recall from Chapter 7 that one function of a CRM is to increase the value of existing customers. One way to do that is to connect the CRM to the customer's SRM so that recurring purchases are automated. The SRM examines inventory, determines that items are required, and automatically creates the order via its connection to the supplier's CRM.

The Ethics Guide *on page 310 discusses some of the ethical issues involved in supply chain information sharing.*

According to the Hackett Group, by focusing purchases to a few vendors and by automating the procurement process, companies can operate with a procurement cost about 70 percent lower than the average.[5]

Some companies initially are uncomfortable with the idea of linking their supply chain information systems to those of other organizations. They may fear a loss of corporate data or a loss of autonomy or control, which could occur if the information sharing is not done well.

Figure 8-16
ERP II in One Section of the Supply Chain

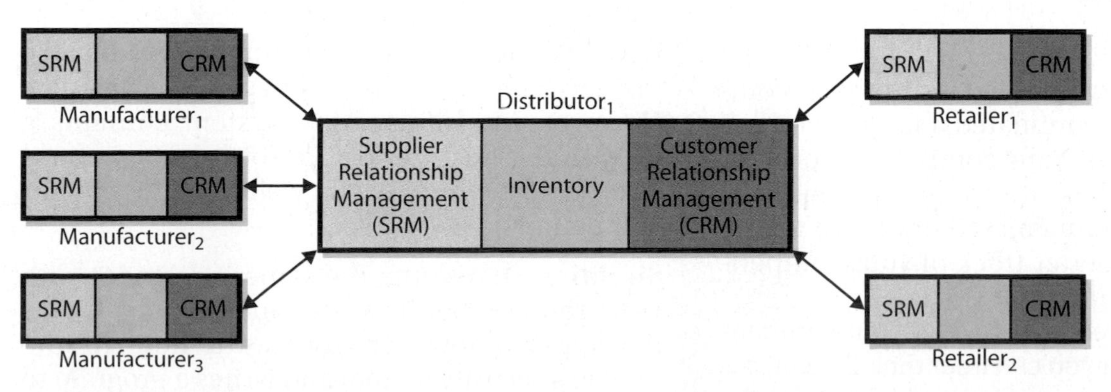

[5]The Hackett Group, *Achieving World-Class Source to Settlement Through Best Practices*, Miami, Florida, March 2003, *http://thehackettgroup.com* (accessed October 2004).

Ethics

GUIDE

The Ethics of Supply Chain Information Sharing

Suppose that you work for a distributor that has developed information systems to read inventory data both up and down the supply chain. You can query the finished goods inventories of your manufacturers and the store inventories of your retailers. These systems were developed to increase supply chain efficiency and profitability. Consider the following situations:

Situation A: You notice that the store inventories of all retailers are running low on items in a particular product family. You know the retailers will soon send rush orders for some of those items, and in anticipation, you accumulate an oversupply of those items. You query the manufacturers' inventory data, and you find that the manufacturers' finished goods inventories are low. Because you believe you have the only supply of those items, you increase their price by 15 percent. When the retailers ask why, you claim extra transportation costs. In fact, all of the increase is going straight to your bottom line.

Situation B: Unknown to you, one of your competitors has also accumulated a large inventory of those same items. Your competitor does not increase prices on those items, and consequently you sell none at your increased price. You decide you need to keep better track of your competitors' inventories in the future.

You have no direct way to read your competitors' inventories, but you can infer their inventories by watching the decrease of inventory levels on the manufacturer side and comparing that decrease to the sales on the retail side. You know what's been produced, and you know what's been sold. You also know how much resides in your inventory. The difference must be held in your competitor's inventories. Using that process, you now can estimate your competitors' inventories.

Situation C: Assume that the agreement that you have with the retailers is that you are able to query all of their current inventory levels, but only for the orders they have with you. You are not supposed to be able to query orders they have with your competitors. However, the information system contains a flaw, and by mistake you are able to query everyone's orders, your own as well as those of your competitors.

Situation D: Assume the same agreement with your retailers as in situation C. One of your developers, however, notices a hole in the retailer's security system and writes a program to exploit that hole. You now have access to all of the retailers' sales, inventory, and order data. ■

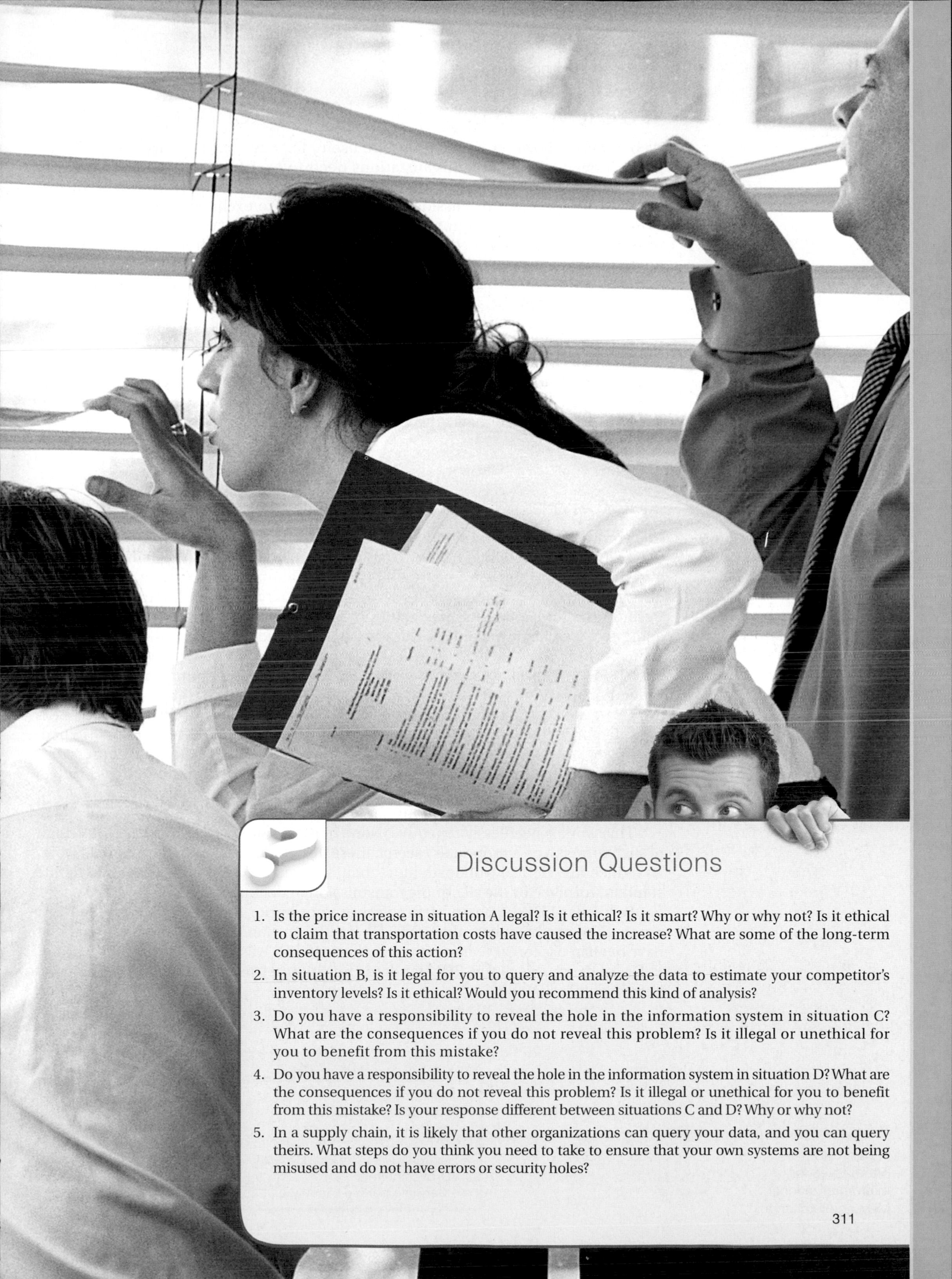

Discussion Questions

1. Is the price increase in situation A legal? Is it ethical? Is it smart? Why or why not? Is it ethical to claim that transportation costs have caused the increase? What are some of the long-term consequences of this action?
2. In situation B, is it legal for you to query and analyze the data to estimate your competitor's inventory levels? Is it ethical? Would you recommend this kind of analysis?
3. Do you have a responsibility to reveal the hole in the information system in situation C? What are the consequences if you do not reveal this problem? Is it illegal or unethical for you to benefit from this mistake?
4. Do you have a responsibility to reveal the hole in the information system in situation D? What are the consequences if you do not reveal this problem? Is it illegal or unethical for you to benefit from this mistake? Is your response different between situations C and D? Why or why not?
5. In a supply chain, it is likely that other organizations can query your data, and you can query theirs. What steps do you think you need to take to ensure that your own systems are not being misused and do not have errors or security holes?

Q6 How Do Organizations Exchange Data?

Web commerce-server applications are useful for B2C, but they are not sufficient for B2B needs. In general, organizations need to exchange data and messages in more general and flexible ways than they can do with commerce servers. As you can see from the previous discussion, they many need to exchange orders, order confirmations, requests for quotations (bids), item inventory status data, accounts payable and accounts receivable data, and a myriad of other types of data and documents.

Figure 8-17 summarizes alternatives for exchanging data and messages. The most basic are telephone calls and documents exchanged via fax or postal mail. Another alternative is to exchange messages and documents via email and FTP. None of these requires information technology beyond what you already know.

The next three alternatives do involve additional technology. *Electronic Data Interchange (EDI)* is a standard for exchanging documents from machine to machine, electronically. Another alternative is *eXtensible Markup Language (XML)*, a standard markup language that offers advantages over EDI and that most believe will eventually replace EDI.

Electronic Data Interchange (EDI)

Electronic Data Interchange (EDI) is a standard of formats for common business documents. To understand the need for EDI, consider the supply chain in Figure 8-10, and suppose that there are 5 distributors and 10 manufacturers. Further, suppose that each distributor wants to send orders electronically to all of the manufacturers. Because the transmissions are electronic, the distributors and manufacturers must agree on a format for the orders. This format will include how many data fields will be sent, the order they will be sent in, how many characters will be sent in each data field, and so forth. This is not difficult work; it merely requires a common design for the order transmissions.

However, if each distributor designs a *different* electronic order format for each manufacturer, then a total of 5 times 10, or 50, different formats must be designed. When you consider that the companies might wish to exchange not only orders, but also requests for quotations, order confirmations, order shipping notices, and so forth, you can see that the distributors and manufacturers would have to develop thousands of different document formats.

This work is needlessly repetitive. None of these companies considers the design of such forms to be a proprietary secret; these designs are just necessary clerical work. To reduce this clerical workload, more than 30 years ago companies began to define standard formats for the electronic transmission of documents.

Particular EDI document definitions are not important for this discussion. Just realize that when you hear the term *EDI*, it refers to standard document formats that have been in use for 30 years or more. In the past, EDI was used over point-to-point or PSDN networks. Recently, EDI standards for the Internet, called **EDI over Internet**, have been developed.

Message and Data Exchange
– Telephone – Paper (fax, postal mail) – Email – FTP – Electronic Data Interchange (EDI) – EDI over Internet – eXtensible Markup Language (XML)

Figure 8-17
Alternatives for Interorganizational Message Exchange

EDI has value and will be used for many more years. Gradually, however, most believe EDI will be replaced by XML, a more promising technology.

eXtensible Markup Language (XML)

At this point, you may be asking a burning question—namely, why not use HTML for document interchange? Why mess around with EDI or anything else when the greatest success story in modern history involves the sharing of Web pages over the Internet? Why not use HTML to create purchase orders, price quotations, or other business documents? They could then be transmitted using HTTP, just as Web pages are.

In fact, organizations have used HTML to share documents. However, doing so presents several problems. We will first summarize those problems and then describe a successor markup language called XML that overcomes them.

What's Wrong with HTML?

Three problems with HTML are:

- HTML tags have no consistent meaning.
- HTML has a fixed number of tags.
- HTML mixes format, content, and structure.

The first problem is that tags are used inconsistently. For example, in standard use heading tags should be arranged in outline format. The highest-level heading tag should be an h1; within h1, there should be one or more h2 tags; and within the h2 tags there should be h3 tags; and so forth, for as many heading levels as the author of a document wants.

Unfortunately, there is no feature of HTML that forces consistent use. An h2 tag can appear anywhere—above an h1 heading, below an h4 heading, or anyplace else. An h2 tag can represent a level-two heading, but it can also be used just to obtain a particular type of formatting. If I want the words "Prices guaranteed until Jan. 1, 2008" to appear in the formatting of a level-two heading, I can code:

```
<h2>Prices guaranteed until Jan. 1, 2008</h2>
```

This statement is not intended to be a level-two heading, but it will be given the font size, weight, and color that such headings have.

The possibility of tag misuse means that we cannot depend on tags to infer the document's structure. An h2 tag may not be a heading at all. This limitation means that organizations cannot use HTML tags to reliably exchange documents.

A second problem with HTML is that it defines a fixed set of tags. If two businesses want to define a new tag, say <PriceQuotation>, there is no way in HTML for them to define it. HTML documents are limited to the predefined tags.

The third problem with HTML is that HTML mixes the structure, formatting, and content of a document. Consider the following line of HTML code:

```
<h2 align="center"><font color="#FF00FF">Price of Item</font></h2>
```

This heading mixes the structure (h2) with the formatting (alignment and color) with the content (Price of Item). Such mixing makes HTML difficult to work with. Ideally, the structure, format, and content should be separate.

How Does XML Fix These Problems?

To overcome the problems in HTML, the computer industry designed a new markup language called the **eXtensible Markup Language (XML)**. XML is the product of a committee that worked under the auspices of the **World Wide Web Consortium (W3C)**, a body that sponsors the development and dissemination of Web standards. By the way, W3C publishes excellent tutorials, and you can find an XML tutorial on its Web site, *http://w3.org*.

XML provides a superior means for organizations to exchange documents. It solves the problems mentioned for HTML, and it has become a significant standard for computer processing. For example, all Microsoft Office 2007 products save their documents in XML format. XML is also a key part of standards for Web services (described on page 316), and it is particularly important for supply chain management, as you will see.

XML solves the problems of HTML by requiring that content, structure, and format be placed into separate documents. Further, document designers can create their own tags and specify the precise arrangement of those tags in a document called an XML schema, which is explained in the following section. Explaining how XML documents are formatted is beyond the scope of this text. Google *XSLT* for information on that topic.

How Can Supply Chains Use XML?

XML has the potential to improve, sometimes drastically, the efficiency of supply chain processes and activities. To understand how, consider REI and its relationship to its distributors. Suppose REI wants to transmit counts of inventory items to all of its suppliers. To do so, REI designs an XML document called *ItemCount.* (For now, think of an XML document as a sequence of tags and data, like HTML documents.) Once it has designed the document, REI records the structure of that document in what is called an **XML schema**. Such a schema is just another XML document, but one that records the structure (or schema) of the *ItemCount* document. Call that schema *ItemCount_schema.*

Next, REI prepares inventory count documents according to its design. Before sending those documents to its distributors, REI double-checks that the documents are valid by comparing them to the schema. Fortunately, hundreds of programs are reality available that can validate an XML document against its schema. For example, both Internet Explorer and Mozilla Firefox can validate any XML document. This validation feature means significant cost savings, because human labor is not required to check documents.

Before sending *ItemCount* documents to the distributors, REI shares the *ItemCount_schema* document with them, possibly by publishing it on a Web site that the distributors have permission to access. When a distributor receives an *ItemCount* document from REI, it uses the *ItemCount_schema* to validate the received document. In this way, the distributors ensure that they receive correct and complete documents and that no part of the document has been lost in transmission. Again, this automated process saves labor because it frees the distributors from manually validating the correctness of the documents they receive. This automated validation can mean enormous labor savings.

How Can Industries Use XML?

Now broaden this idea from two businesses to an entire industry. Suppose, for example, that the real estate industry agrees on an XML schema document for property listings. Every real estate company that can produce data in the format of that schema can then exchange listings with every other such real estate company. Given the schema, each company can ensure that it is transmitting and receiving valid documents.

Figure 8-18 lists some work that is underway on XML standards in various industries.

Industry	Example XML Standards
Accounting	American Institute of Certified Public Accountants (AICPA): Extensible Financial Reporting Markup Language
Automotive	Society of Automotive Engineers (SAE): XML for the Automotive Industry—SAE J2008
Banking	Financial Services Technology Consortium (FSTC): Bank Internet Payment System (BIPS)
Human Resources	HR-XML Consortium
Insurance	ACORD: Property and Casualty
Real Estate	OpenMLS: Real Estate Listing Management System
Workflow	Internet Engineering Task Force (IETF): Simple Workflow Access Protocol (SWAP)

Figure 8-18
XML Industry Standards

Q7 How Can Organizations Connect Computer Programs?

You have learned that companies can use EDI and XML to exchange documents. But, what if two organizations want their computer *programs* to interact? What if a company wants its SRM application program to connect directly to a supplier's CRM application? Or, to the points raised in the Caprice Leinonen interview at the start of the chapter, what if one hospital's information system wants to request data from another hospital's information system? Neither the EDI nor the XML standard, by itself, supports such activity.

The process of a program on one computer accessing programs on a second computer is called **remote computing** or **distributed computing**. Several techniques are used. Two important ones are the use of proprietary designs and Web services.

Distributed Computing Using Proprietary Systems

One way to develop distributed computer programs is to develop proprietary distributed applications. **Proprietary** means that the solution is unique to and is owned by the organizations that develop and pay for the distributed systems. It is a one-of-a-kind solution.

To develop a proprietary design, teams of developers from the companies involved work together using a development process like that described in Chapter 10. The teams determine application requirements, develop a design, and write and test programs according to that design. Such projects are distinguished from other development projects only in the requirement for remote processing.

Consider an example. Suppose the companies in a supply chain decide they want to eliminate the bullwhip effect. To do this, the retailers in the supply chain must share sales data with all companies up the chain. Accordingly, the companies in the supply chain organize a development team consisting of IS personnel from all of the major companies.

The joint development team designs this application to use a particular communications capability, particular operating systems, and particular distributed computing

Many B2B and other interorganizational information systems require meetings among the companies involved to design the joint processes that will be used and eventually to negotiate contracts. You may be asked to participate in such meetings, and, if so, you need to know proper etiquette for such meetings, as described in the Problem Solving-Guide *on page 320.*

techniques. A major portion of the development effort is in selecting which such technologies to use and how to write the programs to use them.

An alternative proprietary method is for one company to develop all of the necessary programs itself and to install some of its programs on another company's computers. In the past, some manufacturers developed order-entry programs that they installed on their customers' computers. These programs call directly into the manufacturer's CRM application. The customers need only install the programs that the manufacturer provides.

Of course, this process is much simpler to describe than it is to do. Inevitably, there are differences on the customers' computers that the manufacturer did not expect, and so the manufacturer has to make special-purpose program versions for different distributors. Sometimes this happens dozens of times, resulting in a software configuration management nightmare for the manufacturer.

Proprietary solutions are difficult and expensive to develop and operate. If they provide sufficient business value, however, the return on investment can make them worthwhile. Even so, considerable management time and attention is necessary. Because of the difficulty, expense, and time involved in developing such solutions, many organizations today are beginning to use another technology that uses a different strategy—XML Web services. We consider it next.

XML Web Service Applications and Service-Oriented Architecture (SOA)

XML Web services, sometimes called simply *Web services*, are a set of standards that facilitate distributed computing using Internet technology. Web services are an implementation of a new processing philosophy called **service-oriented architecture (SOA)**. The key SOA concept is that a computing system uses a *standard method* to declare the services it provides and the interface by which those services can be requested and consumed.

XML Web services are one way, and currently the most accepted way, of implementing an SOA system. As Caprice Leinonen indicated in her interview, SOA will be critically important to health care. XML Web services will be important in other industries as well. Every major software vendor has products that support Web services. For example, Microsoft provides .Net development tools, and IBM provides J2EE development tools. (Because of the standards, by the way, applications developed by these different tools will work together without problem.)

Web Services Concepts

The goal of Web services is to provide a standardized way for programs to access one another remotely, without the need to develop proprietary solutions. Because they are standardized, worldwide, they are immediately accessible. Right now, for example, without a meeting or even a conversation, you can access Amazon.com and use Web services standards to write your own personal front-end to Amazon.com's catalog. (To learn more, see *http://amazon.com/webservices.*) There is no need for developer meetings to create designs for interprogram communication. Everything necessary is already part of the Web services standards.

A number of important standards have been defined to make Web services possible, but a discussion of those standards is beyond the scope of this book. In general, these standards enable programs on one computer to obtain a **service description** that details what programs exist on another computer and how to communicate with those programs.

Once the service user has the service description, it uses the information it contains to invoke the service. In the case of Amazon.com, a service user can invoke the Amazon.com service to find a particular book, to find a set of books, or to provide additional Amazon.com catalog information. Remarkably, it appears to the service user that all of the Amazon.com programs are actually on the service user's computer. If you were the service user, it would be as if you had Amazon.com's catalog programs (and database) on your own machine.

All Web service data are transmitted in XML documents. These documents have XML schemas defined, and all program components of the XML Web services architecture can automatically validate them.

Web Services and the Supply Chain

Web services have the potential to simplify the automation of supply chain interactions. Any organization in the supply chain can develop Web services and publish those services to other organizations in the supply chain. Developers in those other organizations can access the service description and write programs that call the Web services.

Consider an example: Suppose that, to reduce the bullwhip effect, a retailer develops a Web service to share its CRM sales data with companies in the supply chain. Other companies in the supply chain, such as distributors and manufacturers, consume this service to plan their inventory and production activities. As Figure 8-19 shows, the retailer publishes a service description and makes that description available to distributors and manufacturers. Developers in those companies write programs according to the Web service description.

To obtain sales data, the Web service programs of the distributor or manufacturer create a service request. Those Web service programs transmit that request to the service provider at the retailer's computer. The message goes to the retailer and is processed by the Web service programs. Those programs call the CRM application to read data in the CRM database. They then format a response in an XML document and send the response to the service consumer (the distributor or manufacturer).

Because of the standards, no joint development meetings or other coordination activities are required among the organizations to enable the use of these Web services. The developers are all working on the same page, so to speak. They all use the same Web services standards.

Web services not only provide cost savings for the development of interorganizational IS, but they also drastically reduce the time required to achieve operational capability. Furthermore, the use of Web services provides tremendous flexibility. A manufacturer, for example, can combine Web services from several different companies into a single application. The manufacturer can also readily change and adapt those combinations to meet new business requirements.

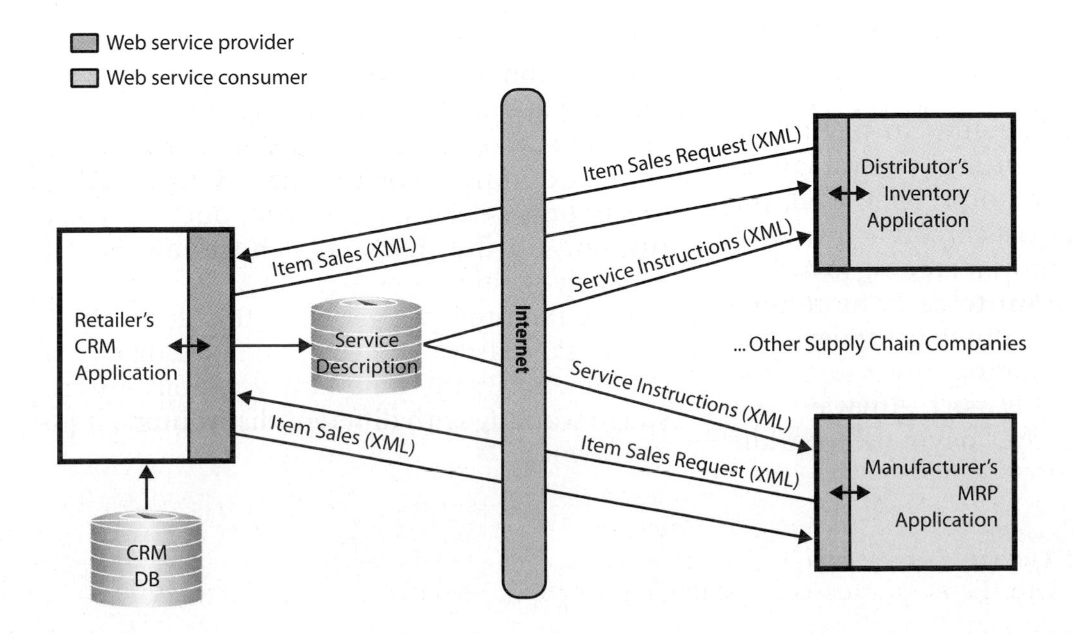

Figure 8-19
Example of Web Services for Sharing Sales Data

Opposing Forces

GUIDE

The Lawyer's Full-Employment Act

I don't think this supply chain profitability thing is likely to work the way it's described here. It sounds like some head-in-the-clouds idea dreamed up by economists.

"First of all, how many products does REI sell? Thousands. And how many distributors does it have? Dozens. How would the company ever know that outages on boots were limiting sales of ski packages? It's got 40-some stores, all over the United States; a Web storefront; and telephone sales. How would REI ever know about patterns like that?

"But, for the sake of argument, let's say it did know. Then what? Suppose REI figured out that every time it runs out of ski boots, on average it loses some number of ski-package sales. Pick any number—say, one out of five. And say that REI makes $200 profit on a ski package. So every time it runs out of ski boots, let's say it loses $40 in profit.

"Knowing that, REI decides to pay a premium to the boot distributor to carry a larger-than-normal inventory of boots. First of all, you wonder why REI doesn't just carry that inventory itself. But anyway, somehow it is going to make a payment to the distributor to carry more boot inventory. All of that, of course, supposes that the distributor is managing inventory that closely, which it probably isn't. Anyway, now REI is going to recoup that payment from the ski, binding, and pole distributor. How—with a check?

"Let's just abandon all sense of reason and say, 'OK, that's what they're going to do.' Now REI has to negotiate an agreement among at least three companies, and probably more if you include the manufacturers. Know what it's like to negotiate an agreement among multiple companies? It takes forever. Just setting up the meetings is tough because everyone's busy, and then the discussions start! And every time you add another company, the required time doubles, at least.

"But, let's suppose that somehow REI does get an agreement. Then what happens? The parties take it to the lawyers. And what may have started as a simple, 1-page agreement becomes a booklet, maybe 20 or 30 pages. Of course none of the people who are trying to get the agreement know 'legalese,' so they have to take it to *their lawyers*, and voilà, you've an ego contest among lawyers and law firms. All of this not only delays the project, but now you're running up the price tag. Those lawyers are expensive.

"By the time you get all of this done, it's no longer ski season, and you're not selling any ski equipment. By the time next year rolls around, you're working with different distributors. It just won't work." ■

Discussion Questions

1. Do you agree that it is unlikely that REI will know that outages of ski boots are limiting sales of ski packages? Describe three different ways the company could find out.
2. Products vary in the contribution that they make to profit. Explain how organizations could use profitability to choose which products they intend to examine for supply chain profitability.
3. Why do you think REI might choose not to carry a larger inventory of ski boots rather than asking the distributor to do so? Under what circumstances would it make sense for REI to carry the larger inventory itself?
4. Suppose REI wants the distributor to carry a larger inventory. Other than sending the distributor a check, how could REI induce the distributor to do so?
5. What steps could these companies take to reduce the time, labor, and expense required to obtain an agreement that would increase supply chain profitability?

Problem-Solving

GUIDE

Interorganizational Information Exchange

Interorganizational information systems—information systems that connect two or more organizations—require collaborative agreements among independent companies and organizations. Such agreements can be successful only if all parties have a clear idea of the goals, benefits, costs, and risks of working together. The creation of collaborative agreements requires many joint meetings in which the parties make their goals and objectives clear and decide how best to share information and other resources.

During your career, you may be asked to participate is such meetings. You should understand a few basic guidelines before participating.

First, when you meet with employees of another company, realize that you must apply stronger limits on your conversation than when you meet with employees in your own firm. For all you know, the company you are meeting with may become your strongest competitor. In general, you should assume that whatever you say to an employee of another company could be general knowledge in your industry the next day.

Of course, the goal of such meetings is to develop a collaborative relationship, and you cannot accomplish that goal without saying something. The best strategy, however, is to reveal exactly what you must reveal and no more.

Before you meet with another company, you and your team should have a clear and common understanding of the purpose of the meeting. Your team needs to agree beforehand on the topics that are to be addressed and those that are to be avoided. Relationships often develop in stages: Two companies meet, establish one level of understanding, meet again with another level of understanding, and so forth, feeling one another out on the way to some type of relationship.

You may be asked to sign a nondisclosure agreement. Such agreements are contracts that stipulate the responsibilities of each party in protecting the other's proprietary information. Such agreements vary in length; some are a page long and some are 30 pages long. You need to understand the policy of your organization with regard to such agreements before the meeting starts. Sometimes, companies exchange their standard nondisclosure agreements before the meeting so that the respective legal departments can review and approve the agreements ahead of time.

In your remarks, stick to the purpose of the meeting. Avoid conversations about your company or about third parties that do not relate to the meeting topic. You never know the agenda of the other party; you never know what other companies they are meeting; and you never know what other information about your company they may want.

Realize that a meeting isn't over until it's over. The meeting is still underway in the hallway waiting for the elevator. It's still underway at lunch. And it's still underway as you share a cab to the airport. By the way, the only two topics in an elevator should be the weather and the number of the floor you want. Don't embarrass yourself or the employees of the other company by discussing in a public place anything other than the weather.

All of these suggestions may seem paranoid, but even paranoid companies have competitors. There is simply no reason, other than carelessness or stupidity, to discuss topics with another company that do not relate to the matter at hand. Your company will assume enough risk just setting up the interorganizational system. Don't add to that risk by making gratuitous comments about your or any other company. ■

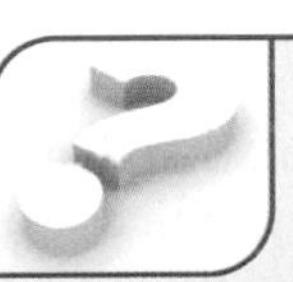

Discussion Questions

1. Suppose you are asked to attend a meeting with your suppliers to discuss the sharing of your sales data. You have no idea as to the specific purpose of the meeting, why you were invited, or what will be expected of you. What should you do?
2. Suppose you flew 1,500 miles for a meeting and at the start of the meeting the other company asks you to sign a nondisclosure statement. You knew nothing about the need to sign such an agreement. What do you do?
3. Some companies have an open, democratic style with lots of collaboration and open discussion. Others are closed and authoritarian, and employees wait to be told what to do. Describe what will happen when employees from two such companies meet. What can be done to improve the situation?
4. Suppose during lunch an employee of another company asks you, "What are you all doing about XML Web services?" Assume that this topic has little to do with the purpose of your meeting. You think about it and decide that it doesn't seem too risky to respond, so you say, "Not much." What information have you conveyed by this statement? What is a better way to respond to the question?
5. Suppose you are in a joint meeting and you are asked, "So who else are you working with on this problem?" Describe guidelines you could use in deciding how to answer this question.
6. Explain the statement, "A meeting isn't over until it's over." How might this statement pertain to other meetings—say, a job interview?

ACTIVE REVIEW

Use this Active Review to verify that you understand the ideas and concepts that answer the chapter's study questions.

Q1 How do companies use e-commerce?

Define *e-commerce* and name and explain categories of e-commerce companies. Explain the terms B2C, B2B, and B2G. Explain differences between merchant and nonmerchant companies. Give examples of each. Explain how e-commerce improves market efficiency and describe economic factors that disfavor e-commerce.

Q2 What technology is needed for e-commerce?

Explain the purpose of each of the elements in Figure 8-5. Describe the difference between HTTP and HTML. Trace the online purchase of a basket of goods, using Figure 8-5 as a guide. Explain the purpose of tags and attributes.

Q3 Why is Web 2.0 important to business?

How did Amazon.com usher in Web 2.0? Explain the term *software as a service* and how it differs from traditional software licensing. Explain the difference in betas between the Web 2.0 and traditional software publishing. Describe the difference in business models between Web 2.0 and traditional software companies. Explain the statement, "If a product requires advertising, then it is not Web 2.0." Explain how use increases value in Web 2.0 and define *mashup*. In what way are Web 2.0 interfaces organic? How does rights management differ between Web 2.0 and traditional software? Summarize three major ways that non-Internet companies can use Web 2.0. Explain the difference between Google's Ad Word and Ad Sense.

Q4 How can information systems enhance supply chain performance?

Define *supply chain* and give an example. Name the four drivers of supply chain performance. Explain the difference between supply chain profitability and organizational profitability. Give an example, other than one in this text, that demonstrates why the two are not maximized in the same way. Explain the bullwhip effect and describe how it can be eliminated.

Q5 How can information systems support supplier relationship management?

Sketch the relationships among SRM, CRM, MRP, MRP II, and ERP. Define SRM and name the three SRM business processes that IS must support. Explain the relationship between SRM and CRM.

Q6 How do organizations exchange data?

Explain how each of the technologies in Figure 8-17 can be used to exchange data and documents. Define EDI and explain how it can be used for the supply chain in Figure 8-10. Describe three problems with HTML and explain how XML fixes these problems. Explain the role of an XML schema document. Describe how industry-standard XML schema documents can be used to facilitate interorganizational data exchange.

Q7 How can organizations connect computer programs?

Using the example of health care, give an example of the need for distributed computing. Explain the term *proprietary system*, and describe how such systems are designed and implemented. Summarize the disadvantages of proprietary systems. Explain the key concept of *service-oriented architecture (SOA)*. Explain how XML Web services might be used for your health-care distributed computing example.

KEY TERMS AND CONCEPTS

Ad Words 302
Ad Sense 302
Attribute 298
Auction 292
Beta program 300
Browser 295
Bullwhip effect 306
Business-to-business (B2B) e-commerce 291
Business-to-consumer (B2C) e-commerce 291
Business-to-government (B2G) e-commerce 292
Channel conflict 294
Clearinghouse 292
Commerce server 295
Database tier 295
Disintermediation 293
Distributed computing 315
E-commerce 297
Electronic Data Interchange (EDI) 312
EDI over Internet 312
Electronic exchange 292
eXtensible markup language (XML) 313
Google's My Maps 301

Hyperlink 297
Hypertext Markup Language (HTML) 297
Hypertext transfer protocol (HTTP) 295
Mashup 301
Merchant companies 291
Nonmerchant companies 291
Price conflict 294
Price elasticity 293
Proprietary 315
Remote computing 315
Server tier 295
Service description 316
Service-oriented architecture (SOA) 316
Social networking 302
Software as a service 299
Supplier relationship management (SRM) 308
Supply chain 304
Supply chain profitability 306
Tag 297
Three-tier architecture 295
User tier 295
Web 2.0 299
Web farm 296
Web page 295
Web server 295
Web storefront 291
World Wide Web Consortium (W3C) 314
Viral marketing 300
XML schema 314
XML Web services 316

USING YOUR KNOWLEDGE

1. Suppose you are a manufacturer of high-end consumer kitchen appliances, and you are about to bring out a new line of mixers that will make an existing model obsolete. Assume you have 500 mixers of that existing model in finished-goods inventory. Describe three different strategies for using an electronic auction for unloading that inventory. Which strategy do you recommend?
2. Search the Microsoft, Oracle, and SAP Web sites for SRM applications. Compare the features and functions you find to those described in this chapter. Are these products commodities, or do they have different features and functions? Is their use of terminology consistent? If not, describe important inconsistencies. Explain why none of these companies are Web 2.0 companies.
3. Visit *http://zillow.com*. Enter the address of someone's home (your parents'?) and obtain an appraisal of it. Check out the appraised values of your neighbors' homes. Do you think this site violates anyone's privacy? Why or why not? Find and describe features that demonstrate that Zillow.com is a Web 2.0 company. Explain why this site might be considered a threat by traditional real estate companies. How might real estate agents use this site to market their services? How might real estate brokers (those who own agencies) use this site to advantage?
4. This chapter contends that over time XML Web services will replace EDI. Search the Web for evidence that either supports or contradicts this contention. Do you find applications that are being converted from EDI to Web services? Are EDI vendors adding Web services applications to their product suites? On a site for a vendor such as SAP, do you see more evidence of EDI or of Web services features and functions?
5. Search the Web for case histories on the use of Web services and supply chain management. You can start by searching for the terms *supply chain* and *Web services*. See where that takes you. Find an article about a major company's use of Web services in the supply chain. Summarize the experience of that company.
6. Amazon.com makes it exceedingly easy for developers to use its Web services. Why do you think Amazon.com does that? What competitive advantage does it receive? Describe another B2C business, in another industry, that might achieve similar benefits by developing an easily used Web service.

COLLABORATION EXERCISES AND CASES

Collaborate with a group of students on the following exercises. Recall from Chapter 2 that collaboration is more than cooperation because it involves iteration and feedback. Post a document, a discussion item, a wiki item, or an idea and obtain feedback from your team members. Similarly, read the ideas of others and comment on them. Try to innovate in both the process by which you collaborate and the work product that you create. Avoid face-to-face meetings. Instead, use collaborative software such as Google Docs & Spreadsheets, Microsoft Groove, or Microsoft SharePoint to facilitate your ideas.

1. Reread the *E-Commerce in Practice* box on page 299. In this exercise, you will compare and evaluate these two publications' strategies for using e-commerce.

   a. These two very similar publications have taken two different approaches for using the Internet to gain revenue from their archives. Describe what you believe are the advantages and disadvantages of each approach.

b. Visit *http://woodenboat.com* and *http://finewoodworking.com*. What do you think is the competitive strategy of these two publications? Justify your response.

c. Given your answer to part b, does competitive strategy explain why they have chosen different ways of using the Internet to gain revenue from their archives?

d. Has *Wooden Boat* chosen its method because it has a store? Is it using its index as bait to attract prospects to the store? Is this technique necessarily any better than a subscription? Why or why not?

e. Under what conditions do you think the *Wooden Boat* strategy is superior?

f. Is *Fine Woodworking* in danger of losing subscriptions to its paper magazine to the online magazine? Does it matter? Might *Fine Woodworking* be attempting to move its readership to an online publication?

g. Under what conditions do you think the *Fine Woodworking* strategy is superior?

2. In this exercise, you will be asked to apply the philosophy and techniques of Web 2.0 to a small business. Use the guidelines in the *Innovation in Practice* box on page 303 to spur your creativity.

Sundog Expeditions (*http://sundogexpeditions.com*) provides river-rafting adventures in Idaho, Oregon, and Alaska. As you might expect, the river-expedition industry is highly competitive. The barrier to entry is low, and many adventure-oriented people use river rafting as a way to make a living doing what they love.

Competitive strategies in this industry are near-perfect examples of Porter's five competitive forces model. Some companies compete on the basis of price for rivers worldwide, whereas others compete on price for certain regions or rivers. Some companies differentiate on quality of food, type of boat (e.g., raft, paddle boat, dory), or some other factor. Of the differentiated companies, some compete worldwide and some compete on particular locations (certain rivers and regions).

Sundog Expeditions is a small company that has chosen a differentiation strategy within the Oregon, Idaho, and Alaska region. The company differentiates itself partly as one of the few rafting companies that offer trips using hard-sided dory boats. But the major differentiation factor for Sundog Expeditions is the quality of the relationships it develops with its customers. Sundog's guides are intelligent, experienced, interesting people who sincerely enjoy their customers and their work. Many of its guides have advanced degrees in biology, history, and other topics relevant to river rafting and outdoor adventures. Guides are part-time employees; keeping the guides happy and satisfied is important to successful implementation of the company's strategy.

The lion's share of Sundog's revenue comes from word-of-mouth and repeat business. Sundog Expeditions would like to increase word-of-mouth using viral marketing and other Web 2.0 principles.

In this exercise, you will be asked to apply Web 2.0 technology and philosophy to further advance Sundog Expedition's competitive strategy.

a. Explain how Sundog Expeditions could advertise using Google Ad Words. In general terms, describe a strategy for changing word bid prices to increase the return on advertising expense.

b. Explain how Sundog Expeditions could earn revenue via Google's Ad Sense. Do you recommend this source of revenue? Why or why not?

c. Using the Web, investigate Web 2.0 advertising vendors other than Google. Compare the best such alternative you find to Google Ad Words and recommend one of the two vendors.

d. Using the suggestions in the *Innovation in Practice* box on page 303, do the following.

(1) Describe four different ways that Sundog Expeditions could use social networking to further implement its competitive strategy.

(2) Describe four different ways that Sundog Expeditions could use mashups to further implement its competitive strategy.

e. Select the three best ideas in your answer to part d. Describe criteria for making the selection and score your ideas based on those criteria.

f. Like most small companies, Sundog Expeditions carefully manages its cash. Explain, at a high level, why you think the ideas in your answer to part e are worth the investment of this critical resource.

g. If you owned Sundog Expeditions, would you implement any of your ideas in part e? Why or why not?

APPLICATION EXERCISES

1. Assume you have been asked to create a spreadsheet to help make a buy-versus-lease decision for the servers on your organization's Web farm. Assume that you are considering the servers for a 5-year period, but you do not know exactly how many servers you will need. Initially, you know you will need 5 servers, but you

might need as many as 50, depending on the success of your organization's e-commerce activity.

a. For the buy-alternative calculations, set up your spreadsheet so that you can enter the base price of the server hardware, the price of all software, and a maintenance expense that is some percentage of the hardware price. Assume that the percent you enter covers both hardware and software maintenance. Also assume that each server has a 3-year life, after which it has no value. Assume straight-line depreciation for computers used less than 3 years, and that at the end of the 5 years you can sell the computers you have used for less than 3 years for their depreciated value. Also assume that your organization pays 2 percent interest on capital expenses. Assume the servers cost $5,000 each, and the needed software costs $750. Assume that the maintenance expense varies from 2 to 7 percent.
b. For the lease-alternative calculations, assume that the leasing vendor will lease the same computer hardware as you can purchase. The lease includes all the software you need as well as all maintenance. Set up your spreadsheet so that you can enter various lease costs, which vary according to the number of years of the lease (1, 2, or 3). Assume the cost of a 3-year lease is $285 per machine per month, a 2-year lease is $335 per machine per month, and a 1-year lease is $415 per machine per month. Also, the lessor offers a 5 percent discount if you lease from 20 to 30 computers and a 10 percent discount if you lease from 31 to 50 computers.
c. Using your spreadsheet, compare the costs of buy versus lease under the following situations. (Assume you either buy or lease. You cannot lease some and buy some.) Make assumptions as necessary and state those assumptions.

    (1) Your organization requires 20 servers for 5 years.
    (2) Your organization requires 20 servers for the first 2 years and 40 servers for the next 3 years.
    (3) Your organization requires 20 servers for the first 2 years, 40 servers for the next 2 years, and 50 servers for the last year.
    (4) Your organization requires 10 servers the first year, 20 servers the second year, 30 servers the third year, 40 servers the fourth year, and 50 servers the last year.
    (5) For the previous case, does the cheaper alternative change if the cost of the servers is $4,000? If it is $8,000?

2. Assume that you have been given the task of compiling evaluations that your company's purchasing agents make of their vendors. Each month, every purchasing agent evaluates all of the vendors that he or she has worked with in the past month on three factors: price, quality, and responsiveness. Assume the ratings are from 1 to 5, with 5 being the best. Because your company has hundreds of vendors and dozens of purchasing agents, you decide to use Access to compile the results.

a. Create a database with three tables: VENDOR (*VendorNumber, Name, Contact*), PURCHASER (*EmpNumber, Name, Email*), and RATING (*EmpNumber, VendorNumber, Month, Year, PriceRating, QualityRating, ResponsivenessRating*). Assume that *VendorNumber* and *EmpNumber* are the keys of VENDOR and PURCHASER, respectively. Decide what you think is the appropriate key for RATING.
b. Create appropriate relationships.
c. Go to this text's companion Web site and import the data in the Excel file **Ch08Ex02**. Note that data for Vendor, Purchaser, and Rating are stored in three separate worksheets.
d. Create a query that shows the names of all vendors and their average scores.
e. Create a query that shows the names of all employees and their averages scores. *Hint:* In this and in part f, you will need to use the *Group By* function in your query.
f. Create a parameterized query that you can use to obtain the minimum, maximum, and average ratings on each criterion for a particular vendor. Assume you will enter *VendorName* as the parameter.
g. Using the information created by your queries, what conclusions can you make about vendors or purchasers?

CASE STUDY 8

You, Inc.

Interorganizational information systems enable small businesses to avoid the time and expense of building infrastructure, thus reducing capital requirements and shortening the time to market. In particular, they can help YOU. Consider the following business opportunity:

People often pay more for new items on eBay than they would pay if they shopped for bargains on the Internet. Either they do not like to e-shop, or perhaps they become entangled in the excitement of an auction, lose a bid, and decide to pay the *BuyItNow* price for a similar item in another auction. Whatever the reason, there is often an inefficiency in the flow of price information among eBay users.

Consider that inefficiency as a business opportunity for your own small business. Assume you are willing to invest no more than $700 in a computer, $49 per month for a DSL line, and a few hours of your time each day. How many of the value-chain activities can you outsource using interorganizational information systems?

Begin with market research. Using your Internet connection to the Web, you can investigate auctions, product categories, and related market segments. Doing this work saves hiring market research firms to produce this information for you. You do not need to conduct extensive and expensive market surveys; the information you need is on the Internet. Suppose you notice that there are opportunities on the sale of high-end motorcycle parts. The Baby Boomers are reliving their childhoods and now have considerable disposable income to spend. They cannot stand to lose an auction and will pay to get what they want, right now. You decide to focus on this opportunity.

Using the Internet, you find sources for motorcycle parts. Sourcing is a typical supply-chain activity; and again, by using the Internet, you have avoided hiring someone else to do this work for you. You search for sites that offer the products you want, have free shipping, and (if possible) for which you do not need to pay taxes.

When you find an item offered at a bargain price, you set up an auction for that item on eBay. You have not yet purchased the item; you just know where you can buy it. You set a price and the terms of the auction so that, at whatever price the item sells, you will make some profit (after deducting the cost of the auction). Avoiding the expense of hiring a photo team to take photos, you download pictures of the item from your vendor and copy those photos into your auction. Your only financial exposure if the item does not sell is the cost of the auction.

Suppose the item sells. You then buy it from the vendor you have located, paying for it using PayPal or a credit card, and you request the vendor to ship the item directly to your customer, a process called *drop shipping*. If you pay with a credit card, it is possible you will receive payment from your customer before you pay for the item you sold. Because the item is new, and because you sell only high-quality items, all service and support are handled by the manufacturer.

Review this scenario in terms of Porter's value chain model. You did market research, but you outsourced all of the data-gathering activities to eBay, PriceGrabber, and so on. You set up the auction on eBay, and thus outsourced the sales infrastructure to eBay. You did the product-sourcing yourself, but again, you had considerable help from the Internet. Because you drop-shipped the item to your customer, you outsourced all inventory, operations, and shipping activities to that vendor. If the customer pays you before you pay your credit card, you can even earn interest on the customer's money. You outsourced service and support to the manufacturer.

Consider support activities: Because you avoided building infrastructure, you have only one part-time employee, yourself; you have no payroll or other compensation needs. You might want insurance, but if you sell enough using eBay you can buy life and medical

Baby Boomer Bike Market

insurance from eBay at attractive terms, so you can outsource those functions as well.

Consider accounting: eBay, PayPal, your credit card company, and the vendor will do most of the work. All you need to do is maintain records to track your income for tax reporting. You can even pay your taxes online if you choose. All of this is possible only because of the prevalence of interorganizational information systems!

Questions

1. Investigate auctions on eBay and, for any category of product in which you have knowledge or interest, compare selling prices to prices of new goods from e-commerce sites. Attempt to find one or more products in which the item sold on eBay costs more than if it had been purchased from a vendor. State the price differential(s). If you find no such products, list the products' eBay prices and vendor prices for five of the products you investigated.
2. Go to *http://ebay.com* and learn how eBay charges for its auctions. You have many options to choose from; select the option(s) that you believe will be best for selling goods using this strategy. Explain why you think that option is the best.
3. Using price comparison sites (such as PriceGrabber, CNET.com, or Froogle), identify three sources for products that you identified in question 1. If you did not find any qualifying products in that question, identify sources for some product in which you have an interest. Seek sources that provide free shipping and to which you do not need to pay taxes.
4. Either by yourself or with a group of classmates, find some product from your answer in question 1 that seems to you to be a good bargain. Set up an auction for that item on eBay, with terms that will enable you to make some profit, even if the product sells at the lowest price.
5. Run the auction. If you make some profit, celebrate, and run it again. If not, state why you did not make a profit and describe what you would do differently to earn some profit.

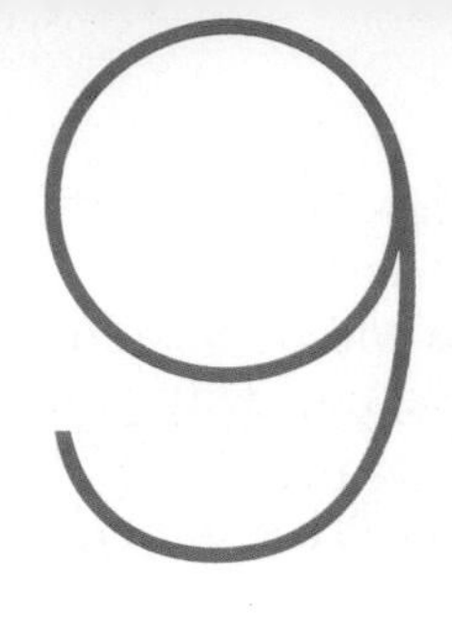

Business Intelligence Systems

STUDY QUESTIONS

Q1 Why do organizations need business intelligence?

Q2 What business intelligence systems are available?

Q3 What are typical reporting applications?

Q4 What are typical data-mining applications?

Q5 What is the purpose of data warehouses and data marts?

Q6 What are typical knowledge-management applications?

Q7 How are business intelligence applications delivered?

Meet Deb Kama

My favorite business books: *Learning to Fly: Practical Lessons from One of the World's Leading Knowledge Companies* by C. Collison and G. Parcell; and *The Fifth Discipline: The Art & Practice of the Learning Organization* by P. Senge

My very first job: Cattle ranch hand.

A guiding principle: Listen, ask questions, and if necessary, gently rock the boat.

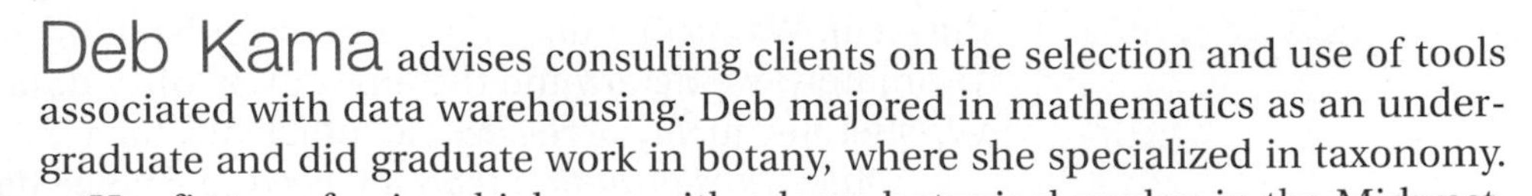

Deb Kama advises consulting clients on the selection and use of tools associated with data warehousing. Deb majored in mathematics as an undergraduate and did graduate work in botany, where she specialized in taxonomy. Her first professional job was with a large botanical garden in the Midwest. From there, she moved to a major financial-services firm in St. Louis where she served as a metadata specialist, data modeler, and data architect for various firm-priority projects. She speaks about the use and management of metadata for data warehouses.

On her early career:

"At the Botanical Garden I was working on a project to describe every plant in North America. We estimated it would take about 32 volumes to publish our survey, and when we looked at the timeline, we realized we'd all be dead before it was done. So, we looked at information technology to help produce the volumes more quickly. However, our work was too far removed from mainstream botany, and in a funding crunch, the department was abolished.

"I interviewed for an IT job—though I knew next to nothing about information technology, and I said so. I did know, however, how to model data. The company was rebuilding its trading system and building a data warehouse for the financial-services industry, and on the basis of my data-modeling skills, they hired me as a data architect."

On patterns in financial services:

"The financial-services industry was totally foreign to me, and so I interviewed people and examined as many documents as I could. Using the modeling skills I'd honed in taxonomy, I produced a model of trading processes, how the markets are used, and the rules that govern trading.

"I began to view financial services as a series of patterns. Every business likes to think it is unique, but it is not. Financial-services companies do the same things, follow the same patterns, as other companies, though there might be differences in terminology. As a data architect, my job was to identify the patterns and document them for use when constructing the data warehouse."

On the flow of data into a data warehouse:

"Today, I advise clients on the selection and use of tools for preparing data for a data warehouse. I concentrate on data-modeling tools, data-profiling tools, and data-transformation tools. Data architects use *data-modeling tools* to record how one particular type of data relates to another type. (Author's note: The entity-relationship model in Chapter 5 is an example of a data-modeling tool.)

"*Data-profiling tools* are like microscopes for looking at data. Imagine you're given a file of terabytes of financial data. You need some way to examine that data. If, for example, a field is numeric, you might want to know the mean, standard deviation, range, or mode, and you might want a graphical frequency

What I want to learn next:
To play slack-key guitar.

Don't do this to me in an interview:
Ask what are my three strengths.

One characteristic of a superior employee:
Lifelong learner—be adaptable, open to change, display initiative, and pursue opportunities for improvement.

diagram. We profile data not only to understand it but also to assess its quality. Ultimately, we determine the amount of 'dirty data' in a data set and then decide whether the quality of the data is sufficiently high for use in our warehouse.

"*Data-transformation tools* are used to change data from one format to another. A data-transformation tool would be used, for example, to roll up sales data from, say, sales by city to sales by state."

On the importance of metadata:

"The data warehousing process sounds a lot simpler than it is. Suppose we want to assess data that is supposed to be the color of something. How hard could that be? Well, how many different values of color do you find in a paint store? *Savory green, bone white, sagebrush opal,* etc. We store the allowed names for color as metadata—data about data. We then use the color metadata to assess the quality of data about paint products.

"Now, suppose you want to compare data from different stores—say, paint products from Lowe's and Home Depot. How does the *savory green* at Lowe's compare to the *savory green* at Home Depot? Are they the same? What if Home Depot doesn't have a color named *savory green* but has one called *dusty green* that is close in color? Somehow, we have to convert Home Depot's *dusty green* into Lowe's *savory green*.

On the storage of metadata:

"We can solve the conversion problem using a data-transformation tool. But the next question is, what do we do with that metadata when we're done? Often, nothing, and that, to me, is a tragedy. That metadata has value, and to leave it buried in some data transformation file is wasteful.

"We have a metadata silo problem. At the data level, people talk about information systems silos—you know, the Sales department has customer data in one system, Marketing has much of that same data in its systems, Operations has customer data in some other system. The result is a lack of data integrity, inefficiency, and an inability to create a complete picture of the customer from the data we have. So organizations develop customer relationship management systems with integrated databases.

"Well, we need to do the same thing for metadata. We need to store it in metadata databases so we can make it available to those who need it. In the case of the color conversion, that metadata would be available to any architect, analyst, or programmer who needed it. Without a metadata database, people construct their own metadata because the right hand doesn't know what the left hand has done."

On the power of metadata:

"Organizations and people can gain incredible leverage by working at the metadata level. Once I understood the basic patterns in financial-services trading, I understood how the various entities relate, and I could readily imagine the consequences of changes in rules or in the introduction of new trading relationships.

"Go back to the color problem. Suppose we've modeled the metadata and classified colors as *cool, hot,* or *neutral.* Using the structure of the metadata, we can analyze sales data for patterns using those categories and learn, say, that sales of *cool-colored* products are plummeting. Early knowledge of that pattern will give us a competitive advantage."

On the future:

"Would I recommend this field? Yes, definitely. Metadata is the future for information workers. In my experience, many information systems are commodities. Commodities can always be outsourced, so that management can concentrate on the crucial driving factors in their businesses. But people and organizations that understand metadata work on another level entirely. They can use the data generated by the commoditized IS to recognize patterns, and they gain a competitive advantage because they perceive changes and opportunities more readily and more quickly."

CHAPTER PREVIEW

The information systems described in Chapters 7 and 8 generate enormous amounts of data. Most of these data are used for operational purposes, such as tracking orders, inventories, payables, and so forth. These operational data have a potential windfall: They contain patterns, relationships, clusters, and other information that can facilitate management, especially planning and forecasting. Business intelligence systems produce such information from operational data.

In addition to information in data, an even more important source of information is employees themselves. Employees come to the organization with expertise, and as they gain experience in the organization they add to that expertise. Vast amounts of collective knowledge exist in every organization's employees. How can that knowledge be shared? Knowledge-management applications address this need, and we will conclude this chapter with a description of the purpose, features, and functions of these applications.

This chapter surveys the most common business intelligence and knowledge-management applications, discusses the need and purpose for data warehouses, and explains how business intelligence applications are delivered to users as business intelligence systems.

Q1 Why Do Organizations Need Business Intelligence?

Today, data communications and data storage are essentially free. Consequently, enormous amounts of data are created and stored every day. A study done at the University of California at Berkeley[1] found that a total of 403 petabytes of new data were created in 2002. That number has grown exponentially; it has been estimated that nearly 2,500 **petabytes**, or 2.5 **exabytes**, of data have been generated in 2007.

The terms petabyte and exabyte are defined in Figure 9-1 (next page). As shown there, the 2.5 exabytes generated in 2007 is equivalent to half the total number of words ever spoken by humans. Or, in slightly more comprehensible terms, 2.5 exabytes of data is 125 times the contents of *all* U.S. research libraries.That is indeed a lot of data, and it represents only the amount generated in 2007!

Somewhere in all that data is **business intelligence**—information containing patterns, relationships, and trends. But that information needs to be found and produced. For example, somewhere in the more than 15+ terabytes of data in the Verizon customer database is evidence that some customers are about to change cell phone companies. Somewhere in that data is evidence that a different pricing scheme would generate more revenue; somewhere in that data is evidence that the district manager in, say, Chicago, is doing a better job than any other district manager. All of that information is in there. The question is: How can Verizon get it out?

Businesses use business intelligence systems to process this immense ocean of data; to produce patterns, relationships, and other forms of information; and to deliver that information on a timely basis to users who need it.

Read the Business Intelligence in Practice *box on page 332 for a description of a typical situation to which business intelligence systems could be applied.*

[1]"How Much Information, 2003," *http://sims.berkeley.edu/research/projects/how-much-info-2003* (accessed May 2005).

Figure 9-1
How Big Is an Exabyte?

Source: Used with permission of Peter Lyman and Hal R. Varian, University of California at Berkeley.

Kilobyte (KB)	*1,000 bytes OR 10^3 bytes* 2 Kilobytes: A typewritten page 100 Kilobytes: A low-resolution photograph
Megabyte (MB)	*1,000,000 bytes OR 10^6 bytes* 1 Megabyte: A small novel OR a 3.5-inch floppy disk 2 Megabytes: A high-resolution photograph 5 Megabytes: The complete works of Shakespeare 10 Megabytes: A minute of high-fidelity sound 100 Megabytes: One meter of shelved books 500 Megabytes: A CD-ROM
Gigabyte (GB)	*1,000,000,000 bytes OR 10^9 bytes* 1 Gigabyte: A pickup truck filled with books 20 Gigabytes: A good collection of the works of Beethoven 100 Gigabytes: A library floor of academic journals
Terabyte (TB)	*1,000,000,000,000 bytes OR 10^{12} bytes* 1 Terabyte: 50,000 trees made into paper and printed 2 Terabytes: An academic research library 10 Terabytes: The print collections of the U.S. Library of Congress 400 Terabytes: National Climactic Data Center (NOAA) database
Petabyte (PB)	*1,000,000,000,000,000 bytes OR 10^{15} bytes* 1 Petabyte: Three years of EOS data (2001) 2 Petabytes: All U.S. academic research libraries 20 Petabytes: Production of hard-disk drives in 1995 200 Petabytes: All printed material
Exabyte (EB)	*1,000,000,000,000,000,000 bytes OR 10^{18} bytes* 2 Exabytes: Total volume of information generated in 1999 5 Exabytes: All words ever spoken by human beings

BUSINESS INTELLIGENCE IN PRACTICE

CARBON CREEK GARDENS

Mary Keeling owns and operates Carbon Creek Gardens, a retailer of trees, garden plants, perennial and annual flowers, and bulbs. “The Gardens,” as her customers call it, also sells bags of soil, fertilizer, small garden tools, and garden sculptures. Mary started the business 14 years ago when she bought a section of land that, because of water drainage, was unsuited for residential development. With hard work and perseverance, Mary has created a warm and inviting environment with a unique and carefully selected inventory of plants. The Gardens has become a favorite nursery for serious gardeners in her community.

“The problem,” she says, “is that I've grown so large, I've lost track of my customers. The other day, I ran into Tootsie Swan at the grocery store, and I realized I hadn't seen her in ages. I said something like, ‘Hi, Tootsie, I haven't seen you for a while,’ and that statement unleashed an angry torrent from her. It turns out that she'd been in over a year ago and had wanted to return a plant. One of my part-time employees waited on her and had apparently insulted her, or at least didn't give her the service she wanted. So, she decided not to come back to The Gardens.

“Tootsie was one of my best customers. I'd lost her, and I didn't even know it! That really frustrates me. Is it inevitable that as I get bigger, I lose track of my customers? I don't think so. Somehow, I have to find out when regular customers aren't coming around. Had I known Tootsie had stopped shopping with us, I'd have called her to see what was going on. I need customers like her.

"I've got all sorts of data in my sales database. It seems like the information I need is in there, but how do it get it out?”

Mary Keeling can benefit from the knowledge in this chapter. You and a group of your classmates will have an opportunity to show how in Collaboration Exercise 1, page 365.

Q2 What Business Intelligence Systems Are Available?

A **business intelligence (BI) system** is an information system that employs business intelligence tools to produce and deliver information. The characteristics of a particular BI system depend on the tool in use, so we will begin by categorizing such tools.

Business Intelligence Tools

A **business intelligence (BI) tool** is one or more computer programs that implement a particular BI technique. We can categorize BI tools in three ways: as reporting tools, as data-mining tools, and as knowledge-management tools.

Reporting tools are programs that read data from a variety of sources, process that data, format it into structured reports, and deliver those reports to the users who need them. The processing of the data is simple: Data are sorted and grouped, and simple totals and averages are calculated, as you will see. Reporting tools are used primarily for *assessment*. They are used to address questions like: What has happened in the past? What is the current situation? How does the current situation compare to the past?

Data-mining tools process data using statistical techniques, many of which are sophisticated and mathematically complex. We will explore data mining in some detail later in this chapter. For now, it is enough to say that *data mining* involves searching for patterns and relationships among data. In most cases, data-mining tools are used to make *predictions*. For example, we can use one form of analysis to compute the probability that a customer will default on a loan or the probability that a customer is likely to respond positively to a promotion. Another data-mining technique predicts products that tend to be purchased together. In one famous example, a data-mining analysis determined that customers who buy diapers are likely to buy beer.[2] That information enabled store managers to locate beer and diapers near each other in store displays.

Although reporting tools *tend to be* used to assess and data-mining tools *tend to be* used to predict, that distinction is not always true. A better way to distinguish between these two BI tools is that reporting tools use simple operations such as sorting, grouping, and summing, and data-mining tools use sophisticated statistical techniques.

Knowledge-management tools are used to store employee knowledge and to make that knowledge available to employees, customers, vendors, auditors, and others who need it. Knowledge-management tools differ from reporting and data-mining tools because the source of their data is human knowledge, rather than recorded facts and figures. Nonetheless, they are important BI tools.

Tools Versus Applications Versus Systems

It will be easier for you to understand this chapter if you distinguish among three terms. As stated, a *BI tool* is one or more computer programs. BI tools implement the logic of a particular procedure or process. A **business intelligence (BI) application** is the use of a tool on a particular type of data for a particular purpose. A *business intelligence (BI) system* is an information system having all five components that delivers the results of a BI application to users who need those results.

Consider an example. Later in this chapter, you will learn about a BI tool called *decision-tree analysis*. That *BI tool* can be used in a *BI application* to assess the risk of default on an existing loan. A *BI system* delivers the results of the decision-tree analysis on a particular loan to a banking officer, who then decides whether to buy or sell that loan and for what price.

Given this introduction, we will now illustrate applications of each type of BI tool.

---

[2]Michael J. A. Berry and Gordon Linoff, *Data Mining Techniques for Marketing, Sales, and Customer Support* (New York: John Wiley, 1997).

Q3 What Are Typical Reporting Applications?

A *reporting application* inputs data from one or more sources and applies a reporting tool to that data to produce information. The resulting information is subsequently delivered to users by a *reporting system*. This section describes operations commonly used by reporting tools and then illustrates two important reporting applications: RFM analysis and OLAP.

Basic Reporting Operations

Reporting tools produce information from data using five basic operations:

- Sorting
- Grouping
- Calculating
- Filtering
- Formatting

Consider the sales data shown in Figure 9-2. This list of raw data contains little or no information; it is just data. We can create information from this data by *sorting* by customer name, as shown in Figure 9-3. In this format, we can see that some customers have ordered more than once, and we can readily find their orders.

This is a step forward, but we can produce even more information by *grouping* the orders, as shown in Figure 9-4 (next page). Notice that the reporting tool not only

CustomerName	CustomerEmail	DateOfSale	Amount
Ashley, Jane	JA@somewhere.com	5 /5 /2007	$110
Corning,Sandra	KD@somewhereelse.com	7 /7 /2007	$375
Ching, Kam Hoong	KHC@somewhere.com	5 /17/2007	$55
Rikki, Nicole	GC@righthere.com	6 /19/2005	$155
Corning,Sandra	SC@somewhereelse.com	2 /4 /2006	$195
Scott, Rex	RS@somewhere.com	7 /15/2007	$56
Corovic,Jose	JC@somewhere.com	11/12/2007	$55
McGovern, Adrian	BL@righthere.com	11/12/2005	$47
Wei, Guang	GW@ourcompany.com	11/28/2006	$385
Dixon,Eleonor	ED@somewhere.com	5 /17/2007	$108
Lee,Brandon	BL@somewhereelse.com	5 /5 /2005	$74
Duong,Linda	LD@righthere.com	5 /17/2006	$485
Dixon, James T	JTD@somewhere.com	4 /3 /2006	$285
La Pierre,Anna	SG@righthere.com	9 /22/2007	$120
La Pierre,Anna	WS@somewhere.com	3 /14/2007	$48
La Pierre,Anna	TR@righthere.com	9 /22/2007	$580
Ryan, Mark	MR@somewhereelse.com	11/3 /2007	$42
Rikki, Nicole	MR@righthere.com	3 /14/2007	$175
Scott, Bryan	BS@somewhere.com	3 /17/2006	$145
Warrem, Jason	JW@ourcompany.com	5 /12/2007	$160
La Pierre,Anna	ALP@somewhereelse.com	3 /15/2006	$52
Angel, Kathy	KA@righthere.com	9 /15/2007	$195
La Pierre,Anna	JQ@somewhere.com	4 /12/2007	$44
Casimiro, Amanda	AC@somewhere.com	12/7 /2006	$52
McGovern, Adrian	AM@ourcompany.com	3 /17/2006	$52
Menstell,Lori Lee	LLM@ourcompany.com	10/18/2007	$72
La Pierre,Anna	DJ@righthere.com	12/7 /2006	$175
Nurul,Nicole	NN@somewhere.com	10/12/2007	$84
Menstell,Lori Lee	VB@ourcompany.com	9 /24/2007	$120
Pham,Mary	MP@somewhere.com	3 /14/2007	$38

Figure 9-2
Raw Sales Data

CustomerName	CustomerEmail	DateOfSale	Amount
Adams, James	JA3@somewhere.com	1/15/2007	$145
Angel, Kathy	KA@righthere.com	9/15/2007	$195
Ashley, Jane	JA@somewhere.com	5/5/2007	$110
Austin, James	JA7@somewhere.com	1/15/2006	$55
Bernard, Steven	SB@ourcompany.com	9/17/2007	$78
Casimiro, Amanda	AC@somewhere.com	12/7/2006	$52
Ching, Kam Hoong	KHC@somewhere.com	5/17/2007	$55
Corning,Sandra	KD@somewhereelse.com	7/7/2007	$375
Corning,Sandra	SC@somewhereelse.com	2/4/2006	$195
Corovic,Jose	JC@somewhere.com	11/12/2007	$55
Daniel, James	JD@somewhere.com	1/18/2007	$52
Dixon, James T	JTD@somewhere.com	4/3/2006	$285
Dixon,Eleonor	ED@somewhere.com	5/17/2007	$108
Drew, Richard	RD@righthere.com	10/3/2006	$42
Duong,Linda	LD@righthere.com	5/17/2006	$485
Garrett, James	JG@ourcompany.com	3/14/2007	$38
Jordan, Matthew	MJ@righthere.com	3/14/2006	$645
La Pierre,Anna	DJ@righthere.com	12/7/2006	$175
La Pierre,Anna	SG@righthere.com	9/22/2007	$120
La Pierre,Anna	TR@righthere.com	9/22/2007	$580
La Pierre,Anna	ALP@somewhereelse.com	3/15/2006	$52
La Pierre,Anna	JQ@somewhere.com	4/12/2007	$44
La Pierre,Anna	WS@somewhere.com	3/14/2007	$48
Lee,Brandon	BL@somewhereelse.com	5/5/2005	$74
Lunden,Haley	HL@somewhere.com	11/17/2004	$52
McGovern, Adrian	BL@righthere.com	11/12/2005	$47
McGovern, Adrian	AM@ourcompany.com	3/17/2006	$52
Menstell,Lori Lee	LLM@ourcompany.com	10/18/2007	$72
Menstell,Lori Lee	VB@ourcompany.com	9/24/2007	$120
Nurul,Nicole	NN@somewhere.com	10/12/2007	$84

Figure 9-3
Sales Data Sorted by Customer Name

CustomerName	NumOrders	TotalPurcha:
Adams, James	1	$145.00
Angel, Kathy	1	$195.00
Ashley, Jane	1	$110.00
Austin, James	1	$55.00
Bernard, Steven	1	$78.00
Casimiro, Amanda	1	$52.00
Ching, Kam Hoong	1	$55.00
Corning,Sandra	2	$570.00
Corovic,Jose	1	$55.00
Daniel, James	1	$52.00
Dixon, James T	1	$285.00
Dixon,Eleonor	1	$108.00
Drew, Richard	1	$42.00
Duong,Linda	1	$485.00
Garrett, James	1	$38.00
Jordan, Matthew	1	$645.00
La Pierre,Anna	6	$1,018.50
Lee,Brandon	1	$74.00
Lunden,Haley	1	$52.00
McGovern, Adrian	2	$99.00
Menstell,Lori Lee	2	$192.00
Nurul,Nicole	1	$84.00
Pham,Mary	1	$38.00
Redmond, Louise	1	$140.00
Rikki, Nicole	2	$330.00
Ryan, Mark	1	$42.00
Scott, Bryan	1	$145.00
Scott, Rex	1	$56.00
UTran,Diem Thi	1	$275.00
Warrem, Jason	1	$160.00

Figure 9-4
Sales Data, Sorted by Customer Name and Grouped by Number of Orders and Purchase Amount

Figure 9-5
Sales Data Filtered to Show Repeat Customers

Repeat Customers

NumOrders	CustomerName	TotalPurchases
6	La Pierre,Anna	$1,018.50
2	Corning,Sandra	$570.00
2	Rikki, Nicole	$330.00
2	Menstell,Lori Lee	$192.00
2	McGovern, Adrian	$99.00

grouped the orders but also *computed* the number of orders for each customer and the total purchase amount per customer.

Suppose we are interested in repeat customers. If so, we can *filter* the groups of orders to select only those customers that have two or more orders. The results of these operations are shown in Figure 9-5. The report in this figure not only has filtered the results, but it also has *formatted* them for easier understanding. Compare Figure 9-5 to 9-2. If your goal is to identify your best customers, the report in Figure 9-5 is far more useful and will save you considerable work.

The five operations just discussed may seem too simple to produce important results, but that is not the case. Reporting tools can produce incredibly interesting and insightful information. We will consider the application of two such tools next.

RFM Analysis

RFM analysis, a technique readily implemented using reporting tools, is used to analyze and rank customers according to their purchasing patterns.[3] RFM considers how *recently* (R) a customer has ordered, how *frequently* (F) a customer ordered, and how much *money* (M) the customer has spent.

To produce an RFM score, the RFM reporting tool first sorts customer purchase records by the date of their most recent (R) purchase. In a common form of this analysis, the tool then divides the customers into five groups and gives customers in each group a score of 1 to 5. The 20 percent of the customers having the most recent orders are given an R score of 1, the 20 percent of the customers having the next most recent orders are given an R score of 2, and so forth, down to the last 20 percent, who are given an R score of 5.

The tool then re-sorts the customers on the basis of how frequently they order. The 20 percent of the customers who order most frequently are given an F score of 1, the next 20 percent of most frequently ordering customers are given a score of 2, and so forth, down to the least frequently ordering customers, who are given an F score of 5.

Finally, the tool sorts the customers again according to the amount spent on their orders. The 20 percent who have ordered the most expensive items are given an M score of 1, the next 20 percent are given an M score of 2, and so forth, down to the 20 percent who spend the least, who are given an M score of 5.

Figure 9-6 shows sample RFM results. The first customer, Ajax, has ordered recently and orders frequently. Ajax's M score of 3 indicates, however, that it does not order the most expensive goods. From these scores, the sales team can conclude that Ajax is a good, regular customer, and that they should attempt to up-sell more expensive goods to Ajax.

---

[3]Arthur Middleton Hughes, "Boosting Response with RFM," *Marketing Tools*, May 1996. See also *http://dbmarketing.com*.

Customer	RFM Score
Ajax	1 1 3
Bloominghams	5 1 1
Caruthers	5 4 5
Davidson	3 3 3

Figure 9-6
Example of RFM Score Data

The second customer in Figure 9-6 could represent a problem. Bloominghams has not ordered in some time, but when it did order in the past it ordered frequently, and its orders were of the highest monetary value. This data suggests that Bloominghams might have taken its business to another vendor. Someone from the sales team should contact this customer immediately.

No one on the sales team should even think about the third customer, Caruthers. This company has not ordered for some time; it did not order frequently; and, when it did order, it bought the least-expensive items, and not many of them. Let Caruthers go to the competition; the loss will be minimal.

The last customer, Davidson, is right in the middle. Davidson is an OK customer, but probably no one in sales should spend much time with it. Perhaps sales can set up an automated contact system or use the Davidson account as a training exercise for an eager departmental assistant or intern.

Online Analytical Processing

Online analytical processing (OLAP), a second type of reporting tool, is more generic than RFM. OLAP provides the ability to sum, count, average, and perform other simple arithmetic operations on groups of data. The remarkable characteristic of OLAP reports is that they are dynamic. The viewer of the report can change the report's format, hence the term *online*.

An OLAP report has measures and dimensions. A **measure** is the data item of interest. It is the item that is to be summed or averaged or otherwise processed in the OLAP report. Total sales, average sales, and average cost are examples of measures. A **dimension** is a characteristic of a measure. Purchase date, customer type, customer location, and sales region are all examples of dimensions.

Figure 9-7 shows a typical OLAP report. Here, the measure is *Net Store Sales*, and the dimensions are *Product Family* and *Store Type*. This report shows how net store sales vary by product family and store type. Stores of type *Supermarket* sold a net of $36,189 worth of nonconsumable goods, for example.

A presentation like that in Figure 9-7 is often called an **OLAP cube**, or sometimes simply a *cube*. The reason for this term is that some software products show these displays using three axes, like a cube in geometry. The origin of the term is unimportant here, however. Just know that an *OLAP cube* and an *OLAP report* are the same thing.

Figure 9-7
OLAP Product Family by Store Type

	A	B	C	D	E	F	G
1							
2							
3	Store Sales Net	Store Type					
4	Product Family	Deluxe Supermarket	Gourmet Supermarket	Mid-Size Grocery	Small Grocery	Supermarket	Grand Total
5	Drink	$8,119.05	$2,392.83	$1,409.50	$685.89	$16,751.71	$29,358.98
6	Food	$70,276.11	$20,026.18	$10,392.19	$6,109.72	$138,960.67	$245,764.87
7	Non-Consumable	$18,884.24	$5,064.79	$2,813.73	$1,534.90	$36,189.40	$64,487.05
8	Grand Total	$97,279.40	$27,483.80	$14,615.42	$8,330.51	$191,901.77	$339,610.90

The OLAP report in Figure 9-7 was generated by SQL Server Analysis Services and is displayed in an Excel pivot table. The data were taken from a sample instructional database, called Food Mart, that is provided with SQL Server.

It is possible to display OLAP cubes in many ways besides with Excel. Some third-party vendors provide more extensive graphical displays. For more information about such products, check for OLAP vendors and products at the Data Housing Review at *http://dwreview.com/OLAP/index.html.*

As stated earlier, the distinguishing characteristic of an OLAP report is that the user can alter the format of the report. Figure 9-8 (next page) shows such an alteration. Here, the user added another dimension, *Store Country* and *Store State*, to the horizontal display. Product-family sales are now broken out by store location. Observe that the sample data only includes stores in the United States, and only in the western states of California, Oregon, and Washington.

With an OLAP report, it is possible to **drill down** into the data. This term means to further divide the data into more detail. In Figure 9-9 (page 340), for example, the user has drilled down into the stores located in California; the OLAP report now shows sales data for the four cities in California that have stores.

Notice another difference between Figures 9-8 and 9-9. The user has not only drilled down, she has also changed the order of the dimensions. Figure 9-8 shows *Product Family* and then store location within *Product Family*. Figure 9-9 shows store location and then *Product Family* within store location.

Both displays are valid and useful, depending on the user's perspective. A product manager might like to see product families first and then store location data. A sales manager might like to see store locations first and then product data. OLAP reports provide both perspectives, and the user can switch between them while viewing the report.

Unfortunately, all of this flexibility comes at a cost. If the database is large, doing the necessary calculating, grouping, and sorting for such dynamic displays will require substantial computing power. Although standard commercial DBMS products do have the features and functions required to create OLAP reports, they are not designed for such work. They are designed, instead, to provide rapid response to transaction-processing applications, such as order entry or manufacturing planning.

Accordingly, special-purpose products called **OLAP servers** have been developed to perform OLAP analysis. As shown in Figure 9-10 (page 341), an OLAP server reads data from an operational database, performs preliminary calculations, and stores the results of those calculations in an OLAP database. Several different schemes are used for this storage, but the particulars of those schemes are beyond this discussion. (Search the Web for the terms *MOLAP, ROLAP,* and *HOLAP* if you want to learn more.) Normally, for performance and security reasons the OLAP server and the DBMS run on separate servers.

For a discussion of security issues relating to reporting tools and reporting systems, see the Security Guide *on page 360.*

Q4 What Are Typical Data-Mining Applications?

Data mining is the application of statistical techniques to find patterns and relationships among data for classification and prediction. As shown in Figure 9-11 (page 341), data mining represents a convergence of disciplines. Data-mining techniques emerged from statistics and mathematics and from artificial intelligence and machine-learning fields in computer science. As a result, data-mining terminology is an odd blend of terms from these different disciplines. Sometimes people use the term *knowledge discovery in databases* (KDD) as a synonym for data mining.

Data-mining techniques take advantage of developments in data management for processing the enormous databases that have emerged in the last 10 years. Of course, these data would not have been generated were it not for fast and cheap computers, and without such computers the new techniques would be impossible to compute.

Most data-mining techniques are sophisticated, and many are difficult to use well. Such techniques are valuable to organizations, however, and some business

	A	B	C	D	E	F	G	H	I
1									
2									
3	Store Sales Net			Store Type					
4	Product Family	Store	Store State	Deluxe Superma	Gourmet Supermar	Mid-Size Groce	Small Grocery	Supermarket	Grand Total
5	Drink	USA	CA		$2,392 83		$227.38	$5,920.76	$8,540.97
6			OR	$4,438.49				$2,862.45	$7,300.94
7			WA	$3,680.56		$1,409.50	$458.51	$7,968.50	$13,517.07
8		USA Total		$8,119.05	$2,392 83	$1,409.50	$685.89	$16,751.71	$29,358.98
9	Drink Total			$8,119.05	$2,392 83	$1,409.50	$685.89	$16,751.71	$29,358.98
10	Food	USA	CA		$20,026 18		$1,960.53	$47,226.11	$69,212.82
11			OR	$37,778.35				$23,818.87	$61,597.22
12			WA	$32,497.76		$10,392.19	$4,149.19	$67,915.69	$114,954.83
13		USA Total		$70,276.11	$20,026 18	$10,392.19	$6,109.72	$138,960.67	$245,764.87
14	Food Total			$70,276.11	$20,026 18	$10,392.19	$6,109.72	$138,960.67	$245,764.87
15	Non-Consumable	USA	CA		$5,064 79		$474.35	$12,344.49	$17,883.63
16			OR	$10,177.89				$6,428.53	$16,606.41
17			WA	$8,706.36		$2,813.73	$1,060.54	$17,416.38	$29,997.01
18		USA Total		$18,884.24	$5,064 79	$2,813.73	$1,534.90	$36,189.40	$64,487.05
19	Non-Consumable Total			$18,884.24	$5,064 79	$2,813.73	$1,534.90	$36,189.40	$64,487.05
20	Grand Total			$97,279.40	$27,483 80	$14,615.42	$8,330.51	$191,901.77	$339,610.90

Figure 9-8
OLAP Product Family and Store Location by Store Type

	A	B	C	D	E	F	G	H	I	J
1										
2										
3	Store Sales Net				Store Type ▼					
4	Store Country ▼	Store Sta	Store City	Product Family ▼	Deluxe Super	Gourmet Supermar	Mid-Size Groce	Small Grocery	Supermarket	Grand Total
5	USA	CA	Beverly Hills	Drink		$2,392.83				$2,392.83
6				Food		$20,026.18				$20,026.18
7				Non-Consumable		$5,064.79				$5,064.79
8			Beverly Hills Total			$27,483.80				$27,483.80
9			Los Angeles	Drink					$2,870.33	$2,870.33
10				Food					$23,598.28	$23,598.28
11				Non-Consumable					$6,305.14	$6,305.14
12			Los Angeles Total						$32,773.74	$32,773.74
13			San Diego	Drink					$3,050.43	$3,050.43
14				Food					$23,627.83	$23,627.83
15				Non-Consumable					$6,039.34	$6,039.34
16			San Diego Total						$32,717.61	$32,717.61
17			San Francisco	Drink				$227.38		$227.38
18				Food				$1,960.53		$1,960.53
19				Non-Consumable				$474.35		$474.35
20			San Francisco Total					$2,662.26		$2,662.26
21		CA Total				$27,483.80		$2,662.26	$65,491.35	$95,637.41
22		OR		Drink	$4,438.49				$2,862.45	$7,300.94
23				Food	$37,778.35				$23,818.87	$61,597.22
24				Non-Consumable	$10,177.89				$6,428.53	$16,606.41
25		OR Total			$52,394.72				$33,109.85	$85,504.57
26		WA		Drink	$3,680.56		$1,409.50	$458.51	$7,968.50	$13,517.07
27				Food	$32,497.76		$10,392.19	$4,149.19	$67,915.69	$114,954.83
28				Non-Consumable	$8,706.36		$2,813.73	$1,060.54	$17,416.38	$29,997.01
29		WA Total			$44,884.68		$14,615.42	$5,668.24	$93,300.57	$158,468.91
30	USA Total				$97,279.40	$27,483.80	$14,615.42	$8,330.51	$191,901.77	$339,610.90
31	Grand Total				$97,279.40	$27,483.80	$14,615.42	$8,330.51	$191,901.77	$339,610.90

Figure 9-9
OLAP Product Family and Store Location by Store Type, Drilled Down to Show Stores in California

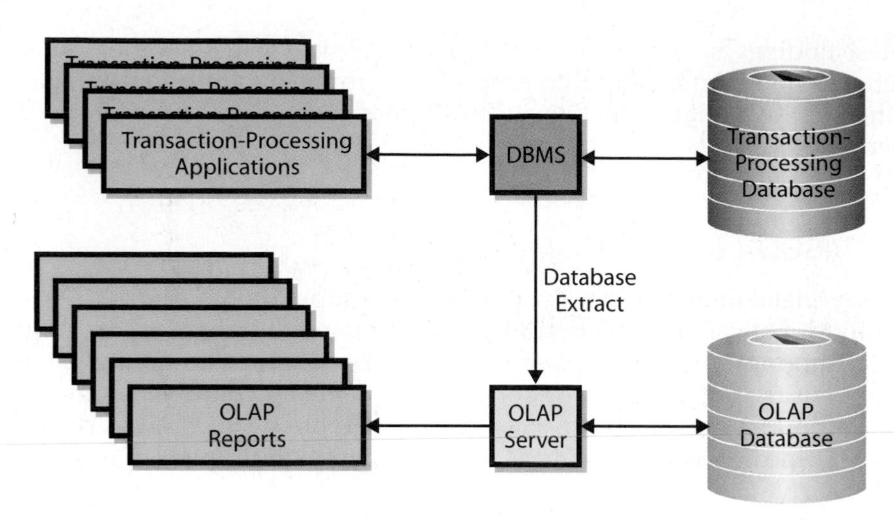

Figure 9-10
Role of OLAP Server and OLAP Database

professionals, especially those in finance and marketing, have become expert in their use. In fact, today there are many interesting and rewarding careers for business professionals who are knowledgeable about data-mining techniques.

Data-mining techniques fall into two broad categories: unsupervised and supervised. We explain both types in the following sections.

Unsupervised Data Mining

With **unsupervised data mining**, analysts do not create a model or hypothesis before running the analysis. Instead, they apply the data-mining technique to the data and observe the results. With this method, analysts create hypotheses *after the analysis*, in order to explain the patterns found.

One common unsupervised technique is **cluster analysis**. With it, statistical techniques identify groups of entities that have similar characteristics. A common use for cluster analysis is to find groups of similar customers from customer order and demographic data.

For example, suppose a cluster analysis finds two very different customer groups: One group has an average age of 33, owns at least two laptops and at least one iPhone, drives a Lexus SUV, and tends to buy expensive children's play equipment. The second group has an average age of 64, owns Arizona vacation property, plays golf, and buys expensive wines. Suppose the analysis also finds that both groups buy designer children's clothing.

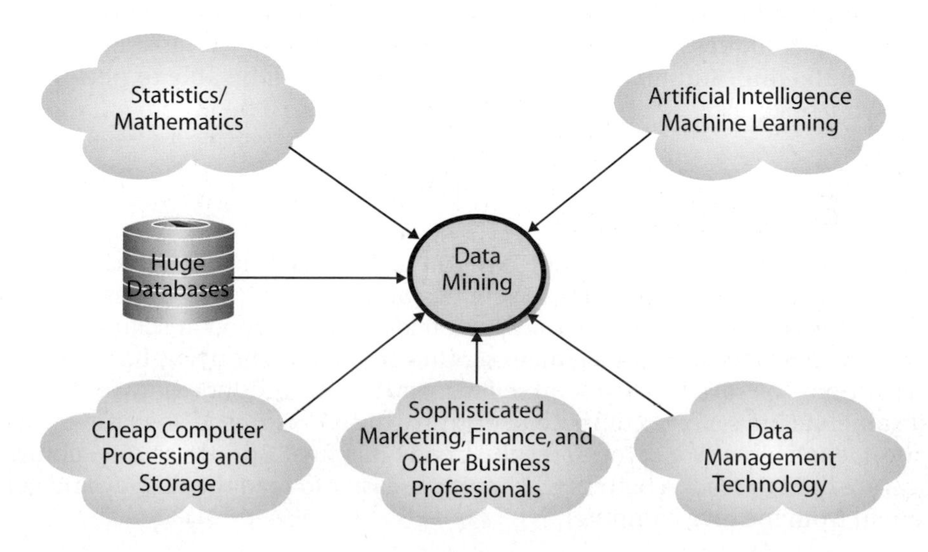

Figure 9-11
Convergence Disciplines for Data Mining

These findings are obtained solely by data analysis. There is no prior model about the patterns and relationship that exist. It is up to the analyst to form hypotheses, after the fact, to explain why two such different groups are both buying designer children's clothes.

Supervised Data Mining

With **supervised data mining**, data miners develop a model *prior to the analysis* and apply statistical techniques to data to estimate parameters of the model. For example, suppose marketing experts in a communications company believe that cell phone usage on weekends is determined by the age of the customer and the number of months the customer has had the cell phone account. A data-mining analyst would then run an analysis that estimates the impact of customer and account age.

One such analysis, which measures the impact of a set of variables on another variable, is called a **regression analysis**. A sample result for the cell phone example is:

```
CellphoneWeekendMinutes =
12 + (17.5 * CustomerAge) + (23.7 * NumberMonthsOfAccount)
```

Using this equation, analysts can predict the number of minutes of weekend cell phone use by summing 12, plus 17.5 times the customer's age, plus 23.7 times the number of months of the account.

As you will learn in your statistics classes, considerable skill is required to interpret the quality of such a model. The regression tool will create an equation, such as the one shown. Whether that equation is a good predictor of future cell phone usage depends on statistical factors, such as t values, confidence intervals, and related statistical techniques.

Neural networks are another popular supervised data-mining technique used to predict values and make classifications such as "good prospect" or "poor prospect" customers. The term *neural networks* is deceiving because it connotes a biological process similar to that in animal brains. In fact, although the original *idea* of neural nets may have come from the anatomy and physiology of neurons, a neural network is nothing more than a complicated set of possibly nonlinear equations. Explaining the techniques used for neural networks is beyond the scope of this text. If you want to learn more, search *http://kdnuggets.com* for the term *neural network.*

In the next sections, we will describe and illustrate two typical data-mining tools—market-basket analysis and decision trees—and show applications of those techniques. From this discussion, you can gain a sense of the nature of data mining. These examples should give you, a future manager, a sense of the possibilities of data-mining techniques. You will need additional coursework in statistics, data management, marketing, and finance, however, before you will be able to perform such analyses yourself.

Data mining and other business intelligence systems are useful, but they are not without problems, as discussed in the Opposing Forces Guide *on page 362.*

Market-Basket Analysis

Suppose you run a dive shop, and one day you realize that one of your salespeople is much better than others at up-selling to your customers. Any of your sales associates can fill a customer's order, but this one salesperson is especially good at selling customers items *in addition to* those for which they ask. One day, you ask him how he does it.

"It's simple," he says. "I just ask myself what is the next product they would want to buy. If someone buys a dive computer, I don't try to sell her fins. If she's buying a dive computer, she's already a diver and she already has fins. But, these dive computer displays are hard to read. A better mask makes it easier to read the display and get the full benefit from the dive computer."

A **market-basket analysis** is a data-mining technique for determining sales patterns. Such an analysis shows the products that customers tend to buy together. In marketing transactions, the fact that customers who buy product *X* also buy product *Y* creates a **cross-selling** opportunity. That is, "If they're buying *X*, sell them *Y*," or "If they're buying *Y*, sell them *X*."

Figure 9-12 shows hypothetical sales data of 1,000 items at a dive shop. The first row of numbers under each column is the total number of times an item was sold. For example, the 270 in the first row of *Mask* means that 270 of the 1,000 items were masks. The 120 under *Dive Computer* means that 120 of the 1,000 purchased items were dive computers.

We can use the numbers in the first row to estimate the probability that a customer will purchase an item. Because 270 of the 1,000 items were masks, we can estimate the probability that a customer will buy a mask to be 270/1,000, or 0.27.

In market-basket terminology, **support** is the probability that two items will be purchased together. To estimate that probability, we examine sales transactions and count the number of times that two items occurred in the same transaction. For the data in Figure 9-12, fins and masks appeared together 150 times, and thus the support for fins and a mask is 150/1,000, or 0.15. Similarly, the support for fins and weights is 60/1,000, or 0.06, and the support for fins along with a second pair of fins is 10/1,000, or 0.01.

These data are interesting by themselves, but we can refine the analysis by taking another step and considering additional probabilities. For example, what proportion of the customers who bought a mask also bought fins? Masks were purchased 270 times, and of those individuals who bought masks, 150 also bought fins. Thus, given that a customer bought a mask, we can estimate the probability that he or she will buy fins to be 150/270, or 0.5556. In market-basket terminology, such a conditional probability estimate is called the **confidence**.

Reflect on the meaning of this confidence value. The likelihood of someone walking in the door and buying fins is 280/1,000, or 0.28. But the likelihood of someone buying fins, given that he or she bought a mask, is 0.5556. That is, if someone buys a mask, the likelihood that he or she will also buy fins almost doubles, from 0.28 to 0.5556. Thus, all sales personnel should be trained to try to sell fins to anyone buying a mask.

Now consider dive computers and fins. Of the 1,000 items sold, fins were sold 280 times, so the probability that someone walks into the store and buys fins is 0.28. But of the 120 purchases of dive computers, only 20 appeared with fins. So the likelihood of

1,000 Items	Mask	Tank	Fins	Weights	Dive Computer
	270	200	280	130	120
Mask	20	20	150	20	50
Tank	20	80	40	30	30
Fins	150	40	10	60	20
Weights	20	30	60	10	10
Dive computer	50	30	20	10	5
No additional product	10	—	—	—	5

Support = P (A & B) Example: P (Fins & Mask) = 150/1,000 = .15

Confidence = P (A | B) Example: P (Fins | Mask) = 150/270 = .5556

Lift = P (A | B)/P (A) Example: P (Fins | Mask)/P (Fins) = .5556/.28 = 1.98

Note: P(Mask | Fins)/P (Mask) = (150/280)/.27 = 1.98

Figure 9-12
Market-Basket Example

someone buying fins, given he or she bought a dive computer, is 20/120 or 0.1666. Thus, when someone buys a dive computer, the likelihood that she will also buy fins falls from 0.28 to 0.1666.

The ratio of confidence to the base probability of buying an item is called **lift**. Lift shows how much the base probability increases or decreases when other products are purchased. The lift of fins and a mask is the confidence of fins given a mask, divided by the base probability of fins. In Figure 9-12, the lift of fins and a mask is 0.5556/0.28, or 1.98. Thus, the likelihood that people buy fins when they buy a mask almost doubles. Surprisingly, it turns out that the lift of fins and a mask is the same as the lift of a mask and fins. Both are 1.98.

Many organizations are benefiting from market-basket analysis today. You can expect that this technique will become a standard CRM analysis during your career.

Decision Trees

A **decision tree** is a hierarchical arrangement of criteria that predict a classification or a value. Here we will consider decision trees that predict classifications. Decision-tree analyses are an unsupervised data-mining technique: The analyst sets up the computer program and provides the data to analyze, and the decision-tree program produces the tree.

A Decision Tree for Student Performance

The basic idea of a decision tree is to select attributes that are most useful for classifying entities on some criterion. Suppose, for example, that we want to classify students according to the grades they earn in the MIS class. To create a decision tree, we first gather data about grades and attributes of students in past classes.

We then input that data into the decision-tree program. The program analyzes all of the attributes and selects an attribute that creates the most disparate groups. The logic is that the more different the groups, the better the classification will be. For example, if every student who lived off campus earned a grade higher than 3.0, and every student who lived on campus earned a grade lower than 3.0, then the program would use the variable *live-off-campus* or *live-on-campus* to classify students. In this unrealistic example, the program would be a perfect classifier, because each group is pure, with no misclassifications.

More realistically, consider Figure 9-13, which shows a hypothetical decision tree analysis of MIS class grades. Again, assume we are classifying students depending on whether their grade was greater than 3.0 or less than or equal to 3.0.

The decision-tree tool that created this tree examined student characteristics such as students' class (junior or senior), their major, their employment, their age, their club affiliations, and other student characteristics. It then used values of those characteristics to create groups that were as different as possible on the classification grade above or below 3.0.

For the results shown here, the decision-tree program determined that the best first criterion is whether the students are juniors or seniors. In this case, the classification was imperfect, as shown by the fact that neither of the senior nor the junior groups consisted only of students with GPAs above or below 3.0. Still, it did create groups that were less mixed than in the *All Students* group.

Next, the program examined other criteria to further subdivide *Seniors* and *Juniors* so as to create even more pure groups. The program divided the senior group into subgroups: those who are business majors and those who are not. The program's analysis of the junior data, however, determined that the difference between majors is not significant. Instead, the best classifier (the one that generated the most different groups) is whether the junior worked in a restaurant.

Examining this data, we see that junior restaurant employees do well in the class, but junior nonrestaurant employees and senior nonbusiness majors do poorly. Performance in the other senior group is mixed. (Remember, these data are hypothetical.)

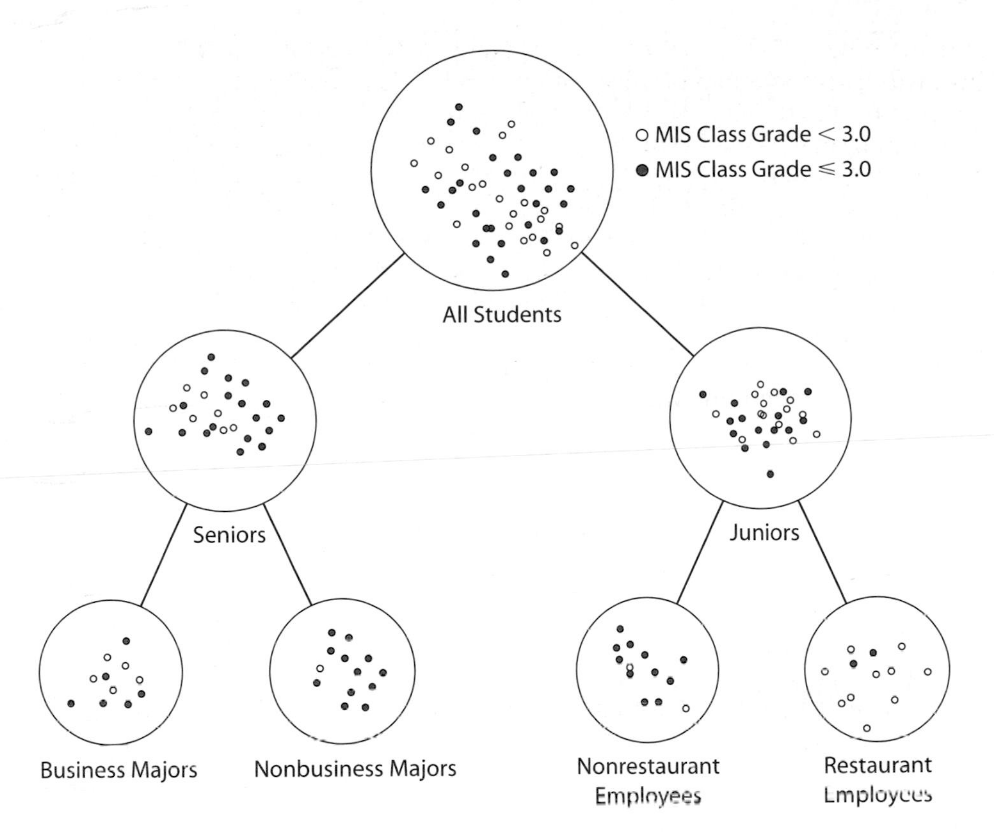

Figure 9-13
Grades of Students from Past MIS Class (Hypothetical Data)

A decision tree like the one in Figure 9-13 can be transformed into a set of decision rules having the format, **If . . . then . . . .** Decision rules for this example are:

- If student is a junior and works in a restaurant, then predict grade > 3.0.
- If student is a senior and is a nonbusiness major, then predict grade ≤ 3.0.
- If student is a junior and does not work in a restaurant, then predict grade ≤ 3.0.
- If student is a senior and is a business major, then make no prediction.

As stated, decision-tree algorithms create groups that are as pure as possible, or, stated otherwise, as different from each other as possible. The algorithms use several metrics for measuring difference among groups. Further explanation of those techniques is beyond the scope of this text. For now, just be sure to understand that maximum difference among groups is used as the criterion for constructing the decision tree.

There are many problems with classification schemes, especially schemes that classify people. The Ethics Guide *on page 346 examines some of these problems.*

Let's now apply the decision-tree technique to a business situation.

A Decision Tree for Loan Evaluation

A common business application of decision trees is to classify loans by likelihood of default. Organizations analyze data from past loans to produce a decision tree that can be converted to loan-decision rules. A financial institution could use such a tree to assess the default risk on a new loan. Sometimes, too, financial institutions sell a group of loans (called a *loan portfolio*) to one another. An institution considering the purchase of a loan portfolio can use the results of a decision-tree program to evaluate the risk of a given portfolio.

Figure 9-14 (page 348) shows an example provided by Insightful Corporation, a vendor of business intelligence tools. This example was generated using its Insightful Miner product. This tool examined data from 3,485 loans. Of those loans, 72 percent had no default and 28 percent did default. To perform the analysis, the decision-tree tool examined six different loan characteristics.

In this example, the decision-tree program determined that the percentage of the loan that is past due (*PercPastDue*) is the best first criterion. Reading Figure 9-14, you can see that of the 2,574 loans with a *PercPastDue* value of 0.5 or less (amount past due

Ethics

GUIDE

The Ethics of Classification

Classification is a useful human skill. Imagine walking into your favorite clothing store and seeing all of the clothes piled together on a center table. T-shirts and pants and socks intermingle, with the sizes mixed up. Retail stores organized like this would not survive, nor would distributors or manufacturers who managed their inventories this way. Sorting and classifying are necessary, important, and essential activities. But those activities can also be dangerous.

Serious ethical issues arise when we classify people. What makes someone a good or bad "prospect"? If we're talking about classifying customers in order to prioritize our sales calls, then the ethical issue may not be too serious. What about classifying applicants for college? As long as there are more applicants than positions, some sort of classification and selection process must be done. But what kind?

Suppose a university collects data on the demographics and the performance of all of its students. The admissions committee then processes these data using a decision tree data-mining program. Assume the analysis is conducted properly and the tool uses statistically valid measures to obtain statistically valid results. Thus, the following resulting tree accurately represents and explains variances found in the data; no human judgment (or prejudice) was involved. ■

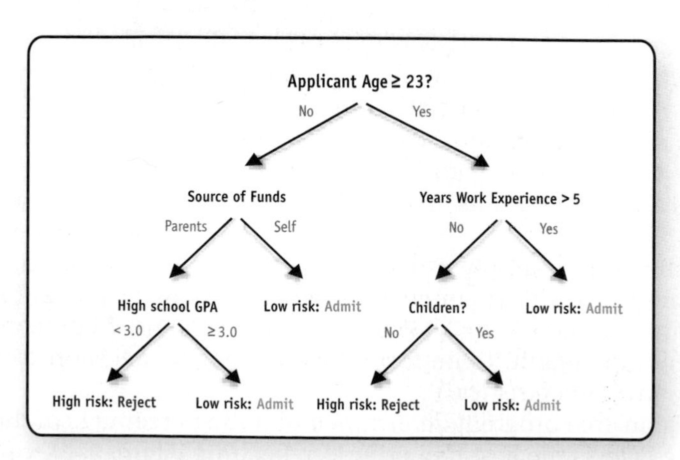

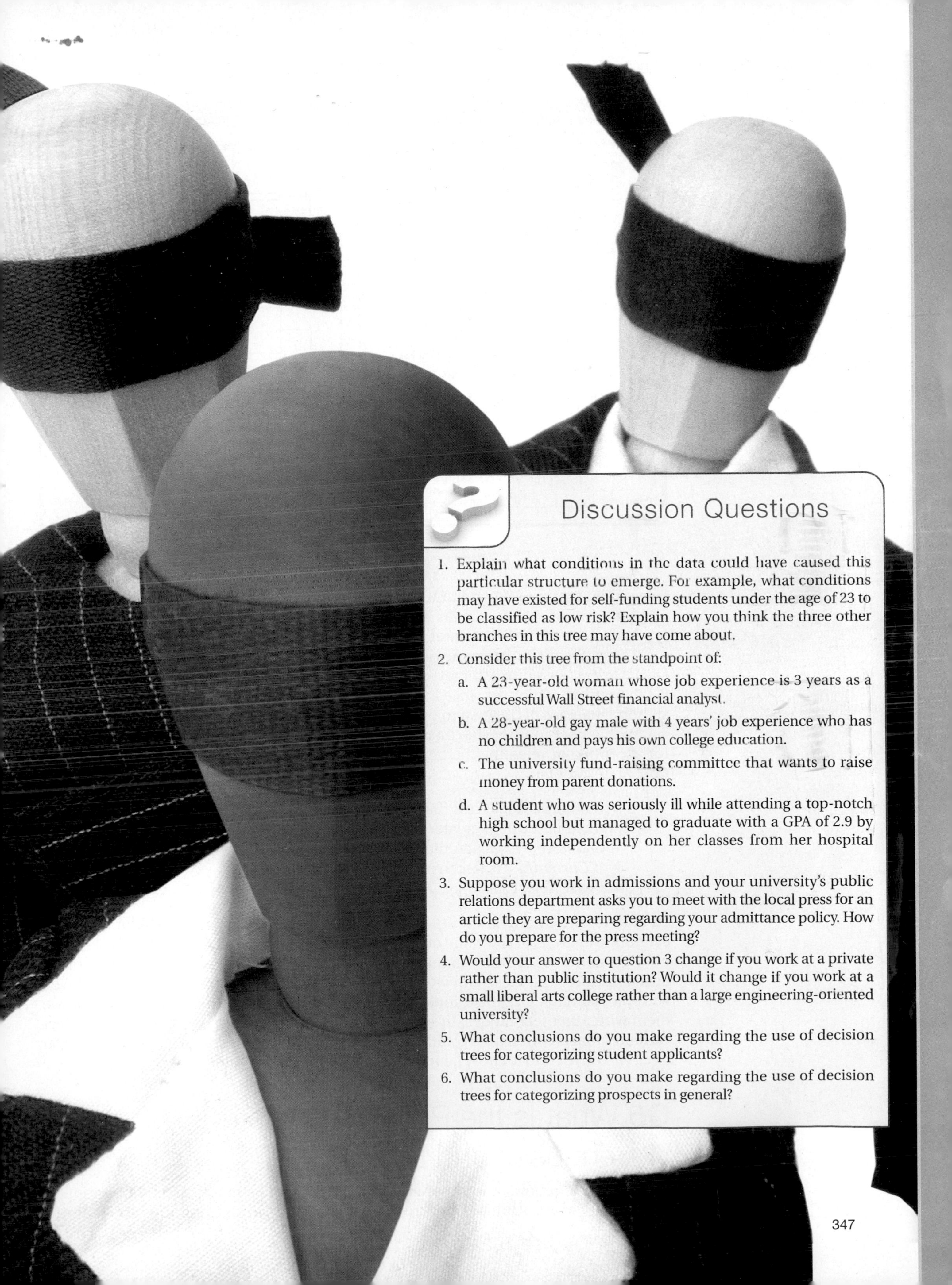

Discussion Questions

1. Explain what conditions in the data could have caused this particular structure to emerge. For example, what conditions may have existed for self-funding students under the age of 23 to be classified as low risk? Explain how you think the three other branches in this tree may have come about.
2. Consider this tree from the standpoint of:
   a. A 23-year-old woman whose job experience is 3 years as a successful Wall Street financial analyst.
   b. A 28-year-old gay male with 4 years' job experience who has no children and pays his own college education.
   c. The university fund-raising committee that wants to raise money from parent donations.
   d. A student who was seriously ill while attending a top-notch high school but managed to graduate with a GPA of 2.9 by working independently on her classes from her hospital room.
3. Suppose you work in admissions and your university's public relations department asks you to meet with the local press for an article they are preparing regarding your admittance policy. How do you prepare for the press meeting?
4. Would your answer to question 3 change if you work at a private rather than public institution? Would it change if you work at a small liberal arts college rather than a large engineering-oriented university?
5. What conclusions do you make regarding the use of decision trees for categorizing student applicants?
6. What conclusions do you make regarding the use of decision trees for categorizing prospects in general?

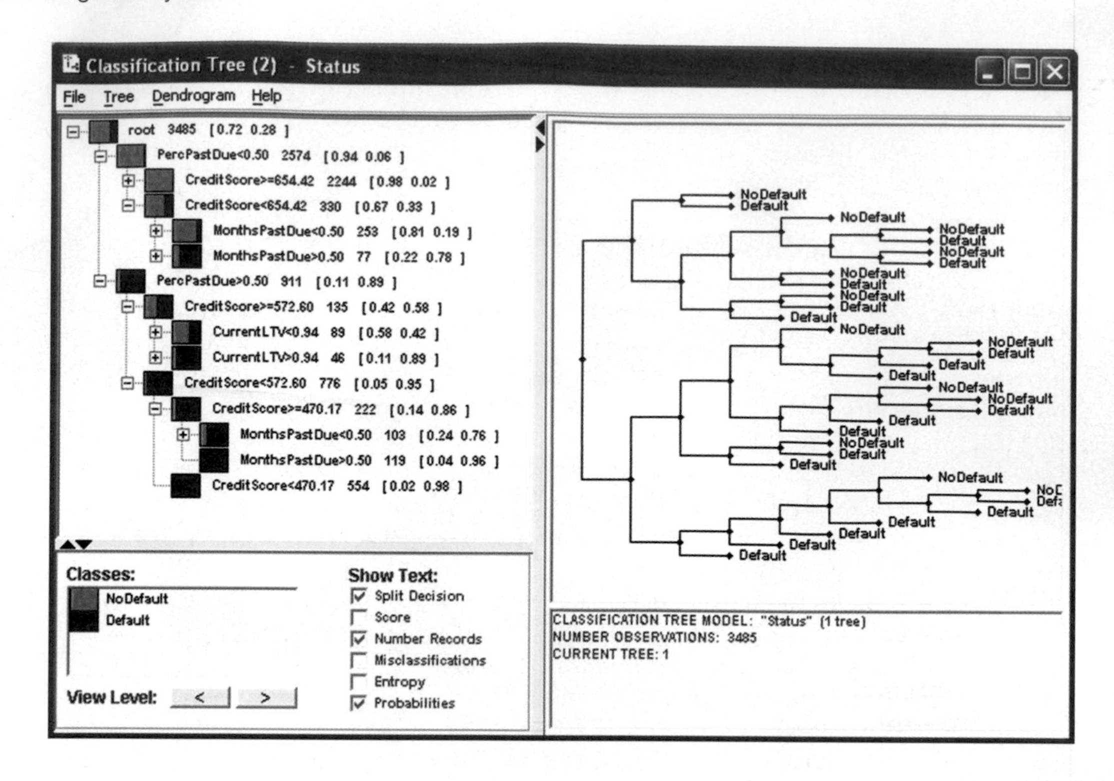

Figure 9-14
Credit Score Decision Tree

is less than half the loan amount), 94 percent were not in default. Reading down several lines in this tree, 911 loans had a value of *PercPastDue* greater than 0.5; of those loans, 89 percent were in default.

These two major categories are then further subdivided into three classifications: *CreditScore* is a creditworthiness score obtained from a credit agency; *MonthsPastDue* is the number of months since a payment; and *CurrentLTV* is the current ratio of outstanding balance of the loan to the value of the loan's collateral.

With a decision tree like this, the financial institution can develop decision rules for accepting or rejecting the offer to purchase loans from another financial institution. For example:

- If percent past due is less than 50 percent, then accept the loan.
- If percent past due is greater than 50 percent *and*
  - If *CreditScore* is greater than 572.6 *and*
    - If *CurrentLTV* is less than .94, then accept the loan.
- Otherwise, reject the loan.

Of course, the financial institution will need to combine these risk data with an economic analysis of the value of each loan to determine which loans to take.

Decision trees are easy to understand and, even better, easy to implement using decision rules. They also can work with many types of variables, and they deal well with partial data. Organizations can use decision trees by themselves or combine them with other techniques. In some cases, organizations use decision trees to select variables that are then used by other types of data-mining tools. For example, decision trees can be used to identify good predictor variables for neural networks.

Q5 What Is the Purpose of Data Warehouses and Data Marts?

Whereas basic reports and simple OLAP analyses can be made directly from operational data, more sophisticated reports and nearly all data-mining applications cannot. One problem is that missing values and inconsistencies in the data can adversely affect results. Also, some analyses necessitate merging operational data with data purchased from outside sources. Yet another problem is data format. Operational data is designed to support fast transaction processing and might need to be reformatted to be useful for BI applications.

To address these problems, many organizations choose to extract operational data into facilities called **data warehouses** and **data marts**, both of which prepare, store, and manage data specifically for data mining and other analyses. (We will explain the differences between data warehouses and data marts in a few pages.)

Figure 9-15 shows the components in a data warehouse. Programs read production and other data and extract, clean, and prepare that data for BI processing. The prepared data are stored in a data-warehouse database using a data-warehouse DBMS, which can be different from the organization's operational DBMS. For example, an organization might use Oracle for its operational processing, but use SQL Server for its data warehouse. Other organizations use SQL Server for operational processing, but use DBMSs from statistical package vendors such as SAS or SPSS in the data warehouse.

video

Data warehouses include data that are purchased from outside sources. A typical example is customer credit data. Figure 9-16 (next page) lists some of the consumer data than can be purchased from commercial vendors today. An amazing (and from a privacy standpoint, frightening) amount of data is available.

Metadata concerning the data—its source, its format, its assumptions and constraints, and other facts about the data—is kept in a data-warehouse metadata database. The data-warehouse DBMS extracts and provides data to BI tools such as data-mining programs.

Problems with Operational Data

Unfortunately, most operational and purchased data have problems that inhibit their usefulness for business intelligence. Figure 9-17 (next page) lists the major problem categories. First, although data that are critical for successful operations must be complete and accurate, data that are only marginally necessary need not be. For example, some systems gather demographic data in the ordering process. But, because such data are not needed to fill, ship, and bill orders, their quality suffers.

Problematic data are termed **dirty data**. Examples are a value of *B* for customer gender and of *213* for customer age. Other examples are a value of *999–999–9999* for a

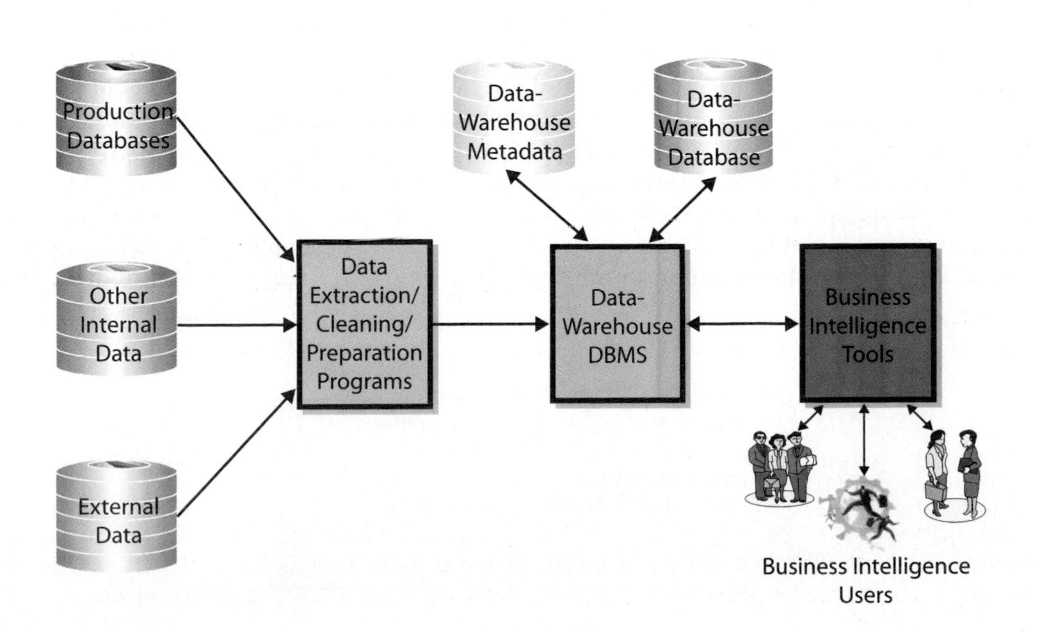

Figure 9-15
Components of a Data Warehouse

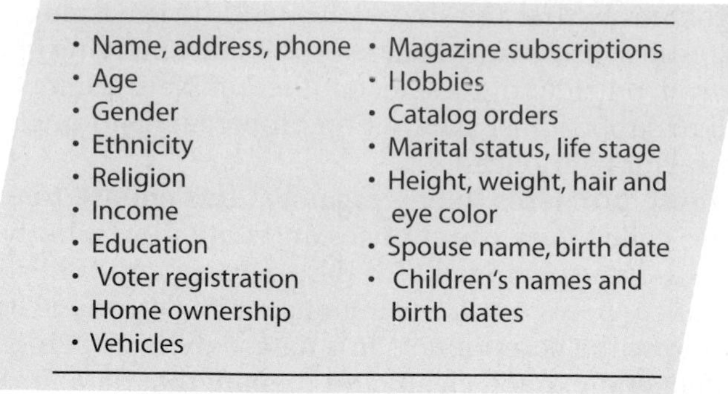
- Name, address, phone
- Age
- Gender
- Ethnicity
- Religion
- Income
- Education
- Voter registration
- Home ownership
- Vehicles
- Magazine subscriptions
- Hobbies
- Catalog orders
- Marital status, life stage
- Height, weight, hair and eye color
- Spouse name, birth date
- Children's names and birth dates

Figure 9-16
Consumer Data Available for Purchase from Data Vendors

U.S. phone number, a part color of *gren*, and an email address of *WhyMe@GuessWhoIAM.org*. All of these values can be problematic for data-mining purposes.

Purchased data often contain *missing* elements. Most data vendors state the percentage of missing values for each attribute in the data they sell. An organization buys such data because for some uses, some data are better than no data at all. This is especially true for data items whose values are difficult to obtain, such as *Number of Adults in Household, Household Income, Dwelling Type*, and *Education of Primary Income Earner*. For data-mining applications, though, a few missing or erroneous data points can be worse than no data at all because they bias the analysis.

Inconsistent data, the third problem in Figure 9-17, is particularly common for data that have been gathered over time. When an area code changes, for example, the phone number for a given customer before the change will not match the customer's number after the change. Likewise, part codes can change, as can sales territories. Before such data can be used, they must be recoded for consistency over the period of the study.

Some data inconsistencies occur from the nature of the business activity. Consider a Web-based order-entry system used by customers worldwide. When the Web server records the time of order, which time zone does it use? The server's system clock time is irrelevant to an analysis of customer behavior. Coordinated Universal Time (formerly called Greenwich Mean Time) is also meaningless. Somehow, Web server time must be adjusted to the time zone of the customer.

Another problem is *nonintegrated data*. Suppose, for example, that an organization wants to perform an RFM analysis but wants to consider customer payment behavior as well. The organization wants to add a fourth factor (which we will call *P*) and scale it from 1 to 5 on the basis of how quickly a customer pays. Unfortunately, however, the organization records such payment data in an Oracle financial management database that is separate from the Microsoft CRM database that has the order data. Before the organization can perform the analysis, the data must somehow be integrated.

For a discussion of extensions of RFM analysis, see the Innovation in Practice *box* *on page 351.*

Data can also have the wrong **granularity**—it can be too fine or too coarse. For the former, suppose we want to analyze the placement of graphics and controls on an order-entry Web page. It is possible to capture the customers' clicking behavior in what is termed **clickstream data**. Those data, however, include everything the customer does at the Web site. In the middle of the order stream are data for clicks on the news, email, instant chat, and a weather check. Although all of that data may be useful for a study of consumer computer behavior, it will be overwhelming if all we

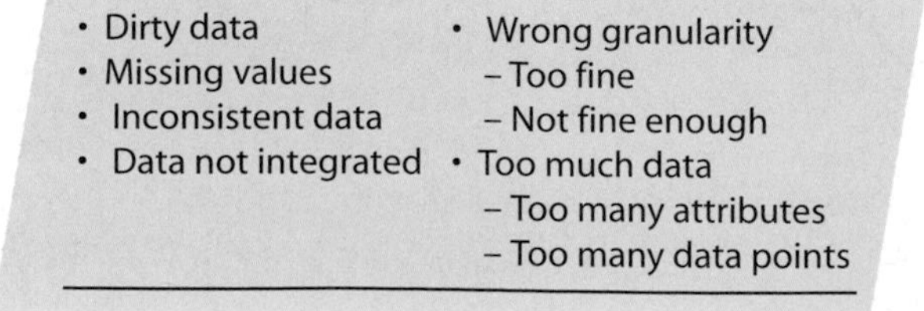
- Dirty data
- Missing values
- Inconsistent data
- Data not integrated
- Wrong granularity
  - Too fine
  - Not fine enough
- Too much data
  - Too many attributes
  - Too many data points

Figure 9-17
Problems of Using Transaction Data for Analysis and Data Mining

INNOVATION IN PRACTICE

INNOVATING RFM

The methodology of RFM analysis can be extended to apply to different analysis scenarios. The text suggests adding a *P* criterion, for how fast a customer pays. To do so, a company would compute the value *D*, the number of days that expire between the issuing of an invoice and the arrival of the payment. In the case of partial payments, *D* would be based on the date of the last payment.

Given that calculation, a company could sort customers according to the decreasing value of *D*, and as with the standard RFM analysis it could assign a *P* value of 1 to the 20 percent of customers who pay the fastest, a *P* value of 2 to the 20 percent who pay the next fastest, and so forth, down to 5. In this way, customers would be given a four-value score based on RFMP. A customer who has a score of [1, 1, 1, 1] is indeed a valuable customer. One who has a value of [1, 1, 1, 5] would be less valuable.

This *P* extension suggests that there may be other possible uses for the RFM-ranking methodology. It could be used to rank suppliers, inventory parts, employees, customer-service representatives, airlines, or hotels.

You and a team of your classmates will be given a chance to develop and evaluate such extensions in Collaboration Exercise 2, on page 366.

want to know is how customers respond to an ad located differently on the screen. To proceed, the data analysts must throw away millions and millions of clicks.

Data can also be too coarse. For example, a file of order totals cannot be used for a market-basket analysis. For market-basket analysis, we need to know which items were purchased with which others. This does not mean the order-total data are useless. They can be adequate for an RFM analysis, for example; they just will not do for a market-basket analysis.

In general, it is better to have too fine a granularity than too coarse. If the granularity is too fine, the data can be made coarser by summing and combining. Only analysts' labor and computer processing are required. If the granularity is too coarse, however, there is no way to separate the data into constituent parts.

The final problem listed in Figure 9-17 is to have *too much data*. As shown in the figure, we can have either too many attributes or too many data points. Think of tables as discussed in Chapter 5. We can have too many columns or too many rows.

Consider the first problem: too many attributes. Suppose we want to know the factors that influence how customers respond to a promotion. If we combine internal customer data with purchased customer data, we will have more than a hundred different attributes to consider. How do we select among them? Because of a phenomenon called the **curse of dimensionality**, the more attributes there are, the easier it is to build a model that fits the sample data but that is worthless as a predictor. There are other good reasons for reducing the number of attributes, and one of the major activities in data mining concerns efficient and effective ways of selecting attributes.

The second way to have too much data is to have too many data points—too many rows of data. Suppose we want to analyze clickstream data on CNN.com. How many clicks does that site receive per month? Millions upon millions! In order to meaningfully analyze such data we need to reduce the amount of data. There is a good solution to this problem: statistical sampling. Organizations should not be reluctant to sample data in such situations.

Data Warehouses Versus Data Marts

So, how is a data warehouse different from a data mart? In a way, you can think of a *data warehouse* as distributor in a supply chain. The data warehouse takes data from the data manufacturers (operational systems and purchased data), cleans and processes the data, and locates the data on the shelves, so to speak, of the data warehouse. The people who work with a data warehouse are experts at data management, data cleaning, data transformation, and the like. However, they are not usually experts in a given business function.

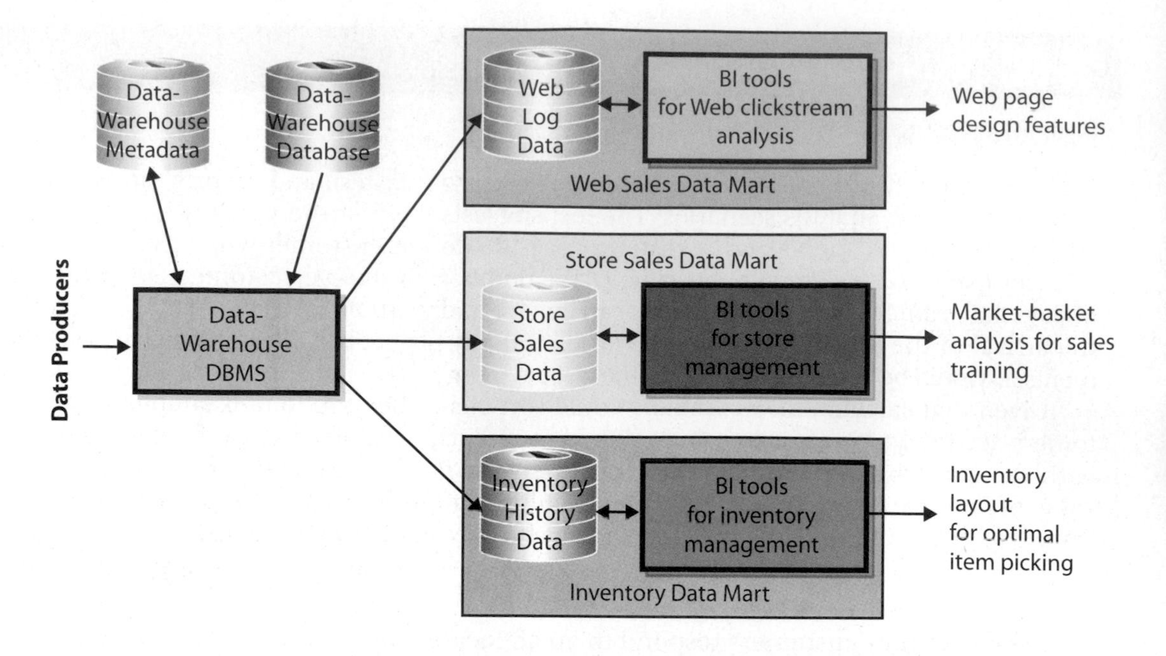

Figure 9-18
Data Mart Examples

A *data mart* is a data collection, smaller than the data warehouse, that addresses a particular component or functional area of the business. If the data warehouse is the distributor in a supply chain, then a data mart is like a retail store in a supply chain. Users in the data mart obtain data that pertain to a particular business function from the data warehouse. Such users do not have the data management expertise that data warehouse employees have, but they are knowledgeable analysts for a given business function.

Figure 9-18 illustrates these relationships. The data warehouse takes data from the data producers and distributes the data to three data marts. One data mart is used to analyze clickstream data for the purpose of designing Web pages. A second analyzes store sales data and determines which products tend to be purchased together. This information is used to train salespeople on the best way to up-sell to customers.

The third data mart is used to analyze customer order data for the purpose of reducing labor for item picking from the warehouse. A company like Amazon.com, for example, goes to great lengths to organize its warehouses to reduce picking expenses.

As you can imagine, it is expensive to create, staff, and operate data warehouses and data marts. Only large organizations with deep pockets can afford to operate a system like that shown in Figure 9-18. Smaller organizations operate subsets of this system; they may have just a simple data mart for analyzing promotion data, for example.

Q6 What Are Typical Knowledge-Management Applications?

Knowledge management (KM) is the process of creating value from intellectual capital and sharing that knowledge with employees, managers, suppliers, customers, and others who need it. Whereas reporting and data mining are used to create new information from data, knowledge-management systems concern the sharing of knowledge that is known to exist, either in libraries of documents or in the heads of employees.

KM applications enable employees and others to leverage organizational knowledge to work smarter. Santosus and Surmacz cite the following as the primary benefits of KM:

1. KM fosters innovation by encouraging the free flow of ideas.
2. KM improves customer service by streamlining response time.
3. KM boosts revenues by getting products and services to market faster.

4. **4.** KM enhances employee retention rates by recognizing the value of employees' knowledge and rewarding them for it.
5. **5.** KM streamlines operations and reduces costs by eliminating redundant or unnecessary processes.[4]

In addition, KM preserves organizational memory by capturing and storing the lessons learned and best practices of key employees.

There are three major categories of knowledge assets: data, documents, and employees. We addressed information derived from data in the reporting and data-mining sections of this chapter. In this section, we will consider KM as it pertains to sharing of document content and employee knowledge.

Sharing Document Content

In Chapter 2, we discussed content management in the context of collaboration systems. The focus on content for KM applications is slightly different. Whereas collaboration systems are concerned with document creation and change management, KM applications are concerned with maximizing content use. In this section, we focus on two key technologies for sharing content: indexing and RSS.

Indexing

Indexing is the single most important content function in KM applications. KM users need an easily accessible and robust means of determining whether content they need exists, and, if so, a link to obtain that content. Users need keyword search that provides quick response and high document relevancy. The higher the relevancy, the more productive users will be.

The largest collection of documents ever assembled exists on the Internet, and the world's best-known indexing engine is operated by Google. When you "google" a term, you are tapping into the world's largest content-indexing system. Google's limitation is that it can index only publicly accessible documents.

When organizations protect their content by placing it behind firewalls, Google's indexing software cannot find it. If you want to access documents published in, say, *Forbes Magazine*, you will have to use an indexing service that has an indexing agreement with Forbes. Similarly, organizations must develop their own indexing systems, or license indexing systems from others, in order to make their own protected content available to their employees and other authorized users.

RSS

Real Simple Syndication, or *RSS*, is a standard for subscribing to content sources. (Actually, as of 2008, there are *seven* different RSS standards; not all of them mean *real simple syndication*, but we will ignore that issue here. Google *RSS standards* to learn more.)

You can think of RSS as an email system for content. With a program called an **RSS reader**, you can subscribe to magazines, blogs, Web sites, and other content sources. The RSS reader will periodically check the sources to which you subscribe to determine whether any content has changed. If so, the RSS reader will place a summary of the change and link to the new content in what is essentially an RSS inbox. You can process your RSS inbox just like your email inbox. You read content changes, delete them in your RSS inbox, and, depending on your reader's features, forward notices of changes to others via email.

Figure 9-19 (next page) shows the interface of a typical RSS reader. The left-hand pane shows the RSS sources to which this user is subscribed. Entries are grouped into

---

[4]Megan Santosus and John Surmacz, "The ABCs of Knowledge Management," *CIO Magazine*, May 23, 2001, *http://cio.com/research/knowledge/edit/kmabcs.html* (accessed July 2005).

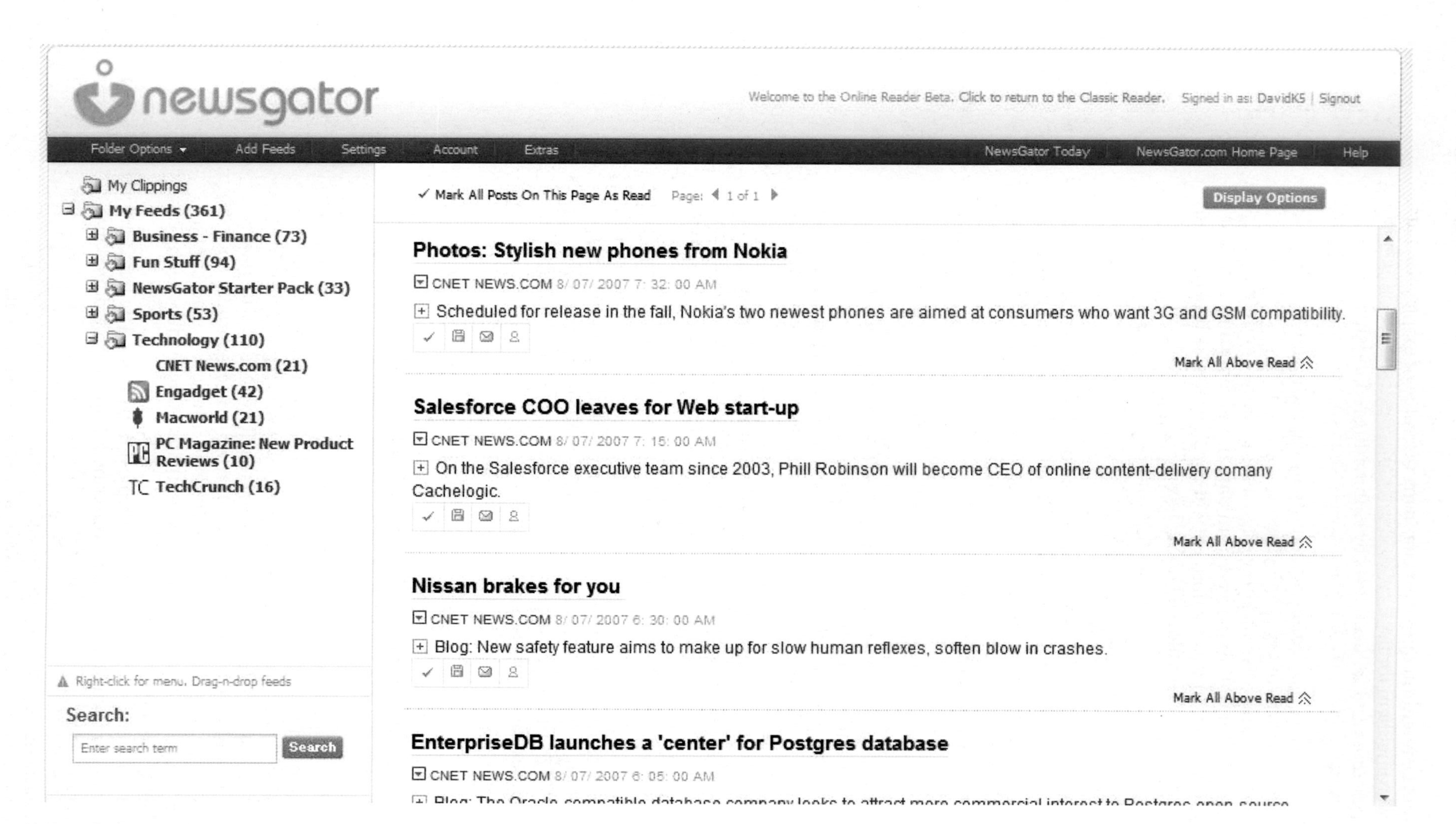

Figure 9-19
Interface of a Typical RSS Reader

categories such as business, technology, and sports. In order to subscribe, the data source must provide what is termed an **RSS feed**. This simply means that the site posts changes according to one of the RSS standards.

Today, the employees in many organizations share their knowledge via personal blogs. Figure 9-20 shows the blog posts of one of the key employees on the Microsoft SharePoint team. Blogs like this include RSS feeds so that you can subscribe to them using an RSS reader. You can also configure SharePoint and other content-management systems to provide an RSS feed on lists or document libraries. Users who subscribe to those feeds will be notified whenever content changes.

Content-sharing systems are flexible and organic. They are closer to Web 2.0 applications than are applications such as reporting and data mining. In fact, some people would say that content-sharing systems *are* Web 2.0 applications.

Expert Systems

Expert systems attempt to capture human expertise and put it into a format that can be used by nonexperts. Expert systems are rule-based systems that use If... then rules similar to those created by decision-tree analysis. However, decision trees' If... then rules are created by mining data. The If . . . then rules in expert systems are created by interviewing experts in a given business domain and codifying the rules stated by those experts. Also, decision trees typically have fewer than a dozen rules, whereas expert systems can have hundreds or thousands of rules.

Problems of Expert Systems

Many expert systems were created in the late 1980s and early 1990s, and some of them have been successful. They suffer from three major disadvantages, however. First, they are difficult and expensive to develop. They require many labor hours from both experts in the domain under study and designers of expert systems. This expense is compounded by the high opportunity cost of tying up domain experts. Such experts are normally some of the most sought-after employees in the organization.

Second, expert systems are difficult to maintain. Because of the nature of rule-based systems, the introduction of a new rule in the middle of hundreds of others can have unexpected consequences. A small change can cause very different outcomes.

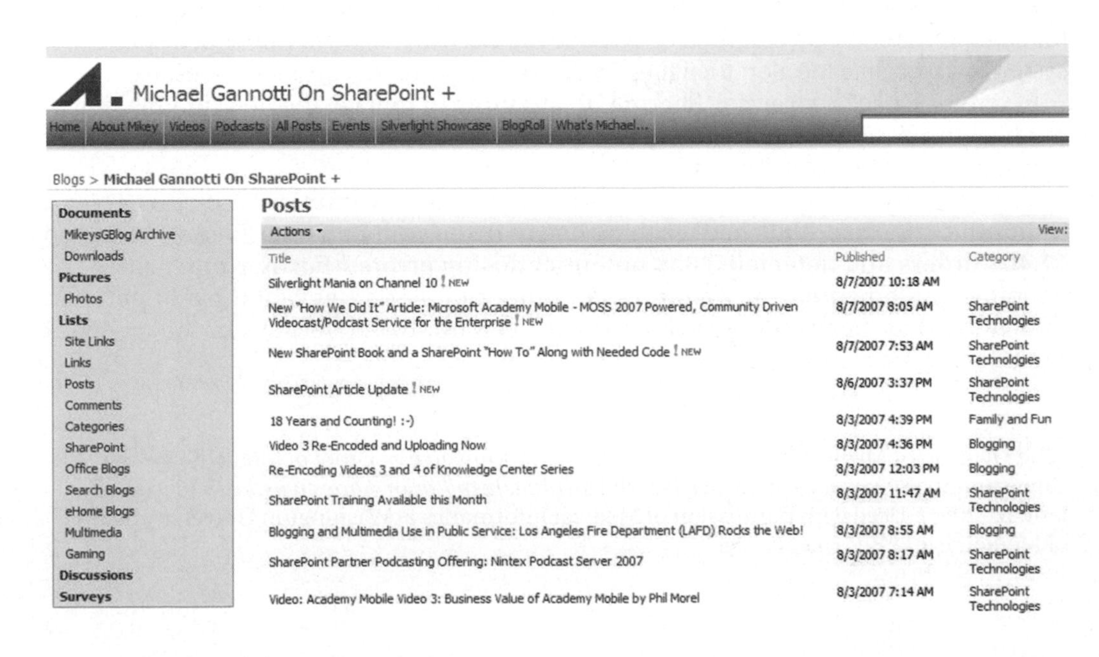

Figure 9-20
Blog Posts of SharePoint Team Member (Michael Gannotti)

Source: Microsoft Office SharePoint Designer 2007. Reprinted with permission from Microsoft Corporation.

Unfortunately, such side-effects cannot be predicted or eliminated. They are the nature of complex rule-based systems.

Finally, expert systems have been unable to live up to the high expectations set by their name. Initially, proponents of expert systems hoped to be able to duplicate the performance of highly trained experts, such as doctors. It turned out, however, that no expert system has the same diagnostic ability as knowledgeable, skilled, and experienced doctors. Even when expert systems were developed that came close in ability, changes in medical technology required constant changing of the expert system, and the problems caused by unexpected consequences made such changes very expensive.

Today, however, there are successful, less-ambitious expert systems. Typically these systems address more restricted problems than duplicating a doctor's diagnostic ability. We consider one next.

Expert Systems for Pharmacies

The Medical Informatics group at Washington University School of Medicine in St. Louis, Missouri, develops innovative and effective information systems to support decision making in medicine. The group has developed several expert systems that are used as a safety net to screen the decisions of doctors and other medical professionals. These systems help to achieve the hospital's goal of state-of-the-art, error-free care.

Medical researchers developed early expert systems to support, and in some cases to replace, medical decision making. MYCIN was an expert system developed in the early 1970s for the purpose of diagnosing certain infectious diseases. Physicians never routinely used MYCIN, but researchers used its expert system framework as the basis for many other medical systems. For one reason or another, however, none of those systems has seen extensive use.

In contrast, the systems developed at Washington University are routinely used, in real time, every day. One of the systems, DoseChecker, verifies appropriate dosages on prescriptions issued in the hospital. Another application, PharmADE, ensures that patients are not prescribed drugs that have harmful interactions. The pharmacy order-entry system invokes these applications as a prescription is entered. If either system detects a problem with the prescription, it generates an alert like the sample shown in Figure 9-21.

A pharmacist screens an alert before sending it to the doctor. If the pharmacist disagrees with the alert, it is discarded. If the pharmacist agrees there is a problem with either the dosage or a harmful drug interaction, she sends the alert to the doctor. The doctor can then alter the prescription or override the alert. If the doctor does not respond, the system will escalate the alert to higher levels until the potential problem is resolved.

Neither DoseChecker nor PharmADE attempts to replace the decision making of medical professionals. Rather, they operate behind the scenes, as a reliable assistant helping to provide error-free care.

Apparently, the systems work. According to the Informatics Web site, "Over a 6-month period at a 1,400 bed teaching hospital, the system {DoseChecker} screened 57,404 orders and detected 3,638 potential dosing errors." Furthermore, since the hospital implemented the system, the number of alerts has fallen by 50 percent, indicating that the prescribing process has been improved because of the feedback provided by the alerts.[5]

---

[5]The Division of Medical Informatics at Washington University School of Medicine for the Department of Pharmacy at Barnes Jewish Hospital. *http://informatics.wustl.edu* (accessed January 2005). Used with permission of Medical Informatics at Washington University School of Medicine and BJC Healthcare.

Pharmacy Clinical Decision Support
Version 2.0

Developed by The Division of Medical Informatics at Washington University School of Medicine for the Department of Pharmacy at Barnes Jewish Hospital.

Data as of: Mar 10 2000 4:40 AM **Alert #: 13104** **Satellite: CHNE**

Patient Name	Registration	Age	Sex	Weight(kg)	Height(in)	IBW(kg)	Location
SAMPLE,PATIENT	9999999	22	F	114	0	0	528

Creatinine Clearance Lab Results (last 3):

Collection Date	Serum Creatinine	Creatinine Clearance
Mar 9 2000 9:55 PM	7.1	14

DoseChecker Recommendations and Thoughts:

Order	Start Date	Drug Name	Route	Dose	Frequency
295	Mar 10 2000 12:00 AM	MEPERIDINE INJ 25MG	IV	25 MG	Q4H
Recommended Dose/Frequency:				**0.0 MG**	**PER DAY**
Comments:	0 <= CrCl < 20. Mependine should not be used for more than 48 hours or at doses > 600 mg per day in patients with renal or CNS disease. Serious consideration should be given to using an alternative analgesic in this patient population.				

Figure 9-21
Alert from Pharmacy Clinical Decision Support System

Source: The division of Medicine at Washington University School of Medicine for the Department of Pharmacy at Barnes Jewish Hospital Informatics. wustl.edu. Used with permission of Medical Informatics at Washington University School of Medicine and BJC Healthcare.

Q7 How Are Business Intelligence Applications Delivered?

By now you should have a good understanding of the potential power and utility of business intelligence applications. However, to make a practical difference the results of the BI analyses need to be delivered to people who can use them. For that, some sort of BI server is needed. Figure 9-22 (next page) summarizes the components of a generic business intelligence system. A *data source* is processed by a *BI tool* to produce *application results*. A **BI application server** delivers those results in a variety of formats to *devices* for consumption by *BI users*.

What Are the Management Functions of a BI Server?

BI servers provide two major functions: management and delivery. The management function maintains metadata about the authorized allocation of BI results to users. The BI server tracks what results are available, what users are authorized to view those results, and the schedule upon which the results are provided to the authorized users. It adjusts allocations as available results change and users come and go.

BI servers vary in complexity and functionality, and their management function varies as well. Some BI servers are simply Web sites from which users can download, or **pull**, BI application results. For example, a BI Web server might post the results of an RFM analysis for salespeople to query to obtain RFM scores for their customers.

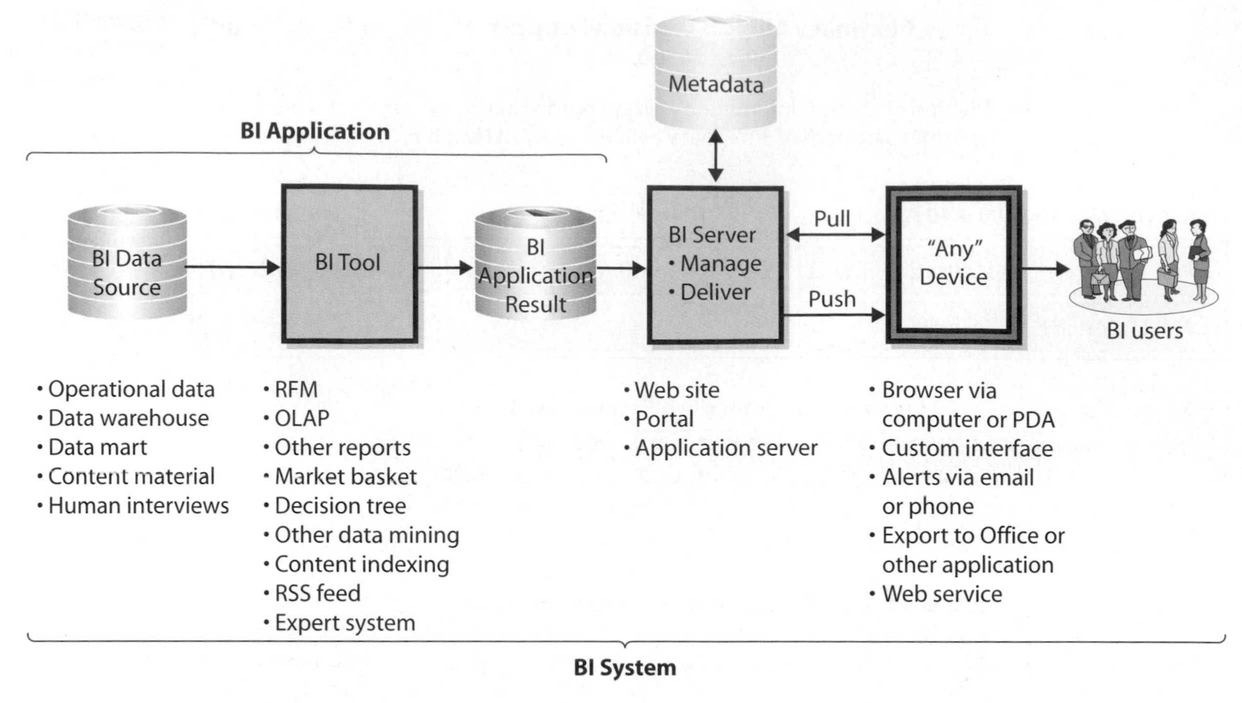

Figure 9-22
Components of Generic Business Intelligence System

The management function for such a site would simply be to track authorized users and restrict access to the site to them.

Another option is for the BI server to operate as a portal server, or as part of one. **Portal servers** are like Web servers except they have a customizable user interface. You have probably used a portal, though you may not have realized it. If you establish an account with iGoogle, for example, you will be given the opportunity to customize the interface to your particular interests. You might, for example, choose to see the weather in certain cities, the values of particular stocks and markets, the results of particular sports events, and so forth. Whenever you sign on to iGoogle, it will present your customized interface. Figure 9-23 shows a sample portal.

Some organizations establish similar portal servers for use by employees within the company. Such portals might provide common data such as local weather, but it would also have links to company news, and, for our purposes, to BI application

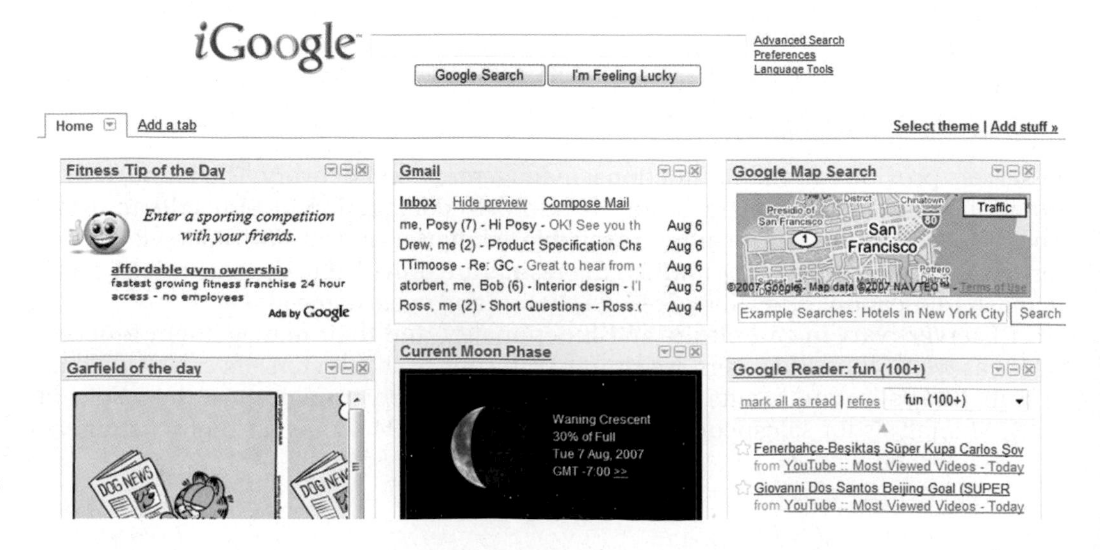

Figure 9-23
Sample Portal, Provided by iGoogle

Source: iGoogle™. GOOGLE is a trademark of Google Inc.

results such as reports on daily sales, operations, new employees, and so forth. Results of data-mining applications could be presented as well.

To implement such a portal, the organization provides authorized user accounts on the portal server and allows users to place reports, data-mining results, or other BI application results on their customized pages. Of course, selections are limited to results that the user is authorized to see. For example, a bank might publish a loan evaluation application based on a decision-tree analysis. Authorized bankers can place that evaluation application on their portal interface and invoke it when necessary. Management functions for BI portals are to track the available BI results, the users and their authorities, and, like all portal servers, the customizations in each users' interface.

A BI application server extends the functionality provided by portals to support user subscriptions to particular BI application results. For example, a user can subscribe to a daily sales report, requesting that it be delivered each morning. Or, the user might request that RFM analyses be delivered whenever a new result is posted on the server. Users can also subscribe to **alerts**, which are messages delivered via email or phone whenever a particular event occurs. A sales manager might want to be alerted, for example, whenever sales in his region exceed $1 million during the week. The BI application server **pushes** the subscribed results to the user.

A **report server** is a special case of a BI application server that serves only reports. BI application servers track results, users, authorizations, page customizations, subscriptions, alerts, and data for any other functionality provided.

As shown in Figure 9-22, all management data needed by any of the BI servers is stored in metadata. The amount and complexity of such data depends, of course, on the functionality of the BI server.

What Are the Delivery Functions of a BI Server?

BI servers use metadata to determine what results to send to which users and, possibly, on which schedule. Today, the expectation is that BI results can be delivered to "any" device. In practice, *any* is interpreted to mean computers, PDAs, phones, other applications such as Microsoft Office, and as an XML service.

As stated, alerts are simply messages transmitted via email or phone that notify a user that a particular condition has occurred. The condition might be expected, such as the arrival of a new report on the BI server. Or, it might be unexpected, such as an **exception alert** that notifies the user of an exceptional event, such as a dramatic fall in a stock price or exceptionally high sales volume.

A BI system, like all information systems, has hardware, software, data, procedures, and people. So far, we have discussed all of the components except procedures. The particular procedures that BI users follow depends on the nature of the BI system. In general, however, such systems tend to be more flexible than operational systems, such as order entry, CRM, or ERP. BI users tend to be engaged in nonstructured, nonroutine work. In such an environment, procedures are limited to basic operational instructions, such as how to obtain a user account, how to subscribe to a particular BI product, and how to obtain a result. The interpretation of the BI results is not normally prescribed by procedure.

There are, however, a few exceptions. The sales force might develop procedures for using RFM scores. "Always do this for a [2, 1, 1]," or "Never spend time on a [5, 5, 5]" are examples. Similarly, users might have instructions for using the results of market-basket analyses. "If the user orders a widget, attempt to up-sell a widget bracket" is an example.

In most cases, however, the use of a particular BI application result is nonroutine and is determined by the users' unique requirements.

Semantic Security

Security is a very difficult problem—and risks grow larger every year. Not only do we have cheaper, faster computers (remember Moore's Law). We also have more data, more systems for reporting and querying that data, and easier, faster, and broader communication. All of these combine to increase the chances that we inadvertently divulge private or proprietary information.

Physical security is hard enough: How do we know that the person (or program) that signs on as Megan Cho really is Megan Cho? We use passwords, but files of passwords can be stolen. Setting that issue aside, we need to know that Megan Cho's permissions are set appropriately. Suppose Megan works in the HR department, so she has access to personal and private data of other employees. We need to design the reporting system so that Megan can access all of the data she needs to do her job, and no more.

Also, the delivery system must be secure. An application server is an obvious and juicy target for any would-be intruder. Someone can break in and change access permissions. Or, a hacker could pose as someone else to obtain reports. Application servers help the authorized user, resulting in faster access to more information. But, without proper security reporting servers also ease the intrusion task for unauthorized users.

All of these issues relate to physical security. Another dimension to security is equally serious and far more problematic: semantic security. **Semantic security** concerns the unintended release of protected information through the release of a combination of reports or documents that are independently not protected.

Take an example from class. Suppose I assign a group project, and I post a list of groups and the names of students assigned to each group. Later, after the assignments have been completed and graded, I post a list of grades on the Web site. Because of university privacy policy, I cannot post the grades by student name or identifier; so instead, I post the grades for each group. If you want to get the grades for each student, all you have to do is combine the list from Lecture 5 with the list from Lecture 10. You might say that the release of grades in this example does no real harm—after all, it is a list of grades from one assignment.

But go back to Megan Cho in HR. Suppose Megan evaluates the employee compensation program. The COO believes salary offers have been inconsistent over time and that they vary too widely by department. Accordingly, the COO authorizes Megan to receive a report that lists *SalaryOfferAmount* and *OfferDate*, and a second report that lists *Department* and *AverageSalary*.

Those reports are relevant to her task and seem innocuous enough. But Megan realizes that she could use the information they contain to determine individual salaries—information she does not have and is not authorized to receive. She proceeds as follows.

Like all employees, Megan has access to the employee directory on the Web portal. Using the directory, she can obtain a list of employees in each department, and using the facilities of her ever-so-helpful report-authoring system, she combines that list with the department and average-salary report. Now she has a list of the names of employees in a group and the average salary for that group.

Megan's employer likes to welcome new employees to the company. Accordingly, each week the company publishes an article about new employees who have been hired. The article makes pleasant comments about each person and encourages employees to meet and greet them.

Megan, however, has other ideas. Because the report is published on the Web portal, she can obtain an electronic copy of it. It's an Acrobat report, and using Acrobat's handy Search feature, she soon has a list of employees and the week they were hired.

She now examines the report she received for her study, the one that has *SalaryOfferAmount* and the offer date, and she does some interpretation. During the week of July 21, three offers were extended: one for \$35,000, one for \$53,000, and one for \$110,000. She also notices from the "New Employees" report that a director of marketing programs, a product test engineer, and a receptionist were hired that same week. It's unlikely that they paid the receptionist \$110,000; that sounds more like the director of marketing programs. So, she now "knows" (infers) that person's salary.

Next, going back to the department report and using the employee directory, she sees that the marketing director is in the marketing programs department. There are just three people in that department, and their average salary is \$105,000. Doing the arithmetic, she now knows that the average salary for the other two people is \$102,500. If she can find the hire week for one of those other two people, she can find out both the second and third person's salaries.

You get the idea. Megan was given just two reports to do her job. Yet she combined the information in those reports with publicly available information and is able to deduce salaries, for at least some employees. These salaries are much more than she is supposed to know. This is a semantic security problem. ■

Discussion Questions

1. In your own words, explain the difference between access security and semantic security.
2. Why do reporting systems increase the risk of semantic security problems?
3. What can an organization do to protect itself against accidental losses due to semantic security problems?
4. What legal responsibility does an organization have to protect against semantic security problems?
5. Suppose semantic security problems are inevitable. Do you see an opportunity for new products from insurance companies? If so, describe such an insurance product. If not, explain why not.

Opposing Forces

GUIDE

Data Mining in the Real World

I'm not really a contrarian about data mining. I believe in it. After all, it's my career. But data mining in the real world is a lot different from the way it's described in textbooks.

"There are many reasons it's different. One is that the data are always dirty, with missing values, values way out of the range of possibility, and time values that make no sense. Here's an example: Somebody sets the server system clock incorrectly and runs the server for a while with the wrong time. When they notice the mistake, they set the clock to the correct time. But all of the transactions that were running during that interval have an ending time before the starting time. When we run the data analysis, and compute elapsed time, the results are negative for those transactions.

"Missing values are a similar problem. Consider the records of just 10 purchases. Suppose that two of the records are missing the customer number and one is missing the year part of transaction date. So you throw out three records, which is 30 percent of the data. You then notice that two more records have dirty data, and so you throw them out, too. Now you've lost half your data.

"Another problem is that you know the least when you start the study. So you work for a few months and learn that if you had another variable; say the customer's Zip code, or age, or something else, you could do a much better analysis. But those other data just aren't available. Or, maybe they are available, but to get the data you have to reprocess millions of transactions, and you don't have the time or budget to do that.

"Overfitting is another problem, a huge one. I can build a model to fit any set of data you have. Give me 100 data points and in a few minutes, I can give you 100 different equations that will predict those 100 data points. With neural networks, you can create a model of any level of complexity you want, except that none of those equations will predict new cases with any accuracy at all. When using neural nets, you have to be very careful not to overfit the data.

"Then, too, data mining is about probabilities, not certainty. Bad luck happens. Say I build a model that predicts the probability that a customer will make a purchase. Using the model on new-customer data. I find three customers who have a .7 probability of buying something. That's a good number, well over a 50–50 chance, but it's still possible that none of them will buy. In fact, the probability that none of them will buy is $.3 \times .3 \times .3$, or .027, which is 2.7 percent.

"Now suppose I give the names of the three customers to a salesperson who calls on them, and sure enough, we have a stream of bad luck

and none of them buys. This bad result doesn't mean the model is wrong. But what does the salesperson think? He thinks the model is worthless and can do better on his own. He tells his manager who tells her associate, who tells the Northeast Region, and sure enough, the model has a bad reputation all across the company.

"Another problem is seasonality. Say all your training data are from the summer. Will your model be valid for the winter? Maybe, but maybe not. You might even know that it won't be valid for predicting winter sales, but if you don't have winter data, what do you do?

"When you start a data-mining project, you never know how it will turn out. I worked on one project for 6 months, and when we finished, I didn't think our model was any good. We had too many problems with data: wrong, dirty, and missing. There was no way we could know ahead of time that it would happen, but it did.

"When the time came to present the results to senior management, what could we do? How could we say we took 6 months of our time and substantial computer resources to create a bad model? We had a model, but I just didn't think it would make accurate predictions. I was a junior member of the team, and it wasn't for me to decide. I kept my mouth shut, but I never felt good about it. Fortunately, the project was cancelled later for other reasons.

"However, I'm only talking about my bad experiences. Some of my projects have been excellent. On many, we found interesting and important patterns and information, and a few times, I've created very accurate predictive models. It's not easy, though, and you have to be very careful. Also, lucky!" ■

Discussion Questions

1. Summarize the concerns expressed by this contrarian.
2. Do you think the concerns raised here are sufficient to avoid data-mining projects altogether?
3. If you were a junior member of a data-mining team and you thought that the model that had been developed was ineffective, maybe even wrong, what would you do? If your boss disagrees with your beliefs, would you go higher in the organization? What are the risks of doing so? What else might you do?

Use this Active Review to verify that you understand the ideas and concepts that answer the chapter's study questions.

Q1 Why do organizations need business intelligence?

Identify the economic factors that have caused so much data to be created. Define *petabyte* and *exabyte*. Explain the opportunities that all of this data presents to business.

Q2 What business intelligence systems are available?

Define *business intelligence system* and *business intelligence tool*. Name and describe the use of three categories of BI tools. Define *business intelligence application* and use an example to explain the differences among BI tools, applications, and systems.

Q3 What are typical reporting applications?

Name and describe five basic reporting operations. Explain why the report in Figure 9-5 is more useful than the list in Figure 9-2. Define *RFM analysis* and explain the actions that should be taken with customers who have the following scores: [1, 1, 1,], [5, 1, 1,], [1, 1, 3], and [1, 4, 1]. Explain OLAP and describe its unique characteristics. Explain the roles for measure and dimension in an OLAP cube. Illustrate an OLAP cube with a single measure and five dimensions, two dimensions on one axis and three on another. Show how drill down applies to your example.

Q4 What are typical data-mining applications?

Define *data mining* and explain how its use typically differs from reporting applications. Explain why data-mining tools are difficult to use well. Describe the differences between unsupervised and supervised data mining. Use an example to illustrate cluster analysis and regression analysis. Define *neural networks* and explain why the term is a misnomer.

Define *support, confidence,* and *lift* and illustrate these terms using the data in Figure 9-12. Describe a good application for market-basket analysis results. Describe the purpose of decision trees and explain how the data in Figure 9-14 is used to evaluate loans for possible purchase.

Q5 What is the purpose of data warehouses and data marts?

Describe the need and functions of data warehouses and data marts. Name and describe the role of data warehouse components. List and explain the problems that can exist in data used for data mining and sophisticated reporting. Use the example of a supply chain to describe the differences between a data warehouse and data mart.

Q6 What are typical knowledge-management applications?

Define *knowledge management* and describe its primary benefits. Explain how KM document sharing differs from content management. Explain the importance of indexing and describe when Google indexing is useful and when it is not. Explain the statement, "RSS is like email for content." Define *RSS reader* and *RSS feed* and explain how they interact. Define *expert system* and explain why expert systems have a checkered reputation. Describe the purpose of the expert systems in use at the Washington University School of Medicine.

Q7 How are business intelligence applications delivered?

Name the components of a business intelligence system and briefly describe the nature or purpose of each. Explain the management functions of a BI server and describe three types of servers defined in this chapter. Explain the difference between push and pull systems. Describe the devices that receive BI results. Summarize the nature of procedures used in BI systems.

KEY TERMS AND CONCEPTS

Alert 359
BI application server 357
Business intelligence 331
Business intelligence (BI) application 333
Business intelligence (BI) system 333
Business intelligence (BI) tool 333
Clickstream data 350
Cluster analysis 341
Confidence 343
Cross-selling 343
Curse of dimensionality 351
Data mart 349
Data mining 338
Data-mining tool 333
Data warehouse 349
Decision tree 344
Dimension 337
Dirty data 349
Drill down 338
Exabyte 331
Exception alert 359
Expert systems 355
Granularity 350
If . . . then . . . decision rule 345
Indexing 353
Knowledge management (KM) 352
Knowledge-management tool 333
Lift 344

USING YOUR KNOWLEDGE

1. Reflect on the differences between reporting systems and data-mining systems. What are their similarities and differences? How do their costs differ? What benefits does each offer? How would an organization choose between these two BI tools?
2. Suppose you are a member of the Audubon Society, and the board of the local chapter asks you to help them analyze its member data. The group wants to analyze the demographics of its membership against members' activity, including events attended, classes attended, volunteer activities, and donations. Describe two different reporting applications and one data-mining application that they might develop. Be sure to include a specific description of the goals of each system.
3. Suppose you are the director of student activities at your university. Recently, some students have charged that your department misallocates its resources. They claim the allocation is based on outdated student preferences. Funds are given to activities that few students find attractive, and insufficient funds are allocated to new activities in which students do want to participate. Describe how you could use reporting and/or data-mining systems to assess this claim.
4. Google *RSS reader* and download an RSS product. Set up feeds to your reader to the five most important business sources you know. Add feeds to your reader about technology and about one of your hobbies. Have at least 15 feeds, total. Run your RSS feeder for 3 days, and list the top five most interesting or informative items your reader made available that you would otherwise not have known about. Document your results by naming your reader, listing your sources, and describing the five most interesting items.

COLLABORATION EXERCISES AND CASES

Collaborate with a group of students on the following exercises. Recall from Chapter 2 that collaboration is more than cooperation because it involves iteration and feedback. Post a document, a discussion item, a wiki item, or an idea and obtain feedback from your team members. Similarly, read the ideas of others and comment on them. Try to innovate in both the process by which you collaborate and the work product that you create. Avoid face-to-face meetings. Instead, use collaborative software such as Google Docs & Spreadsheets, Microsoft Groove, or Microsoft SharePoint to facilitate your ideas.

1. In this exercise, you will apply the knowledge of this chapter to the lost-customer problem at Carbon Creek gardens. Begin by rereading the problem description in the *Business Intelligence in Practice* box on page 332.

   a. Mary wants to know when she's lost a customer. One way to help her would be to produce a report, say in PDF format, showing the top 50 customers from the prior year. Mary could print that report, or we could place it on a private section of her Web site so that she could download it from wherever she happens to be.

      Periodically—say, once a week—Mary could request a report that shows the top buyers for that week. That report could also be in PDF format, or it could just be produced onscreen. Mary could compare the two reports to determine who is missing. If she wonders whether a customer such as Tootsie has been ordering, she could request a query report on Tootsie's activities.

      Describe the advantages and disadvantages of this solution.

   b. Describe the best possible application of an OLAP tool at Carbon Creek. Can it be used to solve the lost-customer problem? Why or why not? What is the best way, if any, for Mary to use OLAP at The Gardens? If none, say why.

   c. Describe the best possible application of decision-tree analysis at Carbon Creek. Can it be used to solve the lost-customer problem? Why or why not? What is the best way, if any, for Mary to use decision-tree analysis at The Gardens? If none, say why.

   d. Describe the best possible application of RFM analysis at Carbon Creek. Can it be used to solve the lost-customer problem? Why or why not? What is the best way, if any, for Mary to use RFM at The Gardens? If none, say why.

e. Describe the best possible application of market-basket analysis at Carbon Creek. Can it be used to solve the lost-customer problem? Why or why not? What is the best way, if any, for Mary to use market-basket analysis at The Gardens? If none, say why.

f. Which of the applications of BI tools in this exercise will provide Mary the best value? If you owned Carbon Creek Gardens and you were going to implement just one of these applications, which would you choose? Why?

2. In this exercise, you will be asked to extend RFM analysis in creative and innovative ways.

a. As a team, explain how RFM analysis works. Also explain how the RFMP analysis described in the *Innovation in Practice* box on page 351 works.

b. As a team, evaluate the effectiveness of RFM analysis. What seem to be the chief strengths of this technique? Under what conditions would its results be misleading? Describe, in general terms, when you would use this technique and when you would not.

c. As a team, evaluate the effectiveness of RFMP analysis. What action should you take with a [1, 1, 1, 5] customer? What action should you take with a [3, 3, 3, 1] customer? What about a [5, 5, 5, 1] customer? Under what circumstances, if any, is RFMP preferred over RFM?

d. Devise a version of the RFM analysis to rank suppliers. What criteria would you use to rank them? Explain how you would use the supplier-ranking scores produced by your analysis.

e. Devise a version of the RFM analysis to rank salespeople. What criteria would you use to rank them? Explain how you would use the salesperson-ranking scores produced by your analysis.

f. Apply the RFM methodology for the ranking of an entity other those already considered. Strive to create the most innovative and useful application of RFM methodology possible.

g. Describe what you think is the proper domain for RFM ranking systems. What kinds of problems or data are best suited for this type of analysis? What kinds are worst suited?

APPLICATION EXERCISES

1. OLAP cubes are very similar to Microsoft Excel *pivot tables*. For this exercise, assume that in your organization's purchasing agents rate vendors similar to the situation in Application Exercise 2 in Chapter 8 on page 325.

a. Open Excel and import the data in the worksheet named *Vendors* from the Excel file **Ch09Ex01**, which you can find on the text's Web site. The spreadsheet will have the following column names: *VendorName, EmployeeName, Date, Year,* and *Rating.*

b. Under the *Insert* ribbon in Excel, click *Pivot Table.* A wizard will open. Select *Excel* and *Pivot table* in the first screen. Click *Next.*

c. When asked to provide a data range, drag your mouse over the data you imported so as to select all of the data. Be sure to include the column headings. Excel will fill in the range values in the open dialog box. Place your pivot table in a separate spreadsheet.

d. Excel will create a field list on the right-hand side of your spreadsheet. Drag and drop the field named *VendorName* onto the words "Drop Row Fields Here." Drag and drop *EmployeeName* on to the words "Drop Column Fields Here." Now drag and drop the field named *Rating* on to the words "Drop Data Items Here." Voilà! You have a pivot table.

e. To see how the table works, drag and drop more fields on the various sections of your pivot table. For example, drop *Year* on top of *Employee.* Then move *Year* below *Employee.* Now move *Year* below *Vendor.* All of this action is just like an OLAP cube, and, in fact, OLAP cubes are readily displayed in Excel pivot tables. The major difference is that OLAP cubes are usually based on thousands or more rows of data.

2. It is surprisingly easy to create a market-basket report using table data in Access. To do so, however, you will need to enter SQL expressions into the Access query builder. Here, you can just copy SQL statements to type them in. If you take a database class, you will learn how to code SQL statements like those you will use here.

a. Create an Access database with a table named *Order_Data* having columns *OrderNumber, ItemName,* and *Quantity,* with data types Number (*LongInteger*), Text (50), and Number (*LongInteger*), respectively. Define the key as the composite (*OrderNumber, ItemName*).

b. Import the data from the Excel file **Ch09Ex02** into the *Order_Data* table.

c. Now, to perform the market-basket analysis, you will need to enter several SQL statements into Access. To do so, click the queries tab and select *Create Query* in Design view. Click *Close* when the Show Table dialog box appears. Right-click in the gray section above the grid in the *Select Query* window. Select *SQL View*. Enter the following expression exactly as it appears here:

```
SELECT  T1.ItemName as FirstItem,
        T2.ItemName as SecondItem
FROM    Order_Data T1, Order_Data T2
WHERE   T1.OrderNumber = T2.OrderNumber
  AND   T1.ItemName <> T2.ItemName;
```

Click the red exclamation point in the toolbar to run the query. Correct any typing mistakes and, once it works, save the query using the name *TwoItemBasket*.

d. Now enter a second SQL statement. Again, click the queries tab and select *Create Query* in Design view. Click *Close* when the Show Table dialog box appears. Right-click in the gray section above the grid in the *Select Query* window. Select *SQL View*. Enter the following expression exactly as it appears here:

```
SELECT    TwoItemBasket.FirstItem,
          TwoItemBasket.SecondItem,
          Count(*) AS SupportCount
FROM      TwoItemBasket
GROUP BY  TwoItemBasket.FirstItem,
          TwoItemBasket.SecondItem;
```

Correct any typing mistakes and, once it works, save the query using the name *SupportCount*.

e. Examine the results of the second query and verify that the two query statements have correctly calculated the number of times that two items have appeared together. Explain further calculations you need to make to compute support.

f. Explain the calculations you need to make to compute lift. Although you can make those calculations using SQL, you need more SQL knowledge to do it, and we will skip that here.

g. Explain, in your own words, what the query in part c seems to be doing. What does the query in part d seem to be doing? Again, you will need to take a database class to learn how to code such expressions, but this exercise should give you a sense of the kinds of calculations that are possible with SQL.

CASE STUDY 9

Knowledge Management at 3M

3M Company develops and manufactures diversified products for many industries, including industrial, consumer and leisure, safety, office, electronics, health care, and transportation. In 2006, its revenues totaled nearly $23 billion, with a net income of $3.85 billion. That same year, 3M employed 75,000 employees.

3M is a global company with different business divisions that focus on different industry segments. It is known for strong interdivision cooperation. It sells through many channels, including distributors, dealers, jobbers, and retailers; some products are even sold directly to consumers. 3M has 12 sales offices in the United States and 185 more offices internationally.

Sources: http://3m.com (accessed August 2007); *http://finance.yahoo.com* (accessed January 2005).

Questions

1. To gain an appreciation of the complexity of this company, visit its Web site at *http://3m.com*. Assume that you are a U.S. customer. Access the 3M site and locate the Material Safety Data Sheet (MSDS) for the product having the 3M ID Number 62–1838–5430–6. What is this product? What is the purpose of the MSDS?
2. Access a 3M site for any country other than the United States. Is the product in question 1 sold in the country you visited? If so, is there an MSDS for that product in that country?
3. Access the U.S. 3M site for "Manufacturing & Industry, Abrasives & Sandpaper." Visit the sections of the site for "Products," "Documentation," and "Where to Buy." Summarize how 3M could use OLAP analysis. Specify measures, dimensions, and cubes. What information would 3M obtain from this analysis? What value does the dynamic aspect of an OLAP analysis add?
4. Do you think the abrasives division could effectively use an RFM analysis? If so, specify how it could perform such an analysis. If not, explain why not.
5. Do you think the abrasives division could effectively use a market-basket analysis? If so, what would it do with the information? If not, why not?
6. Suppose that you want to learn which 3M product is the best for gluing fiberglass to teak (wood). Teak is particularly oily and is difficult to glue. Access the 3M site and attempt to determine which 3M adhesive is best suited for this task. Describe your experience.
7. Repeat question 6, but use Google instead. Describe your experience.
8. Somewhere in 3M there is a person who knows, off the top of his or her head, what product(s) to use to glue fiberglass to teak. Is there any way to find out who that person is? Does 3M know who that person is? What type of BI system might 3M set up to help customers find such experts?
9. The 3M site is oriented around divisions and products. If you know the product you want, you can learn all about that product. But it is poorly organized with regards to problems and needs. 3M is a very successful company. Why do you think the site is constructed in this manner?

PART 3 THE INTERNATIONAL DIMENSION

Global IS and the Value Chain

STUDY QUESTIONS

Q1 How do global information systems benefit the value chain?

Q2 Why do global information systems impact functional and cross-functional systems differently?

Q3 How do global information systems affect supply chain profitability?

Q4 What is the economic impact of global manufacturing?

Q5 Should information systems be instruments for exporting cultural values?

Q1 How Do Global Information Systems Benefit the Value Chain?

Because of information systems, any or all of the value chain activities in Figure 7-2 (page 252) can be performed anywhere in the world. An international company can conduct sales and marketing efforts locally, for every market in which it sells. 3M, for example, sells in the United States with a U.S. sales force, in France with a French sales force, and in Argentina with an Argentinean sales force. Depending on local laws and customs, those sales offices may be owned by 3M, or they may be locally owned entities with which 3M contracts for sales and marketing services. 3M can coordinate all of the sales efforts of these entities using the same CRM system. When 3M managers need to roll up sales totals for a sales projection, they can do so using an integrated, worldwide system.

Manufacturing of a final product is frequently distributed throughout the world. Components of the Boeing 787 are manufactured in Italy, China, England, and numerous other countries and delivered to Everett, Washington, for final assembly. Each manufacturing facility has its own inbound logistics, manufacturing, and outbound logistics activity, but those activities are linked together via information systems.

For example, Rolls Royce manufactures an engine and delivers that engine to Boeing via its outbound logistics activity. Boeing receives the engine using its inbound logistics activity. All of this activity is coordinated via shared, interorganizational information systems. Rolls Royce's CRM is connected with Boeing's SRM, using techniques described in Chapter 8.

Because of the abundance of low-cost, well-educated, English-speaking professionals in India, many organizations have chosen to outsource their service and support functions to India. Some accounting functions are outsourced to India as well.

Because of time differences, virtual companies operate around the globe 24/7. Boeing engineers in Los Angeles can develop a design for an engine-support strut and send that design to Rolls Royce in England at the end of their day. The design will be waiting for Rolls Royce engineers at the start of

their day. They review the design, make needed adjustments, and send it back to Boeing in Los Angeles, where the reviewed, adjusted design arrives at the start of the workday in Los Angeles. The ability to work around the clock by moving work into other time zones has greatly increased productivity.

Q2 Why Do Global Information Systems Impact Functional and Cross-Functional Systems Differently?

As you learned in Chapter 7, functional information systems support business processes within a given value chain activity or business function. Because the systems operate independently, the organization suffers from a lack of data integration. Sales and marketing data, for example, are not integrated with operations or manufacturing data.

This lack of integration has *advantages*, however, for international organizations and international systems. Because the order-processing functional system for a hypothetical U.S. company is separate from and independent of the manufacturing systems of its Taiwanese suppliers, it is unnecessary to accommodate language, business, and cultural differences in a single system. U.S. order-processing systems can operate in English and reflect the practices and culture of the United States. Taiwanese manufacturing information systems can operate in Chinese and reflect the business practices and culture of Taiwan. As long as there is an adequate data interface between the two systems, they can operate independently, sharing data when necessary.

Cross-functional, integrated systems such as ERP solve the problems of data isolation by integrating data into databases that provide a comprehensive and organization-wide view. However, because they are integrated, cross-functional systems do not readily accommodate differences in language, business practices, and cultural norms.

For example, consider SAP's ERP system. SAP software is developed and licensed by SAP, a German software company. Because SAP addresses a global market, SAP software was localized long ago into English and numerous other foreign languages. Suppose that a multinational company with operations in Spain, Italy, Taiwan, Singapore, and Los Angeles uses SAP. Should this company allow the use of different language versions of SAP? As long as the functionality of the versions is the same, no harm occurs by doing so.

But what if employees enter data in different languages? If this is allowed, much of the value of an integrated database is lost. If you speak English, what good are customer contact data recorded in Spanish, Italian, Chinese, and English? Data isolation entered the ERP system via the back door.

Inherent processes are even more problematic. As you learned in Chapter 7, each software product assumes that the software will be used by people filling particular job functions and performing their actions in a certain way. ERP vendors justify this standardization by saying that their procedures are based on industry-wide best practices and that the organization will benefit by following these standard processes. That statement may be true, but some inherent processes might conflict with cultural norms. If they do, it will be very difficult for management to convince employees to follow those inherent processes. Or at least it will be difficult in some cultures to do so.

Inherent processes are standardizing business processes worldwide. Over time, conflicting cultural differences will be eliminated, and the world of commerce will become uniform, worldwide. One can debate whether this standardization is beneficial or harmful. See question Q5 on page 372.

Q3 How Do Global Information Systems Affect Supply Chain Profitability?

In short, global information systems increase supply chain profitability. As stated in Chapter 8, supply chain performance is driven by four factors: facilities, inventories, transportation, and information. Every one of these drivers is positively affected by global information systems. Because of global IS, facilities can be located anywhere in the world. If Amazon.com finds it economically advantageous to warehouse books in Iceland, it can do so. If Rolls

Royce can manufacture its engine turbine blades more cheaply in Poland, it can do so.

Furthermore, information systems reduce inventories, and hence save costs. They can be used to reduce or eliminate the *bullwhip effect,* a phenomenon in which the variability in the size and timing of orders increases at each stage of the supply chain. (For more on this topic, see Chapter 8, page 306.) They also support JIT inventory techniques worldwide. Using information systems, the order of a Dell computer from a user in Bolivia triggers a manufacturing system at Dell, which, in turn, triggers the order of a component from a warehouse in Taiwan—all automatically.

To underscore this point, consider the inventories that exist at this moment in time, worldwide. Every component in one of those inventories represents a waste of the world's resources. Any product or component sitting on a shelf is not being used and is adding no value to the global economy. In a perfect world, a customer would think, "I want a new computer," and that thought would trigger systems all over the world to produce and assemble necessary components, instantly. Given that we live in a world bound by time and space, instantaneous production is unreachable. But the goal of worldwide information systems for supply chain inventory management is to come as close to instantaneous as possible.

Consider transportation, the third driver. When you order a book from Amazon.com, you are presented with at least four shipping options. You can choose the speed and attendant price that is appropriate for your needs. Similar systems for businesses allow them to choose the delivery option that optimizes the value they generate. Further, automated systems enable suppliers and customers to track the shipment's location, 24/7, worldwide.

Finally, global information systems produce comprehensive, accurate, and timely information. As you learned in Chapter 9, information systems produce data at prodigious rates, worldwide. This data facilitates operations as just discussed, but it also produces information for planning, organizing, deciding, and other analyses.

Next time you walk into Wal-Mart, think about the impact global information systems had in producing, ordering, and delivering the thousands of items you see.

Q4 What Is the Economic Impact of Global Manufacturing?

Henry Ford pioneered modern manufacturing methods, and in the process he reduced the price of automobiles to the point that they were no longer the playthings of the very rich, but were affordable to the general population. In 1914, Ford took the unprecedented step of unilaterally increasing his workers' pay from $2.50 per day for 10 hours' work to $5 per day for 8 hours' work. As a consequence, many of his workers could soon afford to purchase an automobile. By paying his workers more, Ford increased demand.

The increase in demand was not due only to purchases by his workers, of course. Because of what economists call the *accelerator effect,* a dollar spent will contribute two or three dollars of activity to the economy. Ford's workers spent their increased pay not just on autos, but also on goods and services in their local community, which benefited via the accelerator effect. That benefit enabled non–Ford workers to afford an auto, too. Further, because of the positive publicity he achieved with the pay increase, the community was strongly disposed to purchase a Ford automobile.

Consider those events in light of global manufacturing. For example, if Boeing manufactures airplanes entirely in the United States, the U.S. economy will be the sole beneficiary of that economic activity. If an Italian airline chooses to buy a Boeing plane, the transaction will be a cost to the Italian economy. There will be no accelerator effect, and the transaction will have no consequence on Italians' propensity to fly.

However, if Boeing purchases major components for its airplanes from Italian companies, then that purchase will generate an accelerator effect for the Italian economy. By buying in Italy, Boeing contributes to Italy's economy, and ultimately increases Italians' propensity to fly. That foreign-component purchase will, of course, reduce economic activity in the United States, but if it induces Italians to purchase sufficiently more Boeing airplanes, then it is possible that the loss will be compensated by the increase in airplane sales volume. That purchase will also benefit Boeing's image among Italians and increase the likelihood of sales to the Italian government.

The same phenomenon pertains to Dell computers, Cisco routers, and Microsoft software. It also explains why Toyota manufactures cars in the United States.

Q5 Should Information Systems Be Instruments for Exporting Cultural Values?

The question of whether information systems *should be* instruments for exporting cultural values is complex. As discussed under question Q2, it is undeniable

that information systems *do* export cultural values. When an organization installs an ERP system, it installs inherent processes. According to ERP vendors, everyone ultimately benefits, because these processes encode each industry's "best practices." But what is deemed a best practice depends heavily on culture. Speed and efficiency might be highly valued in one culture, whereas warm and engaging interpersonal relationships might be highly valued in another. The inherent process, however, will simply encode the cultural values of the designers of the system.

One might say that exporting such cultural values is innocent, and, ultimately, if someone does not like the procedures in place at his or her employer he or she can choose to work elsewhere. But what about values such as freedom of speech? In the spring of 2006, the Chinese government asked MSN to shut down IP support for blog sites that it deemed offensive. The sites, located in China, were criticizing the Chinese government. Had the sites been located in the United States, the First Amendment of the Constitution would have protected the blogs.

The question for MSN was whether it should comply with the Chinese government's request. The values of most—if not all—of the people who constructed the MSN system would support freedom of speech. But the site was operating in China, and as a sovereign government China has the right to enact laws as it sees fit. MSN chose to shut down the sites, and many in the United States criticized that decision. Google experienced similar criticism when, under pressure from China and other countries, it agreed not to allow searching on terms such as *democracy*.

But consider a site that offers online gambling. Gambling is legal in many countries and is considered culturally positive in some. Most European nations allow online gambling. The U.S. federal government, however, outlawed online sports betting, and no state has licensed any form of online games of chance. If a Chinese company were to offer either form of online gambling from a site in the United States, the U.S. government or a state would certainly shut it down.

Is this a double standard? Does the United States want the right to shut down information systems that violate its laws, but disallow other nations from doing the same? Some would say the comparison fails because gambling is a vice and freedom of speech is a basic human right. But, not every nation or culture agrees.

Information systems project human values. The question is, "Whose values?"

ACTIVE REVIEW

Use this Active Review to verify that you understand the ideas and concepts that answer the study questions in the International Dimension.

Q1 How do global information systems benefit the value chain?

Using Figure 7-2 (page 252) as a guide, explain how each primary value chain activity can be performed anywhere in the world. Explain how global, virtual companies operate 24/7. Using the answers to this question, explain three ways that 3M benefits from global information systems.

Q2 Why do global information systems impact functional and cross-functional systems differently?

In your own words, explain the difference between functional and cross-functional systems. Explain the problem of functional systems that cross-functional systems overcome. Explain how this problem can actually be an advantage for global information systems. Describe how different languages, business practices, and cultural norms pose a problem for cross-functional systems. Describe how inherent processes standardize business processes worldwide. State whether you think standardization is beneficial or harmful.

Q3 How do global information systems affect supply chain profitability?

State the short answer to this study question. Identify the four drivers of supply chain profitability. Discuss how global information systems affect each driver. Explain how inventories represent waste. Summarize the ways that global information systems help to fill the shelves at Wal-Mart.

Q4 What is the economic impact of global manufacturing?

Summarize the impact that Henry Ford's act of increasing his workers' pay had on Ford auto sales. Describe how the accelerator effect contributed to the increase in demand. Explain how this same phenomenon pertains to Boeing acquiring major subsystems from manufacturers in Italy or to Toyota building autos in the United States.

Q5 Should information systems be instruments for exporting cultural values?

Describe how information systems export cultural values. Explain how the term *best practice* encodes a cultural bias. State whether you think MSN should have shut down the IP addresses for the blogs in China. Explain the costs and benefits to MSN of its decision. Describe the difference between MSN shutting down the Chinese blog and the United States shutting down an online sports-betting site. If you see no difference, explain why.

CASE 3-1

PART 3

Dun and Bradstreet Sells Reports Using E-Commerce

Dun and Bradstreet (D&B) collects and publishes corporate and financial data and data analysis about public and private companies. Customers use D&B's products to assess the creditworthiness of potential customers, to find and evaluate customer leads, to select potential suppliers, and to facilitate supplier negotiations. In business for over 160 years, D&B stores data about 80 million businesses in over 200 countries worldwide. To provide the latest, most up-to-date information, D&B updates its databases more than one million times a day.

Throughout the years, D&B has used the latest technology to deliver its reports. In the beginning, reports were on paper and delivered via mail. Later, reports were faxed to customers, and still later they were delivered via private communications networks. With the advent of the Internet, however, D&B has an even more effective delivery medium: Web-based e-commerce.

Figure 1 below, shows a search page from the D&B Web site (*http://dnb.com*). The user has selected a credit report and is using the form shown to find a credit report available for Georgia-Pacific, a building-products company located in the state of Georgia in the United States. Available reports are shown in the response in Figure 2, on the next page. These reports can be purchased online via the D&B commerce server.

Consider the advantages to D&B of delivering these reports via the Web. First, the site is up and running 24/7, including holidays. Second, to purchase a report the user enters all customer data, saving D&B data entry and related administrative costs. Furthermore, by using Web-based e-commerce, D&B can change or extend its product offerings simply by making a few changes to its commerce server database. There is no need to create, print, inventory, or mail a new catalog. Finally, the commerce server records

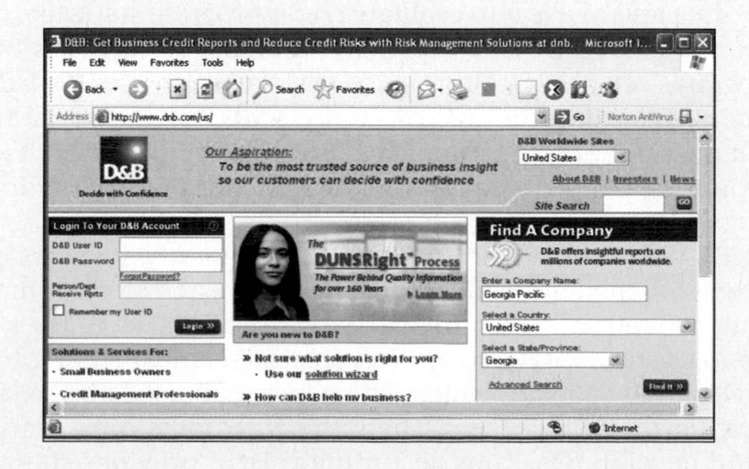

Figure 1
D&B Web Storefront

Source: Used with permission of D&B Corporation

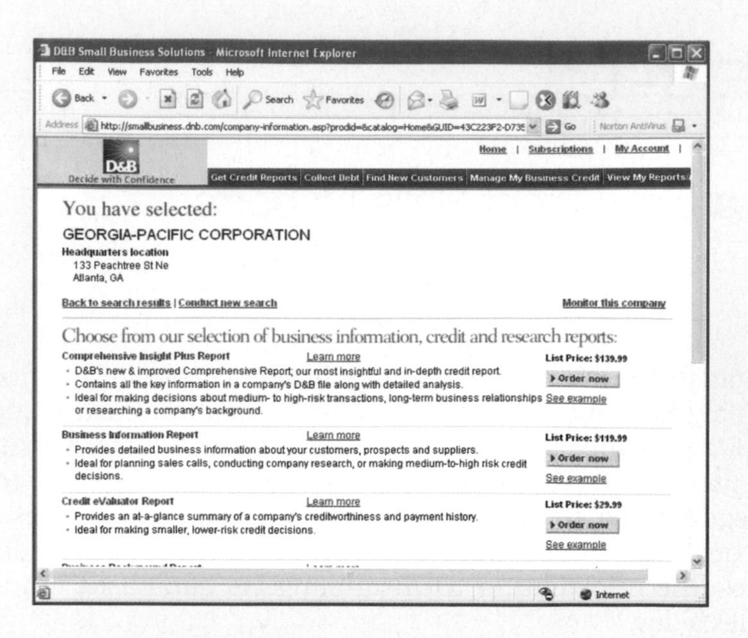

Figure 2
Example of D&B Product Offerings

Source: Used with permission of D&B Corporation

customer purchase data that can be mined for information to guide future product offerings (as you learned in Chapter 9). Thus, by using e-commerce technology, D&B sells 24/7, saves costs, distributes more current data, and gains marketing information.

Some customers are willing to buy company reports using the commerce server described above. For others, this process is too slow and cumbersome. For example, consider the customers that use D&B data to assess creditworthiness. Because of competitive pressure, some companies must make credit assessments immediately, in real time, while interacting with their customers. For such applications, buying a prewritten report over the D&B commerce server will not suffice.

Instead, these customers want to use automated processes to access the D&B databases. They want to write credit-analysis programs that obtain needed data from D&B in real time. Consider, for example, the needs of a computer distributor or retailer. The distributor's customers can place large orders using the distributor's Web storefront. The equipment price for a medium-sized network could total $40,000 or $50,000, and before accepting the order the distributor needs to assess the customer's creditworthiness. In situations like this, the distributor wants its commerce server programs to access D&B data and to use it to evaluate credit programmatically.

To meet this need, D&B developed a version of Web services that its customers' programs can access. Although the D&B version uses XML documents for data exchange, it does not use all of the XML Web service standards. In particular, it does not provide a standard service description nor use standard services protocols. Instead, the D&B service provides a proprietary interface for customers.

Still, D&B's Web services do use XML. Consequently, its users can realize the advantages of schema validation, and both D&B and its customers can use XML standards to reformat documents automatically.

In order to use the D&B Web services, customers must enter into an agreement with D&B that specifies which data will be accessed and what and how they will pay for that data access. Then, the customers must learn the D&B interface and develop programs accordingly. D&B provides some technical assistance to customer program developers.

By using Web services to obtain data, customers obtain the latest, up-to-the-minute data. This advantage is important, because D&B makes over a million updates to its database every day. Furthermore, D&B Web services provide a single, consistent interface for customers to use. Customers save on costs because they need to develop D&B access programs only once; all applications can use those programs to obtain D&B data. Finally, D&B customers can use the Web services interface to request alerts when particular data are updated. Alerts enable customers to update their own databases with the most current data.

Sources: Sean Rhody, "Dun and Bradstreet," *Web Services Journal*, Vol. 1, Issue 1, *http://sys-con.com/webservices* (accessed December 2004); Dun and Bradstreet, "Data Integration Toolkit," *http://globalaccess.dnb.com* (accessed August 2007).

QUESTIONS

1. Summarize the difference between obtaining D&B data by purchasing reports from the D&B Web server and by obtaining D&B data via Web services.
2. Explain how schema validation improves the quality of the data exchange. How can D&B and its Web services customers use schema validation to advantage?
3. As stated, D&B did not describe its Web services in the standard way. What are the consequences to D&B? What are the consequences to D&B's customers? D&B could upgrade its Web services to use these standards. If you worked at D&B, how would you decide whether to make that upgrade? Consider the consequences of the upgrade on both new and existing D&B Web services customers.
4. Besides credit reporting, D&B customers use D&B data to find and assess customer prospects and to determine potential sources of suppliers. Explain how Web services could be used for these applications as well as for credit analysis.
5. D&B is an international organization that provides data to customers worldwide. What advantages does the use of Web services provide for non–U.S. customers?
6. How does the D&B Web services interface give D&B a competitive advantage over other data providers?

CASE 3-2

Laguna Tools

Laguna Tools is a privately held reseller of high-end woodworking equipment. Based in Irvine, California, Laguna imports table saws, lathes, planers, jointers, and combination machines from top-quality European manufacturers. It resells those machines in the United States and Canada. Laguna is especially known for the comprehensive line of band saws that are constructed to its own specifications by factories in Italy and Poland.

Laguna's competitive strategy is to provide the highest-quality tools for woodworking professionals, including cabinet makers, artists, and wood fabricators. It also sells to high-end, "carriage trade" amateur woodworkers. With prices ranging from $2,000 to $20,000 per machine, Laguna's machines are among the most expensive woodworking equipment sold.

Most woodworking shops have a need for multiple machines. A common shop has table saw, band saw, jointer, planer, shaper, lathe, and mortise machines. Accordingly, once a customer orders one machine from Laguna, he or she becomes a particularly valuable asset. The machines are of such quality that a company or individual who buys one is quite likely to buy a second.

Laguna advertises in popular woodworking magazines, and it uses its Web site at *http://lagunatools.com* to gather leads. The company follows up on all leads with phone conversations and promotional literature. (So, out of courtesy to the company, do not fill out the customer information form on its Web site unless you are in the market for very high-quality machinery.)

QUESTIONS

1. What information should Laguna keep in its database of prospective customers?
2. What information should Laguna keep about customers who order?
3. When a salesperson is talking with a potential or actual customer, what data should he or she have available during the conversation?
4. Describe how Laguna could use an RFM analysis. What should it do with a [1, 1, 1] customer? What should it do with a [2, 2, 5] customer? What should it do with a [5, 1, 1] customer?
5. Explain how Laguna could use a market-basket analysis. What information must Laguna have to effectively use a market-basket analysis?
6. Explain how Laguna could use an OLAP analysis. Identify possible measures, dimensions, and cubes. What information would the company obtain from the OLAP analysis?
7. Examine your answers to the questions above and specify whether you think RFM, market-basket, or OLAP analysis would be the most useful to Laguna.

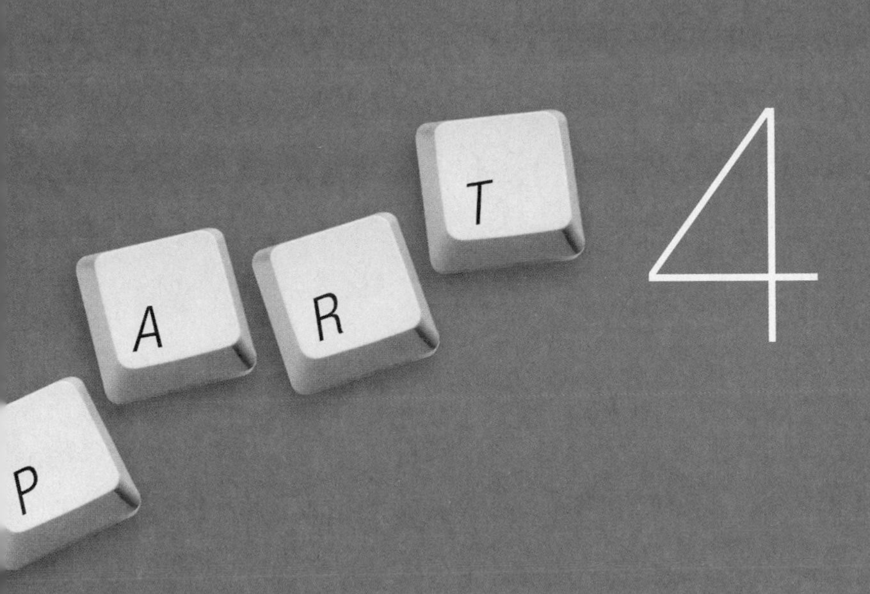

Managing Information Systems Resources

The three chapters in this part address information systems management. In Chapter 10, you will learn processes for developing and maintaining new information systems. It is particularly important for you to learn the users' roles in this process because MIS concerns the *development* and use of IS. Chapter 11 discusses information systems management and the functions of the IS department, as well as the role of outsourcing. Finally, Chapter 12 describes the management of information systems security, a topic that has always been important but has become more so in light of the Sarbanes-Oxley Act.

10 Systems Development

STUDY QUESTIONS

- Q1 What is systems development?
- Q2 Why is systems development difficult and risky?
- Q3 How do businesses use the systems development life cycle (SDLC) process?
- Q4 How do businesses use the rapid application development (RAD) process?
- Q5 How do businesses use object-oriented development (OOD)?
- Q6 How do businesses use extreme programming (XP)?
- Q7 How do the four development methodologies compare?

Meet Don Gray

My favorite business book:
Diffusion of Innovations by Everett Rogers;
Roget's Thesaurus

Don't do this to me in an interview:
Start by telling me how smart you are . . . unless you really are that smart.

What I do when I'm not working:
Walk my dogs, read, bike, hike.

Don Gray is a veteran of more than 25 years of software development experience, coming into software development via the backdoor. He studied accounting as an undergraduate, passed the CPA exam, and worked in tax accounting. After a year, he decided he was more interested in developing computer software than he was in doing taxes. He obtained a customer-support job working for Accountants Microsystems, a software company that licensed tax-preparation software to professional accountants. He worked his way through a variety of jobs, from tech support, to software testing, to software maintenance programming, to development programming, to systems design and the development of sophisticated software systems.

In the last 10 years, he worked as a development manager and vice-president of development for Wall Data, CyberSafe, and Work Wise corporations. In those positions, he managed groups of 40 to 50 developers, PQA test engineers, and technical writers. He led the development of a software product that was named Best-of-Breed by *PC Magazine* and another product that was named Product of the Year by *Network Magazine*. Today, Don works as an entrepreneur investigating and creating new technology for developing computer programs for multiple-CPU computers.

On software development:

"It's complicated. We need a process by which we can define responsibilities, establish roles for team members, and coordinate work. Everyone needs to know what we're doing and why. A development process helps us create efficient and effective ways of accomplishing work and enables us to measure progress.

"Developing systems always involves some degree of customization. Even if you buy software off-the-shelf, you need to integrate that software into your business. It's not like buying a car or an Xbox—those are essentially closed systems. You buy them and use them in predefined ways. Software is never that way because your employees must integrate it with your business processes. Plus there are always different ways of achieving your requirements.

"Take a simple example, say email. You can license an Exchange Server from Microsoft; you can select an open source email server product; or you can let a company like Google process your company's email. Which is the best choice? It depends on what you want to do, on your budget, on your company's culture, and on your expectations.

"A systems development process helps ensure that the solution developed matches the company's needs and that the process and solution makes good use of the company's resources."

On the need for different development processes:

"Why do we need multiple development processes? Because we need to match the development activity to the project's size, complexity, technology, and risks. Say you want to build a dog house. You don't need much of a

My mottos:

"Don't compromise yourself. You are all you've got."—Janis Joplin

"One day soon, humans will be the pets of robots."—Don Gray

What I want to learn next:

A functional programming language for massively parallel systems development.

One characteristic of a superior employee:

Does what needs to be done to achieve success and not just what you direct him or her to do.

Don Gray

process . . . you look at your dog, think about the style of doghouse you want, buy some lumber, and get started. But what if you want to build a house for your family? Now you need to formalize your plans, take them to the city for permit approval, down to the bank for financing, and so forth.

"Next, suppose you want to build the new Tacoma Narrows Bridge. You have a huge project involving many phases of work, complicated planning, and considerable risk . . . financial risk to both the contractor and government as well as physical risk to the public who will use the bridge.

"You need different processes for these projects. Again, it's not just size, it's also the constraints you face. When we developed new tax software, it had to be ready for the tax season. It wouldn't do any good to have a great new product available *after* tax season was over. Managing schedule risk was very important. On other projects, cost management is more important. On other projects, you need to manage technical risk."

On the "user from hell":

"Who is the 'user from hell'? Well, in every software development project, you balance requirements, cost, and schedule. I'd say the user from hell is the one who fixes all three of these. That user wants *everything* and is inflexible about cost or schedule changes. At some point, something may have to give. With systems development, there are so many complexities that you can't know everything at the start.

"My advice to business users is to be careful what you ask for. Most developers want to accommodate you. Software is just bits; given enough time and money, almost any requirement can be met. The main question is, 'Do you really need what you're asking for?' Do you truly need 99.9999 reliability? Do you really need a maximum response time under 5 seconds? Do you really need to keep 7 years of data online? We can do it, but every requirement has cost and schedule implications."

On schedule slippage:

"Why is software always late? Well, first, it isn't *always* late. If we've done something before and if we kept good records, then we should be able to deliver on time. But most software projects are custom-developments; they're 'one-offs' of something we haven't done before. We may be using new technology and that technology may not behave the way it is advertised. We need to learn that technology and possibly learn new development techniques.

"Also, the requirements are always a mess. Users seldom know what they want, or they may be unable to communicate it. Requirements change. Management changes, and the new management brings different priorities. The business environment changes.

"It's not just software, though. Look at the development of any new, large, complicated product. Boeing and Airbus have both experienced long delays in delivery of new airplanes. On the 787, Boeing had to learn how to work with new composite materials and how to integrate work product from around the world. Any large, complicated product that uses new technology is subject to schedule slippage. Plan on it."

On systems analysts:

"Systems analysis is fascinating work. A good systems analyst needs to understand business so that he or she can talk to the business users about requirements. At the same time, a systems analyst needs to be able to talk to technical people, understand what's possible and what isn't, and how requirements, cost, and schedule are related. He or she needs to be good at analyzing trade-offs.

"Systems analysts need superb communications skills; they straddle technology and business. Most importantly, they need to be good problem solvers and to be patient with ambiguity and change. In any complex project, there will be many twists and turns in the road. Systems analysts need to be able to take those in stride, be flexible and fluid, and keep the ball moving along even if the pathway is contorted and confusing."

CHAPTER PREVIEW

This chapter introduces processes for developing information systems. We begin by discussing the nature of development work and the challenges inherent in systems development. We then survey four different development methodologies: the classical systems development life cycle (SDLC), rapid application development (RAD), object-oriented development (OOD), and extreme programming (XP).

Throughout these discussions, we will indicate the roles that you, as a future business professional and manager, should play. Pay particular attention to these discussions. Your goal should be to learn not only how to become an effective consumer of computer expertise and services, but also how to serve as an active user representative on a development project.

Q1 What Is Systems Development?

video

Systems development, or **systems analysis and design** as it is sometimes called, is the process of creating and maintaining information systems. Notice that this process concerns *information systems*, not just computer programs. Developing an *information system* involves all five components: hardware, software, data, procedures, and people. Developing a *computer program* involves software programs, possibly with some focus on data and databases. Figure 10-1 shows that systems development has a broader scope than computer program development.

Because systems development addresses all five components, it requires more than just programming or technical expertise. Establishing the system's goals, setting up the project, and determining requirements require business knowledge and management skill. Tasks such as building computer networks and writing computer programs require technical skills, but developing the other components requires nontechnical, human relations skills. Creating data models requires the ability to interview users and understand their view of the business activities. Designing procedures, especially those involving group action, requires business knowledge and an understanding of group dynamics. Developing job descriptions, staffing, and training all require human resource and related expertise.

Thus, do not suppose that systems development is exclusively a technical task undertaken by programmers and hardware specialists. Rather, it requires coordinated teamwork of both specialists and nonspecialists with business knowledge.

Information Systems Are Never Off-the-Shelf

In Chapter 4, you learned three sources for software: off-the-shelf, off-the-shelf with adaptation, and tailor-made. Although all three sources pertain to software, only two of them pertain to information systems. Unlike software, *information systems are never off-the-shelf.* Because information systems involve your company's people and procedures, you must construct or adapt procedures to fit your business and people, regardless of how you obtain the computer programs.

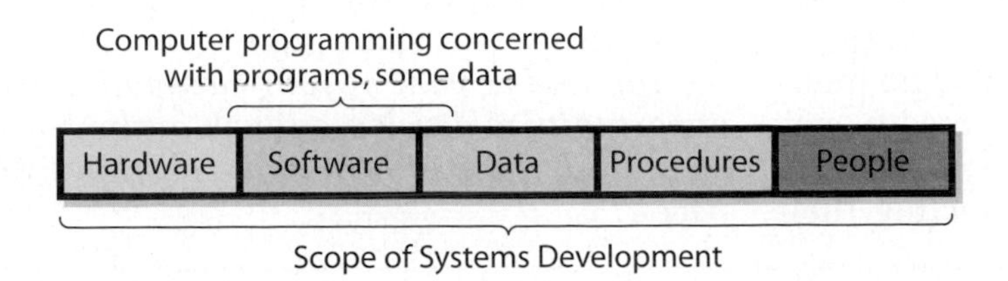

Figure 10-1
Systems Development vs. Program Development

As a future business manager, you will have a key role in information systems development. In order to accomplish the goals of your department, you need to ensure that effective procedures exist for using the information system. You need to ensure that personnel are properly trained and are able to use the IS effectively. If your department does not have appropriate procedures and trained personnel, you must take corrective action. Although you might pass off hardware, program, or data problems to the IT department, you cannot pass off procedural or personnel problems to that department. Such problems are your problems. The single most important criterion for information systems success is ***for users to take ownership of their systems***.

Information Systems Maintenance

Systems development is defined as a process for creating and *maintaining* information systems. Before we continue, you need to understand that, in truth, *maintenance* is a poor term to use in conjunction with information systems. It implies activities to keep a system running—such as someone changing the oil or putting air in the tires—which is an incorrect image. For information systems, *maintenance* means one of two things: either fixing a system to make it do what it should have done in the first place or adapting it to changing requirements. Although neither of those actions is well described by the term *maintenance*, that term is fixed in the industry, and so we will use it in this text. Understand, however, that in the context of IS, **maintenance** means to fix or adapt.

To further set the stage for some of the issues involved in systems development, read the Systems Development in Practice *box below.*

SYSTEMS DEVELOPMENT IN PRACTICE

BAKER, BARKER, AND BICKEL

Baker, Barker, and Bickel met in June 2007 at a convention of resort owners and tourism operators. They sat next to each other by chance while waiting for a presentation; after introducing themselves and laughing at the odd sound of their three names, they were surprised to learn that they managed similar businesses. Wilma Baker lives in Santa Fe, New Mexico, and specializes in renting homes and apartments to visitors to Santa Fe. Jerry Barker lives in Whistler Village, British Columbia, and specializes in renting condos to skiers and other visitors to the Whistler/Blackcomb Resort. Chris Bickel lives in Chatham, Massachusetts, and specializes in renting homes and condos to vacationers to Cape Cod.

The three agreed to have lunch after the presentation. During lunch, they shared frustrations about the difficulty of obtaining new customers. As the conversation developed, they began to wonder if there was some way to combine forces (i.e., they were seeking a competitive advantage from an alliance). So, they decided to skip one of the next day's presentations and meet to discuss ways to form an alliance. Ideas they wanted to discuss further were sharing customer data, developing a joint reservation service, and exchanging property listings.

As they talked, it became clear they had no interest in merging their businesses; each wanted to stay independent. They also discovered that each was very concerned, paranoid even, about protecting their existing customer base from poaching. Still, the conflict was not as bad as it first seemed. Barker's business was primarily the ski trade, and winter was his busiest season; Bickel's business was mostly Cape Cod vacations, and she was busiest during the summer. Baker's high season was the summer and fall. So, it seemed there was enough difference in their high seasons that they would not necessarily cannibalize their businesses by selling the others' offerings to their own customers.

The question then became how to proceed. Given their desire to protect their own customers, they did not want to develop a common customer database. The best idea seemed to be to share data about properties. That way they could keep control of their customers but still have an opportunity to sell time at the others' properties.

They discussed several alternatives. Each could develop her or his own property database, and the three could then share those databases over the Internet. Or, they could develop a centralized property database that they would all use. Or, they could find some other way to share property listings.

You and a team of your classmates will have an opportunity to develop a rough outline of a development project for BBB in Collaboration Exercise 1 on page 415.

Q2 Why Is Systems Development Difficult and Risky?

Systems development is difficult and risky. Many projects are never finished. Of those that are finished, some are 200 or 300 percent over budget. Still other projects finish within budget and schedule, but never satisfactorily accomplish their goals. (See Case Study 10 on page 417, for more statistics on development failures.)

You might be amazed to learn that systems development failures can be so dramatic. You might suppose that with the experience of developing thousands of systems over the years, by now there would be some methodology for successful systems development. In fact, there *are* systems development methodologies that can result in success, and we will discuss four of them in this chapter. But, even when competent people follow one of these methodologies, the risk of failure is still high.

In the following sections, we will discuss the following major challenges to systems development:

- The difficulty of determining requirements
- Changes in requirements
- Scheduling and budgeting difficulties
- Changing technology
- Diseconomies of scale

The Difficulty of Requirements Determination

First, requirements are difficult to determine. After you read the *Systems Development in Practice* box, think about the system that Baker, Barker, and Bickel want to develop. What does it mean to share property listings? Specifically, what property data need to be shared? What should the data entry forms look like? What reports do the owners need? How do they want to query the data? Are the data the same for each company, or do they vary from one to another?

Further, how will one of the agencies go about reserving another agency's property? How will such reservations be communicated to the other agency? How will payments be processed? The questions go on and on. Each of the development processes that we will describe in this chapter is designed to ensure that such questions are both asked and answered.

Changes in Requirements

Even more difficult, systems development aims at a moving target. Requirements change as the system is developed. The bigger the system and the longer the project, the more the requirements change.

When requirements change, what should the development team do? Stop work and rebuild the system in accordance with the new requirements? If they do that, the system will develop in fits and starts and might never be completed. Or, should the team finish the system, knowing that it will be unsatisfactory the day it is implemented and will therefore need immediate maintenance?

Scheduling and Budgeting Difficulties

Other challenges involve scheduling and budgeting. How long will it take to build a system? That question is not easy to answer. Suppose you are building the property-tracking system for Baker, Barker, and Bickel. How long will it take to create the data model? Even if you know how long it takes to build one complete data model, Baker,

Barker, and Bickel might disagree with each other. How many times will you need to rebuild the data model until they agree?

Data modeling is just one element of the project. Suppose Baker, Barker, and Bickel decide to use a public switched data network to connect their three companies. How long will it take to lease the lines to connect to the PSDN vendor? How long will it take to negotiate a contract? How long will it take to determine what hardware and software are required? How long will it take to get the system up and running?

Then, consider the applications. How long will it take to build the forms, reports, queries, and application programs? How long will it take to test all of them? What about procedures and people? What procedures need to be developed, and how much time should be allowed to create and document them, develop training programs, and train the personnel?

Further, how much will all of this cost? Labor costs are a direct function of labor hours; if you cannot estimate labor hours, you cannot estimate labor costs. Moreover, if you cannot estimate how much a system costs, then how do you perform a financial analysis to determine if the system generates an appropriate rate of return?

Changing Technology

Yet another challenge is that while the project is underway technology continues to change. For example, while you are developing Baker, Barker, and Bickel's property-sharing system, Microsoft, Sun, and IBM are extending XML Web services and creating other SOA standards (see Chapter 8). You learn that some of this new technology could drastically shorten your development time, halve the costs, and result in a better system. That is, it will do those things if it actually works the way vendors say it will.

Even if you believe the new technology is a viable answer, do you want to stop your development to switch to the new technology? Would it be better to finish developing according to the existing plan?

Diseconomies of Scale

Unfortunately, as development teams become larger, the average contribution per worker decreases. This is true because as staff size increases, more meetings and other coordinating activities are required to keep everyone in sync. There are economies of scale up to a point, but beyond a workgroup of, say, 20 employees, diseconomies of scale begin to take over.

A famous adage known as **Brooks's Law** points out a related problem: *Adding more people to a late project makes the project later.*[1] Brooks's Law is true not only because a larger staff requires increased coordination, but also because new people need training. The only people who can train the new employees are the existing team members, who are thus taken off productive tasks. The costs of training new people can overwhelm the benefit of their contribution.

In short, managers of software development projects face a dilemma: They can increase work per employee by keeping the team small, but in doing so they extend the project's timeline. Or, they can reduce the project's timeline by adding staff, but because of diseconomies of scale they will have to add 150 or 200 hours of labor to gain 100 hours of work. And, due to Brooks's Law, once the project is late, both choices are bad.

Furthermore, schedules can be compressed only so far. According to one other popular adage, "Nine women cannot make a baby in 1 month."

[1]Fred Brooks was a successful senior manager at IBM in the 1960s. After retiring from IBM, he wrote a classic book on IT project management called *The Mythical Man-Month*. Published by Addison-Wesley in 1975, the book is pertinent today and should be read by every IT or IS project manager. It's an enjoyable book, too.

Is Systems Development Really So Bleak?

Is systems development really as bleak as the list of challenges makes it sound? Yes and no. All of the challenges just described *do* exist, and they are all significant hurdles that every development project must overcome. As noted previously, once the project is late and over budget, no good choice exists. "I have to pick my regrets," said one beleaguered manager of a late project.

The IT industry has over 50 years of experience developing information systems, and over those years methodologies have emerged that successfully deal with these problems. In the next four sections, we will consider four different systems development processes:

- Systems development life cycle (SDLC)
- Rapid application development (RAD)
- Object-oriented systems development (OOD)
- Extreme programming (XP)

You may be wondering why there are *four* different methodologies. Why not just one? As Don Gray said in the opening interview, information systems differ in scope and complexity, and no single process works for all projects. Some information systems are heavy on the hardware and software components; they are nearly automated. Others, such as collaboration or knowledge-sharing systems, are heavy on procedures and people. Some projects have vastly complex databases, and so on. The variations are nearly endless.

Also, the scale of information systems varies widely. Personal systems support one person with a limited set of requirements. Workgroup systems support a group of people, normally with a single application. Enterprise systems support many workgroups with many different applications. Interenterprise systems support many different organizations with different organizational cultures; some support users in different countries with different cultural heritages.

So, given the variety of possible systems, it is not surprising that there are different development processes. Different processes are appropriate for different types of systems. We begin with the classical systems development process.

Q3 How Do Businesses Use the Systems Development Life Cycle (SDLC) Process?

The **systems development life cycle (SDLC)** is the classical process used to develop information systems. The IT industry developed the SDLC in the "school of hard knocks." Many early projects met with disaster, and companies and systems developers sifted through the ashes of those disasters to determine what went wrong. By the 1970s, most seasoned project managers agreed on the basic tasks that need to be performed to successfully build and maintain information systems. These basic tasks are combined into phases of systems development.

Different authors and organizations package the tasks into different numbers of phases. Some organizations use an eight-phase process, others use a seven-phase process, and still others use a five-phase process. In this text, we will use the following five-phase process:

1. System definition
2. Requirements analysis
3. Component design
4. Implementation
5. System maintenance (fix or enhance)

Figure 10-2 (next page) shows how these phases are related. Development begins when a business-planning process identifies a need for a new system. We will address IS

Figure 10-2
Phases in the SDLC

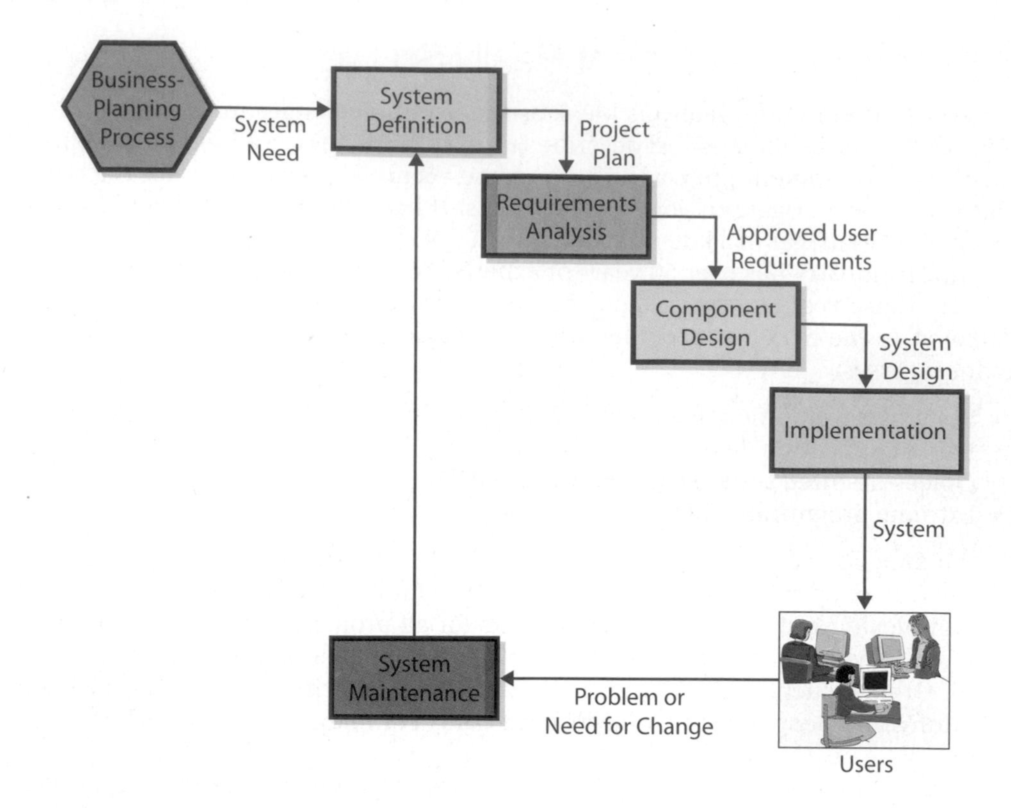

planning processes in the next chapter. For now, suppose that management has determined, in some way, that the organization can best accomplish its goals and objectives by constructing a new information system.

Developers in the first SDLC phase, system definition, use management's statement of the system need to define and plan the new system. The resulting project plan is the input to the second phase, requirements analysis. Here, developers identify the particular features and functions of the new system. The output of that phase is a set of approved user requirements, which become the primary input used to design system components. In the fourth phase, developers implement, test, and install the new system.

Over time, users will find errors, mistakes, and problems. They will also think of new features that they need. The need for these changes is input into a system maintenance phase. The maintenance phase starts the process all over again, which is why the process is considered a cycle.

In the following sections, we will consider each phase of the SDLC in more detail.

How Is System Definition Accomplished?

In response to the need for the new system, the organization will assign a few employees, possibly on a part-time basis, to define the new system, to assess its feasibility, and to plan the project. Typically, someone from the IS department leads the initial team, but the members of that initial team are both users and IS professionals.

Define System Goals and Scope

As shown in Figure 10-3, the first step is to define the goals and scope of the new information system. Recall from Chapters 2 and 3 that information systems are developed to facilitate collaboration; to aid in decision making, problem solving, and project management; and to gain a competitive advantage. At this step, the team defines the goal or purpose of the new system in terms of one or more of these reasons.

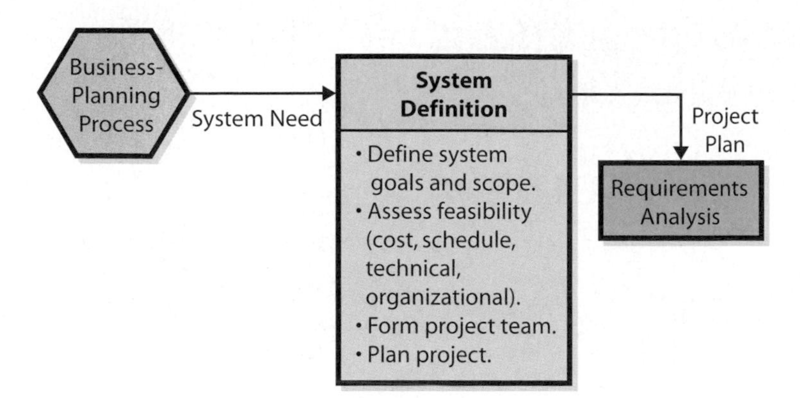

Figure 10-3
SDLC: System Definition Phase

Consider the property listing sharing system for Baker, Barker, and Bickel. What is the purpose of that system? Each owner wants to protect his or her customer base but use the alliance to expand his or her product offerings. This goal is both achieving a competitive advantage and solving the problem of not having enough customers.

During project definition, the project's scope is delineated. Baker, Barker, and Bickel partially defined the scope when they said they do not want to merge their businesses nor their business operations. Also, they do not want to share customer data with each other. They want to share property listings in such a way that each agency preserves its own customer base.

There is one aspect of Baker, Barker, and Bickel's project definition that we have not addressed. How will the members of the alliance compensate each other? What incentive does Baker have to lease one of Barker's properties? And what incentive does Barker have to allow Baker to do so? An important issue like this needs to be part of the project's goals and scope. For our purposes in illustrating systems development, the particular arrangement is unimportant. It needs to be defined, however. For now, we will assume that when Baker leases one of Barker's properties, they split the commission on the lease 50–50.

Assess Feasibility

Once we have defined the project's goals and scope, the next step is to assess feasibility. This step answers the question, "Does this project make sense?" The aim here is to eliminate obviously nonsensible projects before forming a project development team and investing significant labor.

Feasibility has four dimensions: **cost**, **schedule**, **technical**, and **organizational feasibility**. Because IS development projects are difficult to budget and schedule, cost and schedule feasibility can be only an approximate, back-of-the-envelope analysis. The purpose is to eliminate any obviously infeasible ideas as soon as possible.

For example, if Baker, Barker, and Bickel believe that they must have some type of integrated, Web-based database, they can ask a consultant how much such databases generally cost to develop. If the answer is a minimum of $30,000, then they can decide if they can reasonably expect to receive benefits to justify this expense. If they do not expect sufficient benefits, they can cancel the project or agree to accomplish their goals using some other system, say by using email messages.

For a discussion of ethical issues relating to cost estimates, see the Ethics Guide *on page 390.*

Like cost feasibility, *schedule feasibility,* is difficult to determine because it is difficult to estimate the time it will take to build the system. However, the team makes the best schedule estimates that it can, possibly adding schedule padding, such as 30 percent, and then decides if it can accept that estimated delivery date. At this stage of the project, the company should not rely on either cost or schedule estimates; the purpose of these estimates is simply to rule out any obviously unacceptable projects.

Ethics

GUIDE

Estimation Ethics

A *buy-in* occurs when a company agrees to produce a system or product for less than it knows the project will require. An example for Baker, Barker, and Bickel would be if a consultant agreed to build the system for $50,000 when good estimating techniques indicate it will take $75,000. If the contract for the system or product is written for "time and materials," the customer will ultimately pay the $75,000 for the finished system. Or, the customer will cancel the project once the true cost is known. If the contract for the system or product is written for a fixed cost, then the developer will eat the extra costs. The latter strategy is used if the contract opens up other business opportunities that are worth the $25,000 loss.

Buy-ins always involve deceit. Most would agree that buying in on a time-and-materials project, planning to stick the customer with the full cost later, is unethical and wrong. Opinions on buying in on a fixed-priced contract vary. Some would say buying in is always deceitful and should be avoided. Others say that it is just one of many different business strategies.

What about in-house projects? Do the ethics change if an in-house development team is building a system for use in house? If team members know there is only $50,000 in the budget, should they start the project if they believe its true cost is $75,000? If they do start, at some point senior management will either have to admit a mistake and cancel the project or find the additional $25,000. Project sponsors can make all sorts of excuses for such a buy-in. For example, "I know the company needs this system. If management doesn't realize it and fund it appropriately, then we'll just force their hand."

These issues become even stickier if team members disagree about how much the project will cost. Suppose one faction of the team believes the project will cost $35,000, another faction estimates $50,000, and a third thinks $65,000. Can the project sponsors justify taking the average? Or, should they describe the range of estimates?

Other buy-ins are more subtle. Suppose you are a project manager of an exciting new project that is possibly a career-maker for you. You are incredibly busy, working 6 days a week and long hours each day. Your team has developed an estimate for $50,000 for the project. A little voice in the back of your mind says that maybe not all costs for every aspect of the project are included in that estimate. You mean to follow up on that thought, but more pressing matters in your schedule take precedence. Soon you find yourself in front of management, presenting the $50,000 estimate. You probably should have found the time to investigate the estimate, but you didn't. Is your behavior unethical?

Or, suppose you approach a more senior manager with your dilemma. "I think there may be other costs, but I know that $50,000 is all we've got. What should I do?" Suppose the senior manager says something like, "Well, let's go forward. You don't know of anything else, and we can always find more budget elsewhere if we have to." How do you respond?

You can buy in on schedule as well as cost. If the marketing department says, "We have to have the new product for the trade show," do you agree, even if you know it's highly unlikely? What if marketing says, "If we don't have it by then, we should just cancel the project." Suppose it's not impossible to make that schedule, it's just highly unlikely. How do you respond? ■

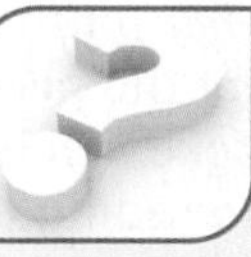

Discussion Questions

1. Do you agree that buying in on a cost-and-materials project is always unethical? Explain your reasoning. Are there circumstances in which it could be illegal?
2. Suppose you learn through the grapevine that your opponents in a competitive bid are buying in on a time-and-materials contract. Does this change your answer to question 1?
3. Suppose you are a project manager who is preparing a request for proposal on a cost-and-materials systems development project. What can you do to prevent buy-ins?
4. Under what circumstances do you think buying in on a fixed-price contract is ethical? What are the dangers of this strategy?
5. Explain why in-house development projects are always time-and-materials projects.
6. Given your answer to question 5, is buying in on an in-house project always unethical? Under what circumstances do you think it is ethical? Under what circumstances do you think it is justifiable, even if it is unethical?
7. Suppose you ask a senior manager for advice as described in the guide. Does the manager's response absolve you of guilt? Suppose you ask the manager and then do not follow her guidance. What problems result?
8. Explain how you can buy in on schedule as well as costs.
9. For an in-house project, how do you respond to the marketing manager who says that the project should be cancelled if it will not be ready for the trade show? In your answer, suppose that you disagree with this opinion—suppose you know the system has value regardless of whether it is done by the trade show.

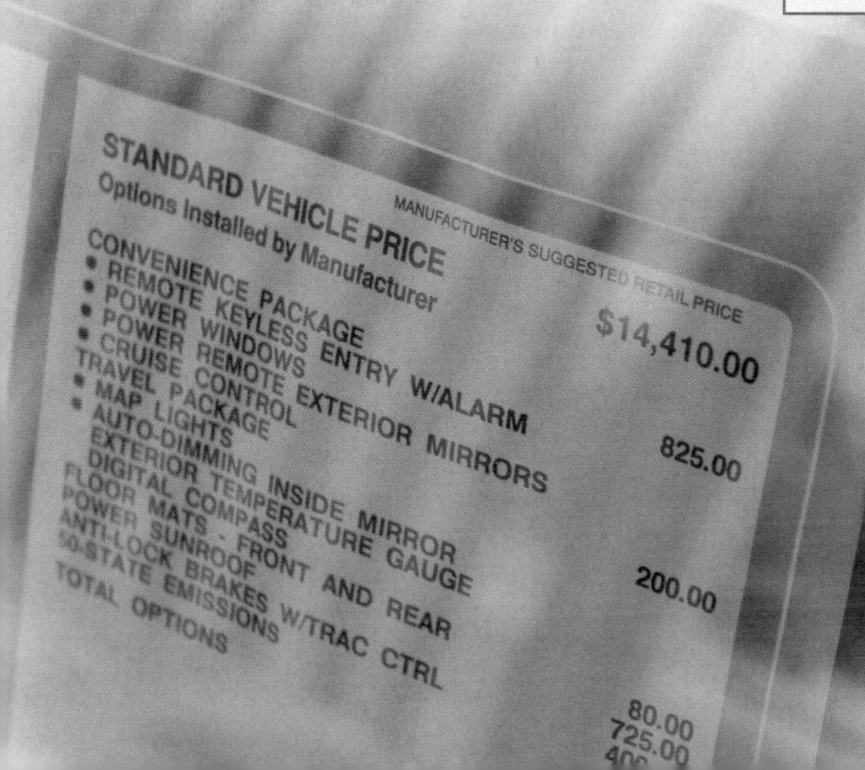

Technical feasibility refers to whether existing information technology is likely to be able to meet the needs of the new system. For a small system, like that for Baker, Barker, and Bickel, technical feasibility is certain. For larger, more complicated projects with demanding performance requirements, feasibility might not be certain. Technical feasibility is used mostly to eliminate projects based on naïve notions about what IT can do. Examples today are systems that require human-like computer robots and so forth.

Finally, *organizational feasibility* concerns whether the new system fits within the organization's customs, culture, charter, or legal requirements. For example, if Baker, Barker, or Bickel has an investor who has a conflict with one of the other person's businesses, the proposed system might be organizationally infeasible. Or, if the combined sales listings would violate antitrust law, the new system would be organizationally infeasible.

Form a Project Team

If the defined project is determined to be feasible, the next step is to form the project team. Normally the team consists of both IT personnel and user representatives. The project manager and IT personnel can be in-house personnel or outside contractors. We will describe various means of obtaining IT personnel using outside sources and the benefits and risks of outsourcing when we discuss IS management in the next chapter.

Typical personnel on a development team are a manager (or mangers for larger projects), system analysts, programmers, software testers, and users. As Don Gray said in the opening interview, **systems analysts** are IS professionals who understand both business and technology. They are active throughout the systems development process and play a key role in moving the project through the systems development process. Systems analysts integrate the work of the programmers, testers, and users. Depending on the nature of the project, the team may also include hardware and communications specialists, database designers and administrators, and other IT specialists.

The team composition changes over time. During requirements definition, the team will be heavy with systems analysts. During design and implementation, it will be heavy with programmers, testers, and database designers. During integrated testing and conversion, the team will be augmented with testers and business users.

User involvement is critical throughout the system development process. Depending on the size and nature of the project, users are assigned to the project either full or part time. Sometimes users are assigned to review and oversight committees that meet periodically, especially at the completion of project phases and other milestones. Users are involved in many different ways. The important point is for users to have active involvement and to take ownership of the project throughout the entire development process.

The first major task for the assembled project team is to plan the project. Members of the project team specify tasks to be accomplished, assign personnel, determine task dependencies, and set schedules. You will learn more about project planning in your operations management classes, if you have not done so already.

What Is the Users' Role in the Requirements Phase?

The primary purpose of the requirements analysis phase is to determine and document the specific features and functions of the new system. For most development projects, this phase requires interviewing dozens of users and documenting potentially hundreds of requirements. Requirements definition is thus expensive. It is also difficult, as you will see.

Determine Requirements

Determining the system's requirements is the most important phase in the systems development process. If the requirements are wrong, the system will be wrong. If the requirements are determined completely and correctly, then design and implementation will be easier and more likely to result in success.

Examples of requirements are the contents of a report or the fields in a data entry form. Requirements include not only what is to be produced, but also how frequently and how fast it is to be produced. Some requirements specify the volume of data to be stored and processed.

If you take a course in systems analysis and design, you will spend weeks on techniques for determining requirements. Here, we will just summarize that process. Typically, systems analysts interview users and record the results in some consistent manner. Good interviewing skills are crucial; users are notorious for being unable to describe what they want and need. Users also tend to focus on the tasks they are performing at the time of the interview. Tasks performed at the end of the quarter or end of the year are forgotten if the interview takes place mid-quarter. Seasoned and experienced systems analysts know how to conduct interviews to bring such requirements to light.

As listed in Figure 10-4, sources of requirements include existing systems as well as the forms, reports, queries, and application features and functions desired in the new system. Security is another important category of requirements.

If the new system involves a new database or substantial changes to an existing database, then the development team will create a data model. As you learned in Chapter 5, that model must reflect the users' perspective on their business and business activities. Thus, the data model is constructed on the basis of user interviews and must be validated by those users.

Sometimes the requirements determination is so focused on the software and data components that other components are forgotten. Experienced project managers ensure consideration of requirements for all five IS components, not just for software and data. Regarding hardware, the team might ask: Are there special needs or restrictions on hardware? Is there an organizational standard governing what kinds of hardware can, or cannot, be used? Must the new system use existing hardware? What requirements are there for communications and network hardware?

Similarly, the team should consider requirements for procedures and personnel: Do accounting controls require procedures that separate duties and authorities? Are there restrictions that some actions can be taken only by certain departments or specific personnel? Are there policy requirements or union rules that restrict activities to certain categories of employees? Will the system need to interface with information systems from other companies and organizations? In short, requirements need to be considered for all of the components of the new information system.

These questions are examples of the kinds of questions that must be asked and answered during requirements analysis.

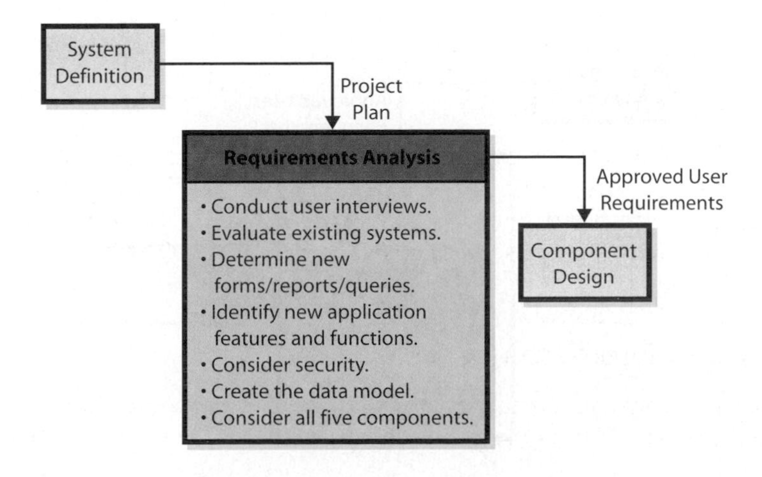

Figure 10-4
SDLC: Requirements Analysis Phase

Obtain User Approval

Once the requirements have been specified, the users must review and approve them before the project continues. The easiest and cheapest time to alter the information system is in the requirements phase. Changing a requirement at this stage is simply a matter of changing a description. Changing a requirement in the implementation phase may require weeks of reworking applications components and the database.

How Are the Five Components Designed?

Each of the five components is designed in this stage. Typically, the team designs each component by developing alternatives, evaluating each of those alternatives against the requirements, and then selecting from among those alternatives. Accurate requirements are critical here; if they are incomplete or wrong, then they will be poor guides for evaluation.

Figure 10-5 shows that design tasks pertain to each of the five IS components.

Hardware Design

For hardware, the team determines specifications for the hardware that they want to acquire. (The team is not designing hardware in the sense of building a CPU or a disk drive.)

For the Baker, Barker, and Bickel system, for example, various hardware communications alternatives are possible:

1. They can use PC and LANs connected over the public Internet.
2. They can lease three separate point-to-point leased lines.
3. They can lease time on some type of PSDN.
4. They can create a VPN over the Internet.

The development team evaluates each of these alternatives against the requirements using criteria like those in Figure 6-16 (page 205).

Program Design

Program design depends on the source of the programs. For off-the-shelf software, the team must determine candidate products and evaluate them against the requirements. For off-the-shelf with alteration programs, the team identifies products to be acquired off-the-shelf and then determines the alterations required. For custom-developed programs, the team produces design documentation for writing program code.

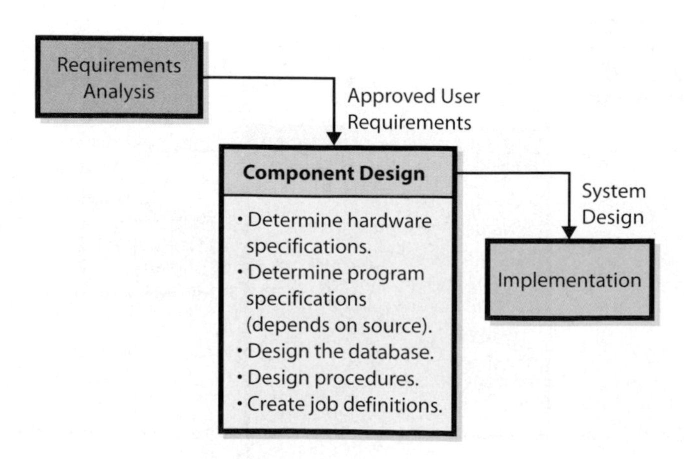

Figure 10-5
SDLC: Component Design Phase

Database Design

If developers are constructing a database, then during this phase they convert the data model to a database design using techniques like those described in Chapter 5. If developers are using off-the-shelf programs, then little database design needs be done; the programs will handle their own database processing.

Procedure Design

For a business information system, the system developers and the organization must also design procedures for both users and operations personnel. Procedures need to be developed for normal, backup, and failure recovery operations, as summarized in Figure 10-6. Usually teams of systems analysts and key users design the procedures.

Design of Job Descriptions

With regard to people, design involves developing job descriptions for both users and operations personnel. Sometimes new information systems require new jobs. If so, the duties and responsibilities for the new jobs need to be defined in accordance with the organization's human resources policies. More often, organizations add new duties and responsibilities to existing jobs. In this case, developers define these new tasks and responsibilities in this phase. Sometimes, the personnel design task is as simple as statements like, "Our admin (currently Jason) will be in charge of making backups." As with procedures, teams of systems analysts and users determine job descriptions and functions.

How Is an Information System Implemented?

Once the design is complete, the next phase in the SDLC is implementation. Tasks in this phase are to build, test, and convert the users to the new system (see Figure 10-7, on the next page). Developers construct each of the components independently. They obtain, install, and test hardware. They license and install off-the-shelf programs; they write adaptations and custom programs as necessary. They construct a database and fill it with data. They document, review, and test procedures, and they create training programs. Finally, the organization hires and trains needed personnel.

	Users	Operations Personnel
Normal processing	• Procedures for using the system to accomplish business tasks.	• Procedures for starting, stopping, and operating the system.
Backup	• User procedures for backing up data and other resources.	• Operations procedures for backing up data and other resources.
Failure recovery	• Procedures to continue operations when the system fails. • Procedures to convert back to the system after recovery.	• Procedures to identify the source of failure and get it fixed. • Procedures to recover and restart the system.

Figure 10-6
Procedures to Be Designed

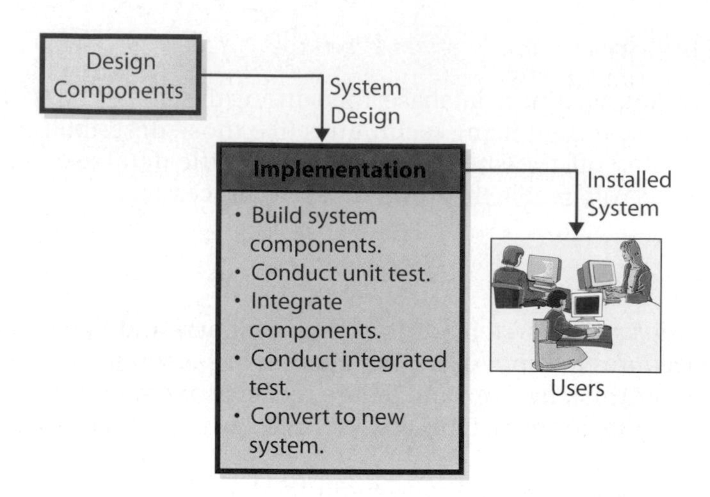

Figure 10-7
SDLC: Implementation Phase

System Testing

Once developers have constructed and tested all of the components, they integrate the individual components and test the system. So far, we have glossed over testing as if there is nothing to it. In fact, software and system testing are difficult, time-consuming, and complex tasks. Developers need to design and develop test plans and record the results of tests. They need to devise a system to assign fixes to people and to verify that fixes are correct and complete.

A **test plan** consists of sequences of actions that users will take when using the new system. Test plans include not only the normal actions that users will take, but also incorrect actions. A comprehensive test plan should cause every line of program code to be executed. The test plan should thus cause every error message to be displayed. Testing, retesting, and re-retesting consume huge amounts of labor. Often, developers can reduce the labor cost of testing by writing programs that invoke system features automatically.

Today, many IT professionals work as testing specialists. Testing, or **product quality assurance (PQA)** as it is often called, is an important career. PQA personnel usually construct the test plan with the advice and assistance of users. PQA test engineers themselves perform testing, and they also supervise user test activity. Many PQA professionals are themselves programmers who write automated test programs.

In addition to IT professionals, users should be involved in system testing. Users participate in the development of test plans and test cases. They also can be part of the test team, usually working under the direction of PQA personnel. Users have the final say on whether the system is ready for use. If you are invited to participate as a user tester, take that responsibly seriously. It will become much more difficult to fix problems after you have begun to use the system in production.

Beta testing (in the classic, non-Web 2.0 sense—see page 300) is the process of allowing future system users to try out the new system on their own. Software vendors such as Microsoft often release beta versions of their products for users to try and to test. Such users report problems back to the vendor. Beta testing is the last stage of testing. Normally products in the beta test phase are complete and fully functioning; they typically have few serious errors. Organizations that are developing large new information systems sometimes use a beta-testing process just as software vendors do.

System Conversion

Once the system has passed integrated testing, the organization installs the new system. The term **system conversion** is often used for this activity because it implies the process of *converting* business activity from the old system to the new.

Organizations can implement a system conversion in one of four ways: pilot, phased, parallel, and plunge. IS professionals recommend any of the first three, depending on the circumstances. In most cases, companies should avoid "taking the plunge"!

With **pilot installation**, the organization implements the entire system on a limited portion of the business. An example would be for Baker to try the system when renting Bickel's properties. The advantage of pilot implementation is that if the system fails, the failure is contained within a limited boundary. This reduces exposure of the business and also protects the new system from developing a negative reputation throughout the organization(s).

As the name implies, with **phased installation** the new system is installed in phases across the organization(s). With the Baker, Barker, and Bickel example, phased installation would be to try only a portion of the system, say that for sending property descriptions to each other, for all three agencies. Once a given piece works, then the organization installs and tests another piece of the system, until the entire system has been installed. Some systems are so tightly integrated that they cannot be installed in phased pieces. Such systems must be installed using one of the other techniques.

With **parallel installation**, the new system runs in parallel with the old one until the new system is tested and fully operational. Parallel installation is expensive because the organization incurs the costs of running both systems. Users must work double time, if you will, to run both systems. Then, considerable work is needed to determine if the results of the new system are consistent with those of the old system.

However, some organizations consider the costs of parallel installation to be a form of insurance. It is the slowest and most expensive style of installation, but it does provide an easy fallback position if the new system fails. In truth, few organizations can afford parallel implementation, and it is rarely done today.

The final style of conversion is **plunge installation** (sometimes called **direct installation**). With it, the organization shuts off the old system and starts the new system. If the new system fails, the organization is in trouble: Nothing can be done until either the new system is fixed or the old system is reinstalled. Because of the risk, organizations should avoid this conversion style if possible. The one exception is if the new system is providing a new capability that is not vital to the operation of the organization.

The Baker, Barker, and Bickel system is an example of such an exception. There is no old system; the agencies are not currently renting each other's properties. If the new system fails, it just means that they will continue not to rent each others' properties. In cases like this, the plunge method can be justified. Otherwise, avoid it.

Figure 10-8 summarizes the tasks for each of the five components during the design and implementation phases. Use this figure to test your knowledge of the tasks in each phase.

Figure 10-8
Design and Implementation for the Five Components

	Hardware	Software	Data	Procedures	People
Design	Determine hardware specifications.	Select off-the-shelf programs. Design alterations and custom programs as necessary.	Design database and related structures.	Design user and operations procedures.	Develop user and operations job descriptions.
Implementation	Obtain, install, and test hardware.	License and install off-the-shelf programs. Write alterations and custom programs. Test programs.	Create database. Fill with data. Test data.	Document procedures. Create training programs. Review and test procedures.	Hire and train personnel.
	Integrated Test and Conversion				

Unit test each component (applies to Implementation row)

Note: Cells shaded tan represent software development.

What Are the Tasks for System Maintenance?

The last phase of the SDLC is maintenance. As noted earlier, maintenance is a misnomer; the work done during this phase is either to *fix* the system so that it works correctly or to *adapt* it to changes in requirements.

Figure 10-9 shows tasks during the maintenance phase. First, there needs to be a means for tracking both failures[2] and requests for enhancements to meet new requirements. For small systems, organizations can track failures and enhancements using word-processing documents. As systems become larger, however, and as the number of failure and enhancement requests increases, many organizations find it necessary to develop a tracking database. Such a database contains a description of the failure or enhancement. It also records who reported the problem, who will make the fix or enhancement, what the status of that work is, and whether the fix or enhancement has been tested and verified by the originator.

Typically, IS personnel prioritize system problems according to their severity. They fix high-priority items as soon as possible, and they fix low-priority items as time and resources become available.

With regard to the software component, software developers group fixes for high-priority failures into a **patch** that can be applied to all copies of a given product. As described in Chapter 4, software vendors supply patches to fix security and other critical problems. They usually bundle fixes of low-priority problems into larger groups called **service packs**. Users apply service packs in much the same way that they apply patches, except that service packs typically involve fixes to hundreds or thousands of problems.

By the way, you may be surprised to learn this, but all commercial software products are shipped with known failures. Usually vendors test their products and remove the most serious problems, but they seldom, if ever, remove all of the defects they know about. Shipping with defects is an industry practice; Microsoft, Adobe, Oracle, RedHat, and many others all ship products with known problems.

Because an enhancement is an adaptation to new requirements, developers usually prioritize enhancement requests separate from failures. The decision to make an enhancement includes a business decision that the enhancement will

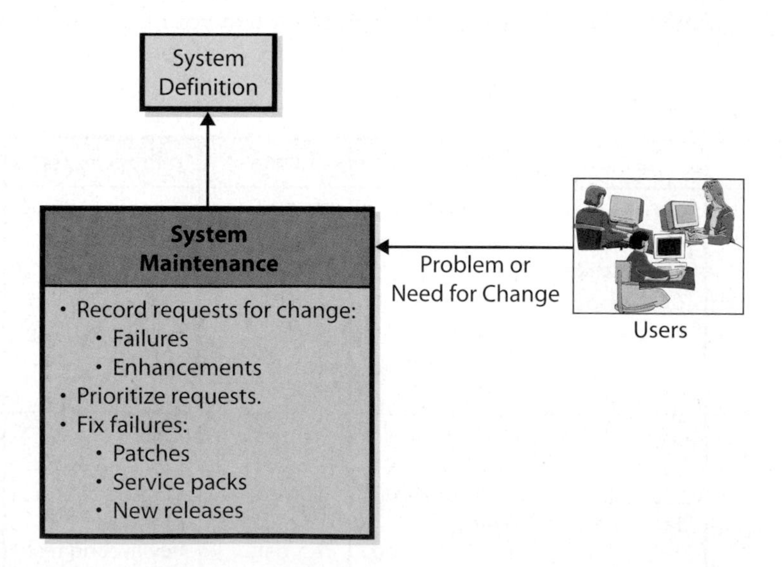

Figure 10-9
SDLC: System Maintenance Phase

[2]A *failure* is a difference between what the system does and what it is supposed to do. Sometimes you will hear the term *bug* used instead of failure. As a future user, call failures *failures*, for that's what they are. Don't have a *bugs list*, have a *failures list*. Don't have an *unresolved bug*, have an *unresolved failure*. A few months of managing an organization that is coping with a serious failure will show you the importance of this difference in terms.

generate an acceptable rate of return. Although minor enhancements are made using service packs, major enhancement requests usually result in a complete new release of a product.

As you read this, keep in mind that although we usually think of failures and enhancements as applying to software, they can apply to the other components as well. There can be hardware or database failures or enhancements. There can also be failures and enhancements in procedures and people, though the latter is usually expressed in more humane terms than failure or enhancement. The underlying idea is the same, however.

As stated earlier, note that the maintenance phase starts another cycle of the SDLC process. The decision to enhance a system is a decision to restart the systems development process. Even a simple failure fix goes through all of the phases of the SDLC; if it is a small fix, a single person may work through those phases in an abbreviated form. But each of those phases is repeated, nonetheless.

What Are the Problems with the SDLC?

Although the industry has experienced notable successes with the SDLC process, there have also been many problems with it, as discussed next.

The SDLC Waterfall

One of the reasons for SDLC problems is due to the **waterfall** nature of the SDLC. Like a series of waterfalls, the process is supposed to operate in a sequence of not-repeated phases. For example, the team completes the requirements phase and goes over the waterfall into the design phase, and on through the process. (Look back to Figure 10-2, page 388.)

Unfortunately, systems development seldom works so smoothly. Often, there is a need to crawl back up the waterfall, if you will, and repeat work in a prior phase. Most commonly, when design work begins and the team evaluates alternatives, they learn that some requirements statements are incomplete or missing. At that point, the team needs to do more requirements work, yet that phase is supposedly finished. On some projects, the team goes back and forth between requirements and design so many times that the project seems to be out of control.

Requirements Documentation Difficulty

Another problem, especially on complicated systems, is the difficulty of documenting requirements in a usable way. I once managed the database portion of a software project at Boeing in which we invested more than 70 labor-years into a requirements statement. The requirements document was 20-some printed volumes that stood 7 feet tall when stacked on top of one another.

When we entered the design phase, no one really knew all the requirements that concerned a particular feature. We would begin to design a feature only to find that we had not considered a requirement buried somewhere in the documentation. In short, the requirements were so unwieldy as to be nearly useless. Additionally, during the requirements analysis interval, the airplane business moved on. By the time we entered the design phase, many requirements were incomplete and some were obsolete. Projects that spend so much time documenting requirements are sometimes said to be in **analysis paralysis**.

Scheduling and Budgeting Difficulties

For a new, large-scale system, schedule and budgeting estimates are so approximate as to become nearly laughable. Management attempts to put a serious face on the need for a schedule and a budget, but when you are developing a large multiyear,

The Opposing Forces Guide *on page 410 explains the difficulties with project estimation.*

multimillion-dollar project, estimates of labor hours and completion dates are approximate and fuzzy. The employees on the project, who are the source for the estimates, know how little they know about how long something will take and how much they guessed. They know that the total budget and timeline is a summation of everyone's similar guesses. Many large projects live in a fantasy world of budgets and timelines.

In truth, the software community has done much work to improve software development forecasting. But for large projects with large SDLC phases, just too much is unknown for any technique to work well. So, development methodologies other than the SDLC have emerged for developing systems through a series of small, manageable chunks. Rapid application development, object-oriented development, and extreme programming are three such methodologies.

Q4 How Do Businesses Use the Rapid Application Development (RAD) Process?

James Martin, one of the pioneers in information systems, popularized the term *rapid application development* in the title of his 1991 book. The basic idea of **rapid application development (RAD)** is to break up the design and implementation phases of the SDLC into smaller chunks and to design and implement those chunks using as much computer assistance as possible. Figure 10-10 shows the process Martin envisioned.

Like SDLC, RAD has a requirements phase, but it interweaves the design and implementation phases. That is, developers design, implement, and fix a piece of the new system until the users are satisfied with that piece. Then, developers move on to design, implement, and fix another section of the system, and so forth, until the entire system has been developed in pieces. This process, sometimes called **incremental development**, reduces development challenges by using a divide-and-conquer strategy.

The RAD requirements analysis can be less detailed and less complete than with SDLC, because the users are actively involved during design and implementation. In effect, during the design/implement/fix process, the users provide detailed requirements in context.

What Distinguishes RAD?

The main RAD characteristics are as follows:

1. The design/implement/fix development process (as just discussed)
2. Continuous user involvement throughout
3. Extensive use of prototypes
4. Joint application design
5. Use of CASE tools

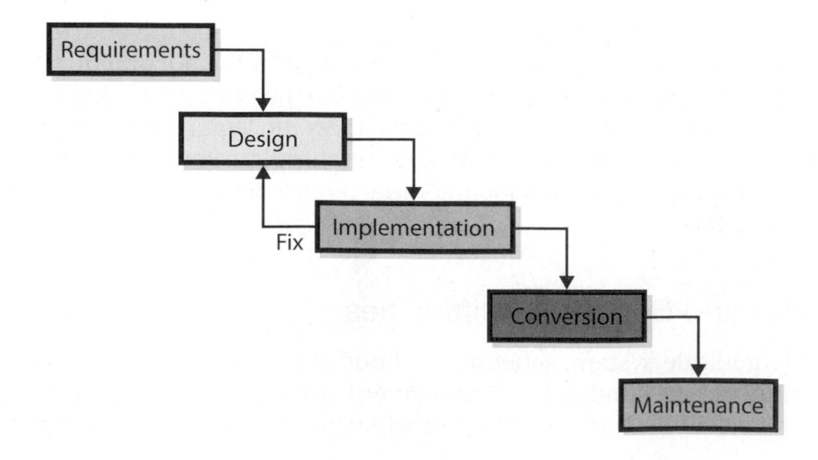

Figure 10-10
Martin's RAD Process

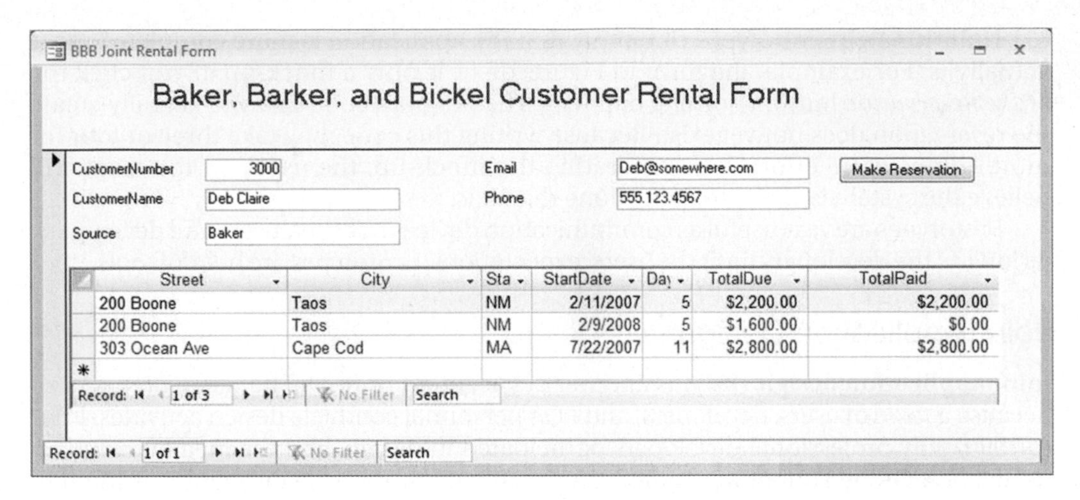

Figure 10-11
Example of a Prototype Form

With RAD, users are actively involved throughout the development process and become key members of the development team. Having users as part of the team not only increases the accuracy and completeness of the requirements, it also promotes a better environment for conversion. The new system will be installed not by strangers, but rather with the active participation of involved users.

The final three characteristics are discussed in detail in the following sections.

Prototypes

Another RAD characteristic is the use of prototypes. A **prototype** is a mock-up of an aspect of the new system. A prototype could be a mock-up of a form, report, query, or other element of the user interface. Figure 10-11 shows a prototype of a data entry form for the Baker, Barker, and Bickel property rental system. This particular form was generated using Microsoft Access, which developers frequently use as a prototyping tool.

Prototypes vary in functionality and utility. Some prototypes are just visual mock-ups of eventual system components. Others are working prototypes from which users can activate some of the system's features. Furthermore, some prototypes are just demonstrations—they are designed to be thrown away. Other prototypes are kept and evolve into the final form, report, or other system component.

Prototypes help users evaluate requirements because they show actual data in context. A user reviewing the form in Figure 10-11, for example, might realize that the system should sort the data in the grid by *StartDate*. This requirement would be difficult to know or specify without the prototype. Prototypes also can provide an opportunity for users to test the user interface. The user can employ the form in Figure 10-11 to enter, modify, or delete data.

Prototypes are more understandable for users than data models. For example, the prototype in Figure 10-12 illustrates that each customer has many rentals, and it implies that each rental has at most one customer. It also shows that the same customer can rent the same property on different dates. We can show the same facts using a data model, as shown in Figure 10-12, but the form is usually easier for users to understand.

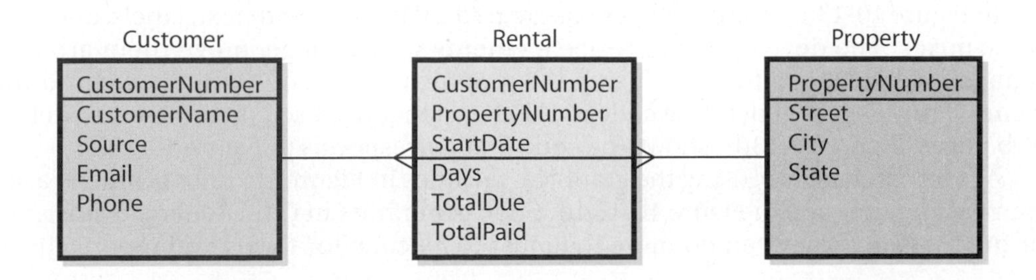

Figure 10-12
Data Model of Prototype Form in Figure 10-11

Unfortunately, prototypes can imply that the application is more complete than it actually is. For example, the form in Figure 10-11 is only a mock-up. If you click the *Make Reservation* button, nothing happens. The program code that will actually create the reservation does not yet exist. Because writing this code may take three or four (or more) times more effort than generating the mock-up, the users on the team will believe the system is closer to being done than it is.

Prototypes are very useful as communication devices between users and developers. As long as the developers limit the users' expectations, prototypes are helpful tools.

Joint Application Design

Joint application design (JAD) is another key element of RAD. The term *joint* is used because a *team* of users, developers, and PQA personnel conducts design activities. Prior to 1990, only professional developers participated in design, and the idea of including users and PQA personnel was radical. JAD came about because developers wanted to incorporate feedback and testing earlier in the development process. Ultimately, developers decided that the best place to get feedback was during design creation.

A *JAD session* is a design meeting of short duration, perhaps an afternoon or a day or two at most. During the session, attendees develop the design of a particular component of the system. The goal is to keep the scope of the component small enough that the design can be completed in a short period.

Organizations vary in the degree of structure given to JAD sessions. Some organizations have strict guidelines for both the JAD process and for the documents created both before and after the JAD sessions. Other organizations are less formal in process and documentation. If you are invited as a user to a JAD session, learn the rules and expectations ahead of time. Also, devote time and attention to the meeting; such meetings are important.

CASE and Visual Development Tools

CASE stands for **computer-assisted software engineering** or **computer-assisted systems engineering**, depending on who is using the term. The first meaning focuses on program development; the second focuses on development of systems having the five components. You will encounter both meanings.

For either meaning, the basic idea is to use a computer system, called a **CASE tool**, to help develop computer programs or systems. CASE tools vary in their features and functions. Some such tools address the entire systems development process from requirements to maintenance; others address just the design and implementation phases. Either way, most CASE tools have a **repository**, which is a database that contains documents, data, prototypes, and program code for the software or system under development.

Most CASE products have tools for creating prototypes, and many have **code generators**, which are programs that generate application code for commonly performed tasks. The idea is to improve developer productivity by having the tool generate as much code as possible. The developer can then add code for application-specific features.

To give you an idea of how a code generator works, examine Figure 10-13, which illustrates the use of Microsoft FrontPage, a product used to generate Web pages. FrontPage is not a CASE tool, but because it has code-generation capabilities we will use it for illustration.

In Figure 10-13(a), the developer has created a Web page with text, labels, and data entry boxes. The developer can resize elements on the page, move them around, change colors, and so forth, all using the graphical tools and symbols. Behind the scenes, FrontPage is generating code in HTML, a language used by browsers to define Web pages. Figure 10-13(b) shows the code that corresponds to Figure 10-13(a).

As you can imagine, using the graphical facilities in Figure 10-13(a) is much easier than writing the code in Figure 10-13(b). Code generators in CASE tools provide similar functionality. They can do more than just write code for forms and reports, how-

Baker, Barker, & Bickel

Reservations Query Form

Start Date:

End Date:

Number Bedrooms: 1 2 3 4

Maximum Daily Rate:

Figure 10-13(a)
Visual Web Page Development

ever. Some CASE tools, for example, generate code for common actions like reading, inserting, updating, and deleting rows of tables in a relational database.

Visual development tools also are used in RAD projects to improve developer productivity. Figure 10-14 (next page) shows the use of Microsoft's Visual Studio.Net. The window in the bottom center has code for processing the form shown in the top center. Visual Studio.Net wrote the program code shown here. The developer starts with that code as a skeleton and adds features and functions to it.

By the way, even though we are introducing visual development tools here, in the discussion of RAD, do not be misled into thinking that such tools are used only in RAD projects. They are used for software development projects of all types.

```
<meta name="ProgID" contents="FrontPage.Editor.Document">
<title>IS300   Classes</title>
<meta name="MicroSoft Border" content="1">
<link rel="File-List" href="Figure%206-13_files/filelist.xml">
</head>
<body>
<h1 align="center"><font face="Comic Sans MS" size="7">Baker, Barker, &amp; Bickle</font></h1>
<p align="center"><b><font face="Comic Sans MS" size="5" color="#FF0000">
Reservations Query Form<font>/b></p>
<blockquote>
<p align="left"><b><font face="Comic Sans MS" color="#ff0000" size="5">     </font> </b></p>
<p align="left"><b><font face="Comic Sans MS" size="5" color="#0000FF">
Start Date:              </font></b>
<input type="text" name="T1" size="20"></p>
   <p align="left"><b><font face="Comic Sans MS" size="5" color="#0000FF">End
    Date:                 
    </font></b><input type="text" name="T1" size="20"><b><font face="Comic Sans MS" size="5"color="#0000FF">   
    </font></b></p>
    <p align="left"><b><font face="Comic Sans MS" size="5" color="#0000FF">
    Number Bedrooms:       </font>
    <font face="Comic Sans MS"><font size="5" color="#008000">
    <input type="radio" Value="V1" checked name="R1"> 1 </font>
    <font size="5" color="#008000">
    <input type="radio" Value="V1" checked name="R1"> 2
    <input type="radio" Value="V1" checked name="R1"> 3
    <input type="radio" Value="V1" checked name="R1"> 4 </font></font></b></p>
    <p align="left"><!-[if gte vml 1]><v:rect id="_x0000_s1027"
  alt="" style='position:absolute;left:3.75pt;top:8.25pt;width:663.75pt;
  height:347.25pt;z-index:-1' strokecolor="#930" strokeweight="3pt"/><![endif]--><![if !vml]><span
style='mso-ignore:vglayout;position:absolute;z-index:-1;left:3px;top:9px;
width:899px;height:467px'><img width=889 height=467
src="Figure%206-13_files/image001.gif" v:shapes="_x0000_s1027"></span><![endif]>
<b><font face="Comic Sans MS" size="5" color="#0000FF">Maximum
  Daily Rate:</font></b></p>
</blockquote>

</body>

</html>
```

Figure 10-13(b)
Code Behind Visual Web Page

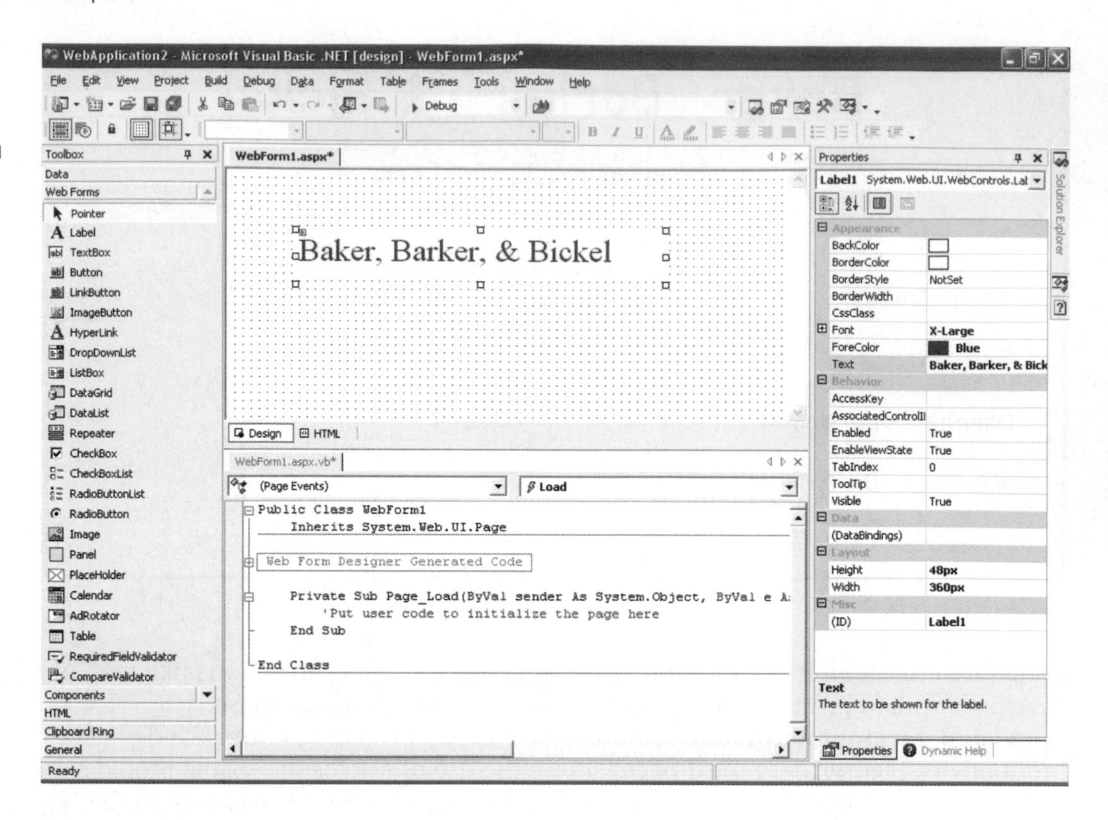

Figure 10-14
Visual Programming Tool Example

Source: Microsoft product screen shot reprinted with permission from Microsoft Corporation.

Q5 How Do Businesses Use Object-Oriented Development (OOD)?

A third development methodology, called **object-oriented development (OOD)**, arose from the discipline of object-oriented programming. As you will see, OOD has a number of characteristics in common with RAD, but it extends those concepts as well. OOD use began after RAD, in the early to mid-1990s.

Object-oriented development arose in response to the judgment that there is too much freedom in computer programming. Fred Brooks, author of *The Mythical Man-Month,* wrote that computer programs are logical poetry. Just as there are a myriad of ways to write poetry, so, too, there are a myriad of ways to write computer programs. Unlike poetry, however, programs must work together. A large system like Windows has thousands of programs that work together in a unified way. To create such a product, programmers must follow consistent practices; if they do not, chaos results.

OOD develops programs using the techniques of **object-oriented programming (OOP)**, which is a discipline for designing and writing computer programs. Programs developed using OOP are easier and cheaper to fix and adapt than those developed using traditional techniques. For this reason and various others, almost every software vendor today writes programs using OOP. Microsoft Windows and Office, for example, were written using OOP techniques.

Developers of business applications have been slower to adopt OOP, in part because they must integrate new programs with existing, non-OOP programs. Still, OOP sees increased use for business applications each year and will soon be the standard for such applications, too.

A series of diagramming techniques called the **Unified Modeling Language (UML)** facilitates OOP development. UML has dozens of different diagrams for all phases of system development. In fact, one complaint about UML is that there are so many diagrams that projects bog down in diagramming to the detriment of finishing the system. UML proponents argue that use of the diagrams is optional and that good project managers will select which ones to use.

UML itself does not require or promote any particular development process. There is, however, one methodology, called the **unified process (UP)**, that was designed for use with UML. We will summarize that process here. Be aware, however, that UML and UP are just examples of OOD diagrams and processes. Your organization may use different techniques. Also note that although UP is primarily a process for developing computer programs and not information systems, the ideas of UP can be broadened to include development of systems having the five components.

The Unified Process

Figure 10-15 shows the basic UP phases. Three of the five phases are similar to phases in the SDLC:

- The *inception* phase is similar to the first part of the SDLC definition phase.
- The *transition* phase is similar to the conversion phase in SDLC implementation.
- The *maintenance* phase is similar to maintenance in the SDLC.

The remaining two phases—*elaboration* and *construction*—are very different from SDLC, as you will see.

Elaboration Phase

During the elaboration phase, developers construct and test the framework and architecture of the new system. The result is a working system with basic capabilities. Elaboration includes requirements determination, design, programming, and testing.

With UML and UP, developers express requirements in the form of *use cases*. A **use case** is simply a description of an application of the new system. Figure 10-16 (next page) shows a sample use case for the Baker, Barker, and Bickel property reservation system. As shown, a use case consists of one or more scenarios that describe how the system will be used. The main success scenario describes how the system is used to create the desired outcome. This is the so-called *happy scenario*. Alternative scenarios describe other situations. They can be other versions of success or scenarios for different cases of failure.

Use cases drive the elaboration iterations. For example, in one iteration developers would implement scenario 1 in the use case in Figure 10-16. With subsequent iterations, they would implement other scenarios. Each iteration terminates with a functioning, tested system. Developers will not implement all of the use cases or use-case scenarios in an iteration, but those that they do implement will work.

According to the UP, the elaboration phase addresses the aspects of the system that have the most risk and uncertainty. Developers save the creation of features and functions for which there is little risk for the construction phase.

In today's world, security is an important source of system requirements. Developers need to address security needs, regardless of the style of development used. For the SDLC

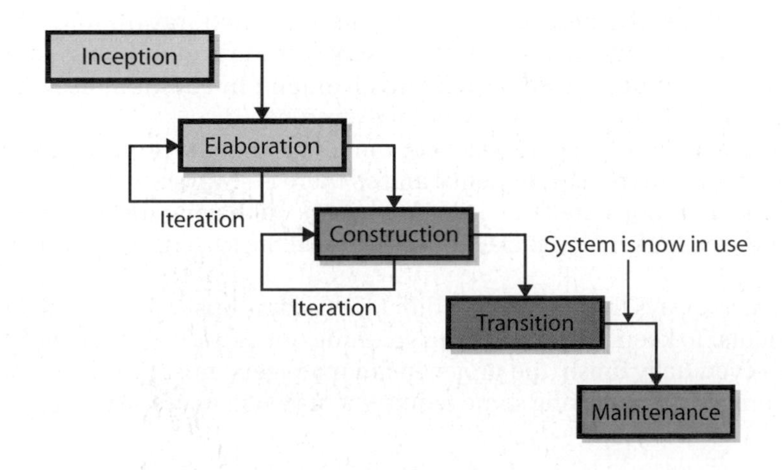

Figure 10-15
Stages in the Unified Process

Figure 10-16
Use Case Example

Baker Reserves Barker or Bickel Property

Main success scenario:

1. Customer calls Baker and wants to make a reservation in Barker or Bickel's territory. Customer states needs. Baker agent queries system for properties meeting those needs. Customer states dates desired. Agent checks availability for those dates. Property is available. Agent states prices and customer agrees to terms. Agent takes credit card information. Agent sends notification to the relevant Barker or Bickel and confirmation to customer.

Alternative scenarios:

2. Property is found and dates are available. Customer wants to think about it. Agent sends more information to customer and holds property reservation for 48 hours.
3. Property is found, and dates are available. Customer says price is too high.
   a. Agent seeks another property.
   b. Agent asks customer for budget and seeks price change from external agent at Barker or Bickel.
      (1) Price change is OK and customer accepts terms.
      (2) Price change is not OK. Agent seeks another property.
4. Property is found and dates are not available.
   a. Agent seeks another property.
   b. Customer changes dates required.

and RAD, developers obtain security requirements during requirements analysis. For UP, developers normally would address security during the elaboration phase.

Construction Phase

The Innovation in Practice *box on page 407 discusses the steps Sears, Roebuck and Company took to standardize the development process and offers you an opportunity to assess that decision.*

During the UP construction phase, developers design, implement, and test the easier, lower-risk features and functions that were not addressed during elaboration. Just as with the elaboration phase, construction consists of multiple iterations, each of which ends with a tested, working version of the system. Once developers have constructed all features and functions, the system is ready for deployment.

As noted earlier, the last two UP phases, transition and maintenance, are similar to phases in the SDLC, and we will not consider them further. The key differences in OOD are in the elaboration and construction phases.

UP Principles

Figure 10-17 summarizes the principles that underlie the UP. We have already discussed the first five. Considering the sixth principle, UP continuously involves users throughout the development process. Because the elaboration and construction phases proceed in iterations, and because users provide requirements for each iteration, there is a continuous need for user involvement. In addition, users provide test criteria and may even perform incremental testing.

One of the dangers of incremental development is that the project is never finished. Users add more and more requirements, and so there is always a need for another iteration. Continual iterations are less likely if the users are paying for the system (as they would be at Baker, Barker, and Bickel) or if they need the system to solve a troublesome problem.

But, there is always the chance that different user groups will insist on different sets of requirements. To keep the project from spinning out of control and to ensure that the system does eventually finish, the project team managers must prioritize requirements and have a process for deferring some requirements when necessary.

INNOVATION IN PRACTICE

SEARS STANDARDIZES DEVELOPMENT

Sears, Roebuck and Company (now owned by Sears Holdings) sells home merchandise, apparel, and auto products throughout the United States and Canada. Sears operates 2,300 retail outlets and sells over the Web at *http://sears.com* and *http://landsend.com*. It also offers products through a variety of specialty catalogs. Additionally, Sears operates the largest home-product repair service in the United States, making more than 14 million service calls per year.

At one point, Sears employed over 1,000 IT professionals who were using a variety of different system development methodologies, including SDLC, RAD, and versions of UP. This variety of different development methodologies resulted in systems having inconsistent quality and timeliness. According to John Morrison, IT Methodology Consultant at Sears:

> One of our central challenges was the use of multiple methodologies throughout IT. Associates were interpreting these methodologies in different ways. . . . [A]t the start of every project, the team had to establish roles for the project, decide which artifacts were going to be used. . . . [W]ithout a consistent, repeatable methodology, you have no way to pass on the process knowledge you've acquired.

To solve this problem, Sears created a single, consistent, enterprise-wide development process. This process was backed by software development tools licensed from IBM and based on a version of the unified process called the Rational Unified Process (RUP)® methodology. These tools provided Sears's developers the ability to manage requirements, development documentation, defects and testing results, and changes to requirements. RUP was chosen as the standard because teams within Sears had obtained success using it on isolated projects.

The results initially were encouraging. IT personnel were more effective because they needed to learn only one development process. Furthermore, the improved management of development projects reduced the costs related to system defects and failures by 20 percent. The IT department expected further cost savings as developers gained more experience with the methods and tools.

This case appeared in the first edition of this textbook as an example of what organizations *should* do. Today, it is less clear that a single development methodology is the best idea. It might be best for developing enterprise-wide, business-critical applications, but in the Web 2.0 world, it might not be the best idea for all applications development. Some applications might be best developed using the SDLC and others developed using RAD or XP (see question Q6).

When are standards important, and when do they get in the way? When rail tracks were first laid across America, the railroads benefited by having a single, standard width of train track. But, would the art world benefit if artists were required to use the same width of paintbrush or identical colors of paint? Clearly not. So, when are standards appropriate? Sometimes innovation occurs when people decide that the old ways, the old rules, and the old processes no longer pertain, or at least pertain differently.

Source: "Sears Builds Enterprise-wide Solution Delivery Framework," *http://306.ibm.com/software/success/cssdb.nsf/CS/MGER-5S3N9N?OpenDocument&Site=software* (accessed June 2005).

In Collaboration Exercise 2 (page 416), you and a team of your classmates will have an opportunity to consider, and maybe second-guess, Sears's standardization decision.

1. Develop incrementally.
2. State requirements with use cases.
3. Address high-risk functions early.
4. Build cohesive architecture early.
5. Test and verify quality early and often.
6. Involve users continuously.
7. Manage requirements.
8. Manage change requests.

Figure 10-17
UP Principles

Source: Larman, Craig, *Applying UML and Patterns: An Introduction to Object-Oriented Analysis and Design and the Unified Process* 2nd Edition, © 2002. Adapted by permission of Pearson Education, Inc, Upper Saddle River, NJ.

Similar comments apply to managing changes. As developers complete iterations, the users may want to change aspects of the system that have already been developed. Some changes are unavoidable and should be expected. If developers and the organization allow too many changes, however, the system can go into paralysis and never move forward.

Most successful UP projects prioritize change requests and implement them in accordance with that priority. To ensure that requests are not lost or duplicated, developers use some sort of change-tracking system.

Q6 How Do Businesses Use Extreme Programming (XP)?

We conclude our discussion of systems development methodologies with a short discussion of **extreme programming (XP)**, which is an emerging technique for developing computer programs. It is not useful for developing large systems that require new business processes and procedures. Organizations have used it successfully, however, in developing application programs.

Extreme programming represents the ultimate in iterative development. Programmers create only features and functions of the new program that they can complete in 2 weeks or less. If many programmers are working on the project, each person's work must be done in such a way that all of their work can be combined and assembled at the end of that period. Users and PQA professionals test the developed code continuously through the process.

In addition to this extremely iterative style, XP is distinguished by three key characteristics: It (1) is customer centric, (2) it uses just-in-time design, and (3) it involves paired programming.

Customer-Centric Nature

With XP, the customer or user of the new program is a critical part of the development team. The customer works full time on the project and consults closely with programmers and test engineers. The customer actively and personally defines requirements to the development team, fleshing out requirement details as they are needed by the programmers. The customer also helps testing personnel develop test plans and automated tests and performs application testing on a regular and recurring basis.

JIT Design

As you learned in Chapter 7, the acronym JIT means *just-in-time*. The JIT design of XP means that programmers defer program design until the last possible moment. Programmers create the minimal design they need to accomplish the requirements of the current iteration, and nothing more. Unlike other development techniques, developers prepare no overarching program design until the code to be written requires it.

As the project proceeds and as an existing design becomes unworkable, the development team discards that design and creates a new design. (The new design might be more or less complex than the discarded one, depending on the nature of the developing system.) Developers then alter existing programs as necessary to conform to the new design. Such a design technique means that developers will change and adapt programs dozens of times during the development process. Although this reprogramming may be expensive, the JIT design process means that the final programs will be as simple as possible.

Paired Programming

Paired programming is the most unconventional characteristic of XP. With it, two programmers work together, side by side, on the very same computer. They look over each other's shoulders, and they continuously communicate as they program on that single machine. According to XP proponents, studies show that two programmers working in this way can do at least as much work as two programmers working separately, and the resulting program code has fewer errors and is more easily maintained.[3] According to the same source, 90 percent of programmers who have tried paired programming for 3 weeks or more prefer it.

At each iteration of the project, one of the programmers moves to a different team. In this way, many different programmers see the same code. Over time, the jointly developed code attains a consistent look and feel. Also, the project never becomes dependent on one programmer for her specialized expertise. Many programmers know many different sections of code.

Extreme programming is not suited for every project or for every organization, but it does offer at least the promise of advantages over traditional programming methods.

Q7 How Do the Four Development Methodologies Compare?

Figure 10-18 compares the four different development techniques described in this chapter. Both the SDLC and RAD address information *systems* consisting of the five components. OOD with UP and XP are primarily concerned with the development of computer *programs*. Software development vendors such as Google or Oracle are more likely to use the latter two techniques. Companies that are developing organizational information systems, say, an inventory or order entry system, are more likely to use the SDLC and RAD.

User involvement is crucial to systems success, as described in the Reflections Guide *on page 412.*

You should be familiar with each of these techniques because you may be asked to participate as a user or customer of one of these systems. If so, take that responsibility seriously.

Systems Development Methodology	Scope	Advantages	Disadvantages
SDLC	All five components	• Comprehensive. • Addresses both business and technical issues. • Tried and tested.	• Requirements analysis may lead to analysis paralysis. • Waterfall nature unrealistic.
RAD	All five components	• Iterative nature reduces risk. • JAD improves design. • Use of prototypes and CASE tools increases productivity.	• Requirements analysis may lead to analysis paralysis. • Less suited to very large projects.
OOD with UP	Primarily object-oriented programs	• Use cases are effective requirements documents. • Risk moved forward to elaboration phase. • Each iteration terminates with a working system.	• Less useful for business systems development than for program development. • Danger of sinking into elaboration black hole.
Extreme Programming (XP)	Programs	• Customer (user) is always involved. • Paired programming improves quality and reduces risk. • Most useful when requirements evolve with systems development.	• Focus is on programming. • JIT design can require wasteful redesign. • Less useful when system involves many users having different, possibly conflicting, requirements.

Figure 10-18
Comparison of Development Techniques

[3]Ron Jeffries, "What Is Extreme Programming?" *XP Magazine,* November 11, 2001, *http://xprogramming.com/xpmag/whatisxp.htm#pair* (accessed May 2005).

Opposing Forces

GUIDE

The Real Estimation Process

I'm a software developer. I write programs in an object-oriented language called C++. I'm a skilled object-oriented designer, too. I should be—I've been at it 12 years and worked on major projects for several software companies. For the last 4 years, I've been a team leader. I lived through the heyday of the dot-com era and now work in the IT department of a giant pharmaceutical company.

"All of this estimating theory is just that—theory. It's not really the way things work. Sure, I've been on projects in which we tried different estimation techniques. But here's what really happens: You develop an estimate using whatever technique you want. Your estimate goes in with the estimates of all the other team leaders. The project manager sums all those estimates together and produces an overall estimate for the project.

"By the way, in my projects, time has been a much bigger factor than money. At one software company I worked for, you could be 300 percent over your dollar budget and get no more than a slap on the wrist. Be 2 weeks late, however, and you were finished.

"Anyway, the project managers take the project schedule to senior management for approval, and what happens? Senior management thinks they are negotiating. 'Oh, no,' they say, 'that's way too long. You can surely take a month off that schedule. We'll approve the project, but we want it done by February 1 instead of March 1.'

"Now, what's their justification? They think that tight schedules make for efficient work. You know that everyone will work extra hard to meet the tighter timeframe. They know Parkinson's Law—'the time required to perform a task expands to the time available to do it.' So, fearing the possibility of wasting time because of too-lenient schedules, they lop a month off our estimate.

"Estimates are what they are; you can't knock off a month or two without some problem, somewhere. What does happen is that projects get behind, and then management expects us to work longer and longer hours. Like they said in the early years at Microsoft, 'We have flexible working hours. You can work any 65 hours per week you want.'

"Not that our estimation techniques are all that great, either. Most software developers are optimists. They schedule things as if everything will go as planned, and things seldom do. Also, schedulers usually don't allow for vacations, sick days, trips to the dentist, training on new technology, peer reviews, and all the other things we do in addition to writing software.

"So we start with optimistic schedules on our end, then management negotiates a month or two off, and voilà, we have a late project. After a while, management has been burned by late projects so much that they mentally add the month or even more back onto the official schedule. Then both sides work in a fantasy world, where no one believes the schedule, but everyone pretends they do.

"I like my job. I like software development. Management here is no better or worse than in other places. As long as I have interesting work to do, I'll stay here. But I'm not working myself silly to meet these fantasy deadlines." ■

Discussion Questions

1. What do you think of this developer's attitude? Do you think he's unduly pessimistic or do you think there's merit to what he says?
2. What do you think of his idea that management thinks they're negotiating? Should management negotiate schedules? Why or why not?
3. Suppose a project actually requires 12 months to complete. Which do you think is likely to cost more: (a) having an official schedule of 11 months with at least a 1-month overrun or (b) having an official schedule of 13 months and following Parkinson's Law, having the project take 13 months?
4. Suppose you are a business manager and an information system is being developed for your use. You review the scheduling documents and see that little time has been allowed for vacations, sick leave, miscellaneous other work, and so forth. What do you do?
5. Describe the intangible costs of having an organizational belief that schedules are always unreasonable.
6. If this developer worked for you, how would you deal with his attitude about scheduling?
7. Do you think there is something different when scheduling information systems development projects than when scheduling other types of projects? What characteristics might make such projects unique? In what ways are they the same as other projects?
8. What do you think managers should do in light of your answer to question 7?

Reflections

GUIDE

Dealing with Uncertainty

In the mid-1970s, I worked as a database disaster repairman. As an independent consultant, I was called by organizations that licensed the then-new database management systems but had little idea of what to do with them.

One of my memorable clients had converted the company's billing system from an older-technology system to the new world of database processing. Unfortunately, after they cut off the old system, serious flaws were found in the new one, and from mid-November to mid-January the company was unable to send a bill. Of course, customers who do not receive bills do not pay, and my client had a substantial cash flow problem. Even worse, some of its customers used a calendar-year tax basis and wanted to pay their bills prior to the end of the year. When those customers called to find the amount they owed, accounts receivable clerks had to say, "Well, we don't know. The data's in our computer, but we can't get it out." That was when the company called me for database disaster repair.

The immediate cause of the problem was that the client used the plunge conversion technique. But looking deeper, how did that organization find itself with a new billing system so full of failures?

In this organization, management had little idea about how to communicate with IT, and the IT personnel had no experience in dealing with senior management. They talked past one another.

Fortunately, this client was, in most other respects, a well-managed company. Senior management only needed to learn to manage their IS projects with the same discipline as they managed other departments. So, once we had patched the billing system together to solve the cash flow problem, the management team began work to implement policies and procedures to instill the following principles:

- Business users, not IS, would take responsibility for the success of new systems.
- Users would actively work with IS personnel throughout systems development, especially during the requirements phase.
- Users would take an active role in project planning, project management, and project reviews.
- No development phase would be considered complete until the work was reviewed and approved by user representatives and management.
- Users would actively test the new system.
- All future systems would be developed in small increments.

I cannot claim that all future development projects at this company proceeded smoothly after the users began to practice these principles. In fact, many users were slow to take on their new responsibilities; in some cases, the users resented the time they were asked to invest in the new practices. Also, some were uncomfortable in

these new roles. They wanted to work in their business specialty and not be asked to participate in IS projects about which they knew little. Still others did not take their responsibilities seriously; they would come to meetings ill prepared, not fully engage in the process, or approve work they did not understand.

However, after that billing disaster, senior management understood what needed to be done. They made these practices a priority, and over time user resistance was mostly overcome. When it was not overcome, it was clear to senior management where the true problem lay. ■

Discussion Questions

1. In general terms, describe how the billing system might have been implemented using pilot conversion. Describe how it might have been implemented using parallel conversion.
2. If you were the billing system project manager, what factors would you consider when deciding the style of conversion to use?
3. If the billing system had been converted using either pilot or parallel, what would have happened?
4. Explain in your own words the benefits that would accrue using the new principles.
5. Summarize the reasons that users resisted these new principles. What could be done to overcome that resistance?
6. Suppose you work in a company where users have little to no active involvement in systems development. Describe likely consequences of this situation. Describe five actions you could take to correct this situation.

ACTIVE REVIEW

Use this Active Review to verify that you understand the ideas and concepts that answer the chapter's study questions.

Q1 What is systems development?

Define *systems development* and explain how it pertains to the five components. Summarize the nature of systems development work and the types of personnel involved. Explain why information systems are never off-the-shelf and what that means for you as a future manager. Explain the term *maintenance* as it pertains to systems development.

Q2 Why is systems development difficult and risky?

Explain the risks of systems development. List five major challenges to systems development and summarize each. State Brooks's Law and explain how it pertains to systems development. Explain why there are four different development methodologies.

Q3 How do businesses use the systems development life cycle (SDLC) process?

Briefly describe the origins of the SDLC. Name the five phases of the SDLC. List the primary tasks in each phase. Explain the role for business users in each phase. Name and explain four dimensions of feasibility. Describe the knowledge needed by systems analysts and summarize their responsibilities. Define *test plan* and *PQA*. Name and describe four types of systems conversion. Explain major tasks in systems maintenance and define *patch* and *service pack*. Summarize the three major problems with the SDLC.

Q4 How do businesses use the rapid application development (RAD) process?

Describe the basic idea of RAD and explain how it differs from the SDLC. Define *incremental development*. Name five RAD characteristics and briefly explain each. Define *prototype* and explain its uses and risks. Give two definitions for the term *CASE*. Explain the role of code generators and visual development tools.

Q5 How do businesses use object-oriented development (OOD)?

Explain the statement, "There is too much freedom in computer programming." Define *OOP* and *UML*. Explain the term *UP* and describe its five stages. Compare UP to the SDLC. Summarize the major UP principles.

Q6 How do businesses use extreme programming (XP)?

Define *extreme programming* and explain its scope of use. Explain how XP is the ultimate in iterative development. Name and describe three key characteristics of XP. Define *JIT design* and explain how it differs from traditional program design. State how most programmers with experience with paired programming feel about it.

Q7 How do the four development methodologies compare?

State the primary scope of each of the four development methodologies discussed in this chapter. Explain the advantages and disadvantages of each. (Use Figure 10-18 as a guide.)

KEY TERMS AND CONCEPTS

USING YOUR KNOWLEDGE

1. Reread the Singing Valley Collaboration Exercise at the end of Chapter 3 (page 86). If you have not already answered that question, do so now, but develop just one innovative idea. Consider that idea from the standpoint of a systems development project. Develop a brief plan for this project using the SDLC. List major tasks that need to be performed at each stage.
2. Reread the Microsoft Surface *Innovation in Practice* box (page 114) and its related Collaboration Exercise (Chapter 4, Collaboration Exercise 2, page 137). Describe one innovative application of Surface at your university. Consider that application from the standpoint of a systems development project. Develop a brief plan for this project using the SDLC. List major tasks that need to be performed at each stage.
3. Reread the choir-sheet-music-tracking problem in the *Innovation in Practice* box on page 158. Chapter 5 focused on the development of a database for that problem. Now consider that application from the standpoint of a systems development project. Develop a brief plan for this project using the SDLC. Pay particular attention to the systems components other than the database that need to be developed. List major tasks that need to be performed at each stage.
4. Reread the Sundog Expeditions collaboration project at the end of Chapter 8 (page 324). Suppose that Sundog Expeditions wants to expand its current Web site to include social networking. Consider that addition from the standpoint of a systems development project. Develop a brief plan for this project using the SDLC. List major tasks that need to be performed at each stage.

COLLABORATION EXERCISES AND CASES

Collaborate with a group of students on the following exercises. Recall from Chapter 2 that collaboration is more than cooperation because it involves iteration and feedback. Post a document, a discussion item, a wiki item, or an idea, and obtain feedback from your team members. Similarly, read the ideas of others and comment on them. Try to innovate in both the process by which you collaborate and the work product that you create. Avoid face-to-face meetings. Instead, use collaborative software such as Google Docs & Spreadsheets, Microsoft Groove, or Microsoft SharePoint to facilitate your ideas.

1. In this exercise, you will be asked to develop an outline of a development process for Baker, Barker, and Bickel. Begin by rereading the *Systems Development in Practice* box on page 384.

   Because we do not know Baker, Barker, and Bickel's detailed requirements, you cannot develop a plan for a specific system. In general, however, they first need to decide how elaborate an information system they want to construct. Consider the following three alternatives:

   (1) They could build a simple system centered on email. With it, each company sends property descriptions to the others via email. Each independent company then forwards these descriptions to its own customers, also using email. When a customer makes a reservation for a property, that

request is then forwarded back to the property manager via email.

(2) They could construct a more complex system using a Web-based, shared database that contains data on all their properties and reservations. Because reservations tracking is a common business task, it is likely that they can license an existing application with this capability.

(3) Same as alternative 2, except assume they do not license an existing product, but develop their own database and applications instead.

a. Of the four development methodologies discussed in this chapter, only the SDLC is appropriate for alternatives 1 and 2, but the SDLC, RAD or OOP could be used for alternative 3. Explain why this is so.

b. Using Figure 10-3 as a guide, perform the steps required for the systems definition phase for alternative 1. You cannot form a project team to complete the project, so, instead, describe the personnel that would need to be on such a team. With regard to planning, specify the tasks that would need to be performed for the requirements, design, and implementation stages.

c. Perform the steps required for the systems definition phase for alternative 2. Again, you cannot form a project team to complete the project, so, instead, describe the personnel that would need to be on such a team. With regard to planning, specify the tasks that would need to be performed for the requirements, design, and implementation stages.

d. Perform the steps required for the systems definition phase for alternative 3. Assume you use the SDLC. Again, just describe the personnel that would need to be on such a team. With regard to planning, specify the tasks that would need to be performed for the requirements, design, and implementation stages.

e. Explain how the development process would be different if they used RAD instead of the SDLC for alternative 3. Which process would you recommend?

f. Given what you know about the BBB alliance and the work you envision in your answers to parts b, c, and d, which alternative do you think makes the most sense? Why? What other information might you need to answer this question? How would you go about finding that information?

g. Clearly, the development of any of these alternatives will be a collaborative effort. Chapter 2 briefly introduced Google Docs & Spreadsheets, Microsoft Groove, and Microsoft SharePoint. Which of these tools would be most appropriate for BBB to use when developing this system? Why? In your answer, use your own experience with these tools, if you have been using them. Explain why the use of one of these tools would be better than email with attachments or FTP.

2. In this exercise, you will be asked to answer the question of when standards are appropriate and when they are a hindrance. Begin by rereading the *Innovation in Practice* box on page 407.

a. Summarize the problem that Sears wanted to solve when it standardized on a single development methodology.

b. Summarize the advantages that Sears obtained by standardizing on a single development process.

c. Using the knowledge you have gained in this class, construct a list of 10 different information systems. Strive to make your systems as different from one another in function, scale, scope (single user vs. interenterprise) as possible. Consider all of the types of IS in Chapters 2, 3, 7, 8, and 9 as well as any other IS you can imagine.

d. For each of the systems in your list in your answer to part c, describe the purpose of the system, the types and numbers of users, and briefly summarize the character of each component.

e. Which of the four development methodologies described in this chapter would be best for each of the systems in your answers to parts c and d? Explain your rationale.

f. Review the Sears case again, paying particular attention to the problems described when using multiple development methodologies. Do you think an organization developing the 10 systems you described should standardize on a single development methodolgy? In your answer, compare the advantages and disadvantages of standardized versus nonstandardized development.

g. Generalize your learning from this exercise to other business processes. For example, when should an organization have a standard sales process? A standard purchasing process? A standard hiring process?

h. When are standards useful, and when are they a hindrance? Discuss this question in your group and summarize the different perspectives. If your group can come to a common answer, state it. If not, explain why you could not come to a common answer.

APPLICATION EXERCISES

1. Suppose you are given the task of keeping track of the number of labor hours invested in meetings for systems development projects. Assume your company uses the traditional SDLC and that each phase requires two types of meetings: *Working meetings* involve users, systems analysts, programmers, and PQA test engineers. *Review meetings* involve all of those people, plus level-1 and level-2 managers of both user departments and the IS department.

   a. Import the data in the Word file **Ch10Ex01** from this text's Web site into a spreadsheet.
   b. Modify your spreadsheet to compute the total labor hours invested in each phase of a project. When a meeting occurs, assume you enter the project phase, the meeting type, the start time, the end time, and the number of each type of personnel attending. Your spreadsheet should calculate the number of labor hours and should add the meeting's hours to the totals for that phase and for the project overall.
   c. Modify your spreadsheet to include the budgeted number (in the source data) of labor hours for each type of employee for each phase. In your spreadsheet, show the difference between the number of hours budgeted and the number actually consumed.
   d. Change your spreadsheet to include the budgeted cost and actual cost of labor. Assume that you enter, once, the average labor cost for each type of employee, as stipulated in the source data.

2. Use Access to develop a failure-tracking database application. Use the data in the Excel file **Ch10Ex02** for this exercise. The data includes columns for the following:

   FailureNumber
   DateReported
   FailureDescription
   ReportedBy (the name of the PQA engineer reporting the failure)
   ReportedBy_email (the email address of the PQA engineer reporting the failure)
   FixedBy (the name of the programmer who is assigned to fix the failure)
   FixedBy_email (the email address of the programmer assigned to fix the failure)
   DateFailureFixed
   FixDescription
   DateFixVerified
   VerifiedBy (the name of the PQA engineer verifying the fix)
   VeifiedBy_email (the email address of the PQA engineer verifying the fix)

   a. The data in the spreadsheet is not normalized. Normalize the data by creating a *Failure* table, a *PQA Engineer* table, and a *Programmer* table. Add other appropriate columns to each table. Create appropriate relationships.
   b. Create one or more forms that can be used to report a failure, to report a failure fix, and to report a failure verification. Create the form(s) so that the user can just pull down the name of a PQA engineer or programmer from the appropriate table to fill in the *ReportedBy*, *FixedBy*, and *VerifiedBy* fields.
   c. Construct a report that shows all failures sorted by reporting PQA engineer and then by *Date Reported*.
   d. Construct a report that shows only fixed and verified failures
   e. Construct a report that shows only fixed but unverified failures.

CASE STUDY 10

Slow Learners, or What?

In 1974, when I was teaching at Colorado State University, we conducted a study of the causes of information systems failures. We interviewed personnel on several dozen projects and collected survey data on another 50 projects. Our analysis of the data revealed that the single most important factor in IS failure was a lack of user involvement. The second major factor was unclear, incomplete, and inconsistent requirements.

At the time, I was a devoted computer programmer and IT techie, and, frankly, I was surprised. I thought that the significant problems would have been technical issues.

I recall one interview in particular. A large sugar producer had attempted to implement a new system for paying sugar beet farmers. The new system was to be implemented at some 20 different sugar beet collection sites, which were located in small farming communities, adjacent to rail yards. One of the benefits of the new system was significant cost savings, and a major share of those savings occurred because the new system eliminated the need for local comptrollers. The new system was expected to eliminate the jobs of 20 or so senior people.

The comptrollers, however, had been paying local farmers for decades; they were popular leaders not just within the company, but in their communities as well. They were well liked, highly respected, important people. A system that caused the elimination of their jobs was, using a term from this chapter, *organizationally infeasible*, to say the least.

Nonetheless, the system was constructed, but an IS professional who was involved told me, "Somehow, that new system just never seemed to work. The data were not entered on a timely basis, or they were in error, or incomplete; sometimes the data were not entered at all. Our operations were falling apart during the key harvesting season, and we finally backed off and returned to the old system." Active involvement of system users would have identified this organizational infeasibility long before the system was implemented.

That's ancient history, you say. Maybe, but in 1994 the Standish Group published a now famous study on information systems failures. Entitled "The CHAOS Report," the study indicated that the leading causes of IS failure are, in descending order, (1) lack of user input, (2) incomplete requirements and specifications, and (3) changing requirements and specifications (*http://standishgroup.com*). That study was completed some 20 years after our study.

More recently, in 2004, Professor Joseph Kasser and his students at the University of Maryland analyzed 19 system failures to determine their cause. They then correlated their analysis of the cause with the opinions of the professionals involved in the failures. The correlated results indicate the first-priority cause of system failure was "Poor requirements"; the second-priority cause was "Failure to communicate with the customer" (*http://softwaretechnews.com/technews2–2/trouble.html*).

In 2003, the IRS Oversight Board concluded the first cause of the IRS BSM failure (see Case Study 1, page 26) was "inadequate business unit ownership and sponsorship of projects. This resulted in unrealistic business cases and continuous project scope 'creep.'"

For over 30 years, studies have consistently shown that leading causes of system failures are a lack of user involvement and incomplete and changing requirements. Yet, failures from these very failures continue to mount.

Sources: http://standishgroup.com;softwaretechnews.com/technews2–2/trouble.html (accessed May 2005).

Questions

1. Using the knowledge you have gained from this chapter, summarize the roles that you think users should take during an information systems development project. What responsibilities do users have? How closely should they work with the IS team? Who is responsible for stating requirements and constraints? Who is responsible for managing requirements?
2. If you ask users why they did not participate in requirements specification, some of the common responses are the following:

   a. "I wasn't asked."

   b. "I didn't have time."

   c. "They were talking about a system that would be here in 18 months, and I'm just worried about getting the order out the door today."

   d. "I didn't know what they wanted."

   e. "I didn't know what they were talking about."

   f. "I didn't work here when they started the project."

   g. "The whole situation has changed since they were here; that was 18 months ago!"

   Comment on each of these statements. What strategies do they suggest to you as a future user and as a future manager of users?
3. If you ask IS professionals why they did not obtain a complete and accurate list of requirements, common responses are:

   a. "It was nearly impossible to get on the users' calendars. They were always too busy."

   b. "The users wouldn't regularly attend our meetings. As a result, one meeting would be dominated by the needs of one group, and another meeting would be dominated by the needs of another group."

   c. "Users didn't take the requirement process seriously. They wouldn't thoroughly review the requirements statements before review meetings."

   d. "Users kept changing. We'd meet with one person one time and another person a second time, and they'd want different things."

e. "We didn't have enough time."
f. "The requirements kept changing."

Comment on each of these statements. What strategies do they suggest to you as a future user and a future manager of users?

4. If it is widely understood that one of the principal causes of IS failures is a lack of user involvement, and if that factor continues to be a problem after 30 years of experience, does this mean that the problem cannot be solved? For example, everyone knows that you can maximize your gains by buying stocks at their annual low price and selling them at their annual high price, but doing so is very difficult. Is it equally true that although everyone knows that users should be involved in requirements specification, and that requirements should be complete, it just can't be done? Why or why not?

11 Information Systems Management

STUDY QUESTIONS

- Q1 What are the functions of the IS department?
- Q2 How do organizations plan the use of IS?
- Q3 What tasks are necessary for managing computing infrastructure?
- Q4 What tasks are necessary for managing enterprise applications?
- Q5 What are the advantages and disadvantages of outsourcing?
- Q6 What are your user rights and responsibilities?

Meet Darwin John

Characteristic of a superior employee:
One who learns.

My management style:
My primary style (I strongly believe we must have one or more backup styles) is low key, yet very focused.

My life mission:
Learning and serving, also then my work. I don't separate them much.

Darwin John has been a chief information officer (CIO) for more than 30 years and, indeed, was one of the first people ever to earn that title. He set the mold for CIOs that many others have followed. Mr. John entered business as an engineer, working for Thiokol Chemical Corporation, but soon moved into information systems through a series of jobs with Honeywell, General Mills, and Scott Paper. It was Scott Paper that first named him CIO, and since then he has worked in that same capacity for the Church of Jesus Christ of Latter-day Saints and the Federal Bureau of Investigation (FBI). Today, he continues as an advisor to the FBI and maintains an active consulting practice advising major organizations.

At Scott Paper, he led a project that required the conversion of more than 40 percent of Scott's installed systems. The project was key to Scott's operations, and the execution of the development plan exposed Scott to considerable risk. Failure could "bring the company to its knees," in the words of one board member. With Mr. John's leadership, the project was a resounding success, and the Scott board of directors voted him and his team a special commendation. Much of the development of the new system was outsourced, and from that experience, as well as subsequent projects throughout his career, Mr. John has learned how to make outsourcing work.

On outsourcing:

"There are four key elements, headlines if you will, on successful outsourcing. First, look at your business strategically and decide what critical capacities you need to have in-house. Never outsource those. You can outsource anything else, but not those.

"Second, separate the management of the work from the management of the contract. Let the outsourcing staff be a full member of your project team. Pull off the contract managers on both sides and put them in a separate group.

"Then it comes down to relationships. Make sure your outsourcing partner knows what drives you and your success and understand what drives them. Look for alignment in objectives.

"And, fourth, develop effective communication; everything depends on good communication."

On relationships:

"They are critical. My success is a function of the quality of my relationships, relationships that are grounded in trust and respect. As a CIO, I would determine who my strategic partners were, and I would make sure that every 18 months or so, either we visited them or they visited us to conduct a confidential conversation

My pet peeve:
Employees who are focused on or think primarily at an operational level.

One favorite motto:
Success is a function of being good at learning and good at changing.

Quote I like:
"If two employees think exactly alike, then we have no need for one of them." —L. Aldrid Christensen

about where we were going, what we needed, what we wanted to accomplish. At the same time, we would seek to understand their strategy, where they were headed, what was driving their business.

"I would tell them, 'Never come in here and try to sell me the latest box or gizmo. I'm not interested in that conversation.' Then and today, I'm interested only in finding strategic alignments between organizations.

"Everything is easier if you have a relationship of trust and respect. I dealt equitably with our partners, and I believe they dealt equitably with us."

On the role of CIO:

"The CIO is a leader, an integration point, and a member of the leadership team. There is no such thing as an information systems strategic plan. There is a strategic plan for the organization, and information systems is a plank in that plan.

"The CIO must earn his or her way onto the leadership team of the enterprise. You cannot succeed based on the power of your title. You succeed based on your relationships and your power to influence.

"Your hard skills, your technical expertise—whatever it is—will get you in the door. But your soft skills—your ability to build relationships, to collaborate, to communicate—those skills enable you to succeed. I tell my employees, 'Soft is hard and hard is easy.' By that I mean it is hard to learn and develop the people-oriented skills, but learning the technical skills is easy."

On learning:

"Among the practices that most helped me when I was a CIO was dividing my time according to what I called the 'third-third-third' model. As best I could, I tried to limit one-third of my work time to minding the store and looking after day-to-day operations. I devoted another third to fostering strong relationships with peers and customers. The final third—and in my view the most critical—I set aside for learning.

"The first time I was named CIO, the personal computer hadn't even been invented. Think about that. Since then we've had the PC, LANs, WANs, the Internet, and now Web 2.0. And there is no indication that it will slow down; in fact it will probably accelerate. You must form the habit of learning throughout your life."

On a career in information systems:

"Would I advise someone to major in information systems? Well, yes and no. Yes, because it's where the action is. You can look at any enterprise and it always comes down to three resources: people, dollars, and information. Because of the amazing changes in technology, the ever-evolving ways of producing and consuming information, the IS field is the place to be.

"But, as I learned from the late Peter Drucker, you're asking me the wrong question. The question should be, 'What are your interests and abilities?' Determine those first. Then ask, 'Do my interests and abilities fit with some interesting job in the information systems field?' If so, by all means I would recommend a career in IS.

"Again, it comes down to alignment. Align who you are with the job that you seek. If you do that, and if you focus on learning the hard-to-learn soft skills, financial and even more important rewards will come your way without fail."

CHAPTER PREVIEW

As you learned in Chapters 7 through 9, information systems are a critical component of organizational success. But as you also learned in Chapters 4 through 6, they are complex. Considerable work is required to transform raw information technology into effective information systems that allow organizations to accomplish their goals and objectives.

This chapter surveys the means by which organizations manage this delicate combination of criticality and complexity. We begin with a survey of the major functions of the IS department and the relationship of the IS department to the enterprise. Then we will consider each of the major functions in greater detail: planning the use of IT/IS, creating and managing the computing infrastructure, creating and managing enterprise IS, and protecting organizational information assets.

Outsourcing is the process of hiring outside vendors to provide business services and related products. For information systems, outsourcing refers to hiring outside vendors to provide information systems, products, and applications. We will examine the pros and cons of outsourcing and describe some of its risks. Finally, we will conclude this chapter by discussing the relationship of users to the IS department. In this last section, you will learn both your own and the IS department's rights and responsibilities.

The purpose of this chapter is not to teach you how to manage information systems. Such management, in truth, requires many years of experience. Instead, the goal of this chapter is to give you an appreciation for the scale and complexity of the IS management task and to help you become an effective consumer of IS services.

Q1 What Are the Functions of the IS Department?

The major functions of the information systems department are as follows:

- Plan the use of IT to accomplish organizational goals and strategy.
- Develop, operate, and maintain the organization's computing infrastructure.
- Develop, operate, and maintain enterprise applications.
- Protect information assets.
- Manage outsourcing relationships.

We will consider each of these functions in greater detail in the next sections of this chapter.

Figure 11-1 (next page) shows typical top-level reporting relationships. As you will learn in your management classes, organizational structure varies depending on the organization's size, culture, competitive environment, industry, and other factors. Larger organizations with independent divisions will have a group of senior executives like those shown here for each division. Smaller companies may combine some of these departments. Consider the structure in Figure 11-1 as a typical example.

The title of the principal manager of the IS department varies from organization to organization. A common title is **chief information officer**, or **CIO**. Other common titles are *vice president of information services, director of information services*, and, less commonly, *director of computer services*.

In Figure 11-1, the CIO, like other senior executives, reports to the *chief executive officer* (CEO), though sometimes these executives report to the *chief operating officer* (COO), who in turn reports to the CEO. In some companies, the CIO reports to the *chief financial officer* (CFO). That reporting arrangement might make sense if the primary information systems support only accounting and finance activities. In

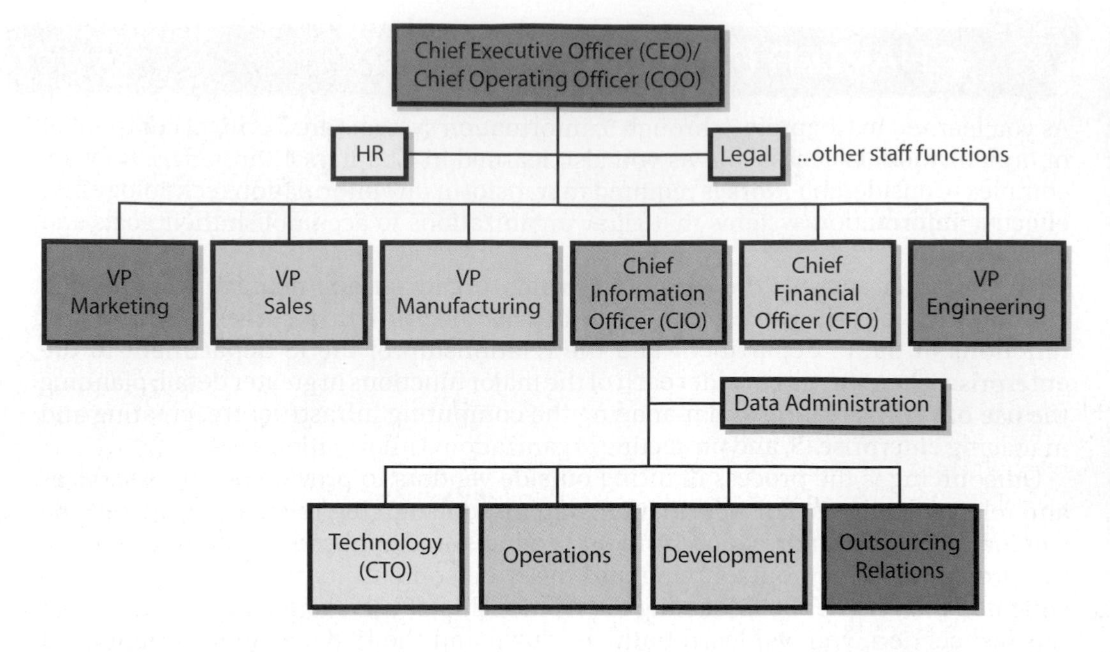

Figure 11-1
Typical Senior-Level Reporting Relationships

organizations such as manufacturers that operate significant nonaccounting information systems, the arrangement shown in Figure 11-1 is more common and effective.

The structure of the IS department also varies among organizations. Figure 11-1 shows a typical IS department with four groups and a data administration staff function.

Most IS departments include a *technology* office that investigates new information systems technologies and determines how the organization can benefit from them. For example, today many organizations are investigating Web 2.0 opportunities and planning how they can use those capabilities to better accomplish their goals and objectives. An individual called the **chief technology officer**, or **CTO**, often heads the technology group. The CTO evaluates new technologies, new ideas, and new capabilities and identifies those that are most relevant to the organization. The CTO's job requires deep knowledge of information technology and the ability to envision and innovate applications in the organization.

As new technologies proliferate at an increasing pace, the job of CTO has never been more exciting or more challenging. For more, read the Innovation in Practice *box on page 425.*

The next group in Figure 11-1, *operations*, manages the computing infrastructure, including individual computers, computer centers, networks, and communications media. This group includes system and network administrators. As you will learn, an important function for this group is to monitor the user experience and respond to user problems.

The third group in the IS department in Figure 11-1 is *development*. This group manages the process of creating new information systems as well as maintaining existing information systems. (Recall from Chapter 10 that in the context of information systems, maintenance means either removing problems or adapting existing information systems to support new features and functions.)

The size and structure of the development group depends on whether programs are developed in-house. If not, this department will be staffed primarily by systems analysts who work with users, operations, and vendors to acquire and install licensed software and to set up the system components around that software. If the organization develops programs in-house, then this department will include programmers, test engineers, technical writers, and other development personnel.

The last IS department group in Figure 11-1 is *outsourcing relations*. This group exists in organizations that have negotiated outsourcing agreements with other com-

INNOVATION IN PRACTICE

iPHONE MEETS WEB 2.0

In the interview that opens this chapter, Darwin John says, "The first time I was named CIO, the personal computer hadn't even been invented." In fact, when he began his career, punch cards were used to input data into computers. Monitors were converted teletype machines (which were used to send *telegrams*). In those days, the IT department had absolute control over information systems use and data. The only removable devices were 11-inch reels of tape, and no one could walk out of the computer room with such a tape without causing a stir (and a demand for a signed tape-release-permission form).

Mr. John has indeed seen change. In May 2007, Apple started selling the iPhone, the latest in personal communications/entertainment/Internet access devices. With iPhones and similar devices, the idea of data control is ludicrous. Users mix up their business contacts from the organization's CRM with their favorite music and their pictures to Mom and Dad—all on the same, easily broken, easily stolen, easily lost device.

In the article "Why the iPhone Is the Single Most Important Thing to Happen to CIOs This Year," Ben Worthen says:

> The iPhone combines music and movies, i.e. the personal, with email and voicemail, i.e. the professional. That's the way life has been trending; knowledge workers have two identities and they inhabit both 24/7. The iPhone not only recognizes this, but caters to it. The message is clear: if the work and the personal parts of your lives are no longer separate why should the devices that you use in those roles be?[1]

The iPhone is impressive, the latest in cell and PDA devices, but it is just another development in a long line of hardware advances. However, the merger of professional and personal lives sounds important. Are the iPhone and similar gear enabling a new sociology? A new set of behaviors?

Meanwhile, Web 2.0 phenomena such as social networking; organic interfaces; mashups; and context-based advertising, such as Google's Ad Words and Ad Sense are changing users' expectations of what computers can do and be.

What a wonderful time to be a CTO! Suppose, for example, you were CTO for a company like 3M, Procter and Gamble, or Toyota U.S.A. What would you be telling your senior management? What opportunities do iPhones and Web 2.0 present to your organization?

You and a team of your classmates will have an opportunity to address this in Collaboration Exercise 1, page 451.

[1]*CIO Magazine, advice.cio.com/why-the-iphone-is-the-single-most-important-thing-to-happen-to-cios-this-year* (accessed August 2007).

panies to provide equipment, applications, or other services. You will learn more about outsourcing later in this chapter.

Figure 11-1 also includes a *data administration* staff function. The purpose of this group is to protect data and information assets by establishing data standards and data management practices and policies.

There are many variations on the structure of the IS department shown in Figure 11-1. In larger organizations, the operations group may itself consist of several different departments. Sometimes, there is a separate group for data warehousing and data marts.

As you examine Figure 11-1, keep the distinction between IS and IT in mind. *Information systems (IS)* exist to help the organization achieve its goals and objectives. Information systems have the five components we have discussed throughout this text. *Information technology (IT)* is simply technology. It concerns the products, techniques, procedures, and designs of computer-based technology. IT must be placed into the structure of an IS before an organization can use it. In the next few sections, we will consider in greater detail each of the functions in Figure 11-1.

Figure 11-2
Planning the Use of IS/IT

- Align information systems with organizational strategy; maintain alignment as organization changes.
- Communicate IS/IT issues to executive group.
- Develop/enforce IS priorities within the IS department.
- Sponsor steering committee.

Q2 How Do Organizations Plan the Use of IS?

We begin our discussion of IS functions with planning. Figure 11-2 lists the major IS planning functions.

Align Information Systems with Organizational Strategy

The purpose of an information system is to help the organization accomplish its goals and objectives. In order to do so, all information systems must be aligned with the organization's competitive strategy.

Recall the four competitive strategies from Chapter 3: An organization can be a cost leader either across an industry or within an industry segment. Alternatively, an organization can differentiate its products or services either across the industry or within a segment. Whatever the organizational strategy, the CIO and the IS department must constantly be vigilant to align IS with it. To underline this statement, see Mr. John's comments in the chapter-opening interview about the importance of alignment.

Maintaining alignment between IS direction and organizational strategy is a continuing process. As strategies change, as the organization merges with other organizations, as divisions are sold, IS must evolve along with the organization.

Unfortunately, however, IS infrastructure is not malleable. Changing a network requires time and resources. Integrating disparate information systems applications is even slower and more expensive. This fact often is not appreciated in the executive suite. Without a persuasive CIO, IS can be perceived as a drag on the organization's opportunities.

Communicate IS Issues to the Executive Group

This last observation leads to the second IS planning function in Figure 11-2. The CIO is the representative for IS and IT issues within the executive staff. She provides the IS perspective during discussions of problem solutions, proposals, and new initiatives.

For example, when considering a merger, it is important that the company consider integration of information systems in the merged entities. This consideration needs to be addressed during the evaluation of the merger opportunity. Too often, such issues are not considered until after the deal has been signed. Such delayed consideration is a mistake; the costs of the integration need to be factored into the economics of the purchase. Involving the CIO in high-level discussions is the best way to avoid such problems.

Develop Priorities and Enforce Them Within the IS Department

The next two IS planning functions in Figure 11-2 are related. The CIO must ensure that priorities consistent with the overall organizational strategy are developed and communicated to the IS department. At the same time, he must also ensure that the department evaluates proposals and projects for using new technology in light of those communicated priorities.

Technology is seductive, particularly to IS professionals. The CTO may enthusiastically claim, "With SOA services we can do this and this and this." Although true, the question that the CIO must continually ask is whether those new possibilities are consistent with the organization's strategy and direction.

Thus, the CIO must not only establish and communicate such priorities, but enforce them as well. The department must evaluate every proposal, at the earliest stage possible, as to whether it is consistent with the goals of the organization and aligned with its strategy.

Furthermore, no organization can afford to implement every good idea. Even projects that are aligned with the organization's strategy must be prioritized. The objective of everyone in the IS department must be to develop the most appropriate systems possible, given constraints on time and money. Well thought out and clearly communicated priorities are essential.

Sponsor the Steering Committee

The final planning function in Figure 11-2 is to sponsor the steering committee. A **steering committee** is a group of senior managers from the major business functions that works with the CIO to set the IS priorities and decide among major IS projects and alternatives.

The steering committee serves an important communication function between IS and the users. In the steering committee, information systems personnel can discuss potential IS initiatives and directions with the user community. At the same time, the steering committee provides a forum for users to express their needs, frustrations, and other issues they have with the IS department.

Typically, the IS department sets up the steering committee's schedule and agenda and conducts the meetings. The CEO and other members of the executive staff determine the membership of the steering committee.

One other task related to planning the use of IT may be to help set the organization's computer-use policy. For more on computer-use issues, read the Ethics Guide *on page 428.*

Q3 What Tasks Are Necessary for Managing Computing Infrastructure?

Managing the computing infrastructure is the most visible of all of the IS department's functions. In fact, the only interaction most employees have with the IS department is when they receive a computer or when they have problems using it. To many employees, the IS department is the "computer department"; they have little idea of the other important jobs the IS department performs behind that equipment.

This section focuses on the major tasks for this management function. We begin with another alignment issue. This issue, however, does not concern alignment with strategic direction, but rather alignment with infrastructure design.

Align Infrastructure Design with Organizational Structure

The structure of the IS infrastructure must mirror the structure of the organization. A highly controlled and centralized organization needs highly controlled and centralized information systems. A decentralized organization with autonomous operating units requires decentralized information systems that facilitate autonomous activity.

Consider Figure 11-3 (page 430), which shows a distributed printing company that grew through a process of acquisition. This company expanded to new geographic

Ethics

GUIDE

Using the Corporate Computer

Suppose you work at a company that has the following computer use policy:

> *Computers, email, and the Internet are to be used primarily for official company business. Small amounts of personal email can be exchanged with friends and family, and occasional usage of the Internet is permitted, but such usage should be limited and never interfere with your work.*

Suppose you are a manager and you learn that one of your employees has been engaged in the following activities:

1. Playing computer games during work hours
2. Playing computer games on the company computer before and after work hours
3. Responding to emails from an ill parent
4. Watching DVDs during lunch and other breaks
5. Sending emails to plan a party that involves mostly people from work
6. Sending emails to plan a party that involves no one from work
7. Searching the Web for a new car
8. Reading the news on CNN.com
9. Checking the stock market over the Internet
10. Bidding on items for personal use on eBay
11. Selling personal items on eBay
12. Paying personal bills online
13. Paying personal bills online when traveling on company business
14. Buying an airplane ticket for an ill parent over the Internet
15. Changing the content of a personal Web site
16. Changing the content of a personal business Web site
17. Buying an airplane ticket for a personal vacation over the Internet ■

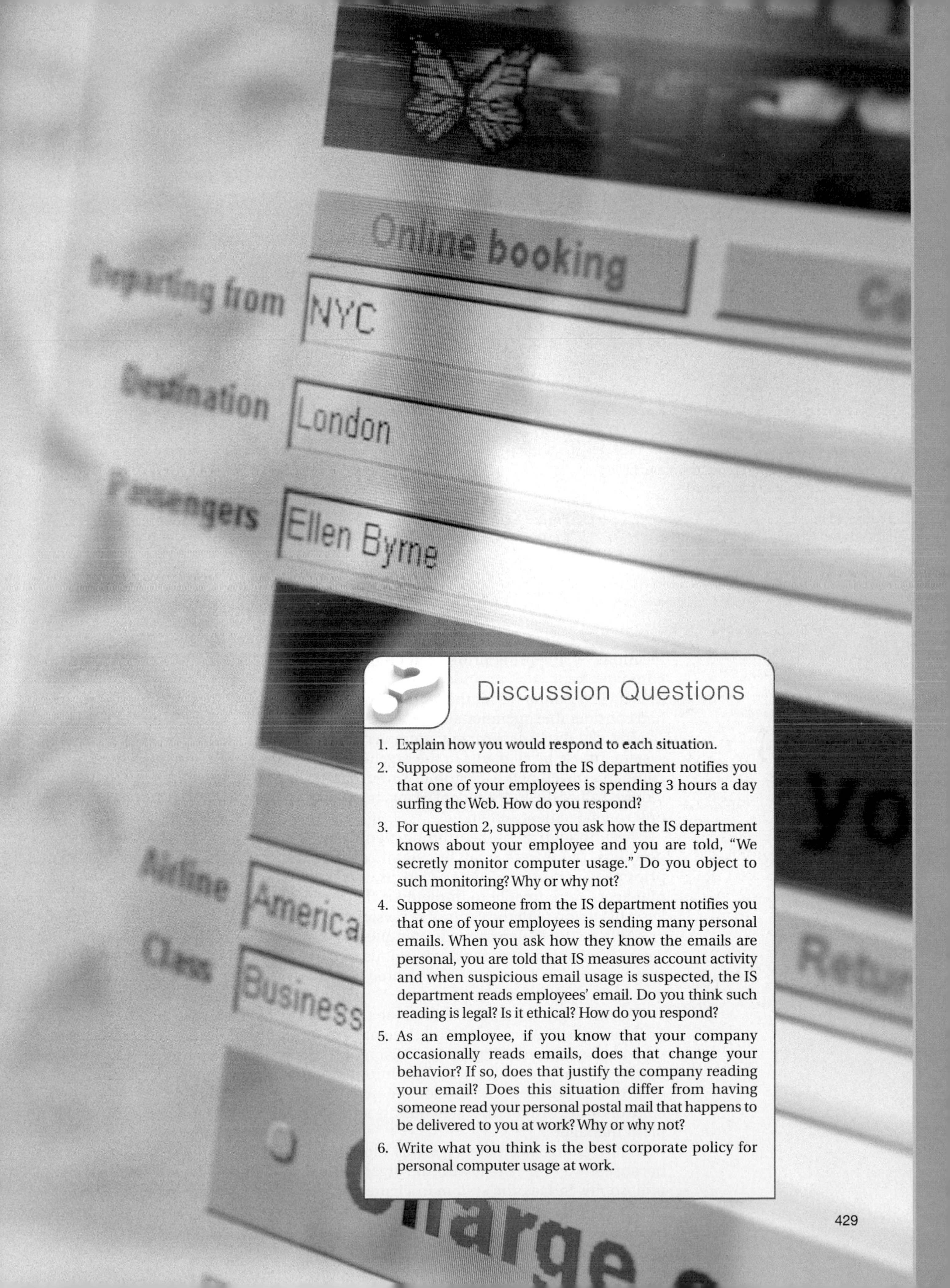

Discussion Questions

1. Explain how you would respond to each situation.
2. Suppose someone from the IS department notifies you that one of your employees is spending 3 hours a day surfing the Web. How do you respond?
3. For question 2, suppose you ask how the IS department knows about your employee and you are told, "We secretly monitor computer usage." Do you object to such monitoring? Why or why not?
4. Suppose someone from the IS department notifies you that one of your employees is sending many personal emails. When you ask how they know the emails are personal, you are told that IS measures account activity and when suspicious email usage is suspected, the IS department reads employees' email. Do you think such reading is legal? Is it ethical? How do you respond?
5. As an employee, if you know that your company occasionally reads emails, does that change your behavior? If so, does that justify the company reading your email? Does this situation differ from having someone read your personal postal mail that happens to be delivered to you at work? Why or why not?
6. Write what you think is the best corporate policy for personal computer usage at work.

- Plants acquired by acquisition
- Existing IS legacy from past
- Separate order entry, production, and billing
- Highly distributed organization

Figure 11-3
Distributed Check-Printing Company

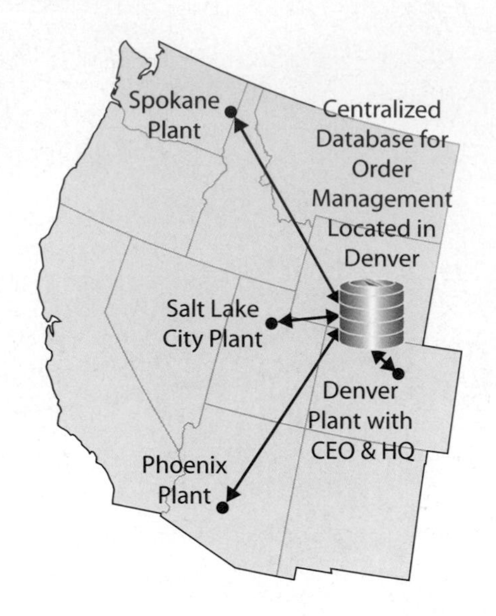

Figure 11-4
Problematic Centralized IS

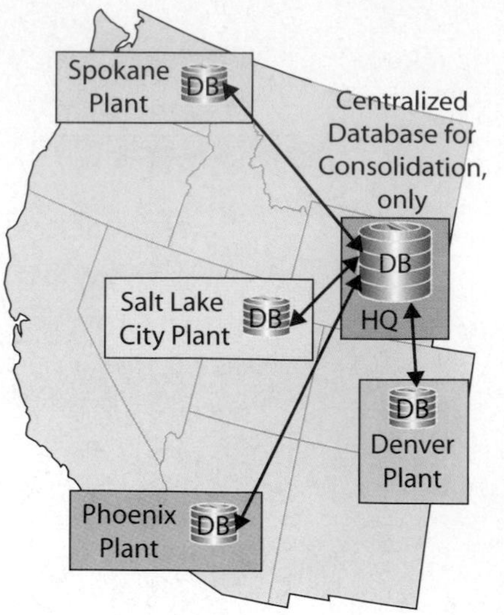

Figure 11-5
Decentralized Order-Management System

locations by acquiring printers in different cities. As each entity was acquired, the company kept it as an independent operating center. The company held plant managers accountable for the performance of their own facilities, and these managers had considerable operational independence.

Initially, the IS department attempted to develop a centralized order-management system for use by all plants in the organization. Figure 11-4 shows this situation. The company developed a customer order database at a data center in Denver and required all of the independent plants to process their orders through the centralized order-management system.

Even though all of the printing plants had been producing essentially the same products, there were small but significant differences in the ways that each plant prioritized and processed its orders. However, with the centralized system, the plant managers were unable to implement their own production-scheduling processes. Dissatisfaction with the centralized system was rampant.

At first, the IS department attempted to remedy the problems, but within a few weeks it was clear that the autonomous managers were never going to be satisfied with a centralized system. They wanted control over all aspects of the ordering and manufacturing process.

Accordingly, the IS department abandoned the concept of a single, centralized order-entry system and instead developed a set of distributed order-management systems, as shown in Figure 11-5. Each of these systems was under the control of the local plant manager. The distributed systems did send order and production data to a centralized facility for the production of consolidated reports, but the control of the order entry, scheduling, and manufacturing remained with the local plant managers.

The system in Figure 11-5 was more successful than the centralized system because it was consistent with the organization's underlying management style and philosophy. In fact, the system in Figure 11-4 should never have been developed. At the time it was envisioned, the IS department was buried deep in the accounting department, and it had little visibility to the rest of the company. After this problem developed, the company raised IS in the management hierarchy and instituted a steering committee. Close collaboration between the CIO and the steering committee prohibited the design of any future system that was so greatly misaligned with the organization.

Create, Operate, and Maintain Computing Infrastructure

Three more tasks in managing the computing infrastructure are to:

- Create and maintain infrastructure for end-user computing.
- Create, operate, and maintain networks.
- Create, operate, and maintain data centers, data warehouses, and data marts.

Those are *huge* tasks.

They are enormous jobs even for a mid-sized company like that shown in Figure 11-5. Consider just end-user computing. Almost every employee in that company has a computer. Each computer has a set of programs. From time to time, those computers need to be upgraded, and the software that resides on them needs to be upgraded as well. When Microsoft ships a new version of Windows or Office, the IS department immediately has user requests for the new version. (Also, it is likely to receive requests *not* to receive the new version.) How do you install a new version of Windows on 1,000 computers? On 5,000? Keep in mind that you have limited resources and cannot afford to send a trained technician to every user's computer.

Alternatively, suppose the steering committee decides the company needs to invest in a new XML-based supply chain management application. A different variation of your computer network protocol is required to support the new capability. This requirement means that you have to install a new version of your networking software on every computer, regardless of whether the computer will be involved in the SCM. How do you proceed?

Suppose you develop an automated process to upgrade all of the users' computers at night, when they are not in use. Your automated procedure works fine until it encounters a computer that has been modified by its user. She decided, secretly, to use Linux rather than Windows. Because of the difference, your automated upgrade program crashes. The IS department has to send a specialist to Phoenix to find out what went wrong with the install.

We will not address the management of the network and data centers here. The subject is too large and complicated and is not directly related to your future business career. Suffice it to say that when you see a diagram like that in Figure 9-18 (page 352), keep in mind that the IS department has to create, operate, and maintain the computers, software, and personnel in the data warehouse and all of the data marts.

Establish Technology and Product Standards

The failure of the network software upgrade points out the need for technology and product standards. The IS department cannot afford to allow every computer user to have her own personal configuration. Doing so not only would mean difficulties for upgrading computers and programs, but it also might mean that some users' computers become incompatible with others. For example, a document created using WordPerfect on a Macintosh might not be readable by a computer that uses Microsoft Word on a Windows machine. For this example, there is a way to import and export such documents, but the IS department has higher priorities for its budget than training users how to do it.

Sometimes when users request computer resources or services, the IS department can seem more like a liability than an asset. To understand why this might be, read the Information Systems Management in Practice *box below.*

Users' computing needs vary according to the work they do. In response, most IS departments have developed a set of three or four different standard configurations. The most basic configuration might have just email and a Web browser. Another configuration might have Microsoft Office programs as well, and a third might have an extended version of Office, email, and some analysis software. A fourth configuration might be created for software development personnel.

No standard will please all of the users, all of the time. The IS department needs to work with the steering committee and other user groups to ensure the standards are effective for most of the users.

Track Problems and Monitor Resolutions

The IS department provides the computing infrastructure as a service to users. As in any service organization, a system must exist to record user problems and monitor their resolution. This system is no different from other customer service applications we have discussed.

In a well-run IS department, when a user reports a problem the department assigns a tracking number, and the problem enters a queue for service. Normally, problems are prioritized on the basis of how critical they are to the user's work. Higher-priority items are serviced first. When the item is placed in the queue, the user is told its priority and given an approximate date for resolution. When the problem is fixed, it is removed from the queue. If the problem is still not resolved, it reenters the queue at a higher priority.

The CIO and the manager of the computer operations group monitor the queue, the average length of time an item remains in the queue, the number of nonresolutions, and so forth. In the future, if you, as a user, encounter such a system, it may seem overly bureaucratic. In fact, it is a sign of good IS management.

INFORMATION SYSTEMS MANAGEMENT IN PRACTICE

OBTAINING DEPARTMENTAL COMPUTING RESOURCES

Suppose you are a department manager, say in purchasing or customer support, and one day one of your employees walks into your office very frustrated. Sitting down, he begins:

"I don't get it. I just don't get it. When we want new computers, the IS department selects the computer for us. Well, no, in truth it forces those computers down our throats. We have to take the computer and the related paraphernalia that they choose. I guess that's OK, in principle, but do you know what they're charging us? Mega-bucks! My budget was charged $1,700 for a computer I know I can buy from Dell for $750. It's ridiculous. And, I'll bet Dell could get it to me faster.

"Also, our choices are so narrow. Sure, we can pick how much memory we want, how fast a CPU, and how much storage, but always within the limits they set. And *they* pick the software. If I want to use WordPerfect, I'm out of luck because they don't support WordPerfect. Or what if I want to use a Macintosh? Forget it! No way are they gonna let me use anything that isn't on their list!

"I wish they would just let us to buy the computers that we want to buy and negotiate our own deals. After all, it's coming out of our budget. I could get a better deal than they do, and be able to pick the software I want on top of it. Why don't we just start ordering from Dell? What do you think?"

As a manager, how do you respond? Why does the IS department require users to acquire computers from them? Just to protect their turf? Or is there some other reason? Does it make sense to propose that your department buy from Dell? Is it worthwhile for your employee to prepare a presentation detailing the money that you could save? To whom would you present such a proposal? How will the IS department respond? What is your best response to this employee?

You and a team of your classmates will have an opportunity to answer these questions in Collaboration Exercise 2, page 451.

Manage Computing Infrastructure Staff

Finally, the IS department also must manage the computing infrastructure staff. The department's employees must be organized, hired, trained, directed, evaluated, and promoted, just as with any other corporate function.

The organization of a typical IS operations department is shown in Figure 11-6. This generic chart has subdepartments for the network, computer center, data warehouse, and user support. In a large organization, these functions might be further divided as well. In particular, a separate department might staff the help-desk function. Sometimes operations groups have specialists for particular applications. There might be, for example, an ERP support group.

Typical job types are shown beneath each subgroup. As you can imagine, each of these specialists needs recurring training. The operations staff must constantly update its knowledge to keep up with upgrades in both hardware and software products. Consider the need for training, coupled with the need for 24/7 operations, coupled with the problems that can occur when a change is first made to, say, the network. Scheduling employees in such an environment is a complex task and a constant problem.

Q4 What Tasks Are Necessary for Managing Enterprise Applications?

In addition to managing the computing infrastructure, the IS department manages enterprise applications as well. The definition of what constitutes an enterprise application varies among organizations. In some organizations, the IS department manages every application, including individual and workgroup applications. In others, individuals and workgroups manage their own applications, with support from the IS department. In the latter case, the term **enterprise applications** is interpreted to mean some functional applications, and all cross-functional applications including CRM, ERP, EAI, and SCM.

Develop New Applications

Figure 11-7 (next page) lists major application management functions. As shown, the IS department manages the development of new applications. The process of

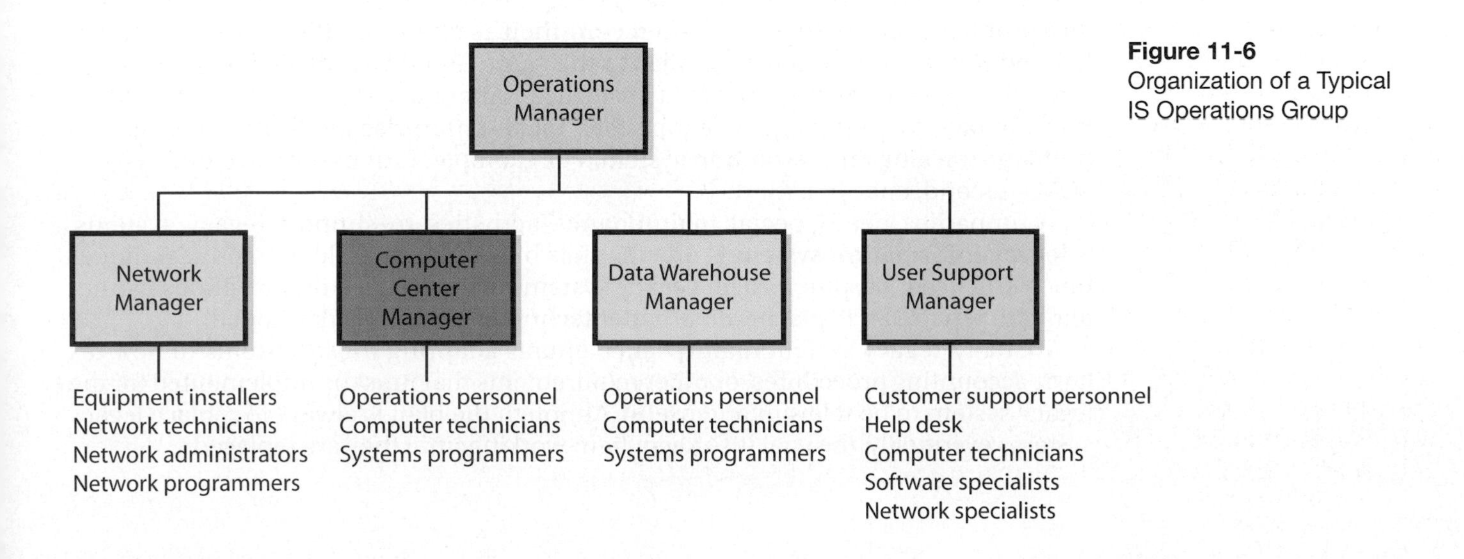

Figure 11-6
Organization of a Typical IS Operations Group

Figure 11-7
Managing Enterprise Applications

- Manage development of new applications.
- Maintain legacy systems.
- Adapt systems to changing requirements.
- Track user problems and monitor fixes.
- Integrate applications.
- Manage development staff.

creating a new application begins when the IS department aligns its priorities with the organization's strategy. Using priorities that arise from that alignment, the IS department develops system plans and proposals and submits them to the steering committee (and possibly other executive groups) for approval. Once the company has selected and approved a system for development, it then initiates a development process.

We discussed application development processes in the last chapter, and we will not repeat that discussion here. Realize, however, that all development processes are variations on the theme of *requirements, design*, and *implementation*. The nature and amount of systems development work depends on the degree to which applications components are outsourced.

In all cases, however, the company will conduct the requirements phase in-house. Each organization has its own strategy, priorities, and direction, and those unique requirements need to be developed and documented, even if major portions of the system will be outsourced.

The rest of the work to be done depends on the degree of reliance on outsource vendors. We discuss variations of outsource scope in the outsourcing section later in this chapter.

Maintain Systems

In addition to managing the development of new applications, the IS department has the responsibility for system maintenance. As stated in Chapter 10, *maintenance* means either to fix the system to do what it was supposed to do in the first place or to adapt the system to changed requirements. Either way, the IS department prioritizes maintenance work and implements changes in accordance with those priorities and budget. It might do the maintenance work in-house or outsource it.

Developing information systems is a service that is provided to the rest of the enterprise. Accordingly, the IS department must have a means to track user issues and problems, prioritize them, and record their resolution. Although such a tracking and monitoring system is similar to the same function provided for infrastructure management, the department usually uses different systems for these two functions. In fact, for larger organizations each major enterprise application has its own problem-tracking and resolution system. For example, ERP might have one system, SCM a second, and HR a third.

Companies need special maintenance activities to support legacy systems. A **legacy information system** is one that has outdated technologies and techniques but is still used, despite its age. Legacy systems arise because organizations cannot afford to replace an IS just because better technology has been developed.

Usually, legacy system maintenance entails adapting those systems to new tax laws, accounting procedures, or other requirements that must be implemented for the legacy system to be relevant and useful. Although the plan is always to replace legacy systems eventually, the goal is to keep them working until they are replaced.

Integrate Enterprise Applications

The third element in Figure 11-7 concerns enterprise application integration. As discussed at the end of Chapter 7, EAI requires developers to create intermediary layers of software, and possibly intermediary databases, to enable the integration of disparate systems. Because such work requires knowledge of many different systems, including legacy systems, companies usually conduct such work in-house rather than outsource it.

Manage Development Staff

The last management function in Figure 11-7 is to manage the development staff. Figure 11-8 shows the structure of a typical development group. Of course, this structure will be simpler for smaller organizations or for organizations that do little in-house development. As stated in Chapter 10, a computer programmer or developer typically is both a software designer as well as a programmer.

Sustaining-application developers work on existing applications. Typically, sustaining developers have fewer years of experience or less knowledge than new-application developers. Figure 11-8 shows sustaining developers and new-application developers as belonging to separate development teams. This arrangement varies considerably depending on the complexity of both sustaining and new development projects.

Product quality assurance (PQA) engineers specialize in the testing of software. In many cases, PQA engineers also are programmers who develop automated testing suites. Because applications must be thoroughly tested when they are modified, test automation is a great boon to productivity.

The final group in Figure 11-8 is *technical writers* who develop product installation instructions, help text, and other support documentation.

Administer Data

Data and database administration functions sound similar, but actually are quite different. Typically, the term **data administration** describes a function that pertains

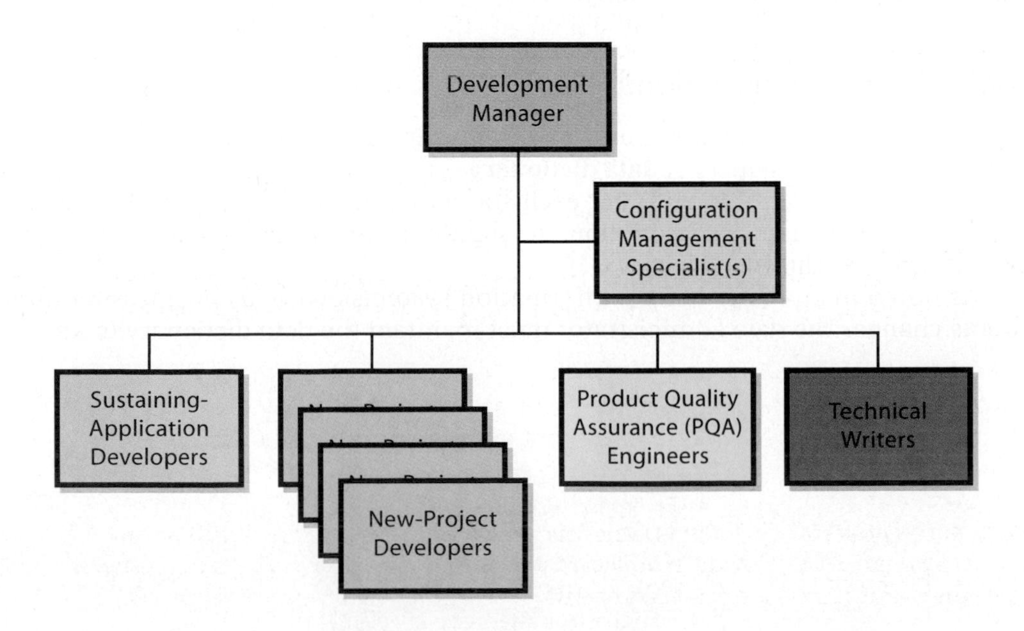

Figure 11-8
Organization of a Typical IS Development Group

to *all* of an organization's data assets. The term **database administration** describes a function that pertains to a *particular* database. A typical larger organization would have one data administrator and several database administrators—say, one for the ERP database, one for the SCM database, one for HR database, and possibly others as well.

The terminology *data administrator* and *database administrator* implies that there is a single person for each role. Normally, each data or database administrator has a staff of several employees. The manager of the group is called the *data administrator* or *database administrator*, and the staff members work in the office of data administration or database administration.

We discussed database administration in Chapter 5. Here we will address the organization-wide function of data administration and the four primary responsibilities shown in Figure 11-9.

Define Data Standards

Data standards are definitions, or metadata, for data items shared across the organization. They describe the name, official definition, usage, relationship to other data items, processing restrictions, version, security restrictions, format and other features of data items that are shared across the organization. Sometimes data standards include the *data owner*, which is a department within the organization that is most concerned with that data item and that controls changes to the definition of that data item.

On the surface, setting data standards may seem like an unnecessary clerical operation. It is not. In fact, the lack of documented and known data standards causes considerable duplication of effort, data inconsistency, wasted labor, and processing errors.

To understand why, consider a data item as simple as *sku_description*. *SKU* stands for stock-keeping unit, and *sku_description* is a data item for holding the description of each part. But what is it? Without a data standard, one application might include component parts in the description, whereas another might place the component parts in a different data item. Without a standard definition, two different applications will refer to the same item with different names. For example, is a *sku_description* the same as *sku_item_desc*? Assume you are a sustaining developer and you encounter a data item named *sku_desc_2005*. How does that data item relate to the data item *current_sku_description*? Without a data standard, developers will waste considerable time trying to reconcile these differences.

Maintain the Data Dictionary

To resolve problems like those for the SKU descriptions, almost every organization maintains a data dictionary. A **data dictionary** is a file or database that contains data definitions. It contains an entry for each standard data item. Typically, the entries include the item's name, a description, the standard data format, remarks, and possibly examples, as shown in Figure 11-10.

As noted many times before, information systems evolve as business requirements change. The data administrator must maintain the data dictionary to keep it

Enterprise-wide function to:
- Define data standards.
- Maintain data dictionary.
- Define data policies.
- Establish disaster-recovery plan.

Figure 11-9
Data Administration Responsibilities

Data Item Name	Data Item Description	Standard Data Format	Remarks	Example
sku_description	A description of a stock-keeping unit.	Character; length 1,000	Does not include component parts.	3/16-inch flathead screw, 20 tpi, stainless steel
sku_desc_2005	A description of a stock-keeping unit prior to the parts reorganization in August 2005.	Character; length 500	No longer used. All descriptions should have been converted to the current_sku_description.	
current_sku_description	A description of a stock-keeping unit after the parts reorganization in August 2005.	Character; length 1,000	Does not include component parts.	3/16-inch flathead screw, 20 tpi, stainless steel

Note: Other fields are common. Some data dictionaries record the data owner, aliases for the data item, security requirements, and additional data.

Figure 11-10
Example of Data Dictionary Fields

current. Obsolete entries must be removed, new items inserted, and changes recorded. Without maintenance, the data dictionary, an essential tool, loses its value. Notice, for example, the two versions of *sku_description* in Figure 11-10: How does *sku_description* relate to *current_sku_description*? They appear identical. Should one of them be removed? What if one of them were slightly different from the other? From this example you can see the need for management of the data dictionary.

Define Data Policies

Data administration also is concerned with the creation and dissemination of data policies. Such policies vary in scope. Examples of broad policies are:

- "We will not share identifying customer data with another organization."
- "We will not share nonidentifying customer data with another organization without the approval of the legal department."
- "Employee data are never to be released to anyone other than the employee without the approval of the human resources department."

Narrower data policies pertain to particular data items. An example is: "We will maintain data about past employees for at least 7 years after their last day of work."

Of course, the data administrator does not create the data policies on his own, out of the blue. Instead, the data administrator works with senior executives, the legal department, functional department managers, and others to determine them. Once the company has created data policies, the data administrator then communicates them to appropriate departments and employees. Data policies also are dynamic; they need to be changed as new corporate policies and new systems are developed and as new laws are created.

Plan for Disaster Recovery

Disaster-recovery planning is the creation of systems for recovering data and systems in the event of a catastrophe such as an earthquake, flood, terrorist event, or other significant processing disruption. We will address this function further in the next chapter when we discuss computer security.

As you can tell from the preceding discussion, managing information systems is a broad and complicated task. Some organizations choose to outsource one or more IS functions. We will consider that alternative in the next section.

Q5 What Are the Advantages and Disadvantages of Outsourcing?

Outsourcing is the process of hiring another organization to perform a service. Outsourcing is done to save costs, to gain expertise, and to free up management time.

The father of modern management, Peter Drucker, is reputed to have said, "Your back room is someone else's front room." For instance, in most companies, running the cafeteria is not an essential function for business success; thus, the employee cafeteria is a "back room." Google wants to be the worldwide leader in search and Web 2.0 applications, all supported by ever-increasing ad revenue. It does not want to be known for how well it runs cafeterias. Using Drucker's sentiment, Google is better off hiring another company, one that specializes in food services, to run its cafeterias.

Because food service is some company's "front room," that company will be better able to provide a quality product at a fair price. Hiring that company will also free Google's management from attention on the cafeteria. Food quality, chef scheduling, plastic fork acquisition, waste disposal, and so on, will all be another company's concern. Google can focus on search, Web 2.0, and advertising revenue growth.

Outsourcing Information Systems

Many companies today have chosen to outsource portions of their information systems activities. Figure 11-11 lists popular reasons for doing so. Consider each major group of reasons.

Management Advantages

First, outsourcing can be an easy way to gain expertise. Suppose, for example, that an organization wants to upgrade its thousands of user computers on a cost-effective basis. To do so, the organization would need to develop expertise in automated software installation, unattended installations, remote support, and other measures that can be used to improve the efficiency of software management. Developing such expertise is expensive, and it is not in the company's strategic direction. Efficient installation of software to thousands of computers is not in the "front room." Consequently, the organization might choose to hire a specialist company to perform this service.

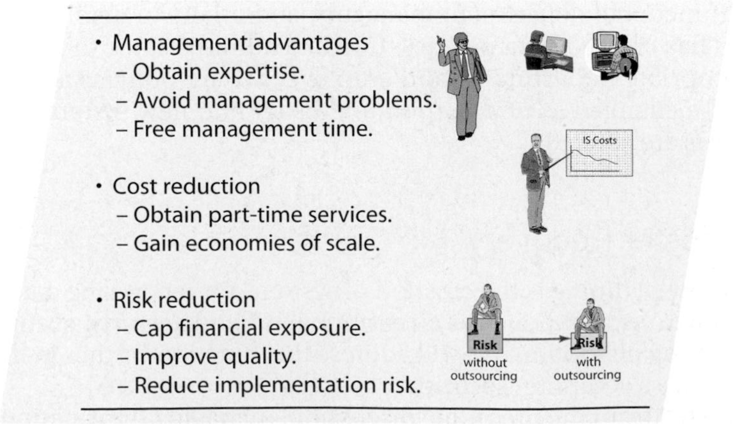

- Management advantages
  - Obtain expertise.
  - Avoid management problems.
  - Free management time.
- Cost reduction
  - Obtain part-time services.
  - Gain economies of scale.
- Risk reduction
  - Cap financial exposure.
  - Improve quality.
  - Reduce implementation risk.

IS Costs

Risk without outsourcing

Risk with outsourcing

Figure 11-11
Popular Reasons for Outsourcing IS Services

Another reason for outsourcing is to avoid management problems. Suppose Carbon Creek Gardens (Chapter 9, page 365) decides to share its inventory with its suppliers using XML Web services. How will Mary Keeling hire the appropriate staff? She doesn't know if she needs a C++ programmer or an HTML programmer. Even if she could find and hire the right staff, how would she manage them? How would she create a good work environment for a C++ programmer, when she does not know what such a person does? To avoid such management problems, Carbon Creek would hire an outside firm to develop and maintain the Web service.

Similarly, some companies choose to outsource to save management time and attention. Suppose the public TV station discussed in Chapter 5 sells educational DVDs over the Web and needs a Web farm to process the workload. Even if the station's IT staff know how to manage a Web farm, acquiring the appropriate computers, installing the necessary software, tuning the software for better performance, and hiring and managing the staff will all require significant management time.

Note, too, that the management time required is not just that of the direct manager of the activity. It is also time from more senior managers who approve the purchase and hiring requisitions for that activity. And, those senior managers will need to devote the time necessary to understand enough about Web farms to approve or reject the requisitions. Outsourcing saves both direct and indirect management time.

Cost Reduction

Other common reasons for choosing to outsource concern cost reductions. With outsourcing, organizations can obtain part-time services. An office of 25 attorneys does not need a full-time network administrator. It does need network administration, but only in small amounts. By outsourcing that function, the office of attorneys can obtain network administration in the small amounts needed.

Another benefit of outsourcing is to gain economies of scale. If 25 organizations develop their own payroll applications in-house, then when the tax law changes 25 different groups will have to learn the new law, change their software to meet the law, test the changes, and write the documentation explaining the changes. However, if those same 25 organizations outsource to the same payroll vendor, then that vendor can make all of the adjustments once, and the cost of the change can be amortized over all of them (thus lowering the cost that the vendor must charge).

Risk Reduction

Another reason for outsourcing is to reduce risk. First, outsourcing can cap financial risk. In a typical outsourcing contract, the outsource vendor will agree to provide, say, computer workstations with certain software connected via a particular network. Typically, each new workstation will have a fixed cost, say, $2,500 per station. The company's management team might believe that there is a good chance that they can provide workstations at a lower unit cost, but there is also the chance that they will get in over their heads and have a disaster. If so, the cost per computer could be much higher than $2,500. Outsourcing caps that financial risk and leads to greater budgetary stability.

Second, outsourcing can reduce risk by ensuring a certain level of quality, or avoiding the risk of having substandard quality. A company that specializes in food service knows what to do to provide a certain level of quality. It has the expertise to ensure, for example, that only healthy food is served. So, too, a company that specializes in, say, Web-server hosting, knows what to do to provide a certain level of service for a given workload.

Note that there is no guarantee that outsourcing will provide a certain level of quality or quality better than could be achieved in-house. Google might get lucky and hire only great chefs. The TV station might get lucky and hire the world's best Web farm manager. But, in general, a professional outsourcing firm knows how to avoid giving everyone food poisoning or having 2 days of downtime on the Web servers. And, if that minimum level of quality is not provided, it is easier to hire another vendor than it is to fire and rehire internal staff.

Finally, organizations choose to outsource IS in order to reduce implementation risk. Hiring an outside vendor reduces the risk of picking the wrong hardware or the wrong software, using the wrong network protocol, or implementing tax law changes incorrectly. Outsourcing gathers all of these risks into the risk of choosing the right vendor. Once the company has chosen the vendor, further risk management is up to that vendor.

Not everyone agrees on the desirability of outsourcing, as described in the Opposing Forces Guide *on page 446.*

International Outsourcing

Many firms headquartered in the United States have chosen to outsource overseas. Microsoft and Dell, for example, have outsourced major portions of their customer support activities to companies outside the United States. India is a popular source because it has a large, well-educated, English-speaking population that will work for 20 to 30 percent of the labor cost in the United States. China and other countries are used as well. In fact, with modern telephone technology and Internet-enabled service databases, a single service call can be initiated in the United States, partially processed in India, then Singapore, and finalized by an employee in England. The customer knows only that he has been put on hold for brief periods of time.

International outsourcing is particularly advantageous for customer support and other functions that must be operational 24/7. Amazon.com, for example, operates customer service centers in the United States, India, and Ireland. During the evening hours in the United States, customer service reps in India, where it is daytime, handle the calls. When night falls in India, customer service reps in Ireland handle the early morning calls from the east coast of the United States. In this way, companies can provide 24/7 service without requiring employees to work night shifts.

International IS/IT outsourcing is not without controversy, however. It is one thing to shift a job of making a tennis shoe to Singapore, or even to hire customer support representatives in India. But there was consternation and wringing of hands when IBM stated that it was shifting nearly 5,000 computer-programming jobs to India. Some perceive the moving of such high-tech, high-skill jobs overseas as a threat to U.S. technology leadership. Others say it is just economic factors guiding jobs to places where they are most efficiently performed.

By the way, as you learned in Chapter 1, the key protection for your job is to become someone who excels at nonroutine symbolic analysis. Someone with the ability to find innovative applications of new technology also is unlikely to lose his or her job to overseas workers.

What Are the Outsourcing Alternatives?

Organizations have found hundreds of different ways to outsource information systems and portions of information systems. Figure 11-12 organizes the major categories of alternatives according to information systems components.

Some organizations outsource the acquisition and operation of computer hardware. Electronic Data Systems (EDS) has been successful for more than 20 years as an outsource vendor of hardware infrastructure. Figure 11-12 shows another alternative, outsourcing the computers in a Web farm.

Acquiring licensed software, as discussed in Chapters 4 and 10, is a form of outsourcing. Rather than develop the software in-house, an organization licenses it from another vendor. Such licensing allows the software vendor to amortize the cost of software maintenance over all of the users, thus reducing that cost for all users.

Another outsourcing alternative is to outsource an entire system. PeopleSoft (now owned by Oracle) attained prominence by outsourcing the entire payroll function. In

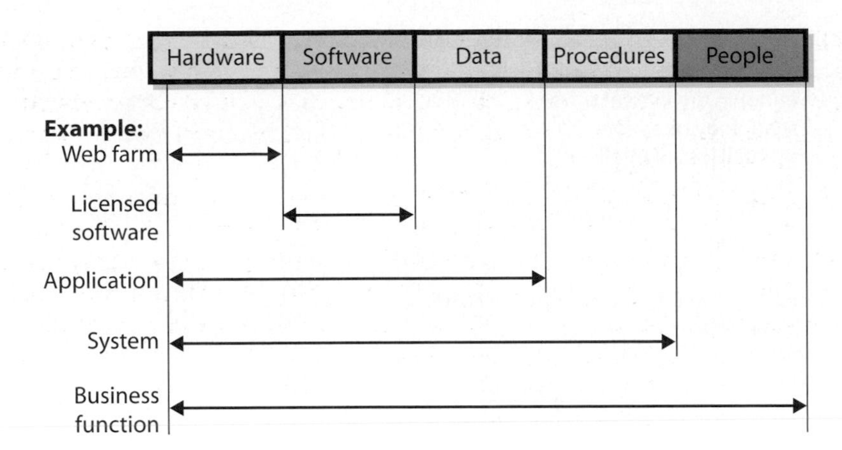

Figure 11-12
IS/IT Outsourcing Alternatives

such a solution, as the arrow in Figure 11-12 implies, the vendor provides hardware, software, data, and some procedures. The company need provide only employee and work information; the payroll outsource vendor does the rest.

A Web storefront is another form of application outsourcing. Amazon.com, for example, provides a Web storefront for product vendors and distributors who choose not to develop their own Web presence. In this case, rather than pay a fixed fee for the storefront service, the product vendors and distributors pay Amazon.com a portion of the revenue generated. Such Web-service hosting has become a major profit center for Amazon.com.

Finally, some organizations choose to outsource an entire business function. For years, many companies have outsourced to travel agencies the function of arranging for employee travel. Some of these outsource vendors even operate offices within the company facilities. More recently, companies have been outsourcing even larger and more important functions. In 2005, for example, Marriott International chose Hewitt Associates to handle its human resources needs for the next 7 years. (See Case Study 11, page 452.) Such agreements are much broader than outsourcing IS, but information systems are key components of the applications that are outsourced.

What Are the Risks of Outsourcing?

With so many advantages and with so many different outsourcing alternatives, you might wonder why any company has any in-house IS/IT functions. In fact, outsourcing presents significant risks, as listed in Figure 11-13 (next page).

Loss of Control

The first risk of outsourcing is a loss of control. Outsourcing puts the vendor in the driver's seat. Each outsource vendor has methods and procedures for its service. The organization and its employees will have to conform to those procedures. For example, a hardware infrastructure vendor will have standard forms and procedures for requesting a computer, for recording and processing a computer problem, or for providing routine maintenance on computers. Once the vendor is in charge, employees must conform.

When outsourcing the cafeteria, employees have only those food choices that the vendor provides. Similarly, when obtaining computer hardware and services, the employees will need to take what the vendor supports. Employees who want equipment that is not on the vendor's list will be out of luck.

The outsource vendor chooses the technology that it wants to implement. If the vendor, for some reason, is slow to pick up on a significant new technology, then the hiring organization will be slow to attain benefits from that technology. An organization

Figure 11-13
Outsourcing Risks

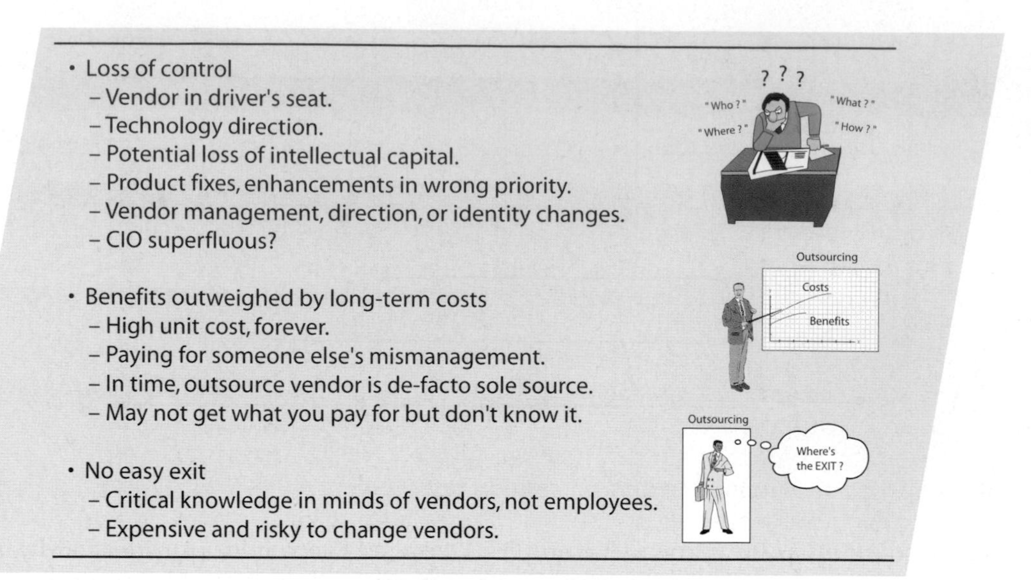

can find itself at a competitive disadvantage because it cannot offer the same IS services as its competitors.

Another concern is a potential loss of intellectual capital. The company may need to reveal proprietary trade secrets, methods, or procedures to the outsource vendor's employees. As part of its normal operations, that vendor may move employees to competing organizations, and the company may lose intellectual capital as that happens. The loss need not be intellectual theft; it could simply be that the vendor's employees learned to work in a new and better way at your company, and then they take that learning to your competitor.

Similarly, all software has failures and problems. Quality vendors track those failures and problems and fix them according to a set of priorities. When a company outsources a system, it no longer has control over prioritizing those fixes. Such control belongs to the vendor. A fix that might be critical to your organization might be of low priority to the outsource vendor.

Other problems are that the outsource vendor may change management, adopt a different strategic direction, or be acquired. When any of those changes occur, priorities may change, and an outsource vendor that was a good choice at one time might be a bad fit after it changes direction. It can be difficult and expensive to change an outsource vendor when this occurs.

The final loss-of-control risk is that the company's CIO can become superfluous. When users need a critical service that is outsourced, the CIO must turn to the vendor for a response. In time, users learn that it is quicker to deal directly with the outsource vendor, and soon the CIO is out of the communication loop. At that point, the vendor has essentially replaced the CIO, who has become a figurehead. However, employees of the outsource vendor work for a different company, with a bias toward their employer. Critical managers will thus not share the same goals and objectives as the rest of the management team. Biased, bad decisions can result.

Benefits Outweighed by Long-Term Costs

The initial benefits of outsourcing can appear huge. A cap on financial exposure, a reduction of management time and attention, and the release of many management and staffing problems are all possible. (Most likely, outsource vendors promise these very benefits.) Outsourcing can appear too good to be true.

In fact, it *can be* too good to be true. For one, although a fixed cost does indeed cap exposure, it also removes the benefits of economies of scale. If the Web storefront takes off, and suddenly the organization needs 200 servers instead of 20, the using organization will pay 200 times the fixed cost of supporting one server. It is likely, however, that because of economies of scale, the costs of supporting 200 servers are far less than 10 times the costs of supporting 20 servers.

Also, the outsource vendor may change its pricing strategy over time. Initially, an organization obtains a competitive bid from several outsource vendors. However, as the winning vendor learns more about the business and as relationships develop between the organization's employees and those of the vendor, it becomes difficult for other firms to compete for subsequent contracts. The vendor becomes the *de facto* sole source and, with little competitive pressure, might increase its prices.

Another problem is that an organization can find itself paying for another organization's mismanagement, with little recourse. Over time, if the outsource vendor is mismanaged or suffers setbacks in other arenas, costs will increase. When this occurs, an outsourcing arrangement that initially made sense no longer makes sense. But the cost and risk of switching to another vendor are high.

Don Gray, the software manager interviewed in Chapter 10, has considerable expertise in offshore software development. He warns that a common problem is the offshore vendor's lack of management expertise: "If you contracted for 200 hours of programmer time, you will probably get that time. What you may not get, however, is the expertise required to manage that time well."[2] By choosing to employ an outsource vendor, the organization loses all visibility into the management effectiveness of the outsource vendor. The organization contracting with the outsource vendor might be paying for gross inefficiency, and might not know it. Ultimately, such a situation will result in a competitive disadvantage with organizations that are not subsidizing such inefficiency.

No Easy Exit

The final category of outsourcing risk concerns ending the agreement. There is no easy exit. For one, the outsource vendor's employees have gained significant knowledge of the company. They know the server requirements in customer support, they know the patterns of usage, and they know the best procedures for downloading operational data into the data warehouse. Consequently, lack of knowledge will make it difficult to bring the outsourced service back in-house.

Also, because the vendor has become so tightly integrated into the business, parting company can be exceedingly risky. Closing down the employee cafeteria for a few weeks while finding another food vendor would be unpopular, but employees would survive. Shutting down the enterprise network for a few weeks would be impossible; the business would not survive. Because of such risk, the company must invest considerable work, duplication of effort, management time, and expense to change to another vendor. In truth, choosing an outsource vendor can be a one-way street.

Choosing to outsource is a difficult decision. In fact, the correct decision might not be clear, but time and events could force the company to decide.

Sometimes you just do not know the right decision about outsourcing, or indeed many courses of action, but you must decide. The Problem-Solving Guide *on page 448 considers some of those situations.*

Q6 What Are Your User Rights and Responsibilities?

We conclude this chapter with a summary of your rights and responsibilities with regard to the IS department. The items in Figure 11-14 (next page) list what you are entitled to receive and indicate what you are expected to contribute.

[2]Don Gray, conversation with author, August 2007.

You have a right to:
- Computer hardware and programs that allow you to perform your job proficiently
- Reliable network and Internet connections
- A secure computing environment
- Protection from viruses, worms, and other threats
- Contribute to requirements for new system features and functions
- Reliable systems development and maintenance
- Prompt attention to problems, concerns, and complaints
- Properly prioritized problem fixes and resolutions
- Effective training

You have a responsibility to:
- Learn basic computer skills
- Learn standard techniques and procedures for the applications you use
- Follow security and backup procedures
- Protect your password(s)
- Use computer resources according to your employer's computer use policy
- Make no unauthorized hardware modifications
- Install only authorized programs
- Apply software patches and fixes when directed to do so
- When asked, devote the time required to respond carefully and completely to requests for requirements for new system features and functions
- Avoid reporting trivial problems

Figure 11-14
User Information Systems Rights and Responsibilities

Your User Rights

You have a right to have the computing resources you need to perform your work as proficiently as you want. You have a right to the computer hardware and programs that you need. If you process huge files for data-mining applications, you have a right to the huge disks and the fast processor that you need. However, if you merely receive email and consult the corporate Web portal, then your right is for more modest requirements (leaving the more powerful resources for those in the organization who need them).

You have a right to reliable network and Internet services. *Reliable* means that you can process without problems almost all of the time. It means that you never go to work wondering, "Will the network be available today?" Network problems should be a rare occurrence.

You also have a right to a secure computing environment. The organization should protect your computer and its files, and you should not normally even need to think about security. From time to time, the organization might ask you to take particular actions to protect your computer and files, and you should take those actions. But such requests should be rare and related to specific outside threats.

You have a right to participate in requirements meetings for new applications that you will use and for major changes to applications that you currently use. You may choose to delegate this right to others, or your department may delegate that right for you, but if so, you have a right to contribute your thoughts through that delegate.

You have a right to reliable systems development and maintenance. Although schedule slippages of a month or two are common in many development projects, you should not have to endure schedule slippages of 6 months or more. Such slippages are evidence of incompetent systems development.

Additionally, you have a right to receive prompt attention to your problems, concerns, and complaints about information services. You have a right to have a means to report problems, and you have a right to know that your problem has been received and at least registered with the IS department. You have a right to have your problem resolved, consistent with established priorities. This means that an annoying problem that allows you to conduct your work will be prioritized below another's problem that interferes with his ability to do his job.

Finally, you have a right to effective training. It should be training that you can understand and that enables you to use systems to perform your particular job. The organization should provide training in a format and on a schedule that is convenient to you.

Your User Responsibilities

You also have responsibilities toward the IS department and your organization. Specifically, you have a responsibility to learn basic computer skills and to learn the basic techniques and procedures for the applications you use. You should not expect hand-holding for basic operations. Nor should you expect to receive repetitive training and support for the same issue.

You have a responsibility to follow security and backup procedures. This is especially important because actions that you fail to take might cause problems for your fellow employees and your organization as well as for you. In particular, you are responsible for protecting your password(s). In the next chapter, you will learn that this is important not only to protect your computer, but, because of intersystem authentication, it is important to protect your organization's networks and databases as well.

You have a responsibility for using your computer resources in a manner that is consistent with your employer's policy. Many employers allow limited email for critical family matters while at work, but discourage frequent and long casual email. You have a responsibility to know your employer's policy and to follow it.

You also have a responsibility to make no unauthorized hardware modifications to your computer and to install only authorized programs. As described earlier in this chapter, one reason for this policy is that your IS department constructs automated maintenance programs for upgrading your computer. Unauthorized hardware and programs might interfere with these programs. Additionally, the installation of unauthorized hardware or programs can cause you problems that the IS department will have to fix.

You have a responsibility to install computer patches and fixes when asked to do so. This is particularly important for patches that concern security and backup and recovery. When asked for input to requirements for new and adapted systems, you have a responsibility to take the time necessary to provide thoughtful and complete responses. If you do not have that time, you should delegate your input to someone else.

Finally, you have a responsibility to treat information systems professionals professionally. Everyone works for the same company, everyone wants to succeed, and professionalism and courtesy will go a long way on all sides. One form of professional behavior is to learn basic computer skills so that you avoid reporting trivial problems.

Opposing Forces

GUIDE

Is Outsourcing Fool's Gold?

People are kidding themselves. It sounds so good—just pay a fixed, known amount to some vendor, and all your problems go away. Everyone has the computers they need, the network never goes down, and you never have to endure another horrible meeting about network protocols, HTTPs, and the latest worm. You're off into information systems nirvana. . . .

"Except it doesn't work that way. You trade one set of problems for another. Consider the outsourcing of computer infrastructure. What's the first thing the outsource vendor does? It hires all of the employees who were doing the work for you. Remember that lazy, incompetent network administrator that the company had—the one who never seemed to get anything done? Well, he's baaaaak, as an employee of your outsource company. Only this time he has an excuse, 'Company policy won't allow me to do it that way.'

"So the outsourcers get their first-level employees by hiring the ones you had. Of course, the outsourcer says it will provide management oversight, and if the employees don't work out, they'll be gone. What you're really outsourcing is middle-level management of the same IT personnel you had. But there's no way of knowing whether the managers they supply are any better than the ones you had.

"Also, you think you had bureaucratic problems before? Every vendor has a set of forms, procedures, committees, reports, and other management 'tools.' They will tell you that you have to do things according to the standard blueprint. They have to say that because if they allowed every company to be different, they'd never be able to gain any leverage themselves, and they'd never be profitable.

"So now you're paying a premium for the services of your former employees, who are now managed by strangers who are paid by the outsource vendor, who evaluates those managers on how well they follow the outsource vendor's profit-generating procedures. How quickly can they turn your operation into a clone of all their other clients? Do you really want to do that?

"Suppose you figure all this out and decide to get out of it. Now what? How do you undo an outsource agreement? All the critical knowledge is in the minds of the outsource vendor's employees, who have no incentive to work for you. In fact, their employment contract probably prohibits it. So now you have to take an existing operation within your own company, hire employees to staff that function, and relearn everything you ought to have learned in the first place.

"Gimme a break. Outsourcing is fool's gold, an expensive leap away from responsibility. It's like saying, 'We can't figure out how to manage an important function in our company, so you do it!' You can't get away from IS problems by hiring someone else to manage them for you. At least you care about *your* bottom line." ■

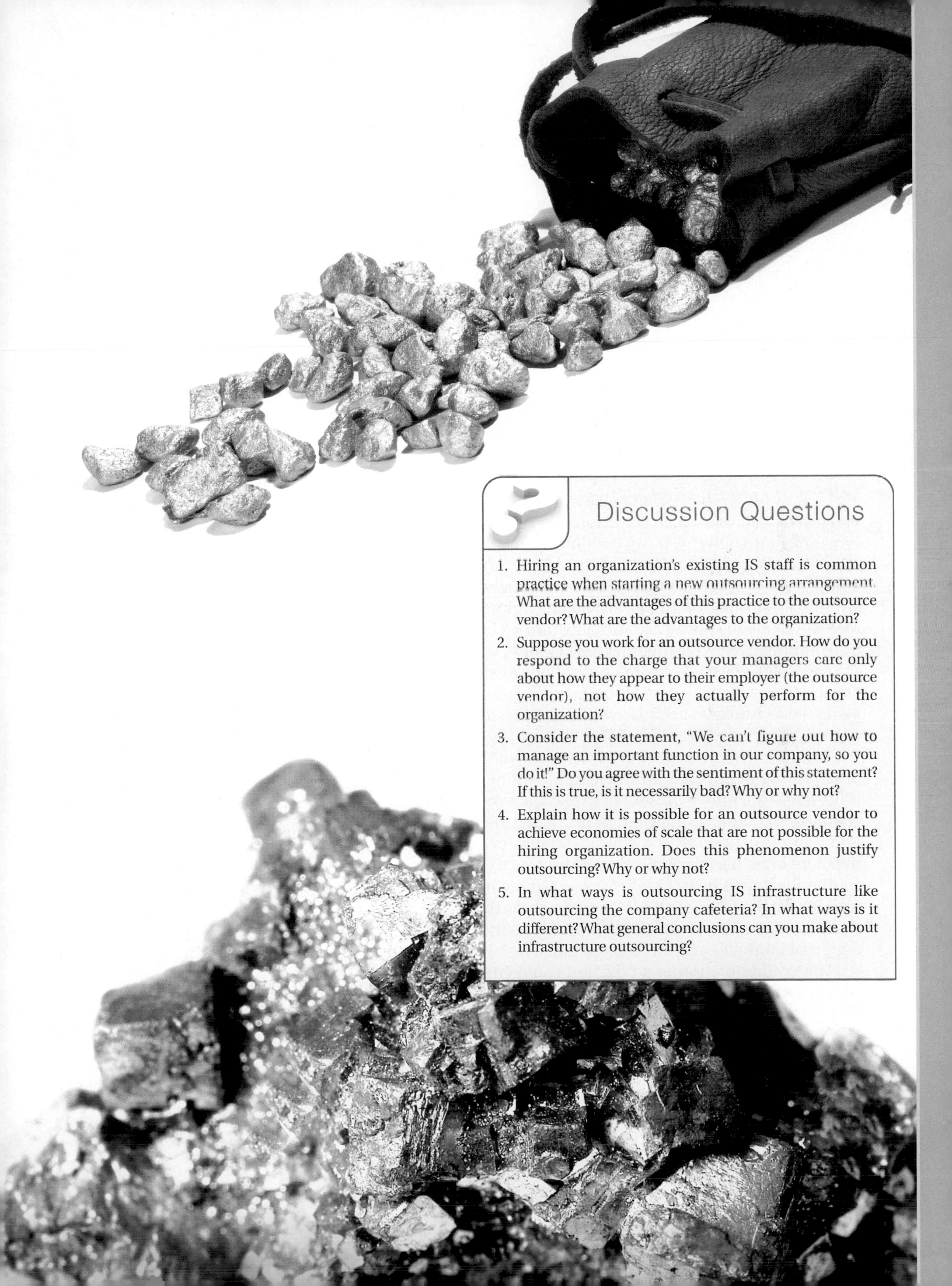

Discussion Questions

1. Hiring an organization's existing IS staff is common practice when starting a new outsourcing arrangement. What are the advantages of this practice to the outsource vendor? What are the advantages to the organization?
2. Suppose you work for an outsource vendor. How do you respond to the charge that your managers care only about how they appear to their employer (the outsource vendor), not how they actually perform for the organization?
3. Consider the statement, "We can't figure out how to manage an important function in our company, so you do it!" Do you agree with the sentiment of this statement? If this is true, is it necessarily bad? Why or why not?
4. Explain how it is possible for an outsource vendor to achieve economies of scale that are not possible for the hiring organization. Does this phenomenon justify outsourcing? Why or why not?
5. In what ways is outsourcing IS infrastructure like outsourcing the company cafeteria? In what ways is it different? What general conclusions can you make about infrastructure outsourcing?

Problem-Solving

GUIDE

What If You Just Don't Know?

What if you have to make a decision and you just don't know which way to go? For complex issues like outsourcing, it can be difficult to know what the right decision is. In many cases, more analysis won't necessarily reduce the uncertainty.

Consider outsourcing as a typical, complex, real-life decision problem. The question is, will outsourcing save your organization money? Will the cap on financial exposure be worth the loss of control? Or, is your organization avoiding managing the IS function because you would just like to have the whole IS mess out of your hair?

Suppose the CIO is adamantly opposed to the outsourcing of computer infrastructure. Why is that? He is obviously biased, because such outsourcing will mean a huge cut in his department and a big loss of control for him. It might even mean he loses his job. But is that all there is to it? Or does he have a point? Are the projected savings real? Or are they the result of a paper analysis that misses many of the intangibles? For that matter, does that analysis miss some of the tangibles?

You could do another study; you could commission an independent consultant to examine this situation and make a recommendation. However, is that avoiding the issue, yet again? Further, what if there is no time? The network is down for 2 days for the third time this quarter, and you've got to act. You've got to do something. But what? Take it to the board of directors? No, they don't know. That's just another way of avoiding a tough decision. You've got to decide.

In some ways, higher education does you a disservice. In school, you're taught that a bit more study, another report, or a little more analysis will help you find a better answer. But many decisions don't work that way. There might not be the time or money for another study or another study might just cloud the issue more. Or maybe it's just not possible to know. What will be the price of Google stock on January 1, 2010? You just don't know. ■

Discussion Questions

1. Suppose you are the CIO and you are opposed, on what you perceive as legitimate grounds, to an outsourcing proposal. Suppose you know that everyone on the steering committee thinks you're biased because your department will shrink. What can you do to increase your credibility?
2. Suppose you're on the steering committee and you know that the CIO is biased about the outsourcing proposal. What questions can you ask to assess the degree to which his bias is influencing his position?
3. Describe a situation where you were in a biased situation and you needed to convince others to believe you, despite your bias. What did you do? Did it work?
4. Suppose you have to make a decision and you feel you don't know what you need to know to make that decision with confidence. Does it help to consider the cost of a mistake? How? Does it help to consider the cost of undoing your mistake? How?
5. Some executives say there's always more time than you think. You can always find a temporizing measure to buy yourself more time. Others say that it is critical to be decisive; make decisions when you have to, with the best knowledge you have; and get on with the next issue. Which view do you take with regard to the situation described here? Why?
6. One theory holds that some people are just better decision makers—that when given very little data, some people just have the knack for making good decisions. Others contend that there is no such difference; some people are just luckier. Or, some people have the knack for managing their affairs so that they never have to make a decision with little information. What do you think?
7. In the scenario presented, the CEO is frustrated and wants to get the IS mess out of her hair. How do her emotions cause her to second-guess her decision process? What role do you think emotions should play in a decision?

ACTIVE REVIEW

Use this Active Review to verify that you understand the ideas and concepts that answer the chapter's study questions.

Q1 What are the functions of the IS department?

List the five primary functions of the IS department. Define *CIO* and explain the CIO's typical reporting relationships. Name the four groups found in a typical IS department and explain the major responsibilities of each. Define *CTO* and explain typical CTO responsibilities. Explain the purpose of the data administration function.

Q2 How do organizations plan the use of IS?

Explain the importance of strategic alignment as it pertains to IS planning. Explain why maintaining alignment can be difficult. Describe the CIO's relationship to the rest of the executive staff. Describe the CIO's responsibilities with regard to priorities. Explain challenges to this task. Define *steering committee* and explain the CIO's role with regard to it.

Q3 What tasks are necessary for managing computing infrastructure?

Explain how alignment pertains to computing infrastructure. Give an example of good and poor alignment. Name and explain three resource categories that the IS department must create, operate, and maintain. Explain, using examples, why these tasks are huge. Describe the rationale and importance of setting technology and product standards. Explain how a well-managed IS department deals with problem reports. Describe typical job categories within the IS department's operations staff.

Q4 What tasks are necessary for managing enterprise applications?

Define *enterprise application*. Using Figure 11-7 as a guide, summarize the tasks required for managing enterprise applications. Define *legacy information system*. Describe the work responsibilities for each of the types of employee in Figure 11-8. Explain the difference between database administration and data administration. Define *data dictionary* and explain its role and importance. Give an example of a data policy. Explain the term *disaster-recovery planning*.

Q5 What are the advantages and disadvantages of outsourcing?

Define *outsourcing*. Explain how Drucker's statement, "Your backroom is someone else's front room" pertains to outsourcing. Summarize the management advantages, cost advantages, and risks of outsourcing. Explain why international outsourcing can be particularly advantageous. Describe skills you can develop that will protect you from having your job outsourced. Summarize the outsourcing risks concerning control, long-term costs, and exit strategy.

Q6 What are your user rights and responsibilities?

Explain in your own words the meaning of each of your user rights as listed in Figure 11-14. Explain in your own words the meaning of each of your user responsibilities in Figure 11-14.

KEY TERMS AND CONCEPTS

USING YOUR KNOWLEDGE

1. According to this chapter, information systems, products, and technology are not malleable; they are difficult to change, alter, or bend. How do you think senior executives other than the CIO view this lack of malleability? For example, how do you think IS appears during a corporate merger?
2. Suppose you represent an investor group that is acquiring hospitals across the nation and integrating them into a unified system. List five potential problems and risks concerning information systems. How do you think IS-related risks compare to other risks in such an acquisition program?

3. What happens to IS when corporate direction changes rapidly? How will IS appear to other departments? What happens to IS when the corporate strategy changes frequently? Do you think such frequent changes are a greater problem to IS than to other business functions? Why or why not?

4. Consider the following statement: "In many ways, choosing an outsource vendor is a one-way street." Explain what this statement means. Do you agree with it? Why or why not?

COLLABORATION EXERCISES AND CASES

Collaborate with a group of students on the following exercises. Recall from Chapter 2 that collaboration is more than cooperation because it involves iteration and feedback. Post a document, a discussion item, a wiki item, or an idea and obtain feedback from your team members. Similarly, read the ideas of others and comment on them. Try to innovate in both the process by which you collaborate and the work product that you create. Avoid face-to-face meetings. Instead, use collaborative software such as Google Docs & Spreadsheets, Microsoft Groove, or Microsoft SharePoint to facilitate your ideas.

1. In this exercise, you will be given a chance to be CTO of a major corporation. In particular, you will be asked to consider the application of iPhone and Web 2.0 technology to your organization. Before you start, read the entire assignment, because later questions may influence your answer to part a.

   a. First, as a team, select the company for which you will be CTO. Choose any company that you find interesting, but select one that is likely to have staffed the CTO position. A company that has at least $200 million sales is a good candidate. You can get a two-fer if you select an organization for which you might want to work; besides getting credit for this assignment, you will be gaining knowledge to use to arrange or conduct job interviews for your team.

   b. Define the job of the CTO. Use the description in this chapter, but augment that description with knowledge from the Internet. Besides basic definitions of CTO, read interviews with practicing CTOs. A good place to start is *http://CIO.com.*

   c. Given your answers to parts a and b, write your own CTO job description. List your major responsibilities; make them particular to the company that you chose in part a.

   d. Summarize the capabilities of an iPhone. Explain how devices like this enable the merger of personal and professional lives. Describe how you think this might be important to particular customers for your company. Consider specific people and situations such as young professionals with children, doctors on call, truck drivers out on the road, or dance instructors in the studio. Again, choose people who are likely to be customers of your company.

   e. Summarize what you consider to be the top three characteristics of Web 2.0. Use the discussion in Chapter 8, but use Web resources as well.

   f. Now consider the combination of iPhone-like devices and Web 2.0 in the context of your company. Identify and describe five innovative applications of these technologies. Use Figure 3-11 (page 72) and explain how your applications generate competitive advantages.

   g. Explain how you can use the knowledge you have gained in this exercise in a job interview either (1) with the company you choose in part a or (2) with another company.

   h. If directed to do so, create a PowerPoint presentation of your answers to parts a through g. Deliver your presentation to your classmates, as directed by your professor.

2. Suppose you are the manager cited in the *Information Systems Management in Practice* box on page 432. An employee has come into your office and has complained about the cost of computers and the limitations placed on employees by the IS department. In this exercise, you will have a chance to brainstorm possible responses with your team.

   a. One approach is to take the side of the IS department. Discuss with your team how you would do this. How would you justify the department's stance? Write a paragraph of ideas that you would express to your employee. List three possible objections he might make in response. How would you counter those responses?

   b. Another approach would be to work with your employee to develop a proposal for a different scheme—perhaps one that recognizes the need for standardization but that allows employees more leeway to acquire computers on their own. Working with your team, develop such a proposal. Document that proposal for presentation to the IS department.

c. Yet a third approach would be to discuss this matter with the IS department and ask someone there to respond to your employee. Explain advantages and disadvantages of this approach.

d. Of the three approaches identified, which do you, as a team, prefer? If you can come to agreement on a single answer, explain your thought process. If, as a team, you cannot agree on a single answer, explain each answer and its rationale.

e. Suppose your employee develops a proposal for a different scheme and the IS department rejects that proposal. What do you do if you agree more with your employee than with the IS department?

f. Generalize your answer to part e. As a mid-level manager, you may be placed into a position where you are enforcing policy from higher management with which you disagree. How will you respond in that circumstance?

APPLICATION EXERCISE

1. Suppose you have just been appointed manager of a help desk with an IS department. You have been there for just a week, and you are amazed to find only limited information to help you manage your employees. In fact, the only data kept concerns the processing of particular issues, called *Tickets*. The following data is kept:

Ticket#, Date_Submitted, Date_Opened, Date_Closed, Type (new or repeat), Reporting_Employee_Name, Reporting_Employee_Division, Technician_Name Problem_System, and Problem_Description

You can find sample Ticket data in the Excel file **Ch11Ex01** on this text's Web site.

As a manager, you need more information. Among your needs are information that will help you learn who are your best- and worst-performing technicians, how different systems compare in terms of number of problems reported and the time required to fix those problems, how different divisions compare in terms of problems reported and the time required to fix them, which technicians are the best and worst at solving problems with particular systems, and which technicians are best and worst at solving problems from particular divisions.

a. Use either Access or Excel, or a combination of the two, to produce the information listed above from the data in the Excel file **Ch11Ex01**. In your answer, you may use queries, formulas, reports, forms, graphs, pivot tables, pivot charts, or any other type of Access or Excel display. Choose the best display for the type of information you are producing.

b. Explain how you would use these different types of information to manage your department.

c. Specify any additional information that you would like to have produced from this data to help you manage your department.

d. Use either Access or Excel or a combination to produce the information in part c.

CASE STUDY 11

Marriott International, Inc.

Marriott International, Inc., operates and franchises hotels and lodging facilities throughout the world. Its 2006 revenue was just over $12.2 billion. Marriott groups its business into segments according to lodging facility. Major business segments are full-service lodging, select-service lodging, extended-stay lodging, and timeshare properties. Marriott states that its three top corporate priorities are profitability, preference, and growth.

In the mid-1980s, the airlines developed the concept of *revenue management*, which adjusts prices in accordance with demand. The idea gained prominence in the airline industry, because an unoccupied seat represents revenue that is forever lost. Unlike a part in inventory, an unoccupied seat on today's flight cannot be sold tomorrow. Similarly, in the lodging industry, today's unoccupied hotel room cannot be sold tomorrow. So, for hotels, revenue management translates to raising prices on Monday when a convention is in town and lowering them on Saturday in the dead of winter when few travelers are in sight.

Marriott had developed two different revenue-management systems, one for its premium hotels and a second for its lower-priced properties. It developed both of these systems using pre–Internet technology; systems upgrades required installing updates locally. The local updates were expensive and problematic. Also, the two systems required two separate interfaces for entering prices into the centralized reservation system.

In the late-1990s, Marriott embarked on a project to create a single revenue-management system that could be used by all of its properties. The new system, called One Yield, was custom developed in-house, using a process similar to those you learned about in Chapter 10. The IT professionals understood the importance of user involvement, and they formed a joint IT–business user team that developed the business case for the new system and jointly managed its development. The team was careful to provide constant communication to the system's future users, and it used prototypes to identify problem areas early. Training is a continuing activity for all Marriott employees, and the company integrated training facilities into the new system.

One Yield recommends prices for each room, given the day, date, current reservation levels, and history. Each hotel property has a revenue manager who can override these recommendations. Either way, the prices are communicated directly to the centralized reservation system. One Yield uses Web-based technology so that when the company makes upgrades to the system, it makes them only at the Web servers, not at the individual hotels. This strategy saves considerable maintenance cost, activity, and frustration.

One Yield computes the theoretical maximum revenue for each property and compares actual results to that maximum. Using One Yield, the company has increased the ratio of actual to theoretical revenue from 83 percent to 91 percent. That increase of 8 percentage points has translated into a substantial increase in revenues.

Source: Case based on information from *www.cio.com/article/119209/The_Price_is_Always_Right* (accessed August 2007). Used through the courtesy of *CIO*. Copyright 2005/2007 CXO Media Inc.

Questions

1. How does One Yield contribute to Marriott's objectives?
2. What are the advantages of having one revenue-management system instead of two? Consider both users and the IS department in your answer.
3. At the same time it was developing One Yield in-house, Marriott chose to outsource its human relations information system. Why would it choose to develop one system in-house but outsource the other? Consider the following factors in your answer.
   - Marriott's objectives
   - The nature of the systems
   - The uniqueness of each system to Marriott
   - Marriott's in-house expertise
4. How did outsourcing HR contribute to the success of One Yield?
5. Summarize the reasons why a company would choose to outsource rather than develop a system in-house.

12 Information Security Management

STUDY QUESTIONS

- Q1 What are the threats to information security?
- Q2 What is senior management's security role?
- Q3 What technical safeguards are available?
- Q4 What data safeguards are available?
- Q5 What human safeguards are available?
- Q6 How should organizations respond to security incidents?
- Q7 What is the extent of computer crime?

Meet Ross Buchholz

My motto:
Treat the customer as you want to be treated—no matter who the customer or what the situation.

One characteristic of a superior employee:
Ability to clearly and concisely communicate to customers, peers, team, and executives.

My pet peeve:
Complaining about problems but not offering a solution.

Ross Buchholz is the manager of operations for RagingWire Enterprise Solutions, a privately held corporation that outsources data center operations and disaster-recovery backup sites for *Fortune* 500 companies. Ross, who holds a degree in microbiology and genetic engineering, took an indirect route to his present position, from auto parts to biotech to disaster recovery.

On college:

"After high school, I had no interest in going to college, primarily because that was what my father most wanted me to do. I was determined to live my life, my way. So, I worked a couple of low-level jobs—one at a paint store and another at an auto parts store. After 6 or 7 months as an auto parts clerk, I happened, by accident, to see my manager's paycheck. He'd been working there 20 years and he was making $3 an hour more than I was!

"That was a defining moment, an epiphany. I knew I didn't want that to happen to me, so I made a plan to get into college. I liked biological sciences and decided to major in microbiology and genetics. While I was in college, I worked full-time as a student tech in a professor's lab on campus because I knew that I needed to get first-hand experience outside of the classroom to compete for jobs when I graduated. After I'd earned my degree, I joined a startup biotech company in Boston, Exelixis Pharmaceuticals, as an associate research scientist."

On the transition to IT:

"I enjoyed research; we were doing genetics using *Drosophila*, the fruit fly, the one that reproduces so fast. But, I'd always enjoyed computers, too. In the lab, people would ask me questions about their computers, how to do things, and after a while I became the go-to guy for computer problems. I started thinking that I might want to work in IT as much as in biology. Also, there's a glass ceiling in science. If you don't have a Ph.D., there's only so far you can go, and I knew I didn't want to spend that much more time in school at that point in my life.

"Eventually I joined the IT Department at Exelixis and worked on all sort of projects. I helped convert the company from Macs to PCs, developed conversion tools, performed audits of computer hardware and software to identify the best suite for the organization, and started to get introduced to IT security at the networking firewall level.

"It was a great company to work for, but we needed to get out of high-cost San Francisco, so we moved to Sacramento. I continued to work remotely for Exelixis—but when my first child was born, I didn't want even the amount of commuting involved in the remote arrangement, so I quit.

"I'm really glad I moved into IT. I like it, and with IT you'll always have a job. In fact, had I stayed in biology at Exelixis, I would have been laid off because they decided to change directions and closed my department."

On RagingWire:

"RagingWire provides outsourcing services for IT organizations at major corporations. I began as a help-desk technician supporting a *Fortune* 500 company and

My guiding principle:
Suck it up and do it right the first time. Quality work always results in fewer cycles.

My very first job:
Cleaning and salting cow hides.

My management style:
Non-micro manager. I expect employees to understand their jobs and not need hand-holding. If they need help or direction, then I expect them to come and ask or to bring it up in group meetings.

Ross Buchholz

knew if I worked hard, there would be many opportunities available. We have what is termed *five nines reliability*; that means our data center is operational a minimum of 99.999 percent of the time. That doesn't just mean that the computers run 99.999 percent of the time; it means all our services such as power, cooling, Internet connectivity, *and* our computers run 99.999 percent of the time. To get that reliability, we have to envision multiple disaster scenarios and plan for them all. As an example, with Internet connectivity we plan for an event that would take two of our three providers offline yet we would still be able to offer uninterrupted service to our customers.

"Over 5 years, I worked my way up to become manager of the help-desk center, and a year and a half ago I was asked to take over as manager of operations."

On disaster recovery:

"We provide a wide range of services, including backup and recovery. Some of our clients want to use our data center just if a disaster disables their own primary data center. On the other hand, some clients want uninterrupted backup. We register our site as a second IP address for their URL. If their site goes down, DNS automatically sends their traffic to our computers. For example, suppose that Big Company has the URL *www.BigCompany.com.* We register the IP address in our DNS servers as a secondary IP address for that URL. When their primary DNS site goes down, as soon as the Internet's domain name system detects the failure, it automatically sends their traffic to us.

"From our perspective, that could happen at any time. We get *zero* advance notice. So, we run duplicates of all their systems. We have the same databases, the same servers, the same firewalls, and, every 15 minutes or so, we make a copy of changes to their data. So, at most, 15 minutes of processing will be lost. Few, if any, of their customers will see any unusual performance."

What business people need to know about IS:

"Managers and other business professionals need a basic understanding of technology, how things work, how the technology pieces fit together. I see that when we negotiate contracts. Customers don't understand the terminology and they make assumptions. They think they are getting something they aren't. Their lack of knowledge can lead to disappointment and problems. Business people need to be able to ask good questions, get involved up front, and truly understand what they're buying."

On good employees:

"Ninety percent of the problems I see each day are problems I've never seen before. That percentage isn't as high for my employees because many of their problems are routine, but still, in this business our people must work effectively under uncertainty and pressure. You need to be able to keep your head, think things through, see the big picture, how one thing leads to another. You also need to be able to talk to customers, find out what they really want. Maybe they don't know what they're doing, so you have to be able to talk them through their problem, find out what really needs to be done, and then do that.

"This morning, one of our customers called to ask us to recover certain files. We did what they asked, but it turned out they really needed to recover more files than they knew. So, when they didn't get the result they expected, we had to figure out why, and do for them what they didn't know how to ask for themselves.

"The other requirement is teamwork. We can't have indispensable stars. When someone figures out how to fix a problem, they need to enter their solution into our knowledge base so the next person who runs into that problem benefits from their experience. Really, that's your legacy—the knowledge you create and leave for others. When someone has a problem and they find a great explanation of that very problem in the knowledge base, with an easy-to-follow solution, you know the person who wrote it up was thinking of the team. You're grateful they're around.

"And, you have to be willing to work. Some weeks I work 50 hours and some weeks I work 70. It depends on what happens, what problems come up, what our customers need. It sounds trite, but it's true: work hard. For me, though, it's almost always fun and interesting."

CHAPTER PREVIEW

This chapter describes the common sources of security threats and explains management's role in addressing those threats. It also defines the major elements of an organizational security policy. Given that management background, it then presents the most common types of technical, data, and human security safeguards. We then discuss how organizations should respond to security incidents, and, finally, examine common types of computer crime.

The primary focus of this chapter is on management's responsibility for the organization's security policy and for implementing human security safeguards. These are the aspects of security that will most concern you as a future business professional.

Q1 What Are the Threats to Information Security?

We begin by describing security threats. We will first summarize the sources of threats and then describe specific problems that arise from each source.

What Are the Sources of Threats?

Three sources of security problems are human error and mistakes, malicious human activity, and natural events and disasters.

Human errors and mistakes include accidental problems caused by both employees and nonemployees. An example is an employee who misunderstands operating procedures and accidentally deletes customer records. Another example is an employee who, in the course of backing up a database, inadvertently installs an old database on top of the current one. This category also includes poorly written application programs and poorly designed procedures. Finally, human errors and mistakes include physical accidents, such as driving a forklift through the wall of a computer room.

The second source of security problems is *malicious human activity*. This category includes employees and former employees who intentionally destroy data or other system components. It also includes hackers who break into a system and virus and worm writers who infect computer systems. Malicious human activity also includes outside criminals who break into a system to steal for financial gain, and it also includes terrorism.

Natural events and disasters are the third source of security problems. This category includes fires, floods, hurricanes, earthquakes, tsunamis, avalanches, and other acts of nature. Problems in this category include not only the initial loss of capability and service, but also losses stemming from actions to recover from the initial problem.

What Are the Types of Security Problems?

Figure 12-1 (next page) summarizes threats by type of problem and source. Five types of security problems are listed: unauthorized data disclosure, incorrect data modification, faulty service, denial of service, and loss of infrastructure. We will consider each type.

Unauthorized Data Disclosure

Unauthorized data disclosure can occur by human error when someone inadvertently releases data in violation of policy. An example at a university would be a new department administrator who posts student names, numbers, and grades in a public place,

Figure 12-1
Security Problems and Sources

		Source		
		Human Error	**Malicious Activity**	**Natural Disasters**
Problem	**Unauthorized data disclosure**	Procedural mistakes	Pretexting Phishing Spoofing Sniffing Computer crime	Disclosure during recovery
	Incorrect data modification	Procedural mistakes Incorrect procedures Ineffective accounting controls System errors	Hacking Computer crime	Incorrect data recovery
	Faulty service	Procedural mistakes Development and installation errors	Computer crime Usurpation	Service improperly restored
	Denial of service	Accidents	DOS attacks	Service interruption
	Loss of infrastructure	Accidents	Theft Terrorist activity	Property loss

when the releasing of names and grades violates state law. Another example is employees who unknowingly or carelessly release proprietary data to competitors or to the media.

The popularity and efficacy of search engines has created another source of inadvertent disclosure. Employees who place restricted data on Web sites that can be reached by search engines might mistakenly publish proprietary or restricted data over the Web.

Of course, proprietary and personal data can also be released maliciously. **Pretexting** occurs when someone deceives by pretending to be someone else. A common scam involves a telephone caller who pretends to be from a credit card company and claims to be checking the validity of credit card numbers: "I'm checking your MasterCard number; it begins 5491. Can you verify the rest of the number?" All MasterCard numbers start with 5491; the caller is attempting to steal a valid number.

Read the Security Management in Practice *box on page 459 for more detailed examples of phishing.*

Phishing is a similar technique for obtaining unauthorized data that uses pretexting via email. The *phisher* pretends to be a legitimate company and sends an email requesting confidential data, such as account numbers, Social Security numbers, account passwords, and so forth. Phishing compromises legitimate brands and trademarks

Spoofing is another term for someone pretending to be someone else. If you pretend to be your professor, you are spoofing your professor. **IP spoofing** occurs when an intruder uses another site's IP address as if it were that other site. **Email spoofing** is a synonym for phishing.

Sniffing is a technique for intercepting computer communications. With wired networks, sniffing requires a physical connection to the network. With wireless networks, no such connection is required: **Drive-by sniffers** simply take computers with wireless connections through an area and search for unprotected wireless networks. They can monitor and intercept wireless traffic at will. Even protected wireless networks are vulnerable, as you will learn. Spyware and adware are two other sniffing techniques discussed later in this chapter.

Other forms of computer crime include breaking into networks to steal data such as customer lists, product inventory data, employee data, and other proprietary and confidential data.

SECURITY MANAGEMENT IN PRACTICE

PHISHING FOR CREDIT CARD ACCOUNTS

Before you read further, realize that the graphics in this case are *fake*. They were not produced by a legitimate business, but were generated by a phisher. A *phisher* is an operation that spoofs legitimate companies in an attempt to illegally capture credit card numbers, email accounts, driver's license numbers, and other data. Some phishers even install malicious program code on users' computers.

Phishing is usually initiated via an email. Go to *http://fraudwatchinternational.com* and select the *Phishing Alerts* tab. You will see a list of recent phishing attacks. You will find messages that appear to be from legitimate businesses but are not.

To understand how email is used to initiate a phishing attack, consider the email in Figure 1. This bogus email is designed to cause you to click on the "See more details here" link. When you do so, you will be connected to a site that will ask you for personal data, such as credit card numbers, card expiration dates, driver's license number, Social Security number, or other data. In this particular case, you will be taken to a screen that asks for your credit card number (see Figure 2).

The Web page in Figure 2 is produced by a nonexistent company and is entirely fake, including the link "Inform us about fraud." The only purpose of this site is to illegally capture your card number. It might also install spyware, adware, or other malware to your computer.

If you were to get this far, you should immediately close your browser, restart your computer, and go shower and brush your teeth! You should also run antimalware scans on your computer to determine if the phisher has installed program code on your computer. If so, use the antimalware software to remove that code.

How can you defend yourself from such attacks? First, you know that you did not purchase two first class tickets to Cozumel. (Had you by odd circumstance just purchased airline tickets to Cozumel, you should contact the legitimate vendor's site *directly* to determine if there had been some mix up.) Because you have not purchased such tickets, suspect a phisher.

Second, notice the implausibility of the email. It is exceedingly unlikely that you can buy two first-class tickets to any foreign country for $349. Additionally, note the misspelled word in the last line and the poor grammar ("cortact with us"). All of these facts should alert you to the bogus nature of this email.

Third, do not be misled by legitimate-looking graphics. Phishers are criminals; they do not bother to respect international agreements on legitimate use of trademarks. The phisher might use names of legitimate companies such as Visa, MasterCard, Discover, and American Express on the Web page, and the presence of those names might lull you into thinking this is legitimate. The phisher is *illegally using* those names. In other instances, the phisher will copy the entire look and feel of a legitimate company's Web site.

Phishing is a serious problem. To protect yourself, be wary of unsolicited email, even if the email appears to be from a legitimate business. If you have questions about an email, contact the company directly (*not* using the addresses provided by the phisher!) and ask about the email. And above all, never give confidential data such as account numbers, Social Security numbers, driver's license numbers, or credit card numbers in response to *any unsolicited email.*

Although it is clear what you should not do in response to phishing, it is less clear what legitimate businesses can do. You and a team of your classmates will have a chance to address this issue in Collaboration Exercise 1, on page 491.

Your Order ID: "17152492"
Order Date: "09/07/05"
Product Purchased: "Two First Class Tickets to Cozumel"
Your card type: "CREDIT"
Total Price: "$349.00"

Hello, when you purchased your tickets you provided an incorrect mailing address.

<u>*See more details here*</u>
Please follow the link and modify your mailing address or cancel your order. If you have questions, feel free to contact us at *account@usefulbill.com*

Figure 1
Fake Phishing Email

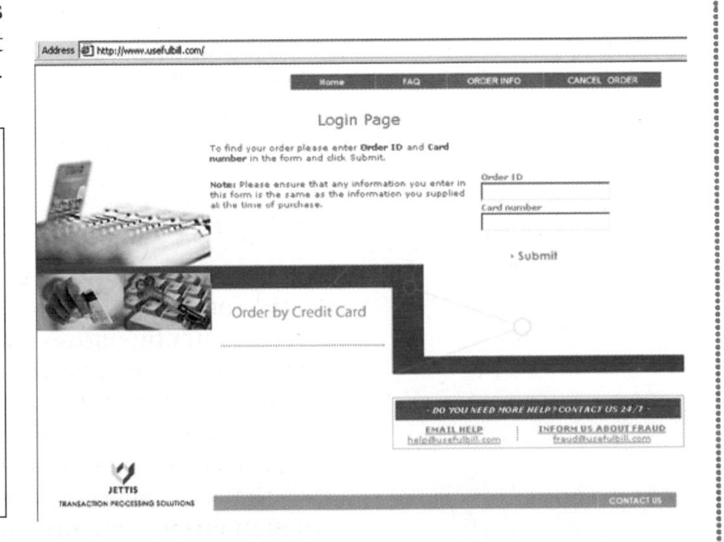

Figure 2
Fake Phishing Screen

Finally, people might inadvertently disclose data during recovery from a natural disaster. During a recovery, everyone is so focused on restoring system capability that they might ignore normal security safeguards. A request like "I need a copy of the customer database backup" will receive far less scrutiny during disaster recovery than at other times.

Incorrect Data Modification

The second problem category in Figure 12-1 is *incorrect data modification*. Examples include incorrectly increasing a customer's discount or incorrectly modifying an employee's salary, earned days of vacation, or annual bonus. Other examples include placing incorrect information, such as incorrect price changes, on the company's Web site or company portal.

Incorrect data modification can occur through human error when employees follow procedures incorrectly or when procedures have been designed incorrectly. For proper internal control on systems that process financial data or that control inventories of assets, such as products and equipment, companies should ensure separation of duties and authorities and have multiple checks and balances in place.

A final type of incorrect data modification caused by human error includes *system errors*. An example is the lost-update problem discussed in Chapter 5 (pages 156–157).

Hacking occurs when a person gains unauthorized access to a computer system. Although some people hack for the sheer joy of doing it, other hackers invade systems for the malicious purpose of stealing or modifying data. Computer criminals invade computer networks to obtain critical data or to manipulate the system for financial gain. Examples are reducing account balances or causing the shipment of goods to unauthorized locations and customers.

Finally, faulty recovery actions after a disaster can result in incorrect data changes. The faulty actions can be unintentional or malicious.

Faulty Service

The third problem category, *faulty service*, includes problems that result because of incorrect system operation. Faulty service could include incorrect data modification, as just described. It also could include systems that work incorrectly by sending the wrong goods to the customer or the ordered goods to the wrong customer, incorrectly billing customers, or sending the wrong information to employees. Humans can inadvertently cause faulty service by making procedural mistakes. System developers can write programs incorrectly or make errors during the installation of hardware, software programs, and data.

Usurpation occurs when unauthorized programs invade a computer system and replace legitimate programs. Such unauthorized programs typically shut down the legitimate system and substitute their own processing. Faulty service can also result from mistakes made during the recovery from natural disasters.

Denial of Service

Human error in following procedures or a lack of procedures can result in **denial of service**. For example, humans can inadvertently shut down a Web server or corporate gateway router by starting a computationally intensive application. An OLAP application that uses the operational DBMS can consume so many DBMS resources that order-entry transactions cannot get through.

Denial-of-service attacks can be launched maliciously. A malicious hacker can flood a Web server, for example, with millions of bogus service requests that so occupy the server that it cannot service legitimate requests. As you learned in Chapter 4 (page 125), computer worms can infiltrate a network with so much artificial traffic that legitimate traffic cannot get through. Finally, natural disasters may cause systems to fail, resulting in denial of service.

Loss of Infrastructure

Human accidents can cause *loss of infrastructure*. Examples are a bulldozer cutting a conduit of fiber-optic cables and the floor buffer crashing into a rack of Web servers.

Theft and terrorist events also cause loss of infrastructure. A disgruntled, terminated employee can walk off with corporate data servers, routers, or other crucial equipment. Terrorist events also can cause the loss of physical plants and equipment.

Natural disasters present the largest risk for infrastructure loss. A fire, flood, earthquake, or similar event can destroy data centers and all they contain. The devastation of the Indian Ocean tsunami in December 2004 and of Hurricanes Katrina and Rita in the fall of 2005 are potent examples of the risks to infrastructure from natural causes.

You may be wondering why Figure 12-1 does not include viruses, worms, and Trojan horses. The answer is that viruses, worms, and Trojan horses are *techniques* for causing some of the problems in the figure. They can cause a denial-of-service attack, or they can be used to cause malicious, unauthorized data access, or data loss.

What Are the Components of an Organization's Security Program?

All of the problems listed in Figure 12-1 are real and as serious as they sound. Accordingly, organizations must address security in a systematic way. A **security program**[1] has three components: senior-management involvement, safeguards of various kinds, and incident response.

The first component, *senior-management involvement*, has two critical security functions: First, senior management must establish the security policy. This policy sets the stage for the organization's response to security threats. However, because no security program is perfect, there is always risk. Management's second function, therefore, is to manage risk by balancing the costs and benefits of the security program.

Safeguards are protections against security threats. A good way to view safeguards is in terms of the five components of an information system, as shown in Figure 12-2. Some of the safeguards involve computer hardware and software. Some involve data; others involve procedures and people. In addition to these safeguards, organizations must also consider disaster-recovery safeguards. An effective security program consists of a balance of safeguards of all these types.

The final component of a security program consists of the organization's *planned response to security incidents*. Clearly, the time to think about what to do is *not* when the computers are crashing all around the organization. We begin the discussion of the security program with the responsibilities of senior management.

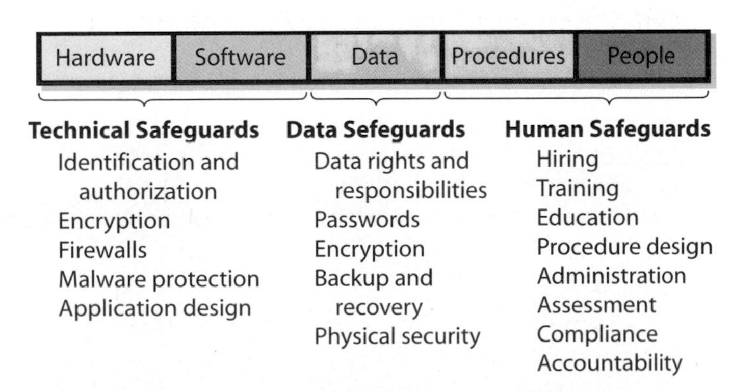

Figure 12-2 Security Safeguards as They Relate to the Five Components

[1]Note that the word *program* is used here in the sense of a management program that includes objectives, policies, procedures, directives, and so forth. Do not confuse this term with a computer program.

Q2 What Is Senior Management's Security Role?

Management has a crucial role in information systems security. Management sets the security policy, and only management can balance the costs of a security system against the risk of security threats. The National Institute of Standards and Technology (NIST) published an excellent security handbook that addresses management's responsibility. It is available online at *http://csrc.nist.gov/publications/nistpubs/800–12/handbook.pdf.* We will follow its discussion in this section.

The *NIST Handbook* of Security Elements

Figure 12-3 lists elements of computer security described in the *NIST Handbook*. First, computer security must support the organization's mission. There is no "one size fits all" solution to security problems. Security systems for a diamond mine and security systems for a wheat farm will differ.

According to the second point in Figure 12-3, when you manage a department you have a responsibility for information security in that department, even if no one tells you that you do. Do appropriate safeguards exist? Are your employees properly trained? Will your department know how to respond when the computer system fails? If these issues are not addressed in your department, raise the issue to higher levels of management.

Security can be expensive. Therefore, as shown in the third principle of Figure 12-3, computer security should have an appropriate cost-benefit ratio. Costs can be direct, such a labor costs, and they can be intangible, such as employee or customer frustration.

According to the fourth principle in Figure 12-3, security responsibilities and accountabilities must be explicit. General statements like "everyone in the department must adequately safeguard company assets" are worthless. Instead, managers should assign specific tasks to specific people or specific job functions.

Because information systems integrate the processing of many departments, security problems originating in your department can have far-reaching consequences. If one of your employees neglects procedures and enters product prices incorrectly on your Web storefront, the consequences will extend to other departments, other companies, and your customers. Understanding that computer system owners have security responsibilities outside their own departments and organizations is the fifth principle of computer security.

As the sixth principle in Figure 12-3 implies, there is no magic bullet for security. No single safeguard, such as a firewall, a virus-protection program, or increased employee

1. Computer security should support the mission of the organization.
2. Computer security is an integral element of sound management.
3. Computer security should be cost-effective.
4. Computer security responsibilities and accountability should be made explicit.
5. System owners have computer security responsibilities outside their own organizations.
6. Computer security requires a comprehensive and integrated approach.
7. Computer security should be periodically reassessed.
8. Computer security is constrained by societal factors.

Figure 12-3
Elements of Computer Security

Source: National Institute of Standards and Technology. *Introduction to Computer Security: The NIST Handbook*, Publication 800–12, p. 9.

training, will provide effective security. The problems described in Figure 12-1 require an integrated security program.

Once a security program is in place, the company cannot simply forget about it. As the seventh principle in Figure 12-3 indicates, security is a continuing need, and every company must periodically evaluate its security program.

Finally, social factors put some limits on security programs. Employees resent physical searches when arriving at and departing from work. Customers do not want to have their retinas scanned before they can place an order. Computer security conflicts with personal privacy, and a balance may be hard to achieve.

What Are the Elements of a Security Policy?

As stated, senior management has two overarching security tasks: defining a security policy and managing computer-security risk. Although management may delegate the specific tasks, it maintains the responsibility for the organization's security and must approve and endorse all such work.

A **security policy** has three elements: The first is a general statement of the organization's *security program*. This statement becomes the foundation for more specific security measures throughout the organization. In this statement, management specifies the goals of the security program and the assets to be protected. This statement also designates a department for managing the organization's security program and documents. In general terms, it specifies *how* the organization will ensure enforcement of security programs and policies.

The second security policy element is the *issue-specific policy*. For example, management might formulate a policy on personal use of computers at work and email privacy. The organization has the legal right to limit personal use of its computer systems and to inspect personal email for compliance. Employees have a right to know such policies.

Management sets security policies to ensure compliance with security law, as discussed in the Ethics Guide *on page 464.*

The third security policy element is the *system-specific policy*, which concerns specific information systems. For example, what customer data from the order-entry system will be sold or shared with other organizations? Or, what policies govern the design and operation of systems that process employee data? Companies should address such policies as part of the standard systems development process.

How Is Risk Managed?

Management's second overarching security task is risk management. **Risk** is the likelihood of an adverse occurrence. Management cannot manage threats directly, but it *can* manage the likelihood that threats will be successful. Thus, management cannot keep hurricanes from happening, but it can limit the security consequences of a hurricane by creating a backup processing facility at a remote location.

Companies can reduce risks, but always at a cost. It is management's responsibility to decide how much to spend, or stated differently, how much risk to assume.

Unfortunately, risk management takes place in a sea of uncertainty. Uncertainty is different from risk. Risk refers to threats and consequences that we know about. **Uncertainty** refers to the things we do not know that we do not know. For example, an earthquake could devastate a corporate data center on a fault that no one knew about. An employee might have found a way to steal inventory using a hole in the corporate Web site that no expert knew existed. Because of uncertainty, risk management is always approximate.

Risk Assessment

The first step in risk management is to assess what the threats are, how likely they are to occur, and what the consequences are if they occur. Figure 12-4 (page 466) lists factors to consider. First, what are the assets that are to be protected? Examples are

Ethics

GUIDE

Security Privacy

Some organizations have legal requirements to protect the customer data they collect and store, but the laws may be more limited than you think. The **Gramm-Leach-Bliley (GLB) Act**, passed by Congress in 1999, protects consumer financial data stored by financial institutions, which are defined as banks, securities firms, insurance companies, and organizations that provide financial advice, prepare tax returns, and provide similar financial services.

The **Privacy Act of 1974** provides protections to individuals regarding records maintained by the U.S. government, and the privacy provisions of the **Health Insurance Portability and Accountability Act (HIPAA)** of 1996 gives individuals the right to access health data created by doctors and other health-care providers. HIPAA also sets rules and limits on who can read and receive your health information.

The law is stronger in other countries. In Australia, for example, the Privacy Principles of the Australian Privacy Act of 1988 govern not only government and health care data, but also records maintained by businesses with revenues in excess of AU$3 million.

To understand the importance of the limitations, consider online retailers that routinely store customer credit card data. Do Dell, Amazon.com, the airlines, and other e-commerce businesses have a legal requirement to protect their customers' credit card data? Apparently not—at least not in the United States. The activities of such organizations are not governed by the GLB, the Privacy Act of 1974, or HIPAA.

Most consumers would say, however, that online retailers have an ethical requirement to protect a customer's credit card and other data, and most online retailers would agree. Or at least the retailers would agree that they have a strong business reason to protect that data. A substantial loss of credit card data by any large online retailer would have detrimental effects on both sales and brand reputation.

Let's bring the discussion closer to home. What requirements does your university have on the data it maintains about you? State law or university policy may govern those records, but no federal law does. Most universities consider it their responsibility to provide public access to graduation records. Anyone can determine when you graduated, your degree, and your major. (Keep this service in mind when you write your resume.)

Most professors endeavor to publish grades by student number and not by name, and there may be state law that requires that separation. But what about your work? What about the papers you write, the answers you give on exams? What about the emails you send to your professor? The data are not protected by federal law, and they are probably not protected by state law. If your professor chooses to cite your work in research, she will be subject to copyright law, but not privacy law. What you write is no longer your personal data; it belongs to the academic community. You can ask your professor what she intends to do with your coursework, emails, and office conversations, but none of that data is protected by law.

The bottom line: Be careful with your personal data. Large, reputable organizations are likely to endorse ethical privacy policy and to have strong and effective safeguards to effectuate that policy. But individuals and small organizations might not. If in doubt, ask. ■

Discussion Questions

1. As stated, when you order from an online retailer, the data you provide is not protected by U.S. privacy law. Does this fact cause you to reconsider setting up an account with a stored credit card number? What is the advantage of storing the credit card number? Do you think the advantage is worth the risk? Are you more willing to take the risk with some companies than with others? Why or why not?
2. Suppose you are the treasurer of a student club, and you store records of club members' payments in a database. In the past, members have disputed payment amounts; therefore, when you receive a payment, you scan an image of the check or credit card invoice and store the scanned image in a database.

   One day, you are using your computer in a local wireless coffee shop and a malicious student breaks into your computer over the wireless network and steals the club database. You know nothing about this until the next day, when a club member complains that a popular student Web site has published the names, bank names, and bank account numbers for everyone who has given you a check.

   What liability do you have in this matter? Could you be classified as a financial institution because you are taking students' money? (You can find the GLB at *http://ftc.gov/privacy/glbact.*) If so, what liability do you have? If not, do you have any other liability? Does the coffee shop have a liability?
3. Suppose you are asked to fill out a study questionnaire that requires you to enter identifying data as well as answers to personal questions. You hesitate to provide the data, but the top part of the questionnaire states, "All responses will be strictly confidential." So, you fill out the questionnaire.

   Unfortunately, the person who is conducting the study visits the same wireless coffee shop that you visited (in question 2), and the same malicious student breaks in and steals the study results. Your name and all of your responses appear on that same student Web site. Did the person conducting the study violate a law? Does the confidentiality assurance on the form increase that person's requirement to protect your data? Does your answer change if the person conducting the study is (a) a student, (b) a professor of music, or (c) a professor of computer security?
4. In truth, only a very talented and motivated hacker could steal databases from computers using a public wireless network. Such losses, although possible, are unlikely. However, any email you send or files you download can readily be sniffed at a public wireless facility. Knowing this, describe good practice for computer use at public wireless facilities.
5. Considering your answers to the above questions, state three to five general principles to guide your actions as you disseminate and store data.

Figure 12-4
Risk Assessment Factors

1. Assets	5. Consequences
2. Threats	6. Likelihood
3. Safeguards	7. Probable loss
4. Vulnerability	

computer facilities, programs, and sensitive data. Other assets are less obvious. Phishing threatens an organization's customers as well its trademark and brand. Employee privacy is another asset that can be at risk.

Given the list of assets to be protected, the next action is to assess the threats to which they are exposed. The company should consider all of the threats in Figure 12-1; there may be other threats as well.

The third factor in risk assessment is to determine what safeguards are in place to protect company assets from the identified threats. According to the *NIST Handbook*, a **safeguard** is any action, device, procedure, technique, or other measure that reduces a system's vulnerability to a threat.[2] No safeguard is ironclad; there is always a *residual risk* that the safeguard will not protect the assets in all circumstances.

A **vulnerability** is an opening or a weakness in the security system. Some vulnerabilities exist because there are no safeguards or because the existing safeguards are ineffective. Because of residual risk, there is always some residual vulnerability even to assets that are protected by effective safeguards.

Consequences, the fifth factor listed in Figure 12-4, are the damages that occur when an asset is compromised. Consequences can be tangible or intangible. *Tangible* consequences are those whose financial impact can be measured. The costs of *intangible* consequences, such as the loss of customer goodwill due to an outage, cannot be measured. Normally, when analyzing consequences, companies estimate the costs of tangible consequences and simply list intangible consequences.

The final two factors in risk assessment are likelihood and probable loss. *Likelihood* is the probability that a given asset will be compromised by a given threat, despite the safeguards. **Probable loss** is the "bottom line" of risk assessment. To obtain a measure of probable loss, companies multiply likelihood by the cost of the consequences. Probable loss also includes a statement of intangible consequences.

Risk-Management Decisions

Given the probable loss from the risk assessment just described, senior management must decide what to do. In some cases, the decision is easy. Companies can protect some assets by use of inexpensive and easily implemented safeguards. Installing virus-protection software is an example. However, some vulnerability is expensive to eliminate, and management must determine if the costs of the safeguard are worth the benefit of probable loss reduction. Such risk-management decisions are difficult because the true effectiveness of the safeguard is seldom known, and the probable loss is subject to uncertainty.

Uncertainty, however, does not absolve management from security responsibility. Management has a fiduciary responsibility to the organization's owners, and senior managers must make reasonable and prudent decisions in light of available information. They must consider the factors listed in Figure 12-4 and take cost-effective action to reduce probable losses, despite the uncertainty.

The next sections discuss safeguards. We begin with technical safeguards, then data safeguards, then human safeguards, and, finally, safeguards against natural disasters.

[2] *NIST Handbook, csrc.nist.gov/publications/nistpubs/800–12/handbook.pdf*, p. 61 (accessed July 2005).

Q3 What Technical Safeguards Are Available?

Technical safeguards involve the hardware and software components of an information system. Figure 12-5 lists primary technical safeguards. We have discussed all of these in prior chapters. Here we will just supplement those prior discussions.

Identification and Authentication

Every information system today should require users to sign on with a user name and password. The user name *identifies* the user (the process of **identification**), and the password *authenticates* that user (the process of **authentication**).

Passwords

All forms of computer security involve passwords. Review the material on strong passwords and password etiquette in Chapter 3 (page 80).

Despite repeated warnings to the contrary, users tend to be careless in their use of passwords. For example, you can find yellow sticky notes holding written passwords adorning the computers in many companies. In addition, users tend to be free in sharing their passwords with others. Finally, many users choose ineffective, simple passwords. With such passwords, intrusion systems can very effectively guess passwords. These deficiencies can be reduced or eliminated using smart cards and biometric authentication.

Smart Cards

A **smart card** is a plastic card similar to a credit card. Unlike credit, debit, and ATM cards, which have a magnetic strip, smart cards have a microchip. The microchip, which holds far more data than a magnetic strip, is loaded with identifying data. Users of smart cards are required to enter a **personal identification number (PIN)** to be authenticated.

Biometric Authentication

Biometric authentication uses personal physical characteristics such as fingerprints, facial features, and retinal scans to authenticate users. Biometric authentication provides strong authentication, but the required equipment is expensive. Often, too, users resist biometric identification because they feel it is invasive.

Biometric authentication is in the early stages of adoption. Because of its strength, it likely will see increased usage in the future. It is also likely that legislators will pass laws governing the use, storage, and protection requirements for biometric data.

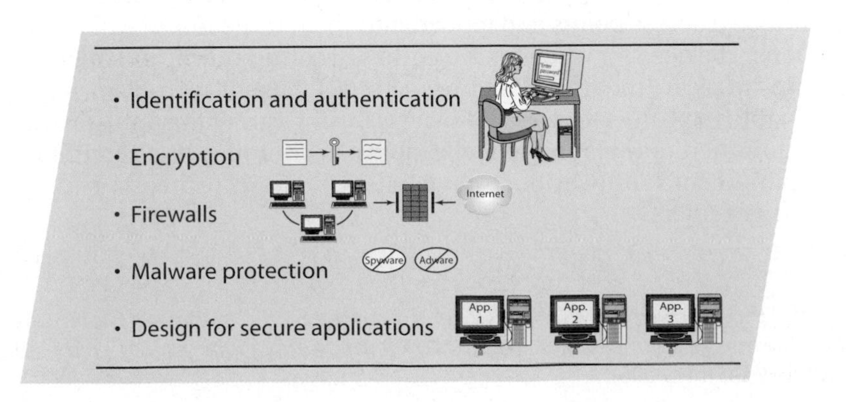

Figure 12-5
Technical Safeguards

You can remember authentication methods by understanding they fall into three categories: what you know (password or PIN), what you have (smart card), and what you are (biometric).

Single Sign-on for Multiple Systems

Information systems often require multiple sources of authentication. For example, when you sign on to your personal computer, you need to be authenticated. When you access the LAN in your department, you need to be authenticated again. When you traverse your organization's WAN, you will need to be authenticated to even more networks. Also, if your request requires database data, the DBMS server that manages that database will authenticate you yet again.

It would be annoying to enter a name and password for every one of these resources. You might have to use and remember five or six different passwords just to access the data you need to perform your job. It would be equally undesirable to send your password across all of these networks. The further your password travels, the greater the risk it can be compromised.

Instead, today's operating systems have the capability to authenticate you to networks and other servers. You sign on to your local computer and provide authentication data; from that point on, your operating system authenticates you to another network or server, which can authenticate you to yet another network and server, and so forth.

A system called **Kerberos** authenticates users without sending their passwords across the computer network. Developed by the Massachusetts Institute of Technology (MIT), Kerberos uses a complicated system of "tickets" to enable users to obtain services from networks and other servers. Windows, Linux, Unix, and other operating systems employ Kerberos and thus can authenticate user requests across networks of computers using a mixture of these operating systems.

Despite all that we know about the need for protecting passwords, compliance with password-protection guidelines is still lacking, as the Opposing Forces Guide *on page 486 demonstrates.*

This discussion indicates another reason why you must protect your user name and password. Once you have authenticated yourself on your local system, your operating system will authenticate you to networks and other servers. Someone who obtains your name and password will gain access not only to your computer, but via intersystem authentication, to many other computers and servers as well. The bottom line: Protect your passwords!

Wireless Access

For a wired network, a potential intruder must obtain physical access to the network. For a wireless network, however, no direct connection is needed. Drive-by sniffers can walk or drive around business or residential neighborhoods with a wireless computer and locate dozens, or even hundreds, of wireless networks. The wireless network will broadcast whether it is protected. If it is not, the sniffer can use it to obtain free access to the Internet or to connect to LANs that are connected to the access point.

In 2004, in a short ride through the Back Bay section of Boston, Massachusetts, a security consultant found 2,676 wireless connections, most of which were residential. Of those, almost half were unprotected.[3] Anyone with a wireless device could have connected to those unprotected access points and tapped into the Internet for free or taken more disruptive actions. The need for wireless security has become known, and more private wireless networks are secure today than they were in 2004. It is still a problem, however.

It is possible to protect wireless networks. Businesses with sophisticated communications equipment use elaborate techniques—techniques that require the support of highly trained communications specialists. Common protections use VPNs and special security servers.

[3]Bruce Mohl, "Tap into Neighbors' Wi-Fi? Why Not, Some Say," *The Boston Globe*, July 4, 2004, *boston.com/business/technology/articles/2004/07/04/tap_into_neighbors_wifi_why_not_some_say?pg=1* (accessed July 2005).

For the less sophisticated SOHO market, wireless networks are less secure. The IEEE 802.11 Committee, the group that develops and maintains wireless standards, first developed a wireless security standard called **Wired Equivalent Privacy (WEP)**. Unfortunately, WEP was insufficiently tested before it was deployed, and it has serious flaws. In response, the IEEE 802.11 committee developed improved wireless security standards known as **WPA (Wi-Fi Protected Access)** and a newer, better version, called **WPA2**. Unfortunately, only newer wireless devices can use these techniques.

Wireless security technology is changing rapidly. By the time you read this, even newer security standards will have been developed. Search the Internet for the term *wireless network security* to learn about the latest standards. In the meantime, on any wireless network you use take the time to enable the highest level of security that you can and be aware that, at present, especially on SOHO networks, wireless networks are not nearly as secure as wired networks.

Encryption

The second technical safeguard in Figure 12-5 is **encryption**. We described some encryption techniques in Chapter 6 (page 206). To review, senders use a key to encrypt a plaintext message and then send the encrypted message to a recipient, who then uses a key to decrypt the message. Figure 12-6 lists five basic encryption techniques.

With **symmetric encryption**, both parties use the same key. With **asymmetric encryption**, the parties use two keys, one that is public and one that is private. A message encoded with one of the keys can be decoded with the other key.

Technique	How It Works	Characteristics
Symmetric	Sender and receiver transmit message using the same key.	Fast, but difficult to get the same key to both parties.
Asymmetric	Sender and receiver transmit message using two keys, one public and one private. Message encrypted with one of the keys can be decrypted with the other.	Public key can be openly transmitted, but needs certificate authority (see below). Slower than symmetric.
SSL/TLS	Works between Levels 4 and 5 of the TCP-OSI architecture. Sender uses public/private key to transmit symmetric key, which both parties use for symmetric encryption—for a limited, brief period.	Used by most Internet applications. A useful and workable hybrid of symmetric and asymmetric.
Digital signatures	Sender hashes message, and uses private key to "sign" a message digest, creating digital signature; sender transmits plaintext message and digital signature. Receiver rehashes the plaintext message and decrypts the digital signature with the user's public key. If the message digests match, receiver knows that message has not been altered.	Ingenious technique for ensuring plaintext has not been altered.
Digital certificates	A trusted third party, the certificate authority (CA), supplies the public key and a digital certificate. Receiver decrypts message with public key (from CA), signed with CA's digital signature.	Eliminates spoofing of public keys. Requires browser to have CA's public key.

Figure 12-6
Basic Encyption Techniques

Asymmetric encryption is slower than symmetric encryption, but it is easier to implement over a network.

Secure Socket Layer (SSL) is a protocol that uses both asymmetric and symmetric encryption. SSL is a protocol layer that works between Level 4 (transport) and Level 5 (application) of the TCP–OSI protocol architecture. With SSL, asymmetric encryption transmits a symmetric key. Both parties then use that key for symmetric encryption for the balance of that session. Because SSL lies between Levels 4 and 5, most Internet applications, including HTTP, FTP, and email programs, can use it.

Netscape originally developed SSL. After a brief skirmish in the marketplace, Microsoft endorsed its use and included it in Internet Explorer and other products. SSL version 1.0 had problems, most of which were removed in version 3.0, which is the version Microsoft endorsed. A later version, with more problems fixed, was renamed **Transport Layer Security (TLS)**.

By either name, SSL or TLS, this is the protocol used whenever you see *https://* in your browser's address bar. As stated in Chapter 6, never send any sensitive data over the Internet unless you see the *s* after *http*.

Using SSL/TLS, the client verifies that it is communicating with the true Web site, and not with a site that is spoofing the true Web site. However, to ease the burden on users, the opposite is not done. Web sites seldom verify the true identity of users. Hence, programs can spoof legitimate users and fool Web sites. Because the consequences affect the Web site and not the client, such spoofing has no effect on the consumer. It is a problem that Web site owners must address, however.

Digital Signatures

Because encryption slows processing, most messages are sent over the Internet as plaintext. By default, email is sent as plaintext. This means, by the way, that you ought not to send your Social Security number, credit card numbers, or any other such numbers in email.

Because email is plaintext, it is possible that someone can intercept your email and change the message unbeknownst to you. For example, suppose a purchasing agent sends an email to one of its vendors with the message, "Please deliver shipment 1000 to our Oakdale facility." It is possible for a third party to intercept the email, remove the words "our Oakdale facility," substitute its own address, and send the message on to its destination.

Digital signatures ensure that plaintext messages are received without alterations. Figure 12-7 summarizes their use. The plaintext message is first *hashed.* **Hashing** is a method of mathematically manipulating the message to create a string of bits that characterize the message. The bit string, called the **message digest**, has a specified, fixed length, regardless of the length of the plaintext. According to one popular standard, message digests are 160 bits long.

Hashing is a one-way process. Any message can be hashed to produce a message digest, but the message digest cannot be unhashed to produce the original message.

Hashing techniques are designed so that if someone changes any part of a message, rehashing the changed message will create a different message digest. For example, the email message with the words "our Oakdale facility" and the same message but with the interceptor's address will generate two different message digests.

Authentication programs use message digests to ensure that plaintext messages have not been altered. The idea is to create a message digest for the original message and to send the message and the message digest to the receiver. The receiver hashes the message it received and compares the resulting message digest to the message digest that was sent with the message. If the two message digests are the same, then the receiver knows that the message was not altered. If they are different, then the message was altered.

For this technique to work, the original message digest must be protected when it is transmitted. Accordingly, as Figure 12-7 shows, the message digest (*MD* in this figure) is encrypted using the sender's private key. The result is called the message's

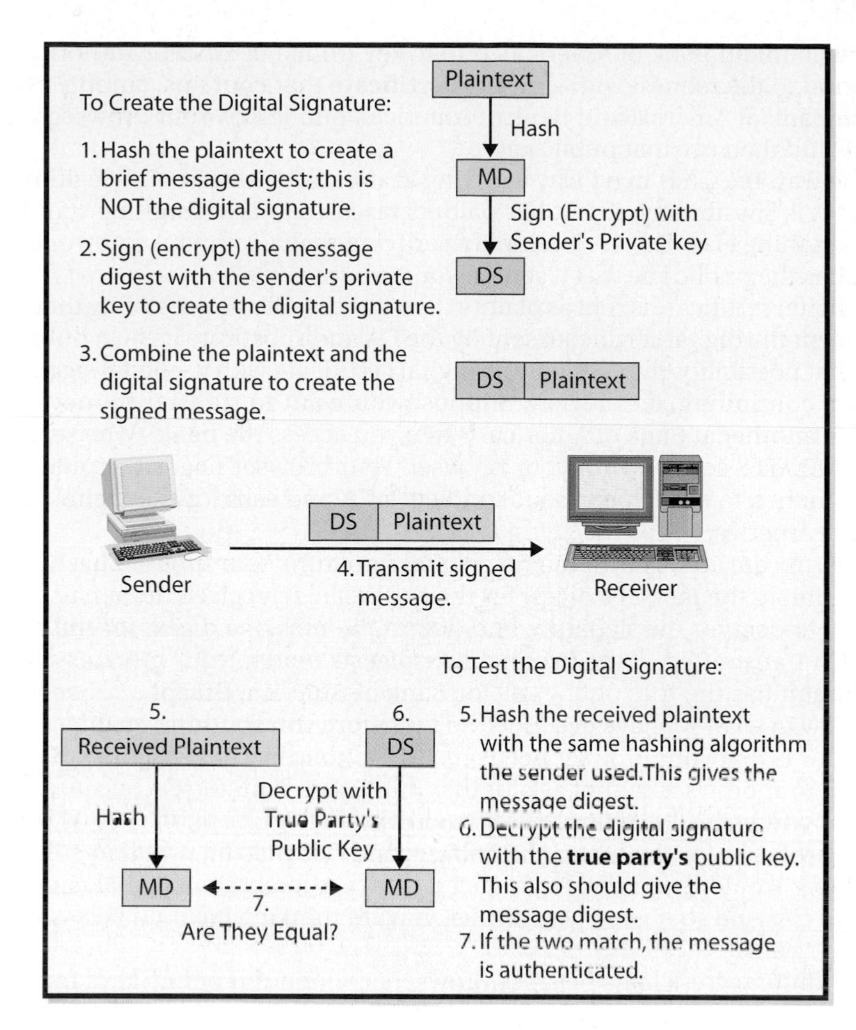

Figure 12-7
Digital Signatures for Message Authentication

Source: Panko, Ray, *Corporate Computer and Network Security*, 1st Edition, © 2004. Reprinted by permission of Pearson Education, Inc., Upper Saddle River, NJ.

digital signature. Applying one's private key to the message digest is called *signing* the message. As shown in step 4 of Figure 12-7, the system sends the signed message to the receiver.

The receiver hashes the plaintext message that arrived, to produce a message digest for the received message. It then decrypts the digital signature with the sender's public key (called the *true party's* public key, in this figure) and compares the message digest for the received message with the original message digest. If they are the same, then the message was not altered. If the message digests differ, then the receiver knows that someone altered the message somewhere along the line.

Only one problem remains: How does the receiver obtain the true party's public key? The receiver cannot ask the sender for its public key, because the sender could be spoofing. For example, if someone is spoofing Bank of America, the spoofer will send the spoofer's public key while claiming that it is sending the public key for Bank of America. The receiver cannot know the received public key is not the true Bank of America public key. Digital certificates prevent such spoofing.

Digital Certificates

When using public keys, a message recipient must know that it has the true party's public key. As just explained, a program that asks a sender to transmit its public key could be fooled. To solve this problem, trusted, independent third-party companies, called **certificate authorities (CAs)**, supply public keys.

Thus, for your browser to obtain the public key for Bank of America, either to conduct a secure session using SSL/TLS or to authenticate a digital signature, your browser will obtain Bank of America's public key from a certificate authority. The CA will respond to the request with a **digital certificate** that contains, among other data, the name Bank of America and Bank of America's public key. Your browser will verify the name and then use that public key.

By the way, the CA is in no way verifying that Bank of America is a legitimate concern, that it is law abiding, that it has paid its taxes, that its accounting standards are high, or anything else. The CA is simplify verifying that a company known as Bank of America has the public key that it sent to your browser.

The digital certificate is sent as plaintext, so there is still the possibility that an entity can intercept the digital certificate sent by the CA and substitute its own public key. To prevent that possibility, the CA signs the digital certificate with its digital signature.

Before continuing, let's review. Suppose you want to transfer money from one account to another at Bank of America. When you access the bank's Web server, it initiates an SSL/TLS session with your browser. Your browser needs the public key for Bank of America to participate, so it contacts a CA and asks for the digital certificate for Bank of America.

The certificate arrives with the CA's digital signature. Your browser hashes the certificate to obtain the message digest for the certificate it received. It then uses the CA's public key to decrypt the signature and obtain the message digest for the certificate that the CA transmitted. If the two message digests match, your browser can rely on the fact that it has the true public key for Bank of America. Except . . . See if you can find the flaw in what we have described so far before you continue reading.

The flaw is that your browser needs the CA's public key to authenticate the digital certificate. Your browser cannot ask for that public key from the CA because someone could be spoofing the CA. Your browser could obtain the CA's public key by requesting a digital certificate for the first CA from a second CA, but the problem still remains. Your browser would then need to contact a third CA to obtain a digital certificate for the second CA. And so it goes. Meanwhile, you are thinking it would be easier to walk down to the bank.

The infinite regress halts because browsers contain the public keys for the common CAs in their program code. As long as you receive your browser from a reputable source, you can rely on the public keys it uses when authenticating digital certificates from the CAs it uses.

Firewalls

Firewalls are the third technical safeguard listed in Figure 12-5. A **firewall** is a computing device that prevents unauthorized network access. A firewall can be a special-purpose computer or it can be a program on a general-purpose computer or on a router.

Organizations normally use multiple firewalls. A **perimeter firewall** sits outside the organizational network; it is the first device that Internet traffic encounters. In addition to perimeter firewalls, some organizations employ **internal firewalls** inside the organizational network. Figure 12-8 shows the use of a perimeter firewall that protects all of an organization's computers and a second internal firewall that protects a LAN.

A **packet-filtering firewall** examines each packet and determines whether to let the packet pass. To make this decision, it examines the source address, the destination addresses, and other data.

Packet-filtering firewalls can prohibit outsiders from starting a session with any user behind the firewall. They can also disallow traffic from particular sites, such as known hacker addresses. They also can prohibit traffic from legitimate, but unwanted addresses, such as competitors' computers. Firewalls can filter outbound traffic as well. They can keep employees from accessing specific sites, such as competitors' sites, sites with pornographic material, or popular news sites.

A firewall has an **access control list (ACL)**, which encodes the rules stating which packets are to be allowed and which are to be prohibited. As a future manager, if you have particular sites with which you do not want your employees to communicate,

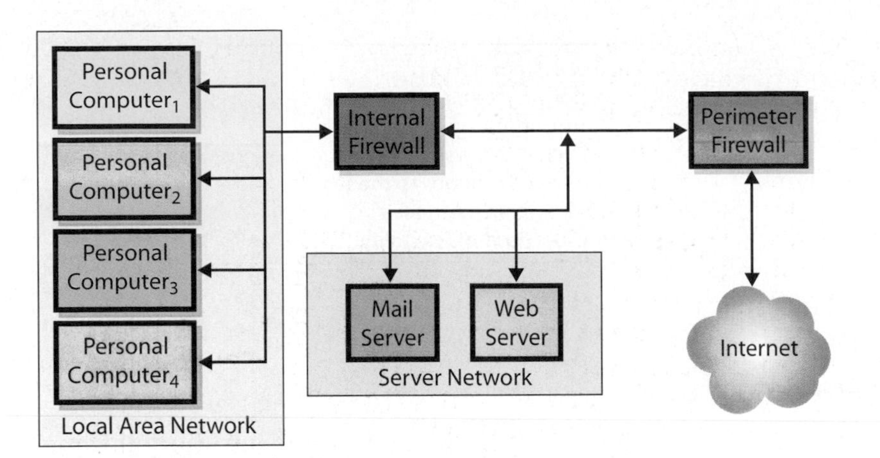

Figure 12-8
Use of Multiple Firewalls

you can ask your IS department to establish rules to enforce your policy in the ACL for the routers that protect your network. Most likely, your IS organization has a procedure for making such requests.

Packet-filtering firewalls are the simplest type of firewall. Other firewalls filter on a more sophisticated basis. If you take a data communications class, you will learn about them. For now, just understand that firewalls help to protect organizational computers from unauthorized network access.

No computer should connect to the Internet without firewall protection. Many ISPs provide firewalls for their customers. By nature, these firewalls are generic. Large organizations supplement such generic firewalls with their own. Most SOHO routers include firewalls, and Windows XP and Vista have built-in firewalls as well. Third parties also license firewall products.

Malware Protection

The next technical safeguard in our list in Figure 12-5 is malware. The term **malware** has several definitions. Here we will use the broadest one: *Malware* is viruses, worms, Trojan horses, spyware, and adware. We discussed viruses, worms, and Trojan horses in Chapter 4 (page 125); you should review that material now if you have forgotten their definitions.

Spyware and Adware

Spyware programs are installed on the user's computer without the user's knowledge or permission. Spyware resides in the background and, unknown to the user, observes the user's actions and keystrokes, monitors computer activity, and reports the user's activities to sponsoring organizations. Some malicious spyware captures keystrokes to obtain user names, passwords, account numbers, and other sensitive information. Other spyware supports marketing analyses, observing what users do, Web sites visited, products examined and purchased, and so forth.

Adware is similar to spyware in that it is installed without the user's permission and that it resides in the background and observes user behavior. Most adware is benign in that it does not perform malicious acts or steal data. It does, however, watch user activity and produce pop-up ads. Adware can also change the user's default window or modify search results and switch the user's search engine. For the most part, it is just annoying, but users should be concerned any time they have unknown programs on their computers that perform unknown functions.

Figure 12-9 (next page) lists some of the symptoms of adware and spyware. Sometimes these symptoms develop slowly over time as more and more malware components are installed. Should these symptoms occur on your computer, remove the spyware or adware using antimalware programs.

Figure 12-9
Spyware and Adware Symptoms

- Slow system start up
- Sluggish system performance
- Many pop-up advertisements
- Suspicious browser homepage changes
- Suspicious changes to the taskbar and other system interfaces
- Unusual hard-disk activity

Malware Safeguards

Fortunately, it is possible to avoid most malware using the following malware safeguards:

1. *Install antivirus and antispyware programs on your computer.* Your IS department will have a list of recommended (perhaps required) programs for this purpose. If you choose a program for yourself, choose one from a reputable vendor. Check reviews of antimalware software on the Web before purchasing.
2. *Set up your antimalware programs to scan your computer frequently.* You should scan your computer at least once a week and possibly more. When you detect malware code, use the antimalware software to remove them. If the code cannot be removed, contact your IS department or antimalware vendor.
3. *Update malware definitions.* **Malware definitions**—patterns that exist in malware code—should be downloaded frequently. Anti-malware vendors update these definitions continuously, and you should install these updates as they become available.
4. *Open email attachments only from known sources.* Also, even when opening attachments from known sources, do so with great care. According to professor and security expert Ray Panko, about 90 percent of all viruses are spread by email attachments.[4] This statistic is not surprising, because most organizations are protected by firewalls. With a properly configured firewall, email is the only outside-initiated traffic that can reach user computers.

   Most antimalware programs check email attachments for malware code. However, all users should form the habit of *never* opening an email attachment from an unknown source. Also, if you receive an unexpected email from a known source or an email from a known source that has a suspicious subject, odd spelling, or poor grammar, do not open the attachment without first verifying with the known source that the attachment is legitimate.
5. *Promptly install software updates from legitimate sources.* Unfortunately, all programs are chock full of security holes; vendors are fixing them as rapidly as they are discovered, but the practice is inexact. Install patches to the operating system and application programs promptly.
6. *Browse only in reputable Internet neighborhoods.* It is possible for some malware to install itself when you do nothing more than open a Web page. Don't go there!

Malware Is a Serious Problem

America Online (AOL) and the National Cyber Security Alliance conducted a malware study using Internet users in 2004. They asked the users a series of questions and then, with the users' permission, they scanned the users' computers to determine how accurately the users understood malware problems on their own computers. This fascinating study can be found online at *http://staysafeonline.info/news/ safety_study_v04.pdf.*

[4]Ray Panko, *Corporate Computer and Network Security* (Prentice Hall, 2004), p. 165.

Question	User Response	Scan Results
Do you have a virus on your computer?	Yes: 6%	Yes: 19%
	No: 44%	No: 81%
	Don't know: 50%	
Average (maximum) number of viruses on infected computer		2.4 (213)
How often do you update your antivirus software?	Last week: 71%	Last week: 33%
	Last month: 12%	Last month: 34%
	Last 6 months: 5%	Last 6 months: 6%
	Longer than 6 months: 12%	Longer than 6 months: 12%
Do you think you have spyware or adware on your computer?	Yes: 53%	Yes: 80%
	No: 47%	No: 20%
Average (maximum) number of spyware/adware components on computer		93 (1,059)
Did you give permission to someone to install these components on your computer?	Yes: 5% No: 95%	

Figure 12-10
Malware Survey Results

Source: AOL/NCSA Online Safety Study, conducted by America Online and the National Cyber Security Alliance. October 2004, *http://staysafeonline.info/news/safety_study_v04.pdf* (accessed March 2005).

Figure 12-10 shows a few important results from this study. Among the users, 6 percent thought they had a virus, but 18 percent actually did. Further, half of those surveyed did not know if they had a virus. Of those computers having viruses, an average of 2.4 viruses were found; the maximum number of viruses found on a single computer was 213!

When asked how often they update their antivirus definitions, 71 percent of the users reported that they had done so within the last week. Actually, only one-third of the users had updated their definitions that recently.

Figure 12-10 shows similar results for spyware. The average user computer had 93 spyware components. The maximum number found on a computer was 1,059. Note that only 5 percent of the users had given permission for the spyware to be installed.

Although the problem of malware will never be eradicated, you can reduce its size by following the six safeguards just listed. You should take these actions as a habit, and you should ensure that employees you manage take them as well.

Design Secure Applications

The final technical safeguard in Figure 12-5 concerns the design of applications. As a future IS user, you will not design programs yourself. However, you should ensure that any information system developed for you and your department includes security as one of the application requirements.

Q4 What Data Safeguards Are Available?

Data safeguards are measures used to protect databases and other organizational data. Figure 12-11 (next page) summarizes some important data safeguards. First, the organization should specify user data rights and responsibilities. Second, those rights should be enforced by user accounts that are authenticated at least by passwords.

Figure 12-11
Data Safeguards

- Data rights and responsibilities
- Rights enforced by user accounts authenticated by passwords
- Data encryption
- Backup and recovery procedures
- Physical security

The organization should protect sensitive data by storing it in encrypted form. Such encryption uses one or more keys in ways similar to that described for data communication encryption. One potential problem with stored data, however, is that the key might be lost or that disgruntled or terminated employees might destroy it. Because of this possibility, when data are encrypted, a trusted party should have a copy of the encryption key. This safety procedure is sometimes called **key escrow**.

Another data safeguard is to periodically create backup copies of database contents. The organization should store at least some of these backups off premises, possibly in a remote location. Additionally, IT personnel should periodically practice recovery, to ensure that the backups are valid and that effective recovery procedures exist. Do not assume that just because a backup is made the database is protected.

Physical security is another data safeguard. The computers that run the DBMS and all devices that store database data should reside in locked, controlled-access facilities. If not, they are subject not only to theft, but also to damage. For better security, the organization should keep a log showing who entered the facility, when, and for what purpose.

In some cases, organizations contract with other companies to manage their databases. If so, all of the safeguards in Figure 12-11 should be part of the service contract. Also, the contract should give the owners of the data permission to inspect the premises of the database operator and to interview its personnel on a reasonable schedule.

Q5 What Human Safeguards Are Available?

Human safeguards involve the people and procedure components of information systems. In general, human safeguards result when authorized users follow appropriate procedures for system use and recovery. Restricting access to authorized users requires effective authentication methods and careful user account management. In addition, appropriate security procedures must be designed as part of every information system, and users should be trained on the importance and use of those procedures. In this section, we will consider the development of human safeguards first for employees and then for nonemployee personnel.

Human Safeguards for Employees

Figure 12-12 lists security considerations for employees. The first is the creation of appropriate position definitions.

Position Definitions

It is impossible to have effective human safeguards unless job tasks and responsibilities are clearly defined for each employee position. In general, job descriptions should provide a separation of duties and authorities. For example, no single individual should be allowed to approve expenses, write checks, and account for the disbursement. Instead, one person should approve expenses, another person pay them, and a

Figure 12-12
Security Policy for In-House Staff

- Position definition
  - Separate duties and authorities.
  - Determine least privilege.
  - Document position sensitivity.

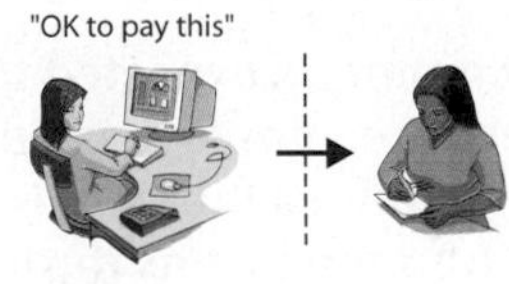

- Hiring and screening

- Dissemination and enforcement (responsibility, accountability, compliance)

- Termination
  - Friendly

  - Unfriendly

third account for the transaction. Similarly, in inventory, no single person should be allowed to authorize an inventory withdrawal, remove the items from inventory, and account for the removal.

Given appropriate job descriptions, users' computer accounts should give users the least possible privilege necessary to perform their jobs. For example, users whose job description does not include modifying data should be given accounts with read-only privilege. Similarly, user accounts should prohibit users from accessing data they do not need. Because of the problem of semantic security (Chapter 9, page 360), access to seemingly innocuous data should be limited if the employee does not need that data for his or her job.

Finally, the security sensitivity should be documented for each position. Some jobs involve highly sensitive data (e.g., employee compensation, salesperson quotas, and proprietary marketing or technical data). Other positions involve no sensitive data. Documenting *position sensitivity* enables security personnel to prioritize their activities in accordance with the possible risk and loss.

Hiring and Screening

Security considerations should be part of the hiring process. Of course, if the position involves no sensitive data and no access to information systems, then screening for information systems security purposes will be minimal. When hiring for high-sensitivity positions, however, extensive interviews, references, and background investigations are appropriate. Note, too, that security screening applies not only to new employees, but also to employees who are promoted into sensitive positions.

Dissemination and Enforcement

Obviously, employees cannot be expected to follow security procedures if they do not know about them. Therefore, employees need to be trained on security policies, procedures, and the responsibilities they will have.

Employee security training begins during new-employee training, with the explanation of general security policies and procedures. That general training must be amplified in accordance with the position's sensitivity and responsibilities. Promoted employees should receive security training that is appropriate to their new positions. The company should not provide user accounts and passwords until employees have completed required security training.

Enforcement consists of three interdependent factors: responsibility, accountability, and compliance. First, the company should clearly define the security *responsibilities* of each position. The design of the security program should be such that employees can be held *accountable* for security violations. Procedures should exist so that when critical data are lost, it is possible to determine how the loss occurred and who is accountable. Finally, the security program should encourage security *compliance*. Employee activities should regularly be monitored for compliance, and management should specify disciplinary action to be taken in light of noncompliance.

Management attitude is crucial: Employee compliance is greater when management demonstrates, both in word and deed, a serious concern for security. If managers write passwords on staff bulletin boards, shout passwords down hallways, or ignore physical security procedures, then employee security attitudes and employee security compliance will suffer. Note, too, that effective security is a continuing management responsibility. Regular reminders about security are essential.

Termination

Companies also must establish security policies and procedures for the termination of employees. Most employee terminations are friendly and occur as the result of promotion, retirement, or when the employee resigns to take another position. Standard human resources policies should ensure that system administrators receive notification in advance of the employee's last day, so that they can remove accounts and passwords. Procedures for recovering keys for encrypted data and any other security assets must be part of the employee's out-processing.

Unfriendly termination is more difficult because employees may be tempted to take malicious or harmful actions. In such a case, system administrators might need to remove user accounts and passwords prior to notifying the employee of her termination. Other actions may be needed to protect the company's information assets. A terminated sales employee, for example, might attempt to take the company's confidential customer and sales-prospect data for future use at another company. The terminating employer should take steps to protect those data prior to the termination.

The human resources department should be aware of the importance of giving IS administrators early notification of employee termination. No blanket policy exists; the information systems department must assess each case on an individual basis.

Human Safeguards for Nonemployee Personnel

Business requirements may necessitate opening information systems to nonemployee personnel—temporary personnel, vendors, partner personnel (employees of business partners), and the public. Although temporary personnel can be screened, to reduce costs the screening will be abbreviated from that for employees. In most cases, companies cannot screen either vendor or partner personnel. Of course, public users cannot be screened at all. Similar limitations pertain to security training and compliance testing.

In the case of temporary, vendor, and partner personnel, the contracts that govern the activity should call for security measures appropriate to the sensitivity of the data and the IS resources involved. Companies should require vendors and partners to perform appropriate screening and security training. The contract also should mention specific security responsibilities that are particular to the work to be performed. Companies should provide accounts and passwords with the least privilege and remove those accounts as soon as possible.

The situation differs with public users of Web sites and other openly accessible information systems. It is exceedingly difficult and expensive to hold public users accountable for security violations. In general, the best safeguard from threats from public users is to *harden* the Web site or other facility against attack as much as possible. **Hardening** a site means to take extraordinary measures to reduce a system's vulnerability. Hardened sites use special versions of the operating system, and they lock down or eliminate operating systems features and functions that are not required by the application. Hardening is actually a technical safeguard, but we mention it here as the most important safeguard against public users.

Finally, note that the business relationship with the public, and with some partners, differs from that with temporary personnel and vendors. The public and some partners use the information system to receive a benefit. Consequently, safeguards need to protect such users from internal company security problems. A disgruntled employee who maliciously changes prices on a Web site potentially damages both public users and business partners. As one IT manager put it, "Rather than protecting ourselves from them, we need to protect them from us." This is an extension of the fifth principle in Figure 12-3.

Account Administration

The third human safeguard is account administration. The administration of user accounts, passwords, and help-desk policies and procedures are important components of the security system.

Account Management

Account management concerns the creation of new user accounts, the modification of existing account permissions, and the removal of unneeded accounts. Information system administrators perform all of these tasks, but account users have the responsibility to notify the administrators of the need for these actions. The IS department should create standard procedures for this purpose. As a future user, you can improve your relationship with IS personnel by providing early and timely notification of the need for account changes.

The existence of accounts that are no longer necessary is a serious security threat. IS administrators cannot know when an account should be removed; it is up to users and managers to give such notification.

Password Management

Passwords are the primary means of authentication. They are important not just for access to the user's computer, but also for authentication to other networks and servers to which the user may have access. Because of the importance of passwords, NIST recommends that employees be required to sign statements similar to that shown in Figure 12-13 (next page).

When an account is created, users should immediately change the password they are given to a password of their own. In fact, well-constructed systems require the user to change the password on first use.

Additionally, users should change passwords frequently thereafter. Some systems will require a password change every 3 months or perhaps more frequently. Users grumble at the nuisance of making such changes, but frequent password changes reduce not only the risk of password loss, but also the extent of damage if an existing password is compromised.

Figure 12-13
Sample Account Acknowledgment Form

Source: National Institute of Standards and Technology, *Introduction to Computer Security The NIST Handbook*, Publication 800–12, p. 114.

I hereby acknowledge personal receipt of the system password(s) associated with the user IDs listed below. I understand that I am responsible for protecting the password(s), will comply with all applicable system security standards, and will not divulge my password(s) to any person. I further understand that I must report to the Information Systems Security Officer any problem I encounter in the use of the password(s) or when I have reason to believe that the private nature of my password(s) has been compromised.

Some users create two passwords and switch back and forth between those two. This strategy results in poor security, and some password systems do not allow the user to reuse recently used passwords. Again, users may view this policy as a nuisance, but it is important.

Help-Desk Policies

In the past, help desks have been a serious security risk. A user who had forgotten his password would call the help desk and plead for the help-desk representative to tell him his password or to reset the password to something else. "I can't get this report out without it!" was (and is) a common lament.

The problem for help-desk representatives is, of course, that they have no way of determining that they are talking with the true user and not someone spoofing a true user. But, they are in a bind: If they do not help in some way, the help desk is perceived to be the "unhelpful desk."

To resolve such problems, many systems give the help-desk representative a means of authenticating the user. Typically, the help-desk information system has answers to questions that only the true user would know, such as the user's birthplace, mother's maiden name, or last four digits of an important account number. Often, too, the method by which the new password can be obtained is sent to the user in an email. Email, as you learned, is sent as plaintext, however, so the new password itself ought not to be emailed. If you ever receive notification that your password was reset when you did not request such a reset, immediately contact IS security. Someone has compromised your account.

All such help-desk measures reduce the strength of the security system, and, if the employee's position is sufficiently sensitive, they might create too large a vulnerability. In such a case, the user may just be out of luck. The account will be deleted, and the user must repeat the account-application process.

Systems Procedures

Figure 12-14 shows a grid of procedure types—normal operation, backup, and recovery. Procedures of each type should exist for each information system. For example, the order-entry system will have procedures of each of these types, as will the Web storefront, the inventory system, and so forth. The definition and use of standardized procedures reduces the likelihood of computer crime and other malicious activity by insiders. It also ensures that the system's security policy is enforced.

Procedures exist for both users and operations personnel. For each type of user, the company should develop procedures for normal, backup, and recovery operations. As a future user, you will be primarily concerned with user procedures. Normal-use procedures should provide safeguards appropriate to the sensitivity of the information system.

Backup procedures concern the creation of backup data to be used in the event of failure. Whereas operations personnel have the responsibility for backing up system databases and other systems data, departmental personnel have the need to back up data on their own computers. Good questions to ponder are, "What would happen if I

	System users	Operations personnel
Normal operation	Use the system to perform job tasks, with security appropriate to sensitivity.	Operate data center equipment, manage networks, run Web servers, and related operational tasks.
Backup	Prepare for loss of system functionality.	Back up Web site resources, databases, administrative data, account and password data, and other data.
Recovery	Accomplish job tasks during failure. Know tasks to do during system recovery.	Recover systems from backed up data. Role of help desk during recovery.

Figure 12-14
Systems Procedures

lost my computer or iPhone tomorrow?" "What would happen if someone dropped my computer during an airport security inspection?" "What would happen if my computer were stolen?" Employees should ensure that they back up critical business data on their computers. The IS department can help in this effort by designing backup procedures and making backup facilities available.

Finally, systems analysts should develop procedures for system recovery. First, how will the department manage its affairs when a critical system is unavailable? Customers will want to order, and manufacturing will want to remove items from inventory even though a critical information system is unavailable. How will the department respond? Once the system is returned to service, how will records of business activities during the outage be entered into the system? How will service be resumed? The system developers should ask and answer these questions and others like them and develop procedures accordingly.

As the Innovation in Practice *box on page 482 indicates, iPhones and similar devices are causing new security threats that companies will need to address.*

Security Monitoring

Security monitoring is the last of the human safeguards we will consider. Important monitoring functions are activity log analyses, security testing, and investigating and learning from security incidents.

Many information system programs produce *activity logs*. Firewalls produce logs of their activities, including lists of all dropped packets, infiltration attempts, and unauthorized access attempts from within the firewall. DBMS products produce logs of successful and failed log-ins. Web servers produce voluminous logs of Web activities. The operating systems in personal computers can produce logs of log-ins and firewall activities.

None of these logs add any value to an organization unless someone looks at them. Accordingly, an important security function is to analyze these logs for threat patterns, successful and unsuccessful attacks, and evidence of security vulnerabilities.

Additionally, companies should test their security programs. Both in-house personnel and outside security consultants should conduct such testing.

Another important monitoring function is to investigate security incidents. How did the problem occur? Have safeguards been created to prevent a recurrence of such problems? Does the incident indicate vulnerabilities in other portions of the security system? What else can be learned from the incident?

Security systems reside in a dynamic environment. Organization structures change. Companies are acquired or sold; mergers occur. New systems require new security measures. New technology changes the security landscape, and new threats arise. Security personnel must constantly monitor the situation and determine if the existing security policy and safeguards are adequate. If changes are needed, security personnel need to take appropriate action.

Security, like quality, is an ongoing process. There is no final state that represents a secure system or company. Instead, companies must monitor security on a continuing basis.

INNOVATION IN PRACTICE

iPHONE CONTROL?

In Chapter 11, you were asked to take the role of CTO and describe the opportunities presented by iPhones and similar devices. As you learned, such devices offer many new opportunities for delivering information systems services, while enabling employees to blend their personal and professional lives.

However (with technology there is always a however), consider iPhones from a security standpoint. iPhones are easily lost, stolen, or broken. Employees use them wherever they happen to be, hence it is difficult, if not impossible, to know what employees have been doing with organizational systems. Who knows what might happen? Employees could be selling downloaded customer data to the competition over public networks at Starbucks. An employee's teenage son could be moving inventory around your warehouses using the ERP interface on your employee's iPhone. Or, an employee could use her iPhone to take a picture of your secret prototype product and mail it to Mom and Dad, who mail it to their neighbor, who puts it on his personal blog site for all the world to see. All of that could be perfectly innocent, or not.

Meanwhile back at headquarters, the corporate officers are signing Sarbanes-Oxley documents. What is the contingent liability of iPhones for system access or data downloading?

What is the IS department to do? Refuse iPhone access to corporate systems? Not likely, at least not for long. Once the iPhone and other devices catch on, there will be no closing that door. IT professionals can demand improved device security, they can develop policies and procedures, but they cannot keep employees from using the devices they like.

The military and other high-security data centers have a policy that any electronic device that enters a secure area never leaves that area. If you enter such a data center with a laptop or even a memory stick, you will never see it again. (You sign documents agreeing to this policy before you are allowed to enter the area.) What would happen if someone entered such a data center with an iPhone? Recall that iPhones have cameras and cell phone access to the Internet.

One technology might offer some control. **Digital rights management (DRM)** refers, in most cases, to technology and products for protecting entertainment content. However, the term **E-DRM**, or **enterprise-DRM** refers to the use of such technology for protecting documents. With it, documents can be restricted for viewing by certain people; they can expire; the ability to print them can be limited; and other restrictions can be created as well.

Clearly, iPhones and similar devices represent a serious security threat. You and a team of your classmates will have an opportunity to solve this problem in Collaboration Exercise 2, on page 492.

Q6 How Should Organizations Respond to Security Incidents?

Every organization needs to be prepared for security incidents. Publicly traded companies are required by the Sarbanes-Oxley Act to do so. Other organizations should do so as a matter of good management. When an incident occurs, whether from an act of nature or from a human threat, time is of the essence. Employees need to know what to do and how to do it. In this section we will consider backup and recovery sites and incident response plans.

Disaster-Recovery Backup Sites

A computer *disaster* is a substantial loss of computing infrastructure caused by acts of nature, crime, or terrorist activity. As stated several times, the best way to solve a problem is not to have it. The best safeguard against a natural disaster is appropriate location. If possible, place computing centers, Web farms, and other computer facilities in locations not prone to floods, earthquakes, hurricanes, tornados, or avalanches. Even in those locations, place infrastructure in unobtrusive buildings, basements, backrooms, and similar locations well within the physical perimeter of the organization.

- Locate infrastructure in safe location.
- Identify mission-critical systems.
- Identify resources needed to run those systems.
- Prepare remote backup facilities.
- Train and rehearse.

Figure 12-15
Disaster Preparedness Tasks

Also, locate computing infrastructure in fire-resistant buildings designed to house expensive and critical equipment.

However, sometimes business requirements necessitate locating the computing infrastructure in undesirable locations. Also, even at a good location, disasters do occur. Therefore, many businesses prepare backup processing centers in locations geographically removed from the primary processing site.

Figure 12-15 lists major disaster-preparedness tasks. After choosing a safe location for the computing infrastructure, the organization should identify all mission-critical applications. These are applications without which the organization cannot carry on and which, if lost for any period of time, could cause the organization's failure. The next step is to identify all resources necessary to run those systems. Such resources include computers, operating systems, application programs, databases, administrative data, procedure documentation, and trained personnel.

Next, the organization creates backups for the critical resources at the remote processing center. In the opening interview, Ross Buchholz described how RagingWire can take over another company's processing with no forewarning. Such a capability is sometimes called a **hot site**. Hot sites are expensive; organizations pay $250,000 or more per month for such services. **Cold sites**, in contrast, provide computers and office space. They are cheaper to lease, but customers install and manage systems themselves. The total cost of a cold side, including all customer labor and other expenses, might not necessarily be less than the cost of a hot site.

Once the organization has backups in place, it must train and rehearse cutover of operations from the primary center to the backup. In the case of a hot site, employees must know how to ensure the handoff occurred without problem, how to run systems while the hot site is active, and how to recover processing when the primary site is again operational. For cold sites, employees must know how to apply backups, how to start systems, and how to run systems from the cold site location. As with all emergency procedures, periodic refresher rehearsals are mandatory.

Backup facilities are expensive; however, the costs of establishing and maintaining that facility are a form of insurance. Senior management must make the decision to prepare such a facility, by balancing the risks, benefits, and costs.

Incident-Response Plan

The last component of a security plan that we will consider is incident response. Figure 12-16 lists the major factors. First, every organization should have an incident-response plan as part of the security program. No organization should wait until some

- Have plan in place
- Centralized reporting
- Specific responses
  - Speed
  - Preparation pays
  - Don't make problem worse
- Practice!

Figure 12-16
Factors in Incident Response

asset has been lost or compromised before deciding what to do. The plan should include how employees are to respond to security problems, whom they should contact, the reports they should make, and steps they can take to reduce further loss.

Consider, for example, a virus. An incident-response plan will stipulate what an employee should do when he notices the virus. It should specify whom to contact and what to do. It may stipulate that the employee should turn off his computer and physically disconnect from the network. The plan should also indicate what users with wireless computers should do.

The plan should provide centralized reporting of all security incidents. Such reporting will enable an organization to determine if it is under systematic attack or whether an incident is isolated. Centralized reporting also allows the organization to learn about security threats, take consistent actions in response, and apply specialized expertise to all security problems.

When an incident does occur, speed is of the essence. Viruses and worms can spread very quickly across an organization's networks, and a fast response will help to mitigate the consequences. Because of the need for speed, preparation pays. The incident-response plan should identify critical personnel and their off-hours contact information. These personnel should be trained on where to go and what to do when they get there. Without adequate preparation, there is substantial risk that the actions of well-meaning people will make the problem worse. Also, the rumor mill will be alive with all sorts of nutty ideas about what to do. A cadre of well-informed, trained personnel will serve to dampen such rumors.

Finally, organizations should periodically practice incident response. Without such practice, personnel will be poorly informed on the response plan, and the plan itself might have flaws that become apparent only during a drill.

Q7 What Is the Extent of Computer Crime?

We do not know the full extent of computer crime. Unfortunately, there is no national census of computer crime, and many organizations are reluctant to admit losses due to adverse publicity. We can rely only on surveys taken of sample organizations. One of the oldest and most respected surveys is the one conducted by the Federal Bureau of Investigation and the Computer Security Institute (known as the FBI/CSI survey).

The FBI/CSI survey has been conducted since 1995, and the organizations involved in the survey are balanced among for-profit and not-for-profit businesses and government agencies. They are also balanced for size of organization, from small to very large. You can obtain a copy of the most recent survey from the site *http://gocsi.com* (registration required).

The 2006 survey addressed computer crime that occurred in 2005 among 616 different organizations. According to the survey, the total loss due to computer crime among these organizations was $52.5 billion. However, for fear of adverse public relations, privacy, or other reasons, many organizations will not report computer crimes they have experienced. In the 2006 survey, in fact, only 313 organizations were willing (or able) to report the size of their loss. Keep in mind this number reflects only the losses of the companies in the survey; we have no idea of the total losses of *all* companies. We can say that there was *at least* $52 billion of loss due to computer crime, but the actual number is likely many, many times larger.

Figure 12-17 lists the top four categories of computer crime. Notice the survey reports the percentage of incidents using the full 616 respondents, but the size of loss is just that attributed to the 313 respondents who reported their losses.

The top four losses were from virus attacks, unauthorized access, laptop theft, and theft of proprietary data. *Unauthorized access* is unfortunately a very broad term that includes attacks and infiltration of computer systems as well as misuse of computer systems by employees. Employees who make personal airline reservations from their computers against organizational policy are included in this category.

Source	Percent Attacked in Prior 6 Months (of 616 respondents)	Total Loss (313 respondents)
Viruses	52 percent	$15.6 billion
Unauthorized access	32 percent	$10.6 billion
Theft of laptop or mobile device	47 percent	$6.6 billion
Theft of proprietary data	9 percent	$6.0 billion

Figure 12-17
Computer Crime, 2006 FBI/CSI Survey

Source: Data from *2006 CSI/FBI Computer Crime and Secuity* www.gocsi.com (accessed August 2007).

However, guard your laptop! Nearly 50 percent of the companies reported theft of laptops or other mobile computer equipment, and a total of $6.6 billion of such devices were lost. The final category was losses due to theft of proprietary data. Such losses must have been huge; only 9 percent of the respondents reported such theft, but the total of such losses was $6 billion.

It is not clear from the survey results how much of the loss of proprietary data was due to data lost on stolen laptops. However, every 6 months or so the press reports another incident in which individual identities were exposed to risk when some employee lost his or her laptop containing proprietary data. As a business professional, make it your practice not to carry out of your office on a laptop any data that you do not need. In general, store proprietary data on servers or removable devices that do not travel with you. If you are required to carry proprietary data on your laptop, outside of your offices, then guard that data appropriately. Behave as if your laptop is a case containing rare gems; in fact, the data it contains may be worth more than a case of rare gems!

That's it! You've reached the end of this text. Take a moment to consider how you will use what you learned, as described in the Reflections Guide *on page 488.*

Opposing Forces

GUIDE

Security Assurance, Hah!

If I have to go to one more employee meeting about security policy, I'm going to scream. The managers talk about threats, and safeguards, and risk, and uncertainty, and all the things they want us to do to improve security. Has any manager ever watched people work in this department?

"Walk through the cubicles here and watch what is happening. I'll bet half the employees are using the password they were assigned the day they started work. I'll bet they've never changed their password, ever! And for the people who have changed their passwords, I'll bet they've changed them to some simpleton word like 'Sesame' or 'MyDogSpot' or something equally absurd.

"Or, open the top drawer of any of my coworkers' desks and guess what you'll find? A little yellow sticky with entries like OrderEntry: 748QPt#7ml, Compensation: RXL87MB, System: ti5587Y. What do you suppose those entries are? Do you think anyone who worked here on a weekend wouldn't know what to do with them? And the only reason they're in the desk drawers is that Martha (our manager) threw a fit when she saw a yellow sticky like that on Terri's monitor.

"I've mentioned all this to Martha several times, but nothing happens. What we need is a good scare. We need somebody to break into the system using one of those passwords and do some damage. Wait—if you enter a system with a readily available password, is that even breaking in? Or is it more like opening a door with a key you were given? Anyway, we need someone to steal something, delete some files, or erase customer balances. Then maybe the idiotic management here would stop talking about security risk assurance and start talking about real security, here on the ground floor!" ■

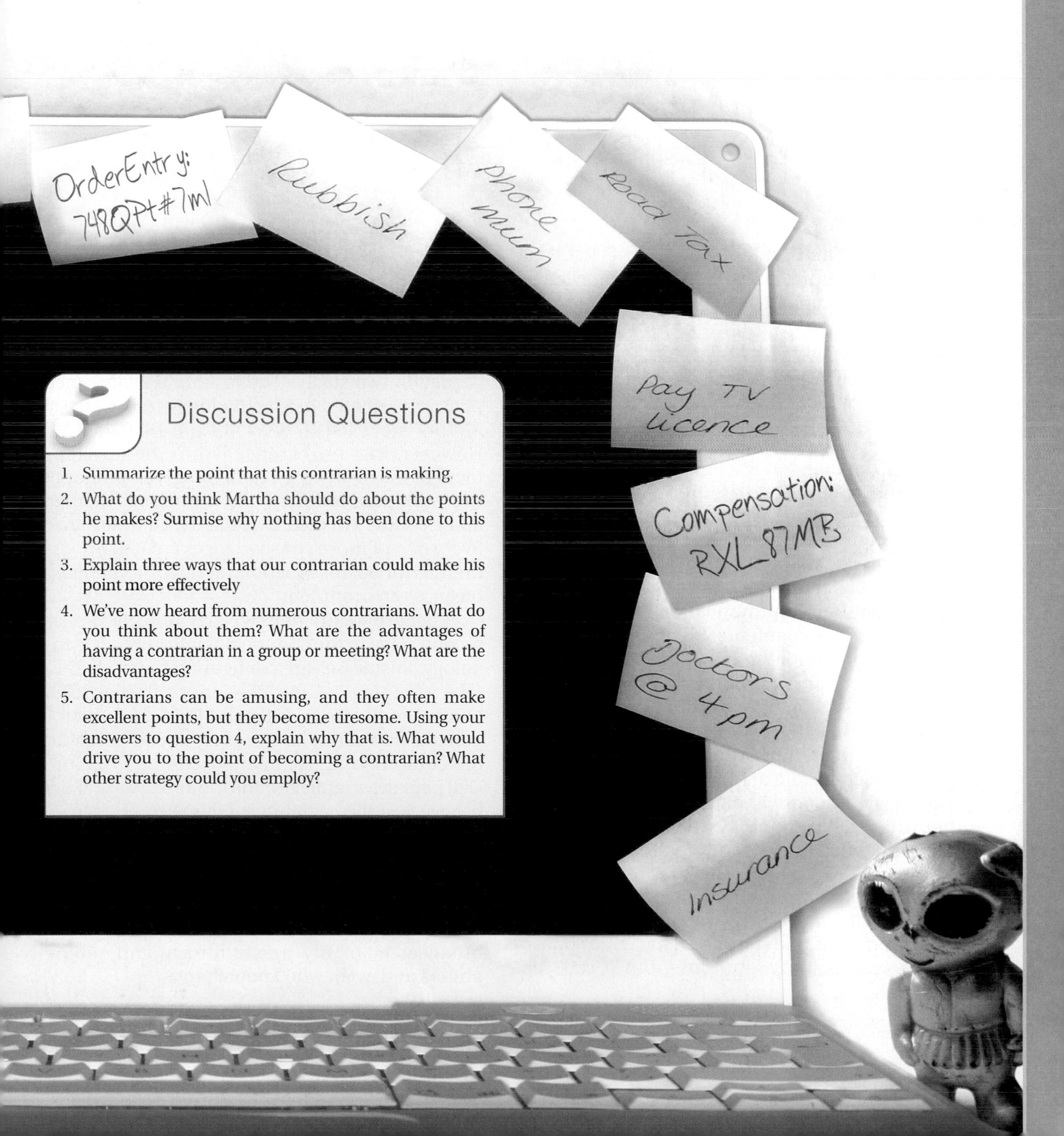

Discussion Questions

1. Summarize the point that this contrarian is making.
2. What do you think Martha should do about the points he makes? Surmise why nothing has been done to this point.
3. Explain three ways that our contrarian could make his point more effectively
4. We've now heard from numerous contrarians. What do you think about them? What are the advantages of having a contrarian in a group or meeting? What are the disadvantages?
5. Contrarians can be amusing, and they often make excellent points, but they become tiresome. Using your answers to question 4, explain why that is. What would drive you to the point of becoming a contrarian? What other strategy could you employ?

The Final, Final Word

Congratulations! You've made it through the entire book. With this knowledge you are well prepared to be an effective user of information systems. And with work and imagination, you can be much more than that. Many interesting opportunities are available to those who can apply information in innovative ways. Your professor has done what she can do, and the rest, as they say, is up to you.

I believe that, today, computer communications and data storage are free—or so close to free that the cost is not worth mentioning. What are the consequences? I do not know, and my nearly 40 years in the IT business make me wary of predictions that extend beyond next year. But I know that free communication and data storage will cause fundamental changes in the business environment. When a company like Getty Images (page 94) can produce its product at zero marginal cost, something's fundamentally different. Further, Getty Images is not the only business with this opportunity.

I suspect the rate of technology development will slow in the next 5 years. Businesses are still digesting the technology that already exists. According to Harry Dent, technology waves always occur in pairs.[5] The first phase is wild exuberance, in which new technology is invented, its capabilities flushed out, and its characteristics understood. That first phase always results in overbuilding, but it sets the stage for the second phase in which surviving companies and entrepreneurs purchase the overbuilt infrastructure for pennies on the dollar and use it for new business purposes.

The automotive industry, for example, proceeded in two stages. The irrational exuberance phase culminated in a technology crash; General Motors' stock fell 75 percent from 1919 to 1921. However, that exuberance led to the development of the highway system, the development of the petroleum industry, and a complete change in the conduct of commerce in the United States. Every one of those consequences created opportunities for business people alert to the changing business environment.

I believe we are poised today to see a similar second stage in the adoption of information technology. Businesses are configuring themselves to take advantage of the new opportunities. Dell builds computers to order and pays for the components days after the customer has paid Dell for the equipment. I use my new computer before Dell pays the supplier for the monitor. Web 2.0 is, I believe, just the beginning of this second stage.

Fiber-optic cable will come to my home (and yours) when telecom companies buy today's dark fiber for pennies on the dollar and light it up. With fiber-optic cable to my house, goodbye video store! Hello DK Enterprises—Internet broadcaster of my music library and sailing photos and, well, who knows?

[5]Harry Dent, *The Next Great Bubble Boom* (New York: The Free Press, 2004), pp. 40 ff.

So, as you finish your business degree, stay alert for new technology-based opportunities. Watch for the second wave and catch it. If you found this course interesting, take more IS classes. Enroll in a database class or a systems development class, even if you don't want to be an IS major. If you're technically oriented, take a data communications class or a security class. If you enjoy this material, become an IS major. If you want to program a computer, great, but if you do not, then don't. There are tremendous opportunities for nonprogrammers in the IS industry. Look for novel applications of IS technology to the emerging business environment. Hundreds of them abound! Find them and have fun! ■

Discussion Question

How will you further your career with what you've learned in this class? Give that question serious thought, and write a memo to yourself to read from time to time as your career progresses.

ACTIVE REVIEW

Use this Active Review to verify that you understand the ideas and concepts that answer the chapter's study questions.

Q1 What are the threats to information security?

List five sources of security threats and describe each. List three security problem types and describe each. Give one example of each of the 15 threats shown in Figure 12-1. Name and describe the three components of an organization's security program. Explain how safeguard types relate to the five components of an information system.

Q2 What is senior management's security role?

Broadly describe senior management's security role. Explain the meaning of each element in Figure 12-3. State three elements of a security policy and explain each. Define *risk* and *uncertainty* and explain the difference between them. Define *safeguard* and *vulnerability* and explain their relationship. Describe two types of consequences. Define *likelihood* and *probable loss* and explain their relationship. Explain computer security risk-management decisions that senior management must make. Explain why uncertainty does not absolve management from security responsibility.

Q3 What technical safeguards are available?

Define *technical safeguard* and explain which of the five components are involved in such safeguards. Explain the use of identification and authentication and describe three types of authentication. List the characteristics of a strong password. Describe the purpose of Kerberos. Explain the security problem posed by wireless networks and describe safeguards that exist for the SOHO market.

Describe symmetric and asymmetric encryption and explain how they are used for SSL/TLS. Explain digital signatures and describe how they are used to detect message modification. Define *digital signature* and *hashing*. Explain the role of digital certificates for preventing the spoofing of public keys. Define *certificate authority*, explain its role, and describe the potential infinite regress when using certificate authorities. Explain how that infinite regress is avoided. Define *firewall, perimeter firewall, internal firewall*, and *packet-filtering firewall*. Explain the role for an access control list. Name the five types of malware as defined in this text and briefly describe each. Describe the six antimalware techniques presented.

Q4 What data safeguards are available?

Define *data safeguards* and give four examples. Explain each.

Q5 What human safeguards are available?

Name the components involved in human safeguards. Name and describe four human safeguards that pertain to employees. Explain how human safeguards pertain to nonemployee personnel. Summarize account administration safeguards. Describe six types of procedures for system users and system operations personnel. Explain three security monitoring functions.

Q6 How should organizations respond to security incidents?

Explain why organizations need to prepare for security incidents ahead of time. Describe ways of avoiding natural disasters; explain the role for remote processing. Define *hot site* and *cold site* and explain the difference, using in your explanation the example cited by Ross Buchholz. Explain the importance of an incident-response plan and the need for centralized reporting. Explain why a rapid, but controlled, incident response is needed and why practice is important.

Q7 What is the extent of computer crime?

Explain why we do not know the true extent of compute crime. Characterize the FBI/CSI computer crime survey. Name the top four categories of computer crime and give rough percentages of the frequency of each type. As an employee, name the single most important thing you can do to reduce computer crime.

KEY TERMS AND CONCEPTS

Access control list (ACL) 472
Adware 473
Asymmetric encryption 469
Authentication 467
Biometric authentication 467
Certificate authority (CA) 471
Cold site 483
Denial of service 460
Digital certificate 472
Digital rights management (DRM) 482
Digital signature 470
Drive-by sniffer 458
Email spoofing 458
Encryption 469
Enterprise-digital rights management (E-DRM) 482
Firewall 472

USING YOUR KNOWLEDGE

1. Search online to find the cheapest way possible to purchase your own credit report. Several sources to check are *http://equifax.com*, *http://experion.com*, and *http://transunion.com*. Assume you can afford to purchase that report (and, if you can, do purchase it).
   a. You should review your credit report for obvious errors. However, other checks are appropriate. Search the Web for guidance on how best to review your credit records. Summarize what you learn.
   b. What actions should you take if you find errors in your credit report?
   c. Define *identity theft*. Search the Web and determine the best course of action if someone thinks he has been the victim of identity theft.
2. Consider the 15 categories of threat in Figure 12-1. Describe the three most serious threats to each of the following businesses:
   a. A local workout studio
   b. A neighborhood accounting firm
   c. A dentist's office
   d. A Honda dealership
3. Describe a potential technical safeguard for each of the threats you identified in your answer to question 2.
4. Describe a potential data safeguard for each of the threats you identified in your answer to question 2. If no data safeguard is appropriate to a business, explain why.
5. Describe a potential human safeguard for each of the threats you identified in your answer to question 2.
6. Describe how each of the businesses in question 2 should prepare for security incidents.
7. How likely are the threats you identified in question 2? If you owned these businesses, which of the items you described in questions 2 through 6 would you implement? If you choose not to implement an item, explain why.

COLLABORATION EXERCISES AND CASES

Collaborate with a group of students on the following exercises. Recall from Chapter 2 that collaboration is more than cooperation because it involves iteration and feedback. Post a document, a discussion item, a wiki item, or an idea and obtain feedback from your team members. Similarly, read the ideas of others and comment on them. Try to innovate in both the process by which you collaborate and the work product that you create. Avoid face-to-face meetings. Instead, use collaborative software such as Google Docs & Spreadsheets, Microsoft Groove, or Microsoft SharePoint to facilitate your ideas.

1. In this exercise you will be asked to determine a policy for organizations to use to protect themselves from phishing attacks. To begin, reread the *Security Management in Practice* box on page 459.
   a. As you might guess, phishing is a serious threat to legitimate brands. Go to the FraudWatch site (*http://fraudwatchinternational.com*) and click on Phishing Alerts. Examine a dozen or more of these alerts and describe five or six techniques that phishers use. The particular attacks on this list depend on when you access it, but generally, you will find a

who's who of business organizations on that list. Describe the techniques that you found.

b. Discuss with your group the danger that such attacks present to legitimate brands. Describe monetary and nonmonetary losses that occur from phishing.

c. Describing phishing attacks and attendant losses is the easy part. The hard part is determining what to do about it. Discuss the following issues with your group.

   (1) How does an organization know that it has been phished? How will the organization be informed? What damage will have occurred by then?
   (2) What should an organization do, once it knows that a phishing attack is underway?
   (3) What steps can companies take to forewarn their customers about phishing attacks?
   (4) How realistic is it for organizations to sue phishers? What aspects of phishing hamper both legal and law enforcement measures?
   (5) Phishing is an industry-wide problem. How can organizations better solve the problem or mitigate its consequences by working together?
   (6) What role do organizations like FraudWatch International serve? Can such organizations prevent phishing?
   (7) Search the Web to determine if it is possible to buy phishing insurance. Describe any such insurance policies you find.

d. Given the knowledge of this exercise, what do you think organizations can do to protect themselves from phishing attacks? Name and describe the top five actions they should take.

e. Document your conclusions in your answer to part d in a memo to a senior marketing manager. Describe the risks, the potential damage, and possible responses. Recommend an organizational policy regarding phishing attacks.

2. In this exercise, you will have an opportunity to determine a security and control policy regarding iPhone use. Begin by rereading the *Innovation in Practice* box on page 482.

   a. Summarize the security problem presented by iPhones and similar devices. Consider the use of such devices in conjunction with corporate IS, data downloads, email, chat, and voice. Use Figure 12-1 as a guide to potential threats.

   b. One possible limitation on iPhone use would be to specify that such devices can be used to download data but not to enter any data into corporate systems. Which of the threats you identified in part a would be controlled by such a policy? In the opinion of your team, would it be worth creating such a policy? Why or why not?

   c. Suppose the IS department were to state that iPhones and similar devices will not have access to the corporate network. What are the consequences of such a policy? If a sales rep claimed that such a policy put her at a competitive disadvantage, would there be merit to the claim? Why or why not? If there is merit to this claim, might it still be worth implementing such a policy?

   d. Google the terms *E-DRM* and *rights management services*. Describe the capabilities of these technologies. What limitations can be created? What type(s) of content can be protected?

   e. At present (December 2007), the iPhone runs only the Macintosh operating system. Microsoft Office documents cannot be processed on an iPhone. How does this fact reduce the potential risk of these devices to organizations? Describe the limitations of a security policy that depends on this limitation.

   f. Setting aside operating systems issues, E-DRM has the potential of offering a solution to the iPhone and similar device control problem. However, at this writing, E-DRM applies only to documents, not data. Describe, at a high level, changes that would need to be made in thick-client applications to use similar technology to limit data access. Describe, at a high level, changes that would need to be made to browsers to use E-DRM-like technology for thin-client applications.

   g. Suppose that E-DRM technology can be extended for both documents and data. What opportunities does that create for you? Describe ways you could use this knowledge in a job interview.

APPLICATION EXERCISES

1. Develop a spreadsheet model of the cost of a virus attack in an organization that has three types of computers: employee workstations, data servers, and Web servers. Assume that the number of computers affected by the virus depends on the severity of the virus. For the purposes of your model, assume that there are three levels of virus severity: *Low-severity* incidents affect fewer than 30 percent of the user workstations and none of the data or Web servers. *Medium-severity* incidents affect

up to 70 percent of the user workstations, up to half of the Web servers, and none of the data servers. *High-severity* incidents can affect all organizational computers.

Assume 50 percent of the incidents are low severity, 30 percent are medium severity, and 20 percent are high severity.

Assume employees can remove viruses from workstations themselves, but that specially trained technicians are required to repair the servers. The time to eliminate a virus from an infected computer depends on the computer type. Let the time to remove the virus from each type be an input into your model. Assume that when users eliminate the virus themselves, they are unproductive for twice the time required for the removal. Let the average employee hourly labor cost be an input to your model. Let the average cost of a technician also be an input into your model. Finally, let the total number of user computers, data servers, and Web servers be inputs into your model.

Run your simulation 10 times. Use the same inputs for each run, but draw a random number (assume a uniform distribution for all random numbers) to determine the severity type. Then, draw random numbers to determine the percentage of computers of each type affected, using the constraints detailed earlier. For example, if the attack is of medium severity, draw a random number between 0 and 70 to indicate the percentage of infected user workstations and a random number between 0 and 50 to indicate the percentage of infected Web servers.

For each run, calculate the total of lost employee hours, the total dollar cost of lost employee labor hours, the total hours of technicians to fix the servers, and the total cost of technician labor. Finally, compute the total overall cost. Show the results of each run. Show the average costs and hours for the 10 runs.

2. Suppose that you have been asked to develop a database to facilitate the creation of ACLs for your organization's firewall. Assume that managers submit all blocking requests and that each request is reviewed by a data communications specialist.

Your database is to keep track of managers, their requests for blocking IP addresses, and each specialist's review of the request. For each request, track the date of the request, the IP address to be blocked, and whether the block applies to incoming, outgoing, or both types of access.

Assume that your database is to track the name and email of the manager who made each request. Assume that a manager can make many requests, but that a particular blocking request is made by one manager. Finally, assume that all requests are reviewed by data communications specialists. After a review, the specialist grants the block, refuses the block, or places the block into a pending status (waiting for more information). Your database is to track the name and email of the specialist who made the review. A specialist can review many requests, but each request is reviewed by at most one specialist.

Create appropriate tables and fill them with data. Create a data entry form to enter requests and a second data entry form to enter reviews. Create the following reports:

- All data for all requests sorted by IP address
- All data for all requests sorted by request date
- All pending requests
- All requests for a particular specialist, sorted by request date
- All requests for a particular manager, sorted by request date

CASE STUDY 12

The ChoicePoint Attack

ChoicePoint, a Georgia-based corporation, provides risk-management and fraud-prevention data. Traditionally, ChoicePoint provided motor vehicle reports, claims histories, and similar data to the automobile insurance industry; in recent years, it broadened its customer base to include general business and government agencies. Today, it also offers data for volunteer and job-applicant screening and data to assist in the location of missing children. ChoicePoint has over 4,000 employees, and its 2004 revenue was $918 million.

In the fall of 2004, ChoicePoint was the victim of a fraudulent spoofing attack in which unauthorized individuals posed as legitimate customers and obtained personal data on more than 145,000 individuals. According to the company's Web site:

> These criminals were able to pass our customer authentication due diligence processes by using stolen identities to create and produce the documents needed to appear legitimate. As small business customers of ChoicePoint, these fraudsters accessed products that contained basic telephone directory-type data (name and address information) as well as a combination of Social Security numbers and/or driver's license numbers and, at times, abbreviated credit reports.

> They were also able to obtain other public record information including, but not limited to bankruptcies, liens, and judgments; professional licenses; and real property data.

ChoicePoint became aware of the problem in November 2004, when it noticed unusual processing activity on some accounts in Los Angeles. Accordingly, the company contacted the Los Angeles Police Department, which requested that ChoicePoint not reveal the activity until the department could conduct an investigation. In January, the LAPD notified ChoicePoint that it could contact the customers whose data had been compromised.

This crime is an example of a failure of authentication and not a network break-in. ChoicePoint's firewalls and other safeguards were not overcome. Instead, the criminals spoofed legitimate businesses. The infiltrators obtained valid California business licenses, and until their unusual processing activity was detected appeared to be legitimate users.

In response to this problem, ChoicePoint established a hotline for customers whose data were compromised to call for assistance. They also purchased a credit report for each of these people and paid for a 1-year credit-report-monitoring service. In February 2005, attorneys initiated a class-action lawsuit for all 145,000 customers with an initial loss claim of $75,000 each. At the same time, the U.S. Senate announced that it would conduct an investigation.

Ironically, ChoicePoint exposed itself to a public relations nightmare, considerable expense, a class-action lawsuit, a Senate investigation, and a 20 percent drop in its share price because it contacted the police and cooperated in the attempt to apprehend the criminals. When ChoicePoint noticed the unusual account activity, had it simply shut down data access for the illegitimate businesses, no one would have known. Of course, the 145,000 customers whose identities had been compromised would have unknowingly been subject to identity theft, but it is unlikely that such thefts could have been tracked back to ChoicePoint.

ChoicePoint offers a wide array of data products for industries, businesses, and consumers. ChoicePoint's homepage states, "ChoicePoint is the nation's leading provider of identification and credential verification services." Figure 1, below, shows just the Consumer Solutions from ChoicePoint's Web site at *http://choicepoint.com* as of February 2005. ChoicePoint provides some of these services directly; partners and data providers offer other of these services by links at the ChoicePoint site.

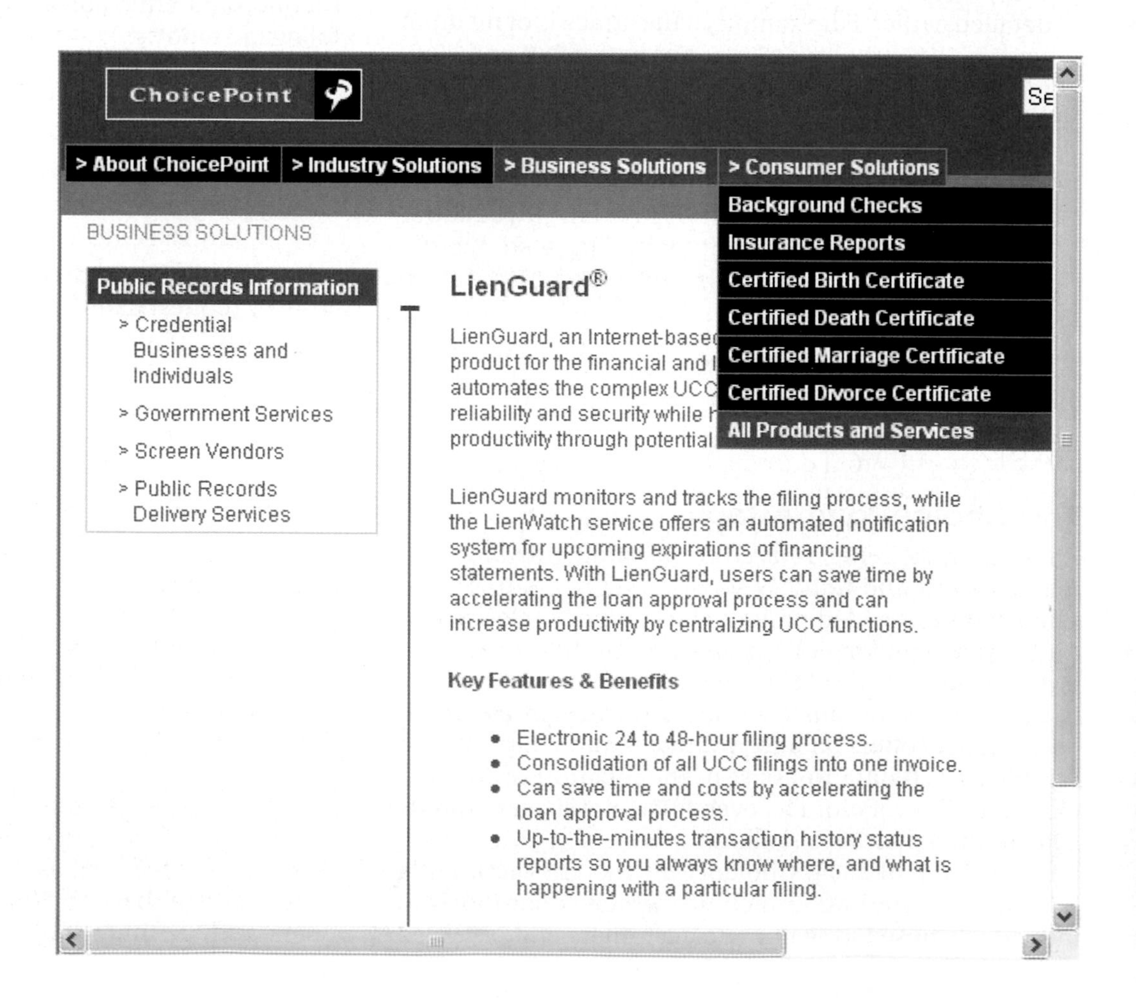

Figure 1
ChoicePoint Consumer Services

Source: Used with permission of ChoicePoint.com.

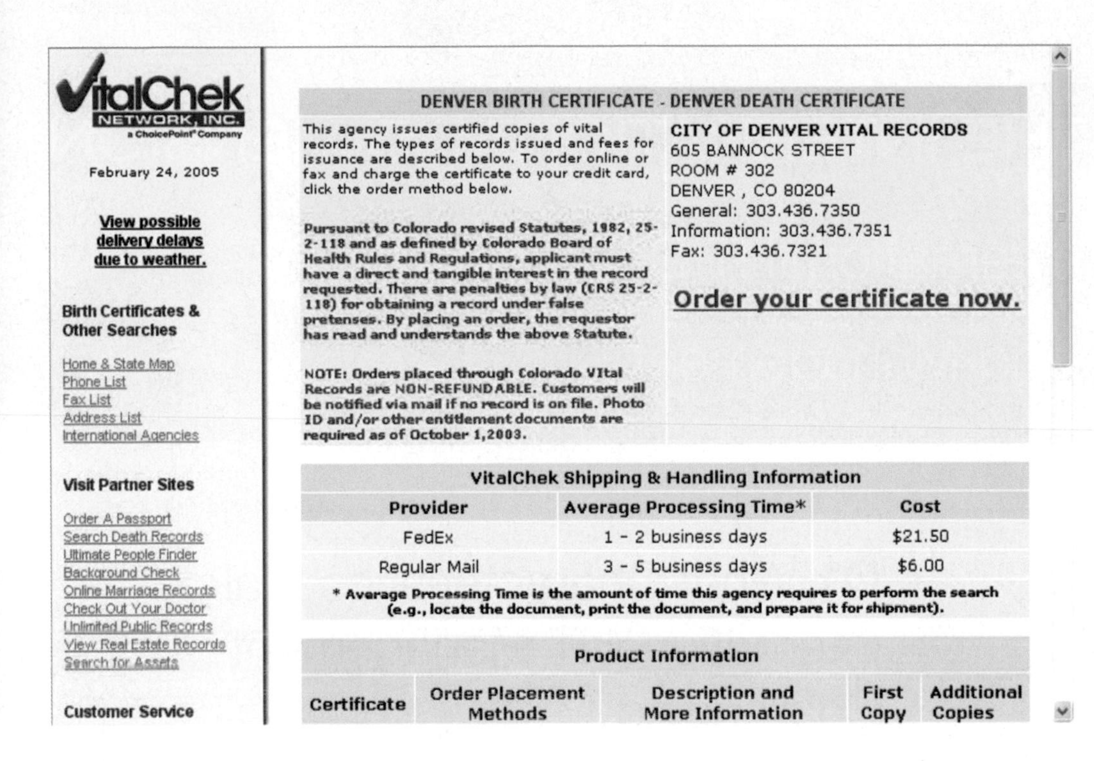

VitalChek
NETWORK, INC.
a ChoicePoint® Company

February 24, 2005

View possible delivery delays due to weather.

Birth Certificates & Other Searches

Home & State Map
Phone List
Fax List
Address List
International Agencies

Visit Partner Sites

Order A Passport
Search Death Records
Ultimate People Finder
Background Check
Online Marriage Records
Check Out Your Doctor
Unlimited Public Records
View Real Estate Records
Search for Assets

Customer Service

DENVER BIRTH CERTIFICATE - DENVER DEATH CERTIFICATE

This agency issues certified copies of vital records. The types of records issued and fees for issuance are described below. To order online or fax and charge the certificate to your credit card, click the order method below.

Pursuant to Colorado revised Statutes, 1982, 25-2-118 and as defined by Colorado Board of Health Rules and Regulations, applicant must have a direct and tangible interest in the record requested. There are penalties by law (CRS 25-2-118) for obtaining a record under false pretenses. By placing an order, the requestor has read and understands the above Statute.

NOTE: Orders placed through Colorado Vital Records are NON-REFUNDABLE. Customers will be notified via mail if no record is on file. Photo ID and/or other entitlement documents are required as of October 1,2003.

CITY OF DENVER VITAL RECORDS
605 BANNOCK STREET
ROOM # 302
DENVER , CO 80204
General: 303.436.7350
Information: 303.436.7351
Fax: 303.436.7321

Order your certificate now.

VitalChek Shipping & Handling Information

Provider	Average Processing Time*	Cost
FedEx	1 - 2 business days	$21.50
Regular Mail	3 - 5 business days	$6.00

*** Average Processing Time is the amount of time this agency requires to perform the search (e.g., locate the document, print the document, and prepare it for shipment).**

Product Information

Certificate	Order Placement Methods	Description and More Information	First Copy	Additional Copies

Figure 2
Ordering a Birth Certificate Via a ChoicePoint Partner

Source: Used with permission of ChoicePoint.com.

For example, a user who clicks on Certified Birth Certificate in Figure 1 will be asked to provide a state. ChoicePoint then links to other data providers to process the request. Figure 2, above, shows the link activated for obtaining the birth certificate for someone in Denver, Colorado.

Notice the red type in the form in Figure 2. Apparently, Colorado law restricts access to birth certificates to those who have a "direct and tangible" interest. It would seem unlikely that this Web site enforces this law. The law and this language possibly exist to provide a basis for legal action when fraudulent use of a birth certificate occurs.

As a data utility, ChoicePoint maintains relationships with many different entities. It obtains its data from both public and private sources. It then sells access to this data to its customers. Much of the data, by the way, can be obtained directly from the data vendor. ChoicePoint adds value by providing a centralized access point for many data needs. In addition to data sources and customers, ChoicePoint maintains relationships with partners such as the City of Denver's vital records department, as shown in Figure 2. Finally, ChoicePoint also has relationships to the subjects on which it maintains data.

Source: http://choicepoint.com/news/statement_0205_1.html#sub1 (accessed February 2005). Used with permission of ChoicePoint.com.

Questions

1. ChoicePoint exposed itself to considerable expense, many problems, and a possible loss of brand confidence because it notified the Los Angeles Police Department, cooperated in the investigation, and notified the individuals whose records had been compromised. It could have buried the theft and possibly avoided any responsibility. Comment on the ethical issues and ChoicePoint's response. Did ChoicePoint choose wisely? Consider that question from the viewpoint of customers, law enforcement personnel, investors, and management.
2. Given ChoicePoint's experience, what is the likely action of similar companies whose records are compromised in this way? Given your answer, do you think federal regulations and additional laws are required? What other steps could be taken to ensure that data vendors notify people harmed by data theft?
3. Visit *http://choicepoint.com.* Summarize the products that ChoicePoint provides. What seems to be the central theme of this business?
4. Review the security policy material in this chapter and reflect on an appropriate program policy for ChoicePoint. Describe why ChoicePoint needs a security policy and who and what should be governed by such a policy. Consider not only employees, but also data subjects, customers, data sources, and partners.
5. Suppose that ChoicePoint decides to establish a formal security policy on the issue of inappropriate release of personal data. Summarize the issues that ChoicePoint should address.

PART 4 THE INTERNATIONAL DIMENSION

International IT Development and Management

STUDY QUESTIONS

- Q1 What characteristics make international IT management challenging?
- Q2 Why is international information systems development difficult?
- Q3 What are the challenges of international project management?
- Q4 What are the challenges of international IT management?
- Q5 How does the international dimension affect computer security risk management?
- Q6 What challenges exist for investigating international computer crime?

Q1 What Characteristics Make International IT Management Challenging?

Size and complexity make international IT management challenging. International information systems are larger and more complex. Projects to develop them are larger and more complicated to manage. International IT departments are bigger and composed of people from many cultures with many different native languages. International organizations have extensive IS and IT assets, and those assets are exposed to more risk and greater uncertainty. Security incidents are more complicated to investigate.

We will consider each of these impacts in more detail in the following questions. The bottom line, however, is that size and complexity make international IT management challenging.

Q2 Why Is International Information Systems Development Difficult?

Before considering this question, realize that the factors that affect international information systems development are more challenging than those that affect international software development. If the *system* is truly international, if many people from many different countries will be using the system, then the development project is exceedingly complicated. For example, consider the effort required for a multinational company like 3M to create an integrated, worldwide CRM. Such a project is massive!

In contrast, creating localized software (one or more programs that are available in different human-language versions) is challenging, but not nearly as daunting. As stated in the International Dimension for Part 2, localizing a program is a

matter of designing it to accept program menus, messages, and help text from external files and to translate those files. Of course, different character sets, different sorting orders, different currency symbols, and other complications must be accounted for, but these challenges are surmountable with good software design and development.

Think about the five components of an information system. Running hardware in different countries is not a problem, and localizing software is manageable. Databases pose some problems, namely determining the language, currency, and units of measure used to record data, but these problems are surmountable. A substantial problem arises, however, when we consider procedures.

An international system is used by people who live and work in cultures that are vastly different from one another. The way that customers are treated in Japan differs substantially from the way they are treated in Spain, which differs substantially from the way they are treated in the United States. Therefore, the procedures for using a CRM will be correspondingly different.

Consider the phases of the SDLC. During systems definition, we are supposed to determine the purpose and scope of the system. As you know by now, information systems should facilitate the organization's competitive strategy by supporting business processes. But what if the underlying processes differ? Again, customer support in Japan and customer support in Spain might involve completely different processes and activities.

Even if the purpose and scope can be defined in some unified way, how are requirements to be determined? Again, if the underlying business processes differ, then the specific requirements for the information system will differ. Managing requirements for a system in one culture is difficult, but managing requirements for international systems can be many times more difficult.

The two responses to such challenges are to either define a set of standard business processes or to develop alternative versions of the system that support different processes in different countries. Both responses are problematic. The first response requires conversion of the organization to different work processes, and, as you learned in Chapter 7, such conversion can be exceedingly difficult. People resist change, and they will do so with vehemence if the change violates cultural norms.

The second response is easier to implement, but creates system design challenges. It also means that, in truth, there is not one system, but many.

Despite the problems, both responses are used. For example, SAP, Oracle, and other ERP vendors define standard business processes via the inherent procedures in their software products. Many organizations attempt to enforce those standard procedures. When it becomes organizationally infeasible to do so, organizations develop exceptions to those inherent procedures and develop programs to handle the exceptions. This choice means high maintenance expenses, as explained in Chapter 7.

Q3 What Are the Challenges of International Project Management?

Managing a global information systems development project is difficult because of project size and complexity. Requirements are complex, many resources are required, and numerous people are involved. Team members speak different languages, live in different cultures, work in different time zones, and seldom meet face-to-face.

Figure 1 summarizes the major challenges. Project integration is more difficult, because international development projects require the complex integration of results from distributed work groups. Also, task dependencies can span teams working in different countries, increasing the difficulty of task management.

Requirements definition for international IS is more difficult for the reasons discussed in Q2. Time management is more difficult because teams in different cultures and countries work at different rates. Some cultures have a 35-hour workweek, and others have a 60-hour workweek. Some cultures expect 6-week vacations, and others expect 2. Some cultures thrive on efficiency of labor, and others thrive on considerate working relationships. There is no standard rate of development for an international project.

In terms of cost, different countries and cultures pay vastly different labor rates. Using critical path analysis, managers may choose to move a task from one team to another. Doing so, however, may substantially increase costs. Thus, management may choose to accept a delay rather than move work to an

Management Issue	Challenge
Project integration	Complex integration of results from distributed work groups. Management of dependencies of tasks from physically and culturally different workgroups.
Requirements	Need to support multiple versions of underlying business processes. Possibly substantial differences in requirements and procedures.
Time	Development pace and workweek vary among cultures and countries.
Cost	Cost of development varies widely among countries. Two members performing the same work in different countries may be paid substantially different rates. Moving work among teams may dramatically change costs.
Quality	Quality standards vary among cultures. Different expectations of quality may result in an inconsistent system.
Human resources	Worker expectations differ. Compensation, rewards, work conditions vary widely.
Communications	Geographic, language, and cultural distance among team members impedes effective communication.
Risk	Development risk is higher. Easy to lose control.
Procurement	Complications of international trade.

Figure 1
Challenges for International IS Project Management

available (but more expensive) team. The complex tradeoffs that exist between time and cost become even more complex for international projects.

Quality and human resources also are more complicated for international projects. Quality standards vary among countries. The IT industry in some nations, such as India, has invested heavily in development techniques that increase program quality. Other nations, such as the United States, have been less willing to invest in quality. In any case, the integration of programs of varying quality results in an inconsistent system.

Worker expectations vary among cultures and nations. Compensation, rewards, and worker conditions vary, and these differences can lead to misunderstandings, poor morale, and project delays.

Because of these factors, effective team communication is exceedingly important for international projects, but because of language and culture differences and geographic separation such communication is difficult. Effective communication also is more expensive. Consider, for example, just the additional expense of maintaining a team portal in three or four languages.

If you consider all of the factors in Figure 1, it is easy to understand why project risk is high for international IS development projects. So many things can go wrong. Project integration is complex; requirements are difficult to determine; cost, time, and quality are difficult to manage; worker conditions vary widely; and communication is difficult. Finally, project procurement is complicated by the normal challenges of international commerce.

Q4 What Are the Challenges of International IT Management?

Chapter 11 defined the four primary responsibilities of the IT department: plan, operate, develop, and protect information systems and IT infrastructure. Each of these responsibilities becomes more challenging for international IT organizations.

Regarding planning, the principal task is to align IT and IS resources with the organization's competitive strategy. The task does not change character for

international companies; it just becomes more complex and difficult. Multinational organizations and operations are complicated, and the business processes that support their competitive strategies also tend to be complicated. Further, changes in global economic factors can mean dramatic changes in processes and necessitate changes in IS and IT support. Technology adoption can also cause remarkable change. The increasing use of cell phones in developing countries, for example, changes the requirements for local information systems. The rising price of oil will also change international business processes. So, planning tasks for international IT are becoming larger and more complex.

Three factors create challenges for international IT operations. First, conducting operations in different countries, cultures, and languages adds complexity. Go to the Web site of any multinational corporation, say *http://mmm.com* or *http://lenovo.com,* and you will be asked to click on the country in which you reside. When you click, you are likely to be directed to a Web server running in some other country. Those Web servers need to be managed consistently, even though they are operated by people living in different cultures and speaking different languages.

The second operational challenge of international IS is the integration of similar, but different, systems. Consider inventory. A multinational corporation might have dozens of different inventory systems in use throughout the world. To enable the movement of goods, many of these systems need to be coordinated and integrated.

Or, consider customer support that operates from three different support centers in three different countries. Each support center may have its own information system, but the data among those systems will need to be exported or otherwise shared. If not, then a customer who contacts one center will be unknown by the others.

The third complication for operations is outsourcing. Many organizations have chosen to outsource customer support, training, logistics, and other backroom activities. International outsourcing is particularly advantageous for customer support and other functions that must be operational 24/7. Amazon.com, for example, operates customer service centers in the United States, India, and Ireland. Many companies outsource logistics to United Parcel Service (UPS), because doing so offers comprehensive, worldwide shipping and logistical support. The organization's information systems usually need to be integrated with outsource vendors' information systems, and this may need to be done for different systems, all over the world. The challenges for the development of international information systems were addressed in questions Q1 and Q2.

The fourth IT department responsibility is protecting IS and IT infrastructure. We consider that function in the next question.

Q5 How Does the International Dimension Affect Computer Security Risk Management?

Computer security risk management is more difficult and complicated for international information systems. First, IT assets are subject to more threats. Infrastructure will be located in sites all over the world, and those sites differ in the threats to which they are exposed. Some will be subject to political threats, others to the threat of civil unrest, others to threats from terrorists, and still others will be subject to threats of natural disasters of every conceivable type. Place your data center in Kansas, and it is subject to tornados. Place your data center internationally, and it is potentially subject to typhoons/hurricanes, earthquakes, floods, volcanic eruption, or mudslides. And, do not forget epidemics that might affect the data center employees.

Second, the likelihood of a threat is more difficult to estimate for international systems. What is the likelihood that the death of Fidel Castro will cause civil unrest and threaten your data center in Havana? How does an organization assess that risk? What is the likelihood that a computer programmer in India will insert a Trojan horse into code that she writes on an outsourcing contract?

In addition to risk, international information systems are subject to far greater uncertainty. As discussed in Chapter 12, uncertainty reflects likelihood that something that "we don't know we don't know" will cause an adverse outcome. Because of the multitude of cultures, religions, nations, beliefs, political views, and crazy people in the world, uncertainty about risks to IS and IT infrastructure is high. Again, if you place your data center in Kansas, you have some idea of the magnitude of the uncertainty to which you are exposed, even if you do not know exactly what it is. Place a server in a country on every continent of the world, and you have no idea of the potential risks to which they are exposed.

Regarding safeguards, technical and data safeguards do not change for international information systems. Because of greater complexity, more safeguards or far more complex ones might be needed, but the technical and data safeguards described in Chapter 12 all work for international systems. Human safeguards are another matter. For example, can an organization depend on the control of separation of duties and authorities in a culture in which graft is an accepted norm? Or, what is the utility of a personal reference in a culture in which it is considered exceedingly rude to talk about someone when they are not present? Because of these differences, human safeguards need to be chosen and evaluated on a culture-by-culture basis.

In short, risk management for both international information systems and IT infrastructure is more complicated, more difficult, and subject to greater uncertainty.

Q6 What Challenges Exist for Investigating Global Computer Crime?

Unfortunately, international computer crime is common. Web sites operated in African countries phish for data in the United States. A scam in the United States steals data from a U.S. corporation and sells that data to an illegal operation in South America. Someone kidnaps a U.S. citizen in a foreign country and sends an email ransom demand to relatives in the United States. The email service provider is located in a Mideastern country. In all of these cases, critical evidence is stored in computers located on foreign soil.

With rare exceptions, such as embassies, nations have sovereignty within their borders. A U.S. criminal investigator can obtain evidence only with the consent of the country in which the evidence lies. Most nations have laws, agreements, and treaties for cooperating in criminal investigations, but the formal process for obtaining permission to search is slow and cumbersome. Further, some nations will not cooperate.

For situations in which speed is of the essence, when the data is likely to be moved soon or deleted, the G8 group of nations has developed a 24-hour *point-of-contact system*. This system, which is used by more than 30 nations, requires each country to staff an office that can speed the processing of permission for evidence gathering. For the countries that participate, the system gives international crime investigators a single point of contact.

In some cases, evidence-gathering is facilitated by informal arrangements among individuals in security agencies and organizations. A U.S. investigator may not have permission to search or obtain evidence, but his or her counterpart in another country may be authorized to do so. Informal arrangements are sometimes made, but the law regarding the admissibility of such evidence in court is complicated.

A final consideration is that the U.S. Fourth Amendment can apply in complex ways to searches outside the United States. The law for gathering evidence for computer crimes in the United States is complicated, and it becomes even more so for international investigations. Organizations that suspect they have been the victims of a computer crime, especially international computer crime, should seek legal counsel, first.

ACTIVE REVIEW

Use this Active Review to verify that you understand the ideas and concepts that answer the part's study questions.

Q1 What characteristics make international IT management challenging?

State the two characteristics that make international IT management challenging. Explain how those factors pertain to IS development, IT management, and risk management.

Q2 Why is international information systems development difficult?

Explain the difference between international systems development and international software development. Using the five-component framework, explain why international systems development is more difficult. Describe difficulties that arise during the systems definition and requirements phases in the development of an international IS. Describe two responses to these difficulties, and explain why both are problematic. Give an example of how each is used.

Q3 What are the challenges of international project management?

State two words that characterize the difficulty of international project management. Explain how each of the knowledge areas in Figure 1 are more complicated for international projects. Give an example of one complication for each knowledge area.

Q4 What are the challenges of international IT management?

State the four responsibilities for IT departments. Explain how each of these responsibilities is more challenging for international IT organizations. Describe three factors that create challenges for international IT operations.

Q5 How does the international dimension affect computer security risk management?

Explain why international IT assets are subject to more threats. Give three examples. Explain why the likelihood of international threats is more difficult to determine. Describe uncertainty and explain why it is higher for international IT organizations. Explain how technical, data, and human safeguards differ for international IT organizations. Give two examples of problematic international human safeguards.

Q6 What challenges exist for investigating international computer crime?

Give two examples of international computer crime. Explain the constraints U.S. investigators face when gathering evidence in foreign countries. Explain the role of the 24-hour point-of-contact system. Describe how informal arrangements can facilitate evidence-gathering in foreign countries. State the recommended action for organizations that believe they have been the victim of an international computer crime.

CASE 4-1

PART 4

The Need for Technical Feasibility

The United States Internal Revenue Service (IRS) Business Systems Modernization (BSM) project has been a multiyear attempt to replace the existing tax-processing information systems with systems based on modern technology. Review Case Study 1 (page 26) for a discussion of the underlying need, problems, and suggested problem solutions.

The subsystem that has generated the most controversy and been the cause of the most serious delays is the Customer Account Data Engine (CADE). The heart of CADE is a database of business rules. Unlike most databases that contain facts and figures like *CustomerName, Email, Balance,* and so forth, the CADE database contains business rules, which are statements about how an organization conducts its business. In the context of the IRS, this database contains rules about tax laws and the processing of tax forms. An example of such a rule is:

Rule 10:
IF the amount on line 7 of Form 1040EZ is greater than zero,
THEN invoke Rule 15.

With a rule-based approach, the IRS need only develop programs that access the database and follow the rules. No other programs need to be developed.

Rule-based systems differ substantially from traditional application programs. Using traditional technology, the developers interview the users, determine what the business rules are, and then write computer code that operates in accordance with the rules. The disadvantage of such traditional programming is that only technically trained programmers can decipher the rules in the program code. Also, only trained programmers can add, change, or delete rules.

The advantage of rule-based systems such as CADE is that the business rules are stored in the database and can be read, added, changed, or deleted by personnel with business knowledge but little computer training. Hence, in theory, CADE is more adaptable to changing requirements than a system written with traditional programming languages.

Unfortunately, the technical feasibility of using a rule-based system for a problem as large and complex as IRS tax processing is unknown. It appears, at least from public records, that no one ever tried to estimate that feasibility. The result has been a string of schedule delays and cost overruns. The first CADE release, which processes only the simplest individual tax returns (those using IRS Form 1040EZ), was to be completed by January 2002. It was delayed once until August 2003, and then delayed again to September 2004. At that point, a limited version of this first release was demonstrated.

The database for these simple returns has some 1,200 business rules, but no reliable estimate has yet been developed for the number of rules required for the full system. The lack of an estimate is particularly serious because some experts believe the difficulty and complexity of creating rules increases geometrically with the number of rules. Meanwhile, $33 million was invested in 2003, and another $84 million was spent in 2004.

Given the history of problems, the IRS hired the Software Engineering Institute of (SEI) Carnegie Mellon University to conduct an independent audit of the project. SEI verified that no one knows with any certainty how many business rules will eventually be required. Additionally, according to the SEI report,

> We believe that harvesting the business rules, not coding them, will drive the cost and schedule of future CADE releases. By harvesting, we mean capturing, adjudicating, and cataloging the rules. CADE has invested many resources exploring rules engines, but few resources exploring the rules themselves. The IRS needs to understand and document their business rules as well as the rules' complicated interactions. Some of the delays that have already plagued CADE are a direct result of an imperfect understanding of the business rules. This situation will only grow as the number and complexity of the implemented rules increases.

According to the SEI testimony, without reliable estimates of the number of business rules,

> No one knows how long rule harvesting will take, how many people will be required, the background, training and experience of the people required, or how much it will cost. Based on anecdotal information presented to us, we believe the time will be measured in years and cost will be measured in the tens of millions of dollars.
>
> Until sound, supported cost and schedule estimates for rule harvesting are available, future CADE plans and schedules are only tentative and likely subject to delays and missed milestones.

Sources: U.S. House, Committee on Ways and Means, Subcommittee on Oversight, Statement of M. Steven Palmquist, Chief Engineer for Civil and Intelligence Agencies, Acquisition Support Program, Software Engineering Institute, Carnegie Mellon University, Pittsburgh, Pennsylvania, February 12, 2004; and *http://treas.gov/irsob/documents/special_report1203.pdf* (accessed June 2005).

QUESTIONS

1. Ignoring developments that have occurred since this case was written, what statement can be made about the technical feasibility, cost feasibility, and schedule feasibility of this project?

2. Use your imagination to try to understand how this situation came about. The IRS selected a team of contractors to develop the information systems that would support the modernization effort. Those contractors proposed a rule-based system, but apparently no one asked whether such a system would work on a problem this large. How could that come about? Suppose you were a non-IT manager at the IRS. Would you know to ask? Suppose you were a senior manager at one of the contractors. Would you know to ask? If you did ask and your technical people said, "No problem," what would you do?

3. Suppose you are a senior IRS manager. In defense of your management, you say, "We hired reputable contractors who had extensive experience developing large and complicated systems. When they told us that a

rule-based approach was the way to go, we agreed. Should we be required to second-guess the experts?" Comment on that statement. Do you believe it? Do you think it's a justification?

4. Does it seem remarkable that, according to the SEI review, no one has yet considered the time, cost, and difficulty of harvesting the rules? Clearly, the need to allocate time and labor to that problem was visible from the start of the project. How do you think such an oversight occurred? What are the consequences of that oversight?

5. Suppose it turns out that a rule-based system is infeasible for processing more complicated tax returns. What alternatives are available to the IRS? As a taxpayer, which do you recommend?

6. Google *IRS CADE problems* and read three or four articles and reports on recent developments. Comment on any recent information that sheds light on your answers to questions 1 through 5. What strategy for solving this problem does the IRS seem to be following? How likely is that strategy to succeed?

CASE 4-2

Southwest Video Training

Suppose that you are the manager of telesales for Southwest Video Training, a company that produces, distributes, and sells video training programs. Your company has programs on customer support, leadership, sales training, motivation, and other training topics. Southwest's competitive strategy is to differentiate its product on the basis of quality, and it has succeeded. The company's programs are perceived not only as the highest quality, but also as the most entertaining and effective.

You manage the telesales department. Your salespeople make "warm calls"; that is, they call existing customers or potential customers who have evidenced a strong interest in your programs. Your company uses a licensing model; rather than sell the videos outright, it sells a license to use them. Larger customers buy site licenses that authorize them to copy videos. Otherwise, customers are not allowed to make copies.

One day you're thinking about how useful your database is when it occurs to you how vulnerable you are. A loss of your database would hamper sales for months! You know that someone at the company backs up the database each week, but you don't know where the backup is stored. Are the backups in your building, and, if so, what would happen if your building caught fire and the backups were lost? Lately, you've been reading about incidents in which data utilities lost data to thieves. What protection do you have against that possibility?

Two partners privately own Southwest, and you approach one of them and raise these issues. He states he hasn't thought about it, saying, "I rely on Jeri [an employee who manages the Web storefront] to take care of it." Without criticizing Jeri, you ask whether anyone knows how well-protected the data are. "No, not really," says the partner. "Why don't you look into it? I mean, don't do Jeri's job for her, but tell her about your concerns and see what you learn. Maybe the two of you can work together on it and get back to me." Assume that you have been given this task.

QUESTIONS

1. Use Figure 12-1 to summarize the threats to which Southwest Video is vulnerable.
2. Southwest is a small company, and the partners are careful with their time and with the partnership's money. You are certain that a proposal to create a broad and comprehensive security plan will seem like overkill to the partners, at least initially. So, you decide to focus on the three most important threats. Identify those three from your list in your answer to question 1. Explain why you believe these are the most important threats.
3. For each of the threats in your answer to question 2, identify potential technical safeguards.
4. For each of the threats in your answer to question 2, identify potential data safeguards.
5. For each of the threats in your answer to question 2, identify potential human safeguards.
6. Describe how you think Southwest should prepare for security incidents.

Glossary

10/100/1000 Ethernet A type of Ethernet that conforms to the IEEE 802.3 protocol and allows for transmission at a rate of 10, 100, or 1,000 Mbps (megabits per second). 194

Access A popular personal and small workgroup DBMS product from Microsoft. 152

Access control list (ACL) A list that encodes the rules stating which packets are to be allowed through a firewall and which are to be prohibited. 206, 472

Access device Device, typically special-purpose computers, that connects network sites. The particular device required depends on the line used and other factors. Sometimes switches and routers are employed, but other types of equipment are needed as well. 200

Access point A point in a wireless network that facilitates communication among wireless devices and serves as a point of interconnection between wireless and wired networks. The access point must be able to process messages according to both the 802.3 and 802.11 standards, because it sends and receives wireless traffic using the 802.11 protocol and communicates with wired networks using the 802.3 protocol. 195

Accounting information systems Systems that support accounting functions, such as budgeting, cash management, accounts payable and receivable, and financial reporting. 263

Accurate information Information that is based on correct and complete data and that has been processed correctly as expected. 13

Activity The part of a business process that transforms resources and information of one type into resources and information of another type; can be manual or automated. 68

Ad Sense A Web 2.0 product from Google. Google searches an organization's Web site and inserts ads that match content on that site; when users click on those ads, Google pays the organization a fee. 302

Ad Words A Web 2.0 advertising product from Google. Vendors agree to pay a certain amount to Google for use of particular search words, which link to the vendor's site. 302

Adware Programs installed on the user's computer without the user's knowledge or permission that reside in the background and, unknown to the user, observe the user's actions and keystrokes, modify computer activity, and report the user's activities to sponsoring organizations. Most adware is benign in that it does not perform malicious acts or steal data. It does, however, watch user activity and produce pop-up ads. 473

Alert A form of report, often requested by recipients, that tells them some piece of usually time-related information, such as notification of the time for a meeting. 359

Analog signal A wavy signal. A modem converts the computer's digital data into analog signals that can be transmitted over dial-up Internet connections. 197

Analysis paralysis When too much time is spent documenting project requirements. 399

Antivirus programs Software that detects and possibly eliminates viruses. 126

Application software Programs that perform a business function. Some application programs are general purpose, such as Excel or Word. Other application programs are specific to a business function, such as accounts payable. 120

Architecture An arrangement of protocol layers in which each layer is given specific tasks to accomplish. 219

Asymmetric digital subscriber lines (ADSL) DSL lines that have different upload and download speeds. 199

Asymmetric encryption An encryption method whereby different keys are used to encode and to decode the message; one key encodes the message, and the other key decodes the message. Symmetric encryption is simpler and much faster than asymmetric encryption. 206, 469

Asynchronous communication Information exchange that occurs when all members of a work team do not meet at the same time, such as those who work different shifts or in different locations. 33

Asynchronous transfer mode (ATM) A protocol that divides data into uniformly sized cells, eliminates the need for protocol conversion, and can process speeds from 1 to 156 Mbps. ATM can support both voice and data communication. 201

Attribute (1) A variable that provides properties for an HTML tag. Each attribute has a standard name. For example, the attribute for a hyperlink is *href*, and its value indicates which Web page is to be displayed when the user clicks the link. (2) Characteristics of an entity. Example attributes of *Order* would be *OrderNumber, OrderDate, SubTotal, Tax, Total*, and so forth. Example attributes of *Salesperson* would be *SalespersonName, Email, Phone*, and so forth. 160, 292

Auctions Applications that match buyers and sellers by using an e-commerce version of a standard, competitive-bidding auction process. 292

Authentication The process whereby an information system approves (authenticates) a user by checking the user's password. 467

Availability In measuring computer performance, the frequency and length of service outages. 205

Beta program A prerelease version of software, used for testing. The beta program becomes obsolete when the final version is released. 300

Beta testing The process of allowing future system users to try out the new system on their own. Used to locate program failures just prior to program shipment. 396

Bill of materials (BOM) A list of the materials that comprise a product. 258

Binary digits The means by which computers represent data; also called *bits*. A binary digit is either a zero or a one. 105

Biometric authentication The use of personal physical characteristics, such as fingerprints, facial features, and retinal scans, to authenticate users. 467

Bit The means by which computers represent data; also called *binary digit*. A bit is either a zero or a one. 105

BlackBerry A handheld computer that enables users to make cell phone calls, process emails, and access the Internet. 115

Broadband Internet communication lines that have speeds in excess of 256 kbps. DSL and cable modems provide broadband access. 199

Brooks's Law The famous adage that states: *Adding more people to a late project makes the project later*. Brooks's Law is true not only because a larger staff requires increased coordination, but also because new people need training. The only people who can train the new employees are the existing team members, who are thus taken off productive tasks. The costs of training new people can overwhelm the benefit of their contribution. 386

Browser A program that processes the HTTP protocol; receives, displays, and processes HTML documents; and transmits responses. 295

Bullwhip effect Phenomenon in which the variability in the size and timing of orders increases at each stage up the supply chain, from customer to supplier. 306

Bus Means by which the CPU reads instructions and data from main memory and writes data to main memory. 106

Business intelligence (BI) Information containing patterns, relationships, and trends. 331

Business intelligence (BI) application Software that uses a tool on a particular type of data for a particular purpose. 333

Business intelligence (BI) application server A computer programs that delivers BI (business intelligence) application results in a variety of formats to various devices for consumption by BI users. 357

Business intelligence (BI) system An information system, having all five IS components, that provides the right information, to the right user, at the right time. 333

Business intelligence (BI) tool A computer program that implements a particular BI technique. BI tools include reporting tools, data-mining tools, and knowledge-management tools. 333

Business process A network of activities, resources, facilities, and information that interact to achieve some business function; sometimes called a *business system*. 8

Business process design See *Business process redesign*. 266

Business process redesign The creation of new, usually cross-departmental, business practices during information systems development. Most business process redesign uses technology to enable new, more efficient business processes that require people to work in new ways and to follow different procedures. 69

Business-to-business (B2B) E-commerce sales between companies. 291

Business-to-consumer (B2C) E-commerce sales between a supplier and a retail customer (the consumer). 291

Business-to-government (B2G) E-commerce sales between companies and governmental organizations. 292

Byte (1) A character of data; (2) An 8-bit chunk. 106, 146

Cable modem A type of modem that provides high-speed data transmission using cable television lines. The cable company installs a fast, high-capacity optical fiber cable to a distribution center in each neighborhood that it serves. At the distribution center, the optical fiber cable connects to regular cable-television cables that run to subscribers' homes or businesses. Cable modems modulate in such a way that their signals do not interfere with TV signals. Like DSL lines, they are always on. 199

Cache A file on a domain name resolver that stores domain names and IP addresses that have been resolved. Then, when someone else needs to resolve that same domain name, there is no need to go through the entire resolution process. Instead, the resolver can supply the IP address from the local file. 229

Cache memory A small amount of very fast computer memory that holds the most frequently used data. Typically, the CPU stores intermediate results and the most frequently used computer instructions in the cache. Cache can be thought of as a local, dedicated memory for the CPU and as "elbow room" for processing. 106

Calculation systems The very first information systems. The goal of such systems was to relieve workers of tedious, repetitive calculations. These systems were labor-saving devices that produced little information. 251

CASE tool A tool used to help develop computer programs or systems. CASE tools vary in their features and functions. Some such tools address the entire systems development process from requirements to maintenance; others address just the design and implementation phases. 402

CD-R An optical disk that can record data once. 113

CD-ROM A read-only optical disk. 113

CD-RW A rewritable optical disk. 113

Central processing unit (CPU) The CPU selects instructions, processes them, performs arithmetic and logical comparisons, and stores results of operations in memory. 103

Certificate authority (CA) Trusted, independent third-party company that supplies public keys for encryption. 471

Channel conflict In e-commerce, a conflict that may result between a manufacturer that wants to sell products directly to consumers and the retailers in the existing sales channels. 294

Chief information officer (CIO) The title of the principal manager of the IT department. Other common titles are *vice president of information services, director of information services*, and, less commonly, *director of computer services*. 423

Chief technology officer (CTO) The head of the technology group. The CTO sorts through new ideas and products to identify those that are most relevant to the organization. The CTO's job requires deep knowledge of information technology and the ability to envision how new IT will affect the organization over time. 424

Clearinghouse Entity that provides goods and services at a stated price, prices and arranges for the delivery of the goods, but never takes title to the goods. 292

Clickstream data E-commerce data that describes a customer's clicking behavior. Such data includes everything the customer does at the Web site. 350

Client A computer that provides word processing, spreadsheets, database access, and usually a network connection. 116

Client-server applications Software applications that require code on both the client computer and the server computer. Email is a common example. 122

Cluster analysis An unsupervised data-mining technique whereby statistical techniques are used to identify groups of entities that have similar characteristics. A common use for cluster analysis is to find groups of similar customers in data about customer orders and customer demographics. 341

Code generator A program that generates application code for commonly performed tasks. The idea is to improve developer productivity by having the tool generate as much code as possible. The developer can then add code for application-specific features. 402

Cold site A remote processing center that provides office space, but no computer equipment, for use by a company that needs to continue operations after a disaster. 483

Collaboration The situation in which two or more people work together toward a common goal, result, or product; information systems facilitate collaboration. 31

Columns Also called *fields*, or groups of bytes. A database table has multiple columns that are used to represent the attributes of an entity. Examples are *PartNumber*, *EmployeeName*, and *SalesDate*. 147

Commerce server A computer that operates Web-based programs that display products, support online ordering, record and process payments, and interface with inventory-management applications. 295

Communication A critical factor in collaboration, consisting of two key elements: the abilities of individuals to share information and receive feedback, and the availability of effective systems by which to share information. 31

Communications protocol A means for coordinating activity between two or more communicating computers. Two machines must agree on the protocol to use, and they must follow that protocol as they send messages back and forth. Because there is so much to do, communications tasks are broken up into levels, or layers, of protocols. 218

Competitive strategy The strategy an organization chooses as the way it will succeed in its industry. According to Porter, there are four fundamental competitive strategies: cost leadership across an industry or within a particular industry segment and product differentiation across an industry or within a particular industry segment. 63

Computer hardware One of the five fundamental components of an information system. 5

Computer-assisted software engineering (CASE) A style of program development that uses a tool, called a CASE tool, to help develop computer programs. 402

Computer-assisted systems engineering (CASE) A style of program development that uses a tool, called a CASE tool, to help develop computer systems. 402

Computer-based information system An information system that includes a computer. 6

Conference call A synchronous virtual meeting, in which participants meet at the same time via a voice-communication channel. 34

Confidence In market-basket terminology, the probability estimate that two items will be purchased together. 343

Content management One of the drivers of collaboration effectiveness, which enables multiple users to contribute to and change documents, schedules, task lists, assignments, and so forth, without one user's work interfering with another's. Content management also enables users to track and report who made what changes, when, and why. 31

Contingent liability A liability that could *possibly*, but not necessarily will, occur. Failure to adequately secure a company's data, for example, could produce a contingent liability. 264

Cost [of a business process] The cost of the inputs to a business process plus the cost of the activities involved in the process. 68

Cost feasibility Whether an IS can be developed within budget. 389

Cross-departmental systems The third era of computing systems. In this era, systems are designed not to facilitate the work of a single department or function, but rather to integrate the activities of a complete business process. 252

Cross-functional systems Synonym for *Cross-departmental systems*. 252

Cross-selling The sale of related products; salespeople try to get customers who buy product *X* to also buy product *Y*. 343

Crow's foot A line on an entity-relationship diagram that indicates a 1:N relationship between two entities. 161

Crow's-foot diagram A type of entity-relationship diagram that uses a crow's foot symbol to designate a 1:N relationship. 162

CRT monitor A type of video display monitor that uses cathode ray tubes, the same devices used in traditional TV screens. Because they use a large tube, CRT monitors are big and bulky, about as deep as they are wide. 113

Curse of dimensionality The more attributes there are, the easier it is to build a data model that fits the sample data but that is worthless as a predictor. 351

Custom-developed software Tailor-made software. 121

Customer life cycle Taken as a whole, the processes of marketing, customer acquisition, relationship management, and loss/churn that must be managed by CRM systems. 269

Customer-management systems Information systems that companies use to obtain additional sales from existing customers. Such systems maintain customer contact and order-history data and track product interests, and some maintain information about the customer's credit status with the organization. 255

Customer relationship management (CRM) The set of business processes for attracting, selling, managing, and supporting customers. 269

Customer relationship management (CRM) system An information system that maintains data about customers and all their interactions with the organization. 269

D-sub See *VGA*. 114

Data Recorded facts or figures. One of the five fundamental components of an information system. 5

Data administration A staff function that pertains to *all* of an organization's data assets. Typical data administration tasks are setting data standards, developing data policies, and providing for data security. 435

Data channel Means by which the CPU reads instructions and data from main memory and writes data to main memory. 106

Data dictionary A file or database that contains data definitions. 436

Data integrity problem In a database, the situation that exists when data items disagree with one another. An example is two different names for the same customer. 164

Data marts Facilities that prepare, store, and manage data for reporting and data mining for specific business functions. 349

Data mining The application of statistical techniques to find patterns and relationships among data for classification and prediction. 338

Data model A logical representation of the data in a database that describes the data and relationships that will be stored in the database. Akin to a blueprint. 159

Data standards Definitions, or metadata, for data items shared across the organization. They describe the name, official definition, usage, relationship to other data items, processing restrictions, version, security code, format, and other features of data items that are shared across the organization. 436

Data warehouses Facilities that prepare, store, and manage data specifically for reporting and data mining. 349

Database A self-describing collection of integrated records. 146

Database administration The management, development, operation, and maintenance of the database so as to achieve the organization's objectives. This staff function requires balancing conflicting goals: protecting the database while maximizing its availability for authorized use. In smaller organizations, this function usually is served by a single person. Larger organizations assign several people to an office of database administration. 169, 436

Database application A collection of forms, reports, queries, and application programs that process a database. 154

Database application system Applications, having the standard five components, that make database data more accessible and useful. Users employ a database application that consists of forms, formatted reports, queries, and application programs. Each of these, in turn, calls on the database management system (DBMS) to process the database tables. 152

Database management system (DBMS) A program used to create, process, and administer a database. 152

Database tier In the three-tier architecture, the tier that runs the DBMS and receives and processes SQL requests to retrieve and store data. 295

Data-mining tools Tools that use statistical techniques, many of which are sophisticated and mathematically complex, to process data to look for hidden patterns. 333

DBA Depending on context, either the *database administrator* or the *office of database administration*. 169

DB2 A popular, enterprise-class DBMS product from IBM. 152

Decision tree A hierarchical arrangement of criteria for classifying customers, items, and other business objects. 344

Denial of service Security problem in which users are not able to access an IS; can be caused by human errors, natural disaster, or malicious activity. 460

Dial-up modem A modem that performs the conversion between analog and digital in such a way that the signal can be carried on a regular telephone line. 198

Digital certificate A document supplied by a certificate authority (CA) that contains, among other data, an entity's name and public key. 472

Digital rights management (DRM) Technology and products used to protect entertainment content. 482

Digital signature Encrypted message that uses *hashing* to ensure that plaintext messages are received without alteration. 470

Dimension A characteristic of an OLAP measure. Purchase date, customer type, customer location, and sales region are examples of dimensions. 337

Direct installation See *Plunge installation*. 397

Dirty data Problematic data. Examples are a value of *B* for customer gender and a value of *213* for customer age. Other examples are a value of *999–999–9999* for a U.S. phone number, a part color of *gren*, and an email address of WhyMe@GuessWhoIAM-Hah-Hah.org. All these values are problematic when data mining. 349

Discussion forum A form of asynchronous communication in which one group member posts an entry and other group members respond. A better form of group communication than email, because it is more difficult for the discussion to go off track. 35

Disintermediation Elimination of one or more middle layers in the supply chain. 293

Distributed computing The process of a program on one computer accessing programs on a second computer. 315

Domain name The registered, human-friendly valid name in the domain name system (DNS). The process of changing a name into its IP address is called *resolving the domain name.* 227

Domain name resolution The process of converting a domain name into a public IP address. 229

Domain name resolvers Computers that facilitate domain name resolution by storing the correspondence of domain names and IP addresses. 229

Domain name system (DNS) A system that converts user-friendly names into their IP addresses. Any registered, valid name is called a domain name. 227

Dot pitch The distance between pixels on a CRT monitor; the smaller the dot pitch, the sharper and brighter the screen image will be. 113

Drill down With an OLAP report, to further divide the data into more detail. 338

Drive-by sniffers People who take computers with wireless connections through an area and search for unprotected wireless networks in an attempt to gain free Internet access or to gather unauthorized data. 458

DSL (digital subscriber line) modem A type of modem. DSL modems operate on the same lines as voice telephones and dial-up modems, but they operate so that their signals do not interfere with voice telephone service. DSL modems provide much faster data transmission speeds than dial-up modems. Additionally, DSL modems always maintain a connection, so there is no need to dial in; the Internet connection is available immediately. 198

Dual processor A computer with two CPUs. 104

DVD-R A digital versatile disk that can record data once. 113

DVD-ROM A read-only digital versatile disk. 113

DVD-RW A rewritable digital versatile disk. 113

DVI A type of signal interface for LCD devices; it provides a better-quality image than the traditional VGA interface, but is more expensive. 114

Dynamic Host Configuration Protocol (DHCP) A service provided by some communications devices that allocates and deallocates a pool of IP addresses. A device that hosts the DHCP service is called a *DHCP server*. On request, a DHCP server loans a temporary IP address to a network device such as a computer or printer. When the device disconnects, the IP address becomes available, and the DHCP server will reuse it when needed. 222

E-commerce The buying and selling of goods and services over public and private computer networks. 297

EDI over Internet Electronic data interchange (EDI) document standards and formats for use in transmitting documents over the Internet. 312

Electronic Data Interchange (EDI) A standard for exchanging documents from machine to machine, electronically. In the past, EDI was used over point-to-point or value-added networks. Recently, EDI systems have been developed that use the Internet as well. 312

Electronic exchanges Sites that facilitate the matching of buyers and sellers; the business process is similar to that of a stock exchange. Sellers offer goods at a given price through the electronic exchange, and buyers make offers to purchase over the same exchange. Price matches result in transactions from which the exchange takes a commission. 292

Email A form of asynchronous communication in which participants send comments and attachments electronically. As a form of group communication, it can be disorganized, disconnected, and easy to hide from. 34

Email spoofing A synonym for *phishing*. A technique for obtaining unauthorized data that uses pretexting via email. The *phisher* pretends to be a legitimate company and sends email requests for confidential data, such as account numbers, Social Security numbers, account passwords, and so forth. Phishers direct traffic to their sites under the guise of a legitimate business. 458

Encryption The process of transforming clear text into coded, unintelligible text for secure storage or communication. 469

Encryption algorithms Algorithms used to transform clear text into coded, unintelligible text for secure storage or communication. Commonly used methods are DES, 3DES, and AES. 206

Enterprise applications IS applications that span more than one department, such as some functional applications, as well as ERP, EAI, and SCM applications. 433

Enterprise application integration (EAI) The integration of existing systems by providing layers of software that connect applications and their data together. 276

Enterprise DBMS A product that processes large organizational and workgroup databases. These products support many users, perhaps thousands, and many different database applications. Such DBMS products support 24/7 operations and can manage databases that span dozens of different magnetic disks with hundreds of gigabytes or more of data. IBM's DB2, Microsoft's SQL Server, and Oracle's Oracle are examples of enterprise DBMS products. 157

Enterprise-DRM (E-DRM) The use of digital rights management (DRM) technology to protect an organization's documents. 482

Enterprise resource planning (ERP) The integration of all the organization's principal processes. ERP is an outgrowth of MRP II manufacturing systems, and most ERP users are manufacturing companies. 272

Entity In the E-R data model, a representation of some thing that users want to track. Some entities represent a physical object; others represent a logical construct or transaction. 164

Entity-relationship data model (E-R model) Popular technique for creating a data model whereby developers define the things that will be stored and identify the relationships among them. 159

Entity-relationship (E-R) diagrams A type of diagram used by database designers to document entities and their relationships to each other. 161

Ethernet Another name for the IEEE 802.3 protocol, Ethernet is a network protocol that operates at Layers 1 and 2 of the TCP/IP–OSI architecture. Ethernet, the world's most popular LAN protocol, is used on WANs as well. 194

Exabyte 10^{18} bytes. 331

Exception alert A message that notifies a system user of an out-of-the-ordinary—exceptional—event. 359

Expert system Knowledge-sharing system that is created by interviewing experts in a given business domain and codifying the rules used by those experts. 355

eXtensible Markup Language (XML) A very important document standard that separates document content, structure, and presentation; eliminates problems in HTML; and offers advantages over EDI. Most believe XML will eventually replace EDI. 313

Extreme programming (XP) An emerging technique for developing computer programs. Programmers create only features and functions of the new program that they can complete in 2 weeks or less. If many programmers are working on the project, each person's work must be done in such a way that all their work can be combined and assembled at the end of that period. Users and PQA professionals test the developed code continuously through the process. Three key XP characteristics are: (1) it is customer centric, (2) it uses just-in-time design, and (3) it involves paired programming. 408

Facilities Structures used within a business process. 68

Fields Also called *columns*; groups of bytes in a database table. A database table has multiple columns that are used to represent the attributes of an entity. Examples are *PartNumber*, *EmployeeName*, and *SalesDate*. 147

File A group of similar rows or records. In a database, sometimes called a *table*. 147

File Transfer Protocol (FTP) A Layer-5 protocol used to copy files from one computer to another. In interorganizational transaction processing, FTP enables users to exchange large files easily. 37, 219

Firewall A computing device located between a firm's internal and external networks that prevents unauthorized access to or from the internal network. A firewall can be a special-purpose computer or it can be a program on a general-purpose computer or on a router. 206, 472

Firmware Computer software that is installed into devices such as printers, print services, and various types of communication devices. The software is coded just like other software, but it is installed into special, programmable memory of the printer or other device. 122

Five-component framework The five fundamental components of an information system—computer hardware, software, data, procedures, and people—that are present in every information system, from the simplest to the most complex. 5

Five-forces model Model, proposed by Michael Porter, that assesses industry characteristics and profitability by means of five competitive forces—bargaining power of suppliers, threat of substitution, bargaining power of customers, rivalry among firms, and threat of new entrants. 63

Flow The movement of resources between or among business activities. 68

Foreign keys A column or group of columns used to represent relationships. Values of the foreign key match values of the primary key in a different (foreign) table. 148

Form Data entry forms are used to read, insert, modify, and delete database data. 154

Frame The container used at Layers 1 and 2 of the TCP/IP–OSI model. A program implementing a Layer-2 protocol packages data into frames. 221

Frame Relay A protocol that can process traffic in the range of 56 kbps to 40 Mbps by packaging data into frames. 201

FTP See *File Transfer Protocol*. 11

Functional application Software that provides features and functions necessary to support a particular business activity (function). 253

Functional systems The second era of information systems. The goal of such systems was to facilitate the work of a single department or function. Over time, in each functional area, companies added features and functions to encompass more activities and to provide more value and assistance. 251

Gigabyte (GB) 1,024MB. 106

Google Docs & Spreadsheets A version-management system for sharing documents and spreadsheet data. Documents are stored on a Google server, from which users can access and simultaneously see and edit the documents. 38

Google's My Maps Web 2.0 product that provides tools with which users can make custom modifications to maps provided by Google; My Maps is an example of a mashup. 301

Gramm-Leach-Bliley (GLB) Act Passed by Congress in 1999, this act protects consumer financial data stored by financial institutions, which are defined as banks, securities firms, insurance companies, and organizations that provide financial advice, prepare tax returns, and provide similar financial services. 464

Granularity The level of detail in data. Customer name and account balance is large-granularity data. Customer name, balance, and the order details and payment history of every customer order is smaller granularity. 350

Hacking Occurs when a person gains unauthorized access to a computer system. Although some people hack for the sheer joy of doing it, other hackers invade systems for the malicious purpose of stealing or modifying data. 460

Hardening a site The process of taking extraordinary measures to reduce a system's vulnerability. Hardened sites use special versions of the operating system, and they lock down or eliminate operating systems features and functions that are not required by the application. Hardening is a technical safeguard. 479

Hardware Electronic components and related gadgetry that input, process, output, store, and communicate data according to instructions encoded in computer programs or software. 103

Hashing A method of mathematically manipulating an electronic message to create a string of bits that characterize the message. 470

Health Insurance Portability and Accountability Act (HIPAA) The privacy provisions of this 1996 act give individuals the right to access health data created by doctors and other health-care providers. HIPAA also sets rules and limits on who can read and receive a person's health information. 464

Horizontal-market application Software that provides capabilities common across all organizations and industries; examples include word processors, graphics programs, spreadsheets, and presentation programs. 120

Hot site A remote processing center run by a commercial disaster-recovery service that provides equipment a company would need to continue operations after a disaster. 483

HTTPs An indication that a Web browser is using the SSL/TLS protocol to ensure secure communications. 206

Human resources information systems Systems that support recruitment, compensation, evaluation, and development of employees and affiliated personnel. 262

Hyperlink A pointer on a Web page to another Web page. A hyperlink contains the URL of the Web page to access when the user clicks the hyperlink. The URL can reference a page on the Web server that generated the page containing the hyperlink, or it can reference a page on another server. 297

Hypertext Markup Language (HTML) A language that defines the structure and layout of Web page content. An HTML tag is a notation used to define a data element for display or other purposes. 297

Hypertext Transfer Protocol (HTTP) A Layer-5 protocol used to process Web pages. 210, 295

Identification The process whereby an information system identifies a user by requiring the user to sign on with a user name and password. 467

Identifier An attribute (or group of attributes) whose value is associated with one and only one entity instance. 160

IEEE 802.3 protocol This standard, also called *Ethernet*, is a network protocol that operates at Layers 1 and 2 of the TCP/IP–OSI architecture. Ethernet, the world's most popular LAN protocol, is used on WANs as well. 194

IEEE 802.11 protocol A wireless communications standard, widely used today, that enables access within a few hundred feet. The most popular version of this standard is *IEEE802.11g*, which allows wireless transmissions of up to 54 Mbps. 195

IEEE 802.16 protocol An emerging wireless communications standard, also know as *WiMax*, that enables broadband wireless access for fixed, nomadic, and portable applications. In fixed mode, it enables access across a several-mile or larger region. See also *WiMax*. 204

If... then . . . decision rules Format for rules derived from a decision tree (data mining) or by interviewing a human expert (expert systems). 345

In-person services According to Reich, jobs that must be provided face-to-face but that are simple and repetitive, primarily requiring good communication skills. Because they are provided in person, such services cannot readily be moved offshore. 17

Incremental development A development process whereby developers design, implement, and fix portions of an application, one-by-one, until the entire program has been developed in pieces. This method reduces development challenges by using a divide-and-conquer strategy. 400

Indexing The most important content function of knowledge-management applications, which uses keyword search to determine whether content exists and provides a link to its location. 353

Information (1) Knowledge derived from data, where *data* is defined as recorded facts or figures; (2) data presented in a meaningful context; (3) data processed by summing, ordering, averaging, grouping, comparing, or other similar operations; (4) a difference that makes a difference. 11

Information system (IS) A group of components that interact to produce information. 5

Information technology (IT) The products, methods, inventions, and standards that are used for the purpose of producing information. 16

Inherent processes The procedures that must be followed to effectively use licensed software. For example, the processes inherent in MRP systems assume that certain users will take specified actions in a particular order. In most cases, the organization must conform to the processes inherent in the software. 267

Input hardware Hardware devices that attach to a computer; includes keyboards, mouse, document scanners, and bar-code (Universal Product Code) scanners. 103

Input resources The resources that a business adds in the course of producing goods or services as part of its value-creating activities. 68

Instruction set The collection of instructions that a computer can process. 118

Internal firewalls A firewall that sits inside the organizational network. 207, 472

International Organization for Standardization (ISO) An international organization that sets worldwide standards. ISO developed a seven-layer protocol architecture called Open Systems Interconnection (OSI). Portions of that protocol architecture are incorporated into the TCP/IP–OSI hybrid protocol architecture. 218

Internet When spelled with a small *i*, as in *internet*, a private network of networks. When spelled with a capital *I*, as *Internet*, the public internet known as the Internet. 192

Internet Corporation for Assigned Names and Numbers (ICANN) The organization responsible for managing the assignment of public IP addresses and domain names for use on the Internet. Each public IP address is unique across all computers on the Internet. 222

Internet Engineering Task Force (IETF) An organization that specifies standards for use on the Internet. Developed the four-layer scheme called the TCP/IP (Transmission Control Program/Internet Protocol) architecture. TCP/IP is part of the TCP/IP–OSI protocol architecture that is used on the Internet and most internets today. 218

Internet Protocol (IP) A Layer-3 protocol. As the name implies, IP is used on the Internet, but it is used on many other internets as well. The chief purpose of IP is to route packets across an internet. 220

Internet service provider (ISP) An ISP provides users with Internet access. An ISP provides a user with a legitimate Internet address; it serves as the user's gateway to the

Internet; and it passes communications back and forth between the user and the Internet. ISPs also pay for the Internet. They collect money from their customers and pay access fees and other charges on the users' behalf. 197

Inventory information systems Operations systems that help control and manage inventory and that support inventory policy. 256

IP address A series of dotted decimals in a format like 192.168.2.28 that identifies a unique device on a network or internet. With the IPv4 standard, IP addresses have 32 bits. With the IPv6 standard, IP addresses have 128 bits. Today, IPv4 is more common, but it will likely be supplanted by IPv6 in the future. With IPv4, the decimal between the dots can never exceed 255. 222

IP spoofing A type of spoofing whereby an intruder uses another site's IP address as if it were that other site. 458

iPhone A handheld computer from Apple that combines a cell phone, an Internet-connection device, and an iPod. 115

IPTV (Internet Protocol television) A technology that uses the TCP/IP–OSI protocol to transmit television and other video signals via a broadband connection and set-top box. 228

Islands of automation The structure that results when functional applications work independently in isolation from one another. Usually problematic because data is duplicated, integration is difficult, and results can be inconsistent. 251

Joint application design (JAD) A key element of rapid application design. A team of users, developers, and PQA personnel conducts design activities during JAD sessions. JAD came about because developers wanted to incorporate feedback and testing earlier in the development process. Ultimately, developers decided that the best place to get feedback was during design creation. 402

Just-barely-sufficient information Information that meets the purpose for which it is generated, but just barely so. 16

Just-in-time (JIT) inventory policy A policy that seeks to have production inputs (both raw materials and work-in-process) delivered to the manufacturing site just as they are needed. By scheduling delivery of inputs in this way, companies are able to reduce inventories to a minimum. 257

Kerberos A system, developed at MIT, that authenticates users without sending their passwords across a computer network. It uses a complicated system of "tickets" to enable users to obtain services from networks and other servers. 468

Key (1) A column or group of columns that identifies a unique row in a table. (2) A number used to encrypt data. The encryption algorithm applies the key to the original message to produce the coded message. Decoding (decrypting) a message is similar; a key is applied to the coded message to recover the original text. 177, 206

Key escrow A control procedure whereby a trusted party is given a copy of a key used to encrypt database data. 476

Kilobyte (K) 1,024 bytes. 106

Knowledge management (KM) The process of creating value from intellectual capital and sharing that knowledge with employees, managers, suppliers, customers, and others who need it. 352

Knowledge-management (KM) tools Computer applications used to store employee knowledge and to make that knowledge available to employees, customers, vendors, and others who need it. The source of KM tools is human knowledge, rather than recorded facts and figures. 333

Layered protocols Different ways of arranging the layers of communication protocols for transmission of data across networks. TCP/IP is one such layered protocol. 218

Latency In measuring computer performance, the transmission delay that occurs due to network congestion during busy periods. 205

LCD monitor A type of video display monitor that uses a technology called *liquid crystal display*. LCD monitors are flat and require much less space than CRT monitors. 113

Lead-generation systems Sales and marketing information systems that send mailings (postal or email) for the purpose of generating sales prospects. 254

Lead-tracking systems Sales and marketing information systems that record data on sales prospects and keep records of customer contacts. 254

Legacy information system An older system that has outdated technologies and techniques but is still used, despite its age. 434

Library In version-control collaboration systems, a shared directory that allows access to various documents by means of *permissions*. 40

License Agreement that stipulates how a program can be used. Most specify the number of computers on which the program can be installed, some specify the number of users that can connect to and use the program remotely. Such agreements also stipulate limitations on the liability of the software vendor for the consequences of errors in the software. 120

Lift In market-basket terminology, the ratio of confidence to the base probability of buying an item. Lift shows how much the base probability changes when other products are purchased. If the lift is greater than 1, the change is positive; if it is less than 1, the change is negative. 344

Linkages Process interactions across value chains. Linkages are important sources of efficiencies and are readily supported by information systems. 67

Linux A version of Unix that was developed by the open-source community. The open-source community owns Linux, and there is no fee to use it. Linux is a popular operating system for Web servers. 120

Local area network (LAN) A network that connects compuers that reside in a single geographic location on the premises of the company that operates the LAN. The number of connected computers can range from two to several hundred. 189

Localizing software The process of making a computer program work in a second language. 236

Logical address Also called an *IP address*, a series of dotted decimals in a format like 192.168.2.28 that identifies a unique device on a network or internet. With the IPv4 standard, IP addresses have 32 bits. IP addresses are called logical addresses because they can be reassigned from one device to another. 222

Loss rate In measuring computer performance, the frequency of problems in the communications network that necessitate data retransmission. 205

Lost-update problem An issue in multi-user database processing in which two or more users try to make changes to the data but the database cannot make all those changes because it was not designed to process changes from multiple users. 157

MAC address Also called a *physical address.* A permanent address given to each network interface card (NIC) at the factory. This address enables the device to access the network via a Level-2 protocol. By agreement among computer manufacturers, MAC addresses are assigned in such a way that no two NIC devices will ever have the same MAC address. 192, 221

Mac OS An operating system developed by Apple Computer, Inc., for the Macintosh. The current version is Mac OS X. Macintosh computers are used primarily by graphic artists and workers in the arts community. Mac OS was developed for the PowerPC, but as of 2006 will run on Intel processors as well. 119

Macro virus Virus that attaches itself to a Word, Excel, PowerPoint, or other type of document. When the infected document is opened, the virus places itself in the startup files of the application. After that, the virus infects every file that the application creates or processes. 125

Main memory A set of cells in which each cell holds a byte of data or instruction; each cell has an address, and the CPU uses the addresses to identify particular data items. 104

Maintenance In the context of information systems, (1) to fix the system to do what it was supposed to do in the first place or (2) to adapt the system to a change in requirements. 384

Malware Viruses, worms, Trojan horses, spyware, and adware. 473

Malware definitions Patterns that exist in malware code. Antimalware vendors update these definitions continuously and incorporate them into their products in order to better fight against malware. 474

Management information system (MIS) An information system that helps businesses achieve their goals and objectives. 5

Managerial decision Decision that concerns the allocation and use of resources. 45

Manufacturing information systems Information systems that support one or more aspects of manufacturing processes, including planning, scheduling, integration with inventory, quality control, and related processes. 256

Manufacturing resource planning (MRP II) A follow-on to MRP that includes the planning of materials, personnel, and machinery. It supports many linkages across the organization, including linkages with sales and marketing via the development of a master production schedule. It also includes the capability to perform what-if analyses on variances in schedules, raw materials availabilities, personnel, and other resources. 259

Many-to-many (N:M) relationship Relationships involving two entity types in which an instance of one type can relate to many instances of the second type, and an instance of the second type can relate to many instances of the first. For example, the relationship between Student and Class is N:M. One student may enroll in many classes, and one class may have many students. Contrast with *one-to-many relationships.* 161

Margin According to Porter, the difference between the value that an activity generates and the cost of the activity. 65

Margin [of a business process] The difference between the value of outputs in a business process and the cost of the process. 68

Market-basket analysis A data-mining technique for determining sales patterns. A market-basket analysis shows the products that customers tend to buy together. 343

Mashup The combining of output from two or more Web sites into a single user experience. 301

Master production schedule (MPS) A plan for producing products. To create the MPS, the company analyzes past sales levels and makes estimates of future sales. This process is sometimes called a *push manufacturing process,* because the company pushes the products into sales (and customers) according to the MPS. 258

Materials requirements planning (MRP) An information system that plans the need for materials and inventories of materials used in the manufacturing process. Unlike MRP II, MRP does not include the planning of personnel, equipment, or facilities requirements. 259

Maximum cardinality The maximum number of entities that can be involved in a relationship. Common examples of maximum cardinality are 1:N, N:M, and 1:1. 162

Measure The data item of interest on an OLAP report. It is the item that is to be summed, averaged, or otherwise processed in the OLAP cube. Total sales, average sales, and average cost are examples of measures. 337

Megabyte (MB) 1,024KB. 106

Memory swapping The movement of programs and data into and out of memory. If a computer has insufficient memory for its workload, such swapping will degrade system performance. 107

Merchant companies In e-commerce, companies that take title to the goods they sell. They buy goods and resell them. 291

Message digest A bit string of a specific, fixed length that is produced by hashing and used to produce digital signatures. 470

Metadata Data that describe data. 149

Microsoft Office Groove A collaboration product that includes version management and other useful tools. Users can access and edits documents at a workspace; the software automatically propagates changes made by one user to other users' computers. 38

Microsoft SharePoint A version-control application that includes many collaboration features and functions, including document check-in/checkout, surveys, discussion forums, and workflow. 40

Microsoft Surface Hardware-software product from Microsoft that enables people to interact with data on the surface of a table. A new product category, Surface is scheduled to be shipped in the winter of 2007–2008. 114

Minimum cardinality The minimum number of entities that must be involved in a relationship. 162

Modem Short for *modulator/demodulator*, a modem converts the computer's digital data into signals that can be transmitted over telephone or cable lines. 197

Moore's Law A law, created by Gordon Moore, stating that the number of transistors per square inch on an integrated chip doubles every 18 months. Moore's prediction has proved generally accurate in the 40 years since it was made. Sometimes this law is stated that the performance of a computer doubles every 18 months. Although not strictly true, this version gives the gist of the idea. 16

MRP I Another name for *Materials requirement planning (MRP)*. 259

MRP II Another name for *Manufacturing resource planning*. 259

Multiparty text chat A synchronous virtual meeting, in which participants meet at the same time and communicate by typing comments over a communication network. 34

Multi-user processing When multiple users process the database at the same time. 156

MySQL A popular open-source DBMS product that is license-free for most applications. 152

Narrowband Internet communication lines that have transmission speeds of 56 kbps or less. A dial-up modem provides narrowband access. 199

Network A collection of computers that communicate with one another over transmission lines. 189

Network Address Translation (NAT) The process of changing public IP addresses into private network IP addresses, and the reverse. 225

Network interface card (NIC) A hardware component on each device on a network (computer, printer, etc.) that connects the device's circuitry to the communications line. The NIC works together with programs in each device to implement Layers 1 and 2 of the TCP/IP–OSI hybrid protocol. 192

Network of leased lines A WAN connection alternative. Communication lines are leased from telecommunications companies and connected into a network. The lines connect geographically distant sites. 199

Neural networks A popular supervised data-mining technique used to predict values and make classifications, such as "good prospect" or "poor prospect." 342

Nonroutine cognitive skills Work skills that include abstract reasoning, problem-solving, communication, and collaboration. 9

Nonmerchant companies E-commerce companies that arrange for the purchase and sale of goods without ever owning or taking title to those goods. 291

Nonvolatile memory Memory that preserves data contents even when not powered (e.g., magnetic and optical disks). With such devices, you can turn the computer off and back on, and the contents will be unchanged. 107

Normal forms A classification of tables according to their characteristics and the kinds of problems they have. 165

Normalization The process of converting poorly structured tables into two or more well-structured tables. 164

Object-oriented development (OOD) A systems development methodology that arose from the discipline of object-oriented programming. OOD develops programs using the object-oriented programming (OOP) techniques. Programs developed using OOP are easier to maintain than those developed using traditional techniques. 404

Object-oriented programming (OOP) A discipline for designing and writing computer programs. Programs developed using OOP are easier and cheaper to maintain than those developed using traditional techniques. 404

Object-relational database A type of database that stores both OOP objects and relational data. Rarely used in commercial applications. 153

Off-the-shelf software Software that can be used without having to make any changes. 121

Off-the-shelf with alterations software Software bought off-the-shelf but altered to fit the organization's specific needs. 121

OLAP See *Online analytical processing*. 337

OLAP cube A presentation of an OLAP measure with associated dimensions. The reason for this term is that some products show these displays using three axes, like a cube in geometry. Same as *OLAP report*. 337

OLAP server Computer server running software that performs OLAP analyses. An OLAP server reads data from an operational database, performs preliminary calculations, and stores the results of those calculations in an OLAP database. 338

Onboard NIC A built-in network interface card. 192

One-of-a-kind application Software that is developed for a specific, unique need, usually for a particular company's operations. 121

One-to-many (1:N) relationship Relationships involving two entity types in which an instance of one type can relate to many instances of the second type, but an instance of the second type can relate to at most one instance of the first. For example, the relationship between *Department* and *Employee* is 1:N. A department may relate to many employees, but an employee relates to at most one department. 161

Online analytical processing (OLAP) A dynamic type of reporting system that provides the ability to sum, count, average, and perform other simple arithmetic operations on groups of data. Such reports are dynamic because users can change the format of the reports while viewing them. 337

Open-source community A loosely coupled group of programmers who mostly volunteer their time to contribute code to develop and maintain common software. Linux and MySQL are two prominent products developed by such a community. 120

Operations information systems Systems that maintain data on finished goods inventory and the movements of goods from inventory to the customer. 255

Operating system (OS) A computer program that controls the computer's resources: It manages the contents of main memory, processes keystrokes and mouse movements, sends signals to the display monitor, reads and writes disk files, and controls the processing of other programs. 106

Operational decisions Decisions that concern the day-to-day activities of an organization. 44

Optical fiber cable A type of cable used to connect the computers, printers, switches, and other devices on a LAN. The signals on such cables are light rays, and they are reflected inside the glass core of the optical fiber cable. The core is surrounded by a *cladding* to contain the light signals, and the cladding, in turn, is wrapped with an outer layer to protect it. 194

Optimal resolution The size of the pixel grid (e.g., 1,024 × 768) on a video display monitor that will give the best sharpness and clarity. This optimal resolution depends on the size of the screen, the dot or pixel pitch, and other factors. 113

Oracle A popular, enterprise-class DBMS product from Oracle Corporation. 152

Organizational feasibility Whether an IS fits within an organization's customer, culture, or legal requirements. 389

Output hardware Hardware that displays the results of the computer's processing. Consists of video displays, printers, audio speakers, overhead projectors, and other special-purpose devices, such as large, flatbed plotters. 105

Output resources The goods or services that result from a business's value-creating activities. 68

Outsourcing The process of hiring another organization to perform a service. Outsourcing is done to save costs, to gain expertise, and to free up management time. 438

Packet A small piece of an electronic message, which has been divided into chunks, which are sent separately and reassembled at their destination. 220

Packet-filtering firewall A firewall that examines each packet and determines whether to let the packet pass. To make this decision, it examines the source address, the destination addresses, and other data. 207, 472

Paired programming The most unconventional characteristic of XP. With it, two programmers work together, side by side, on the very same computer. They look over each other's shoulders, and they continuously communicate as they program on that single machine. According to XP proponents, studies show that two programmers working in this way can do at least as much work as two programmers working separately, and the resulting program code has fewer errors and is more easily maintained. 408

Parallel installation A type of system conversion in which the new system runs in parallel with the old one for a while. Parallel installation is expensive because the organization incurs the costs of running both systems. 397

Parallel workflow A workflow in which activities occur simultaneously. 41

Patch A group of fixes for high-priority failures that can be applied to existing copies of a particular product. Software vendors supply patches to fix security and other critical problems. 126, 398

Payload The program code of a virus that causes unwanted or hurtful actions, such as deleting programs or data, or even worse, modifying data in ways that are undetected by the user. 125

People As part of the five-component framework, one of the five fundamental components of an information system; includes those who operate and service the computers, those who maintain the data, those who support the networks, and those who use the system. 5

Performance guarantees Commitments to certain levels of service quality, made by vendors of communications equipment and services to their customers. Vendors agree to cost penalties if agreed-upon levels of service are not met. 205

Perimeter firewall A firewall that sits outside the organizational network. It is the first device that Internet traffic encounters. 207

Permissions In a version-control system, authorizations to access shared documents stored in various directories. Typical permissions are read-only, read-and-edit, and read-edit-and-delete; some directories have no permission—they are off-limits. 31

Personal DBMS DBMS products designed for smaller, simpler database applications. Such products are used for personal or small workgroup applications that involve fewer than a 100 users, and normally fewer than 15. Today, Microsoft Access is the only prominent personal DBMS. 159

Personal identification number (PIN) A form of authentication whereby the user supplies a number that only he or she knows. 467

Petabyte 10^{15} bytes. 331

Phased installation A type of system conversion in which the new system is installed in pieces across the organization(s). Once a given piece works, then the organization installs and tests another piece of the system, until the entire system has been installed. 397

Phishing A technique for obtaining unauthorized data that uses pretexting via email. The *phisher* pretends to be a legitimate company and sends an email requesting confidential data, such as account numbers, Social Security numbers, account passwords, and so forth. 458

Physical address Also called *MAC address*. A permanent address given to each network interface card (NIC) at the factory. This address enables the device to access the network via a Level-2 protocol. By agreement among computer manufacturers, physical addresses are assigned in such a way that no two NIC devices will ever have the same address. 221

Pilot installation A type of system conversion in which the organization implements the entire system on a limited portion of the business. The advantage of pilot implementation is that if the system fails, the failure is contained within a limited boundary. This reduces exposure of the business and also protects the new system from developing a negative reputation throughout the organization(s). 397

Pixel A small spot on the screen of a video display monitor arranged in a rectangular grid. The number of pixels displayed depends not only on the size of the monitor, but also on the design of the computer's video card. The higher the number of pixels displayed, the better the quality of the display. 113

Pixel pitch The distance between pixels on the screen of an LCD monitor; the smaller the pixel pitch, the sharper and brighter the image will be. 113

Plunge installation A type of system conversion in which the organization shuts off the old system and starts the new system. If the new system fails, the organization is in trouble: Nothing can be done until either the new system is fixed or the old system is reinstalled. Because of the risk, organizations should avoid this conversion style if possible. Sometimes called *direct installation.* 397

Point of presence (POP) The location at which a line connects to a PSDN network. Think of the POP as the phone number that one dials to connect to the PSDN. Once a site has connected to the PSDN POP, the site obtains access to all other sites connected to the PSDN. 201

Point-to-Point Protocol (PPP) A Layer-2 protocol used for networks that involve just two computers, hence the term *point-to-point.* PPP is used between a modem and an ISP as well as on some networks of leased lines. 198

Portal server Program similar to a Web server, but with a customizable user interface. 358

Porter's five competitive-forces model See *Five-forces model.* 63

Pretexting A technique for gathering unauthorized information in which someone pretends to be someone else. A common scam involves a telephone caller who pretends to be from a credit card company and claims to be checking the validity of credit card numbers. Phishing is also a form of pretexting. 458

Price conflict In e-commerce, a conflict that may result when manufacturers offer products at prices lower than those available through existing sales channels. 294

Price elasticity A measure of the sensitivity in demand to changes in price. It is the ratio of the percentage change in quantity divided by the percentage change in price. 293

Primary activities In Porter's value chain model, the fundamental activities that create value—inbound logistics, operations, outbound logistics, marketing/sales, and service. 65

Privacy Act of 1974 Federal law that provides protections to individuals regarding records maintained by the U.S. government. 464

Private IP address A type of IP address used within private networks and internets. Private IP addresses are assigned and managed by the company that operates the private network or internet. 222

Probable loss The "bottom line" of risk assessment; the likelihood of loss multiplied by the cost of the loss consequences (both tangible and intangible). 466

Problem A *perceived* difference between what is and what out to be. 49

Problem-identifier According to Reich, a type of symbolic-analytic worker who processes information to determine that something is not as it should be. 17

Problem of the last mile The difficulty involved in getting the capacity of fast optimal-fiber transmission lines from the street in front of buildings into the homes and smaller businesses located in those buildings. Digging up the street and backyard of every residence and small business to install optical fiber is not affordable; it is hoped that WiMax technology will be able to solve the problem of making the network connections of "the last mile." 203

Problem-solver According to Reich, a type of symbolic-analytic worker who uses technology and other assets to create problem solutions. 17

Procedures Instructions for humans. One of the five fundamental components of an information system. 5

Process-based systems The third era of computing systems. In this era, systems are designed not to facilitate the work of a single department or function, but rather to integrate the activities in an entire business process. 252

Process blueprint In an ERP application, a comprehensive set of inherent processes for all organizational activities, each of which is documented with diagrams that use a set of standardized symbols. 274

Product and brand management systems Marketing information systems that import records of past sales from order processing or accounts receivable systems and compare those data to projections and sales estimates, in order to assess the effectiveness of promotions, advertising, and general success of a product brand. 255

Product quality assurance (PQA) The testing of a system. PQA personnel usually construct a test plan with the advice and assistance of users. PQA test engineers perform testing, and they also supervise user-test activity. Many PQA professionals are programmers who write automated test programs. 396

Program [that implements a protocol] A specific computer product that implements a protocol; for example, Netscape Navigator and Microsoft Internet Explorer are two such programs. 219

Project A dynamic application of people and other resources for the creation of a product or the achievement of some aim. Projects normally have a limited duration—they start and are completed. 50

Project management Use of software to produce charts (such as Gantt charts) that schedule tasks and resources that are dependent on each other. 50

Proprietary As applied to computer applications, the term indicates that a solution is unique to and is owned by the organization that develops and pays for the system. 315

Protocol A standardized means for coordinating an activity between two or more entities. 192

Protocol architecture See *Layered protocols.* 218

Prototype A mock-up of an aspect of a new system; it could be a mock-up of a form, report, query, or other element of the user interface. 400

Public IP address An IP address used on the Internet. Such IP addresses are assigned to major institutions in blocks by the Internet Corporation for Assigned Names and Numbers (ICANN). Each IP address is unique across all computers on the Internet. 222

Public key/private key A special version of asymmetric encryption that is popular on the Internet. With this method, each site has a public key for encoding messages and a private key for decoding them. 206

Public switched data network (PSDN) A WAN connection alternative. A network of computers and leased lines is developed and maintained by a vendor that leases time on the network to other organizations. 200

Pull production planning A manufacturing process whereby products are pulled through manufacturing by demand. Items are manufactured in response to signals from customers or other production processes that products or components are needed. 259

Pull report A report that the user must request. To obtain a pull report, a user goes to a Web portal or a business intelligence (BI) Web server and clicks a link or button to cause the reporting system to produce and deliver the report. 357

Push production planning A manufacturing process in which a company pushes products into sales. The company analyzes past sales levels, makes estimates of future sales, creates a master production schedule, produces products according to that schedule, and pushes them into sales. 259

Push report Reports sent to users according to a preset schedule or whenever a particular event occurs. 359

Quad processor A computer with four CPUs. 104

Query A request for data from a database. 154

Radio frequency identification (RFID) tag A computer chip that transmits data about the container or product to which it is attached. RFID data include not just product numbers, but also data about where the product was made, what the components are, special handling requirements, and, for perishable products, when the contents will expire. RFIDs facilitate inventory tracking by signaling their presence to scanners as they are moved throughout the manufacturing facility. 256

RAM Stands for *random access memory*, which is main memory consisting of cells that hold data or instructions. Each cell has an address that the CPU uses to read or write data. Memory locations can be read or written in any order, hence the term *random access*. RAM memory is almost always volatile. 104

Rapid application development (RAD) A type of application development pioneered by James Martin. The basic idea is to break up the design and implementation phases of the SDLC into smaller chunks and to design and implement those chunks using as much computer assistance as possible. 400

Real Simple Syndication (RSS) A standard for subscribing to content sources; similar to an email system for content. 353

Record Also called *row*, a group of columns in a database table. 147

Reference Model for Open Systems Interconnection (OSI) A protocol architecture created by ISO that has seven layers. Portions of the OSI model are incorporated into the TCP/IP–OSI hybrid architecture that is used on the Internet and most internets. 218

Regression analysis A type of supervised data mining that estimates the values of parameters in a linear equation. Used to determine the relative influence of variables on an outcome and also to predict future values of that outcome. 342

Relation The more formal name for a database table. 148

Relational database Database that carries its data in the form of tables and that represents relationships using foreign keys. 148

Relationship An association among entities or entity instances in an E-R model or an association among rows of a table in a relational database. 160

Relevant information Information that is appropriate to both the context and the subject. 16

Remote computing See *Distributed computing*. 315

Replicated databases Databases that contain duplicated records. Processing of such databases is complex if users want to be able to update the same items at the same time without experiencing *lost-update problems*. 238

Report A presentation of data in a structured or meaningful context. 154

Report server A special case of a business intelligence (BI) application server that serves only reports. 359

Reporting tools A type of business intelligence tool, these programs read data from a variety of sources, process that data, format the data into structured reports, and delivery those reports to the users who need them. 333

Repository A CASE tool database that contains documents, data, prototypes, and program code for the software or system under development. 402

RFM analysis A way of analyzing and ranking customers according to the recency, frequency, and monetary value of their purchases. 356

Risk The likelihood of an adverse occurrence. 463

Root servers Special computers that are distributed around the world that maintain a list of IP addresses of servers that resolve each type of top-level domain. 229

Rotational delay On a disk, the time it takes the data to rotate under the read/write head. The faster the disk spins, the shorter the rotational delay. 112

Router A special-purpose computer that moves network traffic from one node on a network to another. 200

Routine production services According to Reich, jobs that involve relatively low-skilled workers who can read and perform simple calculations, are reliable, and are able to follow simple directions. Because of the low skills required, these jobs pay little, and many have moved offshore. 17

Routing table A table of data used by a router to determine where to send a packet that it receives. 224

Row Also called *record*, a group of columns in a database table. 147

RSS See *Real Simple Syndication*. 353

RSS feed A data source that transmits using an RSS standard. The output of an RSS feed is consumed by an RSS reader. 355

RSS reader A program by which users can subscribe to magazines, blogs, Web sites, and other content sources; the reader will periodically check the sources, and if there has been a change since the last check, it will place a summary of the change and a link to the new content in an inbox. 353

Safeguard Any action, device, procedure, technique, or other measure that reduces a system's vulnerability to a threat. 466

Sales and marketing information system System that supports the basic functions of sales and marketing: lead generation, lead tracking, customer management, sales forecasting, and product and brand management. 253

Sarbanes-Oxley Act of 2002 Law passed by the U.S. Congress in 2002 that governs the reporting requirements of publicly held companies. Among other things, it strengthened requirements for internal controls and management's responsibility for accurate financial reporting. 264

Schedule feasibility Whether IS will be able to be developed on the timetable needed. 389

Scope In the discipline of project management, the characteristics needed to be built into or achieved by an IS; same as the term *requirements*. 50

Seats A measure of a certain number of users of a software product by a company, for licensing purposes. 125

Secure Socket Layer (SSL) A protocol that uses both asymmetric and symmetric encryption. SSL is a protocol layer that works between Levels 4 (transport) and 5 (application) of the TCP–OSI protocol architecture. When SSL is in use, the browser address will begin with https://. The most recent version of SSI is called TLS. 206, 470

Security policy Management's policy for computer security, consisting of a general statement of the organization's security program, issue-specific policy, and system-specific policy. 463

Security program A systematic plan by which an organization addresses security issues; consists of three components: senior management involvement, safeguards of various kinds, and incident response. 461

Seek time On a disk, the time it takes the read/write arm to position the head over the correct circle. Seek time is determined by the make and model of the disk device. 112

Segment The container that a TCP uses to carry messages. The TCP program places identifying data at the front and end of each segment that are akin to the To and From addresses that you would put on a letter for the postal mail. 220

Semantic security Concerns the unintended release of protected information through the release of a combination of reports or documents that are independently not protected. 360

Separation of duties and authorities An internal control that requires that different people be responsible for different portions of activities involving receipt and disbursement of a company's funds. 264

Sequential workflow A workflow in which activities occur in sequence. 41

Server A computer that provides some type of service, such as hosting a database, running a blog, publishing a Web site, or selling goods. Server computers are faster, larger, and more powerful than client computers. 116

Server farm A large collection of server computers that coordinates the activities of the servers, usually for commercial purposes. 116

Server tier In the three-tier architecture, the tier that consists of computers that run Web servers to generate Web pages and other data in response to requests from browsers. Web servers also process application programs. 295

Service description With Web services, an XML file that details what programs exist on another computer and how to communicate with those programs. 316

Service pack A large group of fixes that solve low-priority software problems. Users apply service packs in much the same way that they apply patches, except that service packs typically involve fixes to hundreds or thousands of problems. 398

Service-oriented architecture (SOA) Processing philosophy that advocates that computing systems use a *standard method* to declare the services they provide and the interface by which those services can be requested and used. Web services are an implementation of SOA. 316

Set-top box An external device that receives an IPTV (Internet Protocol television) signal and distributes it to multiple television set or home entertainment centers. 228

SharePoint site A workflow site, created in Microsoft's collaboration tool SharePoint, that enables team members to define workflows for their group. The software that runs the site will send emails to team members requesting reviews, create task lists defined for the workflow, check documents in, mark tasks as complete, email the next person in the workflow, and email copies of all correspondence to the workflow leader, who can use this capability to ensure that all teammates perform the work they are requested to do. 41

Simple Mail Transfer Protocol (SMTP) A Layer-5 architecture used to send email. Normally used in conjunction with other Layer-5 protocols (POP3, IMAP) for receiving email. 219

Site license A license purchased by an organization to equip all the computers on a site with certain software. 123

Skype A company, owned by Yahoo!, that provides voice-over-IP (VoIP) phone service. 228

Smart card A plastic card similar to a credit card that has a microchip. The microchip, which holds much more data than a magnetic strip, is loaded with identifying data. Normally requires a PIN. 467

Sniffing A technique for intercepting computer communications. With wired networks, sniffing requires a physical connection to the network. With wireless networks, no such connection is required. 458

Social networking Connections of people with similar interests. Today, social networks typically are supported by Web 2.0 technology. 302

Software Instructions for computers. One of the five fundamental components of an information system. 5

Software as a service Business model whereby companies (such as Google, Amazon.com, and eBay) provide services based on their software, rather than providing software as a product (by means of software-usage licenses). Software as a service is an example of Web 2.0. 299

SOHO [small office, home office] An acronym for small office/home office. 232

Solution broker According to Reich, a type of symbolic-analytic worker, who links *problem-identifiers* with *problem-solvers*. Solution brokers understand the underlying domain of the problems and solutions and are able to raise money and influence decision makers to create the solution. 17

Special function cards Cards that can be added to the computer to augment the computer's basic capabilities. 104

Spoofing When someone pretends to be someone else with the intent of obtaining unauthorized data. If you pretend to be your professor, you are spoofing your professor. 458

Spyware Programs installed on the user's computer without the user's knowledge or permission that reside in the background and, unknown to the user, observe the user's actions and keystrokes, modify computer activity, and report the user's activities to sponsoring organizations. Malicious spyware captures keystrokes to obtain user names, passwords, account numbers, and other sensitive information. Other spyware is used for marketing analyses, observing what users do, Web sites visited, products examined and purchased, and so forth. 473

SQL Server A popular enterprise-class DBMS product from Microsoft. 152

Steering committee A group of senior managers from a company's major business functions that works with the CIO to set the IS priorities and decide among major IS projects and alternatives. 427

Storage hardware Hardware that saves data and programs. Magnetic disk is by far the most common storage device, although optical disks, such as CDs and DVDs, also are popular. 105

Strategic decision Decision that concerns broader-scope, organizational issues. 46

Strong password A password with the following characteristics: seven or more characters; does not contain the user's user name, real name, or company name; does not contain a complete dictionary word, in any language; is different from the user's previous passwords; and contains both upper- and lowercase letters, numbers, and special characters. 80

Structured decision A type of decision for which there is a formalized and accepted method for making the decision. 47

Structured Query Language (SQL) An international standard language for processing database data. 153

Supervised data mining A form of data mining in which data miners develop a model prior to the analysis and apply statistical techniques to data to estimate values of the parameters of the model. 342

Supplier relationship management (SRM) A business process for managing all contacts between an organization and its suppliers. 308

Supply chain A network of organizations and facilities that transforms raw materials into products delivered to customers. 304

Supply chain profitability The difference between the sum of the revenue generated by the supply chain and the sum of the costs that all organizations in the supply chain incur to obtain that revenue. 306

Support In market-basket terminology, the probability that two items will be purchased together. 343

Support activities In Porter's value chain model, the activities that contribute indirectly to value creation—procurement, technology, human resources, and the firm's infrastructure. 65

Switch A special-purpose computer that receives and transmits data across a network. 192, 221

Switch table A table of data used by a switch to determine where to send frames that it receives. 223

Switching costs Business strategy of locking in customers by making it difficult or expensive to change to another product or supplier. 71

Symbolic-analytic services According to Reich, job skills that deal with information and apply abstract reasoning. These services need not be performed in person, can be performed offshore using modern communications facilities, and are required by high-value organizations. 17

Symmetric encryption An encryption method whereby the same key is used to encode and to decode the message. 206, 469

Symmetrical digital subscriber lines (SDSL) DSL lines that have the same upload and download speeds. 199

Synchronous communication Information exchange that occurs when all members of a work team meet at the same time, such as face-to-face meetings or conference calls. 7

System A group of components that interact to achieve some purpose. 5

System conversion The process of *converting* business activity from the old system to the new. 396

Systems analysis and design The process of creating and maintaining information systems. It is sometimes called systems development. 383

Systems analysts IS professionals who understand both business and technology. They are active throughout the systems development process and play a key role in moving the project from conception to conversion and, ultimately, maintenance. Systems analysts integrate the work of the programmers, testers, and users. 392

Systems development The process of creating and maintaining information systems. It is sometimes called *systems analysis and design*. 383

Systems development life cycle (SDLC) The classical process used to develop information systems. These basic tasks of systems development are combined into the following phases: system definition, requirements analysis, component design, implementation, and system maintenance (fix or enhance). 387

Table Also called a *file*, a group of similar rows or records in a database. 147

Tag In markup languages such as HTML and XML, notation used to define a data element for display or other purposes. 297

TCP/IP–OSI (protocol) architecture A protocol architecture having five layers that evolved as a hybrid of the TCP/IP and the OSI architecture. This architecture is used on the Internet and on most internets. 218

Team survey A form of asynchronous communication in which one team member creates a list of questions and other team members respond. Microsoft SharePoint has built-in survey capability. 35

Technical feasibility Whether existing information technology will be able to meet the needs of a new IS. 289

Technical safeguard Safeguard that involves the hardware and software components of an information system. 467

Terabyte (TB) 1,024GB. 106

Test plan Groups of sequences of actions that users will take when using the new system. 396

Thick client A software application that requires programs other than just the browser on a user's computer—that is, that requires code on both a client and server computers. 122

Thin client A software application that requires nothing more than a browser and can be run on only the user's computer. 122

Three-tier architecture Architecture used by most e-commerce server applications. The tiers refer to three different classes of computers. The user tier consists of users' computers that have browsers that request and process Web pages. The server tier consists of computers that run Web servers and in the process generate Web pages and other data in response to requests from browsers. Web servers also process application programs. The third tier is the database tier, which runs the DBMS that processes the database. 295

Timely information Information that is produced in time for its intended use. 13

Top-level domain (TLD) The last letters in any domain name. For example, in the domain name *www.icann.org* the top-level domain is *.org*. Similarly, in the domain name *www.ibm.com, .com* is the top-level domain. For non–U.S. domain names, the top-level domain is often a two-letter abbreviation for the country in which the service resides. 228

Trade-off In project management, a choice among scarce resources such as scope, time, cost, quality, risk, people, and other resources. Managers may need to trade off a delay in the project due-date to reduce expense and keep critical employees. 50

Transaction processing system (TPS) An information system that supports operational decision making. 45

Transmission Control Program (TCP) TCP operates at Layer 4 of the TCP/IP–OSI architecture. TCP is used in two ways: as the name of a Layer 4 *protocol* and as part of the name of the TCP/IP–OSI protocol architecture. The architecture gets its name because it usually includes the TCP protocol. TCP receives messages from Layer-5 protocols (like http) and breaks those messages up into segments that it sends to a Layer-3 protocol (like IP). 220

Transmission Control Program/Internet Protocol (TCP/IP) architecture A protocol architecture having four layers; forms the basis for the TCP/IP–OSI architecture blend used by the Internet. 218

Transparency The degree to which the user is unaware of the underlying communications system. 205

Transport Layer Security (TLS) A protocol, using both asymmetric and symmetric encryption, that works between Levels 4 (transport) and 5 (application) of the TCP–OSI protocol architecture. TLS is the new name for a later version of SSL. 206, 470

Trojan horse Virus that masquerades as a useful program or file. The name refers to the gigantic mock-up of a horse that was filled with soldiers and moved into Troy during the Peloponnesian Wars. A typical Trojan horse appears to be a computer game, an MP3 music file, or some other useful, innocuous program. 125

Tunnel A virtual, private pathway over a public or shared network from the VPN client to the VPN server. 202

Uncertainty Those things we don't know. 463

Unified Modeling Language (UML) A series of diagramming techniques that facilitates OOP development. UML has dozens of different diagrams for all phases of system development. UML does not require or promote any particular development process. 159, 404

Unified process (UP) A methodology designed for use with the Unified Modeling Language (UML) that uses use cases that describe the application of a new system. 405

Uniform resource locator (URL) A document's address on the Web. URLs begin on the right with a top-level domain, and, moving left, include a domain name and then are followed by optional data that locates a document within that domain. 228

Unix An operating system developed at Bell Labs in the 1970s. It has been the workhorse of the scientific and engineering communities since then. 119

Unshielded twisted pair (UTP) cable A type of cable used to connect the computers, printers, switches, and other devices on a LAN. A UTP cable has four pairs of twisted wire. A device called an RJ-45 connector is used to connect the UTP cable into NIC devices. 193

Unstructured decision A type of decision for which there is no agreed-on decision-making method. 47

Unsupervised data mining A form of data mining whereby the analysts do not create a model or hypothesis before running the analysis. Instead, they apply the data-mining technique to the data and observe the results. With this method, analysts create hypotheses after the analysis to explain the patterns found. 341

Upgrade A license offered by software vendors in the initial purchase of a product that allows users to obtain an updated version of the product for far less than the price of a new copy. 123

Use case A description of an application of a new system that is used with the Unified Modeling Language (UML) and the Unified Process (UP). 405

User tier In the three-tier architecture, the tier that consists of computers that have browsers that request and process Web pages. 295

Usurpation Occurs when unauthorized programs invade a computer system and replace legitimate programs. Such unauthorized programs typically shut down the legitimate system and substitute their own processing. 460

Value According to Porter, the amount of money that a customer is willing to pay for a resource, product, or service. 65

Value chain A network of value-creating activities. 65

Version control Use of software to control access to and configuration of documents, designs, and other electronic versions of products. 40

Version management Tracking of changes to documents by means of features and functions that accommodate concurrent work. The means by which version management is done depend on the particular version-management system used; three such systems are wikis, Google Docs & Spreadsheets, and Microsoft Groove. 37

Vertical-market application Software that serves the needs of a specific industry. Examples of such programs are those used by dental offices to schedule appointments and bill patients, those used by auto mechanics to keep track of customer data and customers' automobile repairs, and those used by parts warehouses to track inventory, purchases, and sales. 120

VGA A traditional type of signal interface for LCD devices; it is less expensive than the newer DVI interface, but does not provide as good an image. 114

Videoconferencing Technology that combines a conference call with video cameras. 34

Video processor A dedicated part of a computer's special CPU and memory for the storing and processing of video images. 114

Viral marketing A marketing method used in the Web 2.0 world in which *users* spread news about products and services to one another. 300

Virtual meeting A meeting in which participants do not meet in the same place and possibly not at the same time. 34

Virtual private network (VPN) A WAN connection alternative that uses the Internet or a private internet to create the appearance of private point-to-point connections. In the IT world, the term *virtual* means something that appears to exist that does not exist in fact. Here, a VPN uses the public Internet to create the appearance of a private connection. 201

Virus A computer program that replicates itself. 125

Visual development tools Tools used in RAD projects to improve developer productivity. An example is Microsoft's Visual Studio.Net. 403

Voice over IP (VoIP) A technology that provides telephone communication over the Internet. 39, 228

Volatile memory Data that will be lost when the computer or device is not powered. 107

Vulnerability An opening or a weakness in a security system. Some vulnerabilities exist because there are no safeguards or because the existing safeguards are ineffective. 466

Waterfall The fiction that one phase of the SDLC can be completed in its entirety and the project can progress, without any backtracking, to the next phase of the SDLC. Projects seldom are that simple; backtracking is normally required. 399

Web farm A facility that runs multiple Web servers. Work is distributed among the computers in a Web farm so as to maximize throughput. 296

Web page Document encoded in HTML that is created, transmitted, and consumed using the World Wide Web. 295

Web server A program that processes the HTTP protocol and transmits Web pages on demand. Web servers also process application programs. 295

Web storefront In e-commerce, a Web-based application that enables customers to enter and manage their orders. 291

Web 2.0 Generally, a loose cloud of capabilities, technologies, business models, and philosophies that characterize the new and emerging business uses of the Internet. 299

Wide area network (WANs) A network that connects computers located at different geographic locations. 189

Wiki A knowledge base maintained by its users; processed on Web sites that allow users to add, remove, and edit content. 37

WiMax An emerging technology based on the IEEE 802.16 standard. WiMax is designed to deliver the "last mile" of wireless broadband access and could ultimately replace cable and DSL for fixed applications and replace cell phones for nomadic and portable applications. See also *IEEE 802.16*. 203

Windows An operating system designed and sold by Microsoft. It is the most widely used operating system. 118

Wired Equivalent Privacy (WEP) A wireless security standard developed by the IEEE 802.11 committee that was insufficiently tested before it was deployed in communications equipment. It has serious flaws. 469

Wireless NIC (WNIC) Devices that enable wireless networks by communicating with wireless access points. Such devices can be cards that slide into the PCMA slot or they can be built-in, onboard devices. WNICs operate according to the 802.11 protocol. 195

Workflow A process or procedure by which content is created, edited, used, and disposed. 32

Workflow control Use of software and IS to monitor the execution of a work team's processes; ensures that actions are taken at appropriate times and prohibits the skipping of steps or tasks. 32

Workspace In Microsoft Groove, an electronic "space" consisting of tools and documents that enable users to collaborate. 38

World Wide Web Consortium (W3C) A body that sponsors the development and dissemination of Web standards. 314

Worm A virus that propagates itself using the Internet or some other computer network. Worm code is written specifically to infect another computer as quickly as possible. 125

Worth-its-cost information Information for which there is an appropriate relationship between the cost of the information and its value. 16

Wi-Fi Protected Access (WPA and WPA2) An improved wireless security standard developed by the IEEE 802.11 committee to fix the flaws of the Wired Equivalent Privacy (WEP) standard. Only newer wireless hardware uses this technique. 469

XML schema An XML document that specifies the structure of other XML documents. An XML schema is metadata for other XML documents. For example, a SalesOrder XML schema specifies the structure of SalesOrder documents. 314

XML Web services Sometimes called *Web services*; a set of standards that facilitate distributed computing using Internet technology. The goal of Web services is to provide a standardized way for programs to access one another remotely, without the need to develop proprietary solutions. 316

Index

Page numbers in **bold** represent definitions; those in *italic* represent figures.

D